MUSIC AND CULTURE IN AMERICA, 1861–1918

EDITED BY
MICHAEL SAFFLE

GARLAND PUBLISHING, INC.
A MEMBER OF THE TAYLOR & FRANCIS GROUP
NEW YORK AND LONDON
1998

Library of Congress Cataloging-in-Publication Data

Music and culture in America, 1861–1918 / edited by Michael Saffle.
       p.   cm. — (Essays in American music ; vol. 2) (Garland
reference library of the humanities ; vol. 1952)
   Includes index.
   ISBN 0-8153-2125-2 (alk. paper)
   1. Music—United States—19th century—History and criticism.
2. Music—United States—20th century—History and criticism.   3. Music
and society.   I. Saffle, Michael Benton, 1946– . II. Series. III. Garland
reference library of the humanities ; vol. 1952.
ML200.M87   1998
780'.973'09034—dc21   97-49479
                                           CIP
                                           MN

Cover illustration details a page from *Pacific Coast Musical Review* of 1911.

Printed on acid-free, 250-year-life paper
Manufactured in the United States of America

CONTENTS

Series Foreword   vii

Introduction   ix

William Steinway and Music in New York,
   1861-1871
   Edwin M. Good   3

Mrs. Potiphar at the Opera: Satire,
   Idealism, and Cultural Authority in
   Post–Civil War New York
   Karen Ahlquist   29

Concert Singers, Prima Donnas, and Entertainers:
   The Changing Status of Black Women
   Vocalists in Nineteenth-Century America
   Thomas L. Riis   53

Somewhere Between Beer and Wagner:
   The Cultural and Musical Impact of German
   Männerchöre in New York and New Orleans
   Mary Sue Morrow   79

The Indianapolis Männerchor: Contributions
   to a New Musicality in Midwestern Life
   Suzanne G. Snyder   111

Why American Art Music First Arrived in
   New England
   Nicholas E. Tawa   141

Promoting the Local Product: Reflections on
the California Musical Press, 1874-1914
Michael Saffle 167

Music in Lancaster, Kentucky, 1885-1910:
Local Talent, Touring Artists,
and the Opera House
Ben Arnold 197

Jacob Guth in Montrose: A Town Band in
Central Pennsylvania, 1888-1897
Kenneth Kreitner 231

When Cairo Met Main Street: Little Egypt,
Salome Dancers, and the World's Fairs
of 1893 and 1904
Charles A. Kennedy 271

Inventing Tradition: Symphony and Opera in
Progressive-Era Los Angeles
Catherine Parsons Smith 299

The Operettas of Charles Hutchinson Gabriel
Clyde W. Brockett 323

The Missing Title Page: Dvořák and
the American National Song
John C. Tibbetts 343

Index 367

Contributors 383

SERIES FOREWORD

Essays in American Music celebrates the rich and varied heritage of this country's music by bringing together articles written by distinguished scholars, researchers, and teachers about significant and unique musical events, persons, and places. Altogether the historiography of American music has advanced considerably since the first calls went out in the early 1800s for the collecting of historical data, and today readers may choose from a vast body of literature on American music, including several excellent histories and surveys, numerous critical studies and facsimile editions, monographs on individual musicians, topical studies, reference works (including bibliographies), indexes, encyclopedias and dictionaries as well as articles in journals devoted specifically to American music.

The content of the subjects addressed in the essays contained in this series offers evidence for the fact that there is still much to discover about this country's musical past. The purpose of this series is to provide a sampling of areas of research currently under pursuit and, nearing the onset of the twenty-first century, to provide a stimulus for future research into American music.

The volumes in the series progress chronologically, beginning with the period prior to 1865. Volume two focuses on 1861-1918; volume three will cover 1900-1950; and subsequent volumes will examine the remainder of the twentieth century. All of the contributors to the series are recognized authorities in their respective areas of investigation and represent prominent organizations devoted to the study of American music, including, for example, the College Music Society, the Sonneck Society for American Music, the Hymn Society in the United States and Canada, and others. Within the space allotted to them, all contributors have provided essays on topics of their choice and were encouraged to apply their own critical points of view.

James R. Heintze
Michael Saffle

INTRODUCTION

Music and Culture in America, 1861-1918 reflects the development of our nation's intellectual and artistic heritage during the decades that separated the beginning of the Civil War from the end of World War I. It was during those years that America became an international military and industrial power, that her cities grew to "modern" size, and that many of her cultural institutions—the Metropolitan Opera is one example, the *New York Times* and Harvard University are others—were recognized around the world as "authorities" to contend with.

The essays comprising the present volume are arranged by subject in roughly chronological order, although certain essays refer as well to the 1840s, the 1850s, the 1930s, and even the 1940s. Whatever its subject or purview, however, each essay sheds light on musical and cultural issues associated with that phase of our history often referred to (however insufficiently or imprecisely) as the "Brown Decades," the "Gilded Age," and the "Gay Nineties."

Edwin M. Good examines musical life in New York City during and immediately after the Civil War as reflected in the diaries of piano manufacturer William Steinway. Many of Good's observations complement those of Karen Ahlquist, whose discussion of satire, idealism, and cultural authority in New York after 1865 tells us much about the ways in which American attitudes toward "culture" were molded more than a century ago.

Men's choral societies (or Männerchöre) were an important part of nineteenth-century musical life in both Europe and the United States. Mary Sue Morrow compares the activities of New York and New Orleans societies before as well as after the Civil War. Suzanne G. Snyder discusses Männerchor activities in and around Indianapolis between the 1870s and the first decade of the twentieth century.

Thomas L. Riis deals with an important and complex topic in our nation's history: the place of African-American women vocalists on the operatic and music-hall stages. Charles A.

Kennedy describes the influence of Little Egypt and the hootchie-kootchie on American musical taste, especially insofar as it was molded by the Chicago and St. Louis World's Fairs of 1893 and 1904.

Most of the art music identified throughout the present volume is European in origin. Nicholas E. Tawa examines the birth of American art music in nineteenth-century New England and summarizes the careers of five of its composers: Chadwick, Foote, MacDowell, Paine, and Parker.

Music was not merely composed and performed throughout post–Civil War America; it was also reviewed and criticized by the press. Michael Saffle explains how California music magazines encouraged local music-making in 1870s San Francisco and throughout the Pacific coast during the 1890s, 1900s, and 1910s. Catherine P. Smith describes the creation and reception of a "Progressive Era" musical tradition in Los Angeles before as well as after the turn of the century.

American musical culture is a product of our small towns as well as of our great cities. Ben Arnold examines the ups and downs of "Gilded Age" musical life in Lancaster County, Kentucky. Kenneth Kreitner describes the activities of one Jacob Guth and the band he directed in 1880s Montrose, Pennsylvania, and examines a collection of partbooks that tells us much about our instrumental heritage. Clyde Brockett evaluates the little-known operettas of Charles Hutchinson Gabriel and explains their significance for the history of our nation's musical stage.

Finally, John C. Tibbetts informs us about Antonín Dvořák's American sojourn and its implications not only for Dvořák himself, but for his American pupils and our nation's cultural development.

I would like to express my sincere appreciation to James Heintze of The American University, Washington, D.C., for his suggestions and patience. I would also like to thank each and every contributor to this volume; their researches have enriched our understanding of American musical and cultural history. Finally, I would like to thank the staff of Garland Publishing for their encouragement and assistance.

Michael Saffle

Music and Culture in America, 1861–1918

WILLIAM STEINWAY AND MUSIC IN NEW YORK, 1861-1871

Edwin M. Good

William Steinway (1835-1896) was the fourth son and sixth child of Henry Engelhardt (sometimes spelled "Engelhard"; 1797-1871) and Julianna Thiemer (1804-1877) Steinway (originally Steinweg). When William was fifteen years old, the Steinways left their ancestral home in Seesen, Germany (in the Harz Mountains of the Duchy of Braunschweig), and settled in New York. The Steinway men, including William, found positions in various New York piano-manufacturing firms. In 1853, when William was age eighteen, Henry Sr. and his two sons, Charles (1829-1865) and Henry Jr. (1830-1865),[1] formed Steinway & Sons as a partnership and began to manufacture pianos. Success soon followed, with a gold medal at an American Mechanics Fair in New York in 1855, several patents, and—as production and sales expanded—the need for manufacturing space greater than the lofts and small buildings in downtown New York that the company had occupied since 1853. In 1860, Steinway & Sons built a large factory on Fourth Avenue (now Park Avenue) between 52nd and 53rd Streets. Both the size of the building and its location in what was then the outskirts of the city testified to a forward look and very high ambition. Henry Jr. handled design and construction and took out Steinway's first seven patents, and Charles was in charge of the factory.

William joined the partnership on attaining the age of twenty-one, on 5 March 1856. Before that he had worked in the factory mainly as a bellyman (i.e., a specialist in making soundboards), and his name is listed in the Steinway & Sons number books as bellyman for all of the company's first instruments. At some point, which we do not yet know, William was put in charge of finances and sales—perhaps because his command of English was evidently extremely fine. We do not know whether his brothers were as good at English as he was.[2]

On 20 April 1861 William began to keep a diary,[3] which he maintained sedulously almost to his life's end with very few gaps in it.[4] The occasion of beginning the diary was his imminent marriage (on 23 April) to Regina Roos (1843-1882) in Buffalo—indeed, he wrote with a flourish across the top of the first page: "DAILY DIARY OF WILLIAM STEINWAY & WIFE!" The diary was written in English, but William quoted German song titles, cables, and telegrams in German.[5]

As the years went along, William's responsibilities in the company increased. Tragically, both Henry Jr. and Charles died in March 1865, just before the end of the Civil War, Henry in New York and Charles in Germany. Henry Sr., then sixty-eight years old, was apparently no longer active in the company's operations, and Albert (1840-1877), the fifth son, was an officer in the Union Army and not yet a partner.[6] William had evidently been basically in charge of the company for most of a year, and everything now devolved upon him and upon Albert. William had just turned thirty, and Albert was not quite twenty-five.

On 28 April, three days after receiving the news of Charles's death, William urgently requested the eldest brother, Theodore (1825-1889), then engaged in an increasingly profitable piano-making business in Braunschweig, to drop everything and remove to New York. On 31 May William records receiving a letter from Theodore saying that he will come. The only letter we have from Theodore at this time is undated, and it seems negative. Theodore says that he does not wish to come but will if it becomes absolutely necessary.[7] Perhaps we have not read it correctly or perhaps there was another letter, now lost, in which Theodore agreed to come in the fall. Or William may have engaged in wishful thinking. In the event, Theodore sold the Braunschweig business to his associates, Grotrian, Helfferich, and Schultz, and arrived in New York on 26 October, thus becoming the partner responsible for design and construction. Albert also became a partner, taking charge of the factory, and William continued to handle the commercial and financial affairs.[8]

As the person in financial and commercial charge of what rapidly became New York's largest manufacturer of pianos—and, by the early 1870s, the nation's largest[9]—William Steinway was, whether he wished to be or not, a participant in the New York musical scene. Evidently he wished to be, as his activities were numerous.

The diary gives evidence that Steinway had connections to a number of New York's major pianists quite early in our period. Merely to name some of them and the earliest dates in the diary when William mentions their playing Steinways will indicate the rising importance of Steinway pianos[10]: William Mason (8 November 1862), John Nelson Pattison (20 December 1862), Robert Goldbeck (21 March 1863), Sebastian Bach Mills (7 November 1863),[11] Alfred H. Pease (8 February 1864), Carl Wolfssohn (7 January 1865),[12] Edward Dannreuther (11 September 1865), Bernardus Boekelmann (1 October 1866), Leopold de Meyer (1 October 1867),[13] Oscar Pfeiffer (21 November 1867), Anna Mehlig (5 February 1870), and Marie Krebs (23 November 1870). This is, of course, only a partial list of pianists whom William mentions, but some of them (e.g., Louis Moreau Gottschalk [1829-1869] and James Wehli) played Chickerings, and we cannot be sure whose instruments others played.

Some of these pianists remained faithful to Steinway for their entire careers. William Mason (1829-1908) and Sebastian Bach Mills (1838-1898) were major New York–based performers, and both were not only committed to Steinway but were personal, lifelong friends of William.[14] The company's inventory books list from year to year the names of musicians in New York to whom Steinway loaned or rented pianos, and it is a notable list. Theodore Thomas (1835-1905) was a regular recipient and arranged on one occasion for the use of Steinways when Anna Mehlig (1846-1928) was on tour with his orchestra.[15]

International Recognition for Steinway & Sons

Two international events assisted in giving Steinway & Sons even wider notice. An exhibition held in London in 1862 was the first opportunity for the fledgling company to put its instruments under the scrutiny of the world's piano experts. The company had already had success at local exhibitions, but London was a much wider chance.[16] Steinway won a medal for the recently patented cross-strung grand. It was only one of eight gold medals awarded, but it recognized what we now know was Steinway's contribution in bringing the grand piano to what can effectively be called modernity. Interestingly, William never mentioned the London success in the diary. Henry Jr. represented the company in London, and William refers both to shipping pianos to London and to Henry's departure and return. But if the diary were our sole source of information, we would not know that Steinway & Sons won a notable prize. Though the prize called Steinway's innovation of the cross-strung grand to the attention of the international piano industry and drew some imitation, it probably did not make much of an impression on the New York scene.

The other event was also an international exposition, this one held in Paris in 1867. At the Paris exposition, the Americans swept the field. Steinway & Sons and Chickering & Sons won the two highest prizes in the piano competition. Who won the highest is still in dispute. Both companies quite noisily claimed the first prize and denigrated the other's arguments to the contrary.

Theodore Steinway represented the company in Paris, and William was intensely aware of the importance of what was happening there.[17] But he could not worm information out of Theodore. On 17 May William was in Buffalo when he wrote in the diary: "Receive Cable telegram early in the morning that we had received Gold Medal." He does not even say from whom the cable (no doubt sent via the transatlantic cable) came. On the next day he says that he has decided not to publicize the medal until he receives further information. On 29 May he writes to Europe, no doubt pleading with Theodore for information. On 29 June he records: "Official list of Medals awarded to Americans, we heading the list." But it is not clear that this information comes from Theodore.

On 2 July the gloom deepens: "Chickering gets Cabletelegram that in addition to a gold Medal he has cross of the legion of honor. Great Jubilee at their store, we feel in despair about absence of news from Theodore." C. Frank Chickering (1827-1891), who was present with the Chickering exhibit in Paris, was given the Croix de la Legion d'Honneur, a very high French decoration. The news sent the Chickering workmen out to parade in the streets of Boston. In Steinway Hall, William knew only that, six weeks and four days after the first news of Steinway's gold medal, there was still no word from Theodore.

The next day the other shoe fell: "At noon our telegram comes stating that we got gold Medal before Chick[ering]. Our flag up, and telegraphing to our principal Agents. I write long letter to Theodore." And on 4 July: "Work all day, write and telegraph. We receive telegram, societé [*sic*] des Beaux Arts medal to us." The medal of the Société des Beaux Arts was a special medal apart from the exposition's awards, as was Frank Chickering's Cross of the Legion of Honor.

Steinway took the Beaux Arts medal as the evidence of its primacy, and Chickering & Sons took the Legion of Honor as the evidence that it had really won, and there was very little room for a rational decision between them. But that did not stop the two companies from doing all they could to advance their claims. On 5 July William wrote: "Chickering commences to blow in his Advertisements. We do the same." Only on 11 July, just under eight weeks since the first arrival of news from Paris, does William receive a communication that we know is from Theodore, a telegram that apparently says, "Victory of the Overstrung System."[18]

That may stand for the effect of the Paris victory—and I propose no decision on whether Steinway won first prize or Chickering did; at this remove, it doesn't matter. The American piano industry had proven its worth to the European musical community, and Steinway & Sons had demonstrated a leadership in the American industry that had far-reaching effects. Steinway's increased visibility in Europe led directly to increased exports, the establishment of a London sales office, the appointment of sales agents in other major European cities, and ultimately the decision in 1880 to open a factory in Germany. To be sure, an administration unable and unwilling to exploit the opportunities presented by the Paris medal could have missed doing what Steinway did.[19] I think William's commercial acumen and the family's ambition, as well as good contacts in Germany and elsewhere, were responsible for the company's continuing success and its attainment of preeminence in the eyes of the musical world. As I have said elsewhere, "Once the public had been persuaded that [the Steinway system] was the norm, it had become the norm."[20]

At any rate, Steinway's Paris success could not help giving the piano something of a boost in New York itself. On 14 May 1870, William boasted of shipping sixty-five pianos in a week, the most ever. By that year, Steinway & Sons was manufacturing (and selling) about two thousand pianos in a year, a very large number indeed. The success of a local firm out in the wider world surely had some impact on New York as well.

Steinway Hall

The heyday of Steinway's centrality in the New York scene began on 31 October 1866, with the concert officially inaugurating Steinway Hall. Until it was closed in 1890, Steinway Hall, seating twenty-five hundred persons, was a major venue for concerts. Carnegie Hall, with its larger capacity, supplanted it in 1891. The Academy of Music, just down 14th Street from Steinway Hall, was larger, frequently presenting operas as well as concerts, and the Metropolitan Opera House, opening in 1883, became the major opera house.

William's diary entry for 31 October 1866 has entirely to do with the opening of Steinway Hall: "Inauguration Concert; by the Bateman Concert Troupe. Everybody is delighted with the acoustic qualities. House filled to overflowing Great Success. Supper afterwards, jolly time til 3 A.M."[21] H. L. Bateman's troupe performed several concerts in the early weeks of the hall's opening; on the inaugural occasion the performers were: Euphrosyne Parepa-Rosa (1836-1874), soprano; Pasquale Brignoli (1824-1884), tenor; Ferranti, a basso buffo; Fortuna, baritone; the pianist Sebastian Bach Mills; the violinist Carl Rosa (1842-1889); John Liptrot Hatton (1809-1886), composer and accompanist; and, says George Odell, "an orchestra led by Theodore Thomas."[22]

Steinway Hall also played host in its first season to the New York Philharmonic. The interior of the Academy of Music, where the Philharmonic normally played, had burned on 22 May 1866, and on 29 July William recorded in the diary his signing what we take to be the contract for the Philharmonic's occupying Steinway Hall. The first concert took place on 17 November. Carl Bergmann conducted, and Carl Wolfssohn, the pianist, and soprano Nathalie Seelig were soloists. The program included

Columbus, an overture by George F. Bristow, the American composer and critic.[23]

Pianists were staple fare in the Philharmonic's concerts. Sophie Groschel played the first movement of the Mozart D-minor Concerto (K. 466) on 15 December, William Mason played a Beethoven concerto (we have not found out which one) on 26 January 1867,[24] and Sebastian Bach Mills gave the American premiere of Liszt's E-flat Major Concerto on 20 April—William's comment about the last was "splendid."

These performances, of course, had to be played on Steinway pianos. On 24 November 1866 William had a bit of a set-to with George F. Bristow on that subject. James Wehli, a very fine pianist whom William had heard and admired before, had been engaged as soloist in the Philharmonic's December concert, but Wehli, like Louis Moreau Gottschalk, was devoted to Chickerings, and William notes in the margin: "refuse to Bristow to let Wehli use a Chickering grand." George F. Bristow (1825-1898) was a somewhat successful composer with distinctly nationalistic leanings, and he was also a violinist in the New York Philharmonic. Here came Bristow with the effrontery to request of William Steinway that Wehli play a Chickering in Steinway Hall, on the very premises of Steinway & Sons, manufacturers and sellers of pianos![25] William may have been an enthusiastic supporter of the Philharmonic and an admirer of Wehli's pianistic gifts, but he permitted no illusions about the proprietorship of Steinway Hall. Wehli's performance had to be cancelled, as the Philharmonic had nowhere else to play and was contracted to play at Steinway Hall. The Philharmonic substituted Sophie Groschel on short notice, and perhaps for that reason she played only one movement of the Mozart D-minor Concerto.[26]

Steinway was not, of course, the first piano firm to build its own concert hall. Erard and Pleyel in Paris had done it many years before, and Chickering followed Steinway's lead in 1875, bringing Hans von Bülow (1830-1894) on an American tour, during which he played the world premiere of Tchaikovsky's First Concerto in Boston and performed at the inauguration of Chickering Hall in New York.[27]

William Steinway and the New York Liederkranz
In addition to assisting others in their performances, both by making and selling pianos and by managing a major concert venue, William himself performed. He played the piano, of course, but he was not a performing pianist (we find no indication that any family members were).[28] Like a great many German men, those of the Steinway family were enthusiastic singers, all of them joining the New York Liederkranz, the largest of the German singing societies in the city.[29] William was perhaps the most enthusiastic, a very fine tenor who, as he relates several times in the diary, was able when in good voice to sing "high C" with ease. On a number of occasions, he sang solos with the Liederkranz, perhaps most notably on 20 April 1861, when the diary's first entry reads: "Philharmonic Concerts Liederkranz performs Walpurgis night Wm. sings tenor solo." Mendelssohn's cantata *Die erste Walpurgisnacht*, Op. 60, has a quite demanding tenor role.

The Liederkranz was an active group, giving public and private concerts several times a year, fairly often singing with the New York Philharmonic, the Brooklyn Philharmonic, and Theodore Thomas's orchestra. German singing societies were a staple of the New York musical scene in those days, and there were a great many of them. Perhaps best known, in addition to the Liederkranz, were the Arion Society (a splinter from the Liederkranz),[30] the Aschenbrödel Verein, the Germania Männerchor, the New York Allgemeiner Sängerbund, the New Yorker Sängerrunde, and Teutonia. I have gathered the names of seventy-seven such societies in New York, from the Allemania Männerchor to the Zoellner Männerchor (in Brooklyn), and I doubt that I have them all. Many of them participated in large festivals and competitions of singing societies.

William describes several such festivals. From 15-20 July 1865, a huge festival in New York engaged eighty-two groups from all over the Northeast, including Montréal. Postponed from its first planned presentation in 1861, the festival occupied front page space in the *New York Times* and included several mass concerts, a prize concert (the Philadelphia Sängerbund won first prize), and a steamboat excursion on the East and Hudson Rivers and a picnic at Jones Wood. A banner year for such affairs was 1866, no doubt because the Civil War had interrupted all festivities. In late June one was held in Providence, Rhode Island, where the Liederkranz apparently won, and in late July 1866, part of the group went to a festival in Louisville, Kentucky, and most of its members attended one in Philadelphia, but without winning. A big festival in Baltimore in 1869 saw the Liederkranz walk away with the first prize.

It is not surprising to see the programs of such groups as these filled with the chestnuts of German four-part male chorus literature. William gives many song titles, most of which I have been unable to track down, perhaps because they were sung so much that folks simply got tired of them and they disappeared. Now and again one finds surprising evidence that these groups could indeed be very ambitious. Mendelssohn's *Die erste Walpurgisnacht* is an instance, and not the only one. We read in the diary that the Liederkranz performed Félicien David's *Le Désert* in 1862 and Niels Gade's cantata *Comala* in 1863; a performance of Schubert's operetta *Die Verschworenen, D. 787* (1823), was planned and postponed in 1864 and realized in 1866. That one-act work, based on Aristophanes' *Lysistrata*, had only recently been discovered, was first performed in Vienna in 1861, and was published only in 1889.[31] This presentation in the Liederkranz clubhouse (31-33 East 4th Street) must have been the first in North America, and the Liederkranz must have worked from manuscript copies. According to the Liederkranz history it was played again 19 May 1867, though William does not refer to that performance in the diary.[32]

William was active not only vocally but also organizationally in the Liederkranz. He first became president of the society in 1867, and was frequently returned to that office. Indeed, he had accepted the presidency in the year he died, and the entire period from 1867 to 1896 could be called the "William Steinway era" of the Liederkranz. The group moved its location twice in those years. William was a principal mover in the choice of sites, fundraising, and architectural decisions.

William's Observation of the Musical Scene

It is impressive to see how assiduously William followed the musical life in New York—not as a performer or an officer of the company and the Liederkranz but as a patron and occasional commentator. For example, I count fifty-five references in the diary to his attendance or that of family members at orchestra concerts from 1861 through 1871. William himself or his family members attended concerts or recitals by soloists or troupes of artists 100 times in those ten years and operas or opera concerts 117 times.[33] Chamber music concerts were few—only five, all of them chamber music soirées by Theodore Thomas and William Mason. He mentions thirteen benefit concerts and five religious or choral ones (not by the Liederkranz or other singing societies). Six concerts took place in beer-halls, not so disreputable a venue then, especially among the Germans in New York, as it might be now.[34] William refers to twenty-four private concerts or soirées in people's homes during 1861-1871. And he attended musical entertainments of various kinds, including "minstrels," a total of eight times. He was not a habitué of Bryant's or Leon and Kelly's Minstrels, but he was not above such entertainments now and again.[35]

Apart from his attendance at and participation in Liederkranz or other singing-society programs, William attended or mentioned family members attending 333 different performances between 1861 and 1871. New York was an active city for the arts in general, especially, then as now, for the theater and for music. William was also a frequent visitor to the theater, especially but not exclusively in German. Those activities we shall have to leave aside.

The theater that he most enjoyed was opera. We might have predicted that, given his own pleasure and success at singing. Any tenor who can sing "high C" ("with ease," as he says a couple of times) will probably listen critically and with pleasure to other tenors. And sopranos. And other singers. William occasionally expressed his opinion of singers and other musicians, and he pays modestly more attention to tenors than to others. He commented on tenors William Candidus (who became his brother-in-law in 1865, marrying Wilhelmine Steinway Vogel), Theodor Habelmann, Franz Himmer, and Theodor Wachtel, among others. But William also commented on Kristina Nilsson and Carlotta Patti,[36] among other women, and we know that he heard such stellar sopranos as Euphrosyne Parepa-Rosa, Clara Louise Kellogg, Johanna Rotter, and others.

I noted above that William or members of his family attended the opera 117 times in ten years. Over that period they saw sixty different operas, presented by various troupes. There seem to have been no resident repertory opera companies in New York, though several companies performed there regularly. Max Maretzek and Max Strakosch brought fine troupes in mostly Italian opera, and Carl Anschütz was the impresario and conductor of a troupe that presented German opera (sometimes opera translated into German). They were the most visible groups in this time.

By far the most popular operas, judged by William's own attendance, were Gounod's *Faust*, which he saw twelve times in those ten years (six times in 1864 alone),[37] Weber's *Der Freischütz*, which he saw six times, von Flotow's *Martha* and Lortzing's *Czar und Zimmermann*, both of which he saw four times.[38] Changing tastes—and the ways some tastes do not change—may be illustrated by the operas he saw three times in the ten years: Adolphe Adam's *Le Postillon de Lonjumeau*, which I warrant few if any who read these words have heard; Mozart's *Don Giovanni* and *Die Zauberflöte*; Donizetti's *Daughter of the Regiment* and *Lucrezia Borgia*; Rossini's *Barber of Seville*; Meyerbeer's *Les Huguenots*; and Offenbach's *La Belle Hélène*.

When we count the operas by composer, we come up with a somewhat different picture. William saw or reported on seven Offenbach works: *Orphée aux enfers, La Grande-Duchesse de Gérolstein* (which was first performed in New York only five months after the Paris premiere), *La Belle Hélène, Geneviève de Brabant, La Périchole, La Vie parisienne*, and *Barbe-bleu*.[39] Six of the operas he saw or reported on were by Donizetti: *Betly, Daughter of the Regiment, Roberto Devereux, Lucrezia Borgia, Il Poliuto*, and *Don Sebastien*—but no *Lucia di Lammermoor*, no *Don Pasquale*,[40] and no *Elixir of Love* (our current favorites). Six were by Verdi: *Rigoletto, Macbeth, Il trovatore, Un Ballo in Maschera, La forza del destino*, and *La traviata*. There were five by Mozart: *Die Zauberflöte, Die Entführung aus dem Serail, Le nozze di Figaro, Don Giovanni*, and *Der Schauspieldirektor*); and four by Auber: *Le Maçon* (in its German version *Maurer und Schlosser*), *Fra Diavolo, Le Muette de Portici* (also in German, *Die Stumme von Portier*), and *Le domino noir*—none now staples of the operatic repertory. Of what we now consider staples, we find two Wagner operas (*Tannhäuser* and *Lohengrin*), two by Bellini (*Norma* and *La Sonnambula*), two by Gounod (*Faust* and

Romeo et Juliette), two by Rossini (*Barber of Seville* and *William Tell*), two by Weber (*Der Freischütz* and *Oberon*), Beethoven's *Fidelio*—which William saw only once in these years—and Nicolai's *Merry Wives of Windsor*—which he also saw only once.

But we find also such forgotten works as Flotow's *Stradella*, Balfe's *Enchantress*, Boieldieu's *Jean de Paris* and *La dame blanche* (both in German, of course), Achille Peri's *Judith*, *Crispino e la Comare* by the brothers Ricci, William Vincent Wallace's longtime favorite *Lurline*, and Victor Massé's *Les noces de Jeannette*,[41] as well as two operas by Errico Petrella (a now-forgotten composer once touted as Verdi's equal), *Ione* and *Carnival of Venice*,[42] and a comic opera entitled *Incognito oder Der Fürst wider Willen* by a composer named Kipper whose first name I have been unable to find. This last was performed only once (perhaps for good reason), and at that by the Liederkranz at a social evening on 27 April 1864.[43]

Such catalogs make somewhat wearisome reading. Nevertheless, to ponder this one is to recognize several things about the New York operatic scene during the decade following 1861. It was tremendously varied, to begin with. I would be surprised if New Yorkers in the decade of the 1980s were able to see sixty different operas (and these are only the ones William or his family members attended).[44]

A somewhat surprising indication from William's diary—not one that I, at least, expected to find—is that the New York operatic scene during the Civil War might have been no less active than in the years just after it. William's activities, indeed, suggest. He began his diary on 20 April 1861, very soon after the Civil War began. During 1861 he mentions only two opera performances, one of which (28 October 1861) was in the fall of the 1861-1862 season. In 1862 he mentions ten opera performances through June and sixteen (including one opera concert) from September through December. In 1863 he refers to nineteen performances, all but one of which (including an opera concert) took place between September and December. The year 1864 was even more active, with twenty-three performances: eight between 1 January and 15 April, and fifteen between September and December.

William's opera- and concert-going fell off in 1865, no doubt at least in part because of his brothers' deaths and all of the stress surrounding those events. He saw two operas in February of that year, one in May, and only five in the autumn. The next years were much lighter than the earlier ones, again perhaps for personal reasons (children of his were born in 1865, 1866, and 1869, for instance, no doubt increased his evenings at home), and he attended only three operas in 1866, three in 1867, five in 1868, and six in 1869. His activity picked up again in 1870 (twelve performances) and 1871 (ten, including an opera concert). I suspect, however, that this drop in William's operagoing activity had to do more with his own personal situation than with the state of opera in New York.

We need another angle on the matter to decide it. Sampling the opera seasons for 1864 and the 1869-1870 season by a good look at Odell's narratives of them,[45] I find that things did, as one might expect, pick up after the Civil War. In 1864, two opera companies presented winter and autumn seasons. A group managed by Leonard Grover and conducted by Carl Anschütz presented five operas in German in January 1864, with four new ones (as well as an old one) in September: *Faust, Fidelio, La dame blanche* (*Die weisse Dame*), *Tannhäuser*, and *The Merry Wives of Windsor* in January, as well as *Faust, Martha, Robert le Diable, La Juive*, and *Don Giovanni* in September.

The other group was Max Maretzek's troupe, which worked almost entirely in Italian. Here we have twenty different works, thirteen of which were played in February and March, and seven (in addition to seven repeated works) from October to December. Some were staples of the repertory: *Don Giovanni, Faust, Norma, Un Ballo in Maschera, Lucia di Lammermoor, Il trovatore, La traviata, Rigoletto,* and *The Daughter of the Regiment.* Others were works occasionally heard today: *Martha* and *La Sonnambula.* Still others were works that have now virtually disappeared from the stage: *Ione, I due Foscari, Il Poliuto, I Puritani, Lucrezia Borgia, Robert le Diable, Linda di Chamounix, Don Sebastien* (Donizetti's last opera), and *Fra Diavolo.*

Two weeks of opera starring Caroline Richings offered six works at Niblo's Saloon in late February and March: *Le postillon de Lonjumeau, Linda di Chamounix, The Daughter of the Regiment, La Sonnambula, The Bohemian Girl,* and *The Enchantress.* Two works preceded this offering at Niblo's, between 13 January and 5 Febuary: *The Bohemian Girl* and

Wallace's *Maritana* (also given at about the same time at the Park Theatre, Brooklyn). The same company added to those two operas *Fra Diavolo* and Balfe's *Rose of Castile* at the Olympic Theatre in July. Apart from *The Daughter of the Regiment*, this is a testimonial to vanished glories.

The Théâtre Français presented eight different works of a very light sort, five of them relatively early works by Offenbach (*Le mariage aux lanternes, Les deux Aveugles, Tromb-al-ca-zar, Le Violoneux*, and *Ba-ta-clan*), and the other minor works by minor composers (Massé's *Les noces de Jeannette*, Flotow's *Pianella*, and *Les pantins de Violette*—Adam's last work). In addition, Barnum's Museum offered *Linda di Chamounix* in December. This is not terribly impressive: six companies offering thirty-eight works by eighteen composers. Still, considering that it was wartime we ought not to be critical.

The 1869-1870 New York opera season was livelier. The Academy of Music saw twenty-seven different operas by five different opera companies, as well as a production of Weber's *Der Freischütz* by the Arion Society, one of the local German singing societies. A minor company led by one Dryane opened the season from 22 September to 9 October, with four productions: *La Juive, Les Mousquetaires de la Reine* (both by Halévy), *Lucia di Lammermoor*, and *Robert le Diable*. In November and December and again in late January and February, Max Maretzek's company held forth in a season of 15 different works ranging from the sublime (*Il trovatore, Rigoletto*, and *Un Ballo in Maschera*) through the decent (*Norma, Faust, Fra Diavolo, La Muette de Portici, William Tell*, and *La Sonnambula*) to the ridiculous (*Crispino e la Comare* and Ferrari's *Pipele*). From 14 March to 2 April, and again on 13-14 May, the Parepa-Rosa group presented eight operas, including *The Marriage of Figaro, Martha, Don Giovanni, Maritana, Oberon, The Bohemian Girl*, and *The Black Domino*. A ten-day presentation by the Strakosch group from 19 to 29 April brought *The Magic Flute* and *Faust*, and from 16 to 25 May a group led by one Albites sang four Italian operas: *Il trovatore, Martha, Il Poliuto*, and *Un Ballo in Maschera* (all having been presented at the Academy under the above auspices as well).

The Stadttheatre, the principal German-language theater for both plays and operas, presented a long season of operas sung in

German (frequently translated) under the direction of Hermann Grau[46] from 17 September to 22 April, interspersed with plays. This group gave eighteen different operas, five of them by Offenbach (*La Belle Hélène, La Vie parisienne, Orphée aux enfers, La Grande-Duchesse de Gérolstein,* and *Barbe-bleu,* all translated); others not given elsewhere included *Fidelio,* Boieldieu's *La dame blanche,* Flotow's *Stradella,* and von Suppé's *Die schöne Galatea.* There was also such standard fare as *The Magic Flute, Faust* (of course), *Don Giovanni, Fra Diavolo, Robert le Diable,* and *Martha.*

In the Théâtre Français a season of English opera by the Parepa-Rosa forces offered between 11 September and 2 October Balfe's *The Puritan's Daughter* (for the first time in North America), *The Bohemian Girl, La Sonnambula, Maritana, Martha,* and *Fra Diavolo.* This was followed by a few days of German opera under Carl Anschütz's direction; these productions included *Faust, Martha, The Magic Flute,* and *Robert le Diable* (are these titles beginning to sound familiar?). A distinct novelty (Odell acknowledges himself astonished and bemused) was six performances of *Askold's Grave* (*Askol'dova mogila,* 1835), an opera by the Russian composer Alexey Nikolayevitch Verstovsky (1799-1862), the performances in Russian beginning on 15 December. February and March saw a few performances of Offenbach (*La Grande-Duchesse de Gérolstein, Geneviève de Brabant, Barbe-bleu, La Périchole*) and others: Adam's *Le Sourd* and Boieldieu's *La dame blanche*—all, this time, in French. But even the French-language press bemoaned the slim pickings.

Finally there was Jim Fisk's Grand Opera House, where Caroline Richings and her troupe essayed a season from 15 November to 11 December. Some familiar titles included *Maritana, The Bohemian Girl, Fra Diavolo, Il trovatore, La Sonnambula, Martha,* and *Faust*; some less familiar included *Les Huguenots* (in English, no less), and Auber's *The Crown Diamonds.*

Eleven different companies, not including the Arion Society, presented opera in "seasons" ranging in length from four days (the Anschütz group at the Théâtre Français) to seven months of opera (the Grau troupe at the Stadttheater). They offered from one (the Russian group) to eighteen (Grau's group) different works each, the average being seven. In sum, forty-three different works were given during the year. That is a lively scene, and the fact that William attended only nine times shows that he was very much taken up with other activities. It seems, then, that the Civil War presented a somewhat lessened operatic activity, which was improved (or perhaps improving) in the years after. But William turns out not to be our best witness to that, given the activities in which he himself participated.

New York concert activity, of course, expanded considerably when Steinway Hall was built, and William became, effectively, an impresario. It is interesting to watch his attendance at the Steinway Hall concerts both immediately after the hall opened and later. He was present at everything in the first weeks—or at least he refers to everything, and often enough to the size of the house to give us to understand his personal presence. Between 31 October and 17 December 1866, William refers to thirty-three performances and public rehearsals in Steinway Hall.[47] For the first couple of weeks, H. L. Bateman's troupe, which inaugurated the hall on 31 October, had exclusive use of it, with concerts in the evenings of 1-2 and 5-9 November and matinées on 3 and 10 November. Thereafter came a Sunday concert every week, usually featuring a well-known soloist and Theodore Thomas's orchestra.

Popular concerts were presented on Mondays and Wednesdays, and a series of matinées devoted to the music of Beethoven and presented by pianist Carl Wolfssohn began on 10 November. Other artists who appeared on these and other, related occasions included soprano Marie Abbot (assisted by Matilda Toedt, contralto); Fred Steins, basso; Alfred H. Pease, pianist; George W. Morgan, organist; William Dressler; John M. Abbot;[48] Henry Tucker; and such professionals as John Nelson Pattison, pianist; and George W. Morgan, organist.[49] The "occasions" included a benefit for Morgan on 17 December.[50] At the same time public rehearsals for and presentations of two concerts by the New York Philharmonic took place: the former on 3 and 10 November and 8 and 15 December, and the latter on 17 November and 15 December.

(It is worth observing that, in the midst of William's activity associated with the opening of Steinway Hall, occurred another Steinway debut: on 13 December 1866 Paula Theoda Steinway was born, "a fine healthy girl, who screams lustily as soon as born." Paula was William and Regina's second child—the first, George, having been born in June 1865.)

In contrast to his careful monitoring of the first months of Steinway Hall's existence in 1866 (and his enthusiasm for its musical life), William displayed lackluster interest in music during 1867. He attended the opening concert of the season on 1 October of that year, which presented the first appearance in New York in two decades of Leopold de Meyer, "the Lion Pianist," who had made something of a splash in the 1840s.[51] De Meyer was assisted by Jenny Kempton, soprano; Carl Rosa, violinist; G. W. Colby, pianist; and Theodore Thomas's orchestra. During the rest of that month, however, William attended only the Sunday concert on 13 October and Theodore Thomas's orchestra concert on 26 October. In November three performances brought him out: two by pianist Oscar Pfeiffer (21 and 24 October) and one on the latter day by tenor Ignatz Pollak. Pfeiffer was assisted by Eliza Lumley-Blath, contralto; J. R. Thomas, baritone; and others; and on 24 October by Euphrosyne Parepa-Rosa, soprano; Carl Rosa; W. R. Johnson, organist; and G. W. Colby. I have found no information on Pollak's concert; in fact, I doubt that it was at Steinway Hall.[52]

On 2 December 1867 William attended, as might be expected, the concert by the Liederkranz in Steinway Hall, which he says was a "complete success." The other artists on this occasion were Alida Topp, pianist; Johanna Rotter, soprano; Eliza Lumley-Blath, contralto; Wenzel Kopta, violinist; and Fred Steins, basso.[53] The only other occasion on which William went to Steinway Hall that month was not a musical one. Charles Dickens gave the first series of his famous readings at the hall on 9-10, 12, and 13 December. William met Dickens at the hall on 8 December, attended the readings on the two following days, and reported gratifyingly large ticket sales on 11 December for the following days. The same day, however, William was struck by an attack of gout that laid him low for a week, and he was unable to get to the other two Dickens readings.[54]

So much for the fall of 1867 and William's attendance at Steinway Hall. To be sure, there was doubtless much to keep him busy, what with two infant children and some expansion of business at Steinway & Sons. That was the year when Steinway and Chickering won the top prizes for pianos at the Paris exposition, and the commercial results for Steinway, at any rate, were considerable. But William does not complain in the diary of excessive work at this time, though later a characteristic phrase is "excessively busy." Indeed, the fall of 1867 contains an unusual number of days without any entry at all except the date and day of the week. William's lack of concert-going zeal is difficult to explain. He did attend some other musical performances: *Les Huguenots* at the Academy of Music on 10 October; Offenbach's *La Grande-Duchesse de Gérolstein* at the French opera on 11 October; a Liederkranz concert featuring Alida Topp, pianist, on 3 November; and Max Maretzek's premiere production in the United States of Gounod's *Romeo et Juliette* at the Academy of Music on 15 November. Even that is considerably less than we might have expected. Perhaps there was something in the air that he didn't mention because he could not recognize it.

In more general terms, William's observation of the musical scene focused more on singers than his position in a piano company might by itself indicate. As I pointed out above, William himself was an enthusiastic and evidently very good singer—a fact that his position in Steinway & Sons does not and could not explain. During the years I am considering in this essay, he expressed his opinion of nine pianists—some of them extremely good (e.g., William Mason, Anna Mehlig, Sebastian Bach Mills, and James Wehli) and others now completely forgotten (e.g., a certain Miss Stobaios, whose first name I have been unable to discover, John Nelson Pattison, and Theodore Ritter). In the same time period, he commented in his diary on some nineteen singers, including such stars as Carlotta Patti, Kristina Nilsson, Theodor Wachtel, and Theodor Habelmann, and such nonentities as Franz Himmer, an F. Schoenfeld, and a Miss Ludecus. It is interesting to observe that eight of these nineteen singers were tenors, William's own classification. But we have already had reason to guess from the importance of opera in his life that William's heart was in song, even though his livelihood was in the piano.

Conclusions from all this material are hardly possible. William Steinway did not participate in or observe the entire New York scene during these or any years. The partial coverage may nevertheless be interesting as the sample of the scene that one culturally knowledgeable and involved person enjoyed. We must eagerly await the next installment of Vera Brodsky Lawrence's fascinating and exhaustive work on George Templeton Strong, which will allow us a better comparison of two quite different views of New York's musical life.[55] That the angles were different may be deduced from the fact that William never refers to Strong in the diary. I cannot conclude that the two did not know each other; it would seem somewhat odd if they never even met, given their somewhat similar tastes. William actually had dealings with both Marshall S. Bidwell and Charles E. Strong, partners in George Templeton Strong's law firm. Moreover, Strong lived on the edge of Gramercy Park, where William lived from 1874 onwards (although only at the very end of Strong's life). Still, Strong represented old New York, and William represented the high cultural side of Manhattan's Upper East Side "Little Germany" neighborhood, and perhaps his failure to mention Strong points to a social gulf between them.

It is worth emphasizing, moreover, that this material is only a sample of what William's diary holds for 1861-1871, let alone for the rest of his life (he died in November 1896). I set out these gleanings as entries into work in progress that remains very far from completion. If they are scrappy and frustratingly inconclusive, that may be part of what anyone's life is. The fact that the view of William's life in these pages is dominated by the view that he had of it renders even more emphatic its partial quality. I myself am as anxious as anyone else to discover what is to be found in the rest of William Steinway's diary. After several years of work on it, I feel that I am only beginning to make his acquaintance.

Arlington, Virginia

---

[1] The eldest son, C. F. Theodore (1825-1889), had not joined the exodus from Germany but remained in Germany, for a time in Seesen and in Wolfenbüttel, and later in the city of Braunschweig, where he continued the piano-making that Henry Sr. had carried on before leaving Seesen. He also retained the Steinweg form of the family name. The names of the others had, of course, been anglicized in New York, Charles having been Karl, and Henry Jr., Heinrich like his father. William likewise had been Wilhelm.

[2] In a later autobiography William claimed that he had learned his English in the school in Seesen. If that is an accurate memory, we must be amazed either at the quality of English instruction in that little German town or at William's linguistic ability to pick up the language after coming to New York. Most of the documents we have from the other brothers are in German, and Theodore's English, of which we have occasional examples, was more or less rudimentary. There is some indication that Henry, Sr., not only did not learn English but refused to do so, and he may have been illiterate, able perhaps to write his name but possibly no more. The language generally used in the Steinway factory was German into the twentieth century. But William, dealing with English-speaking customers and other businessmen, had to be fluent in English. He remained fluent in German as well, as many letters and other documents show.

[3] The diary is the principal source of the information that forms the basis of this article. I am engaged, with Cynthia Adams Hoover of the Smithsonian Institution and a group of volunteer researchers, in editing and annotating the diary with a view to publishing it. It has been made available to us through the enthusiasm and kindly cooperation of Henry Z. Steinway, its owner and former president of Steinway & Sons.

[4] The last entry in the diary is dated 8 November 1896, and William died on 30 November. In the early years, a good many days have no entry except the date and the day (sometimes marginal marks that almost certainly record sexual activity between William and his wife), and on a few occasions later in his life a serious illness—usually a heavy attack of gout—kept him from making any entries for some time. An attack of gout, for instance, put him completely out of commission and prevented any entries in his diary between 5-25 January 1875.

[5] In the early years, William wrote the German words in the old script, which is sometimes nearly illegible. As he got older, he used that script much less.

[6] We judge this from the fact that the partners signed the annual inventory, and Albert's signature does not appear until the signing in 1866 of the inventory taken for the year 1865.

[7] This is No. 49 in a collection of Steinway documents, mostly letters, of which photocopies are at the Smithsonian and originals are in the La Guardia-Wagner Archives at La Guardia Community College, Long Island City.

[8] I can summarize further company developments. Henry Sr. died in 1871, and the partnership became a closely held corporation in 1876, of which William was president and treasurer until his death. Albert died rather suddenly in 1877. During the late 1870s, several nephews came into the company, and in 1880, William and Theodore between them having

established a factory in Hamburg, Germany, Theodore returned to Braunschweig, where he lived until his death in 1889.

[9]Chickering & Sons in Boston had been the largest, but by 1870 Steinway was making about two thousand pianos a year, Chickering about fifteen hundred (see Good, *Giraffes, Black Dragons, and Other Pianos* [Stanford, CA: Stanford University Press, 1982], 203).

[10]Steinway & Sons made its first grand in 1857 and received the patent for the cross-strung grand frame in 1859. Grands, of course, were the staple of concert pianism, and Steinway aimed at that exposure very early in its career.

[11]On 31 October 1862 appears this entry: "Chas. to New Haven for Mills concert," which suggests that Mills was playing Steinways by then, for one would not expect a family member to go to New Haven otherwise.

[12]Wolfssohn (1834-1907) lived in Philadelphia but played often in New York.

[13]De Meyer (1816-1883) was not, of course, a New York pianist but a famous European, "the Lion Pianist," touring under Steinway's auspices. It was his first American tour in twenty years.

[14]On the wall of Henry Z. Steinway's room in Steinway Hall on 57th Street today is a large oil portrait of William Mason, presented by his family to the Steinways. Mills occasionally played other pianos than Steinway (William refers to his performance once on a Steck grand), but he and William were relatively close, and Mills played at a party in March 1872 that William gave to celebrate the engagement of his niece, Louisa Vogel, to Gustav Deppermann. (Another performer at that party was Pablo de Sarasate.)

[15]Diary, 3 June 1870.

[16]On the importance of these international fairs to the development of the piano trade, see Good, 175-76.

[17]In *Giraffes*, 181, I stated mistakenly that William was present at the Paris exposition. It was in reading the diary that I discovered that error (among others).

[18]The diary entry reads: "Telegram from Theodore Victory of the Overstrung System." It is not clear whether "Victory of the Overstrung System" quotes Theodore's cable or summarizes it. Chickering's winning grand did not have cross-stringing, for which the company would have had to pay royalties to Steinway as the patentee.

[19]I would say, with some regret, that Chickering failed precisely to take advantage of its chance to make a larger splash on the world scene. I have not studied the company closely enough to diagnose wherein the failure lay.

[20]Good, 218.

[21]The entry is a sample of William's style. The entire diary is rather terse in this way, not at all philosophic, not reflective. William sets down what happened, who he saw at what occasions, and very little else. Rarely, as here, he remarks briefly on his own or others' reactions to things. It is a major reason why editing the diary necessitates adding annotations to flesh out the document's own very bare bones. William probably wrote it for himself, as an *aide mémoire*, and could remind himself of details and feelings by reading the facts.

[22]George Clinton Densmore Odell, *Annals of the New York Stage* (New York: Columbia University Press, 1936), Vol. VIII, 229. The orchestra was probably Theodore Thomas's own. Parepa sang "Bel raggio" from Rossini's *Semiramide*, "The Nightingale's Trill" (no doubt a coloratura showpiece), and, with Brignoli, the duet "Da quel di" from Donizetti's *Linda di Chamounix*. Mills played the first movement of Robert Schumann's piano concerto.

[23]Odell, VIII, 237. The Philharmonic played five concerts in the season in those days (though William mentions only four in the diary for 1866-1867). There were two public rehearsals for the 17 November concert. The orchestra's sojourn in Steinway Hall was not profitable, as Howard Shanet points out in *Philharmonic: A History of New York's Orchestra* [New York: Doubleday, 1975], 128-29). Though rent was only $1,000 instead of $2,750 at the Academy, the smaller seating capacity of Steinway Hall brought receipts from ticket sales down from $13,900 in 1865-1866 to $9,500 in 1866-1867. When the orchestra returned to the rebuilt Academy for the 1867-1868 season, receipts went higher than ever. See also Shanet, 435, note 74.

[24]William's entry is "Mason plays Beethoven: Concerto very finely." "Finely" is one of his very few English inelegances.

[25]The auditorium was in the same building on East 14th Street as the Steinway showrooms. Indeed, the best way to get to it was through those rooms.

[26]William and Bristow later locked horns over the piano-manufacturers' competition at the Philadelphia Centennial Exhibition in 1876. Bristow, who was one of the jurors, favored Weber over Steinway in the competition, though he, with the other jurors, signed a certificate in 1877 that avowed Steinway's "Highest degree of excellence in all their styles." See Cynthia Adams Hoover, "The Great Piano Wars of the 1870s," *A Celebration of American Music: Words and Music in Honor of H. Wiley Hitchcock*, ed. Ott et al. (Ann Arbor, MI: University of Michigan Press, 1990), esp. 142-47.

[27] Chickering's sponsorship of von Bülow was also in imitation of Steinway's sponsorship of the great United States tour by Anton Rubinstein (1829-1894) in 1872-1873. Such sponsorship of artists was also nothing new.

[28] Unlike such European pianist-manufacturers as Muzio Clementi and Henri Herz, American makers seldom played very much. One exception was Albert Weber (1828-1879), who is said by Dolge to have been a very fine pianist, though he did not, so far as I have discovered, perform in public, except in church on the organ. See Alfred Dolge, *Pianos and Their Makers* (Covina, CA: Corvina Publishing, 1911; reprint New York: Dover, 1972), 296-98.

[29] See the article in this volume by Mary Sue Morrow, which has a good deal to say about the Liederkranz. I am grateful to her and to the editor for the opportunity to see her article before mine was finished.

[30] The occasion of the schism, in 1854, was, at least in part, the Liederkranz's revolutionary decision to allow women into the society for the purpose of presenting works both for female chorus and for mixed voices. The gentlemen of the Arion wanted no such thing! But they also complained about the food at the club. See *History of the Liederkranz of the City of New York, 1847 to 1947, and of the Arion, New York,* compiled by the History Committee (New York: Dreschel, 1948), 8.

[31] *New Grove*, s.v. "Schubert, Franz."

[32] *History of the Liederkranz*, 12. The cast included Johanna Rotter, soprano, and F. Wack (Odell, VIII, 212).

[33] The instances where William mentions that family members attended a concert or opera and he did not are quite rare, and the "opera concerts" as distinguished from operas number only three.

[34] Many of the German beer-halls regularly presented quite respectable concerts along with their food and drink. Theodore Thomas himself, that pillar of musical probity, presented summer concerts at places like the Terrace Garden.

[35] All of these performances are in addition to the times that William himself performed privately or publicly.

[36] William later met and became friends with Adelina Patti, but he does not seem to have heard her in the years covered by this essay. We do not know whether he heard Jenny Lind in her famous Barnum tour. He never says so.

[37] See Dizikes, *Opera in America* (New Haven: Yale University Press, 1993), 175. *Faust* was first performed in the U.S. in Philadelphia, in German, on 18 November 1863, and was given in Italian under Max Maretzek's direction on 25 November 1863, with Clara Louise Kellogg as

Margarita. It "became the most popular opera in America for the next half century," claims Dizikes, and he may have understated the time. Some dissenting voices were heard: George Templeton Strong, the famous diarist, and William Henry Fry, the American composer, agreed in thinking that Gounod could not write melodies, and orchestra musicians found the music disconcertingly hard to play. Dizikes, 189, quotes a wonderful sentence from Edith Wharton's *Age of Innocence* on Kristina Nilsson's singing *Faust* in Italian: "An unalterable and unquestioned law of the musical world required that the German text of French operas sung by Swedish artists should be translated into Italian for the clearer understanding of English-speaking audiences."

[38] William saw *Czar und Zimmermann* three times within a month: on 26 September, 17 October, and 20 October 1862. He next saw it only in 1870, having perhaps been surfeited eight years earlier!

[39] Several of these works, let it be noted, were presented in German translation. I give the French titles in the interests of ease of reference.

[40] But William several times sang the duet "Tornami a dir che m'ami" for tenor and soprano from this opera.

[41] William does not mention it by name, but he saw it at the Academy of Music on a double bill with the first American performance of Donizetti's *Betly* on 28 October 1861. Clara Louise Kellogg (1842-1916), the famous American soprano, was the prima donna, and Pasquale Brignoli (1824-1884) was the tenor. See Odell, VII, 427.

[42] See *New Grove*, s.v. "Petrella, Errico."

[43] William said in the diary that it was "done very well." But perhaps it was not worth doing.

[44] A quick count of operas broadcast from 1931 to 1950 from the Metropolitan Opera in New York as listed in Paul Jackson, *Afternoons at the Old Met: Metropolitan Opera Broadcasts, 1931-1950* (Portland, OR: Amadeus, 1992), 508-28, showed that seventy different operas were broadcast in those nineteen years. It is hard to assess the comparability of the numbers.

[45] I am, of course, aware that not everything that Odell lists took place as stated. Nevertheless, the picture that emerges from Odell, VIII, 559-693, covering the 1869-1870 season, is not totally misleading.

[46] Odell calls him only H. Grau, but William refers to him by name in the diary on 30 December 1872.

[47] For a reason I do not know, he refers to nothing between 17 December 1866 and 1 January 1867, though programs were presented then.

[48] The last named no doubt the principal artist's husband; see Odell, VIII, 230.

[49] Odell, VIII, 230.

[50] Like all such concerts, this was probably a potpourri of different artists doing different artistic things. I say "probably" because Odell, VIII, 230, identifies the concert as a "benefit" for Morgan, which usually meant that the beneficiary also performed, along with a troupe of assisting artists, whereas William calls it "Morgans Organ Concert," which suggests (but does not necessitate) an unassisted performance. Solo recitals in those days were not unknown, but they were very rare.

[51] See the mostly humorous account of de Meyer's American tour in the 1840s in Harold Schonberg, *The Great Pianists* (New York: Simon & Schuster, 1963), 179-87. Schonberg quotes *Dwight's Journal of Music* on the 1868 tour as saying that de Meyer was "more extravagant than ever," referring to de Meyer's frequent clowning and other idiosyncratic behavior. Bernard Ullmann, who had been Henri Herz's agent in a controversy with de Meyer in 1845, claimed in *Dwight's Journal* (as Schonberg notes) that Steinway had paid de Meyer $15,000 to play Steinway pianos. The truth of that matter would be hard to uncover. Ullmann was the agent of Hans von Bülow in the latter's 1875-1876 tour for Chickering, and he tried then, too, to introduce controversy with Steinway. No doubt it was one of the ways you played the game in those days.

[52] Odell does not mention the concert, which is, of course, no evidence that it did not take place. And I have not found any newspaper announcement, though one would be expected in the *New York Times* or the *New York Herald*.

[53] Odell, VIII, 336, ungraciously says of Ms. Lumley-Blath, "good name for a contralto." Report of the concert is in Odell, VIII, 370. Fred Steins was in considerable demand for such assisting roles in concerts. He was a lifelong close friend of William, his name appears frequently in the diary, and they often sang together, both in Liederkranz events and in private.

[54] William did not reveal his opinion of the Dickens readings, which garnered tremendous interest and great attention. Gout, by the way, was a longtime problem for William. He had his first serious attack of what seems gout at age thirty (he called it rheumatism, and tended later, when gout had definitely been diagnosed, to use the two terms more or less interchangeably), and it plagued him for the rest of his life. His diet did nothing to mitigate it, being very rich.

[55] *Resonances: 1836-1850* (New York and Oxford: Oxford University Press: 1988), the first volume of Lawrence's work *Strong on Music: The New York Musical Scene in the Days of George Templeton Strong, 1836-1875*, is much more than a commentary on Strong's activities, but gives complete information about what was happening musically in New York. I expect a great deal of help from her in the next volume(s).

MRS. POTIPHAR AT THE OPERA: SATIRE, IDEALISM, AND CULTURAL AUTHORITY IN POST–CIVIL WAR NEW YORK

Karen Ahlquist

> While lull'd by Sound, and undisturb'd
> by Wit,
> Calm and Serene you indolently sit;
> And from the dull Fatigue of Thinking
> free,
> Hear the facetious Fiddles Repartie.
> Our homespun authors must forsake the
> field,
> And Shakespeare to the soft Scarlatti
> yield.
> Joseph Addison, 1707[1]

> The opera seems to many philosophers
> an illogical absurdity, and it invites
> delightful satire. But the human mind is
> very complex.
> George William Curtis, 1875[2]

> Literary criticism is always impelled
> sooner or later to become social
> criticism.
> Van Wyck Brooks, 1956[3]

With debates on artistic canons at the forefront of scholarly life and even in public consciousness, the issue of the European patrimony in American culture looms larger than ever. Social factors are particularly contested. With regard to music, Ralph Locke argues that explanations of the canon's origin and growth in nineteenth-century America are sometimes framed in terms of "a small social elite concerned primarily either with assuring themselves a pleasant evening's entertainment or, worse, with celebrating their worldly position and lording it over the lower classes." He contrasts these explanations with "overwhelming evidence of the responsiveness and the personal devotion that marked the listening experiences of many nineteenth- and early twentieth-century listeners of different backgrounds."[4] In this essay, I wish to grant outright the existence of this "responsiveness and personal devotion" to music among at least some Americans. After all, it should be hard to imagine a musical culture developing without genuine interest among its participants.[5] But as Locke emphasizes, explanations based on "exclusivist motives" can easily overwhelm more evenhanded accounts. He even finally asks current musicologists: "Why should our scholarly attitudes toward such [previous] music lovers' motives, or toward the motives of those that supplied them with this music [i.e., patrons], be heavily colored by a cynical mistrust?"[6]

Why indeed?

Such explanations are hardly new; an anti-elite tradition in American art criticism can be documented from colonial times and to England as well. Opera, of course, is the *bête noir* of an anti-elite critic. Yet with the rehabilitation in recent years of nineteenth-century bel canto opera, it seems that a look at this tradition is in order. This essay deals with the roots of anti-elite opera criticism. Noting how easy it has been to accept a negative stance toward opera and its audience as true and natural, it will note critical agendas not only when we disagree with them today (as in the case of Addison and Steele on Handel) but also when we are more inclined to agree (could Edith Wharton have been wrong about Gilded Age operagoers?). Thus the issue of elite culpability in creating the "class character" of operagoing is here beside the point. Instead, I will focus on the critical approach itself, looking for the intellectual rationales behind the social assessments of opera and asking two questions: What is the position of the critic relative to the object of criticism? and, When opera is successfully derided as elite, who benefits?

The great growth of "serious" musical life in mid-to-late nineteenth-century America has been well studied.[7] Led by German immigrant "missionaries" such as Theodore Thomas and the Damrosch family, promoting serious music—or more aptly, serious attitudes toward music—filled a social, institutional, moral, and aesthetic space the previous musical culture had left open for it. A large and growing German immigrant population provided both performers and audience members to support this new endeavor. But immigration was only a precondition and, as such, only part of the story. Perhaps more interesting (because more complex) is the Anglo-American population's willingness to accept this music wholeheartedly, and, of greater import here, with their spokesmen's endorsement. Intellectuals—i.e., educated commentators on music— played an important role in establishing the success and high prestige of German music in late nineteenth-century American society. With strong anti-elite biases inherited from England up against a newly blossoming musical life, intellectuals had to rationalize democratic principles of long-standing with a new musical idealism. In so doing, they came to see the German tradition as a solution to the problem of creating an American musical life worthy of the term "culture."

American musical anti-elitism can be traced to its English counterpart.[8] Perhaps most famously, eighteenth-century intellectuals such as Joseph Addison, Richard Steele, and Jonathan Swift mocked opera audiences in the name of British chauvinism and the superiority of the word over music's essential frivolity. Opera, performed by Italian companies in Italian and featuring the castrato hero, seemed to exaggerate foreignness at a time when Englishness was increasingly being defined in anticontinental terms. Opera and its advocates were linked with the Hanoverian monarchy and its first minister, Robert Walpole. Lacking political clout, opera's critics aimed to enhance their position by out-Englishing the monarchial party. Thus as Richard Leppert observes, in 1711 one such critic, John Dennis, "virtually accuses English supporters of Italian opera of being enemies of the state":

> If they are so fond of the Italian Musick, why do they not take it from the Hay-Market [Theatre] to their Houses, and hug it like their secret Sins there? ... Is there not an implicit Contract between all the People of every Nation, to espouse one another's Interest against all Foreigners whatsoever?... Why ... should they prefer Italian Sound to British Sense, Italian Nonsense to British Reason, the Blockheads of Italy to their own Countrymen, who have Wit; and the Luxury, and Effeminacy of the most profligate Portion of the Globe to the British Virtue?[9]

Dennis's denigration of Italian opera epitomizes the classic British anti-opera perspective. Linking opera to the cliché of the unintelligent and immoral Italian, critics likewise denigrated music ("Italian Sound") as lacking the intellectual content found in words. From a non-elite social position, they censured opera as an official culture favored by a political and social in-crowd either incapable of recognizing opera's inferiority or willing to put up with it to enhance their positions.

These critics are perhaps most famous by today's standards for being wrong about opera and about Handel. But their insistence that they were intellectually superior to the opera audiences was—and still is—powerful and compelling. Placing the "critical center" below the upper class, Addison and the others distinguished between intellectual superiority and high social position and undermined a simple high-low equation between a repertoire's formality and the intellectual status of its audience. In asserting their view of the social role and class reach of various forms of musical culture, they linked social and musical criticism and asserted their own critical authority.[10]

This blend of anti-elitism and musical deprecation was not unique to Handel's London. Rather, it crossed the Atlantic and took hold. As in England, musical life in colonial America and the early Republic was extensive and varied. Polemics against music were fewer in colonial America than in England and came from fewer quarters. While the Puritan critique (sometimes centered on instrumental music) was substantial, it did not reach far beyond the New England churches that inherited the issue from the Mother Country.[11] Despite the critique, many eighteenth-century Americans, like the English, accepted music as entertainment. There is evidence that domestic music-making was pursued by eighteenth-century Americans as a sign of genteel aspiration. Moreover, the immediate post-Revolutionary period even brought a growing concert life that included large-scale performances of European music (notably Handel). Yet one can also find evidence of an anti-genteel attitude that included music among other signs of overrefinement, to be distinguished from good breeding. John Adams, for example, linked it with monarchy as against hardy republicanism:

> A monarchy would probably, somehow or other make me rich, but it
> would produce so much Taste and Politeness, so much Elegance in

Dress, Furniture, Equipage, so much Musick and Dancing, so much Fencing and Skaiting, so much Cards and Backgammon, so much Horse Racing and Cockfighting, so many Balls and Assemblies, so many Plays and Concerts that the very Imagination of them makes me feel vain, light, frivolous and insignificant.[12]

Adams's seeming fear of leisure for its own sake puts music in good company. His comment probably also says more about his outlook on life in general than on music in particular. But in denigrating signs of economic and social advantage, he does foster the notion of popular activity as republican and, therefore, more genuine than such "vain, light, and frivolous" activities as concerts. And of course music formed a major part of a growing popular culture that was broadly accessible, pro-American, and, by the 1830s, self-consciously pro-Jacksonian "common man."[13] John Adams's antimonarchical attitudes had become virulently anti-"aristocratic." Not simply wealth (indeed, it can be argued that Americans have always admired wealth, especially when self-made), but signs of a lack of humble origin could bring on condemnation of "fashionable" elitism. The charges against opera in America as it struggled to establish itself were vigorously put forth. For example, the institution of opera separate from theater in nineteenth-century New York makes a telling case study, a colorful and often-told story in which an entrepreneurial spirit dedicated to "naturalizing" opera in New York stood in conflict with the old anti-elite interpretation of opera as a haven for the wealthy and ostentatious.[14] The opera season managed by Giocomo Montresor (1832), the Italian Opera House (1833-35) and, more famously, the Astor Place Opera House (1849-52) inspired commentary—much of it anonymous writings in the city's burgeoning press—worthy of Addison and Steele. As in Handel's London, mocking opera audiences made for easy fun. On the Montresor company, imported by a group of wealthy New Yorkers with help from Mozart's now-aged librettist Lorenzo da Ponte, the aptly-named *Spirit of the Times* gloated:

Another circumstance has created some talk with the gossips.... The Opera House was not *crammed* on Monday night. Those not initiated into the mysteries of the *ton* cannot conceive the sensation such an event creates in "good society." What? The patrons of the Opera to suffer the mortification of not rendering popular to any extent, what

their judgment approves? Are the *elite* to be told that MISS
KEMBLE is more attractive than PEDROTTI?[15]

In this telling commentary, the *Spirit* took delight in the failure of an
enterprise organized and sanctioned by members of the upper class.
Further, it hinted that the *bon ton* was either too naive or too arrogant
to notice that its tastes did not suit all New Yorkers. Equating opera's
social setting with the genre itself, the *Spirit* rejected the latter on
account of the former.

Non-elite New Yorkers would be needed to make opera
succeed. In 1835, a writer for the *American Musical Journal*
summarized the tension between opera as private, upper-class
entertainment and its need—both ideological and financial—for a
broader public:

> If the proprietors of the [Italian Opera House] are determined to keep
> it for their own amusement, as a sort of private establishment, it is
> incumbent on them to assume the entire management and the whole
> responsibility. No one will have any right to complain of such a
> course. But if, on the contrary, they really wish to establish
> permanently the Opera in this city, then such changes in the present
> arrangement as experience indicate to be necessary to effect this
> object should be disinterestedly and at once adopted.[16]

These "changes in the present arrangement" put the finger on the
overriding issue facing opera's proponents in New York before the
Academy of Music succeeded in 1854: access. Opera needed to be
available to the "common man" at prices he could afford. In those
circumstances, opera would succeed or fail on the votes of the broad
theatergoing public. Presumably success with this public would
render opera democratic and hence American. And on these terms
opera established itself as commercial entertainment. Advertising
replaced high prices as the chief method of income production, and
the 4,600-seat auditorium of the Academy of Music held all comers,
including wealthy boxholders and many others. Sometimes taking a
leaf from P. T. Barnum, entrepreneurs such as Max Maretzek,
Bernard Ulmann, and Max Strakosch made concessions to the
extremes of Jacksonian society, offering at the Academy both elite-
derived social panache and broad access.[17]

But while opera's entrepreneurial basis allowed it to be considered "American," it also moved opera beyond the realm of new cultural ideals beginning to permeate thinking on music. The Academy of Music came too late; by the 1850s opera as a commercial endeavor was achieved at the cost of a new respect accorded "serious" music. Reaching America in the 1840s, the new idealism was removed both from the world of everyday culture and from the commercial world that had created opera's success. Neatly summed up in Matthew Arnold's phrase "the best which has been thought and said in the world," cultural idealism responded to the great social upheavals of the nineteenth century and tried to address the problems they created. In *Culture and Anarchy* (1869), the English critic Arnold advocated culture as a way to "see things as they are" and hence "escape the thraldom of the moment." Having studied "the law of perfection," he argued, one could achieve an understanding of "the nature of real good, and [arrive] nearer to a condition of mind out of which really fruitful and solid [reform] operations may spring."[18]

Many educated Americans espoused Arnold's ideals. New York historian Thomas Bender refers to "Brownstone culture," the name derived from the comfortable row homes in which many cultured New Yorkers lived in the last third of the century. The intellectual descendants of Thomas Jefferson's "natural aristocracy," these individuals have been called the "metropolitan gentry" (also Bender's term), "cultured classes," "thoughtful classes," and, somewhat pejoratively, "genteel society."[19] Like Addison and Steele in the *Spectator*, the journalists and essayists among them addressed like-minded readers in magazines of relatively small circulation. But as the term "thoughtful" suggests, their tone is mellower than that of the sharp-tongued eighteenth-century writers or the caustic, anonymous critics of the Jacksonian era. Recognizing the intractability of the great social problems under consideration, they were simultaneously willing to consider alternative solutions and firm in their belief that the best answers would come from them.[20]

The new cultural ideal speaks to this belief. "The men of culture are the true apostles of equality," Arnold asserted.[21] He was, however, no democrat. Rather, he argued that creating and empowering an educated elite of farsighted individuals who would be recognized as such would produce solutions to problems for the good of all. Culture would ideally lead authority away from the wealthy and place it in the hands of intellectuals chosen on merit. The appeal of such a program to an educated member of the middle class is obvious. So are the problems it creates. What, for example, should constitute the "culture" that would place a person in this category? What characteristics does this individual have? What does he *not* have? How should his authority be asserted, especially in a democratic society with a commercial economic base? And finally, how should he approach the problems of the day, and how could culture aid in their solution?

The new cultural ideal was a boon to music. There was no question that music was—or could be—culture. In both Europe and America, increased musical participation and music's enhanced status were everywhere evident. Despite criticism, opera became more widespread and successful as the nineteenth century progressed. Even the more common musical genres such as parlor song, often derided as sentimental, were created and understood as more than just entertainment.[22] As has been well-documented, German immigration fostered the growth of high-cultural musical institutions and an increasing German orientation of organizations such as the New York Philharmonic. So spread the idea of a musical canon—a body of works to be regarded as "the best which has been thought and said" through music. More to the point, however, is the growing idealism among Anglo-American commentators on music, including most prominently the long-influential Boston critic John Sullivan Dwight. In the spirit of Arnold, Dwight extolled the value of music as a cultural pursuit. "Music is an expresson of character," he asserted in 1870, "of the moods, the spirit, the meaning of the man that makes it." To Dwight, great composers were great intellects even if lacking formal education. Through "their sufferings, ... their willing martyrdom to the ideal of their art," they offered an emotional, intellectual, and spiritual experience that ennobled the serious listener, allowing "instincts [to] get attuned into a sympathy with universal law and unity."[23] Like culture on Arnold's model, music helped one reach beyond the mundane affairs of ordinary life, take advantage of "the free play of the mind," and finally understand how society's problems could adequately be addressed.

Intellectuals coming from the old tradition—the one that favored the word over music and censured attempts to use music-making as social pretention—now had to deal with two important changes: a wider range of music in successful public settings, and music's growing prestige. Yet the new musical culture was still subject to charges of elitism. While literary life could be achieved in small, inaccessible venues of salons, dinner parties, and little magazines, music involved public performance, which encompassed "uncultured" genres such as minstrelsy and opera buffa. Its institutional setting, aesthetic character, and level of support were all subject to debate. Thus the new idea of culture pitted traditional American democratic values against the seeming social limitations of the culture itself.

The issue became more acute in New York after the Civil War because of an increasing gulf between wealth and poverty. "Perhaps in no other great city, whether European or American, was social inequality so extreme," Bender writes, calling the situation "the defining circumstance of life in Gilded Age New York." With such a gap between the city's "new and very rich class of crude capitalists" (as Bender calls them) and "the ignorant masses," the problem for a generation of thinkers and writers was to forge an appropriate response.[24] Seeing culture as anticommercial and an alternative to the pursuit of money allowed cultured critics to advocate intellect as a quality of leadership, link intellect with character, distinguish such leaders from the moneyed classes, and (in some cases) imagine expanding the cultured ranks by expanding education. In music, achieving the ideal of a cultured democracy meant carving out a social space and an appropriate repertoire. To succeed as definers of this artistic core and to credibly articulate its social boundaries, cultured critics needed first of all to separate anti-elitism from disdain for music. Music would have to be established as culture on both an aesthetic and a social basis.

From this perspective, deprecating elites at the Italian opera still played a role. But music could itself no longer take the beating given it in Handel's London or in Jacksonian New York. Walt Whitman's change of heart regarding opera shows the influence of musical culture on social commentary. Whitman, a self-styled democrat, "man of the people," and advocate of culture for all classes, was also a typical journalist: colorful, blunt in his assessments, and engaged in the social issues of his day. In 1855 his report on the Academy of Music for the out-of-town readers of *Life Illustrated* presents a voyeuristic approach to elites in the audience:

Look at that woman just stepping to the pavement!... A half-indifferent look she gave to the crowd, every one of whom renders to her his mute admiration, and then she passed on. The gentleman ... is a mean-looking man, forty-five or fifty years old, a very rich banker and capitalist. She was of poor family, and married him for his wealth, and has no love or respect for him. You can see many such couples at the opera.

Whitman gives us the classic critique: the man is implicitly condemned for the pursuit of money, the woman explicitly for the pursuit of social position. Neither has admirable qualities; indeed, Whitman ends his account by asking, "Would not a commoner gathering of every-day people, with friendship, and jokes, and plenty of fun and laughter, be more of a satisfaction?"[25]

Yet after several years of dismissing opera as un-American in its substance, Whitman was finally converted to its cause. In an 1845 manifesto, "Art-Singing and Heart-Singing," he had objected to "the stale, second-hand, foreign method, with its flourishes, its ridiculous sentimentality, its anti-republican spirit, and its sycophantic influence, tainting the young taste of the republic."[26] Ten years later, however, Verdi's music, no longer tainted by un-American, "ridiculous sentimentality," could even transcend his negative social interpretation of the Academy of Music:

The orchestra is full ... and at the signal of the leader they begin.... The crowded tiers—the gas-lights—the rich and novel spectacle—the beautiful women—vanish from your eyes and thoughts with the first beat of the drum. It is the stormy music of Giuseppe Verdi; it is the noble opera of *Ernani*. With the rise of the curtain you are transported afar—such power has music.... If you have the true musical feeling in you, from this night you date a new era in your development, and, for the first time, receive your ideas of what the divine art of music really is.[27]

Whitman accepted a European-based cultural offering as American and worthwhile. But in satirizing upper-class operagoers, he also served as a prototype for a new critical approach. While Addison and Steele and the Jacksonian writers mocked opera—both substance and setting—from beyond its doors, Whitman had become an insider. The distinction is important. It is easy to accuse the eighteenth-century London critics of failing to give opera a fair hearing. But Whitman did give it one. Thus he comes across as thoughtful, dispassionate, and evenhanded. Moreover, in recommending to his out-of-town readers of *Life Illustrated* magazine that they visit the opera themselves, he fostered its success as emanating from the free choice of the citizenry at large. He both recognized the power and worth of complex music and distanced himself from the economic and social elites with which it had long been associated.

But Whitman was not quite a "cultured" writer. For in favoring culture's support by a broad constituency, he implicitly supported its commercial basis. Thus he failed to support an anticommercial attitude that became a central tenet of the new idealism. Cultured writers sought to distinguish between the trappings of success and true good breeding. The origins of such a view precede Matthew Arnold's 1869 statement of it. Emerson, for example, distinguished between economic success and intellectual and moral superiority; he also placed the wealthy beyond the cultured realm.[28] Further, as Karen Halttunen has shown, advice literature addressed to young Americans represented an "effort to establish that it was possible to know something about the character of a stranger" by his outward presentation.[29] That which is authentic cannot be bought. Those who have bought their social position are unable to distinguish authenticity from artificiality, for the profit motive that created their wealth has also disabled their judgment. The wealthy individual will seek a quick fix rather than make a sustained effort for quality. And his manners are merely "fashionable" rather than innately "fine."[30]

Closer than Whitman to the center of the cultured approach to music was the New York–based journalist and essayist George William Curtis (1824-1892). A few years younger than the poet, Curtis was the most prominent journalist after Whitman to deal seriously with both music and broader social and political concerns. Thus (like Whitman) he shows music as still important to a wide readership in the nineteenth century. More politically oriented than Dwight, his lifelong friend and fellow Brook Farmer, Curtis used his forty-year tenure as editor of *Harper's* to advocate full citizenship for southern blacks after the Civil War, women's suffrage, civil service reform, and the eight-hour day for workers. He spoke out against the Tammany Hall political machine and the spoils system, running unsuccessfully as a reform candidate for public office. In demand as a lecturer, he often spoke on relations between education and society. And Bender tells us that in the 1880s, even in competition with Mark Twain and William Dean Howells, he was the favorite American writer of the student body at Harvard.[31]

One of Curtis's main themes was the obligation of the cultured man in public affairs. Refusing to grant value to learning for its own sake, Curtis insisted that "The Duty of the American Scholar" was to join "a class which, by its very character, is dedicated to eternal and not to temporary interests."[32] Above all, temporary interests meant striving for material success; private gain stood opposed to public good. At the time of this early speech, 1856, the great issue of the day was slavery, and before exhorting his hearers at Wesleyan University to fight it tooth and nail, he argued that "it fosters [in the slavemasters] pride, indolence, luxury, and licentiousness, which equally imbrute the human being. Therefore, in the slave States there is no literature, no art, no progressive civilization."[33] With the Civil War's end, other, less urgent issues took the place of the great battle over slavery vs. freedom. Yet Curtis continued to urge "college men" (he saw higher education as the clearest marker of cultured status) to move beyond individual interest and comfort to act on behalf of the general welfare. And like Arnold, he believed that education equipped one to know just what the general welfare would be.

He also claimed to know who would *not* know. Curtis, like other New Yorkers of his generation, believed that social criticism was part and parcel of a literary or journalistic career.[34] An early set of sketches, *The Potiphar Papers* (1853), set the tone for a lighthearted, satirical style of social commentary and an approach to social elites that he later tempered, but never completely abandoned. Peopled with characters such as the dowager Mrs. Settum Downe, the Reverend Cream Cheese, and Mrs. Potiphar herself, *The Potiphar Papers* lampooned the habits of New York's nouveaux riches and exposed what he considered their failures of integrity and moral rectitude.[35] He maintained this approach in his column, "The Editor's Easy Chair," in *Harper's*.[36] Like Whitman, who mocked what he saw as unmerited superior attitudes of the wealthy, Curtis derided failures of common courtesy that led to the inconvenience or even suffering of others. In a typical scene, members of the diamond-studded Hogsflesh family disturb a concert audience by noisily arriving late and taking the best seats in the house.[37] Ill behavior at a cultured public event such as a performance of "good" music could graphically symbolize the ethical failures of the new upper class.

Curtis's equation of high social position and moral inadequacy affected his musical judgments. But it did not overwhelm them; although trained in aesthetics by Dwight, his musical tastes were broader. He liked both Beethoven and Wagner, and saw the need to like the one only at the expense of the other as small-minded.[38] He enjoyed a Strauss waltz and remarked over the "continuing spell of the old and familiar" operas such as *La sonnambula* and *Lucia di Lammermoor*.[39] He even refuted Addison, Steele, and John Dennis by name for their literalistic approach to opera's "absurdities." "The gravity of their censure is hardly less amusing than the absurdity which they attack," he argued, adding, "The critic might as well sneer at a fairy tale."[40] Reluctant to dismiss musical styles out of hand, he judged as cultured an individual who sought in music Arnoldian "eternal and not ... temporary interests." Recognizing excellence marked one's entitlement to a position of cultural and political authority. From this perspective, marginalizing the wealthy was important, for their social standing could only be artificial and their tastes ignorant and vulgar.

Could one imagine Mrs. Potiphar appreciating Wagner? Along with other critics, Curtis answered with a resounding no. Of course Mrs. Potiphar predated the arrival of Wagner's music in New York, even in concert performance.[41] Yet Wagner and Wagnerism were well-suited for a cultural program that excluded her successors in the opera boxes. Wagner himself was an idealist, arguing forcefully for a cultural sphere independent of commercial constraints, the profit motive, and stardom. Even in the opera house, he maintained, entertainment values would no longer do. Wagner's own belief in culture as a social and moral force matched his disdain for the broader public.[42] Further, as Burton Peretti has shown, his character and personality—of humble origin, strong-willed, entrepreneurial, self-made, a creator of heroic characters—could be seen to fit an American democratic model.[43] Wagner offered a new repertoire of great rhetorical and dramatic power that challenged the minds of intellectuals but reached audiences on a visceral level as well. Wagnerism, a program derived from the composer's own writings, fascinated many cultured New Yorkers, advanced the composer's intellectual reputation, and offered an approach to the works themselves. It brought controversy and a richness of interpretative possibilities, and allowed Wagner himself to create the grounds on which his works were to be judged. Leaving nothing to chance, he let it be known that a music drama was not the disparaged elite genre, opera, but something new, to be received on new terms. His theory of drama, radically different from that of traditional Italian opera, argued that the latter's artificiality crippled it as a dramatic form. Although music's status in Anglo-American culture had risen in the nineteenth century, drama's status was of longer standing. Wagner's assertion of dramatic over musical values linked his "reforms" to important, traditional Anglo-American theatrical priorities.

What now could better demonstrate a new meaning of "culture" than the blossoming of a new repertoire? From this perspective, the key event in the early years of the Metropolitan Opera was less its founding in 1883 by big money (which in any case would have been the only way to raise the necessary capital) than the institution of German opera the following year. With the house in financial ruin, Leopold Damrosch (1832-1885), the German founder/conductor of the New York Oratorio and Symphony Societies, proposed a season of opera in German at reduced prices, arguing that the increase in attendance would more than offset losses. The Damrosch rescue mission was successful. Until his death in February 1885, Damrosch brought singers, chorus, and orchestra under control under cost, and the season all told brought in more than twice the revenue of the previous season at little more than half the previous admission charges.[44] German opera, led by Wagner's music dramas, could answer the search for a musical high culture on an educational rather than social class basis. Even the operatic superstar Adelina Patti could not stave off the eventual collapse of the competing Academy of Music in the face of German performances at the Metropolitan.

Not surprisingly, the thoughtful or cultured listeners who supported Wagner took the high ground, linking the economic elite with Italian opera, and placing both in a negative light.[45] As Curtis put it, "There was a universal feeling that the day of the exclusive glory of the Italian genius had passed."[46] It seemed clear to all concerned that the "flimsy and soporific" Italian opera could not hold up the mantle of music as edification.[47] Victory for German music even in the opera house served as an aesthetic and social symbol of the triumph of artistic excellence over claptrap, triviality, and performers' values. And while seven years of German opera (1884-

1891) did not put the class issue to rest, the elite stockholders lost even the perception that they had any power over the aesthetic agenda. While they eventually felt it important to show how much they hated the German regime, as long as it lasted, their distaste merely showed how critically irrelevant they had become.

To the extent that the problem of culture in a democratic society could be solved, German music was the solution. As Peretti points out, Wagner's music could be understood as both serious and broadly accessible.[48] By succeeding at the Metropolitan, Wagner's works replaced the notion of opera as elite entertainment with a model based on the new cultural ideals. His musical, dramatic, and rhetorical power filled a cultural hole created by the social and aesthetic criticism of Italian opera. The double criticism depicted a performance genre such as opera as both a dramatic and a social event. Thus it was essential that it succeed on both counts. In the realm of opera, Wagner's success marked the triumph of the cultural ideal, finally able to work its good over society as its advocates argued.

Yet in 1884, the critics and the criticized were in fact allied in the opera house under Wagner's artistic legacy. From his "inside" position, Curtis continued to censure elite audience members for ill behavior and suggested that they attended for the wrong reasons. The announcement in January 1891 that the Metropolitan would end its German-only policy inspired some of the sharpest barbs of his career. Curtis had many times placed Wagner in the canon of great masters along with Beethoven. He also enjoyed reminding his readers that Adelina Patti was paid $5,000 per performance (he would never say she *earned* that much).[49] He echoed both of these themes in a description of a Patti performance:

> Not Donizetti's night, nor Lucia's night, nor music's night, it was solely Patti's night.... There was no drama, no Lucia, no tragedy. There was a famous prima donna singing; a sole personality no longer fascinating. The curtain fell, the audience waited for "Home, sweet Home," then coolly arose and departed. There was apparently no interest, no real feeling. The singers had none, nor the prima donna, nor the orchestra, nor the audience. The performance gave an opportunity for an "ovation." That was all.[50]

Curtis blamed the Metropolitan stockholders for the coming return of this mode of performance. Accusing them of having only "said that they supplied the money for the maintenance of operas," he threatened that "if the boxes chatter, the parquet will hiss. If for that reason the parquet is closed to lovers of music, the opera itself will disappear."[51] For reasons he did not explain, Curtis considered the cultured parquet audience and the gentry critic better able to shut the opera down than the boxholders who paid its bills. Curtis's "lovers of music"—those who went to the opera for the right reasons—could be distinguished from both the upper class and the public at large.

In this manner the cultured critics circumscribed a narrow social milieu for opera performance, and hence for culture. Rather than democratize its benefits through wider dissemination, they subliminally advocated culture for the intellectual few, who would presumably be equipped to enhance the lives of the many. Thus they strengthened the charge that opera itself is inherently elite. They also reinforced the charge that they were out of touch, that their approach was a tepid and inadequate response to the pressing problems of the day.[52] And it does seem that they were unable to reach beyond the questions of "what is culture" and "who is cultured." George William Curtis supported Theodore Thomas's parks concerts, along with any effort to broaden the audience for "good" music in order to improve the lives of a wider segment of the population. But he devoted far more of the power of his pen to using the issue of audience behavior as a way to mock the boxholders. In so doing, he spoke against the capitalist class—against those who both underwrote the Metropolitan and were held accountable for gaping social inequities. But he never acknowledged the obstacles to extending his cultural ideals to a broader population. Like other critics of a similar cast, he could satisfy his conscience while committing himself to that population in only a limited way.

The problem of music as culture in a democratic society was not solved. In fact, this period may represent the last serious attempt to see "good" music as having value beyond itself. This failure was probably symptomatic of what Stow Persons calls the "decline" of American gentility.[53] The gentry critics succeeded in isolating themselves from the socioeconomic elite above them, but in music, not even Curtis made the great leap to the democracy below. This may have been a prophetic failure for American music history. In isolating his own small "class" as the proper audience for great art, Curtis marked that art, along with those who appreciated it, was marginal to any serious effort to address the day's issues. The agenda forced on the Metropolitan in its German years was aesthetic only, as writers focused on Wagner's music and his place in the canon.

With purely analytical approaches becoming more sophisticated, studying music for its own sake became more attractive. The separation of "serious" new music from the broader population, achieved by modernist intellectuals after Curtis's generation, advanced music's position in new intellectual communities. These individuals had no reason or need to adopt a benign attitude toward the public at large, much less its social elite. Moreover, the growth in the late nineteenth century and into the twentieth of an economically strong, self-consciously popular music shows how much cultural influence would come from other sources. This growth brought—and brings—an "outsider" approach toward opera to the fore, in turn magnifying the anti-elite critique. With insider critics in 1884 favoring the upstart Wagner against the wealthy stockholders, how easy is it a century later to see him—long since enshrined—as merely another staged event of an exclusive culture? If a sympathetic writer like Curtis, who enjoyed Italian opera and remembered its broad appeal at mid-century, could still write it off in 1884 as "a traditional fashion ... largely maintained as a social opportunity under conditions which most favored personal display and made the least intellectual demand," how easy is it for a latter-day Addison or Steele never to know that opera's audience had reached beyond the boxes?[54] And finally, as bel canto opera has once again been appreciated by audiences and scholars on new terms, might we not ask a historical question of the present: when opera is successfully derided as elite, who benefits?

The George Washington University

---

[1] Joseph Addison, Prologue to Edmund Smith, *Phaedra and Hippolitus*, 1707. Quoted in Eric Walter White, *A History of English Opera* (London: Faber & Faber, 1983), 143.

[2] George William Curtis, *Harper's Magazine* 52/1 (December 1875): 142.

[3]Introduction to Randolph Bourne, *The History of a Literary Radical* (New York: S. A. Russell, 1956). Quoted in Thomas Bender, *New York Intellect: A History of Intellectual Life in New York City, from 1750 to the Beginnings of Our Own Time* (New York: Knopf, 1987), 231.

[4]Ralph P. Locke, "Music Lovers, Patrons, and the 'Sacralization' of Culture in America," *19th Century Music* 17 (Fall 1993): 150, 162.

[5]Locke cites studies by Ruth Solie, Joseph Horowitz, Peter J. Rabinowitz, Michael Broyles, Katherine K. Preston, and Vera Lawrence to support this contention. I would point out especially Horowitz's use of a Willa Cather story, "A Wagner Matinée," in which a musically trained woman, long isolated in Nebraska, hears Wagner's music for the first time and is emotionally overcome ("They Stood Up and Screamed: American Wagnerism and the Women's Movement," a paper read for the American Musicological Society, Pittsburgh 1992).

[6]Locke, 160.

[7]George Martin, *The Damrosch Dynasty: America's First Family of Music* (Boston: Houghton Mifflin, 1983); Ezra Schabas, *Theodore Thomas: America's Conductor and Builder of Orchestras, 1835-1905* (Urbana: University of Illinois Press, 1989); and Howard Shanet, *Philharmonic: A History of New York's Orchestra* (Garden City, New York: Doubleday, 1975), Chapters 15-16.

[8]For a fuller account of the English background, along with operatic development and criticism in New York before the Civil War, see Karen Ahlquist, *Democracy at the Opera: Music, Theater, and Culture in New York City, 1815-60* (Urbana: University of Illinois Press; forthcoming).

[9]Dennis, *An Essay upon Publick Spirit*, quoted in Richard Leppert, "Imagery, musical confrontation and cultural difference in early 18th-century London," *Early Music* 14/3 (August 1986): 337. For similar commentary, see John Hollander, *The Untuning of the Sky: Ideas of Music in English Poetry, 1500-1700* (Princeton: Princeton University Press), 383 (Addison); Peter Cosgrove, "Affective Unities: The Esthetics of Music and Factional Instability in Eighteenth-Century England," *Eighteenth-Century Studies* 22/2 (Winter 1988-1989): 143 (Pope); and Roger Fiske, *English Theatre Music in the Eighteenth Century*, 2nd ed. (Oxford: Oxford University Press, 1986), 48-53, 127-28.

[10]For English attitudes toward music, see Linda Phyllis Austern, "'*Sing Again Syren*': The Female Musician and Sexual Enchantment in Elizabethan Life and Literature," *Renaissance Quarterly* 42 (Fall 1989): 420-88; and "Music and the English Renaissance Controversy over Women," *Cecilia Reclaimed: Feminist Perspectives on Gender and Music*, ed. Susan C. Cook and Judy S. Tsou (Urbana: University of Illinois Press, 1994); Richard Leppert, *Music and Image: Domesticity, Ideology and*

Socio-cultural Formation in Eighteenth-Century England (Cambridge: Cambridge University Press, 1988); and J. V. Guerinot and Rodney D. Jilg, *The Beggar's Opera* (Hamden, CT: Archon Books, 1976). On popular culture, see Ronald Paulson, *Breaking and Remaking: Aesthetic Practice in England, 1700-1820* (New Brunswick, NJ: Rutgers University Press, 1989). On elites in Handel's London as patrons and subscribers, see Carole Mia Taylor, *Italian Operagoing in London, 1700-1745* (Ph.D. diss., Syracuse University, 1991). Taylor has analyzed the social makeup of Handel's opera audiences from documentary sources and linked it to developments in his career.

[11]David P. McKay and Richard Crawford, *William Billings of Boston: Eighteenth-Century Composer* (Princeton: Princeton University Press, 1975), 3-9; Kenneth Silverman, *A Cultural History of the American Revolution* (New York: Thomas Y. Crowell, 1976), 39-41, 195-197; Mary Gosselink DeJong, "'Both Pleasure and Profit': William Billings and the Uses of Music," *William and Mary Quarterly* 42/1 (January 1985): 106-13.

[12]Letter to Mercy Warren (1776), quoted in Richard L. Bushman, "American High-Style and Vernacular Culture," *Colonial British America: Essays in the New History of the Early Modern Era*, ed. Jack P. Greene and J. R. Pole (Baltimore: Johns Hopkins University Press, 1984), 354-55.

[13]On the theater, including musical theater, see Susan L. Porter, *With an Air Debonair: Musical Theatre in America, 1785-1815* (Washington: Smithsonian Institution Press, 1991); David Grimsted, *Melodrama Unveiled: American Theater and Culture, 1800-1850* (Berkeley: University of California Press, 1987); and Francis Hodge, *Yankee Theatre: The Image of America on the Stage, 1825-1850* (Austin: University of Texas Press, 1964). On Jacksonian-era popular culture, especially in New York City, see Richard Stott, *Workers in the Metropolis: Class, Ethnicity, and Youth in Antebellum New York City* (Ithaca: Cornell University Press, 1990); Elliott J. Gorn, "'Good-Bye Boys, I die a True American': Homicide, Nativism, and Working-Class Culture in Antebellum New York City," *Journal of American History* 74/2 (September 1987): 388-410; Sean Wilentz, *Chants Democratic: New York City and the Rise of the American Working Class, 1788-1850* (New York: Oxford University Press, 1984); and Christine Stansell, *City of Women: Sex and Class in New York, 1789-1860* (Urbana: University of Illinois Press, 1987).

[14]See Ahlquist, Chapters 3 and 5; Peter Buckley, *"To the Opera House": Culture and Society in New York City, 1820-1860* (Ph.D. diss., State University of New York at Stony Brook, 1984); John Dizikes, *Opera in America, A Cultural History* (New Haven: Yale University Press, 1993); Vera Brodsky Lawrence, *Strong on Music*, Vol. 1 (New York: Oxford University Press, 1988) and 2 (Chicago: University of Chicago Press, 1995); Katherine K. Preston, *Opera on the Road: Traveling Opera Troupes in the United States, 1825-1860* (Urbana: University of Illinois Press, 1993).

[15]*Spirit of the Times*, 1/47 (17 November 1832). Teresa Pedrotti was performing at the same time that actress Fanny Kemble appeared at the Park Theatre.

[16]*American Musical Journal* 1/8 (July 1835): 189.

[17]Ahlquist, Chapter 5.

[18]*Culture and Anarchy*, ed. J. Dover Wilson (Cambridge: Cambridge University Press, 1963), 6, 70 ["best thought"], 44-45ff. ["see things"], 37 ["thraldom"], 200 ["nature"], and passim.

[19]Bender, 208, and Chapter 5. "Cultured" and "thoughtful classes" are from Joseph A. Mussulman, *Music in the Cultured Generation: A Social History of Music in America, 1870-1900* (Evanston: Northwestern University Press, 1971). On the intellectual underpinnings of gentility in the early nineteenth century, see Stow Persons, *The Decline of American Gentility* (New York: Columbia University Press, 1973), 3, 57, and passim.

[20]Bender, 173, 176.

[21]Arnold, 70.

[22]Ahlquist, Chapter 4.

[23]Dwight, "The Intellectual Influence of Music," *Atlantic Monthly* 36/5 (November 1870): 615, 617, 625. See also "Music as a Means of Culture," *Atlantic Monthly* 36/3 (September 1870): 321-31. For comparisons of Dwight's thinking with that of other idealists, see Ora Frishberg Saloman, "American Writers on Beethoven, 1838-1849: Dwight, Fuller, Cranch, Story," *American Music* 8 (1990): 12-28; and Saloman, "Dwight and Perkins on Wagner: A Controversy within the American Cultivated Tradition, 1852-1854," *Music and Civilization: Essays in Honor of Paul Henry Lang* (New York: Norton, 1984), 78-92. See also Michael Broyles, *"Music of the Highest Class": Elitism and Populism in Antebellum Boston* (New Haven: Yale University Press, 1992), 225-26.

[24]Bender, 171. In his history of the American urban middle class, Stuart Blumin agrees that "the most clearly defined social structure in American history, and the deepest awareness among Americans of the classes that divided them, emerged in the years following the Civil War" (258). But he also cautions that writers of the period emphasized the extremes of social "sunshine" and "shadow" (286), a two- rather than the three-part model he advocates. Blumin, *The Emergence of the Middle Class: Social Experience in the American City, 1760-1900* (Cambridge: Cambridge University Press, 1989). The cultured critics discussed here explicitly excluded themselves from the "aristocracy." Yet they were educated and comfortably well-off.

[25]*Life Illustrated* 1/2 [new ser.] (10 November 1855): 9. Reprinted in Walt Whitman, *New York Dissected: A Sheaf of Recently Discovered Newspaper*

Articles by the Author of Leaves of Grass, ed. Emory Holloway and Ralph Adimari (New York: Rufus Rockwell Wilson, 1936), 202.

[26]*Broadway Journal* 2/21 (29 November 1845): 318-19. Reprinted in *The Uncollected Poetry and Prose of Walt Whitman,* ed. Emory Holloway (Garden City, NY: Doubleday, 1921), Vol. I, 104-06.

[27]*Life Illustrated* 1/2 [new ser.] (10 November 1855). See also Robert D. Faner, *Walt Whitman and Opera* (Philadelphia: University of Pennsylvania Press, 1951).

[28]Emerson, "Manners" (1844). Reprinted in *The Collected Works of Ralph Waldo Emerson,* ed. Alfred R. Ferguson and Jean Ferguson Carr (Cambridge, MA: Harvard University Press, 1983), 75-78, 86, and passim. See also Persons, 43-44, 49.

[29]Halttunen, *Confidence Men and Painted Women: A Study of Middle-Class Culture in America, 1830-1870* (New Haven: Yale University Press, 1982), 33. See also Persons, 37-41.

[30]Persons, 39.

[31]Bender, 177-81.

[32]Curtis, *Orations and Addresses of George William Curtis,* 3 vols., ed. Charles Eliot Norton (New York: Harper, 1894), Vol. I, 9.

[33]Curtis, *Orations,* Vol. I, 15. Curtis was married to Anna Shaw, sister of Robert Gould Shaw, who led the first black regiment to fight in the Civil War (recalled in the film *Glory*).

[34]Much of Walt Whitman's journalistic work belongs in this category. Other writers of this type include George G. Foster, Charles Astor Bristed (himself of an old wealthy family), and Donald Grant Mitchell ("Ik Marvel"). See Blumin, 15-16; and David S. Reynolds's illuminating *Beneath the American Renaissance: The Subversive Imagination in the Age of Emerson and Melville* (New York: Knopf, 1988).

[35]Curtis, *The Potiphar Papers* (New York: Putnam, 1853); and Gordon Milne, *George William Curtis and the Genteel Tradition* (Bloomington: Indiana University Press, 1956), 72-73, 199-202.

[36]For a catalog of musical topics in these columns, see Mussulman, Appendix II.

[37]*Harper's* 60/3 (February 1880): 463-64. See also *Harper's* 51/1 (June 1875), 136-38 [a description of rudeness at a Theodore Thomas concert to which he returned several times]; 56/3 (February 1878): 462-63; 66/5 (April 1883): 793-94; 68/4 (March 1884): 641-42; 69/2 (July 1884): 307-08; 69/6 (November 1884): 961-63; and 72/5 (April 1886): 802-03.

[38]*Harper's* 49/1 (June 1874): 131; 65/5 (October 1882): 799; 66/6 (May 1883): 954-55; 68/6 (May 1884): 968-69 [includes opera]; and 74/3 (February 1887): 475-76. Curtis sang and played the flute. See George Willis Cooke, *Introduction to Early Letters of George William Curtis to John S. Dwight: Brook Farm and Concord* (New York: Harper, 1898), 18-19, 73. Many of these early letters were on musical subjects. On his music criticism, see Mussulman, passim.

[39]*Harper's* 59/1 (June 1879): 138.

[40]*Harper's* 68/2 (January 1884): 314.

[41]The first Wagner heard in New York was the *Tannhäuser* overture performed by the orchestra of Louis Antoine Jullien in June 1854 (Shanet, 117). For other early dates and review excerpts, see H. Earle Johnson, *First Performances in America to 1900: Works with Orchestra* (Detroit: Information Coordinators, 1979) and Mark McKnight, "Wagner and the New York Press, 1855-76," *American Music* 5 (1987): 145-55.

[42]Richard Wagner, *Art and Revolution* (1849), trans. William Ashton Ellis (1895), *The Art Work of the Future and Other Prose Works* (Lincoln: University of Nebraska Press, 1993), 30-65. See also William Weber, "Wagner, Wagnerism, and Musical Idealism," *Wagnerism in European Culture and Politics*, ed. David C. Large and William Weber (Ithaca: Cornell University Press, 1984), 28-71.

[43]Peretti, "Democratic Leitmotivs in the American Reception of Wagner," *19th Century Music* 13/1 (Summer 1989): 34-35.

[44]Mussulman, Chapter 9; and Paul E. Eisler, *The Metropolitan Opera: The First Twenty-five Years, 1883-1908* (Croton-on-Hudson, NY: North River Press, 1984), 78-122.

[45]*New York Times*, 18 November 1884, p. 5; *Nation* [Henry T. Finck] 39/1012 (20 November 1884): 446; and 40/1019 (8 January 1885): 29-30.

[46]*Harper's* 70/5 (April 1885): 807.

[47]Henry T. Finck, *Nation* 39/1007 (16 October 1884): 328.

[48]Peretti, 35-6.

[49]*Harper's* 69/6 (November 1884): 962-63; and 72/6 (May 1886): 969-70.

[50]*Harper's* 82/4 (March 1891): 637.

[51]*Harper's* 82/4 (March 1891): 638. Taking a more sanguine position, the *Times* emphasized the stockholders' right to support financially whatever repertoire they chose and speculated that the repertoire would include German opera. Still, the reporter saw the stockholders as "escaping the rigorous claims of culture and enjoying the pleasures of sin for a season"

(16 January 1891, p. 8). For further commentary, see the *New York Times,* 18 January, p. 11; 22 January, p. 4; 25 January, p. 15; and 29 January, p. 5. The *New York Tribune* stated that "such a change ... will bring disaster" (20 January 1891, p. 6).

[52]Bender refers here specifically to civil service reform, which he sees as unable to bring benefits consistent with the intellectual energy put into achieving it. A leader in this movement was George Templeton Strong, the well-known musical diarist and president of the New York Philharmonic in the early 1870s.

[53]On the relationship between gentry isolation and its decline in political influence, see Persons, 121, 277.

[54]*Harper's* 82/5 (April 1891): 797-98.

CONCERT SINGERS, PRIMA DONNAS, AND ENTERTAINERS: THE CHANGING STATUS OF BLACK WOMEN VOCALISTS IN NINETEENTH-CENTURY AMERICA

Thomas L. Riis

In a book titled *The Work of the Afro-American Woman* (1908), the author Mrs. N. F. Mossell lists and describes the numerous accomplishments of African-American women of the nineteenth century.[1] Conspicuous by its absence is any reference to black women singers. This omission may be attributed simply to Mossell's lack of interest or expertise in music, but I imagine that it reflects a larger issue, namely that music as such was not fully regarded as "work," that is, as an accomplishment requiring effort worthy of recognition in the public, male-dominated sphere of life. Part of the problem in accurately assessing the contributions of African-American women to music and the impact of music on them lies in the multiply-marginalized space of the participants—as women, as blacks, as musicians. Interested as Mossell was in documenting the achievements of her sisters, her reticence on this issue suggests an unsureness about what sort of thing musical work might be and doubts about whether women's musical activities were better left undiscussed in the chosen context. As Judith Tick has explained in her thorough discussion of the matter, the association of women with music and the tagging of music as a characteristically feminine activity has a long history in Europe and America.[2] To suggest that black women were accomplished in music, like their white sisters, would have been to pay a mixed compliment at best.

The issue is further complicated because of course music is more than one thing. Questions of class, taste and repertory crowd the picture further and force us to abandon any hope of placing all black women in a single meaningful category of activity, whether we are talking about teaching, composing, performing, or sponsoring musical works. To simplify (perhaps to oversimplify) a discussion, I have chosen to concentrate on an easily isolated group of black women performers—singers—and to consider how black women chose and practiced their art in the nineteenth century.

Female vocal soloists emerged as a special group early on, and so the choice to give them priority here is not arbitrary. In a very basic sense singing was available to everyone; it is not surprising that it was widely taken up by women who sought a career outside the home. Indeed the number of recorded black women instrumentalists in the nineteenth century other than pianists is exceptionally rare.[3] Singing did not require special equipment or tools and so could be practiced without extraordinary wealth. Singing was also culturally coded as an ability that women could demonstrate with dignity and nobility suggestive of Rousseau. The pathos of their situation as an "enslaved" minority (ironically an image that Northern free blacks were best situated to manipulate before 1860) enhanced even more the attraction of a singing career for an African American woman.

Scholars have recently begun to document the extensive involvement of black women in operatic activities at the end of the nineteenth century, but the story of women singing operatic music begins much earlier with the name of Elizabeth Taylor Greenfield, hailed as "the famous songstress, the Black Swan," as early as the 1850s[4] (see page 56). It is worth taking a moment to deconstruct this universally applied sobriquet because it resonates with most of the elements that would consistently be cited as desirable for a black woman singer throughout the century. Swans move with grace and pride. They exude a regal simplicity, an elegant proportion of body and an apparently effortless motion. Oddly, or perhaps not so oddly, they are usually white and they are also fairly silent (at least in nature). But as the familiar phrase "swan song" suggests—the image is derived from ancient bestiary traditions—they finally sing before dying and in doing so they maintain both their beautiful carriage and their pathetic mien.

Therefore they evoke both aesthetic as well as emotional sympathy.

The singer so titled received biographical treatment by James Monroe Trotter in 1881, in his important *Music and Some Highly Musical People*, "sketches of the lives of remarkable musicians of the colored race" (originally published by Lee and Shepard in Boston and Dillingham in New York).[5] Trotter's portrait fulfills all the hopes one could hold for such a seductive yet chaste image. In addition to Greenfield's musical prowess, Trotter stresses her charm, modesty, and naturalness, unspoiled by growing fame. The support that she received from her normally conservative Quaker guardian in her musical studies is presented as a charming anecdote of tolerance when the old lady discovers that the young Elizabeth has been taking singing and guitar lessons behind her back. The whole world, it seems, wishes this "celebrated cantatrice" well. Trotter includes no fewer than a dozen lengthy press clippings to make his case that Greenfield's talent is unique and her vocality overawing.[6] A Buffalo critic summarized her musical gifts:

> She has a voice of great sweetness and power, with a wide range from lowest to the highest notes than we have ever listened to: flexibility is not wanting, and her control of it is beyond example for a new and untaught vocalist.[7]

Greenfield was widely acclaimed for her sweet, relaxed tone, accurate intonation, and amazing lower register, but the critical cultural word in this paragraph is "untaught." Her skills are assumed to be God-given, not the product of schools or effort. And indeed the consistent qualifier in several of the critiques of her performance suggest that she would be even better with more training. This is not a minor point, because even the teachability of black women was far from a settled question in the generations immediately before Greenfield. Her famous predecessor, Phillis Wheatley, who inaugurated African-American literature with her book of poetry in 1773, required the public attestations of eighteen prominent white gentlemen, to insure that a publisher would even consider her work.[8] Such was the skepticism of the most advanced minds of the eighteenth century.

Elizabeth Taylor Greenfield (1809?-1876), known as the "Black Swan," was a pioneering model for African-American concert singers in the nineteenth century.

Nellie E. Brown-Mitchell (1845-1924) made her career by singing first in northern churches and then as the starring performer in the Bergen Concert Company, a touring group of the 1880s.

By the early nineteenth century some progress appears to have been made. Greenfield is usually not viewed as a freak of nature, although the predominant image and the favored critics' metaphor for her is the "rare bird." Her partisans claim that she is unusual if not unique, pleasing if not beautiful in appearance, possesses the bird's gift of song, and, like the bird, is a creature of nature. This superficially complimentary description, stressing her eccentricity, conveniently obscures any larger social facts about African-American women as a group as well as avoids uncomfortable circumstances related to performance and touring that Greenfield must have suffered. Trotter provides no details about a practice piano that was "taken from her" at some point in her London tour or about the circumstances of her being stranded by an unscrupulous agent when she first arrived in Europe—to mention only two suspicious passages in Trotter's hagiography.[9]

Greenfield evidently possessed many skills that she and her manager, Colonel Wood, conveyed effectively. She was a trained instrumentalist as well as a singer, playing the guitar, harp, and piano on her concerts—although singing was always the featured attraction. She often sang a familiar song as a soprano and then as a tenor to underline her prodigious three-octave compass. She performed ballads from the repertoire of the great European touring singers of her time, so that comparison could easily be made with them in her favor. Also, it would seem that Greenfield, probably because of her short height, appeared to be more youthful—and therefore more innocent and "natural"—than her chronological age. Trotter quotes a *Buffalo Commercial Adver-tiser* critique, which begins "Miss Greenfield is about twenty-five years of age" on the occasion of a concert when the singer was over forty.[10] Harriet Beecher Stowe, meeting her in 1853 and being two years her junior, described Greenfield (then forty-four years old) as "a gentle, amiable and interesting young person."[11]

Greenfield's English expedition, a little over a year's visit from April 1853 to July 1854, was widely successful evidently because her talent found sympathetic patronage among the artistically active aristocracy as well as Stowe, who was traveling in England at the time, and Sir George Smart, "organist and composer to Her Majesty's chapel royal" and arbiter of musical taste in London.[12] However, her original plan to devote an extended period to study in Europe never materialized. Greenfield scored points as a successful singer (and, as an acomplished African American performing familiar songs from the white parlor repertory in a sophisticated style, she was a rare bird indeed). However, there are obviously some problems with the picture that Trotter has attempted to paint.

Greenfield performed exclusively for private parties in London, and was advised by persons unknown to eschew public concerts, "until her return to the United States,"[13] probably to avoid overtaxing her voice. But although she taught voice for years and remained active in Philadelphia musical life, her performing career in the United States during her last twenty years is poorly documented. Some sad inferences are clear. After she had ceased to be a "phenomenon," the wonder of the day, and despite critical plaudits, Greenfield was deserted by audiences who had little tolerance or interest in even a very fine performer would could not or would not deliver fresh novelties. Black fans were also highly suspicious of an accomplished member of the race who agreed to appear before segregated audiences or whites-only affairs, and Greenfield had had to fend off criticism for this breach even before her European trip.[14] And of course a mature woman, especially one having been feted for a year in Europe, would have found the rigors of the road and the well-documented exclusions in public accommodations and travel unbearable without considerable resources. Greenfield either found no support or realized her own vocal limitations when she aborted (or was prevented from) any attempts at extended European study. It seems that Greenfield's career was more vexed than Trotter is willing to allow, although her experience may serve as a model for our understanding. Certainly she was imitated by others.

Greenfield blazed a trail that many followed. The generation after hers was graced by two widely recognized concert sopranos, Nellie Brown-Mitchell (1845-1924; see page 57) and Marie Smith Williams, known as "Madame Selika" (1849-1934). Mitchell's career was made by singing in New England churches, and while she eventually performed in New York, Chicago, Baltimore, and Washington, the relatively restricted circle of her early admirers, that is, religious members of her region and race, reminds us that the barriers to be overcome by aspiring black women were still daunting. Brown-Mitchell sang in recitals and concert companies in the 1870s and 1880s, became the featured attraction of the

Bergen Concert Company in 1885, and even toured in the South in 1886, but her legitimacy and principal audience derived from her church background, the least threatening context for whites with respect to the presentation of black culture after the Civil War.[15] Like Greenfield, Brown-Mitchell came from a free northern background and enjoyed the benefits of a middle-class education. Her career prospered up to the turn of the century with a repertory of polite ballads and parlor songs, which allowed her to display what by all accounts was a smooth, sweet, and exceptionally well-controlled voice.[16]

Madame Selika, dubbed "the Queen of Staccato," emerged during the 1880s as an accomplished and glamorous singer of arias by Donizetti, Bellini, Meyerbeer, and Verdi. The elegance of her career signals what was probably the peak of public interest in black concert singers prior to that of our own day. It is no coincidence that this period witnessed a general increase in status for stage performers together with what Lawrence Levine has called the "sacralization" of opera.[17] Opera, as an acceptable arena for women to appear in and as a repertory associated with the elite classes of Europe (and hence upwardly mobile Americans) was eagerly embraced and exploited by Selika. She probably had entertained thoughts of some sort of singing career from an early age. Having been born in Natchez, Mississippi (Elizabeth Greenfield's native town), Selika was nurtured by a wealthy white Cincinnati family who smoothed her way and were able to provide for her training. About 1878 she adopted the name of the heroine from Meyerbeer's *L'Africaine*, after reportedly being called upon at the last minute to perform the role.

At any rate Selika quickly rose in critical favor following her debut in 1876. She worked under the management of William Dupree, made multiple tours of the United States, Europe, and the Caribbean, and finally settled into a teaching career in Cleveland in the 1890s.[18] The sources refer to "problems of management" at about this time, and so once again the mundane but stressful issues of touring costs, accommodations, and possibly audience venues (black performers were often booked into rundown theaters) are implied.[19] Also by the mid-1890s Selika was being unfavorably compared with the younger black singers of the day, most notably Flora Batson Bergen (1870-1906) and Matilda

Sissieretta Joyner Jones (1868-1933).[20] Nevertheless, Selika's career marks another step in the recognition and elevation of a personal achievement and of the accomplishments of African-American women in general in the late nineteenth century. We shall presently examine the wider context for this development.

Still a teenager in the late 1880s, Flora Batson had sung ballads on three continents with a touring troupe when she launched her career on the East Coast, quickly becoming one of Selika's rivals. Batson succeeded Brown-Mitchell in the Bergen Concert Company in 1886 and then went on to marry the managing director of the company, James Bergen. She was evidently a woman of ambition and talent. Comments about her range suggest that, like Greenfield, Batson had a phenomenally large compass that fascinated audiences as much as her beauty of tone or pyrotechnical skill. She was known as the "Double-Voiced Queen of Song" to emphasize her ability to command both the soprano and the baritone tessituras, and was off to a flourishing career when she died suddenly in 1906.[21]

Undoubtedly the most famous of black singers at the end of the century was Sissieretta Jones, frequently identified by her advertising name, "the Black Patti," by writers effecting the common device of associating her with the more well-known white diva, Adelina Patti. Jones's career follows precisely the waning of popularity for black female concert singers and the rise of young vivacious "new" women as vaudeville stars. Before her career ended she enjoyed unparalleled fame and respect throughout the country.[22]

By the late 1890s, when Jones's early successes were still being hailed, the conditions of urban America were such that operatic songs were less often included in the rapidly expanding venues of popular amusement. Opera itself was being increasingly defined as an elite medium. Also in the 1890s new styles appeared in the shape of cakewalks and ragtime songs. Musical comedies were looking conspicuously less European and more "American," that is, fast-paced, colloquial, kinetic, silly (rather than witty), and brash. Would-be concert singers, "serious" entertainers (if that odd contradiction be permitted), faced the possible charge of excessive sobriety and complexity. It was almost a compliment to identify a Broadway show as plotless, chaotic or busy, since so many of them were.[23] For solo singers who hoped to maintain a wide audience it never hurt to speak directly the the listeners, to show the common touch.

Sensible of this change, Jones shifted her emphasis in mid-career, from concert touring to form the Black Patti Troubadours, essentially a traveling variety show, or combination, in which Jones appeared only as part of an elegant operatic finale following the comic playlets and vaudeville specialties of her all-black company. In 1882 Jones had performed a Meyerbeer aria for President and Mrs. Benjamin Harrison in the White House,[24] but by 1896 she had set out on the less exalted but apparently more lucrative path as the star of a traveling troupe producing such skits as "A Filipino Mis-fit" and "At Jolly Coon-ey Island," a clear concession to popular tastes and a signal that the space for black opera singers was being narrowed even further.[25] With the Troubadours she was still performing for both white and black audiences (sometimes at separate times and venues in southern towns), but all of the earlier factors that had limited the possibilities for black women were still in force.

Probably hastened by declining vocalism and illness, as well as changes in audience taste and financial reverses suffered by her managers, Voelckel and Nolan, Jones retired in 1916, never having appeared at the Metropolitan Opera, although her early career had suggested that this pinnacle was technically within her reach.[26] Nevertheless, she had accomplished something that no other black singer had managed. By dint of training and hard work she improved upon a large dose of native talent and made it pay off. She achieved an honest reputation as a first-rate artist. By carefully building and guarding her image and sidestepping many pitfalls she was eventually recognized as a performer who could justly be compared to the other greats of her day regardless of race. Her reward was to receive at least a measure of public support across the board, from whites and blacks of all classes (except, of course, the most virulently racist or antimusical).[27]

Unfortunately Jones's fame was short-lived. Although the black elite of the early twentieth century had supported Jones and the other concert singers of her day and willingly spoke up and turned out to witness the performances of the stars on tour, these angels represented a minority within a minority and lacked real power to change the exclusionary policies of large white cultural establishments. Meanwhile the sizable black, urban middle class was taking to heart a new kind of entertainer: singer/dancer/actresses like Aida Overton Walker (1880-1914).[28]

The year of Greenfield's death (1876) and Selika's debut also saw the first African-American musical comedy (although the generic term was not then in general use), anticipating by twenty-five years the more famous efforts of Aida Walker, who performed in the shows of Williams & Walker and Cole & Johnson. In this early show two women singers, the sisters Anna and Emma Hyers, were the center of attention in a work created for them by Joseph Bradford titled *Out of Bondage*.[29] Still in their twenties and managed by their ambitious father, Sam, the Hyers sisters were already seasoned performers by the time of the show's premiere. They had debuted (1867) in their California home and after intensive training had brought off a successful cross-country tour (1871), which had netted them acclaim as accomplished concert singers. As had been the case for earlier black divas, their remarkable ranges, force, purity of tone, and sensitivity were widely proclaimed. In Salt Lake City, Chicago, Cleveland, and New York, they appeared with the leading African-American male singers of the day, Wallace King and John Luca. Their repertory was wide, including familiar operatic arias, jubilees, spirituals, and ballads, performed as solos, duets, and quartets. Since white concert singers were not performing any black music at the time and even black stars did not normally sing spirituals on their programs, the Hyers sisters probably featured the broadest selection of styles available on the concert stage of their day. They concertized extensively in New England from 1871 to 1875—a wise move, since, judging from the tours of Brown-Mitchell and the Fisk Jubilee Singers, New England could be depended upon to be the most sympathetic and least race-prejudiced area of the country at the time.

In 1876, with "an enlarged company" and a play "written expressly for them," the Hyers set out to create a theater piece about African-American life.[30] A comedy (not a farce) with some historical elements and many musical insertions to highlight the Hyers' specialized talents, *Out of Bondage* proved a popular piece. It consisted of four acts and presented various scenes in the life of one black family during slavery, at the time of Emancipation and the years following, in which the main characters, former slaves, finally become successful concert singers in the North. The dialogue is largely polite and inconsequential, but promotes the values of family loyalty, education, good humor, and music. A concert within the play forms the fourth and final act.

In 1877 the Hyers created a play set in Africa called *Urlina, the African Princess.* In this they also incorporated elements of contemporary burlesque, with Emma, the contralto of the pair, taking the pants role as Prince Zurleska.[31] Aided by comedians Billy Kersands and Sam Lucas, they used the profits from this vehicle to pay their way back to California. Dubbed an "operatic bouffe extravaganza," it fed the current taste for spectacle as well as pantomime and song. In it the Hyers sisters seem to have created a fair success and demontrated a remarkable versatility.[32]

Like the other renowned women performers of their day, the Hyers sisters insisted upon dignified performances. Unlike the men in their companies who were the featured comedians (and had grown up in the blackface minstrel show world), the women, even as they moved into dramatic vehicles, maintained a level of decorum that legitimized their presence on the stage and went far toward protecting their reputations. Women who strayed too far from reserved gestures, modest costumes, and carefully chosen words took grave risks of placing themselves beyond the pale of social redemption. Consequently they set guards on all sides to preserve both the appearance and the reality of proper behavior. In 1879 one San Francisco critic noted that "[the Hyers sisters] are an earnest pair, but really dead earnest is not exactly the spirit in which to approach the burlesque."[33] Black women had to negotiate a narrow space, and excessive flamboyance would have been equally or probably more severely criticized than earnestness.[34]

Two points in the Hyers' career stand out in our tracing of the history of nineteenth-century black women singers. The first is their exceptional ability, which was widely recognized in their traditional roles as singers. The second is that they were able to translate their musical success to the dramatic stage and then later to vaudeville. The rising status of the legitimate stage and the increased respectability of the acting profession in the last two decades of the nineteenth century facilitated this movement.[35] But the Hyers sisters also had something unique to offer that played against type. They were sufficiently intriguing to cause at least some critics to suspend the normal expectations for black women as a group, if they had stereotypical modes in mind. A wonderful summary of this forced new perspective appeared in the *Oregonian* critic's report of *Urlina* and was reprinted in the *San Francisco Pacific Appeal*:

> Operatically and dramatically the piece and the performances can not be judged by any of the legitimate or standard rules of criticism. There is much in the performance which pleases, amuses, and even touches the tender sympathies of the audience. Urlina combines harmoniously the elements of comedy, burlesque and pathos.[36]

Emma continued her career in vaudeville in the 1890s and apparently died at sometime before 1900.[37] Anna Madah travelled with John Isham's shows and to Australia with a minstrel show in 1899. Reportedly she was cast in a Williams & Walker musical before retiring to San Francisco in 1902.[38] Although the Hyers sisters were recalled by black commentator Ike Simond as "the greatest of all colored efforts," for nearly a century they have been lost to the history books.[39]

The career progression from church soloist to concert company singer to musical comedy player probably was the pattern repeated most often for black women vocalists in the late nineteenth century. Church and parlor provided the sites for early training and encouragement, and the concert company was developed as a quasi-educational forum where talented young women could demonstrate what they had learned and where they need not fear for their moral reputations. Both were acceptable venues from the standpoint of racial politics. Audiences were mostly black. The musical comedy was the pinnacle of the popular theater (since joining a white operatic company was still forbidden) and could provide steady employment in relatively prestigious circumstances. Lower middle-class urban women were the most likely candidates for this kind of professional life. Since general economic conditions were more favorable and populations were larger in Atlantic seaboard cities rather than in the countryside, South or West, careers tended to be launched in those cities regardless of the singer's home or place of birth.

Eileen Southern, Josephine Wright, Jo Tanner, and Paula Giddings have begun to document the phenomenal proliferation of female singers and singing teachers in large northern cities, especially in Boston and Washington through the 1880s and 1890s.[40] This growth was obviously part of a bigger picture. The institutionalization of community music-making and concert music was coupled with larger developments in the United States in the Gilded Age, including the building of music conservatories and the immigration of influential German musicians to the United States in these years, but expanded opportunities for participation in the dominant culture's serious "art" traditions was no less important to the African-American community for that.[41] It is essential to keep in mind that the young adults of this period had been part of a post-Emancipation baby boom. As the first children born to former slaves, but not in slavery, they were touched with a sense of optimism, possibility, and progress for the race and had not yet witnessed the reactionary and brutal backlash of lynch law and the legal apparatus known as Jim Crow. The tonic of newly won freedom was still inspiring hundreds of black families to greater efforts, and indeed measurable progress and growth occurred in many arenas of black business and culture, despite rankling threats and abuses from whites and the creation of new legal barricades.[42]

Wright records no fewer than seventeen "prima donnas" among the thirty-three "professional or semi-professional" black women musicians in Boston between 1870 and 1900,[43] and their careers were made possible chiefly through the aid of churches, mostly black and a few white, which supported the heightened aspirations of the young (see page 67). In Washington, a city with a conspicuous black upper class, Doris McGinty has detailed the careers of some one hundred seventy performers from 1900 to 1920, over half of whom are identified as amateur or professional singers.[44] It seems clear that women all over the country at the end of the century were laying claim to a public space (at least a lectern if not a whole stage), to an area becoming as much theirs as the home had already become earlier in the century. The women who sang in public were finding an audience as well as an identity.

For the black elite of the period, presiding over the activities of culture was an essential mark of having arrived, of having shed the cares of poverty and of the domination by whites in the

PROGRAMME.

Part First.

1. TRIO FOR TWO VIOLINS AND PIANO......................*Rhizia*
   DAVID OSWELL, MADALINE TALBOT, AND MRS. WILSON.

2. QUARTET. — "Sighing for Thee."
   AUBER QUARTET, — MESSRS. SMITH, HILL, RUFFIN, AND HENRY.

3. SONG. — "Down by the Sea" (Bass).................*Knowlton*
   JAMES HENRY, Jun.

4. DUET. — "On Mossy Banks".........................*Gilbert*
   MISS P. E. ALLEN AND E. M. PINKNEY.

5. SONG. — "Thou everywhere"..........................*Lachner*
   MRS. WILSON.

6. ROMANCE. — "Alice, where art Thou?"................*Ascher*
   JAMES M. SCOTTRON.

7. QUINTET. — "The Image of the Rose" ....*Reichardt*
   MISS P. E. ALLEN AND QUARTET.

Part Second.

1. THEMA WITH VARIATIONS. — Violin and Piano...........*Rode*
   DAVID T. OSWELL.

2. DUET. — "Take now this Ring"...............*La Sonnambula*
   MRS. WILSON AND JAMES M. SCOTTRON.

3. QUARTET. — "Soldier's Farewell".....................*Kinkel*
   MESSRS. SMITH, HILL, RUFFIN, AND HENRY.

4. SONG. — "Waiting," with Violin Obligato.............*Millard*
   MISS P. E. ALLEN, MRS. D. WILSON, AND DAVID T. OSWELL.

5. MARCH. — Vocal ....*Becker*
   MESSRS. SMITH, PINKNEY, RUFFIN, AND HENRY.

6. QUARTET. — "Man the Life-Boat" (by request).

7. CHORUS. — "Angel of Peace".........................*Keller*
   WITH ORGAN AND PIANO ACCOMPANIMENT.

A program for a public concert given by Boston's Progressive Musical Union on 9 March 1875.

political arena. As segregation on all fronts, especially in northern ones, not only failed to recede but became the rule rather than the exception, the intensity with which a variety of cultural goals developed within black communities was hastened even more. Given their presence throughout the nineteenth century, it is hardly surprising that black singers would have figured strongly in the picture.

The prototypical figure of the singer herself of course had a lot to do with the attractiveness of the profession. Hearkening back to Elizabeth Greenfield again, singers tended to dress elegantly, to speak softly, and to carry themselves with pride and politeness on the stage. At the same time, they could, if necessary, act independently. The men who to some extent controlled their backstage life or their touring schedule were made temporarily invisible. In the practice of her art, the songstress was the center of attention and in control of the stage. She could project an image of grandeur or condescension, of joy or ebullience, of wit, dignity, mystery, or grace. Biographies of white European singers of the time begin to create the myth of the temperamental singer, the diva who must be coddled lest she fly into a rage and fail to perform her vocal magic.[45] On this point the black diva could also identify, turning the persona to her own use. Social slights that she might suffer need not be interpreted racially (and hence dangerously for the singer) but only as actions insufficiently sensitive to her artistic nature. The diva was, after all, an artist, regardless of her race. Ideally she must answer to no one. She had little need to conform to any rules other than those demanded by her own self-esteem and her art. That the larger world had begun to sanctify (or villify) the female opera singer was a distinct advantage, because it secured for the person who fit the role a higher level of mental and emotional satisfaction than almost any other occupation.

Also an increasingly "scientific" American ideology was brought into play in support of these talented singers. It was noted by some critics that Nellie Brown-Mitchell and the Hyers sisters were practitioners and even teachers of the Guilmette Method. The details of the method are never explained in publicity blurbs and indeed are obscure today, but the point of mentioning it at all is clear. An avowedly rational approach to music-making implied that singing was beginning to be understood not merely as a God-given gift, but as a skill that could be enhanced by means of scientific cultivation, by following the correct rules. Such rationalizations emphasized that artistry, no matter how "natural" to the race or the sex, did not just happen, and that black women were capable of learning and applying scientific principles. This idea had radical implications indeed.

Finally, the female opera singer was a kind of *performing object,* a music box so to speak, and she was viewed and understood as a singing body. She need never *speak* on stage. As a performer she need never leave the gauzy realm bordered and suffused by musical time and tone. Although such a characterization may sound baldly dehumanizing, it recognizes that women could create and maintain a shield or framework for self-presentation with much less psychological danger than would be possible in the business or political worlds (where men dominated and expected to continue dominating by means of unseen wealth and their own rhetoric of business speech).[46]

Support for singers also naturally grew out of women's own organizations, the numerous "self-culture" clubs of upper-crust black women, who understood best of all the value of putting up a good appearance, and where speech could be social but not necessarily political. As described by Willard Gatewood:

> Self-culture organizations, which usually took the form of literary or reading clubs, focused on self-development through the study of what were considered great books, art, literature, history, music or philosophy. [A typical] upper-class cultural organization in a large black community ... met once a month throughout the year except during the summer ... and included musical performances as well as literary study.[47]

Of course most of the participants in these affairs had been raised in homes where early exposure of children to the fine arts and the apparatus of serious cultivated styles of music had been a significant concern in child rearing.[48] Almost all early vocal instruction of course had been received at home.

Gatewood also explains that "few other organizations in the black community exhibited a stronger commitment to the idea of 'service to the race' than women's clubs."[49] And it is easy to see how a female singer in alliance with a larger group of supportive women would have embraced the powerfully needed impulse to "uplift" her community in every way possible—to be the best example that she could be in the service of society. Within these groups at least the idea that a woman performer might be doing woman's "work" must have held some currency.

While the woman opera singers might be said to have elevated themselves and their race by associating with high-class music, assuming a commanding persona, adopting a scientific method, and attracting a coterie of appreciative listeners, the achievement of the most famous group of black singers in the nineteenth century, the Fisk Jubilee Singers, reverses the perspective and effect by means of the music itself. By being presented in a polished manner, the spirituals—a repertory clearly associated for the early audiences with the slaves and the common black "folk"—were elevated and made to stand for a new sort of nobility, the plaintive and naturally affective music of a "poor, peeled, despised ... race."[50] The spirituals have been discussed in many other contexts that need not concern us here, but for purposes of this essay, it is worth pointing out that a key creator in the songs that have come to be called "Negro spirituals," the choral arrangements associated with Fisk University and Hampton Institute, as well as dozens of other "student" groups, is Ella Sheppard, accompanist and co-arranger of the earliest Fisk programs.[51]

Sheppard's name is associated with the first group of Fisk students, but she was slightly older than the other students, already thoroughly trained as a pianist. She deserves fuller recognition not only as one of the original members but as one of the shaping forces. When the Fisk oratorio singing society decided to assist in raising money for the financially suffering school, under the direction of George White (a Caucasian), the Fisk students took to the road. The students' concerts generally included secular music and classical selections, but the fame of the spirituals travelling in tandem so to speak with Fisk students, most of whom had been living in slavery a few years before, has given rise to the common misconception that the Fisk Jubilee Singers' repertory consisted exclusively of slave songs. Much to White's surprise it was the reception of their folk songs rather than the classical selections that made the group the musical phenomenon of the decade. A significant contribution to the transformation of the students' traveling repertory may have been made by Sheppard, since she worked so closely with White, who was mindful of the need to supply fresh arrangements of the original folk songs. Comments made in her unpublished diary in the Fisk archives suggest that she was instrumental in assisting if not actually in conceiving the effects achieved by the group during its European touring years, along with its leaders, White and Theodore Seward. Many passages in her diary of 1877-1878 are especially tantalizing:

Monday Leipzig Nov. 19 [18]77
Had rehearsal. Mrs. Prof. Luhdartt & two daughters called. Had trouble with Mrs. W. because she would not allow me to go to Mrs. Smith's to arrange the "medley" which Mr. White sent to be ready for use Wednesday night; she insisted on my remaining to entertain the above friends. After dinner when I had got the use of a piano a 1/2 hr. & could not get the parts of the medley arranged I was furiously angry & declared that the next time I would do what I thought best....

Thurs. Nov. 23 Potsdam
... I think often, now, that I cannot endure my share of the work another day, it is so heavy a responsibility, & so unnoticable that when I've worked myself almost lifeless one doesn't notice I've been doing anything much. O that I could be content to labour in this field my Lord has honored me with, & not murmur or wish for another sphere, to be at rest....[52]

Such entries, together with the published histories and transcriptions of the Fisk Jubilee music, highlight in another way how women's histories and contributions may be lost not through blatant prejudice or intent to harm, since White and Seward were presumably men of good will, but simply because both men and women accepted the auxiliary role of women in so many public circumstances and that women as a matter of habit and self-preservation yielded name, space, and credit to men on many occasions.[53] It is impossible to miss both Sheppard's frustration and her evident musical expertise expressed in the diary. When the Fisk Singers began traveling on their own, in 1882, unaffiliated with the university, women singers other than Sheppard remained in the forefront. Their contributions are still incompletely chronicled. Sheppard herself was not a diva, but her experience should enlighten us on the position of talented black women in public fora during her time.[54]

Besides the many successful individual careers in the nineteenth century, at least one nominal operatic troupe was formed, "The Colored American Opera Company," which briefly held the stage in 1873 with performances of Julius Eichberg's *The Doctor of Alcantara* (1862), a work of modest challenges but some merit. Trotter supplies a positive but measured account of the handful of appearances made by this group in Washington and Philadelphia.[55] Three women sang with the ensemble: Agnes Gray Smallwood (soprano), Lena Miller (contralto), and Mary Coakley (contralto). Neither Trotter nor the critics he quotes make great claims for them, but all favor such adjectives to describe their singing as "pretty," "neat," "admirable," "correct," and "resonant."[56] This early attempt to form a black company was imitated by Theodore Drury in 1889, who presented opera scenes, and from 1900 to 1908 full-fledged operas (including *Faust, Carmen*, and *Aïda*). His leading ladies included Desseria Plato and Estelle Pickney.[57]

This essay has not attempted to discuss all of the black women singers of the nineteenth century, but merely to point out that theirs has been a constant presence during a time in which many struggled to construct and project positive roles and images. That these women modeled their behavior and took their cue from women of the dominant race to some extent does not negate the specific achievements of the women involved. It is satisfying to record that badges of identity with Africa and the oppressed of the world were sought and proudly worn by these black women even within the relatively privileged and historically uninformed American context. Selika and Aïda were favored roles for obvious reasons, but their popularity with American singers was not inevitable. Blacks were shaping their performances within a larger cultural matrix, and women insisted on telling their stories—either through the symbolic Africans of European opera (Selika and Aïda) or the established types found in American stageplays of the time (plantation characters, poor orphans, or "tragic mulattos"[58]), or by imitating the actions of mothers, daughters, and female friends in their own experience.

That black women singers made careers at all is a testimony to their strong wills and steadfastness. Elizabeth Taylor Greenfield had to overcome high walls of disbelief, just as Phillis Wheatley had in the century before her. All of the mid-century concert singers had to cope with incredulous audiences, prejudiced critics, domineering male managers, and physically taxing, blatantly discriminatory travel arrangements.

Their status as women had both advantages and disadvantages for the singers. The appearance of women in minstrel shows was long delayed because of the exclusively male cast of the early traveling troupes,[59] not to mention the dangers of the road itself. But although this circumstance prevented women from acquiring a dose of experience and professional training in the 1840s and 1850s, it also kept them from being associated exclusively with old minstrel stereotypes once they finally appeared on the stage. (It was neither the fault nor the activities of nineteenth-century women, either black or white, that created post-minstrel figures like Aunt Jemima.) Before as well as after the midpoint of the nineteenth century it was essential that women who hoped to prosper act in roles proper to their gender within the realm of the woman's traditional role as mother and guardian of the home. While these restrictions certainly limited the roles that they could eventually assume, women were probably not so greatly disadvantaged by their exclusion from the earliest minstrel show performances.

Even if minstrel roles had been attainable, many black women were already doubly burdened. When they were not literally slaves they often worked full days as domestic servants in the homes of whites and then tended to the needs of their own families as well; they had to be mothers twice over. These conditions obviously left little time for professional work outside the home. However, even with such strictures, home music making was possible for those who had access to a piano or a guitar, though it generally did not include appearances on a public stage. Because music was conceded to be a feminine activity, not a threat to male control, black women could be allowed to participate if they showed talent or interest in a mildly sympathetic environment. By the end of the nineteenth century, the elitism of opera, the elevated status of the opera singer, intensified training (made available within communities and clubs), and the emancipation of thousands of women had also changed the picture substantially. What had been a mere possibility for an unusually talented young woman of 1850 became a genuine career track for many middle-class girls in the 1890s.

Although the popular music industry, and specifically the realm of American musical comedy, was not as receptive of women as men, it eventually provided a place for the bright, vivacious, go-getter at the turn of the century. Discrimination still prevented African-American women from entering the ranks of the Metropolitan Opera until 1955, when Marion Anderson finally crossed the color line there, but a place for the black female singer was established far more securely than for the black male singer by 1900.

The beginning of the twentieth century brought even more changes. The rise of recording technology and the marketing of the blues on disk, two crucial elements in the commodification of black talent early in the second decade of the twentieth century, would soon revolutionize the way Americans and the world heard and viewed black women singers. The effects of these powerful forces cannot be minimized, since they led to the next remarkable chapter of African-American music-making, but we should not forget the early pioneers, these black artists of only a century ago, who did much useful cultural work and proudly provided for younger generations lively and inspiring images of black women. Their suitability and "Americanness" (however that might be construed) ought not to be questioned, since these women followed the highest and bravest path open to them. To fully recognize and explain their activities, however, is still part of our historical task.

University of Colorado, Boulder

---

[1] Mrs. N. F. Mossell, *The Work of the Afro-American Woman* (1908; reprint ed. New York and Oxford: Oxford University Press, 1988).

[2] Judith Tick, *American Women Composers Before 1870* (Ann Arbor, MI, and London: UMI Research Press, 1983), 13-21.

[3] Judith and Howard Sacks, *Way Up North in Dixie* (Washington, D. C.: Smithsonian Institution Press, 1993), gives a rare account of black women fiddlers.

[4]James Monroe Trotter, *Music and Some Highly Musical People* (1881; reprint ed. New York: Johnson Reprint Company, 1968), 66-87.

[5]Trotter, 1.

[6]Trotter, 71-77.

[7]Trotter, 73.

[8]Henry Louis Gates, Foreword to Mossell, *The Work of the Afro-American Woman* (1988), viii-ix.

[9]Trotter, 80, 82.

[10]Trotter, 75.

[11]Trotter, 80. It is also possible that Trotter simply got the birthdate for Greenfield wrong. Others have suggested birth years as late as 1824.

[12]Trotter, 82.

[13]Trotter, 86.

[14]Jo A. Tanner, *Dusky Maidens: The Odyssey of the Early Black Dramatic Actress* (Westport, CT : Greenwood Press, 1992), 23.

[15]Eileen Southern, *Biographical Dictionary of Afro-American and African Musicians* (Westport, CT : Greenwood Press, 1982), 53.

[16]Southern, 53. Also, Caroline Lamar Jones has reported on "female concert singers in the nineteenth century" in an unpublished article given at the NEH Summer Seminar for College Teachers, Afro-American Musicians in the Nineteenth Century; Harvard University, 13 August 1982.

[17]Lawrence Levine, *Highbrow/Lowbrow: The Emergence of Cultural Hierarchy in America* (Cambridge: Harvard University Press, 1988), 83ff.

[18]Tanner, 28-9; and Southern, 334.

[19]*Ibid.*

[20]Tanner, 29.

[21]Tanner, 30.

[22]See Dennis Loranger, "Women, Nature and Appearance: Themes in Popular Songs from the Turn of the Century," *American Music Research Center Journal* 2 (1992): 68-85.

[23]Gerald Bordman, *American Music Theatre: A Chronicle*, 2nd ed. (New York: Oxford University Press, 1992), 118-82.

[24]Elise Kirk, *Music in the White House* (Urbana and Chicago: University of Illinois Press, 1986), 151.

[25]Thomas Riis, *Just Before Jazz* (Washington, D. C.: Smithsonian Institution Press, 1989), 146-47.

[26]The recent research of John Graziano on the life of the Black Patti was presented at the Annual Meeting of the American Musicological Society; Minneapolis, 29 October 1994.

[27]William Lichtenwanger, "Matilda Sissieretta Joyner Jones," *Notable American Women, 1607-1950,* ed. Edward T. James (Cambridge: Belknap Press of the Harvard University Press, 1971), Vol. II, 288-90.

[28]Richard Newman, "'The Brightest Star': Aida Overton Walker in the Age of Ragtime and Cakewalk," *Prospects: An Annual Journal of American Cultural Studies* 18 (1993): 465-81.

[29]*African-American Theater*, ed. Southern (New York and London: Garland Publishing, 1994) is a reprint with musical excerpts of two Hyers plays, *Out of Bondage* (1876) and *Peculiar Sam; or, The Underground Railroad* (1879).

[30]Southern, *African-American Theater,* xvii.

[31]Errol Hill, "The Hyers Sisters: Pioneers in Black Musical Comedy," *The American Stage: Social and Economic Issues from the Colonial Period to the Present,,* ed. Ron England and Tice Miller (Cambridge, Eng.: Cambridge University Press, 1993), 124.

[32]Hill, 121.

[33]Hill, 127.

[34]On the questions of respectability and the dangers of the stage, see Nancy Reich, "Women as Musicians: A Question of Class," *Music and Difference,* ed. Ruth Solie (Berkeley: University of California Press, 1993), 132-33.

[35]Benjamin McArthur, *Actors and American Culture, 1880-1920* (Philadelphia: Temple University Press, 1984), 85ff.

[36]Hill, 122.

[37]Southern, *Biographical Dictionary,* 30.

[38]Southern, *Biographical Dictionary,* 126.

[39]Ike Simond, *Old Slack's Reminiscence and Pocket History of the Colored Profession from 1865 to 1891* (1891, reprint; Bowling Green, Ohio: Popular Press, 1974), 7; and Riis, 9-12.

[40]Southern, "In Retrospect: Black Prima Donnas of the Nineteenth Century," *The Black Perpsective in Music* 7/1 (Spring 1979): 95-106; Josephine Wright, "Black Women in Classical Music in Boston During the Late Nineteenth Century: Profiles of Leadership," *New Perspectives on*

Music: Essays in Honor of Eileen Southern, ed. Wright, with Samuel A. Floyd Jr. (Warren, MI: Harmonie Park Press, 1992), 373-407; Tanner; and Paula Giddings, *When and Where I Enter: The Impact of Black Women on Race and Sex in America* (New York: Morrow, 1984).

[41]H. Wiley Hitchcock, *Music in the United States: A Historical Introduction*, 3rd ed. (Englewood Cliffs, NJ: Prentice-Hall, 1988), provides an excellent brief overview of the period.

[42]C. Vann Woodward, *The Strange Career of Jim Crow*, 3rd ed. (New York: Oxford University Press, 1974) is the most complete record of the systematic creation of the system of segregation following Reconstruction.

[43]Wright, "Black Women in Boston," 377.

[44]Doris McGinty, "Black Women in the Music of Washington, D.C.," *New Perspectives on Music,* ed. Wright and Floyd, 443-49.

[45]Susan Rutherford, "The Voice of Freedom: Images of the Prima Donna," *The New Woman and Her Sisters: Feminism and Theatre, 1850-1914,* ed. Viv Gardner and Susan Rutherford (New York and London: Harvester Wheatsheaf, 1992), 95-114; Bram Dijkstra, *Idols of Perversity: Fantasies of Feminine Evil in Fin-de-Siecle Culture* (New York and Oxford: Oxford University Press, 1986); and Catherine Clement, *Opera, or the Undoing of Women*, trans. Betsy Wing (Minneapolis: University of Minnesota Press, 1988).

[46]Carolyn Abbate has explored this idea of the singing body and other issues of women as performers in "Opera; or, the Envoicing of Women," *Music and Difference*, ed. Solie (Berkeley: University of California Press, 1993), 234-35, 255.

[47]Willard B. Gatewood, *Aristocrats of Color: The Black Elite, 1880-1920* (Bloomington and Indianapolis: Indiana University Press, 1990), 241.

[48]Gatewood, 248.

[49]Gatewood, 269.

[50]Riis, "The Cultivated White Tradition and Black Music in Nineteenth-Century America: A Discussion of Some Articles in Dwight's Journal of Music," *The Black Perspective in Music* 4/2 (Special issue 1976): 174.

[51]Sheppard is mentioned in Trotter, 257, but her story has yet to be fully told. Her unpublished diary rests in the archives of Fisk University.

[52]Ella Sheppard diary, 19 October 1877 to 15 July 1878 [124 pages], Fisk University Archives.

[53]For a fuller discussion of the transcribing of the Fisk Singers songs, see Dena Epstein, "The Story of the Jubilee Singers: An Introduction to Its

Bibliographic History," *New Perspectives on Music,* ed. Wright and Floyd, 151-62.

[54]Rainer E. Lotz, "The Black Troubadours: Black Entertainers in Europe, 1896-1915," *Black Music Research Journal* 10 (Fall 1990): 253-55.

[55]Trotter, 241-52.

[56]Trotter, 248-51.

[57]Southern, *Music of Black Americans,* 2nd ed. (New York: Norton, 1983), 289.

[58]Riis, *Just Before Jazz,* 7-8, 19.

[59]Robert Toll, *Blacking Up* (New York: Oxford University Press, 1974), 139.

SOMEWHERE BETWEEN BEER AND WAGNER: THE CULTURAL AND MUSICAL IMPACT OF GERMAN MÄNNERCHÖRE IN NEW YORK AND NEW ORLEANS[1]

Mary Sue Morrow

German Männerchöre have always held a rather convivial spot in the history of America's musical institutions. Known mainly for their sponsorship of huge choral festivals, the Männerchöre have unquestionably contributed to the growth of choral singing in the United States. They became an increasingly familiar part of the American cultural landscape after the 1840s, founded by the new waves of German immigrants fleeing political and social unrest at home. In the young cities of the Midwest (e.g., Milwaukee, St. Louis), the Männerchöre often provided the "earliest source of musical culture."[2] Their impact was less assured in older cities, where Germans did not constitute an ethnic majority and where cultural patterns had been developing for a century or more. What did happen in those cities? Did the Männerchöre play a major role in establishing or supporting lasting musical institutions or were their activities more insular and ephemeral?

I would like to address these questions by focusing on two cities that shared certain demographic features but offered the Männerchöre very different musical and cultural arenas: New York and New Orleans. As major ports, both cities served as common destinations for German immigrants during the nineteenth century. Though most of the immigrants eventually headed inland, in both New York and New Orleans a substantial number elected to make the city itself their home. The German community in New York was of course much larger in absolute numbers (168,225 as compared to New Orleans' 13,944, according to the 1880 U.S. census), but in both cities it constituted less than 15 percent of the population (14 percent in New York and 7 percent in New Orleans).[3]

In addition, because of immigration patterns, Germans actually dominated the New Orleans immigrant community during the last quarter of the century: The 1890 census reported 34,369 foreign-born out of a total of 242,039 residents, with a breakdown as follows: Germans 11,338; Irish 7,923; French 5,710; Italians 3,622; English 1,624.[4] Thus, though their community may have been proportionally as well as numerically smaller than the one in New York, New Orleans Germans did occupy a significant, though not dominant, position in the city's ethnic roster. In addition, the two German communities also had cultural and social similarities. Both were dominated by prosperous tradesmen,[5] and both had to contend and compete with other, much poorer immigrant communities, especially the Irish and the Italians. And in both, informal singing clubs had begun to appear by the end of the 1830s, before the big surge of German immigration.[6]

The musical scenes of the two cities in 1840 bore little resemblance to each other. In New Orleans, home of the first permanent opera company in the United States, ethnic rivalry between the city's two dominant factions (the French and the English-speaking Americans) determined the developments in the cultural arena, which revolved around opera and theater. The earliest references to opera date back to performances at the St. Peter Street Theater in the 1790s, but that venture eventually succumbed to competition from the Orleans Theater, a French opera house that opened in 1808.[7] By the 1830s, its success had spawned an equally successful American rival, the St. Charles Theater, at that time the largest theater in the United States. The offerings by the two competitors in January 1838, for example, encompassed six different operas by Auber, two by Boieldieu, two by Rossini, and one each by Meyerbeer, Herold, Halévy, Bellini, Bishop, and Isouard, often in multiple performances.[8] Thus, when Männerchöre began to appear in New Orleans, the city's cultural framework had already been set.

TABLE 1

Documented Männerchöre in New York, 1840-1900.*

Organization	Date found in sources
*Liederkranz	founded 1847
*Rheinischer Sängerbund	founded 1847
*New York Sängerrunde	founded 1848
*Gesangverein Schillerbund	founded 1848
Harmonia	founded 1848
Eintracht	1849
Gesangverein der Social-reformer	1849
Loreley Männerchor	1851
*Arion	founded 1854
*Mozart Verein	founded 1854
*Yorkville Männerchor	founded 1856
Melrose Liedertafel	1856
Euphonia	founded 1856
New York Liederkranz	1857
Union Männerchor	1858
Unabhängige Vereine	1858
Bloomingdale Sänger Freundschafts-Bund	1858
Hudson Männerchor	founded 1858
*Beethoven Männerchor	founded 1859
Frauenlob	1860s
New York Quartett-Club	1860s
Sociale Männerchor	1860s
Erato	1860s
Sing Academia	1860s
Colonia Männerchor	1860s
Junger Männerchor	1860s
Teutonia Männerchor	1860s
Helvitia Männerchor	1860s
Kreutzer Quartett-Club	founded 1860
Gesangverein Arminia	founded 1863
Theodor Koerner Liedertafel	founded 1863
Gesangverein Franz Abt Schuler	founded 1866
Harlem Männerchor	founded 1865
Gesangverein Heinebund	founded 1869
*Männergesangverein Eichenkranz	founded 1869
Gesangverein Cordialia	founded 1870
Turner Liedertafel	1870s
Gesangverein der Oesterreicher und Oesterreich	founded 1876
*New York Männerchor	founded 1870
Verein "Ohne Namen"	1874-1876

*Information for the clubs marked with an asterisk was taken from club documents found in the Music Division of the New York Public Library. The remaining clubs were mentioned in Snyder, "The *Männerchor* Tradition in the United States" (see endnote 4), 491-96.

Organization	Date found in sources
Helvetia Männerchor	1880s
*Ehrenritter Gesangverein	1880s
Marschner Quartett Club	1880s
*Socialistische Liedertafel	founded 1880
Liedertafel Egalite	founded 1881
Harlem Eintracht	founded 1882
Männer-Gesang-Verein "Teutonia"	founded 1883
Franz Schubert Männerchor	founded 1883
Arbeiter Liedertafel	founded 1884
Arbeiter Liedertafel, Morrisania	founded 1884
Bremer Gesangverein	founded 1885
Männergesang Verein Schuechterner Quartet	founded 1885
Rheinpfälzer Männerchor	founded 1886
Arbeiter Männerchor	founded 1886
Schottener Männerchor	founded 1886
Männerchor der Möbelarbeiter	founded 1887
Palestrina Verein	1890s
New York Quartett-Club	1890s
Columbia Männerchor	1890s
Central Turnverein	1890s
Bloomingdale Eintracht	1890s
Arbeiter Liederkranz	founded 1890
International Arbeiter Liedertafel	founded 1891

TABLE 2

Documented Männerchöre in New Orleans, 1840-1900[‡]

Organization	Founding date
New Orleans Liederkranz	1845
Turnverein chorus	1851
Deutsche Harmonie Club of New Orleans	unknown
Deutsche Harmonie Club of Carrollton	1869
Deutsche Männergesangsverein	1873
6th District Männergesangsverein	1874
New Orleans Liedertafel	1878
New Orleans Quartett Club	1882
Harugari Männerchor	1882
Frohsinn	1884
Liederkreis of the 4th District	1889
Franz Schubert Gesangsverein	1897

[‡]Information taken from Nau, 104-06, 111; and *Tägliche Deutsche Zeitung*, 20 April 1884, and 16 October 1884. The date given for Frohsinn in Nau and cited in Snyder is incorrect.

Despite its greater population, New York in 1840 had a much less structured musical culture. Its earliest opera seasons were presented by traveling troupes (one from New Orleans) in the 1820s; an attempt to establish an Italian opera house in the 1830s failed after a few years. Although various societies gave occasional concerts in the early decades of the nineteenth century, and while the city did not lack for theaters and pleasure gardens, a stable and permanent musical organization did not appear until 1842, with the founding of the Philharmonic Symphony Society. The first theater devoted exclusively to opera and concerts—the Academy of Music—opened only in 1854, while the first permanent opera company—the Metropolitan— did not come into existence until 1883.[9] Thus the New York Männerchöre arrived on a musical scene ripe for organization and uncluttered by existing institutions.

During the last half of the nineteenth century, the roster of Männerchöre in both cities continued to grow (see Tables 1 and 2, pages 81-82). For the most part, the structure and activities of the clubs followed a predictable pattern: A small group of men formed a core of "active" members who sang in the chorus and often dominated the club's elected officials. (Women sometimes were admitted to a "Damenchor" or used in a mixed chorus, but were not allowed to become members.)[10] The actives were joined and supported by a larger number of "passive" members, who paid their dues for the pleasure of attending the concerts and other functions sponsored by the clubs. "Other functions" are the key words here, because a club's activities nearly always extended beyond the purely musical realm to include such other functions as elaborate balls, picnics, and summer excursions, making them into organizations whose social and cultural aspects assumed at least as much importance as their musical ones. As a result, factors such as the social status and ethnic attitudes of the membership, the relative importance of music and socializing in the club's purpose, and its relationship to the surrounding non-German community all shaped its interaction with the city's music establishment.

That the issue of social status and class distinctions arose at all is actually somewhat ironic, given the fact that Männerchöre had originated in Germany as social associations that brought together men from the working class. And initially, some in the German-American community hoped that the social element would serve as a unifying force, bringing the immigrants together in the alien society of the New World. In 1860, the *Staatszeitung* of New York expressed the view that singing clubs united "the worker, the businessman and the politician" and erased "the social distinctions which divide the German element."[11] But that rosy, utopian view did not take into account the divisive power of money in America's "classless" society, and an elite group of wealthy Männerchöre began to separate from the pack during the last third of the nineteenth century in both New York and New Orleans.[12]

Of the few clubs that made it to the top of the heap in New York, the most prominent were the Liederkranz, founded in 1847; Arion, which split from the Liederkranz in 1854 and finally reunited with it in 1920; and the Beethoven Männerchor.[13] During the 1860s all three built imposing clubhouses in the heart of New York's German district (at that time the Lower East Side.) By the 1880s both the Liederkranz and Arion had outgrown their accommodations and chose to move uptown (both literally and figuratively) to more spacious and prestigious locations on the upper east side (the Liederkranz to East 58th and the Arion to the corner of Park Avenue and 59th Street). The new Liederkranz clubhouse, built at a cost of $325,000—an enormous sum of money in those days—boasted a grand ballroom; dining, reception, and billiard rooms; a library; and a concert hall seating twelve hundred, all lavishly furnished in the best of Victorian overkill.[14]

Such elegant surroundings were supported by a large membership willing to pay substantial dues. Though the Liederkranz started out with a reasonable charge of $2 per year in 1857, it had upped the ante to $24 by 1869, and to $30 by 1885. Arion stayed right by its side, with annual dues of $3 in 1854 but charging $30 by 1886 and $40 by 1894.[15] Such figures must of course be seen in nineteenth-century terms. As money that went to discretionary entertainment, these dues were well beyond the means of a typical factory or government postal worker, whose income in 1890 would have been under a thousand dollars annually.[16] Even if he could have scraped the money together for the dues (and the initiation fee that often equaled a year's dues), an average worker certainly would not have felt comfortable, or probably even welcome, in the luxurious surroundings the clubs offered; nor would he have had the wardrobe or the leisure time that would have allowed him to take advantage of the elaborate club activities. But plenty of men did have the time and money to join, for the Liederkranz and Arion grew to be the largest Männerchöre in New York.

Only thirteen years after its founding, in 1860, the Liederkranz could count 547 members; a quarter of a century later, in 1884, it reached a peak of 1,557 members shortly after it moved into its new clubhouse.[17] Though Arion always remained somewhat smaller, it too reached a peak of over 1,000 in 1886,[18] while the Beethoven Männerchor trailed with a still substantial 500 members in 1870.[19] These numbers included many prominent New Yorkers, mostly but not exclusively of German stock. Carl Schurz, an early member of the Liederkranz, served as ambassador to Spain under Abraham Lincoln and later became a U.S. senator. Theodore Roosevelt joined during his tenure as New York's police commissioner; both William Steinway, manager and part owner of the piano firm, and Oswald Ottendorfer, civic leader and editor of the *Staatszeitung,* served as president.[20]

With the financial resources provided by the substantial dues of a large membership, these elite clubs could support an extensive calendar of entertainment for their membership. All three regularly sponsored summer excursions that ranged from brief outings to Coney Island to weekends in the Catskills; some years brought more elaborate trips, like the Arion journey to Yellowstone National Park in 1897.[21] During the winter, the preferred activity seemed to be dancing, for formal balls dominated the clubs' entertainment calendars. Both the Liederkranz and Arion held lavish events at prestigious locations like the Metropolitan Opera House, taking them beyond the confines of the German community into the wider New York social scene:

> The Liederkranz Ball which occupies one of the most conspicuous places in New York's festive calendar, more than maintained its reputation for gaiety and splendor. Fashion and beauty filled the box tiers and the vast parquet floor of the Metropolitan Opera House was thronged with masqueraders resplendent in the picturesque costumes of historic times.[22]

In the 1890s, Arion began to make use of Madison Square Garden for its balls, but "the increasingly public character of these affairs became so distasteful to club members that they were finally discontinued."[23] In addition, during the 1890s, the younger members of all three clubs, known as Young Arion, the Liederkranz Bachelor's Circle, and the Beethoven Bachelors, joined together to sponsor charity balls that usually raised anywhere from $10,000 to $25,000 for various worthy causes.[24]

None of the New Orleans clubs came close to the wealth of even the less prominent New York elite, but at least one, the Liedertafel, did have elitist aspirations. After modest beginnings, with a treasury of $98.11 and dues at $6.00 per year, the Liedertafel expanded rapidly, reporting a treasury worth $1,669.19 only two years later.[25] Heady with success, club officers voted to move to new quarters in the prestigious Pickwick Club.[26] In doing so, they assumed an annual rent of $1,800 and had to float bonds worth $5,000 to furnish the place in a suitably luxurious style.[27] To pay for the new surroundings, the club launched a membership drive, and by January 1882, it boasted 588 members (plus 40 women in a Damenchor) and an annual cash flow of over $6,000.[28]

These financial triumphs accompanied a steady rise in the club's role in New Orleans society. In 1881, after one of its balls, the *Tägliche Deutsche Zeitung* proclaimed:

> All of the prominent Germans were there, so that we can dispense with naming them.... The dancing lasted until the wee hours of the morning, and as soon as the hangovers are gone, each person will surely say he had attended the nicest and most entertaining Carnival party that ever took place in New Orleans.[29]

The Liedertafel also sponsored charity fund-raisers that benefited the larger New Orleans community, on one occasion taking in $859 at a concert for a local hospital (see pages 87-88).[30] Its social activities likewise began to take on a grander scope. In April 1881, the club rented the steamer *Robert E. Lee* for a cruise on the Mississippi to the plantation home of the former governor Henry Warmouth, who greeted them at dockside and invited the

New Orleans Liedertafel.

GRAND VOCAL AND INSTRUMENTAL

CONCERT

GIVEN

FOR THE BENEFIT OF THE

Charity Hospital.

——AT THE——

GRAND OPERA HOUSE

——ON——

THURSDAY, APRIL 5th, 1883.

A New Orleans Liedertafel concert-program cover.
Courtesy of the New Orleans Historic Collection.

PROGRAMME.

PART I.

I.—*Overture* . . . . *Iphigenie in Aulis* . . . . GLUCK.
ORCHESTRA.

II.—*Andante con moto from the 5th Symphony* . . . . BEETHOVEN.
ORCHESTRA.

III.—*Aria* . . *Le Cheval de Bronze* . . . . . *Soprano Solo* . . . . . AUBER.
Mrs. ALICE SCHWARTZ.

IV.—*Swedish Wedding March* . . . . SOEDERMANN.
ORCHESTRA.

V.—*Fantaisie de Concert* . . . . . *Faust* . . . . ALARD.
Violin Solo with Piano Accompaniment.
Misses MARIE WAYNACK and CECILE MARX.

VI.—*Les Bacchantes* . . . . *Philomene and Baucis* . . . . GOUNOD.

a) OUVERTURE PASTORALE.
b) REVEILLE.
c) MELODRAME.
d) DANCE DES BACCHANTES.

ORCHESTRA.

PART II.

Das Lied von der Glocke · · · · The Lay of the Bell.
Words by SCHILLER. — *Music by* ROMBERG.

Grand Chorus and Solis.

N. O. LIEDERTAFEL and ORCHESTRA.

The PIANO used at this occasion has been kindly furnished by
Mr. LOUIS GRUNEWALD.

The concert program itself.

club officers to dine with him.[31] Such activities also attracted members from outside the German community, as they did in the elite New York clubs. In fact, by 1882, fully one seventh of the Liedertafel's 580 members were not native German speakers, though according to the minutes, they participated only in the entertainments, not the business meetings.[32] Moreover, like exclusive clubs everywhere, those who belonged anxiously controlled and limited access to their activities. In the early days, non-members could purchase tickets to events, though generally through one of the members.[33] After the move to the new quarters, however, regulations restricting and even prohibiting attendance at club functions by nonmembers began to appear.[34] Unlike its New York cousins, however, the Liedertafel could not sustain the position to which it aspired, and by 1887, only six years after the move to the Pickwick Club, it had disappeared from view entirely.[35] Though a variety of causes led to its downfall, the root of the problem was the simple fact that the New Orleans German community simply was not large or wealthy enough to support a club with those aspirations.[36]

Ranging under the elite clubs in both cities were the rank-and-file Männerchöre that catered to comfortably situated workers, businessmen, and professionals; even the largest and best established of them could not begin to compete with the social and financial clout of their wealthier counterparts.[37] Most, for example, rented rather than owned their meeting space; the chronicles of the New York clubs are filled with accounts of the frequent moves most were forced to make, ever in search of a sympathetic landlord with a generously flowing tap.

In New Orleans, Frohsinn bemoaned the fact that it had paid out what was considered to be a considerable sum for rent in 1886 ($735—less than half of what the Liedertafel had spent a few years earlier) but lacked the capital to invest in any property.[38] If a club did manage to purchase a clubhouse, it was on a much more modest scale than those of the Liederkranz or Arion; the property on East 86th Street purchased by the Mozartverein of New York in 1893 cost a mere $21,000.[39] As a rule these clubs had a smaller membership—averaging around two hundred—and lower dues. In 1888, for example, the New York Ehrenritter Gesangsverein demanded only six dollars a year from its members.[40] During that same decade, dues for the New Orleans

Frohsinn were twelve dollars per year, less than half the price of the New York Liederkranz and Arion, though still requiring a comfortable income.[41]

Club treasuries and annual cash flow likewise remained modest. In 1872, for example, the New York Sängerrunde reported assets of $3,210; that year its annual cash flow topped $4,500, but fell to less than a quarter of that only a decade later after a decline in membership.[42] Similarly, when the rented quarters of the New Orleans Frohsinn burned in 1892, the club lost all its possessions, valued at fifteen hundred dollars.[43] The modest size of an 1897 inventory list reveals that it had not been able to fully replace its property:

> 1 square concert piano (original cost $250)
> 2 glass door armoires
> 1 large covered table
> 6 heavy wooden chairs
> 1 ice cooler plus tray and glasses
> 11 pictures
> 1 hat rack
> 1 screen
> 18 cane bottom chairs[44]

Frohsinn's annual income topped five thousand dollars during the peak of its membership in the early 1890s, but dropped dramatically only a few years later when, like the New York Sängerrunde, it began to lose members.[45] Finally, though the Männerchöre of more modest means also held charity fundraisers, the amounts they raised were apt to be well under what the more affluent could conjure up. For example, the New York Eichenkranz regularly reported a fundraising capacity of between two hundred and four hundred dollars.[46]

The excursions of such clubs had a more homespun character, often entailing picnic trips to the surrounding countryside. In New Orleans, escaping to the slightly cooler outlying areas during the heat of the summer proved particularly enticing, and clubs like Frohsinn took advantage of special railway fares for jaunts to resort areas north of Lake Pontchartrain. On one outing to Slidell in August 1884, the planning and welcoming committee took an early train over to make preparations and serenaded the remaining club members and families when they arrived. Each of the committee members had assumed the persona of a well-known literary or musical figure, including Ole Bull, Beethoven, Mozart, Shakespeare, and Schiller. Shakespeare was the leader and conducted his singers with a head of red cabbage stuck on the end of his baton.

By 11:00 A.M., "the party became quite lively," especially "after the picnic baskets were unpacked and the foaming 'nectar of the gods' from the South Brew Company was flowing freely."[47] Then came dancing and bowling, while some opted for a visit to "the magnificent bayou with the Railroad Company's creosote factory," which must indeed have been spectacular in the August heat. The only crisis of the day occurred when the beer ran out an hour before the train was to leave, causing a near riot of indignation. When the club began preparations for a similar excursion the following year, they made a special point of ordering enough beer.

The gulf between the elite and rank-and-file clubs involved more than money, social status, and the sophistication of the entertainment; it concerned ethnic identity as well. While practically all the Männerchöre claimed to be the preservers of German culture in a new land, the rank-and-file tended to be more aggressively Teutonic, often linking their club's existence to the German community's struggle to survive under adverse circumstances.

The history of the New York Sängerrunde refers to the time "in which the 'Rowdythum' of New York was still in full bloom and professional ruffians of the 'French Louis' type, and their followers never lost a chance to harass each German festivity with their presence, whether it was held outside or in closed chambers—that time in which it was often dangerous to speak German out on the street."[48] The history of the Yorkville Männerchor refers to similar "rough and vulgar elements,"[49] while the Mozartverein went a step further and laid the blame for the rowdiness squarely on the Irish.[50] But the cultural paranoia received its fullest expression in the history of the New York Männergesangverein Eichenkranz:

The 1860s, before the glorious victories of the Franco-Prussian war, were not in general favorable times here for the development and cheerful growth of German culture, that is the German love of singing and music, the true cultivation of German customs, and the maintaining of the ideal German life style—in contrast to the eternal quest for the "almighty dollar" and the strict, religious, puritanical bigotry and temperance mania that rules everywhere.

To the Irish the German was, in the political and social realm (particularly in view of the ever-growing Element in the cities) still only the "d... [*sic*] Dutchman, the phlegmatic, pipe-smoking friend of "lager beer, sauerkraut and Limburger cheese," someone who couldn't be compared with the whiskey-drinking sons of the "Emerald Isle," and who in general, according to his [the Irishman's] point of view, had no right to political recognition.[51]

New Orleans also had a substantial Irish population (see the figures earlier), and the relationship between the two communities apparently suffered from the same prejudices, as revealed by an 1890 article in the *Tägliche Deutsche Zeitung*. In that year the city's Männerchöre hosted a meeting of the Nordamerikanischer Sängerbund (discussed later); after the successful close of the festival, the paper's Sunday morning columnist congratulated the participants, contrasting the civilized nature of their drinking habits with those of the Irish (and managing a swipe at the temperance ladies):

This week, New Orleans offered residents of other nationalities a quite singular spectacle: we can only regret that the Christian temperance ladies or the pig-headed prohibitionists didn't send delegations here in order to see the hurly-burly with their own eyes. They would have been able to see how 20,000 Germans—all strapping, robust figures, elegantly and respectably dressed, Moses and the Prophets safely in their pockets—amused themselves for an entire week without somehow losing control; how they smoothly "bent their elbows" from early in the morning until late at night without there ever being a drunk to be seen on the streets; how though New Orleans was delivered up unto them—for better or worse—they did not avail themselves of the rights of the conquerors but in every instance behaved like worthy, well-bred true German men.——What would New Orleans have looked like if the Irish National-Liga or a national political convention had been here

instead! A German regards drinking as a science: he never gets drunk
and is merry without causing a row.[52]

Despite these differences, the musical taste of both elite and
rank-and-file clubs proved to be remarkably similar, although the
smaller clubs did not have the resources to mount productions of
works calling for large forces.[53] Regular concerts almost invariably
included a wide variety of pieces, from the expected choral
numbers to instrumental and vocal solos to symphonic works,
generally played by a hired orchestra.[54] The symphonic and solo
repertoire drew heavily on classic and romantic standards still
heard frequently today, especially the orchestral music of
Beethoven, overtures of Weber and Wagner, and Italian or French
opera arias. But even the combined choral works of Mozart,
Haydn, Beethoven, Schubert, Robert Schumann, and Wagner could
not satisfy the Männerchöre's voracious appetite for musical
fodder, so most clubs tended to feature composers specializing in
the genre, like Joseph Rheinberger, Otto Teich, Wilhelm Paasch,
Julius Otto, Franz Abt, Karl Friedrich Zöllner, Johann Wenzel
Kalliwoda, and others, who churned out a seemingly endless
stream of choral trivia. But again, though individual directors may
have shaped a club's repertoire for better or worse, no distinction
can be made between the musical tastes of the elite and the middle
rank. Both presented "serious" as well as mass-produced music, as
demonstrated by two programs, one from an elite Liederkranz
concert and the second from the fortieth anniversary celebration
of the rank-and-file Sängerrunde[55] (see pages 94 and 95).

Only when we consider the musical outreach of the clubs do
any differences become apparent, for the limited financial
resources and ethnocentric orientation of most Männerchöre
restricted their direct musical impact to the German community
itself. The elite clubs, however, had the money to support the
production of major works and often performed in the major
concert halls and opera houses where their performances would
have been heard by a wider audience. In New York, for example,
the Liederkranz presented the American premiere of Liszt's
Prometheus on 21 October 1871; Bruch's *Scenen aus der Odyssee*
on 25 January 1874; and Brahms's *Ein deutsches Requiem* on 24

The Liederkranz at Carnegie Hall, 7 January 1897

Jubel-Overture	C. M. v. Weber
"Die Ehre Gottes in der Natur" Männerchor und Orchestra	Beethoven
"Ruhe, Süssliebchen" Männerchor	Heinrich Zöllner
Arie aus *Hamlet* Frl. Blauvelt und Orchestra	A. Thomas
Drei Männerchöre "Ritornell" "Der schönste Bursch" "Die Muttersprache"	 R. Schumann Döring Engelsberg
Trauermarsch aus der *Götterdämmerung*	R. Wagner
Concert für Pianoforte in A-dur Herr Joseffy und Orchestra	F. Liszt
Zwei Männerchöre im Volkston "Mei' Muata mag mi' net" "Minnelied"	 Folk song Buente
Altfranzösisches Lied aus der Oper *Der Ueberfall*	H. Zöllner
Frl. Blauvelt und Orchestra	
Zwei Männerchöre mit Sopran-Solo "Ständchen" "Glockenthürmer's Töchterlein" Solo: Frl. Blauvelt	 Liszt Reinthaler
"Die Allmacht" Männerchor und Orchestra Solo: Frl. Blauvelt	Schubert-Liszt

A Sängerrunde Concert in November 1888

Jubel-Overture Orchester	C. von Weber
Männerchor—"In der Lenznacht" New York Sängerrunde	Carl Hirsch
Concert für Violine und Orchester Herr Ferdinand Carri	Max Bruch
"Schlummer Arie" aus *Die Afrikanerin* Frl. Augusta Marschall	Meyerbeer
Männerchor—"Sturm" New York Sängerrunde	Carl Hirsch
Zwei ungarische Tänze Orchester	Johannes Brahms
Jubilate Amen Hymne für Sopran, Männerchor, Piano und Orgel	Johannes Geleke
Piano Solo—Ungarische Rhapsodie (No. 4) Herr Hermann Carri	Franz Liszt
Männerchor—"Festgesang" M.G.V. Eichenkranz, Zollner Männerchor M.G.V. Germania, New York Sängerrunde	Arthur Claassen
Einzug der Gäste in die Wartburg aus *Tannhäuser* Orchester	Rich. Wagner

---

January 1875.[56] The Beethoven Männerchor arranged a performance of *Fidelio* at the Academy of Music on 16 December 1870, followed the next night by *Christus am Oelberg* at the club's new hall.[57] Though it is impossible to ascertain what percentage of the audience came from outside the German community, critics from English-language newspapers like the *New York Tribune* and the *New York Times* did review some of the concerts (see the Appendix, pages 107-109). Thus, even if they did not attend, culturally educated New Yorkers would have at least known of the contributions of the elite Männerchöre.

Not only did the elite clubs sponsor their own concerts, in New York they were frequently asked (especially the Arion and Liederkranz) to assist in concerts of the city's professional ensembles. A few examples should suffice here; others are given in the Appendix. During a strike by the chorus members at the Academy of Music, the manager hired the Liederkranz for a production of Mozart's *Don Giovanni* in January 1858. The critic at the *New York Times* praised the Liederkranz's performance, saying that it "sang with better evidence of musical training than we are accustomed to hear in an Italian opera house," though one suspects that was more of a dig at the Italians than praise for the Germans.[58]

The following year, Arion sang in the first American production of a complete Wagner opera, *Tannhäuser*, given at the German Theater in the Bowery.[59] Both organizations also participated in concerts of the New York Philharmonic Society (the Liederkranz as early as 1850),[60] and in Theodore Thomas's symphony series. In addition, the two clubs also served as hosts and sponsors of many European performers and composers touring America. One Arion concert saw the American premiere of the violinist Fritz Kreisler, and the Liederkranz hosted a wide variety of guests, from Jenny Lind to Richard Strauss.[61]

Both the Liederkranz and Arion made contacts with outside concert organizations through their conductors, who included two of the most influential musical men in New York: Theodore Thomas and Leopold Damrosch. Thomas came to New York from Esens, Germany, at age ten; he joined the New York Philharmonic Society as a violinist in 1854, and later served as its conductor.[62] During his tenure as Liederkranz director (1882-1884 and 1887-1888), he used the Liederkranz chorus in his famous Wagner concerts.[63] Leopold Damrosch immigrated to the United States in 1871 to become the Arion's musical director, a position he held until 1883.[64] During that time he also founded the New York Oratorio Society (in 1873) and the New York

Symphony Society (in 1878), guiding both until his death in 1885.[65] His son Walter continued his father's unceasing efforts to bring new music, and especially new German music, to American audiences. Succinctly put, the elite Männerchöre of New York played a vital role in shaping the city's permanent musical institutions. Performances by rank-and-file clubs—no matter what the program—went unnoticed outside their communities; their names almost never appear in the columns of the *New York Times* or the *New York Tribune*, eloquent if negative testimony to their narrower outreach.

Rank-and-file clubs in New Orleans had a similar fate, especially when they concentrated on the production of operettas and musical farces in the German language, as Frohsinn did. Had the elite Liedertafel survived longer, it might have formalized a German contribution to New Orleans' musical institutions, for it did show signs of moving in that direction when it sponsored a concert at the Grand Opera House. Not only was the program printed in English, and the performance advertised in the English-language *Daily Picayune*, but the repertoire is unusually French for a Männerchor presentation (see page 88). As observed earlier, however, the community's numbers and financial base were working against the Liedertafel as an elite institution. Even more insidious, and ultimately more damaging, was the internal tension between the club members interested mainly in the music and those interested mainly in the entertainment and socializing.[66] The latter usually won.

In 1881, two months after its elaborate riverboat trip, the club's music director, J. Hanno Deiler, resigned in exasperation when club members balked at financially supporting the active members' participation at a national Sängerfest in Chicago.[67] Deiler viewed participation in the Sängerfest activities as a measure of the club's commitment to serious music-making and left the Liedertafel to form the New Orleans Quartett Club.[68] However noble and worthy his musical ideals may have been, this club faced continuing membership and financial crises, causing Deiler to lash out publicly against the "apathy of the common mass of people," who expected a singing club to be "above all an entertainment club," and who tended "to be satisfied with lesser achievements in singing as long as there are plenty of 'entertainments' in return for the monthly dues."[69] Though the

Quartett Club outlasted the society-oriented Liedertafel and managed to limp along into the twentieth century, its members sang mostly to themselves.

Ironically, the only time the larger New Orleans community became substantially involved with the Männerchöre was for the 1890 national Sängerfest of the North American Sängerbund, which Deiler had managed to secure for New Orleans. The *Tägliche Deutsche Zeitung* chronicled every detail of the proceedings, running countless feature articles and publishing a special festival edition a month before the actual event (the cover presented a Valkyrie-*cum*-harp singing to alligators!). Ever supportive of a large party, the city kicked in a splendid welcome, building a special Sängerhalle with a seating capacity of five thousand and amenities like a press room decked out with tropical plants and a well-stocked bar.[70] To accommodate the out-of-town singers, a special hotel had to be constructed. Built in only six weeks, it featured a large double bar flanked by two spacious community rooms and an upstairs sleeping room containing three hundred fifty cots, all neatly arranged in rows with fresh new linens, "so that there was no question of bedbugs." Though the *Tägliche Deutsche Zeitung* did remark that it might prove difficult for a singer to locate his cot among the hundreds there, especially late at night after an evening of carousing, it jovially dismissed the problem, saying "what does it matter, as long as the cot is empty."[71] With an estimated 1,700 German singers in what was still a relatively small city,[72] the rest of the population could hardly have been uninvolved, especially when the out-of-towners played tourist, visiting the local breweries (one had 1,786 visitors in a single day), or purchasing souvenirs (oranges and alligators—both stuffed and live—were the favorites).[73]

In fact, the participation in the actual musical events extended beyond the German community: English-language newspapers like the *Daily Picayune* and the *New Orleans States* announced and reviewed festival activities; the French Opera House staged a special production of Meyerbeer's *Les Huguenots* in honor of the Sängerfest; the city's mayor, Joseph Shakespeare, took German lessons in preparation; most of the concerts were sold out; and the opening evening featured a performance by the local French choral society, the Orpheon Français.[74] As the *Daily*

Picayune observed: "The Saengerfest ... is in a large degree cosmopolitan because the people of New Orleans without regard to nationality have entered heart and soul into the great work."[75] The effect of the event on the city was nonetheless short-lived; the English-language newspapers abandoned the story as soon as the last note was sung; the Sängerhalle and hotel were torn down and the New Orleans Männerchöre left to their own devices until one by one they slipped out of existence.[76]

Although they unquestionably contributed to the city's musical culture by keeping a large segment of the population involved in music at a time when any type of cultivated music was the object of a certain amount of suspicion, the New Orleans clubs had little impact on the city's musical institutions. Hampered by the lack of financial resources, crippled by internal conflicts and the relatively small size of the community, and in competition with the Anglo/French musical establishment, their effect was insular and ephemeral, centering mainly around a onetime grand event. In New York, the climate was right. There the Männerchöre emerged into an unorganized musical world that was ripe for the establishment of permanent institutions and which offered them an arena largely free of cultural competition. With the financial resources of the elite clubs, and the ready-made audience secured by the rank-and-file, they were perfectly positioned to assume the city's musical leadership. Perhaps, though, the different degrees of success depended on intangible factors discernable even today: New York still provides a home for many of the country's most honored musical institutions, and New Orleans still throws a good musical party.

Loyola University

---

[1]I am indebted to the librarians and archivists of the Historic New Orleans Collection and the Music Collection of the New York Public Library for their assistance in my research for this project and to my colleague Dr. Mark McKnight for his comments on the manuscript. The research on the New York clubs was completed while I was attending a 1986 NEH Summer Seminar at New York University on "The Cultural Life of American Cities."

[2]Suzanne Gail Snyder, "The *Männerchor* Tradition in the United States: A Historical Analysis of Its Contribution to American Musical Culture" (Ph.D. diss., University of Iowa, 1991), 6.

[3]Stanley Nadel, *Kleindeutschland: New York City's Germans, 1845-1880* (Ph.D. diss., Columbia University, 1981), 81; and *New Orleans: A Chronological and Documentary History, 1539-1970*, comp. and ed. Martin Siegel (Dobbs Ferry, NY: Oceana Publications, 1975), 29. J. Hanno Deiler, a musician, historian and leading figure in the nineteenth-century New Orleans German community, contended that the census did not accurately reflect the true numbers of the community. He estimated the number to have been closer to 25,000, for a percentage of 11.5%. See his "Germany's Contribution to the Present Population of New Orleans with a Census of the German Schools," *Louisiana Journal of Education* (May 1886): 3. However, an equally avid historian for New York's German community might have been able to make a case for underreporting there as well.

[4]J. Hanno Deiler, *Geschichte der Deutschen Gesellschaft von New Orleans. Festschrift zum Goldenen Jubiläum der Gesellschaft* (New Orleans: by the author, 1897), 50. Because the French and Spanish communities were many generations deep by 1890, the numbers of foreign-*born* residents do not reflect the extent of their ethnic domination.

[5]Nadel, 136; and John Frederick Nau, *The German People of New Orleans, 1850-1900* (Leiden: E. J. Bull, 1958), 7.

[6]Nadel, 237; Deiler, *Zur Geschichte der Deutschen Kirchengemeinden im Staate Louisiana* (New Orleans: by the author, 1894), 23. Deiler cites an item dated 4 October 1840 from the *New Orleans Picayune*: "The German Glee Club will assist at the opening of the new German church in Clio Str. this morning." The wording implies the prior existence of the club. I am indebted to Raymond N. Calvert of New Orleans for bringing this passage to my attention.

[7]Henry A. Kmen, *Music in New Orleans: The Formative Years, 1791-1841*, (Baton Rouge: Louisiana State University Press, 1966), 58, 67. The French Opera House, which opened in 1859, was a direct successor to the Orleans Theater.

[8]Kmen, 137. Kmen documents opera performances from 1796 to 1841 in a valuable appendix to his dissertation, *Singing and Dancing in New Orleans* (Ph.D. diss.: Tulane University, 1961), 272-449. Two other theaters, the St. Philip Street and the Camp Street, also offered opera performances in the early nineteenth century.

[9]*New Grove Dictionary of Music and Musicians*, ed. Stanley Sadie (London: Macmillan, 1980), s.v. "New York," by Irving Kolodin, Francis D. Perkins, and Susan Thiemann Sommer.

[10]In the late nineteenth century, the New Orleans Frohsinn actually took the radical step of allowing widows of former members to join and be present at business meetings, though the minutes make it clear they could not vote—or even participate in the discussion.

[11]*Staatszeitung*, 19 July 1860. Quoted in Nadel, 239.

[12]Elitism also could be found in some of the clubs in other large cities, e.g., St. Louis and Baltimore, but apparently was less common in smaller communities. See the discussion in Snyder, 108-10.

[13]*History of the Liederkranz of the City of New York 1847 to 1947 and of the Arion, New York* (New York: Drechsel Printing Co., 1948), 51; and *Beethoven Männerchor. Ausflug. 1890* ([New York]: n.p.), 7. The only other club that may have been their equal in status was the New York Männerchor; a financial report from 1895-1896 reveals assets worth $171,907.22, dues income of $1,454.50, and a yearly cash flow of over $10,000, quite impressive considering the membership numbered only 334. See the club's *Finanz Bericht und Mitglieder-Liste*. The histories of the New York clubs are located in the Music Collection of the New York Public Library.

[14]*Liederkranz*, 10-15; and *Arion. New York von 1854-1904: Ein Rückblick auf fünfzig Jahre deutschen Strebens in Amerika anlässlich des goldenen Jubiläums des Vereins* (New York: n.p., 1904), 19-23.

[15]*Liederkranz*, 143-44; *Charter und Statuten des Gesang-Vereins Deutscher Liederkranz der Stadt New York* (New York: Keppler & Schwarzman, 1885), 8; and *Arion*, 7, 77. I have no figures for the Beethoven Männerchor.

[16]Paul Douglas, *Real Wages in the United States, 1890-1926* (Boston and New York: Houghton Mifflin, 1930), 140, 193.

[17]*Liederkranz*, 9, 19.

[18]*Arion*, 27.

[19]*Beethoven Männerchor*, 8.

[20]*Liederkranz*, 4, 39. Steinway was also a prominent civic leader, who served as president of the Metropolitan Opera Association, the New York Rapid Transit Commission and a close friend and advisor of President Grover Cleveland. See *The New Grove Dictionary of American Music*, s.v. "Steinway, William" by Cynthia Adams Hoover; and Albert Bernhardt Faust, *The German Element in the United States* (New York: The Stuben

Society of America, 1927): Vol. II, 448-49. See also the essay by Edwin Good in the present volume.

[21] *Liederkranz*, 149.

[22] *Leslie's Weekly*, 8 February 1888, quoted in *Liederkranz*, 20. Snyder gives an extensive description of the whole masked ball phenomenon (Snyder, 122-36).

[23] *Liederkranz*, 23.

[24] *Liederkranz*, 36.

[25] "Liedertafel Constitution, and its Minutes and Correspondence," 31 May 1879 and 8 November 1881. Manuscript Division, Historic New Orleans Collection, New Orleans, Louisiana.

[26] "Liedertafel Minutes," 3 October 1881. The Pickwick Club is still in existence as an exclusive men's club.

[27] "Liedertafel Minutes," 5 December 1881.

[28] "Liedertafel Minutes," 2 January 1882.

[29] "An prominenten Deutschen hatte sich Alles eingefunden, so dass wir auf Nennung verzichten können.... Bis zur frühen Morgenstunde währte der Tanz und wenn der Katzenjammer überwunden, wird sich Jeder sagen müssen, das er dem schönsten und amusantesten Carnevalsfeste, welches je in New Orleans stattfand, beigewohnt hat" [*Tägliche Deutsche Zeitung*, 1 March 1881].

[30] *Tägliche Deutsche Zeitung*, 16 April 1883.

[31] *Tägliche Deutsche Zeitung*, 29 April 1881; 3 May 1881.

[32] "Liedertafel Minutes," 2 January 1882.

[33] "Liedertafel Minutes," 25 January 1879, 12 November 1879, 20 December 1880, 10 January 1881.

[34] "Liedertafel Minutes," 3 April 1882.

[35] By 1887 the Liedertafel was no longer listed in the city directory.

[36] See Snyder, "Singing and Drinking in New Orleans," *The Southern Quarterly* 27 (Winter 1989): 5-24.

[37] At the very bottom of the financial scale were the socialist workers' Männerchöre that sprang up during the latter part of the century in New York. A newspaper published for the fourth Sängerfest of the Arbeiter-Sängerbund in Brooklyn in 1905 lists the names of sixty-two workers' clubs in the Northeast; the ten in New York all had under one hundred

members. See the *Fest-Zeitung für das vierte Bundes-Sängerfest des Arbeiter-Sängerbundes der N. O. Staaten von Amerika am 1, 2, 3, und 4 Juli 1905. Brooklyn, N.Y* (New York: Co-Operative Press, [1905]), 18. Otherwise I found no trace of their activities.

38"Frohsinn, Minutes and Correspondence," 3 February 1887, containing an undated clipping from the *Tägliche Deutsche Zeitung.* Manuscript Division, Historic New Orleans Collection, New Orleans, Louisiana.

39*Mozart Verein, 1854-1904. Fest-Souvenir zum Goldenen Jubiläum* (New York: n.p., 1904), 27.

40*Grundgesetze des Ehrenritter-Gesang-Vereins* (New York: Adolph Volkhard, 1888).

41"Frohsinn Minutes," 12 December 1884.

42*Geschichte der New York*[er] *Sängerrunde von ihrer Gründung Nov. 1848 bis zu ihrem 40 jährigen Stiftungsfest in November 1888* ([New York?], n.p., 1888).

43These included a piano and the club's library of books and scores. See "Frohsinn Minutes," 1 November 1892.

44"Frohsinn Minutes," 10 May 1897.

45"Frohsinn Minutes," 11 January 1892, and 8 January 1897. During these five years the membership dropped from 502 to 209.

46*Geschichte des Männergesangvereins Eichenkranz. Zur Erinnerung an das 25 jährige Jubiläum gefeiert vom 13. bis 15. Oktober 1894* (New York: n.p., 1894), 21.

47This account of the day is taken from the *Tägliche Deutsche Zeitung,* 3 August 1884; and "Frohsinn Minutes," 13 June 1884, 23 July 1884, and 4 June 1885.

48"[I]n welcher das Rowdythum New Yorks noch in voller Blüte stand und professionelle Raufbolde vom Schlage eines "French Louis" mit ihren Anhängern es sich nicht nehmen lassen, jede deutsche Festlichkeit, ob im Freien oder im geschlossenen Raum abgehalten, durch ihre Gegenwart zu stören, jene Zeit in welcher es oft gefährlich war, sich auf offener Strasse der deutschen Sprache zu bedienen" [*Sängerrunde,* n.p.]. Snyder documents the harassment German communities all over the U.S. received during the "Know-Nothing" movement of the 1850s (Snyder, 338-80).

49*Yorkville Männerchor. Fest-Souvenir zum Goldenen Jubiläum, 1856-1906* ([New York?], n.p. [1906]), 6.

50*Mozart Verein,* 15-16.

51"Die sechsiger Jahre vor den herrlichen Siegen des deutschen-franzözsichen Krieges waren hierzulande im Allgemeinen der Entwicklung und dem fröhlichen Gediehen des Deutschthums, d.h. den deutschen Liebe zum Gesang und zur Musik, der treuen Pflege deutscher Sitten, deutscher Geselligkeit und der Aufrechthaltung deutscher idealer Lebensauffassung im Gegensatze zur ewigen Jagd nach dem 'almighty Dollar' und der streng religiös-puritanischen Bigotterie und Temperenzsucht die überall vorherrschte, nicht günstig.

"Dem irischen, besonders in den Städten sich breit machenden Elemente gegenüber war der Deutsche im politischen und socialen Leben noch immer nur der d... [sic] Dutchman, der phlegmatische, pfeifenrauchende Freund von 'Lager, Sauerkraut und Limburger,' der sich mit ihm, dem Whiskey trinkenden Söhne der 'grünen Insel' in keiner Weise vergleichen konnte und überhaupt dessen Ansichten nach kein Anrecht auf politische Anerkennung hatte" [*Eichenkranz*, 9]. Defensiveness about Männerchor drinking habits was a widespread phenomenon. See Snyder, 380-409.

52"New Orleans bot diese Woche den Bewohnern anderer Nationalitäten einen ganz eigenthümlichen Anblick dar; wir bedauern blos, dass die christlichen Temperenzweiber, oder die verbohren Prohibitionisten nicht Deputationen hierher geschickt haben, um sich den Rummel mit eigenen Augen anzusehen! Sie hätten hier sehen können, wie zwanzigtausend Deutsche, alles stramme, kräftige Gestalten, elegant and solid gekleidet, Moses und die Propheten wohlverwahrt in der Tasche, sich eine ganze Woche lang köstlich amüsirten, ohne irgendwie über die Schnur zu hauen; wie sie von früh Morgens bis spät Abends flott kneipten, ohne dass ein Betrunkener in den Strassen zu sehen war; wie sie, obgleich New Orleans ihnen auf Gnade und Ungnade überantwortet war, doch von dem Recht des Eroberers keinen Gebrauch machten, sondern sich bei jeder Gelegenheit als brave gebildete ächt deutsche Männer benahmen.——Wie würde New Orleans wohl aussehen, wenn die irische National-Liga, oder eine politische National-Convention acht Tage darin gewirtschaftet hätten! Der Deutsche betrachtet das Trinken als eine Wissenschaft; er besäuft sich nie und ist heiter, ohne Krakehl zu machen" [*Tägliche Deutsche Zeitung*, 16 February 1890].

53Only the socialist workers' Männerchöre stand apart by virtue of the texts of their choral works, many of which touched on concerns of workers. Often new words were set to familiar operatic choruses. For example, the "Schlachthymn" entitled "Auf Römer Auf" in Wagner's Rienze found its way into the repertoire of the Sozialistischer Liedertafel with the words: "Arise, arise, gather round you proletarian bands/Fight the system that lo these many years has [held us] bewitched in the service of accursed avarice/ the yoke, death to the parasites, and hail to work." (See the "Musical Archives of the Sozialistischer Liedertafel and Arbeiter Männerchor," Music

Division, New York Public Library.) However, such politically charged choruses alternated with ordinary overtures and opera arias on worker's festival concerts, so in one sense, they were no different from their bourgeois brothers.

[54]Mixed genre formats were still common throughout the musical world in the late nineteenth century.

[55]Hermann Mosenthal, *Geschichte des Vereins deutscher Liederkranz in New York* (New York: F. A. Ringler, 1897), 109; and *Sängerrunde* 1888, n.p.

[56]Mark Curtis McKnight, *Music Criticism in the "New York Times" and the "New York Tribune," 1851-1876* (Ph.D. diss., Louisiana State University, 1980), 302-92; and *Liederkranz*, 144-45.

[57]*Beethoven Männerchor*, 8.

[58]*New York Times*, 16 January 1858. Quoted in McKnight, 117.

[59]*Arion*, 41, 72, and McKnight, 148-49.

[60]*Liederkranz*, 142.

[61]*Liederkranz*, 37, 40.

[62]Richard Crawford, *The American Musical Landscape* (Berkeley and Los Angeles: University of California Press, 1993), 81. Thomas also directed the Theodore Thomas Orchestra and the American Opera Company, and was the tireless sponsor of innumerable other professional music events.

[63]*Liederkranz*, 19, 97.

[64]*Arion*, 19, 22.

[65]*New Grove Dictionary of American Music* (London: Macmillan, 1986), s.v. Damrosch, Leopold, by H. E. Krehbiel, Richard Aldrich, H. C. Colles/R. Allen Lott.

[66]The same type of conflict also surfaced in New York clubs, but there the much larger community could support a club for every taste.

[67]"Liedertafel Minutes," 2 June 1881.

[68]The Quartett Club was the first New Orleans Männerchor to formally join the Sängerbund.

[69]*Tägliche Deutsche Zeitung*, 30 March 1890.

[70]*Tägliche Deutsche Zeitung*, 6 February 1890. Nau, 109, gives the capacity as 6,400, citing the *Official Text Book of the Twenty-Sixth American German Choral Union Festival*.

[71]Snyder, 148.

[72] *Tägliche Deutsche Zeitung*, 4 February 1890, and 7 February 1890.

[73] *Tägliche Deutsche Zeitung*, 15 February 1890.

[74] *Tägliche Deutsche Zeitung*, 13 February 1890; *New Orleans States*, 12 February 1890; 13 February 1890; and 15 February 1890.

[75] *Daily Picayune*, 13 February 1890.

[76] The few remaining German clubs of any kind, including Männerchöre, consolidated in 1920 into an umbrella organization known as the Deutsches Haus.

APPENDIX

Selected Liederkranz and Arion Performances
Reaching a Wider Audience

Note: *indicates that the concert was reviewed in the *New York Times* or the *New York Tribune.*

28 Dec. 1849:   Liederkranz with visiting Strauss Orchestra

25 May 1850:   Liederkranz in concert of Philharmonic Society

13 Nov. 1850:   Liederkranz with Jenny Lind at Tripler Hall

6 Dec. 1851:   Liederkranz at Astor Place Opera House
                           Lortzing: *Czar und Zimmermann*

17 Dec. 1851:   Liederkranz at Niblo's Garden
                           Lortzing: *Czar und Zimmermann*

*29 Dec. 1856:   Arion at Broadway Theater
                           Beethoven: *Fidelio*

*15 Jan. 1858:   Liederkranz at Academy of Music
                           Mozart: *Don Giovanni*

27 Jan. 1859:   Arion in Mozart's *Die Zauberflöte*

*4 Apr. 1859:   Arion at New York Stadt Theater
                           Wagner: *Tannhäuser* (U.S. premiere)

28 Dec. 1859:   Liederkranz at Cooper Institute
                           Haydn: *Die Schöpfung*

25 Jan. 1862:   Liederkranz in concert of Philharmonic Society

21 Dec. 1863:   Arion at Academy of Music
                           Gounod: *Faust* (in German)

15 Mar. 1864:   Liederkranz in concert of Philharmonic Society

*11 Mar. 1865:   Liederkranz at fourth of Theodore Thomas's series
                           Palestrina: "Fratus Ergo"
                           Liszt: "Credo"

*13 Jan. 1866:   Liederkranz at third of Theodore Thomas's series
                     Beethoven: "Choral Fantasy"

4 May 1867:   Liederkranz at twenty-fifth anniversary concert of
                         Philharmonic Society
                     Bruch: "Frithjofs-Saga"

18 Apr. 1868:   Arion in concert of Philharmonic Society

*Apr. 1870:   Liederkranz presents:
                     Handel's *Alexandersfest*

*May 1870:   Arion in concert of New York Philharmonic
                     Liszt: *Legende von der heiligen Elisabeth*

*Nov. 1870:   Liederkranz presents:
                     Liszt: *Legende von der heiligen Elisabeth*

*Dec. 1870:   Liederkranz presents Beethoven concert

7 Mar. 1874:   Liederkranz gives concert for Max Bruch
                     Bruch: "Scenen aus der Odyssee"

18 Apr. 1876:   Arion in concert for St. John's Guild
                     Weber: *Der Freischütz*

7 Apr. 1877:   Liederkranz in concert of Thomas Orchestra

8 Sept. 1877:   Arion at Terrace Garden
                     Weber: *Abu Hassan*

13 June 1878:   Liederkranz in concert with Thomas Orchestra

3 May 1879:   Liederkranz in concert of Brooklyn Philharmonic

12 June 1879:   Arion at Terrace Garden
                     Hoffner: *Der Ring des Nibelungen*

1 Apr. 1880:   Arion with New York Symphony and Oratorio
                         Society
                     Berlioz: "Damnation of Faust"

24 Apr. 1884:   Liederkranz in Theodore Thomas's Wagner concerts

1 May 1884:   Liederkranz in Theodore Thomas's Wagner concerts

10 Mar. 1895:   Liederkranz concert at Carnegie Hall with violinist Eugene Ysaye

7 Jan. 1897:   Liederkranz public concert at Carnegie Hall

19 Mar. 1899:   Liederkranz in concert at Carnegie Hall Haydn: *The Creation*

THE INDIANAPOLIS MÄNNERCHOR: CONTRIBUTIONS TO A NEW MUSICALITY IN MIDWESTERN LIFE

Suzanne G. Snyder

> The foundations of musical appre-
> ciation in Indianapolis were laid by
> German musical organizations, such
> as those represented in the great
> Saengerfest gathering in this city this
> year. It was the German immigration
> following the [Eighteen-] Forties ...
> that did more than any other agency to
> familiarize intelligent people with
> better music than "Leather Breeches"
> or "Hell on the Wabash."[1]

The above comment on nineteenth-century musical life in Indianapolis is found in the official souvenir publication of the North American Sängerbund's thirty-second national Sängerfest, held in Indianapolis from 17-20 June 1908. At the time of this festival, Indianapolis possessed no fewer than twenty-eight separate German-American organizations, several of which featured music as part of their activities. The most prominent of these organizations was the Indianapolis Männerchor—a society devoted to the promotion of male choral singing.

Several North American Sängerbund souvenir publications credit Michael Haydn with beginning the "Männerchor," or German secular male-chorus movement. In 1788, Haydn published *Männerquartette ohne Begleitung* ("Male Quartets Without Accompaniment"), the earliest collection of part-songs for male chorus to receive public attention. In 1808 the first German male singing club was organized in Berlin by Carl Friedrich Zelter and numbered the poet Goethe among its members. Calling itself the

"Liedertafel" after the "Round Table" of Arthurian romance, the organization was a prototype for similar societies in other cities. The first major German *Sängerfest* (choral festival) was held in 1845 at Würzburg in Bavaria, and involved male singing societies throughout the German-speaking states of Europe.[2]

Following the 1848 Revolution, many Germans who had supported the unification of the German states under a single constitution were forced to leave their homeland in search of political, artistic, and economic freedom. For the Germans newly arrived in the United States, the Männerchöre served to forge a bond of brotherhood and a sense of common purpose aimed toward facilitating survival in a foreign country. Singing the familiar songs of the *Vaterland* together helped ease the pain of dislocation by providing a link between the old life and the new. The singing societies not only served an important musical and social outlet for the German-American communities, but in many cases also supplied the earliest source of musical culture for the non-German population of the towns and cities in which they were located. The Männerchor tradition thus received impetus in the United States, where—through their Sängerfeste, concert series, opera productions, and general enthusiasm—German immigrants made a significant impact on the musical life of Indianapolis and many other American cities.

The Indianapolis Männerchor's Formation, Early Concerts, and Repertory

The history of the Indianapolis Männerchor began in 1854 when Eduard Longerich, Gottfried Recker, and Adolph Schnellschmidt settled in Indianapolis, having joined the many Germans fleeing Europe. These three gentlemen found lodgings with Recker's brother Hubert, who had arrived in the city shortly before. The four lived in primitive conditions in a sparsely furnished room rented for three dollars a month on the top floor of a three-story building at 75 East Washington Street. Having little money for other amusements, they spent their evenings singing quartets and trios to the accompaniment of a guitar or flute, and later, a melodeon.[3] Soon they were joined by Nicholas Jose, who operated a truck garden at the corner of Orange and State Streets, and by June of the same year the quartet had expanded into a small male chorus consisting of friends who weekly sought musical diversion.[4] Alarmed by the number of men attending the weekly sessions and the energetic singing that issued from the open windows of his building, the landlord raised the rent to four dollars a month.[5] Anton Scherrer's humorous article, commemorating the ninetieth anniversary of the Indianapolis Männerchor in 1944, said of the original chorus:

> All had loud, lusty, locustlike voices. As in the case of the locusts, the sounds seemed to come from the underside of the abdomen which, when you come to think of it, is what makes male-chorus singing the exciting thing it is. (Any resemblance to men and insects living or dead, is a coincidence and not an invitation to start trouble.)[6]

The group's first formal concert was held 28 May 1855 in the ballroom of Washington Hall and was conducted by housepainter Anton Despa. Despa was a replacement for director Eduard Longerich, who had returned to Europe to recover from the swamp malaria that plagued Indianapolis's early years (i.e., before the marshy land had been drained). The cost of admission was one dollar, which included both the concert and the dance that followed. A ball following Männerchor concerts was a tradition practiced with enthusiasm in many German communities across the United States.[7]

A typical nineteenth-century Indianapolis Männerchor concert consisted of two parts separated by an intermission. Longer concerts, such as "A Venetian Night," held outdoors Friday, 12 July 1895, in Cottage Grove Park, were often in three parts; on this particular occasion fireworks were ignited during both ten-minute intermissions and after the concert.[8] Most concerts featured a vocal soloist whose selections were interspersed throughout the program. A "Grand Concert," given by the United German Male Singing Societies of Indianapolis (the Männerchor, Harmony, and Liederkranz Societies and the Turner Singing Club) on Friday, 14 May 1875, presented "Miss Anna Gehl, soprano, and Mr. Edw. Schultze of Chicago, tenor" as guest soloists. Miss Gehl sang a recitative and an aria from Concone's *Judith*, and an aria from Weber's *Der Freischütz*; in his turn, Schultze sang the "Romanza" from Verdi's *Aïda* and Thiessen's

"The Sea Has Its Pearls," the last with piano and cello accompaniment.[9]

On other occasions, particularly when a band or orchestra shared the entertainment, an instrumental soloist would be featured. Hartmann's "My Pretty Jane" was performed on "Venetian Night" by Indianapolis Military Band member Mr. N. R. Rembusch, euphonium. A Männerchor program given Monday, 25 October 1875 at Washington Hall contained a horn solo (a transcription of Beethoven's "Adelaïde," played by Herr Jos. Cameron) and a piano solo (Moscheles's "Andante and Rondo, Op. 85," played by Herr Jno. B. Campbell).[10] In most cases, the music performed at outdoor events, such as the "Venetian Night" concert, was of a lighter nature than that of the Männerchor's regular concert series, as may be seen from the examples given above.

Around the turn of the century, Indianapolis Männerchor programs chiefly contained works by German composers who are both familiar and less well-known to us today. Pieces by Wohlgemuth, Spicker, Heyne, Truhn, and Zimmermann shared the stage with selections by Wagner, Mendelssohn, Robert Schumann, Beethoven, and Mozart. Composers from other European countries were also represented, as pieces by Verdi, Rossini, Tschaikovsky, Saint-Saëns, and Holst are found on concert programs from this period. To a lesser extent, American composers also found their way into Männerchor concerts: Louis Gottschalk's "The Dying Poet" was performed on "Venetian Night," and Charles Wakefield Cadman's "From the Land of the Sky-Blue Water" was discovered among some sheet music, programs, and other items in an old trunk belonging to the Männerchor.[11]

Most of the material used by the Indianapolis Männerchor in the latter half of the nineteenth century was in the form of printed sheet music, bound collections, and original compositions. Much of the sheet music was published by European firms, such as C. F. W. Siegel, Otto Forberg, or F. E. C. Leuckart of Leipzig, and imported to the United States, where the Indianapolis Männerchor obtained it through dealers such as Edward Schuberth & Co. (23 Union Square, New York City), D. Kanner (79 West Fourth Street, Cincinnati), or Wulschner & Son (78-80 North Pennsylvania Street, Indianapolis). Generally, bound collections of printed music that survive can be divided into two categories: those containing a general assortment of German folk songs and Lieder to be used on any occasion, and those containing a number of short works intended for a special event, such as a Sängerfest. The former usually includes all four voices, while the latter is in the form of a partbook (i.e., a book in which only a single vocal part is printed).

An example within the first category of bound collections is *Loreley*, a general selection of 147 songs for male chorus, published by P. J. Tonger of Cologne in 1879 and indexed alphabetically by title, composer, and intended use or subject matter ("Abendlieder," "Grablieder," "Frühlingslieder," etc.).[12] Two other books of songs for male chorus, also published by Tonger, are the first volumes of a Männerchor series called *Tonger's Taschen* ("Pocket") *Albums*. As their title suggests, these are of a size that could be easily slipped into a pocket and carried to a variety of Männerchor functions (e.g., a serenade or a graveside service) and are hardbound to withstand wear. Both books were compiled by Joseph Schwartz, the director of the Cologne Männergesangverein, and are indexed in the same manner as the *Loreley*.

A compilation of fourteen male-chorus works intended for a massed choir performance at the twenty-seventh Sängerfest of the North American Sängerbund (1893, Cleveland, Ohio) exemplifies the second category of bound collections used by the Indianapolis Männerchor. Published by Schirmer in New York, the collection is softbound and in partbook form. The collection includes works by Franz Lachner, Heinrich Zöllner, Gustav Baldamus, and Max von Weinzierl, popular nineteenth-century composers of Männerchor music. Works by Zöllner, Baldamus, and Weinzierl are bound with the "Pilgrim's Chorus" from Richard Wagner's *Tannhäuser* in a similar compilation produced by Breitkopf & Härtel of New York City for the North American Sängerbund's twenty-eighth Sängerfest (1896, Pittsburgh, Pennsylvania).[13]

Four-part choral works for men's voices were purchased by the Indianapolis Männerchor whenever possible. If a popular tune, available only for solo voice, was desired, an arrangement would be made. Two original compositions written for the Indianapolis Männerchor also came to light in the archives. A short unpublished "drinking song" in the key of F major was signed by Franz Belluiger and dated 14 April 1899. The composition appears to be typical of the genre, containing simple, marchlike rhythms and an uncomplicated harmonic structure. A pyramid of voices is built in the last four measures, each voice outlining the F-major triad, and adding emphasis to the words "er lebe hoch!" The other work, entitled "Das deutsche Volkslied," is much lengthier and was written by Walther Donner for the Indianapolis Männerchor with violin, cello, and piano accompaniment. The piece is dated February 1921 and is in manuscript form.[14]

The Formation of Männerchor Federations

In 1856, the Indianapolis Männerchor made its debut at the eighth national Sängerfest in Cincinnati, Ohio, sponsored by the North American Sängerbund. The first federation of German singing societies in the United States and, indeed, in the world, the North American Sängerbund (or NASB) was formed in the spring of 1849, when the societies of three cities on the Ohio River (Cincinnati, Ohio; Louisville, Kentucky; and Madison, Indiana) agreed to hold a regional competitive music festival, the purpose of which was to determine which town had the best German singing group.[15]

The first Sängerfest organized by the North American Sängerbund was held 1-4 June that same year in Cincinnati. Five societies attended, with a total of 118 singers.[16] Present at the first Sängerfest was Hans Balatka (discussed later in connection with the NASB's 1867 Sängerfest), who returned to his home in the Milwaukee, Wisconsin, area to organize its German singing societies into a smaller sister federation called the Northwestern Sängerbund. In 1856, the inaugural Northwestern Sängerfest was held in Milwaukee (19-22 June) with great success. Unfortunately, subsequent attempts at Sängerfeste failed and the Northwestern Sängerbund collapsed. It was revived after the Civil War with a Sängerfest in La Crosse, Wisconsin (15-17 July 1866); the Northwest Sängerbund henceforth called the La Crosse Sängerfest their "first."[17]

Societies affiliated with the North American Sängerbund were mostly drawn from states bordering the Ohio River, including western Pennsylvania. By 1890, a few choruses from cities in the South (the Gesangsektion Turnverein of New Orleans, Louisiana, and the Frohsinn of Mobile, Alabama) were also members of this federation. Sängerfeste held by the North American Sängerbund also frequently attracted Männerchöre of states farther west and north (e.g., the Aurora Sängerbund of St. Louis, and the Germania Männerchor of Saginaw, Michigan), whereas the Northwestern Sängerbund drew societies from the northern Midwest (i.e., Wisconsin, Iowa, Missouri, northern Indiana, and Illinois).[18]

Two other Sängerbünde were formed in the early 1850s: the Northeastern Sängerbund in 1850, and the German-Texan Sängerbund in 1852. A historical sketch of the North American Sängerbund in a later souvenir publication explained the need for these other organizations, stating:

> On account of the great extension of our country and the poor accommodations for traveling—the New York and Erie R[ail] R[oad] did not reach Dunkirk before 1851, and the Baltimore and Ohio did not reach Wheeling before 1853—the foundations of several associations or unions of singers became necessary.[19]

In no respect did the other major federations consider themselves of smaller stature than the North American Sängerbund. The Northeastern Sängerbund, in particular, thought itself the equal of the older federation, at first calling itself the "Allgemeiner Deutscher Sängerbund von Nordamerika" ("General German Singer's Union of North America"). Technically, this was an overstepping of bounds, for at that particular time the Eastern federation's member societies consisted exclusively of those from the Baltimore, Philadelphia, and New York areas. In response, the North American Sängerbund called itself the "Erster deutsche Sängerbund von Nordamerika" ("*First* German Singer's Union of North America") for a number of years until the Eastern federation abandoned the title.[20]

Performing Kreutzer's "Das Felsenkreuz" with only twelve singers at their first North American Sängerbund festival appearance, the Indianapolis Männerchor attracted little attention. Two years later, however, the organization had sufficient membership to organize a convention in which German singing societies from all over the state of Indiana participated. The success of this venture guaranteed other state Sängerfeste, such as one held in Terre Haute in 1860, where the Indianapolis

Männerchor won special recognition under Despa's leadership. Continuing to gain acclaim after the hiatus of the Civil War (during which there were no national Sängerfeste), the Indianapolis Männerchor was awarded the honor prize of a silver tuning fork in 1865 at the thirteenth Sängerfest of the North American Sängerbund in Columbus, Ohio, and a silver goblet and beaker for second prize the following year in Louisville, Kentucky.[21]

The Indianapolis Sängerfest of 1867

In the fall of 1867, the Indianapolis Männerchor played host to the North American Sängerbund's fifteenth Sängerfest. Over forty singing societies attended, representing cities as far east as Allegheny City, Pennsylvania, and as far west as Chicago. Participating Männerchöre from towns and cities within the state of Indiana included the Aurora Sängerbund, Columbus Männerchor, Evansville Liederkranz, Jeffersonville Sängerbund, LaPorte Männerchor, Madison Concordia, Michigan City Teutonia, New Albany Männerchor, Richmond Liederkranz, and the Terre Haute Männerchor. The combined total of Sängerfest participants equaled approximately one thousand singers.[22]

The Männerchor, the only German singing society in Indianapolis at the time, was responsible for the success of the event. Citizens and local officials, who wanted Indianapolis to show itself the equal of other Sängerfest host cities—some of which had included such thriving centers of nineteenth-century culture and commerce as Buffalo, Cleveland, Dayton, Detroit, and Pittsburgh—assisted the Männerchor in the vast preparations necessary. A concert hall erected on the southeast corner of the Court House Square furnished the location for the three concerts held during the first three days of the event. Although a temporary structure, partially financed by a fifteen-hundred-dollar contribution from the city council, the hall was spacious and well-built.[23] Inside, the Sängerfest Hall contained a large stage, a second-story gallery, and two elegant chandeliers; outside, a substantial balcony stood over the main entrance.[24] Above the balcony a frieze depicted Orpheus, the Greek mythological hero who charmed the deities of Hades when he played upon his lyre. The frieze also depicted the patriotic figures of Germania and

Columbia, symbolizing the Sängerfest's joining of the old world with the new.[25]

The contract for decorating the interior of the Sängerfest Hall fell to Mr. George Klein of New York City, whose wife, Francisca, operated a custom-design enterprise that specialized in the coordination of ornamental details for such events.[26] American, German, and Swiss flags and coats of arms adorned the pillars flanking the stage and gallery, while large portraits of famous composers lined the walls at the back and sides of the stage. Likenesses of Handel, Beethoven, Mozart, and Haydn were given the most prominent places at the stage's center, while Schubert, Meyerbeer, and Wagner occupied the east side and Mendelssohn, Gluck, and Franz Abt the west side. Twenty-four burners illuminated the stage, and every gallery pillar contained three burners as well, which, with the two central chandeliers, provided sufficient light for the needs of the singers, instrumentalists, and audience. Festoons of evergreens held up by cherubs, baskets of flowers, both real and artificial, and draped lengths of red, white, and blue bunting completed the trimmings.[27]

The city's storefronts, particularly those in the vicinity of the concert hall, were covered with wreaths, flags, bunting, and inscriptions. The show window of the City Dry Goods Store at 37 East Washington Street, for instance, displayed a large silken shield upon which was the motto "God Bless Our Country."[28] An article in the *Indianapolis Daily Journal* summarized the motivation underlying the months of preparation:

> We are very sure that all who come to the Fifteenth Saengerfest will be impressed with the idea that Indianapolis has done the best possible to give it *eclat*. If we do not spend money as lavishly as larger cities, we are confident that the impression will be made that every arrangement has been made that taste or experience could suggest to make the festival in this city the most successful ever held by this great confederation of singers. This week will witness the greatest musical event in the history of our city.[29]

The opening day of the Sängerfest dawned clear and sunny. A reception committee assembled at Union Depot as early as 5:00 A.M. to fire a salute of welcome as each train approached the station. A slight accident near Lafayette, Indiana, held up the train carrying the Chicago and Detroit societies until 8:00 A.M.; and the Louisville train, bearing the banner of the North American Sängerbund, was also delayed somewhat, but no *Sängergeister* ("singer's spirits") were much dampened as a consequence of these events. With the help of the City Band, the greeters ushered the arriving societies through the colorfully decorated streets to Mozart Hall, where they were given refreshments by the entertainment committee and assisted by the quartermaster's committee in finding their lodging assignments for the week.[30] A number of societies, particularly those with large memberships, were housed in hotels or meeting halls, while many of the smaller groups were quartered in private homes. The whereabouts of each society was published in the local papers to facilitate visitation, a favorite pastime at Sängerfeste during leisure hours.[31]

In the afternoon, all the groups assembled with their bands and banners at Mozart Hall and marched to Sängerfest Hall for the opening concert and remarks by the governor of Indiana, the mayor of Indianapolis, and the festival president. The Louisville societies ceremoniously handed over the flag of the North American Sängerbund to the Indianapolis Männerchor, in whose custody it would remain until the next Sängerfest.[32] The Cincinnati Orchestra provided most of the music for this concert, which consisted of the overtures to Weber's *Der Freischütz,* Rossini's *Semiramide,* and Boildieu's *La Dame blanche,* ending with Wagner's "March" from *Tannhäuser.* The leader of the orchestra was Carl Barus, the Sängerfest's musical director. Barus resided in Cincinnati, where he generated the motivating force behind a number of the city's orchestral and choral groups. No stranger to Sängerfeste, by 1867 Barus had held the post of musical conductor at two national meetings of the North American Sängerbund (Canton, Ohio, in 1854 and Columbus, Ohio, in 1865) and three meetings of the Indiana Sängerbund (1858, 1859, and 1860). In the early 1880s, Barus moved to Indianapolis to become the director of the Indianapolis Männerchor; his contribution to that society's accomplishments will be discussed presently.[33]

A grand fireworks display closed the opening day's festivities, and although the main decoration on the front of the building housing the Seidensticker & Co. law firm caught fire as the result of a stray rocket, the first day of the Sängerfest was heralded a great success.

Two more concerts took place during the following days of the Sängerfest. The first, which occurred Wednesday, 4 September, at 8:00 P.M., showcased the talents and musicality of the individual singing societies. The Evansville Liederkranz displayed "good taste" and a "careful balancing of voices" in their performance of Eisenhofer's "Horch." The Louisville Liederkranz executed Fischer's "Gute Nacht" in "fine style," and the Columbus Männerchor rendered Liszt's "Kriegsgesang" with "great spirit." The accolades of the evening went to the Chicago Concordia's performance of Franz Abt's "Vineta," in which Mr. Bischoff, the society's tenor soloist, distinguished himself with his clear enunciation and fine interpretation. Earning an encore, the Concordia's director led the chorus in an "Ave Maria," which again featured Mr. Bischoff. Two more encores were demanded over the course of the concert, one for the Cincinnati Männerchor's execution of Abt's "Herz o' willst dich bitten," and one for the Germania Männerchor of Chicago's performance of Abt's "Battle Prayer." Both encores were "very properly" refused by Carl Barus and Hans Balatka, the musical directors of the respective groups.[34]

Named the honorary director of the Sängerfest, Hans Balatka had recently moved to Chicago from Milwaukee, where he had organized one of the leading musical societies in the Midwest—the Milwaukee Musikverein. He also founded the Northwest Sängerbund (described earlier), a sister federation of the North American Sängerbund, which included member societies from Wisconsin, Iowa, and Illinois. Balatka was a composer as well as a musician, director, and organizer; his choral work, "The Power of Song," won a silver goblet for best composition at the North American Sängerbund's eighth Sängerfest, held in Cincinnati in 1856.[35]

For the visiting singing societies, the schedule for the second and third days of the Sängerfest consisted of morning rehearsals and evening concerts, with the afternoons free for sight-seeing and visiting each other's "open houses" at their temporary headquarters. Featuring only one massed chorus ("The Star Spangled Banner"), the second day's concert permitted individual societies to display their musicianship and training by performing

short Männerchor pieces. This concert, given 5 September at
8:00 P.M., was attended by so many people that the hall was filled
to overflowing and an estimated five thousand were forced to
listen from the lawn outside the building. This fact is even more
remarkable, given that a sizable audience, unable to obtain tickets
for the concert, had already attended the morning rehearsal for
fifty cents admission. The rehearsal had not gone well. Nearly
half of the singers showed up late or not at all, incurring the
displeasure of Barus, who seemed justifiably "harder to please"
than he had at previous rehearsals that week.[36] Nor had the
audience been well behaved, as we learn from an editorial in the
Indianapolis Daily Journal:

> After each performance, in addition to legitimate applause—which
> should always be with the hands or with a cane, and never with the
> feet—there was a perfect storm of yells, catcalls, and "ki-his," which
> are the disgrace of our Theater. So noisome did this become, that
> Mr. Barus was compelled to stop and request his audience to desist.
> Gentlemen who enjoy the distinction of Messrs. Barus and Balatka
> in the musical world will go away from Indianapolis with a
> decidedly indifferent opinion of our musical taste and education.[37]

The *Journal* continued the discussion of proper concert
comportment with a lecture on the proper use of the *encore:*

> There is another nuisance allied to this [the "ki-his"]; and that is the
> *encore*. In the hands of a tasty [*sic*] and appreciative audience, the
> *encore* is a valuable compliment to performers, but when it is
> persistently used without sense or reason, and apparently for no
> other purpose than to get double the amount of music paid for, it
> degenerates into absolute boorishness. We are sure our good people
> will take these hints kindly, and overpower with good taste and
> common sense the *canaille* which crowd the pits and galleries of our
> places of amusement.[38]

The combined chorus numbers of the final concert had been
made available to member societies of the North American
Sängerbund some months previous to the Sängerfest, so that each
group could learn the music beforehand. Each singer had his own
partbook (which contained only the music for the specific voice
indicated), published by J. Schuberth & Co. of New York.[39] The

seal of the state of Indiana adorned the top of each partbook's front cover, while the bottom featured a drawing of the old state capitol building. The Sängerbund Chorus performed Müller's "Sänger's Gruß" to great applause, and the orchestra, composed of "ten first and ten second violins, eight violas, five violincellos, trombones, cornets, clarionets, flutes, two kettle drums, one snare and one bass drum," played Littholf's *Robespierre* overture with such effect "as to constrain many [listeners] to actually cry out with ardor."[40] Other selections performed by the United Chorus of the Sängerbund included works by Becker, Schneider, and Abt, ending with the "Pilgrim's Chorus" from Wagner's *Tannhäuser.*

A few unscheduled concerts occurred over the course of the Sängerfest. Washington Hall, the headquarters of the Germania Society of Chicago during their stay in Indianapolis, became the setting for one such event. Although described as an "impromptu" by a local newspaper, the Germania Society's concert showed no lack of forethought in the selection of its program. Directed by Hans Balatka and assisted by the twenty-eight-piece Great Western Light Guard Band, which traveled with the chorus from Chicago, the Germania performed Carl Friedrich Zöllner's "Prayer of the Earth," Kunz's "Beautiful Augusta," and a comic song based on Schiller's *Räuber.* A tenor solo, "Robin Adair," and a quartette from Meyerbeer's *Prophète* rounded out the vocal part of the program. The "celebrated" Great Western Light Guard Band supplied overtures by Kreutzer and Johann Christoph Bach, Mendelssohn's "March" from *Athailia,* and Hans Balatka's arrangement of a "Fantasia" from Verdi's *Sicilian Vespers.*[41]

Another Chicago society, the Concordia Männerchor, gave a private concert at their headquarters, Mozart Hall, in the late evening of the Sängerfest's second day. The program's highlight was the "Marching Serenade" featuring a grand chorus and tenor and baritone solos. The Chicago singing societies had a reputation to maintain that preceded them to the Sängerfest. An article published in the *Chicago Tribune,* Friday, 30 August, and reprinted in the *Indianapolis Daily Journal,* Monday, 2 September, announced their projected trip to Indianapolis, saying that

all who have heard them know what our German singing societies can do; and such will not be surprised if their representatives ...

returned to Chicago crowned with the laurels that the goddess of music distributes to her worthy subjects.[42]

Maintaining or establishing reputations in all areas of endeavor seemed to be the order of business throughout the Sängerfest. An ad in the newspaper gave notice of a meeting of "The Heavy Singers in Reutti's saloon, the corner of East and Washington streets, at two o'clock p.m., Sept. 4, 'for mutual practice and enjoyment, and to see who is the champion among the 'heavy weights.'" Singers tipping the scales at two hundred pounds or more were urged to attend.[43] Such an advertisement could not be ignored by the press, one of whom reported:

> The Meeting of [the] Heavy Weights at Reutti's saloon ... was not numerous, but it was large. Two persons were present whose awful ponderosity evidently frightened off those who could but just drop the scale at two hundred. The leader of this couple ... is a German from Chicago named A. Waltenspiel, member of the Brewer's Association, who is dubbed by his companions "Gambrinus," the Beer King, and better known by his pseudonym than by his true name. He is a wonderful development, and his residence in Chicago is an illustration of that "eternal fitness of things" [apparently a tribute to Chicago's beer industry] which a philosopher will discover in almost all earthly dispensations.[44]

Among the substantial number of newspapers covering the Sängerfest's concerts and other events were the *Cincinnati Commercial,* the *Chicago Tribune,* the *Louisville Volksblatt,* the *St. Louis Westliche Post,* the *Newark* [New Jersey] *Advertiser,* and the *New Orleans Times.* Two music journals, the *New York Musik-Zeitung* and the *Indianapolis Musical Review,* also sent representatives to report on the proceedings. To administer to the creature comforts of these patient gentlemen camping out at the Festival Headquarters in Mozart Hall, Indianapolis businesses donated the following items: one gallon each of cherry rum and bourbon, three gallons of whiskey, twenty-four bottles of wine, two boxes of soda water, fourteen boxes of cigars, four dozen boxes of fine cut and plug tobacco, six loaves of bread, a dozen lemons, a box of crackers, and an unspecified amount of Bologna sausage.[45]

In the manner of other Sängerfeste of the North American Sängerbund, the last day of the Sängerfest featured a parade, a picnic on the grounds of Northwestern Christian University, and a Grand Ball at the Sängerfest Hall. In his final article of festival coverage, the *Indianapolis Daily Journal*'s correspondent wrote:

> The Fifteenth Annual Festival of the North American Sängerbund is concluded, and never again, perhaps, will its session be held in Indianapolis.... The remembrance of this Feast will remain vivid for all time so long as the delicious memories of its music shall continue, and our only hope is that the reception the visitors have been accorded in our goodly city will cause them to be as proud and glad of the occasion, as are we who have listened to them, and endeavored to render their sojourn agreeable.[46]

The Indianapolis Sängerfest of 1908

Forty-one years later, in 1908 (17-20 June), Indianapolis hosted the North American Sängerbund's Thirty-second National Sängerfest. Both the city and the Sängerbund had grown substantially in the decades separating the two Sängerfeste. Indianapolis audiences of the early twentieth century had become acquainted with vocal soloists on the order of Nordica, Melba, David Bispham, and Emil Fischer, as well as pianists such as Paderewski, Edward Macdowell, and the young Arthur Rubinstein. Likewise, the male chorus singers of the participating societies were more musically sophisticated than their counterparts of 1867. They were also more numerous. The North American Sängerbund's previous Sängerfest, held in St. Louis in 1903, had attracted 121 singing societies, with a combined total of approximately 3,037 singers. Expectations for the Indianapolis festival were, therefore, heightened both artistically and economically. The Männerchor was in charge of the preparations for the event and was assisted by the Indianapolis Liederkranz (founded in 1872) as well as by the singing sections of the Indianapolis and the Southside Turner Societies, but many other Indianapolis organizations also contributed their efforts in order to realize the increased requirements of a four-day music festival that featured two matinée and three evening concerts.

Although the Sängerfest of 1867 was, for its time, an elaborate event, the 1908 Sängerfest was much more sophisticated in terms of its arrangements. A lengthy commemorative booklet was printed, containing (along with concert programs) two long articles entitled "The History of the German Male Chorus and of the North American Sängerbund" and "A Sketch of Musical Life in Our City, Past and Present," as well as a number of short articles about the various German singing organizations of Indianapolis. Both German and English versions of the two main articles and the programs appeared in print; the shorter articles were printed in German only. The booklet also included short biographies of Walter Damrosch, Louis Ehrgott, and Alexander Ernestinoff, the three major conductors of this Sängerfest. Rendered in the art nouveau style representative of the early twentieth century, the cover of the booklet pictured a draped male figure with a trumpet at his lips, and two draped female figures encircling portraits of Wagner and Beethoven.[47]

For the five concerts of the event, the Sängerfest Committee engaged four soloists: soprano Marie Rappold, contralto Ernestine Schumann-Heink, baritone Adolf Muehlmann, and bass David Bispham. Rappold, a British singer of German parentage, was currently engaged by the New York Metropolitan Opera; during the Sängerfest she sang "Dich theure Halle" from *Tannhäuser* and the "Prayer" from *Tosca*.[48] Schumann-Heink had taken part in every Bayreuth festival from 1896 to 1906 and was known for her Wagnerian roles. Less than a year following the Indianapolis Sängerfest she would create the role of Klytemnestra in Richard Strauss's *Elektra* (25 January 1909).[49] The featured soloist of the second concert at the Indianapolis Sängerfest, Schumann-Heink's numbers included Vitellia's recitative and aria from Mozart's *Titus,* Adriano's recitative and aria from Wagner's *Rienzi,* and Schubert's "Die Allmacht," arranged for orchestra by Louis Victor Saar.[50] Muehlmann and Bispham each performed selections from Wagner operas, and Rappold, Muehlmann, and Bispham also appeared in Max Bruch's dramatic cantata *Das Feuerkreuz* the opening night of the Sängerfest.[51]

The services of conductor Walter Damrosch and the New York Symphony Orchestra were retained for the Sängerfest. The son of Leopold Damrosch, who came to the United States in 1871 to direct the nationally recognized Arion Society of New York City, Walter Damrosch had toured the nation with his "Damrosch Opera Company," bringing opera to many towns and cities for the first time. He conducted the American premiere of *Parsifal* in 1898, and in 1903 he reorganized the New York Symphony, which he was to lead until 1927.[52] The Sängerfest choruses were conducted by Alexander Ernestinoff, the leader of many Indianapolis musical societies. Trained at the Russian Royal Conservatory of Music under Anton Rubinstein, Ernestinoff had spent four years directing German opera in New York before settling in Indianapolis.[53]

The then-recently constructed Coliseum at the state fair grounds provided the setting for the concerts of the 1908 Sängerfest. This event marked the first occasion that the Coliseum was used for purposes other than the exhibition of horses and cattle, but nobody seemed to cast aspersions upon its suitability as a concert facility.[54] An expanse of white canvas the size of a circus tent covered the sawdust arena and upon it chairs were arranged for the audience. The stage, constructed at the west end of the arena and decorated with evergreens, naturally constituted the major attraction. Behind it rose a huge tier of seats occupied by the chorus throughout the five concerts. German and American flags adorned the building's steel columns, upon each of which hung shields bearing the names of the twenty-seven cities sending choruses to the Sängerfest.[55] One experienced Sängerfest-goer commented to the press:

> Except for one building, in which the united [*sic*] German singers met in Europe, six years ago, for their festival ... this is the most beautiful building in every detail I have seen arranged for the purpose of a sængerfest [*sic*], either in Europe or America.[56]

The effect of the Coliseum's transformation was so spectacular and so well publicized by the newspapers that Indianapolis residents flocked to the state fair grounds in droves, by streetcar, automobile, and carriage, to get a glimpse of it. A column in the *Indianapolis News* encouraged the sight-seeing and even recommended automobiles "take advantage" of Meridian Street, which was paved, a route allowing motorists the added enjoyment of glimpsing from afar the lights of the fairgrounds above the heavily wooded wilderness on either side of Thirty-eighth Street.[57]

The Coliseum's acoustical fitness for an event like the Sängerfest was more than adequate; spectators attending rehearsals said that, although his back was to them, they could hear Ernestinoff's spoken instructions to the chorus as clearly as if they themselves had occupied the stage.[58] In the words of the famous conductor Walter Damrosch, who walked around during the rehearsals and listened from various places in the hall, it was "admirably adapted to music." According to the maestro, "There was no point where the slightest tone was not distinctly heard"; and, he added wryly, "In the future when any one speaks to me about building a concert hall I shall say 'Just build me a cattle shed.'"[59]

It was no longer feasible for all the participating societies to perform individually. The 1908 Sängerfest attracted approximately eighty-four societies from out of town, hence only a few groups—the Toledo Männerchor, the St. Louis Liederkranz, and the Milwaukee Männerchor—were permitted that distinction. The greater proportion of Männerchor pieces were sung by the combined societies of various cities. The United Singers of Indianapolis, for instance, performed Mangold's "Waldlied" in the first concert, Wednesday, 17 June, at 8:00 P.M; the United Singers of Chicago and the United Singers of St. Louis sang in the third and last concerts, respectively.

Although Männerchor selections still comprised a portion of the concert programs, male chorus pieces by lesser-known composers such as Hegar, Wiesner, Becker, and Wengert were overshadowed by operatic and symphonic works of Beethoven, Liszt, Mendelssohn, Mozart, Puccini, Saint-Saëns, and Tschaikovsky. If a prize had been awarded to the composer whose works enjoyed the greatest frequency of exposure at the 1908 Sängerfest, the undeniable winner would have been Richard Wagner with a grand total of nine pieces. Wagner's music was performed in each of the five concerts, and four of the five concerts contained two Wagner numbers.[60]

Another feature of the 1908 Sängerfest that sharply contrasted with the festival of 1867 was the inclusion of women and children in the concerts. Indianapolis women joined the city's men to form a mixed chorus of six hundred for the performance of Bruch's cantata *Das Feuerkreuz* the opening night of the Sängerfest. Young New England composer, organist, and conductor Edward Bailey Birge chose 1,600 out of 20,000 children in the Indianapolis public schools to sing Peter Benoit's *Into the World* on the fourth concert, Friday afternoon, 19 June, at 2:30 P.M. *Into the World* was considered one of the best cantatas of the time for children's voices, but the *Indianapolis News* pointed out that it was difficult music for them to learn because of its lack of continuous melody.[61] The afternoon of the concert, the children and their teachers were transported to and from the fairgrounds in sixteen special street cars. Their performance was more than successful; according to the *Indianapolis Star*, "the final note was the signal for an outburst such as has never been witnessed in Indianapolis."[62] The Sängerfest ended with a "Forest Festival" at Germania Park, held that Saturday afternoon.

The Indianapolis Sängerfeste of the North American Sängerbund served a dual purpose. On the one hand, the singing festivals enriched and showcased Indianapolis culture. On the other hand, they celebrated the nation's wealth of German heritage and in so doing promoted a greater German-American cross-cultural understanding. In the words of the North American Sängerbund's president Hanno Deiler, to the people of Indianapolis in 1908:

> Permit me ... on behalf of all Germans in the United States to give my thanks for the tribute which today was paid to the Germans ... for the part that our people can claim to have taken in the settlement and establishment of the welfare of this land, in the propagation of culture, the sciences and arts, in the vocations and in undertakings of all kinds, as well as for the faithful fulfillment of civic duties.... See from your own city of Indianapolis what Germans and the children of Germans have done here, and you will realize what the German element means to the United States.[63]

Other Local Musical and Social Activities of the Indianapolis Männerchor

Participating in Sängerfeste of the North American Sängerbund and presenting its own busy concert and guest artist series did not prevent the Indianapolis Männerchor from singing at the first and last encampments of the Grand Army of the Republic, held in 1866 and 1948 in Indianapolis.[64] An 1886 concert in Tomlinson Hall was attended by General Sherman and served a double purpose: it opened the G. A. R. Campfire and raised money for the construction of the Soldier's and Sailor's Monument, still standing in the middle of Indianapolis's famous downtown "Circle." Other benefit concerts aided the old German-English Independent School of Indianapolis that was situated on the north side of Maryland Street, between Delaware and Alabama Streets, and a gala performance, given in September 1878, netted a total of six hundred dollars to assist yellow fever victims in the South.[65]

The Männerchor was also known for its masked balls and festivities of the pre-Lenten season. These were primarily social events, although concerts and short plays were often a part of the evening's entertainment. Invitations to the carnivals were colorful and often highly original in design. They were mailed well in advance of the event because they contained information regarding the renting of costumes. An invitation to a carnival to be held Friday, 2 February 1883, served as a costume-rental reminder to Männerchor members and their guests:

> Management has secured the services of the celebrated costumer, A. R. Van Horn of Philadelphia; he will arrive in the city on Wednesday, January 24th with five hundred of the most complete, handsome and comical costumes ever seen here. These costumes will be displayed in two large rooms adjoining the English Opera House, from January 24th on.[66]

These outfits portrayed figures of absurd, legendary, allegorical, historical, and satirical origin, ranging anywhere from Teutons in skins to George Washington, Harlequin, and Louis XIV. The prices of such rentals ranged from five to one hundred dollars, depending upon the amounts of velvet and brocade used.

Each Männerchor member received a complimentary ticket for himself and "one lady," with tickets at reasonable prices available for additional "ladies." All tickets were sold in advance, and none was available at the door in order to prevent gate-crashing—a very real possibility, considering the popularity of the masked balls and the unknown identities of costumed guests. Nonmembers could purchase tickets only "upon application of a member of the society."

A set of strict regulations governed the carnivals. To avoid traffic congestion in the unloading of guests, carriages were required to approach the building from the west only. Carnivals began formally at 9:00 P.M. with a Grand March, before which no one was allowed on the dance floor. Between 9:00 and 11:00 P.M., only those in fancy costume or "domino" (a long cloak with wide sleeves, a hood, and a mask) were admitted to the dance floor, and guests were warned that "a simple face mask will not suffice." Carnivals frequently lasted all night, with a supper served at 12:30 A.M.[67]

The participation of women in Indianapolis Männerchor events was not restricted to social events such as carnivals and masked balls. A women's chorus, or "Damenchor," made up of the wives and daughters of Männerchor members, frequently took part in Männerchor concerts. This was the case on Friday, 30 April 1909, when the women's chorus performed Max Gulbins's "Die ihr hoch herniederschaut." The women then joined the men in singing Niels W. Gade's "Frühlingsbotschaft" and the "Sonnengesang" from Edgar Tinel's oratorio *Franciscus*.[68] The mixed chorus also performed Wagner's March from *Tannhäuser* and the "Finale" from Verdi's *Sicilian Vespers* on a concert given 11 December 1879.[69] Participating in various Sängerfeste—including the controversial twentieth Sängerfest of the North American Sängerbund, held in Louisville in 1877—the Indianapolis Männerchor's mixed chorus gained special acclaim.[70]

Apparently, a number of the Sängerbund officials viewed the increased participation of mixed choruses as a threat to the male chorus domination of the traditional Sängerfest. Hans Balatka, the concert director of the twentieth NASB Sängerfest, was brought before a board of delegates on charges of "having too few male choruses and too many operatic selections on the programme."[71] Balatka must have defended his position to the satisfaction of those present, for later Sängerfest programs relied heavily on the attendance of the mixed choruses for performances of such works as Verdi's *Requiem* and the "Pilgrim's Chorus" from *Tannhäuser*.

Max Leckner, at one time the president of the Music Teachers National Association, became the director of the Indianapolis Männerchor in the early 1870s. Establishing a music school, he had the idea to train the members' children for eventual participation in either the Männerchor or the women's chorus.[72] Two classes from the "Singschule des Männerchor" were involved in the Männerchor concert held Monday, 25 October 1875 at Washington Hall. The first class performed the "Jägers-Abschied" by Mendelssohn, while the second sang Robert Schumann's "Marienwürmchen" and "Eine Volksweise."[73] For a number of years, during Leckner's directorship, the Singschule flourished.

A number of operetta productions were also staged by the Männerchor in the second half of the nineteenth century, beginning in 1869. The city had received its first taste of operatic music only eighteen years before in the fall of 1851, when Anna Bishop and M. Bochsa gave a recital of arias in the Masonic Hall, and in the words of Indianapolis historian Berry Robinson Sulgrove, "furnished the curious some idea of what music was that was neither hymn nor ballad, jig nor hornpipe."[74] According to Ona B. Talbot's article on the history of music in Indianapolis, this performance drew mixed reviews from its audience:

> To some it was a revelation of a pleasure of a higher kind than had been customary. Others saw no music in it because there was no "tune" in it and found it ludicrous. The history of music is ever thus.[75]

Seven years later, touring opera companies began to visit the city, presenting major works at English's Opera House or Tomlinson Hall; neither edifice stands today. The Emma Abbot Opera Company and the Grand English Opera Company brought *Fra Diavolo, Orpheus and Euridyce* [sic], *Martha,* and *The Flying Dutchman* to Indianapolis in the 1870s. In 1886, the Mapleson Grand Italian Opera Company introduced Indianapolis audiences to *Carmen, Faust,* and *Lucia di Lammermoor,* and turn-of-the-century opera lovers were treated to the Metropolitan Opera Company's staging of *The Barber of Seville, Don Pasquale,* and *Lohengrin* (the latter featuring Schumann-Heink and David Bispham, both of whom returned to Indianapolis as guest soloists at the thirty-second Sängerfest of the North American Sängerbund in 1906).

The touring companies developed an eager audience for grand opera in Indianapolis, but their visits were infrequent and eventually ceased completely because the city did not have a hall large enough to make it worthwhile to stage lavish productions of works like *Lohengrin*. Tomlinson Hall, in particular, was inconvenient for the presentation of large-scale operas, as the scenery had to be hauled inside through the windows—a factor that kept the Metropolitan Opera Company from giving *Romeo and Juliet* one cold afternoon in 1901 when they had arrived late from St. Louis.[76]

Because major operatic productions were performed so infrequently in Indianapolis, the Männerchor's small-scale operettas featuring their own Männerchor and Damenchor members were greatly appreciated. The first of these productions was mounted on 12 May 1869, when the Männerchor presented the *Dorfbarbier*, a comic opera in three acts by Johann Schenk, one of Beethoven's instructors in Vienna. The Männerchor did not give another operetta until 1882, when the society was under the direction of Carl Barus, who is considered one of the greatest nineteenth-century conductors and musicians to have lived in Indianapolis. The great-grandfather of physicist Bernard Vonnegut and author Kurt Vonnegut Jr., Barus left Europe in 1848 as a result of the turmoil in Germany. After a brief stint as a "Latin farmer" in Saginaw, Michigan (a popular label in mid-nineteenth-century America, "Latin farmer" described the newly arrived immigrant farmer who had years of university training—but little or no knowledge of how to farm), he settled in Cincinnati. There he conducted the Philharmonic Society—one of the earliest orchestras in the Midwest—and the Barus Symphony Orchestra.[77]

Barus's first connection with Indianapolis came in 1858 when he conducted the Männerchor's first state Sängerfest. In 1882, he was persuaded to move to Indianapolis permanently as director of the Indianapolis Männerchor, a position he occupied until 1896. Under his direction the Männerchor reached its height, producing five operettas in the years 1882-1885, as well as the Indianapolis "May Festivals" (musical events modeled after the Cincinnati May Festivals) that brought many guest artists to the city. The Männerchor, as an organization, did not take part in the May Festivals, although many individual members were involved in performances.

Two short works by Kipper, *Der Haifisch* ("The Shark," a comic opera scene) and *Fidelia* (described as a "quodlibet" opera), were given in the same evening in 1882. Flotow's *Stradella* was presented in 1893 (and repeated in 1894), followed the next evening by *Martha*. Millöcker's comic opera *Der Bettelstudent* was produced at Dickson's Grand Opera House on 16, 17, and 18 February 1885. The two Flotow operas and the Millöcker opera netted the Männerchor one hundred and forty-six dollars' profit.[78] The organization was invited to bring *The Beggar Student* to Louisville, which they did, presenting it the next month. An invitation to do the same at Heuck's Opera House in Cincinnati was refused, because "after all, the Männerchor was only an amateur organization, the members of which had businesses and babies to tend to."[79]

Several prominent roles in the Männerchor operetta productions went to John P. Frenzel, a successful Indianapolis banker, who "at age twenty-eight ... was the youngest president of a national bank in the United States."[80] His financial support of the Männerchor enabled the organization to move in 1907 from the East Washington Street building (once the city hall) that they had occupied since 1877, to a new building on Illinois Street, later touted by architects and historians as a supreme example of the American neo-Renaissance style.[81] The new Männerchor Hall was host to a great many guest artists, such as Artur Schnabel, the Flonzaley Quartet, Joseph Szigeti, Pablo Casals, and Efrem Zimbalist, brought to Indianapolis by the personal efforts of Frenzel. When Frenzel died in 1933, leaving no children, he bequeathed ten thousand dollars to the Männerchor. He left the rest of his estate to the Indiana Trust Company, to be used

> in promoting the cultivation of and the education in the art of male chorus singing in the city of Indianapolis, and in accomplishing this objective, give financial support to ... any male chorus ... organized under the laws of the state of Indiana, ... having for its principal object the promotion of ... male chorus singing.[82]

Unfortunately, Frenzel's will was contested, and the Männerchor received nothing. Because he had owned most of the stock in the Männerchor Hall, the society was forced to relocate, eventually moving into the Athenaeum, home of the Indianapolis Turners. The Männerchor Hall building became by turns a dance studio, a hall for USO activities during World War II, and Indiana

University Law School. It was purchased by a local insurance company and demolished to make room for a parking garage in 1974. A few relics were saved from the old building, including some stained-glass windows, later moved to an Italian restaurant in downtown Indianapolis, and four stone angels playing instruments, later donated to the Indianapolis Children's Museum. The cornerstone box was examined by Kenneth Duncan, the first non-German president of the Männerchor, and was then given to the Indianapolis Museum of Art.

The Indianapolis Männerchor is still in existence, calling itself the oldest continuously active male chorus in the United States. Unlike many other German male singing societies, it has survived seven wars without ceasing, even withstanding undercover infiltration by the Federal Bureau of Investigation during World War II. Upholding a glorious tradition of musical endeavor in Indianapolis, the "Gentlemen of Song" recently celebrated their 140th anniversary. The Männerchor's membership, however, like many of the other surviving German singing societies in the United States, has suffered in recent years from a lack of interest, particularly among young men, and is in danger of literally "dying out." Although its days may well be numbered, Indianapolis Männerchor members maintain an optimistic view that the society will experience many more years of tuneful and sociable harmony in the century to come.

Indianapolis, Indiana

---

[1]Ona B. Talbot, "A Sketch of Musical Life in Our City, Past and Present," *Thirty-second National Saengerfest des Nord-Amerikanischen Saengerbundes, Indianapolis, June 17-20, 1908: Official Souvenir* (Indianapolis: Aetna Press, 1908), 54.

[2]"Synopsis of the History of the German Male Chorus and the North American Saengerbund," *Thirty-second National Saengerfest des Nord-Amerikanischen Saengerbundes, Indianapolis, June 17-20, 1908: Official Souvenir* (Indianapolis: Aetna Press, 1908), 10. This article also appears in the German language (pp. 5-9). Subsequent souvenir books of NASB Sängerfeste contain the same article with minor revisions; such revisions are

usually confined to the last few paragraphs, which are updated to include mention of the current Sängerfest.

[3]C. E. Emmerich, *Festschrift zur Feier des Vierzigjährigen Stiftungsfestes des Indianapolis Männerchor am 15., 16. und 17. Juni 1894* (Indianapolis: n.p., 1894), 2.

[4]Anton Scherrer, "Maennerchor," *Indianapolis Times*, 12 May 1944.

[5]Scherrer.

[6]Scherrer.

[7]This custom is still observed in Indianapolis Männerchor concerts today when the concert's location has sufficient floor space for dancing.

[8]Program, "A Venetian Night," Friday, 12 July 1895.

[9]Program, "Grand Concert," Friday, 14 May 1875.

[10]Program, *Abend-Unterhaltung des Maennerchor*, Monday, 25 October 1875.

[11]This trunk was for several years in the care of Männerchor member Paul Meister. Its contents were recently transferred to join an extensive collection of Indianapolis Männerchor material in the Special Collections and Archives of the Indiana University–Purdue University Indianapolis (I.U.P.U.I.) Library, where fourteen boxes of Männerchor music are filed as part of Athenaeum Turners Collection, A78-11.

[12]Aug. Reiser, ed., *Loreley: Sammlung auserlesener Männerchöre* (Cologne: P. J. Tonger, 1879). The Tonger publications mentioned in this paragraph were part of the aforementioned trunk collection.

[13]*Siebenundzwanzigstes Saengerfest des Nord-Americanischen Saengerbundes, Cleveland, Ohio, 1893* (New York: G. Schirmer, n.d.); *Achtundzwanzigstes Sängerfest des Nordamerikanischen Sängerbundes, Pittsburg, Pennsylvania, 1896* (New York City: Breitkopf u. Härtel, n.d.). These two compilations can be found in boxes 41 and 42, respectively, of the Athenaeum Turners Collection, A-78-11, I.U.P.U.I. Library.

[14]The compositions mentioned in this paragraph were part of the trunk collection, now in the I.U.P.U.I. Library.

[15]The first federation of this scope in Europe, the "Allgemeine Deutsche Sängerbund," was founded in Coburg in 1862.

[16]Carl Peltz, "Historical Sketch of the North American Sängerbund," *Andenken an das Goldene Jubilaeum des Nordamerikanischen Saengerbundes* (Cincinnati: North American Saengerbund, 1899), 9.

[17]*Der Nord Stern* [La Crosse, WI], 21 July 1866; see also *Souvenir des 15. Sangesfestes des Sängerbundes des Nordwesterns* (Milwaukee: Northwestern Sängerbund, 1891), 15.

[18]The word *Sängerbund* ("Federation of Singers") was often an individual society's name, as in the case of the Aurora Sängerbund; this is not to be confused with the larger federations of societies (i.e. the North American Sängerbund).

[19]"Synopsis," *Thirty-second National Saengerfest,* 11.

[20]Orlo O. Sprunger, "The North American Saenger's Union" (Master's thesis: Ohio State University, 1951), 13.

[21]Joseph Hermann Keller, *Festschrift zur Feier des goldenen Jubilaeums des Indianapolis Männerchor am 23, 24, und 25 Juni, 1904* (Indianapolis: Gulenberg, 1904), 17.

[22]"Synopsis," *Thirty-second National Saengerfest,* 11. This figure, given henceforth in official souvenir books of the NASB, could well be inaccurate. According to the list of participating societies and members given in the *Indianapolis Daily Journal* (Thursday, 5 September 1867), thirty-six out-of-town organizations attended, with a combined total of 756 singers, including the thirty members of the Indianapolis Männerchor. The addition of nineteen orchestral musicians from Louisville, thirty-two from Cincinnati, and twelve band members from Terre Haute brings the total up to a mere 819.

[23]A copy of a letter certifying the hall's architectural soundness was published in the *Indianapolis Daily Journal,* 2 September 1867. The Young Men's Christian Association used the hall for an evangelical revival 7-8 September after the Sängerfest was over. One or two other groups also held meetings in the building before its dismantlement, see Jacob Piatt Dunn, *Greater Indianapolis,* 2 vols. (Chicago: Lewis Publishing Co., 1910), Vol. 1, p. 63.

[24]Dunn; Talbott, 55; *Indianapolis Daily Journal,* 2-3 September 1867. A picture of the hall can be found George Theodore Probst, *The Germans in Indianapolis, 1840-1918,* rev. and ed. Eberhard Reichmann (Indianapolis: German-American Center & Indiana German Heritage Society, Inc., 1989), 66.

[25]Also represented in the frieze was a figure which the reporter for the local newspaper called "Orion." I have not been able to find a more detailed description of the freize, or this figure in particular, but doubt that it was Orion—the mighty hunter from Greek mythology. The figure's place, opposite that of Orpheus, suggests strongly that it might have been "Arion," another famous musician of mythological origin, for whom many German (and American) singing societies were named. The most famous

Männerchor by the name of "Arion" in the United States was the Arion Society of New York City, organized 23 January 1854. For more information, see the author's article, "Names and Varieties of Männerchöre," *The Sonneck Society Bulletin* 16/1 (Spring 1990), 12-15.

[26]*Daily Journal*, 2 and 6 September 1867.

[27]*Daily Journal*, 2 September 1867.

[28]*Daily Journal*, 3 September 1867.

[29]*Daily Journal*, 2 September 1867.

[30]*Daily Journal*, 4 September 1867.

[31]*Daily Journal*, 5 September 1867.

[32]The banner was described as "blue on one side with a harp and wreath in the center"; the other side "is white with an eagle holding a music book in its claws" [*Daily Journal*, 4 September 1867].

[33]F. O. Jones, ed. *A Handbook of American Music and Musicians* (Canaseraga, N.Y.: F. O. Jones, 1886; repr. New York: Da Capo Press, 1971), 11.

[34]*Daily Journal*, 5 September 1867.

[35]Jones, 11.

[36]*Daily Journal*, 6 September 1867.

[37]*Loc. cit.*

[38]*Loc. cit.*

[39]*Festgesänge für das fünfzehnte Gesangfest des Nordamerikanischen Sängerbundes, Indianapolis, Ind., 1867* (New York: Schuberth & Co., 1867).

[40]*Daily Journal*, 5-6 September 1867.

[41]*Loc. cit.*

[42]*Chicago Tribune*, 30 August 1867; *Indianapolis Daily Journal*, 2 September 1867.

[43]*Daily Journal*, 4 September 1867.

[44]*Daily Journal*, 5 September 1867.

[45]*Daily Journal*, 4 September 1867.

[46]*Daily Journal*, 7 September 1867.

[47]*Thirty-second National Saengerfest*, cover.

[48] *Indianapolis Telegraph und Tribune*, 20 June 1908.

[49] Desmond Shawe-Taylor, "Schumann-Heink [*née* Rössler], Ernestine," *The New Grove Dictionary of American Music*, ed. H. Wiley Hitchcock and Stanley Sadie, 4 vols. (London: Macmillan, 1986), Vol. 4, p. 170.

[50] *Telegraph und Tribune*, 10 June 1908.

[51] *Thirty-second National Saengerfest*, 62-71.

[52] *Baker's Biographical Dictionary of Musicians*, 4th ed. (New York: G. Schirmer, Inc., 1940), 246. The premiere of *Parsifal* was a concert version.

[53] *Thirty-second National Saengerfest*, 47.

[54] *Indianapolis News*, 15 June 1908.

[55] *Indianapolis Star*, 15 June 1908.

[56] *Indianapolis News*, 15 June 1908. Similar sentiments are expressed in an information circular sent to member societies of the North American Sängerbund, see Nord-Amerikanischer Saengerbund Invitation and Programs, Athenaeum Turners Collection, A-78-11, Special Collections and Archives, Indiana University–Purdue University Indianapolis Library.

[57] *Ibid.*

[58] *Indianapolis Star*, 17 June 1908.

[59] *Indianapolis Star*, 17 and 20 June 1908.

[60] *Thirty-second National Saengerfest*, 62-71.

[61] *Indianapolis News*, 20 June 1908.

[62] *Indianapolis Star*, 20 June 1908. This was not the first time a children's chorus had been used in a Sängerfest; the eighteenth Sängerfest of the Northwestern Sängerbund, held in Davenport, Iowa, in July 1898, brought together almost two thousand children from the Davenport public schools to sing "Die Wacht am Rhein" and the "Star Spangled Banner."

[63] *Telegraph und Tribune*, 18 June 1908. Translation by Timothy Parrott.

[64] Shirley Vogler Meister, "Maennerchor Carries on Long Tradition," Indianapolis *Arts Insight* 5/7 (November 1983), 12.

[65] Joseph Hermann Keller, unpublished notes (in the private possession of Männerchor past-president Kenneth Duncan) for a speech made 27 March 1907 at the formal opening of the new Männerchor Hall on Illinois Street.

[66] Carnivals invitation, Friday, 2 February 1883. Maennerchor Invitations and Programs, Oscar Frenzel Collection, A88-26, I.U.P.U.I. Library.

[67]Kenneth Duncan, "A short history of the Indianapolis Männerchor"; p. 2 of unpublished notes, Indianapolis Maennerchor History—Kenneth Duncan, Athenaeum Turners Collection, A88-45 M20, I.U.P.U.I. Library.

[68]Program, *Viertes Concert des Indianapolis Maennerchor*, Friday, 30 April 1909.

[69]Program, *Dritte Unterhaltung des Indianapolis Maennerchor*, Thursday, 11 December 1879.

[70]Keller, notes.

[71]Peltz, "Historical Sketch," 12.

[72]Peltz, 12.

[73]*Abend -Unterhaltung des Maennerchor*, Monday, 25 October 1875.

[74]As quoted in Talbot, 54.

[75]*Loc. cit.*

[76]Talbot, 59.

[77]Shirley Vogler Meister, "Stouthearted Singers," *Indianapolis Magazine* (July 1983), 44.

[78]Scherrer, 17.

[79]*Loc. cit.*

[80]Meister, p. 44.

[81]*Loc. cit.*

[82]"Frenzel Provides for Maintenance of Male Chorus by Large Bequest," *Indianapolis Star*, 9 June 1933.

WHY AMERICAN ART MUSIC FIRST ARRIVED IN NEW ENGLAND

Nicholas E. Tawa

For about 250 years after the first British settlements in the New World, the possibility of a viable native art music was out of the question. Throughout the seventeenth century, the struggle for existence took precedence over all other considerations. The eighteenth century saw the appearance of our first towns and some desultory music-making. A few Americans could and did write music, but conditions were not auspicious for the survival of any sophisticated homegrown art. They were either genteel gentlemen-practitioners like Francis Hopkinson of Philadelphia or poorly trained New England singing-school teachers like William Billings of Boston. The latter, who had undoubted musical talent, worked within the narrow confines determined by the barely literate amateur choruses of the time. He also died a pauper, scarcely any financial rewards having come his way during his lifetime. As W. Dermot Darby writes:

> Billings's merit is that he was the first musician of really independent and original talent that America produced. He was handicapped by lack of technical knowledge and lack of a suitable milieu.... He is a noteworthy figure, but his importance is not overwhelming.[1]

Well into the nineteenth century, American musical ability was acquired by Americans visiting Europe or from foreign musicians visiting America.

American songwriters grew plentiful by the mid-nineteenth century, the chief of whom was Stephen Foster. Yet, again, they could not translate their simple art into something of more ambitious scope. As for art composers, there were William Fry of

Philadelphia, George Bristow of New York, and Louis Moreau
Gottschalk of New Orleans. However, they did not bring forth a
new crop of native composers in any of these cities. Gottschalk
was the only one of the three with any striking creative ability,
but he wrote mainly piano pieces: some unduly sentimental,
others astounding in ideas, and most overly repetitious and
structurally weak. Besides, Gottschalk was a wanderer, incessantly
traveling from city to city and country to country to perform at
the keyboard.

Meanwhile, a greater acceptance of art grew. The violinist
Ole Bull, the singer Jenny Lind, and the orchestra conductor Louis
Antoine Jullien showed all Americans the possibilities inherent in
artworks admirably played. In New England, the growing number
of admirers of John Ruskin's writings gradually overcame their
opposition to sonorous and sense-exciting tones, a legacy of
Puritanism. They began to emphasize the ethical and didactic
force of the art and yearn for artistic music of their own.

Nevertheless, native composers of consequential art music
could not make a first appearance in the United States until
certain conditions had been met. First, during childhood and
adolescence, budding composers needed family or friends to
precipitate an interest in music as a career. Somehow or other, a
thorough musical education had to be obtained. The desire and
determination to continue on a musical course, despite possible
financial difficulties and social disapproval, had to exist. On
balance, the artistic, cultural, and intellectual community needed
to approve and encourage the production of music. Sponsorship
by influential or affluent individuals was necessary. A spirit of
collegiality among the few composers there were would give
strength and encouragement to each. The availability of
competent musicians willing and able to perform whatever new
American works were created, and of audiences willing to listen,
were of paramount importance. Finally, a means to a livelihood,
preferably through music, was certainly a desideratum.

Until the mid-nineteenth century, the conditions outlined
above were not met anywhere in the United States. Composers
were few and usually ill-trained, and they were rarely granted a
hearing. As the amateur composer William Henry Fry observed in
1863:

So rare are the composers of any sort that even in our large cities the men who can detail with the pen, on paper, the abstract sonorousness and expression of musical effects may be set down at one or two—or none—and out of the great cities there is nobody at all.[2]

Fry did not see how ripe Boston was for the steadfast cultivation of art music, but Gottschalk did. This pianist-composer liked to concertize in the city, finding it aristocratic in taste and welcoming to "the sciences and arts." Bostonians, he said, were sophisticated, musical, and financially supportive of music. Gottschalk cited Henry Wadsworth Longfellow, Annie and James T. Fields, and Oliver Wendell Holmes as among the people who befriended him during his visits. "Boston," he stated,

possesses what New York has not yet obtained: two concert halls, which are in no way inferior to any of the largest concert halls in the world.... O Maecenac New Yorkers, who boast of the golden patronage you accord to art, what are your titles? Is it perchance that usurious enterprise which is called the Academy of Music, by which you will draw from the impresario a double tax under the form of exorbitant rent and gratuitous admission?[3]

At last emerged in or near New England the five composers with whom we are concerned in the present book: John Knowles Paine (1839-1906), George Whitefield Chadwick (1854-1931), Edward MacDowell (1860-1908), Horatio Parker (1863-1919), and Arthur Foote (1853-1937). By the end of the century, writers on music acknowledged all five—indeed, let us refer to them below as "the Five"—as our most significant and frequently performed musical creators, each having major works of considerable worth to his credit. (The only non–New Englander, the New York–born MacDowell, had a mother and, later, a wife from New England.)

All five musicians—Paine, Chadwick, MacDowell, Parker, and Foote—absorbed the high moral sense, the dedication to duty, and the determination to do well at whatever they undertook, which was part of the New England character of the time. Even more than just experiencing no conflict with their society, they (along with other New Englanders) loved their region and appreciated its contributions to literature, the arts, and the social and political history of America. Theirs was a background that included the musical endeavors of Billings and Lowell Mason; the writings of Anne Bradstreet, Ralph Waldo Emerson, Nathaniel Hawthorne, and Henry David Thoreau; the paintings of John Singleton Copley; the contributions to political thinking of the Adams family; and the dedication of private wealth to the building and maintenance of libraries, museums, schools for the deaf, and asylums for the insane. After examining what the Five said and did, we conclude that they were proud of and behaved in accordance with their heritage.

Although the musical styles of the Five differed, all of them worked willingly within a traditional framework shared by them and approved by the local musical world. At the same time, they thought similarly about what their artistic responsibilities should be vis-à-vis their society. In short we can regard them as belonging together as an artistic circle, albeit an informal one. Benjamin Lambord, a pupil of MacDowell, testified to this, when he said in 1915:

> For the establishment of that which, for lack of a better name, we call the American-school of composers we ... look to New England. Through the composers known as the Boston group America first assimilated into its musical life the finest traditions of European musical culture and in the labors of these men the American community was taught in some degree to look seriously upon the native composer and his achievement.

Lambord detected no common style among them. A resident of New York, he declared that Americans had to accept Boston as the birthplace of art music in the United States, keeping also in mind the excellence of its permanent professional orchestra, the Boston Symphony, the thorough musical education obtainable at Harvard University and local conservatories of music, and the vigorous cultural life of the community.[4]

Likewise, in 1885 The *Musical Herald* described Boston as the authentic "musical centre" of America. Here, the amount and excellence of the music presentations surpassed those of "any other city in America" and probably equaled those of "any European musical city." A large portion of the public frequented "lectures upon musical history and analysis, which pour enough musical information upon the inhabitants to make each one a critic." It was hardly surprising that musicians found Boston a choice town in which to work.[5]

On the other hand, New York City, however huge and prosperous, was considered inhospitable to composers. Local performers avoided present-day music. Audiences refused to listen to American compositions.[6] Chicagoans behaved similarly. After Longfellow wrote to Amy Fay saying that Boston was "quite music mad," Fay wrote him back from Chicago, in 1880, lamenting the musical insensitivity of Chicagoans. A similar complaint came from conductor Theodore Thomas, who held up Boston as the city to emulate.[7]

It is time to examine more closely the first of the conditions for art music's arrival and its pertinence to New England. We find that music constantly sounded in most of the composers' homes as they grew up. For example, Paine's father, sister, a grandfather, and an uncle were all musicians. Homegrown music-making was a regular occurrence during Paine's young life. His family underwrote his music studies with Hermann Kotzschmar, in Portland, Maine, where Paine himself was born and raised. Paine's sister also helped finance his music studies in Germany, with Karl Haupt and Wilhelm Wieprecht.[8]

Chadwick's parents, uncles, and aunts had attended that old New England institution, the singing school. His father, after removing his family to Lawrence, Massachusetts, worked as an insurance salesman and taught singing, and the young composer's brother instructed him on the piano. Although his father opposed a music profession for his son, Chadwick eventually rejected his father's rule, taught music privately, and pursued his music studies at the New England Conservatory. In 1876 he joined the faculty of Olivet College, Michigan.

Parker's father was an architect. His mother, born in Germany, was a trained musician and proficient in Latin and Greek. She instructed her son on the keyboard and engaged Chadwick to begin his instruction in music theory and composition.[9]

Musicians did not form Foote's background. His father edited the *Salem Gazette,* and his sister, a writer, raised him after the death of his mother. Foote once said: "I had no especial musical inheritance or surroundings." Yet his family enjoyed music and provided him with piano lessons from a local teacher. Later, he entered Harvard College to study with Paine. In 1875, Foote received an M.A. in music from Harvard (the first granted by any American university).[10]

MacDowell's parents were not musicians, but his mother loved music and began him on piano at age eight. He studied with various piano teachers in New York before leaving for Europe with his mother in order to further his studies. We therefore can see that family influences were certainly factors in the turning to music of all five men.

Also to be noted is the importance of women in shaping their careers, not only their mothers and sisters but, later, their wives as well. Another native of Portland, for example, Paine's wife believed completely in her husband, at least according to the composer's friend Henry Finck. Paine's wife also made do with her husband's modest salary that he earned at Harvard; she allowed no one to interrupt him while he composed, disputed his critics, and strove to win him performances.[11]

Parker's wife had been a German music student, so she understood the importance of what her husband was doing. Seeing how busily he worked as a conductor and teacher, after he joined the faculty at Yale University, she endeavored to carve out as much leisure time as she could for his creative work. Their daughter said of her own girlhood: "How often we would come flying into the house, full of enthusiasm over something to be greeted by Mother standing guard. 'Hush,' she would say, 'your father is working.' Her absolute selflessness, devotion and understanding never wavered for an instant. Father and his work came first, last and always."[12]

MacDowell's wife had been her husband's piano student before marrying him. She worried about her husband's excessive sensitivity to the outside world, yet she knew it formed an essential part of his genius. From her came the strength MacDowell needed to survive the lack of recognition he encountered as well as his inability to find a permanent position and the hand-to-mouth existence he experienced during the first years of marriage. MacDowell's wife nursed him as best she could later, when nervous disorders engulfed him, especially after the disastrous denouement of his teaching career at Columbia University.

These wives facilitated the solid establishment of American art music by providing the conditions favorable for creativity. Without them, their husbands might well have succumbed to the many tribulations that assailed them at every turn of their careers.

The second condition identified earlier—the need for thorough musical education—was satisfied after four members of the Five went to Germany for their advanced music education. (Foote, who remained in a Boston completely under the influence of German music and ideas, relied mainly on Paine for his advanced training.)

Like other New Englanders of Puritan ancestry, Paine worked seriously at the pursuit to which he had bound himself. He favored German schooling because it was thoroughgoing and because he esteemed German ideals and the musical contributions of German composers. Giving similar reasons, and not deterred by his poverty, Chadwick too left for Germany, eventually studying under the eminent educator and composer Josef Rheinberger.[13] After traipsing from European teacher to European teacher, MacDowell settled down in Frankfurt, where the noted composer Joachim Raff became his instructor in composition.

However lengthy their stays in Europe, none of the Five forgot that he was an American; none lost his love for his own native land. To this, MacDowell's wife testified, when she spoke of her husband's ceaseless "enthusiasm for his own country." After his return to America, MacDowell particularly cherished the countryside surrounding his Peterborough home and was electrified by sites rich in history. To him, and his musical colleagues, America "was not a [culturally] bare and arid tract."[14]

Most of the Five lived in and around Boston. Even after moving to New Haven in order to tech at Yale University, Parker often returned there. MacDowell spent his most fruitful years in the city (1888-1896). Later, when he left to teach at Columbia University, he visited Boston again and again, because there his works were enthusiastically performed and received.

On good terms with one another, the Five frequent gathered together to discuss music and examine one another's works. Foote and Chadwick mention high-spirited rendezvous during the 1890s at Boston clubs and in each other's homes, where they gathered about the same table in convivial intercourse, whetting each other's wits with thrust and parry rejoicing in each other's successes, and working for them, too, but ever ready with the cooling compress of gentle humor or sarcasm if perchance a head showed an undue tendency to enlarge. And in that invigorating atmosphere of mutual respect and honest criticism they worked with joy and enthusiasm, knowing that if only their work was good enough it would be pretty sure of a hearing sooner or later.

When Parker returned each week to Boston, starting in 1893 (to act as organist and choirmaster at Boston's Trinity Church), "the congenial companionship of his old friends," writes Chadwick, "the active musical life of Boston, his growing reputation, all stimulated [Parker] to further effort."[15]

The third condition for the arrival of music in New England—the will to succeed—was never in doubt. Each of the Five demonstrated an adamant purposefulness and a strength of character that propelled him forward. All were determined to be composers worthy of the name. In order to accomplish this, they studied and absorbed all past musics and became adepts in melody, harmony, rhythm, and form.[16] Like their confrères in the other arts, the Five were certain that "the art of the past could provide useful sources for the development of a national American art. While the reliance on sources or authority would be important, what would be produced would be a unique American art."[17]

Foote, for example, wrote that he and his fellow composers wanted to aspire to the permanent and essential in music and to avoid whatever was fleeting and inferior.[18] Thus the music the Five created would satisfy the needs of their contemporary audience and provide beacons for the future: "We are entrusted with the task of forming the taste of the next generation whether we will or no," said Parker. Besides, "It is our duty to do so."[19]

The hazards were many, because their road was unmarked. The rewards were few. This realization motivated Parker to say:

The many rewards of a serious composer are slender at best, and most precarious, especially in this country.... One who aspires to compose must therefore be prepared to content himself with little beyond his work. The exaltation which attends the continued pursuit of beauty should be his. The communion and fellowship of the great masters of music should comfort and encourage him, but he must seek his rewards in spiritual and not in material things.[20]

Nevertheless, each of the Five found the courage to originate a number of sound artistic compositions, beautifully crafted and, in the eyes of their New England advocates, worthy of comparison with like works from other nations: songs, piano character pieces, chamber music, cantatas, masses, oratorios, operas, suites, concertos, symphonic poems, overtures, and symphonies.

Our next consideration is of major import: the necessity for some sort of artistic, cultural, and intellectual community ready to approve and encourage the production of music. In New England, said Parker, a need for native composers came to exist after the Civil War. To further New England's civilization, its cultural and intellectual leaders sought to bring forth an art of their own, including musical works. They were not "content to import everything bodily."[21] By 1865 the Romantic movement was finally catching on in New England, where music was seen as opening the door to exalted realms and abstracting listeners from the residual torments of postwar existence. The Five successfully tapped into these feelings. They thus truly became the first, in the words of Van Wyck Brooks, to establish a native musical "culture, creating the living chain that we call tradition."[22] To be sure, other composers were active in America. However, none achieved the prominence of the Five and none initiated a continuing line of American composers extending into contemporary times.

Why was Boston the focal point for this important musical activity, so momentous for the cultural future of the United States? In the latter part of the century America experienced tremendous population growth and industrial expansion. Immigrants arrived by the millions. At first, they came mostly from the British Isles and Germany. As the century progressed they came more and more from the Mediterranean basin and Eastern Europe. Most were peasants, with scarcely any education and no money. These immigrants, as well as young men and women from rural America, sped to the cities, looking for work and, to occupy their leisure hours, inexpensive entertainment suited to their uncultivated tastes.

Urban centers burgeoned. While this made possible the support crucial for the survival of art composers, it also gave rise to a feeling of transition and an awareness of the splintering of society. This was especially true for educated New Englanders, including the Five, who favored artistic and intellectual pursuits.

The unfamiliar and rude ways of living evidenced by the urban masses demonstrated lack of refinement to the Five and their Yankee society.[23] Something better had to be offered, something they saw as embodying the ideals and moral code of the older America they cherished. They did accept popular entertainment in moderation, but not for their own lifework. Instead, they trod a different path, toward the advancement of noble goals by means of what they composed. The giving of the best in themselves imbued every piece of music they created. In these ways, the Five hoped to capture the nobler part of the American experience.[24] Fortunately for them, more than elsewhere in the country, Boston had a large cluster of informed persons who also felt their apprehensions and solidly endorsed their elevated calling.

In other places, artists went unnoticed or lacked the trust of their communities. Music especially was seen as a worthless activity separate from real life and qualifying merely as a diversion for a woman's idle hours.[25] A goodly number of the Yankee inhabitants of the Boston area, however, thought differently. Witness their approval of music education in the public schools from 1838 onward. Witness too their turning out in droves for the National Peace Jubilee of 1869. Many of them, with scores in hand, attended what concerts were available in order to get a better grip on the music. In the embryonic phase of art music, composers required people's willing presence at concerts to encourage their further efforts. Music lovers did come, though the concert halls were fuller in some years than in others. On balance, attendance increased from year to year.

Another inducement for producing artistic compositions was the pride that New England society and its cultural leaders took in their intellectual and artistic history, and in their desire to bear a part in and to bring forward that history. Civic pride, said Charles Eliot Norton, required the reassurance of artists in Boston's midst, so that they would aspire to attain superior results. The most noteworthy works of art were never mere individual pronouncements, but rather expressions of a nation's faith and its vital essence. If great enough, a civilization would find artists ready to meet these standards.[26]

John Jay Chapman praised the "sincere men" of Boston who encouraged or constituted themselves into "centers of thought, centers of music, centers of painting." Such men saw the need for native art and music and hoped to offset the influence of the brash America growing daily about them. Chapman appealed to all Americans to abet the few trying to foster their fellow artists.[27]

It appears that the cultural leaders that Norton and Chapman spoke about were less noticeable in New York City. In 1895 an unhappy Antonín Dvořák lamented that mercenary Manhattan businessmen opposed high culture. If an employee took up music, he was dismissed from their employment. Patrons of the art were pitifully few. New York performers and publishers would not touch anything American. Under such conditions how could a viable native art music come into being?[28]

Sponsorship by influential or affluent individuals was needed. Unlike the New York described by Dvořák, Boston had patrons of music who benefited composers in important ways. The lift given American musicians by means of musical soirees was one helping hand that the Five took advantage of, attending as guests, performers, and composers. Little money, however, normally accompanied their presence. To give one example, Clara Kathleen Rogers, a former professional singer, and her husband, the Boston lawyer Henry Munroe Rogers, applied themselves to the fostering of music. Rogers herself writes that one reason for their musical evenings was to assist young musicians, by inviting influential people to come and hear them. She mentions as among her guests the musicians Benjamin Lang and Julius Eichberg, the music critics John Sullivan Dwight and William Foster Apthorp, the music director of the Boston Symphony, writers like Julia Ward Howe, and composers Chadwick, Foote, and MacDowell. Louise Moulton and her husband held similar soirées to which they invited Harvard's academics, writers, and performing musicians as well as the Five.[29]

Celia Thaxter, a good friend of Paine, made an effort to promote MacDowell's music. Thaxter's summer home on Appledore, Isles of Shoals, in the 1890s, became a gathering place for vacationing friends, among them musicians, artists, writers, and music lovers. Macdowell brought out several major piano works here for the first time, with himself at the keyboard. Pianist William Mason, a guest at Appledore, describes the audience listening to MacDowell as "people of intelligence and culture who, under adverse circumstances would not have appreciated the beauty of these intellectual works, but who after closer association were led to perceive their beauty and who learned to love them."[30]

Paine's compositional efforts came to the public's attention—owing, often, to the exertions of his close friend John Fiske, a philosopher and member of the Harvard history faculty. Fiske introduced Paine to prominent local residents, including William James and William Dean Howells, and he defended Paine against charges made by conservative Harvard faculty members that his music courses had no place in a university curriculum. Moreover, Fiske wrote several published articles in praise of Paine's music. As one might expect, Paine was a frequent attendee of Fiske's musical at-homes.[31]

Several noted American musicians also labored on behalf of American music. The Philadelphia-born singer David Bispham, to name one, successfully solicited English music leaders to perform Parker's *Hora Novissima*. The highly regarded pianist, teacher, and conductor Benjamin Lang was one of the first Bostonians to appreciate the young Foote's talents and himself persuaded the budding composer to take up music for his lifework. In addition, Lang conducted the premieres of several choral compositions by the Five. Louise Homer, a friend of Horatio Parker, devoted herself to mastering the title role of Parker's opera *Mona* when the Metropolitan Opera introduced it: "Her passionate desire to make a success of this work was most touching. It occupied her thoughts, almost exclusively, for several months."[32]

Once in a while funds from sponsors were crucial in advancing a career. When Parker desperately needed the wherewithal to finance his studies in Germany, one Mr. Burr advanced him the necessary money. The wealthy J. Montgomery Sears once offered to subsidize MacDowell so that he could devote himself to writing an opera. (Though moved by the gesture, MacDowell refused the proposal, worried that what he might compose would be second-rate.[33]) Regrettably such offers of largess were rare.

The most celebrated Boston patron of artists was Isabella Stewart Gardner. Music sounded constantly in her home, from recitals to full-fledged symphony concerts. Foote—to cite one composer she benefited—engaged in chamber music performances in her home, some of them including his own chamber works. In January 1888 Gardner also lent assistance to local composers by helping found the short-lived Manuscript Club of Boston, under whose auspices new compositions received performances at her home. Two of them were Foote's Suite for Orchestra in E and Parker's String Quartet in F.[34]

Cofounded by Chadwick, the Music Teachers National Association also acted in support of American composers. One event of significance was the first known all-American concert, given at its eighth annual meeting in Cleveland in 1884, which presented the music of Paine, Chadwick, and Foote. The next year, Paine's Violin Sonata was performed. Calixa Lavallée, a Canadian musician living in Boston at that time, was the prime mover in arranging these occasions. Foote states that these concerts provided him with the first real chance to hear his "compositions in large form. At that time an American writing serious music was a rare bird, opportunities for a hearing being hard to get. To these concerts I thus owe the beginning of what reputation I may have."[35]

Fortunately for Foote and his confederates, Boston boasted a surprisingly large number of writers on music who had musical training. Their articles on music, appearing in newspapers and magazines, were widely read by music lovers, not only locally, but throughout the country. The most eminent of these writers was John Sullivan Dwight, influential editor of *Dwight's Journal of Music,* published from 1852 to 1881. His approval of the works of Paine, Chadwick, and Foote, when they were still unknown, were welcome because they brought many of his readers to their side.[36] Dwight championed Paine especially, extolling the merits of his First and Second Symphonies at the time of their premiere.

Several other Boston writers on music also called attention to the Five—attention that was of major consequence in the promotion of music in New England, if not the nation. These highly respected writers included Apthorp, Benjamin Edward Woolf, Louis C. Elson, Howard Malcom Ticknor, Henry Taylor Parker, and Philip Hale.

In Chicago, the two best-known writers on music were George P. Upton, originally from Boston, and W. S. B. Mathews. Both men valued New England's composers and urged their music on Chicagoans. In New York critics Finck and Richard Aldrich had been students of Paine, took an interest in Boston's musical happenings, and introduced its composers to New Yorkers. In addition, Finck, James Gibbons Huneker, and Lawrence Gilman constantly championed MacDowell's compositions.[37]

The availability of competent musicians to perform new music, so essential to the cause of local music production, was nip and tuck for many years in Boston and depended chiefly on foreign-born (and mostly German) performers who came to reside in the city. These musicians were equally an impediment and an aid to the American composer. I cannot overemphasize their importance in stimulating interest in art music and thus paving the way for New England composers like the Five.

From the earliest years of the United States onward, Europeans supplied the majority of the instrumentalists, singers, music directors, music educators, and music publishers of the entire country. In Boston, there was the English organist William Selby, who resided in the city during the 1770s. Two decades later the van Hagens, a Dutch family, concertized, gave music lessons, and published music. Gottlieb Graupner, a German who arrived in Boston about the same time, did likewise. Of greater significance, Graupner founded the Boston Philo-Harmonic Society for the performance of serious orchestral music and cofounded the Handel and Haydn Society, in 1815. In the 1830s the Englishman George Webb taught at Boston's Academy of Music and led the undistinguished orchestras of the Academy, the Music Fund Society, and the Handel and Haydn Society.

Then, beginning in 1848, Boston became the home of large numbers of German musicians fleeing from the turmoil caused by the unsuccessful uprising against autocracy in Central Europe. The appearance in 1849 in Boston of the Germania Musical Society was of major importance to the arrival of art music in New England. It comprised a company of proficient instrumentalists from Berlin who impressed New Englanders wherever they gave concerts. When the group disbanded in 1854, one member, Carl Zerrahn, put together a new orchestra, the Boston Philharmonic, and led it in a series of concerts. He subsequently conducted another series of orchestral concerts underwritten by the Harvard Musical Society and also acted as music director of the Handel and Haydn Society. Zerrahn and his compatriot Bernhard Listemann were Boston's principal orchestral directors prior to the founding of the Boston Symphony in 1881.

At last, through the largess of Henry Lee Higginson, Boston acquired a permanent ensemble of the highest quality, made up of highly skilled German-born instrumentalists and initially conducted by George Henschel, himself German-born and -educated. Like Isabella Stewart Gardner, Higginson wanted the benefits of culture to reach not only his own affluent circle but also the working classes; he believed that great art would alleviate their anxieties and alter the direction of their thinking from earthly sourness of spirit to the sublime. In the words of William James, Higginson's Boston Symphony and Gardner's Fenway Court gave Bostonians "the chance to forget themselves, to become like children again, immersed in wonder."[38]

It was only to be expected that Bostonians would become conditioned to Austro-German art music and come to value it above all other national musics. Moreover, Boston music students flocked to local German instructors. Stimulated by these musicians, a few Bostonians commenced traveling to Central Europe in order to experience directly the art music of the Germanic countries and to engage in serious musical study.

In the latter half of the century, as the Five tried to make their way in the music world, five other musicians—Germans all— stood forth as musicians of high influence in Boston. Julius Eichberg, a violinist, conductor, and composer, arrived in Boston in the late 1850s and established the Boston Conservatory of Music in 1867. Otto Dresel came in 1852 and immediately began to give piano performances, teach, and write newspaper and magazine pieces on music, which Bostonians eagerly read. Franz Kneisel arrived in 1885 to become concertmaster in the Boston Symphony and leader of the Kneisel Quartet, which would premier many an American composition. Wilhelm Gericke was conductor of the Boston Symphony from 1884 to 1889 and again from 1896 to 1898. During Gericke's tenure, many new orchestral compositions by the New England group were given their initial performances. Finally, Arthur P. Schmidt settled in Boston in 1866 and founded a music publishing house and committed himself to issuing works by all five composers, especially those of Foote and MacDowell.

It is obvious that these Germans—Eichberg, Dresel, Kneisel, Gericke, and Schmidt—were instrumental in arousing Bostonians' interest in native composers, in encouraging the increase in performing groups that would play the music of these composers, and in supplying the personnel for these groups. When they also acted as counselors, friends, and supporters of the Five their services were even more valuable.[39]

Another German, of importance to Paine in particular, was Theodore Thomas. In 1869, he had founded his own excellent orchestra and conducted it principally in New York but also in other cities. Eventually Thomas would become the first director of the Chicago Orchestra. He signaled the arrival of the New England composer when he brought his orchestra to Boston and premiered Paine's First Symphony, in 1876, and then took it back to New York for performance there. Thomas's first-rate rendition of the symphony prompted Boston's musical community to look more closely at the works of local composers.

Despite the invaluable services of European musicians, their presence also had an adverse effect. The Germans regarded the music of their countrymen to be superior to that of Americans, an attitude quickly communicated to Americans of some influence in the music world.[40] Paine knew that American respect for his music came more easily after German approval. Parker found all American operatic enterprises dominated by Germans and Italians, so much so that: "One is tempted to say that a knowledge of our language is a hindrance rather than a help in gaining admission to the opera here [New York City]." Chadwick thought entering American works alongside European works in competitions was usually a waste of time. The judges were often foreigners and favored whatever was not American.[41] On balance, however, European musicians did much to further the cause of American composers like Chadwick, Foote, Paine, Parker, and MacDowell.

We should keep in mind that concerts were essential to sustain composers in their creative efforts. In this regard, New England, and especially Boston, had after the Civil War grown more favorably disposed toward American works than had other American cities. This is made quite clear when we read, for example, the commentaries of the New York music critics and the several complaints that MacDowell and Parker made about the "inferior" music public and the denial of performances in New York.[42] All things considered, Boston musical societies were more open-minded than not and inspired hope in native composers that their creations had a reasonable chance of being heard, if not accepted. Fortunately for art music, Boston's performing groups were relatively plentiful and skilled at what they did.

Except for MacDowell, the Five produced many choral and organ compositions to satisfy the demands of the local churches. Consider the appetite for new works among Boston's amateur choral societies. The most prominent of these were the Handel and Haydn Society, founded in 1815; the Apollo Club, 1871; the Boylston Club, 1873; and the Cecilia Society, 1877. As Dwight observed, along with the Handel and Haydn Society, a remarkable attribute of Boston's musical scene was "the springing up and prosperous continuance of so many vocal clubs, composed mainly, but not entirely of amateurs. The three most important— the Apollo, the Boylston, and the Cecilia."[43]

Note what was said of the Handel and Haydn Society when Theodore Thomas invited its members to come to New York, expense free, in 1873. A New York newspaper reported:

> They represent all classes of society—ladies from Beacon street, merchants from State street, shop girls, young lawyers, clerks, mechanics. Their opportunities for study and practice are no better than ours; yet we believe that most of our connoisseurs will be amazed when they find how far the Boston singers are in advance of the highest achievement of any similar organization in New York. They will not only teach our societies how to sing an oratorio, but they will teach our audience how to enjoy one.[44]

Happily for American music, the Handel and Haydn Society did fit into its performances several large native works, including Paine's *St. Peter and the Nativity*, and Parker's *St. John, Hora Novissima*, and *Morven and the Grail*.

The Apollo Club proffered Paine's *The Tempest, The Summons to Love, Phoebus Arise,* and *The Birds*; and Foote's *Farewell to Hiawatha*. An April 1885 concert featured Paine's music to *Oedipus Tyrannus*, Chadwick's "Introduction" and

"Allegro" from his Second Symphony, and Foote's *If Doughty Deeds*. Reporting on the evening, a writer said:

> The American muse has at last been provided with board and lodging. The concert of the Apollo Club ... was a great stride in the right direction. It gave a programme composed entirely of the works of Boston musicians, and as some of these are the leading composers of the country the concert stood out as a representation of American music.... If our composers only knew that they can obtain a hearing for their best works there will be a great impetus given to American composition. Not every one can have the patience ... [to] compose great works without seeing any chance of their performance.[45]

The Boylston Club under Lang's direction performed Paine's *The Realm of Fancy* in 1877. The Cecilia Society, also conducted by Lang, gave the first public performance of Foote's *The Wreck of the Hesperus*, in 1888. As conductor of various Boston groups and the Springfield and Worcester Festivals, Chadwick saw to it that he and his colleagues were liberally represented on his programs. For example, Chadwick championed Parker's vocal compositions, among them *King Trajan* and *The Kobolds*. Famous at the turn of the century were the Norfolk, Connecticut, Festivals of the Litchfield County Choral Union (led by Carl Stoeckel), which boasted a large chorus, an imported orchestra made up of members of the New York Philharmonic, and soloists when needed.[46] Heard here were Parker's *A Star Song, King Gorm the Grim*, and *The Dream of Mary*, and Chadwick's *Noel* and *Land of Our Hearts* for chorus and orchestra as well as his orchestral *Aphrodite, Tam O'Shanter*, and *Anniversary Overture*. In 1880 two orchestras performed Paine's Second Symphony: the Boston Philharmonic and the orchestra of the Harvard Musical Association.

The following year the completely professional Boston Symphony Orchestra gave its first concert. Later this ensemble performed most of the orchestral compositions written by the Five and other American composers. In 1906 Philip Hale published a long list of American compositions played by the orchestra from its inception to the beginning of 1906. Most never received repeat performances, although one or two received several; among these were Chadwick's *Melpomene* Overture (five performances) and Paine's "Prelude" to *Oedipus Tyrannus* (three).[47] Evidently at least some members of the audience wanted more American compositions. A squib sent in 1884 to George Henschel, conductor of the Symphony, read:

> Let no more Wagner themes thy bill enhance
> And give the native workers just one chance,
> Don't give the Dvorak symphony again;
> If you would give us joy, oh, give us Paine![48]

In addition to the Boston Symphony, chamber ensembles like the outstanding Kneisel Quartet volunteered to play new works by Paine, Chadwick, Foote, and Parker, sometimes with not a little persuasion from the composers themselves. (MacDowell did not write chamber music.) In 1886, for example, Chadwick tried persistently but unsuccessfully to get Franz Kneisel to perform a Parker composition. An exasperated Chadwick wrote to Parker: "Kneisel gave for an excuse for not playing your Quartet that so many people wanted to hear the Brahms Sextette that he was obliged to put it on the programme to the exclusion of the great American work!"[49] Nevertheless, compared to what was happening to composers in other parts of the country, the Five had little to complain about.

The last condition for the arrival of American art music in New England concerns the need of composers to earn a living. Unfortunately, art composers made little money through the sale and performance of their music. Nor was subsidization by the wealthy in the cards. To live composers had to teach, work as music directors, or give keyboard performances. All of the Five offered their services as private teachers, although only some of them were successful. After Parker returned from abroad in 1885, he and Arthur Whiting rented a Boston studio and waited for students. None came, and Parker was forced to leave for an organist's position in Brooklyn and a teaching position at St. Paul's School in Garden City, Long Island.[50] On the other hand, Foote hung on and eventually made a fair amount of money from private teaching.

Most of the Five at some point found employment at a college or conservatory of music, at a time when music posts were rapidly opening up both in older institutions and in recently founded schools of music. Composers were attracted to these positions for reasons of dependable incomes, summers free for creative work, and extended sabbaticals. In 1862 Paine won the post of instructor in music at Harvard. Later he became a full professor, owing to the sponsorship of Harvard's president, Charles William Eliot. Eliot himself felt strongly about music:

> When I became president of Harvard University there was no organized department of music in it and it was not customary in New England for highly educated, long-trained men to adopt the profession of music. There were many amateurs but few professional devotees.... I knew how fine an element in culture music was, and I did my best with admirable supporters to develop a department of music at Harvard University, hoping that the influence of that department might spread through all the walks of life.[51]

Later Paine was responsible for the music education of a number of young men who later carved out their own place in the music world—among them Foote himself as well as Daniel Gregory Mason, Edward Burlingame Hill, Frederick Shepherd Converse, and John Alden Carpenter. Other Paine students who in one way or another affected music included Henry Lee Higginson, Henry Finck, Richard Aldrich, M. A. DeWolfe Howe, Archibald Davison, Olin Downes, and Hugo Leichtentritt. Paine also taught at the brand-new New England Conservatory and the College of Music of Boston University.

When he returned from his European studies in 1880, Chadwick taught privately for a while. However, it was not long before he joined the faculty of the New England Conservatory, becoming its director in 1897. Under his administration the school installed a comprehensive theory and composition department, a capable repertory orchestra, and a flourishing opera workshop. Horatio Parker, Frederick Shepherd Converse, Edward Burlingame Hill, Daniel Gregory Mason, Arthur Farwell, Arthur Shepherd, and William Grant Still studied composition under Chadwick. (Note the future composers who studied both with Paine and Chadwick.) As mentioned above, Chadwick also directed the Springfield and Worcester Festivals.

Parker taught first at two New York schools and the National Conservatory of Music, and directed music at three churches. In 1893 he became organist and music director of Boston's Trinity Church, a position he occupied until 1902. In 1894 he was also called to Yale University as professor of music; by 1904, he had become dean of Yale's School of Music. Chadwick said that Parker "organized and conducted a symphony orchestra, which became an indispensable laboratory of the department, since it furnished the necessary experience for composers, conductors, singers, and players who were studying in the school." His contributions to education were praised by H. E. Krehbiel, who refers to the respect Parker brought to music when he linked the musical activities of Yale with those of New Haven's citizens by means of a series of orchestral concerts and a reorganized choral society, and by working assiduously to plan and build an impressive building for concerts, Woolsey Hall.[52]

While he lived in Boston MacDowell taught piano and composition privately and gave piano recitals, performed with chamber music ensembles, and appeared as soloist with the Boston Symphony Orchestra. In 1896, he went to New York to work as professor of music at Columbia University, a position that ultimately proved uncongenial to him.

Foote's principal occupations included private keyboard and composition instruction, the duties of organist at Boston's First Unitarian Church, and participation in Boston's countless chamber music concerts.

New England's hegemony in art music ended in the second decade of the twentieth century. Nevertheless, we must look to New England when we wish to study the first viable actuation of art music in the United States. Through the Five—John Knowles Paine, George Whitefield Chadwick, Edward MacDowell, Horatio Parker, and Arthur Foote—and the support of New Englanders, America first incorporated into its culture the finest musical works and ideas of Europe. Their example taught the American musical establishment to begin taking its own composers seriously and to recognize that music of excellence could come into being in the New World. For these reasons, every American composer and every lover of music that came after is in the debt of the Five.

Brighton, Massachusetts

[1]W. Dermot Darby, in *Music in America*, ed. Arthur Farwell and W. Dermot Darby, The Art of Music 4 (New York: National Society of Music, 1915), 52.

[2]William Treat Upton, *William Henry Fry* (New York: Crowell, 1954), 272-73.

[3]Louis Moreau Gottschalk, *Notes of a Pianist*, ed. Jeanne Behrend (New York: Knopf, 1964), 157, 232-33.

[4]*Music in America*, Art of Music 4, ed. Arthur Farwell and W. Dermot Darby (New York: National Society of Music, 1915), 335, 344.

[5]*The Musical Herald* 6 (1885), 164.

[6]Carl Engel, "Views and Reviews," *Musical Quarterly* 18 (1932): 179; and William Dean Howells, *Imaginary Interviews* (New York: Harper, 1910), 51.

[7]Florence French, *Music and Musicians in Chicago* (Chicago: French, 1899), 33, 34; [Amy Fay], *More Letters of Amy Fay: The American Years, 1879-1916*, selected and ed. S. Margaret William McCarthy (Detroit, MI: Information Coordinators, 1986), 5-7; and Theodore Thomas, *A Musical Autobiography* (1905; reprint New York: Da Capo, 1964), 104.

[8]George Thornton Edwards, *Music and Musicians of Maine* (Portland: Southworth, 1928), 122-23; John C. Schmidt, *The Life and Works of John Knowles Paine* (Ann Arbor, MI: UMI Research Press, 1980), 29; and Walter Raymond Spalding, *Music at Harvard* (1935; reprint, New York: Da Capo, 1977), 150-51.

[9]Louis C. Elson, *The History of American Music*, rev. to 1925 by Arthur Elson (New York: Macmillan, 1925), 297.

[10]Arthur Foote, *An Autobiography*, with an introduction and notes by Wilma Reid Cipolla (1946; reprint New York: Da Capo, 1979), 26; Foote, "A Bostonian Remembers," *Musical Quarterly* 23 (1937): 37; and Wilma Reid Cipolla, in the *American Grove*, s.v. "Foote, Arthur (William)."

[11]Henry T. Finck, *My Adventures in the Golden Age of Music* (New York: Funk & Wagnalls, 1926), 80; M. A. DeWolfe Howe, "John Knowles Paine," *Musical Quarterly* 25 (1939): 261, 266.

[12]Isabel Parker Semler, in collaboration with Pierson Underwood, *Horatio Parker* (New York: Putnam's Sons, 1942), 178. Hereafter "Semler."

[13]Elson, 170-71; and Steven Ledbetter and Victor Fell Yellin, in the *American Grove*, s.v. "Chadwick, George Whitefield."

[14]Marian MacDowell, "MacDowell's 'Peterborough Idea'," *Musical Quarterly* 18 (1932): 35-36, 38.

[15]Foote, "A Bostonian Remembers," 41; and *An Autobiography*, 55. See also George Chadwick, "American Composers," in *History of American Music*, ed. W. L. Hubbard, The American History and Encyclopedia of Music, Vol. VIII (Toledo, OH: Squire, 1908), 13. Finally, see the item in the *New England Magazine Review* 6 (1916): 120-21; and George Chadwick, *Horatio Parker* (New Haven: Yale, 1921), 12. The Parker obituary that appeared in the *Boston Transcript*, 1906, quotes Parker as stating that John Knowles Paine was his mother's teacher in composition, his encourager in music when he first started off as a musician, and his close personal friend over the years (Allan A. Brown Collection, scrapbook of clippings *M165.8, Vol. 7, in the Boston Public Library).

[16]*Music and Public Entertainment*, ed. Parker (Boston: Hall & Locke, 1911): "Introduction," xv.

[17]Richard Guy Wilson, in *The American Renaissance, 1876-1917* (New York: The Brooklyn Museum, 1979): Part I, "The Great Civilization," 12.

[18]*Theory of Music*, ed. Foote; introductions by W. L. Hubbard, Emily Liebling, and W. J. Henderson (New York: Irving Square, c. 1910), 230-31.

[19]Semler, 75.

[20]*Music and Public Entertainment*, "Introduction," xvi.

[21]Semler, 200.

[22]Van Wyck Brooks, "Forward" to Helen Howe, *The Gentle Americans* (New York: Harper & Row, 1965), xv.

[23]For a discussion of the new popular-music culture that arose after the Civil War, see Nicholas E. Tawa, *The Way to Tin Pan Alley* (New York: Schirmer, 1990).

[24]Richard Guy Wilson, "The Great Civilization," in *The American Renaissance, 1876-1917* (New York: The Brooklyn Museum, 1979), 11. See also, Stow Persons, *The Decline of American Gentility* (New York: Columbia University Press, 1973), 99.

[25]Henry Steele Commager, *The American Mind* (New Haven: Yale University Press, 1950), 10.

[26]Kermit Vanderbilt, *Charles Eliot Norton: Apostle of Culture in a Democracy* (Cambridge, MA: Belknap, 1959), 205.

[27]John Jay Chapman, *Memories and Milestones* (New York: Moffat, Yard, 1915), 13.

[28]Antonin Dvořák, "Music in America," *Harper's New Monthly Magazine* 90 (1895): 430-31.

[29]Clara Kathleen Rogers, *The Story of Two Lives* (privately printed at the Plimpton Press, 1932), 30; and Lilian Whiting, *Louise Chandler Moulton, Poet and Friend* (Boston: Little, Brown, 1910), 124-25.

[30]William Mason, *Memories of a Musical Life* (New York: Century, 1901), 253-56.

[31]John Spencer Clark, *The Life and Letter of John Fiske* (Boston: Houghton Mifflin, 1917): Vol. I, 206, 418-20; Vol. II, 83.

[32]Sidney Homer, *My Wife and I* (New York: Macmillan, 1939), 217.

[33]Semler, 40; and T. P. Currier, "Edward MacDowell As I Knew Him," *Musical Quarterly* 1 (1915), 26.

[34]Morris Carter, *Isabella Stewart Gardner and Fenway Court* (Boston: Houghton Mifflin, 1925), 112-13; Honor McCusker, *Fifty Years of Music in Boston* (Boston: Trustees of the Public Library, 1938), 40; and Rogers, *Two Lives*, 187-88.

[35]Foote, *An Autobiography*, 32; and Sumner Salter, "Early Encouragements to American Composers," *Musical Quarterly* 18 (1932): 78-79.

[36]George Willis Cooke, *John Sullivan Dwight* (Boston: Small, Maynard, 1898), 223.

[37]The Allen A. Brown Collection also contains clippings of articles and reviews written by the New York critics, especially when their subject was a composer of the New England group or a performing group from Boston.

[38]Robert Hughes, *Culture of Complaint* (New York: New York Public Library and Oxford University Press, 1993), 180.

[39]Foote, *An Autobiography*, 51-52; and "A Bostonian Remembers," 41. See also George W. Wilson, program notes for the concert of the Boston Symphony, 6-7 February 1891.

[40]In 1938, Elliott Carter was still able to state that anything American in serious music was synonymous with "novelty." Even though many compositions by European composers of secondary rank were frequently heard, those by the New England group and later composers continued to be novelties, rarely heard and subject to condescension. See Carter, "Vacation Novelties, New York," *Modern Music* 15 (1937-38): 96-97.

[41]John C. Schmidt, *The Life and Works of John Knowles Paine* (Ann Arbor, MI: UMI Research Press, 1980), 129; Semler, 160-61; and Victor Yellin, *The Life and Operatic Works of George Whitefield Chadwick* (Ph.D. diss., Harvard University, 1957), 83.

[42]*New York Musical Courier* 20 (1890): 25; and Howard Shanet, *Philharmonic: A History of New York's Orchestra* (Garden City, New York: Doubleday, 1975), 110, 180, 194-95.

[43]John Sullivan Dwight, "Music in Boston," *The Memorial History of Boston*, Vol. IV, ed. Justin Winsor. (Boston: Ticknor, 1881), 452.

[44]H. Earle Johnson, *Hallelujah, Amen!* (Boston: Humphries, 1965), 117-18.

[45]Allan A. Brown Collection, scrapbook of clippings, **M 304.1, Vol. III, The Boston Public Library. In pencil, at the beginning of the clipping is written "Courier."

[46]Semler, 196.

[47]Allan A. Brown Collection, scrapbook of clippings, **M165.9, Vol. VI, The Boston Public Library.

[48]M. A. DeWolfe Howe, *The Boston Symphony Orchestra* (Boston: Houghton Mifflin, 1914), 98.

[49]Semler, 84.

[50]Semler, 69-70.

[51]Finck, 75.

[52]George Wakefield Chadwick, *Horatio Parker* (New Haven: Yale University Press, 1921), 14; and H. E. Krehbiel, in *Grove's Dictionary,* 2nd ed. (1926), s.v. "Parker, Horatio William."

PROMOTING THE LOCAL PRODUCT: REFLECTIONS ON THE CALIFORNIA MUSICAL PRESS, 1874-1914

Michael Saffle

Throughout the nineteenth and early twentieth centuries, American music magazines functioned to a considerable extent as advertising venues for a wide variety of products and services. Among these were musical instruments as well as lessons offered by local music schools and recent sheet-music publications. But advertising was not restricted to paid announcements. Much unpaid "advertising" was religious or pedagogical or intellectual in character. Thus a magazine might promulgate the ideas of its editor or contributors about the place of music in Christian worship, or music and elementary education, or the significance of Western musical history. A great deal of this kind of advertising was—should we call it "sociological"? Certainly it was *social*, because it promoted values associated with certain social strata or classes or races even as it promoted the activities of "appropriate" individuals and organizations.

In effect, then, advertising of one kind or another constituted most (if not, as it sometimes seems, virtually all) of the reading matter in turn-of-the-century American music periodicals. It also constituted most of the *materia musica* published in daily newspapers and the popular press as a whole. Even factual accounts of musical events in places like London or Rome were frequently run in American periodicals for purposes of comparison—which is to say, in order to encourage local music-lovers to perceive themselves as sophisticated. A squib about a New York City production of a Mozart opera, for instance, might be used to alert midwesterners to a production of the same work in their own city or state. Or it might be used to proclaim the appearance in Detroit or Cincinnati or Chicago of the celebrated

singer who helped make that New York production great. Only
during and especially after World War I, with the rise of strictly
"professional" magazines like *The Musical Quarterly*, was
American music journalism replaced by musical scholarship,
thereby achieving a standard of objectivity previously unknown in
our nation's periodical press.

Three especially important and comparatively durable
California music magazines—*Sherman & Hyde's Musical Review*,
the *Pacific Coast Musician*, and the *Pacific Coast Musical
Review*—appeared in print in the western United States between
the 1870s and the beginning of World War I.[1] To a considerable
extent, they were devoted to promoting local musical products:
the music and musicians of America in general, of the Pacific
coast in particular, and especially of the San Francisco Bay Area
and Greater Los Angeles. The purpose of this article is to examine
how these three magazines promoted that local product, and to
draw some conclusions about how such promotion reflects for us
today the musical life of California during the late nineteenth and
early twentieth centuries.

Sherman & Hyde's Musical Review (or simply *Review*, as it was
often referred to in its own pages) appeared in print for the first
time in late December 1873 or early January 1874; the earliest
surviving issue bears the latter date.[2] Like most nineteenth-
century European and American music magazines, it combined
fact and fiction—fact in the form of news, reviews, and feature
articles about music; fiction in the form of short stories,
anecdotes, and poems. Thus the first issue of the *Review*
proclaimed itself a "monthly journal of music, art and literature."
And, like other, contemporary music magazines, the *Review* ran
advertisements both on its own behalf as well as on behalf of local
businesses, music teachers, and other, assorted enterprises.[3]

In no respect was any of this exceptional by nineteenth-
century standards. Robert Schumann's *Neue Zeitschrift für Musik*
(which first appeared in 1834), restricted for years to four pages
per issue, was devised to do the same kinds of things and to appeal
to the same general kind of reader: the enthusiastic, respectable
middle-class citizen. So were other nineteenth-century European
and American music magazines: the *Révue et Gazette Musicale de*

Paris (which first appeared in the 1830s), the *Musical Times* of London (which first appeared in the 1840s), and the journal John Sullivan Dwight published in Boston (which first appeared in 1852).

The first issue of *Sherman & Hyde's Musical Review* opened with an editorial pontificating about the purpose of the magazine and explaining something of its contents. After devoting several paragraphs of praise to their own "sincere love for music" (which they themselves proclaimed proof of "a love for all that is beautiful"), Messrs. Sherman and Hyde proudly described San Francisco as

> a city of 200,000 inhabitants and [one that] possess[es] more than the usual number of musical people and amount of musical talent. Our resident artists compare favorably with those of any city of the same size in the United States. Our singing societies, glee-clubs and choirs would be a credit to any city. Concerts and the opera are nearly always well patronized. Eminent pianists, singers and musicians of all kinds are continually visiting us, and we believe that genuine talent is as much appreciated in San Francisco as in any part of the world.[4]

When these words were printed the *Review*'s publisher, Leander S. Sherman, was twenty-nine years old; an ambitious younger man, he seems to have been capable even from the first of striking an authoritative "older" tone in print.[5]

From these and other observations, we might conclude that the ostensible purpose of the *Review* was to boost local musical activities, even though its editorial staff also proposed furnishing readers with "general news from all parts of the country." And we would be correct in drawing such a conclusion. Nor did the *Review* intend to limit itself to announcements and assessments of musical events, local or exotic:

> To lend variety to our local news we propose devoting a certain space each month, to such of our San Francisco teachers as many choose to avail themselves thereof, believing thereby that we can materially aid them, and add an interesting feature to our magazine.

Finally, the editorial concluded somewhat primly with the observation that a "limited number of [paid] advertisements" would be accepted for publication [in the *Review*],

> but none of [it of] a flaming or too conspicuous character, for we intend that the advertising department shall be a secondary consideration, as we wish it to be distinctly understood that the REVIEW is not an advertising sheet, but a musical newspaper.[6]

It goes almost without saying that the editors of the *Review* intended to run their magazine as a business, and to profit financially from it. Magazines cost a lot to print, and the *Review* was a handsome publication by the standards of its day. Nevertheless, it mostly did not run in a conspicuous manner the ads it did accept, nor did it accept much business from nonmusical firms. The principal exception seems to have been the firm of Sherman & Hyde itself. Located in 1874 at the intersection of Sutter and Kearny Streets,[7] Sherman & Hyde sold pianos, instruments of various kinds, sheet music, and a wide variety of other musical products. The cover of the first issue of the *Review* was entirely taken up with ads for Sherman & Hyde itself—and, rather atypically, for two insurance firms: those of the Hutchinson, Marr & Smith Agency at 314 California Street, and the Hartford Fire Insurance Co. next door at 313 California Street.

After an issue or two, however, the *Review* adopted a newspaperlike front-page layout, complete with masthead, lead story and, often, an accompanying illustration. (A reproduction of a typical *Review* front page appears on page 171.) In keeping with this layout, almost all of the paid advertisements that appeared in these later issues were printed on one of the last two pages in each ten- to twelve-page issue. Most of these ads took the form of short announcements, some of them phrased in quite conservative language. (It is difficult today to tell whether some of them were inserted as paid advertisements, or as "public service.") A few large, boxed ads were also published, however; Houseworth's Photographic Parlors (12 Montgomery Street), for instance, took out one column in praise of its "Miniature to Life-size Portraits" finished in "Water Colors, Indian Ink, Crayon or

MUSICAL AND MISCELLANEOUS DEPARTMEMT.

AMERICAN ARTISTS.

No. 4.

MLLE. EMMA ALBANI.

THIS charming young American artiste, who has for two seasons past fairly shared the laurels and honors of the Royal Italian Opera, Covent Garden, London, with Madame Adelina Patti, has been engaged for the season, and will appear at the New York Academy of Music on Monday evening, Sept. 28th. She is a French Canadian by birth, belonging to the old Arcadian family, La Jeunesse, immortalized in Longfellow's "Evangeline." She was trained in early childhood in the study of music by her father (himself a skilled musician,) and displayed remarkable talents for the divine art from the most tender years. After a short residence at Albany, N. Y., she went to Paris and studied for two years under the famous Duprez. The great tenor then sent her to the renowned maestro, Lamperti, at Milan, who welcomed her with the significant remark, "Ah! there's a fortune in that little throat." Several years of hard study followed, and having overcome her scruples in regard to going on the stage, which at one period were almost insuperable, Lamperti brought her out in opera at Messina. Her success was instantaneous. After engagements at Malta, and at the principal opera houses of Italy, she made her *debut* in London, and became a sterling favorite with the English public. During the last seasons at Covent Garden and St. Petersburgh her name was placed side by side with the Diva, Patti. The care which has been bestowed upon her vocal training, united to her nat-

ural gifts, constitute her one of the foremost singers of the age. Her repertoire is very extensive and varied, comprising the following works:

"Aida" . . . . Verdi
"Lohengrin" . . . . Wagner
"La Stella del Nord" . . . . Meyerbeer
"Flying Dutchman" . . . . Wagner
"Ruy Blas" . . . . Marchetti
"Romeo and Juliet" . . . . Gounod

"William Tell" . . . . Rossini
"I Puritani" . . . . Bellini
"Hamlet" . . . . Thomas
"Mignon" . . . . Thomas
"Ballo in Maschera" . . . . Verdi
"Rigoletto" . . . . Verdi
"Faust" . . . . Gounod
"Linda" . . . . Donizetti

"Don Giovanni" . . . . Mozart
"Traviata" . . . . Verdi
"Trovatore" . . . . Verdi
"Figlia del Reggimento" . . . . Donizetti
"Dinorah" . . . . Meyerbeer
"Sonnambula" . . . . Bellini
"Les Huguenots" . . . . Meyerbeer
"Martha" . . . . Flotow
"Lucretia" . . . . Donizetti
"Il Barbiere" . . . . Rossini
"Lucia" . . . . Donizetti
"Roberto" . . . . Meyerbeer
"Ernani" . . . . Verdi

Although an American by birth, the first appearance of Mlle. Albani during the coming season, under the direction of Messrs. Strakosch, will be her *debut* in this country. No lengthy introduction of her is needed, as her triumphs in Italy, Paris, London, and St. Petersburgh have been watched with sympathetic interest by the *dilettanti* of the New World. The announcement that at the present day Mlle. Albani is regarded in Europe as an artist of the first rank will, therefore, not fall upon unfamiliar ears. The pure beauty of Mlle. Albani's voice, the chaste elegance of her style, and the great personal charm of her presence, amounting to positive magnetism, leave no doubt as to the effect she will produce in her native land. She has just closed a brilliant season at the Royal Italian Opera, Covent Garden, and it was only by the most strenuous exertions and the most liberal offers that the favorite prima donna was prevented from accepting an engagement of a very flattering nature at St. Petersburg, and was secured for America. Her appearance among us will be an event of no trifling importance, heralded as she is by the universal verdict of approval of musical Europe. In welcoming her to her home we shall but honor our own land, and give due recognition to merit.

A front page from *Sherman & Hyde's Musical Review*
(No. 10; October 1874)

—Miss Fanny Marston's concert at Platt's Hall, January 27th, assisted by local talent, was very largely attended, and an attractive programme was presented. Miss Marston sang with her usual taste, and was frequently applauded. We regret that want of space forbids an extended notice regarding those who assisted at the entertainment, but we can say that the concert was enjoyable throughout.

—We regret to learn that Mr. Frank Gilder, not having met with the pecuniary success in his first concert of the popular series, has decided to relinquish his purpose of continuing them for the present. We hope he may receive the necessary encouragement to induce him to continue them, as we have no doubt such an enterprise, if properly managed, could be made profitable, and at the same time offer peculiar attractions, one of the least being the low price of admission.

—A new prima donna has appeared at "the home of the setting sun."—San Francisco. She is the daughter of a Sioux chief, and in quantity and quality of voice is said to equal that copious pale-face, PAREPA ROSA. They rave about her in "Frisco."

The above notice we clip from *Harper's Bazaar* of January 3d. If anyone can give any information concerning the "new prima donna," it will be thankfully received at our office.

—Mr. Alfred Wilkie was the recipient of a benefit, on February 13th, at Pacific Hall, tendered by Madame Anna Bishop and others. A programme, which included Madame Bishop and prominent local talent, was offered, and many of the selections received deserved *encore*. We understand that Mr. Wilkie intends remaining here for the present, and we gladly welcome him among us, as his superb voice will be an acquisition to our musical circles.

—Madame Agatha States announces for her benefit, to take place on the 27th inst., at Platt's Hall, the opera of the *Sicilian Vespers*, including in the cast Signor Orlandini, and others.

—Madame Anna Bishop is to be the recipient of another complimentary concert on the 28th inst., prior to her departure for Australia.

—Miss Mary Wadsworth, the California prima donna, is organizing a concert troupe, to travel through the interior of California and Nevada during the coming month. She includes among the attractions, Signor G. Mancusi, the Italian baritone, Mr. L. Bodecker, pianist, and others.

PERSONALS.

—There is no one who has had the pleasure of being present at the private theatricals and *musicales* lately given, who has not been particularly impressed with the talents of Mrs. Hall McAllister, in the different representations in which that lady has been engaged. The astonishing success attendant on the production of the *Doctor of Alcantara*, which was first given by the Amateurs, as a private entertainment, and afterwards repeated publicly at Platt's Hall, for the benefit of a deserving charity, is still fresh in the minds of our readers, and for which they are especially indebted to Mrs. McAllister. The recent entertainment of the "Cheap and Hungry Club," is also another evidence of her interest in such matters of amusement, and we are informed that she is now engaged in preparing another musical treat for her many friends and admirers. As a lady of the highest personal standing in society; as a warm friend to those who have her private regard; and as a lover of all that pertains to the cultivation of this method of thus publicly expressing our thanks to her for the interest she has invariably manifested in all matters pertaining to musical enterprises, not only by her continued exertions to afford pleasure and enjoyment to those who possess her acquaintance and esteem, but

also by contributing, in a substantial manner, to all the different calls made by others, in the matter of subscription concerts, operas, etc. We hope that the knowledge that her efforts are fully appreciated, may induce her to continue to take precedence in all that pertains to musical culture and growth in the future, as she has done in the past, and we are confident that such knowledge will be to her sufficient recompense for the time and money spent in so doing.

—A performance will be given on Thursday evening, February 19th, at the Opera House, at which time and place an opportunity will be offered to the public of San Francisco, to show, in a liberal and substantial manner, their appreciation of the efforts of one who has probably done more for the advancement and growth of the higher order of music and musical culture, than any one else since the palmy days of '49. A true musician, with talents of the highest order; a man who has never failed to proffer his services for the assistance and benefit of any and all deserving charities; a leader in all our musical entertainments, and a composer of more than ordinary merit. We will certainly be sustained in our opinion by all, when we state that Professor GEORGE T. EVANS is more deserving of a benefit at the hands of our citizens, than anyone whose name has been placed before the public for a similar purpose. Professor Evans has been at the head of the musical profession in our midst for many years, and is so well known as not to require further comment at our hands. He will be assisted on that occasion by the combined orchestras of the Opera House and California Theatre, which he has for so long a time led, and also by the Galton and Lee Troupe, the Amphion Quartette, the Bohemian Glee Club, and others. With the programme that will be offered with so many attractions, we have no doubt that a crowded house will greet him on that occasion, as a slight token of the appreciation in which his talents and worth as a musician are held by the community.

—Professor L. A. Seward, the Organist of Trinity Church, who has been for some time past employed in perfecting his improved method of musical instruction, called "The Objective System," is, we are pleased to learn, meeting with the success so admirable a method deserves. He has received the highest commendations from those to whom its merits have been explained, more especially from the Board of Education and the principals and teachers of our different public and private schools. Professor Seward's recent exhibition of the System at the Denman School, was particularly interesting, attracting the attention of the scholars, who were more than pleased with the ease and facility with which the different transpositions from one key to another were made, as well as the extremely interesting lecture which accompanied the working of the boards. We shall take occasion, in a future number of the REVIEW, to enter into full details of this instructive and simple method of teaching, a perusal of which, we have no doubt, will be found to be worthy of particular attention.

—Professor Charles J. J. Smith, who is favorably known in our community as an accomplished musician, and who, it will be remembered, was the one selected out of all our musical celebrities as the only person capable of performing on the "big drum" in the Camilla Urso Festival, held some years since, has returned to our city, after a prolonged sojourn at the "Hub." Professor S. expresses himself not only as perfectly satisfied with his experience of the "musical metropolis," but that he will be evidently content to remain in San Francisco for the future, as being more congenial to his musical tastes and inclinations. He has resumed the practice of his profession, and we take great pleasure in calling the attention of our readers to the fact of his being an efficient and competent instructor.

—Mr. Henry C. Chauncey, well and favorably known in musical circles as an amateur pianist, is achieving quite a reputation as a composer. One of his latest compositions, the *Alameda Galop*, was produced, for the first time, at the public performances of the *Doctor of Alcantara*, by the Amateurs, and was justly encored. He has now in the hands of the publisher, two other instrumental pieces, one of which, entitled *Bouquet Waltz*,

is to be given on the occasion of the benefit of Professor George T. Evans, on Thursday, 19th instant. We have had the pleasure of hearing the Waltz, as played by Mr. Chauncey, and we are sure that it will become exceedingly popular.

—During the first concert season of Madame Nilsson through the country, she was troubled with a serious cold at one of the Eastern cities. Manager Strakosch requested Brignoli to apologize to the audience. His explanation was as follows: "The manager begs the indulgence of the audience for Miss Nilsson; she is a little horse." The audience greeted this with a burst of laughter, and Brignoli, thinking that he had failed to make himself understood, tried again as follows: "Mr. Strakosch begs the indulgence of the audience for Mdle. Nilsson; she has a little colt."

—We have received from Rev. J. J. Powell, of Cloverdale, an anthem, and several musical compositions by Professor Passmore, of that town, which we have examined and found to possess more than ordinary merit. The words to the anthem were composed by Rev. Mr. Powell, and were very appropriate to the occasion for which they were written. The anthem was sung for the first time on Christmas last, and its production very favorably noticed by the papers.

—Frank Gilder, the celebrated pianist, has concluded to remain here for a short time, and will, during his stay, give lessons in music to a limited number of pupils.

—Mr. E. Caswell, for a long time connected with the largest music house in Canada, is now in the city, and expects to make his home here.

EDITOR'S SANCTUM.

OUR thanks are due to the Press for the complimentary notices of the first number of the REVIEW. We hope, with our present number in enlarged form, to still further merit their favors.

C SHARP, SACRAMENTO, CAL.—Your favors are duly received and fully appreciated. We hope musical items may be on the increase in your city.

REV. J. J. P., CLOVERDALE, CAL.—Package of manuscript received and will be returned as soon as possible. Should be pleased to hear from you often, for the benefit of the readers of the REVIEW.

S. S. P., VIRGINIA CITY, NEV.—There is some talk of a concert troupe visiting your city soon, but at what date has not yet been determined upon.

TEACHER, PETALUMA, CAL.—The Polka you desire is not out of print. We can furnish as many copies as you may desire.

MISS S. E. H.—Your communication is too lengthy and want of space prevents its publication.

W. H. H. H., SANTA CRUZ, CAL.—List of subscribers received. Remember us in regard to musical matters that occur in your part of the State.

A. V.—Getze's is the best Reed Organ Instructor. Price, $2.50.

E. B. M.—You can find the desired information in "Moore's Encyclopedia of Music."

ENQUIRER.—There are several good organs, but only those manufactured by Peloubet, Pelton & Co. bear the trade mark "The Standard."

QUERY.—Mr. A. R. Parsons resides in New York; has lately returned from Europe, where he pursued his studies with the best masters in Leipsig and Berlin.

C. M.—Clark's New Method is a first-class method. It is published by Lee & Walker.

An inside page from *Sherman & Hyde's Musical Review*
(No. 2; February 1874)

Oil Colors, by artists who have always taken first premiums wherever their work has been exhibited for competition."[8]

By far the largest number of back-page advertisements were run by Sherman & Hyde itself. Thus we find in some issues several columns or even an entire three-column page filled with statements like the following:

TO MUSIC TEACHERS!

We have the best selected stock of sheet music on this coast, (over 30,000 folios.) Send your orders direct to us and they will receive prompt attention.

Similar announcements praised the pianos on sale in Sherman & Hyde's showrooms, or thanked the editors of other magazines and newspapers for their flattering comments about the *Review*.[9] A few ads, presented as if they were service announcements, also served commercial purposes:

TO SUBSCRIBERS!

We have no back numbers. Hereafter all subscriptions will have to begin with the current number.

(This statement managed to combine useful, time-saving information with a subliminal, "must buy now" message; the *Review* is so successful, readers, that you cannot afford to wait for copies!) Or even:

TO CANVASSERS!

You can make from ten to fifteen dollars per day by canvassing for the REVIEW. Everybody ought to have it.

There seems no reason to question the veracity of most of the ads and announcements published in the *Review*, with the possible exception of this last one. Even if Sherman & Hyde had been willing to pay salesmen fifty cents for each subscription sold—that is, half of the price of each subscription itself, which was one dollar per year—a solicitor would have had to sell twenty subscriptions to earn even ten dollars per day—a considerable daily wage in 1870s San Francisco.[10]

Most of the *Review* was devoted not to advertising, but to news: announcements of local events, feature articles about celebrities of several kinds, reviews of recent performances, and so on. (A reproduction of an inside page appears on page 172.) Individual issues consisted of several long articles followed by a series of short reports about local musicians and their activities. Almost all of these were positive in tone; one of the *Review*'s function, after all, was to "boost" Bay Area music-making in all its aspects.

Or, at least, *almost* all of them. Most of the concert news to appear in the *Review* was laudatory, but once in a while a critic would proclaim the deficiencies of a local artist or ensemble. A squib in the May 1874 issue, for example, lamented that a recital by one Miss Marian Singer was "sadly marred in some of [its] numbers":

> While disposed to give to Miss Singer all the necessary praise, we think that neither as vocalist or pianist is she entitled to the rank some of her friends claim for her.... She should study another year or two before again appearing in public; taking as her model the fine artistic method of Madame Anna Bishop. [More on Mme. Bishop below.] As a pianist, Miss Singer shows to better advantage, but still the same lack of soul and finish is perceptible and without which she cannot expect to excel.[11]

A few issues of the *Review* ran letters addressed to the editors; often these missives praised the contents of the magazine itself or drew attention to the excellent wares for sale at Sherman & Hyde's emporium. Finally, occasional columns would be fleshed out with anecdotes or "saws," including such inevitabilities of the day as this misogynistic observation:

> There is one particular in which all the writers upon the character of women perfectly agree, and that is their love of sway. Tacitus, speaking of the sex, says emphatically: "Their predominant passion is the love of power and in its exercise they know no bounds."[12]

Perhaps the most interesting features published in the *Review* belonged to their "American Artists" series or resembled it in one of several ways. The series itself was described in the ninth issue in the following words:

Not only will we give sketches and portraits of our greatest and most widely celebrated artists, but from time to time we shall present [to *Review* readers] certain of our deserving ones whose names are not the brightest ones of to-day, but who are destined to attain honorable positions in the future. This is to us at once a duty and a pleasure, and we enter upon it cheerfully, trusting that we may be of some service in introducing to our readers many well deserving aspirants for public favor and appreciation.... [Finally,] we desire to state most emphatically that no article that has thus far appeared [in the *Review*], or which may in future appear in this series, has been, or will be inserted at the request of any person or persons.... We desire to be distinctly understood that every sketch presented will be from material furnished us upon our solicitation.[13]

Among the articles published in this series was a lengthy description of the career of Emma Albani (whose portrait appears on page 171), at the time already renowed for her artistic accomplishments.[14]

Similar articles, most of them published without accompanying illustrations, were also devoted to visiting international celebrities and especially to local performances given by them. In January 1874, for instance, Anna Bishop—born in California but famous around the world—appeared in a San Francisco production of *Norma* organized as a benefit in her honor.[15] Compare what was published about this event in one of the San Francisco daily papers with what was published in the *Review*, and one is likely to conclude that the *Review* not only presented musically sophisticated fare to its readers, but fare that was also clear and easy to read.

First, the comparatively lengthy review published in the *San Francisco Daily Examiner*, the principal newspaper of its time and place:

The complimentary benefit tendered to Madame Anna Bishop at Platt's Hall last night, was a deserved tribute to that distinguished artist. The Hall was crowded in every part, every seat being occupied, and not even standing room remained after eight o'clock. The throng of beauty and fashion in Platt's Hall was never greater than on this occasion. Madame Bishop was in splendid voice, and her performance throughout excited the entire audience to a high pitch of enthusiasm. The wonderful preservation, after two score years of continuous exercise, of her marvelous vocal organ was the theme of general remark and admiration. Her acting was also superb, and her appearance quite prepossessing. Truly it may be said of her that

> "Age cannot wither, nor custom stage,
> Her infinite variety."

The selection of the beautiful and popular opera of Norma was highly judicious. A better choice could not have been made to display the talents of the beneficiary to the best advantage as the High Priestess. The solo "Casta Diva" was superbly rendered by Madame Bishop. The duet in the second act was a great success. "Mira, O! Norma!" was very evenly rendered and won great appreciation, as did the duet in the 1st act. Signor Pietro Baccei's voice, although rather deficient in the first act, gathered strength as the opera proceeded, and as a whole his part was well done. Miss Annie Elzer, as "Adalgisa," received encomiums from every side. Her voice was in splendid trim, and her appearance chaming. Mrs. Geo. T. Evans as "Clotilde," and Signor Rigo as "Orveso," were both excellent in their respective parts. Altogether it was a delightful evening's entertainment."[16]

Significantly, nowhere does the *Examiner*'s critic state clearly that the event was a performance of a complete opera rather than, say, a vocal recital with appearances by a variety of guest artists; he was content to cover the news rather than the musical (and musician-oriented) news.[17] A similar notice, somewhat less effusive in tone, appeared in the *Daily Alta California*; this announcement did in fact state that *Norma* was performed complete.[18]

The *Review*, on the other hand, presents a more complete as well as comprehensible and economical report about what happened:

The opera of "Norma" was produced, according to announcement, at Platt's Hall, on January 22d, for the benefit of Mme. Anna Bishop, the beneficiare appearing in the title role, assisted in the other portions of the cast, by Miss Alzer, Mrs. Geo. T. Evans, Signor Baccei, and others. The attendance was very large, and the opera sung exceedingly well, not only proving a musical success, but also a benefit in truth to an estimable lady and a world-renowned artiste. In this connection we call attention to a short sketch of the career of this fanous cantatrice, which we think well worthy of perusal.[19]

The *Review* went on to describe elsewhere, and in much greater detail, Mme. Bishop's career—beginning in September 1839, when she began her first tour of Continental Europe and moving on to May 1868, when she began her return to New York with a successful series of concerts in Australia, Egypt, Malta, Gibraltar, and London. "It is believed [Mme. Bishop] is the greatest female traveler now living," the *Review* concluded, "having traversed the entire world in filling her professional engagements."[20] The *Review*, then, not only reported a local event, but drew attention to one way that event could be understood in terms of the international musical scene.

Daily papers like the *Examiner*, of course, could not restrict themselves to musical issues; the *Review* could and (largely) did. But the *Review* did more than report musical news; it discussed and evaluated it with an enthusiasm and intelligence altogether missing in the popular press. Compare, for instance, the lengthy and detailed report in the *Review* of San Francisco's first *Magic Flute* (presented on 12 and 13 May 1874 at Platt's Theater), with the shorter, somewhat confusing, and far less "critical" account found in the *Examiner*. The newspaper devoted much of its space to comments about one Joy Wandesforde who, the *Examiner* critic explained, "sang with a clear, strong voice, and executed some very difficult passages with good effect."[21]

The *Review*, on the other hand, observed that Miss Wandesforde's Pamina

> was excellent, both in voice and action, and her rendition creditable alike to teacher and pupil. Should Miss Wandesforde persevere in her musical studies, we are confident that she will some day make quite a reputation for herself. We hope she will not think that she has already arrived at perfect, as it requires long and unwearied attention to study to acquire anything more than ordinary.[22]

We also learn from the *Review* that the performance was organized by one Prof. Mulder Fabbri in order to introduce his students to the public; the *Examiner* remarked merely that the event was "an amateur performance."[23] Among these was Wandesforde; and in praising her accomplishments to date—those of a local student of music—the *Review*'s critic also praised her teacher and his efforts overall. "The very least that can be said of the entire performance," the critic in question concluded, "is that it was exceedingly creditable to all concerned."[24]

In many of its articles and advertisements the *Review* can be understood today as striving primarily or even exclusively to sell products. An article on pianoforte playing thus can be "read" as an advertisement for Sherman & Hyde pianos, albeit a rather soft-spoken one.[25] In other respects, it can be understood as striving to maintain and disseminate attitudes and standards acceptable to its readers—which is to say, attitudes and standards acceptable to a predominantly Christian, almost exclusively white, middle- or upper middle-class California audience.

The inclusion of material outside the interests of such individuals during the *Review*'s first year of publication was unusual but not unknown. Of course, articles about events outside California served mostly to confirm its readers' attitudes and standards; occasionally such reports even pandered to them. In a lengthy essay about New York, for example, a columnist for the *Review* identified only as "Dry Bones" managed several times to imply that San Francisco was at least as sophisticated in its musical accomplishments and tastes as Manhattan, as well as a lot pleasanter to inhabit.[26]

In another of its issues, however, the *Review* did something unusual: it published a lengthy paean of praise to Jewish musicians and music-making associated with a San Francisco synagogue:

MUSIC AT HOME.

— CHOIR OF THE JEWISH TEMPLE EMANU-EL, SUTTER STREET. — As the Jewish holidays have now begun, it will not be inappropriate, we think, to notice the music of this place of worship in order that visitors may take advantage of the fact to hear the music which has been especially prepared for these days of religious observance. The choir is composed of Mrs. H. B. Howell, soprano; Mrs. Kate Chisholm, alto; Mr. S. D. Mayor, tenor; (whose place, during his temporary absence, is supplied by Mr. J. E. Tippett); Mrs. W. C. Campbell, base [*sic*], and Mr. Louis Schmidt, organist....

Mr. Wolff, the newly chosen cantor, is a welcome addition to our singers and one who will well repay anyone to hear. Possessed of a fine baritone voice, under good cultivation and control, with a just appreciation of the requirements of his station and a commendable pride in the singers composing the choir, The Temple Emanu-El [*sic*] can be congratulated on its excellent appointment of this genial gentleman and the selected singers composing their choir.[27]

Insofar as I could determine, no articles about African-American music or musicians appeared in *Sherman & Hyde's Musical Review* during 1874-1875, but the presence of occasional squibs about other ethic (and religious) groups and activities made the magazine a model of 1870s "outreach" as well as a profitable advertising venue for an important San Francisco music business. Unhappily, the *Review*'s readership apparently became impatient with so much attention lavished on local events. In a notice published in the January 1875 issue of their magazine, Messrs. Sherman and Hyde announced that, "since a large proportion of our subscribers reside in the country, and are not interested in detailed criticisms of concerts in this city, we have decided to omit critical notices in the future."[28]

California underwent tremendous changes during the decades that separated the 1870s from the 1900s and 1910s. These changes, as well as others characteristic of the nation as a whole, were reflected in the local musical press. Population growth, for example, meant more readers for magazines and newspapers. Technological developments meant more ways of printing and distributing more kinds of verbal and visual information. Demographic changes meant a readership of somewhat more diverse ethnic and religious backgrounds.

After the turn of the century, magazines like the *Pacific Coast Musician* (or simply *Musician*) and the *Pacific Coast Musical Review* (or simply *Musical Review*) took advantage of these changes. Compared with Sherman & Hyde's publication, these hadsome periodicals reached more people—again, mostly members of the white, male, Protestant middle class—than had previously been possible.[29] They also went in, as we shall see, for both paid and unpaid advertising more systematically and extensively. Music dealers, piano teachers, instrument retailers, and other professionals took out hundreds of ads in both magazines. (A reproduction of a typical page from the *Musician,* complete with advertising, appears on page 180.) Furthermore,

FACULTY COLLEGE OF MUSIC
University of Southern California.
Top line, reading from left to right: Mrs. N. R. Robbins, Mr. W. F. Skeele, Dean, Miss C. A. Trowbridge, Mr. H. Cogswell and Mr. Wm. Mead. Lower line, reading from left to right: Mr. C. E. Pemberton, Miss Macloskey, Miss Madge Patton, Miss L. Arnett and Herr O. Seiling.

KINGSLEY IN ENGLAND.

If you are an organist and are a woman, do not go to England, for all the music of the established church in that country is performed by men and boys.

Bruce Gordon Kingsley, in his talk before the Ebell Club * * * gave some interesting details on cathedral music in England, France and Germany, as he saw and studied conditions.

It seems that away back in ancient days, there was an antipathy against women taking part in church music in England—a prejudice which exists to the present day. The choir boys are boarded, clothed and lodged by the church, in exchange for which they give their musical services. It means work, too—they are made to earn their keep, for choirs frequently are rehearsed twice a day throughout the year.

England leads the world in organ music, but her organists receive very low salaries, as compared with those paid in this country. For instance, the organists at St. Paul's and at Westminster Abbey in London get not more than $1,500 per year, which is quite the top salary. In the big New York churches it is not unusual for organists to receive anywhere from $3,000 to $5,000 per year. Mr. Kingsley's description of a visit he paid to the famous abbey on the Isle of Wight, which has the wonderful choir of monks, was most interesting. There the oldest type of music in existence—reaching back to compositions 450 years before Bach—are performed.—Los Angeles Times.

A page from the *Pacific Coast Musician*
(Volume 1, No. 2; December 1911)

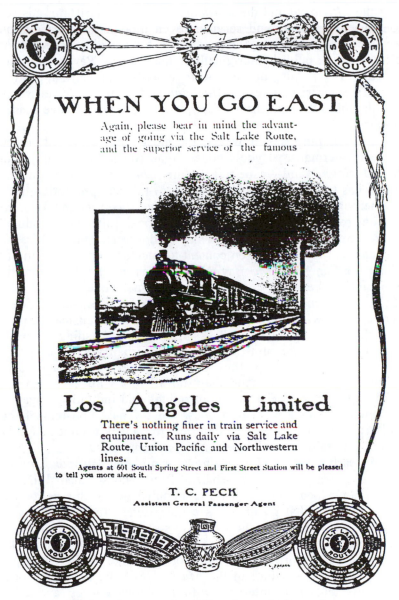

WHEN YOU GO EAST

Again, please bear in mind the advantage of going via the Salt Lake Route, and the superior service of the famous

Los Angeles Limited

There's nothing finer in train service and equipment. Runs daily via Salt Lake Route, Union Pacific and Northwestern lines.

Agents at 601 South Spring Street and First Street Station will be pleased to tell you more about it.

T. C. PECK
Assistant General Passenger Agent

A advertisement for railroad travel from the
Pacific Coast Musical Review
(special "University of California" edition; 1906)

both the *Musician* and the *Musical Review* regularly ran ads for nonmusical products and services, even though their orientation remained "high-class." (A reproduction for an advertisement for railroad travel, published originally in the *Musical Review*, appears on page 181.) Ads, in fact, were essential to self-supporting business enterprises like the *Musician* and *Musical Review*: they paid the bills. Without them, these publications would have ceased to exist.

For our purposes, however, the most noteworthy difference between Sherman & Hyde's house-organ (on the one hand), and the *Musician* and—especially—the *Musical Review* (on the other), has to do not with the quantity of musical promotion, paid or otherwise, but with its *quality*. Both the *Musician* and *Musical Review* redefined the whole idea of "local [musical] product" before promoting it with increasing boldness and vigor. Messrs. Sherman and Hyde had been content to encourage musical activity within the San Francisco Bay Area, at least (as we have already seen) until it began to cost them readers and money. The editors of the *Musician* and—again, especially—of the *Musical Review* were content with nothing less than encouraging musical activity throughout California as well as Oregon and Washington state, until they taken the rural as well as the urban Pacific Coast as their province.[30] More: they did not merely encourage local activity, but exalted it. And they did all this with a vengeance, defending beleaguered local organizations and individuals against all comers, especially eastern ones. For the new boosters of the California musical scene, promoting the local product rapidly became a mission as well as a commercial enterprise.

As early as 1898, a magazine known as the *Musical Courier* sounded the call to arms on behalf of Pacific-coast musical life. In an article on local musical history, a contributor to this periodical boldly claimed that no previous century ever "[bore] witness in America, and perhaps in the world, to so many distinctly different phases in music in any region as in California."[31] Assertions like this one became articles of faith for men like Arthur Metzger who, in his role as editor of the *Musical Review*, defended local musicians and their interests with ferocious energy and even anger. Contributors to the *Musician* were somewhat less vehement, but they nevertheless did a lot to build enthusiasm for

SECOND
EVENT

SECOND
SERIES

GREAT
PHILHAR-
MONIC
COURSE

COMING
EARLY
IN
DECEMBER
TO THE
AUDI-
TORIUM

MANAGEMENT
L. E.
BEHYMER

JAN KUBELIK, the Renowned Bohemian Violin Virtuoso

A cover from the *Pacific Coast Musician*
(No. 1; November 1911)

the burgeoning musical life of California in the years immediately prior to 1914.

Let us begin with the *Musician*. (A reproduction of the cover from a typical issue is reproduced on page 183.) Established in 1911 and edited at first by Frank H. Colby, this periodical resembled in many ways Sherman & Hyde's paper of almost forty years earlier: monthly issues were devoted mostly to musical news and feature stories, although occasional poems and pieces of fiction also appeared in its pages. Too, like Sherman & Hyde's *Review*, the *Musician* was devoted to furthering the cause of "local" artists and artistry, especially in coastal California. Praise was largely heaped upon local artists and ensembles, positive observations the rule rather than the exception. In its first issue, for example, appeared the following notice:

> Just as the Pacific Coast Musician goes to press its editor is in receipt of a live letter under date of Oct. 29 [1911] from that indefatigable purveyor of big things musical, L. E. Behymer, who writes from San Francisco in a way that makes it appear that the compliment to Frisco's cold winds and fogs is a warm musical atmosphere with a stirring enthusiasm in it that is feet-lifting.
>
> Mr. Behymer pays a glowing tribute to San Francisco's substantial appreciation of the best in musical interpretive ability.... About $100,000 have already been subscribed, he writes, for the forthcoming San Francisco season of French opera, of which Los Angeles hopes to get a taste....[32]

Similar endorsements also appeared in issues of the *Musical Review*, and not merely in its opening issues. As late as February 1911, by which time the magazine had become a weekly publication, Metzger ran a lengthy series of editorial endorsements from magazines like the *Musical Courier* of New York and the *Presto* and *Indicator* of Chicago. Metzger himself confessed to being "particularly proud" of the praise he had received, but not for its own sake; rather, as he explains, "Such endorsement repays the editor for a great many hardships that he has encountered during the last ten years of building up a musical journal for the Pacific Coast."[33] The region, rather than the individual or even the publication itself, became the product being promoted.

On more than one occasion the *Musician* and its editor Colby took up the cudgels on behalf of one or another local "cause," a favorite example being the San Francisco Symphony:

> The San Francisco Symphony Orchestra is gradually improving in spite of the usual unjust criticisms that are being hurled about by those who seem to have learned a great deal in the last few days about orchestras and how they should be conducted. Orchestras are like the individual musician—they can not be created in a moment's time—and our organization is fast fulfilling the promises made by Henry Hadley, its praiseworthy conductor.[34]

Individual artists were also singled out for praise. In one issue of the *Musician*, for instance, choral director and teacher Carl Bronson—"busy and popular Los Angeles musician"—was honored with a two-page spread (complete with photographic portrait) and a lengthy list of pupils, almost all of them described as "excellent," "successful," "well known," and so on, and many of them active in places like Pasadena as well as in Los Angeles, New York, Salt Lake City, and even "abroad."[35]

But the *Musician* did more than merely praise artists and institutions; it also criticized, albeit constructively, deficiencies—at least, those it perceived as damaging to California musical life. Thus, on a single page of one 1913 issue may be found the last part of a patriotic article about California government, a "somewhat slangy" humorous poem about Sibelius, a recipe for rhubarb pie (half-buried inside comments about the vocal prowess of one "Miss Blank") and—most interesting of all—the following squib about local musical journalism and its responsibilities to the public:

Our Newspapers and Music

> It is the rule and not the exception to find comments on matters of musical importance being made in the Los Angeles press by writers unfitted because of their utter lack of musical knowledge, to intelligently handle the subject and making [sic] their papers often ridiculous in the eyes of cultured music loving readers. These papers would likely far sooner think of assigning the sporting editor to review a symphony concert than of securing a man of musical culture to "cover" a sporting event. While columns are given up to sports where inches are devoted to music, those inches should be in

the hands of writers capable of intelligently commenting on musical matters if those papers would best serve readers who look to their columns for discriminating information.

Speed the day when the whole Los Angeles press will emulate the big journals of the East and have writers with special musical knowledge to comment on music![36]

Here, as elsewhere, the Atlantic-coast "establishment" is transformed into a stick applied to the backsides of the local "opposition."

In a nutshell, the *Musician*'s message was that California—and sometimes, by extension, American—musical life deserved to be encouraged and defended. Local music deserved better than it often received at the hands of unsympathetic critics. Periodicals like the *Musician* and the *Musical Review* were "inspired by a strenuous desire to give adequate recognition to the musicians residing in the Golden State." The battle-cry was: Onward and Upward! But each artist and merchant was expected to shoulder his or her own weapon. Thus "the musical profession of California [had only] itself" to blame when its supporters replaced their "lamb-like attitudes of artistic toleration" in favor of a "vigorous resistence to everything that appears to retard musical progress in California."[37]

As one author put it:

Have the American people no marked characteristics? They most certainly have. Cannot the American composers find musical ideas to define these traits of character? Most decidedly, yes!

But have they done so? is another questions. That [American composers] have written good music and even great music, cannot be denied, but it has been for the most part patterned after European models.[38]

Jingoism pure and simple? Hardly. The author of this diatribe went on to place artistic quality over national or regional pride: "The important thing is not so much that [each composer] should produce American music as that we should produce *good* music."[39] But jingoism nonetheless. Because, unfortunately, the author in question also believed that "good" American music (which is to say, "cultured" or art music) cannot emerge either from Native American or African-American traditions:

Music composed by [?"real" Americans] is certainly not going to contain the foreign and exotic material of Negro or Indian themes, for these have no affinity with his national life and feeling. What could be more out of place than the use of a Negro or Indian theme, superimposed upon a rich and highly colored background of Wagnerian harmony? And yet that is what many of our composers are doing and labeling it, "American Music." ... Think how young America is in music, compared with Germany, Italy, etc. We are going to produce ... great men of music and establish a strong and individual school of composition, which will indeed be American in every fibre; but we will never do it with the negro and Indian elements as a basis.[40]

To do this author justice, the "Indian" compositions of composers like Edward MacDowell were largely juxtapositions of quasi-authentic folk melodies with Central European harmonic progressions.

But what of women in the scheme of things? The *Musician* apparently ignored them altogether. Not so with other contemporary magazines, the *Musical Review* among them. Established in 1901, the *Musical Review* began as a monthly magazine; by 1909 it had become a weekly periodical of eight or more pages, most of them filled with uncompromising and often highly defensive observations. Alfred Metzger, the publication's editor, showed few prejudices where Pacific coast musical life was concerned. He regularly ran articles not only about women performers, for instance, but about women composers—a scarce commodity in those days, at least in the eyes of the public. (One such article appeared in September 1908 and is reproduced on page 188.) Furthermore, this belligerent editor sometimes devoted whole issues of the *Musical Review*—exclusive, that is, of paid advertising and a certain amount of news—to "causes." These ranged in scope and significance from the price of opera tickets to the importance of an orchestra for San Francisco's musical life, the last a cause that eventually became an obsession both with Metzger and many of his readers.[41] (A typical editorial page from an issue of the *Musical Review* is reproduced on page 189.)

Consider just one issue of the *Musical Review*: that of 2 March 1912. Except for photographs of the "distinguished tenor

A CALIFORNIA COMPOSER.

Enthusiasts of popular music will soon be eagerly straining their ears for the melodies of California's very latest composer of this class of music, a young lady who, though still in her teens, will soon take the laurels off the brows of her well known contemporaries with remarkable ease. This young lady is Miss Edna Williams. Many people possess the advantageous, if peculiar, faculty of being able to play on almost any instrument, or sing without having been taught even the very rudiments of music and this happy individual will be found to possess a very correct pitch and imitative quality. But in the case of Miss Williams it strongly approaches the point of the phenomenal. Though so young, she already composes with a celerity and clearness of purpose that we would look for only in a composer of more experience. She is born with the taste and talent for this style of music and composes it as naturally as if it were not a very unusual thing to do.

But it is the quality of her work that calls for attention. It has, besides possessing every requisite to be thoroughly successful, the individuality which will make a lasting impression. One notes with pleasure that she strives to attain a higher standard of the popular music of today, something which those who entertain the public and the people themselves will fully appreciate. Manuel Lowenstein, a clever young librettist, writes the words to Miss Williams' songs. They will help to make of them the brilliant success that the many friends of both are confident will be the eventual result, he always being in full harmony with the composer. Besides her interesting ability as a composer, Miss Williams is gifted with a full, round contralto voice which, when developed and cultivated, will delight the music lovers. Miss Williams' compositions, which include some delightful two-steps, are being published in the East and will soon be placed for sale throughout the United States.

CHARLOTTE M. VOORSANGER.

MISSES LOIS STEERS AND WYNN COMAN TO THE MUSICAL REVIEW.

Misses Lois Steers and Wynn Coman, the musical impresarios of the great Northwest, write to the Musical Review as follows:

Portland, Ore., July 30, 1906.

We had intended writing you immediately after the earthquake and offering our congratulations upon your fortunate escape which we heard from some mutual friends; but with the two Kubelik concerts, the first on the night following the 'quake, and two days given over to getting off relief supplies, then our hurried departure for New York on the 22nd of April, we scarcely had time to breathe.

We have but just returned, and one of

MISS EDNA WILLIAMS.

the very first letters to be written is to you. It seems almost incredible that you should have gotten out the next issue of the "Review" in such excellent order, and you must accept the firm's congratulations upon that as well as upon your escape.

Thanks for the many kind expressions of your faith in us and of your good will. We are doing all in our power for the betterment of the musical conditions up here, not alone in this, our home town, but throughout our entire territory, which comprises Oregon, Washington, Idaho, Utah, Montana and British Columbia. It is a great pleasure to have our work appreciated.

Mr. Behymer and his wife have been making us a three days' visit and we found them charming people. Although we have been doing business together constantly for the past few years this was our first meeting. You will be glad to learn that it resulted in much that will be highly bene-

From the *Pacific Coast Musical Review*
(Volume 9, No. 5; September 1906)

PACIFIC COAST

Musical Review

SAN FRANCISCO. OAKLAND. LOS ANGELES. PORTLAND. SEATTLE
THE ONLY MUSICAL JOURNAL IN THE GREAT WEST
PUBLISHED EVERY WEEK

ALFRED METZGER - - - - - - EDITOR

San Francisco Office
Sherman, Clay & Co. Building, Kearny and Sutter Sts., Mezzanine
Floor, Kearny-St. Side. Telephone, Kearny 4000.

Oakland, Berkeley, and Alameda Office
1117 Paru St., Alameda, Cal. - Miss Elizabeth Westgate in Charge

Los Angeles Office
1419 S. Grand Ave. - - - Heinrich von Stein in Charge

Portland and Seattle Office
375 Sixteenth St., Portland, Ore. - Miss Edith L. Niles in Charge

Vol XVI.   SATURDAY, JUNE 5. 1909.   No 10

The PACIFIC COAST MUSICAL REVIEW is for sale at the
sheet-music departments of all leading music stores.

Entered as second-class mail matter at the San Francisco Postoffice.

SUBSCRIPTIONS—Annually in advance, including postage:
United States $2.00
Foreign Countries 3.00

IMPORTANT NOTICE
Office Hours from 3 to 5 o'clock every afternoon except Tuesdays
and Saturdays. In case of unforeseen absence of editor during office
hours, leave note on desk making appointment. Always leave name
and address or telephone number.

ADVERTISING RATES:

	One Time.	Annual Contract Per Week.
Inside Pages	$20.00	$15.00
One-Half Page	12.00	8.00
One-Quarter Page	8.00	5.00
One Inch (on Page 7)	2.00	1.50
One Inch (on Page 13)	1.50	1.00
One-Half Inch (on Page 13)..........	.75	.50
Musical Directory	.50	.25

THE CALIFORNIA COMPOSER AND ARTIST.

When the editor of the Pacific Coast Musical Review first entertained any plans to establish a journal devoted to the musical interests of California, such plans were inspired by a strenuous desire to give adequate recognition to the musicians residing in the Golden State. And this desire again emanated from the conviction that visiting artists who come among us but rarely and merely touch our cities in passing, received all the adulation, homage and publicity in the gift of the people, while those artists who reside among us, share their joys and sorrows with us, spend their incomes with us and have a just claim upon our patronage and regard, were passed by unnoticed, not because their talents did not deserve serious recognition, but because they had pitched their tents within this State and had thereby created a prejudice against them, as if living in California was evidence of incompetency. The editor of the Pacific Coast Musical Review, realizing the flagrant injustice of this situation, made up his mind to cast his influence upon the side of the resident artists, and as he was unable to fight these battles in the columns of the daily papers, he decided to establish a musical journal for the very purpose of espousing the cause of the California musician.

It is a strange coincidence that this very policy of defense and encouragement of California artists and students should have proved the biggest obstacle placed in the way of this paper and preventing its progress for quite a time. Instead of rejoicing over the birth of a paper that owed its existence to a fondness and affection for all musicians of merit in California, this manifest display of leniency and trust aroused the ire of many members of the profession and instead of assisting the editor in maintaining a weapon of defense for the California artists, the misguided disciples of art resented the efforts on their behalf and sneeringly spread the report that any one could receive favorable attention in the columns of this paper. These reports became so persistent and so tenacious that it became necessary for this paper, in order to preserve its existence, to adopt an additional policy in behalf of those who deemed leniency in critical opinion sufficient objection to demand the withholding of support from a musical journal. And so we added to our original policy of leniency and encouragement in matters appertaining to California artists a policy of severity and unrelenting condemnation of all musical pretenses among those unworthy of serious notice. And, strange to say, while up to this time much of professional support was withheld from this paper during its course of lenient encouragement, this new policy of combined leniency and severity proved successful, and where the hand-clasp of fondness failed to impress, the whip of critical severity was unexpectedly successful. And while it cost us a great sorrow to be compelled to establish this paper through the fear entertained for it, at the same time we were forced into this policy by the character of the members of the profession who seem to consider the scourge of adverse criticism as the only possible foundation for a successful enterprise.

And so the musical profession of California must blame itself for the fact that the Pacific Coast Musical Review changed its lamb-like attitude of artistic toleration to a vigorous resistence to everything that appears to retard musical progress in California. That notwithstanding the continued proofs of the severity of this paper, there still exist teachers who tell their pupils that everybody can receive favorable mention in this paper is not the result of actual facts, but emanates from a failure to be recognized, and hence in order to console their pupils these teachers tell them that everybody can receive recognition in these pages. We would not pay attention to these child-like reports, if it were not to strengthen the arguments of all those students who read this paper and take pride in reading the recognition of their praiseworthy efforts in these columns. We want to impress upon the minds of our friends the indisputable fact that we only speak encouragingly of those whom we consider worthy of such encouragement. Those whom we consider unworthy are ignored. And because we ignore the unworthy ones it naturally happens that all students noticed by us receive favorable comments. We do not notice inefficiency among students because we do not care to discourage anyone from studying, and pupils are the easiest discouraged followers of the muses. Of course, we only express our personal opinion regarding the merit of performances. We do not express the opinion of one teacher about the efforts of another teacher's pupils. If we did this we might just as well suspend this paper. So anyone desirous of receiving the honest opinion of this paper regarding their efforts, are welcome to it for whatever benefit it may be to them. Those who think its opinion devoid of value because someone else, whom they personally may not consider worthy of favorable comment, receives encouragement in it, should not resent being ignored, for it is very plain that they place their own opinion about their efforts above the opinion of this paper, and consequently the latter becomes superfluous, and it would be a pity to waste printer's ink and paper on its publication.

and vocal teacher" MacKenzie Gordon and the "successful California soprano soloist" Mrs. Chas. H. Farrell, the entire first page and much of the rest of the issue are given up to defending the magazine and those it advocated—among them San Francisco Symphony conductor Henry K. Hadley—from attacks published in the New York musical press, specifically in *Musical America*.[42] Some of these "attacks" were vicious; others did no real damage to either Metzger or his magazine. Against all and sundry, however, Metzger launched vigorous counterattacks. To refute the ridicule heaped upon one of his statements (i.e., that "Beethoven, unlike Mozart, was not a master at the age of twenty or earlier"), and to correct his antagonist's erroneous claim that Beethoven composed the *Egmont* overture at the age of nineteen, Metzger quoted at length—and with the lavish use of interpolated editorial emphasis in the form of capitalized words—from eight contemporary reference works.[43]

That Metzger took criticism personally cannot be doubted; he began one of his refutations by confessing he did.[44] On the other hand, he also took "personally" criticism of his region and colleagues, Hadley among then. One of the nastiest attacks against both Metzger and Hadley was racially motivated: an anonymous note, typed on the edge of a page taken from an issue of the *Musical Review*, called Metzger a "little shrivelled-up Sheeny!" On this occasion, however, Metzger showed admirable restraint: he deplored his assailant's language, but he refused to take sides in such a skirmish, affirming that "it is idiotic to try to raise such an issue"—at least, if one wished to build support within the musical community as a whole.[45]

Metzger was willing to praise American music in general; he was even willing to praise other regions and their musical activities, provided those activities came up to artistic snuff and (it would seem) gave him a stick with which to beat his enemies. A lengthy article published in the *Musical Review*, for example, ostensibly in praise of the Chicago Grand Opera, provided Metzger with an opportunity not only to discuss issues of performance and interpretation, but to rebuke those locals who had snubbed the out-of-town company because of the recent defeat of "the Municipal Opera House scheme": an attempt on the part of some San Francisco residents to establish their own permanent opera house.[46]

One of the finest hours in the life of the *Musical Review* took place in 1906, immediately after the great San Francisco earthquake. Forced for a time to set up offices outside his beloved city,[47] Metzger continued to take an active interest in the fate of San Francisco artists and merchants. His post-disaster means of encouraging musical activity in the Pacific coast as a whole took a more substantial form than mere words, however, albeit one that at first may seem rather odd: Several months after the quake he printed twenty thousand copies of a special "University of California" edition of the *Musical Review* and contributed the proceeds to his own magazine!

Self-serving? Of course. But also others-serving. Advertising rates for this special edition were slashed and, for the first time, the *Musical Review* "set aside its rule and accept[ed] biographical sketches with photo accompanying as paid advertising matter." To insure high quality, Metzger announced that he guaranteed "that every advertiser in this issue belongs to the leading musicians of California."[48] By promoting his own publication and opinions, Metzger also managed to promote the local products of others with imagination and effect.[49]

Virginia Polytechnic Institute and State University

---

[1]These magazines were by no means the only California musical periodicals to be published between the beginning of the Civil War and 1914. Others included the *Pacific Musical Gazette* (1867-1868), *Footlight* (1877-1881), and *Music and Drama* (1882-1901). See Mary Kay Duggan, "Music Publishing and Printing in San Francisco Before the Earthquake & Fire of 1906," *Kemble Occasional* [San Francisco] No. 24 (Autumn 1980): 3. Unfortunately, extant complete runs of pre-World War I California music magazines are quite rare.

[2]Information about *Sherman & Hyde's Musical Review* presented in the present article was gathered from a copy of the twelve 1874 issues preserved today in the collections of the Library of Congress, Washington, D.C., and from 1875 issues quoted in secondary sources. According to standard reference works the *Review* continued to be published into or even throughout 1879, but the present author has never seen copies of post-1875

issues. Interestingly enough, monographs like David Warren Ryder, *The Story of Sherman, Clay & Co., 1870-1952* (San Francisco: privately printed, 1952), ignore the *Review* altogether. NB: Sherman & Hyde, which published the *Review*, became Sherman, Clay & Co. in 1876, when Major Clement Comer Clay bought out the interest of Sherman's partner F. A. Hyde. Leander Sherman seems always to be been the guiding light behind the firm and its successes; there is no reason to think that Hyde had much to do with the *Review*.

[3]Sherman & Hyde (later, Sherman, Clay & Co.) were not the only San Francisco music firm to publish its own magazine. From October 1867 to May 1868 Matthias Gray of the firm of Gray & Herwig, 613 Clay Street, published *The Musical Monthly*; later he went on to become one of California's foremost early publishers of sheet-music. See Duggan, "Music Publishing and Printing in San Francisco Before the Earthquake & Fire of 1906," 4.

[4]Quoted from *Sherman & Hyde's Musical Review* No. 1 (January 1874): 10. Most of the *Review* issues I examined did not consist of numbered pages.

[5]Details about Sherman's life and career in San Francisco may be found in Ryder, *The Story of Sherman,, Clay & Co., 1870-1952*, passim.

[6]*Sherman & Hyde's Musical Review* No. 1 (January 1874): 10.

[7]A photograph of this building, which as a shell survived the Earthquake of 1906, appears in Ryder, *The Story of Sherman, Clay & Co., 1870-1952*, 23.

[8]*Sherman & Hyde's Musical Review* No. 5 (May 1874).

[9]See, for example, the note of thanks to one Mr. Klose, "manager of the *Pacific*, for the favorable notice of our last issue" [*Sherman & Hyde's Musical Review* No. 5 (May 1874)].

[10]Ryder relates an anecdote about one Mr. Leon Lang, for forty years an employee of Sherman, Clay & Co., who learned to live on $37.50 per month, half of his wage for that period of time. After six months' practice he finally succeeded in supporting his wife and himself on this amount (a little more than one dollar per day) and was rewarded with an additional $37.50 each month in salary. The point of the story is that a married couple could live on such a sum only with difficulty [*The Story of Sherman, Clay & Co., 1870-1952*, 25-26].

[11]*Sherman & Hyde's Musical Review* No. 9 (September 1874).

[12]*Ibid.*

[13]*Ibid.*

[14]Emma Albani, born Marie Louise Lajeunesse (1847-1930), described her own career in an autobiography entitled *Forty Years of Song* (London 1911).

[15]Anna Bishop [née Riviere] (1810-1884) appeared regularly on the operatic stages of Europe and the United States before her retirement in 1883.

[16]*San Francisco Daily Examiner* (23 January 1874).

[17]This is not meant to imply that the *Review* as always superior to daily papers like the *Examiner*. Far from it. On both 26 and 27 October 1874, for instance, the *Examiner* announced at some length a regimental band concert that took place on the latter evening. Equally fulsome announcement appeared on 25 October in the *San Francisco Chronicle*, and on 26 October in the *Daily Alta California*. The *Review* reported this event only after the fact [*Sherman & Hyde's Musical Review* No. 11 (November 1874)] and in comparatively little detail.

[18]*Daily Alta California* [San Francisco], Vol. 26, No. 8698 (23 January 1874), 1.

[19]*Sherman & Hyde's Musical Review* No. 2 (February 1874).

[20]*Loc. cit.*

[21]*San Francisco Daily Examiner* (13 May 1874).

[22]*Sherman & Hyde's Musical Review* No. 5 (May 1874).

[23]*San Francisco Daily Examiner* (13 May 1874).

[24]*Sherman & Hyde's Musical Review* No. 2 (February 1874).

[25]See "The Mechanical Element of Pianoforte Playing," *Sherman & Hyde's Musical Review* No. 2 (February 1874). In the same issue, the publishers proclaimed: "PIANOS ON EASY INSTALLMENTS!! We have just received ten of the Becker Bros. Square Grand Pianos, New York—price, $450—which we are selling at the very low price of $350. They are the best cheap piano in the market."

[26]See "Music in New York" and "Whisperings from the Metropolis" [the last dated "August 3d, 1874"], *Sherman & Hyde's Musical Review* No. 8 (August 1874).

[27]*Sherman & Hyde's Musical Review* No. 9 (September 1874). Decades later California music magazines also published regular reports of Jewish artistic endeavors in the San Francisco and Los Angeles areas. See, for example, "Musical Service at Temple Emanu-El," *Pacific Coast Musical Review* 16/10 (5 June 1909): 4-5.

[28]Quoted in Duggan, "Music Publishing and Printing in San Francisco Before the Earthquake & Fire of 1906," 6.

[29]Musical culture in turn-of-the-century San Francisco and Los Angeles was perceived by most "cultured" individuals as indistinguishable from such an audience. (For confirmation, see Catherine P. Smith's essay "Inventing Tradition: Symphony and Opera in Progressive-Era Los Angeles" in the present volume.) On the other hand, population growth and demographic changes all but mandated the tacit admission of ever more individuals of both sexes within the charmed circle of European-oriented "culture" that was the world of art music in early twentieth-century California.

[30]Both the *Musician* and *Musical Review* paid lip service to the notion of a Pacific-coast musical "culture," although they devoted comparatively little space to reporting and evaluating musical activities in such places as Portland, Seattle, and Sacramento.

[31]Josephine Gro, "Music of the Pacific Coast During the Nineteenth Century," *The Musical Courier* 37 (1898): 26.

[32]Additional information about the career of Behymer, a successful turn-of-the-century impresario, may be found in Smith, "Inventing Tradition: Symphony and Opera in Progressive-Era Los Angeles."

[33]Quoted from "The Musical Press and Profession Enthusiastically Endorse the Pacific Coast Musical Review," *Pacific Coast Musical Review* 19/19 (4 February 1911): 8. Many of Alfred Metzger's editorials appeared without bylines; one has only to read them, however, to know they are his.

[34]*Pacific Coast Musician* 1/4 (February 1912): 15. Composer and conductor Henry Kimball Hadley (1871-1937) established the San Francisco Symphony Orchestra and directed it from 1911 to 1915.

[35]See C. H. Keefer, "Carl Bronson: Busy and Popular Los Angeles Musician," *Pacific Coast Musician* 3/7 (July 1914): 21-22.

[36]*Pacific Coast Musician* 2/3 (December 1913): 7.

[37]Quoted from Metzger, "The California Composer and Artist," *Pacific Coast Musical Review* 16/10 (5 June 1901): 3.

[38]Charles E. Pemberton, "American Music," *Pacific Coast Musician* 3/9 (September 1914): 17.

[39]*Loc. cit.*; italics added.

[40]Pemberton, "American Music," 16-17.

[41]See, for example, *Pacific Coast Musical Review* 21/11 (16 December 1911): 5. These issues and several others are discussed here at considerable length and in Metzger's characteristically emphatic tone.

[42]See Metzger, "Pacific Coast Musical Review Not Guilty of an Error: Musical America, a Weekly Publication Printed in New York City, Unjustly Ridicules the Editor of This Paper," *Pacific Coast Musical Review* 22/22 (2 March 1912): 1.

[43]*Loc. cit.*

[44]*Loc. cit.*

[45]*Loc. cit.*

[46]See Metzger, "Chicago Company Gives this City the Most Artistic Ensemble in its History: Certain Society People in Order to Avenge Themselves for the Defeat of the Municipal Opera House Scheme 'Bite Off Their Noses to Spite Their Faces' and Refuse to Attend the Opera Season," *Pacific Coast Musical Review* 26/26 (28 March 1914): 1, 3.

[47]For years Metzger ran advertisements on behalf of Sherman, Clay & Co., successors to Sherman & Hyde in San Francisco. After the earthquake that firm moved temporarily to Oakland, and through its offices Metzger for a time carried on the *Musical Review*'s business. Later he established new quarters for his periodical in the restored Sherman, Clay & Co. building mentioned above.

[48]"To the Musical Profession and the Music Dealers of California," *Pacific Coast Musical Review* 9/4 (August 1906): 41.

[49]I would like to thank Virginia Polytechnic Institute and State University for research monies used in the preparation of this essay. A preliminary version was presented as a paper before the Sonneck Society for American Music at its 1993 national meeting, held at the Asilomar Conference Center, Monterey, California.

MUSIC IN LANCASTER, KENTUCKY, 1885-1910: LOCAL TALENT, TOURING ARTISTS, AND THE OPERA HOUSE

Ben Arnold

Even though it was, at the time, a small frontier town of three thousand inhabitants, Lancaster, Kentucky, enjoyed between 1885 and 1910 a musical life that was exceedingly rich and varied. Near the center of the state, then known as the Dark and Bloody Ground, Lancaster (in Garrard County) suffered many of the pitfalls that befell other similar towns with frequent killings, vandalism, and other rebellious acts on the frontier. Nonetheless, in the midst of this hazardous living, music flourished. From the lawlessness of the 1880s (when the town finally came together to outlaw liquor in the prohibition crusades in 1885) to the turn of the century (which began an era of civic pride with an electric works, a telephone system, and a water works), music could be found in the homes, the churches, the schools, the park, and in the opera house (when it was standing) of turn-of-the-century Lancaster. Local musicians actively participated in bands and orchestras, playing for dances and socials of all types as well as giving concerts both in the opera house and in the town park, touring musicians, vaudeville acts, and minstrel shows frequently came to town.

Of all these local, homespun music-making activities, the Lancaster Brass Band was the most prominent during these years, reaching its zenith between 1892 and 1899. Prior to 1892 bands would start up for a few months before member musicians would leave town, and then the bands would fold. After 1899, local bands seemed unable to compete with the imported bands from surrounding areas.

In January 1892 the ten-member Lancaster Brass Band was organized. They ordered a new set of Conn instruments "and the citizens residing in the neighborhood of the practice room [were] hereby warned."[1] By March the instruments had been paid for and the citizens were warned again that "those 'at outs' with any member of the band had better make peace at once or they will get a serenade."[2] The group began practicing enthusiastically and soon were accused of "making the lives of those in the neighborhood miserable."[3] By May they gave a strawberry supper at the Mason Hotel and invited the public to attend.[4]

The band received a shot in the arm (temporarily at least) when Frank Meister, an excellent E-flat cornet player, moved from Cincinnati to lead the band and run a confectionery.[5] Three months later, however, Meister sold his business and left town, leading many naysayers to claim the band would "fall through."[6] The band survived without Meister and soon was good enough to begin playing in towns outside of Lancaster.

In June 1893 the band went to the nearby town of Harrodsburg to perform for the Kentucky Division of American Wheelman, where eight hundred bicyclist were convening.[7] They were warmly greeted[8] and were such a hit that the directors of the League of the American Wheelmen "chose the Lancaster band as their official band in Kentucky. This insures the boys a number of fine trips, the principal one being to the annual meet and races of the bicyclists at Owensboro next spring. The boys also have a partial engagement to go to Washington with the Knights of Pythias."[9]

By February 1894 the band had grown to sixteen members and were selected by the Knights of Pythias lodge to go to the national encampment at Washington, D.C., in August.[10] In March C. C. Cook, "the famous E-flat cornet player" opened a carriage shop on Buford Street,[11] and in June Professor Crouse, a clarinetist, opened a barber shop over Stormes' Furniture Store.[12] In July they began practicing every day so that they would be prepared to go to Washington with the Knights of Pythias."[13]

Within a month the band had grown so popular in Lancaster that a number of citizens "contributed enough money to erect a bandstand in the park [with plans to have free concerts] every

Friday evening during the warm weather."[14] In April the bandstand was completed. "Of course a few moss backs objected to its being built there[,] but as that class of cattle object to everything their wail amounts to nothing."[15] A few days later Jim Crow Dillion painted the stand,[16] and the Lancaster Concert Band gave its first concert on 9 May. "The park was filled with ladies Wednesday evening, attracted by the open-air concert by the band. Another concert will be given next Wednesday evening. Two uniformed policemen are stationed at the park gates and no objectionable characters are admitted.[17]

The band seldom performed during winter seasons. By April 1895, however, band members had resumed practice: "Rats are getting scarce."[18] They evidently did not practice enough and "could not get in shape to play for the parade [in May]. This is why a foreign band had to be engaged."[19] In June they played between speakers at the second annual contest of the Kentucky Declamatory League held in the circuit court room,[20] but they did little else that summer until August. "The Lancaster brass band has about gotten together again, after a Rip Van Winkle nap."[21] In September they played for the funeral of a former band member, but were, for the most part, inactive.[22]

In March 1896 the band renewed its practicing and gave

an open rehearsal at Masonic Hall [to which they] invited their parents, sisters and brothers. Sweethearts are not in it this time and they will have to wait until the concerts in the park are commenced. The band is in good shape now and it is the intention to give a concert in the park every Friday night as soon as the weather will permit.[23]

The concerts and reading started on May 1.[24] The Lancaster Cornet Band under the direction of J. E. Stormes participated with other local and imported talent in an evening of "select reading and music." Miss Elvira Sydnor Miller from the *Louisville Times* joined with local talent for this event given in the program reproduced below:

1. March	The Tattler
Kreemer	
2. Recitation "Kentucky Down to Date"	Miss Miller

3. Violin Solo "Stabat Mater"	Rossini
Singelee, Opus. 134	Miss Huffman
4. Recitation "Poor Nancy"	Miss Miller
5. Overture "Storm King"	
6. Recitation "Col. Blue Grass of Kentucky"	Miss Miller
7. Soprano Solo "L'Estasi"	Arditi
Mrs. Logan	
8. Recitation "Her Credentials"	Miss Miller
9. March "Yatch Club"	Barker
10. Violin Solos "6th AirVarie"	Dancla, Op. 84
11. Recitation "The Minuet"	Miss Miller
12. Baritone "Wanderer"	Harlow
Mr. Landram	
13. Recitation "The Woman Reporter"	
Miss Miller	
14. Schottische "Where Summer Roses Bloom"	Schroeder
OLD KENTUCKY HOME[25]	

The review the following week claimed the event "was attended by a large and cultivated audience":

The music furnished by the brass band was complimented on all hands by those competent to judge, and the boys are highly elated over the cordial reception and applause given them. The violin playing by Miss Clyde Huffman was heartily applauded and this young lady fully sustained the enviable reputation she enjoys as a performer upon the Queen of Instruments. Mrs. John M. Logan's vocal solo was an enjoyable feature of the evening and she was roundly applauded. The 'Tattler,' Miss Elvira Sydnor Miller, was given a hearty round of applause when she appeared before the audience.[26]

The review also reported a small mishap:

At the concert the other night, one of the ladies was so unfortunate as to lose her place in the music which caused an annoying delay. Imagine [*sic*] the feelings of those interested when a lot of hoodlums began clapping their hands and stamping their feet. Such a rude performance was a disgrace to a civilized community. I was told that this was done especially by young boys. Well, if such was the case, it showed conclusively that their mothers had allowed them to be brought up in the street, and had neglected their duties in teaching them the difference between being a gentleman and a ruffian.[27]

The Knights of Pythias also engaged the band to perform on Decoration Day,[28] and at a concert given June 30, it was reported that "nearly every man, woman and child in town was out last Tuesday night to hear the music."[29] On 31 July 1896 the band played the following program, consisting of marches, polkas, and traditional favorites:

March, Princeton Cadets	Durand
Polka, Henrietta	Beyer
March, Elks	Kremer
Overture, Living Pictures	Delby
Polka, Trokey	Sousa
March, Soldiers Delight	Stahl
Schottische, Sparkle	Seiple
March, Fire King	Thomas
"Old Kentucky Home"[30]	

The band was prominent enough during this time to play again in various other cities. In June 1896, the band took a week-long boat tour on the steamer *Rescue* from High Bridge, to Cherokee Park in Lexington, to Frankfort, and on to Louisville, playing standards like "My Old Kentucky Home":

Our city presents rather a lonely, deserted appearance this week, being deprived of the presence of the entire concert band force and the excellent music which they furnished every evening. The band, consisting of eighteen of the life of the town, went to High bridge last Saturday where they took the steamer, Rescue, for a week's outing. They sail by Frankfort to the Ohio, thence down to Louisville, returning next Sunday.[31]

The only problem reported in the trip was with one of its members. Letcher Owsley.

It has been estimated that out of the eight days trip four of them were consumed in waiting for Letcher Owsley to find his drum or music. Whenever the captain called for music, Letcher's melodious

(?) voice would ring out "wher's my drum?" "wher's my music?" etc., and the whole gang would have to wait for him.[32]

At the 11 August concert,

the Public Square filled with ladies and children. While the boys were lumbering away they received an invitation from the W. C. T. U. to come to Mrs. Gill's where the teacher's entertainment was being held. They went out and were treated to an elegant supper, and the way the choice etables disappeared before that gang was a caution.[33]

In April 1897, the band was "practicing twice a week and working hard,"[34] and gave a charity concert along with other concerned citizens for victims of the Southern Flood.

Saturday morning when the *Louisville Times and Post* were delivered here telling of the great distress among our Southern neighbors, expressions of sympathy were heard on all hands. Mr. John M. Farra suggested giving a public entertainment and sending the proceeds to the suffering people. He then set out in earnest, and coming to The *Record* office, was immediately supplied with enough posters and dodgers to send out all over the county. Several of the band boys had, by this time, joined in and were hastening about town seeing local musical talent. Milton Sneed, the well-known colored musician, tendered his chorus singers and agreed to give an old-fashioned southern darkey cake walk. By night the program was complete. Judge Burnside agreed to let the Court House be used, and the band boys put in Monday and Tuesday fixing a stage, cleaning and filling lamps and making other preparations.

It was agreed to put the admission at 15 cents. The *Record* printed a big batch of tickets and these were given to a number of parties to sell. They went like hot cakes, many people buying more than they had use for.

Tuesday night the band played several pieces in front of the Court House and by 7:30 the building was packed almost to suffocation. We will give the program in the order it was given. First was an overture by the band, which was followed by a chorus sung by ten or twelve of our best singers. Then came a bass solo by Judge Hemphill, which brought forth much applause. Judge is a fine bass singer, and, as we heard some one say, 'He went way down under the stage' in some parts of the song. The solo sung by Mr. John M.

Farra needs no comment here, as everybody knows what a sweet, clear voice he has. The song, "L'Estacie," sung by Mrs. John M. Logan, was applauded to the echo. Mrs. Logan has a splendid voice and Lancaster people are always glad when she is on the program. Mrs. Logan is very obliging and always responds when asked to assist in an entertainment. She never refuses when asked to lend a helping hand. The band then ground out another number, and Mr. R. G. Ward sang a tenor solo. Mr. Ward has the best tenor voice we ever heard, and from the applause he received, we believe everyone else in the large audience thought the same way. Mr. Joe S. Haselden then brought out his graphophone and gave several selections. The funnel attachment enabled everyone in the house to hear distinctly. A quartette then sang "Swinging in the Grape Vine Swing," after which Milton Sneed, dressed as an old, southern negro, sang, "Massa in the cold, cold ground." Sneed has a splendid voice, and the audience gave him great applause. The chorus by the colored girls was one of the most enjoyable numbers on the program. This was led by Miss Bertha Johnston, who possesses a remarkably sweet voice, over which she has perfect control. Those in the chorus were Misses Lucy Hood, Eliza Hood, Della Dunn, Har[r]iet Johnston, Malinda Hayden, and Electrice Anderson, Hattie Hopper.

The evening's entertainment closed with a genuine, old-fashioned colored cake walk. There were four couples taking part, namely, Milton Sneed and Miss Hattie Hocker, Wm. Farris and Miss Bertha Johnson, Clay Green and Miss Eliza Hood, Wm. King and Miss Harriett Johnston. The girls wore pretty dresses, as white as snow, and were fixed up as nicely as the average white girl graduate. . . .

Much praise is due those getting up the entertainment and too much cannot be given the colored people who came forward and, by taking part, showed their desire and willingness to help those rendered helpless and homeless by the great flood in the south. . . .

A letter was written to the *Louisville Times*, enclosing two drafts of $42 each, payable, one to the Governor of Arkansas and the other to the Governor of Mississippi and requesting Mr. Brown, the clever, big-hearted manager of the *Times*, to forward the drafts.[35]

The Lancaster Brass Band also played at the Demorest Gold Medal Contest held at the Court House in May.[36] In June,

the band stand in the park has been made three feet lower and S. H. Bruce is closing in the sides with fancy shingles. It will be handsomely painted and a great improvement. Park Commissioner

Stormes is having everything fixed nicely and the little park will soon be a thing of beauty. If there was some way of preventing loafing boys from tramping out the grass 'twould be a good idea to do so.[37]

In the same month the band played for Crab Orchard Spring's formal opening.[38]

The band performed weekly in June and July, but by mid-August, it was showing signs of fatigue.

The *Record* is asked nearly every day "When is the band going to play in the new stand?" In reply to this oft asked query we will say that it is almost impossible to get some of the members to practice, and, unless at least two nights are spent in working up the music, those who do attend do not feel like attempting to play it on the street. Some of the members are suffering with severe cases of "Girl," and, of course, when they get in this shape it's useless to try to get their attention on anything else.[39]

In August they were asked to play for a Watermelon Feast sponsored by the young ladies of the Missionary Society at the residence of Mrs. Emma Kauffman.[40] In September the band was reported "in fine trim. A clarinet and piccolo were recently added, which help out wonderfully."[41]

At the beginning of December 1897, "the Lancaster band ... laid off practice until after the holidays. Those living near the band room are in consequence, rejoicing."[42] But by mid-January 1898, the

racket resumed. The Lancaster Band after a rest of several months resumed practice Tuesday evening and if some of the members can quit courting long enough, hopes to be in shape to furnish good music next summer.[43]

In March they participated in The "Old Bachelors" Convention, which was an antidote to an earlier Old Maid's Convention. "The convention will be composed of the Lancaster Concert Band—leading local talent, and both Old and Young Bachelors. The entertainment will be side-splitting from the beginning and those who attend will be laughing a year hence. The young men are working hard, and time nor labor will be spared to make the convention a howling success."[44]

After the convention several young men of the community and of the Lancaster band gave a minstrel show.

Lewis Walker acted as interlocutor, with Charley Anderson and Letcher Owsley on the "ends." Anderson and Owsley are certainly first-class minstrels and their work was highly complimented by everybody who saw it. Their "gags" were all new and were sprung on popular, home people, which, of course, made them more enjoyable. The singing of John Farra, Ode Shugars, Virge Kemper, Owsley, Hughes and Anderson was well up, and one of the most enjoyable features of the evening. This in a great measure was due to the lovely piano accompaniments played by Miss May Z. Hughes. This charming little lady very gracefully agreed to help the boys by playing, as they had no orchestra, and had it not been for her kindness, the musical part of the program would have been a flat failure.[45]

In April 1898 the band received uniforms,[46] and in June they assisted local talent in a charity concert. "The young ladies, desiring to answer the appeal for funds to supply our soldiers with hymn books, have arranged a concert to be given at the Court House Monday night next, the proceeds to be used in the noble cause above mentioned. The small sum of 15 cents will be charged, which will entitle you to any seat in the house. The program appears below:

————————

1. Lancaster Concert Band	
2. Opening address	G. B. Swinebroad
3. Duet	Misses Bessie Batson and Stella Huston
4. Reading	Miss Ellen Hiatt
5. Vocal Solo	Miss Olivia Sweeney
6. Piano Solo	Miss May Hughes
7. Reading	Miss Edna Mason
8. Music	Lancaster Concert Band
9. Quartette	
	Miss Lusk, Mrs. Patterson, Messrs. Owsley and Shugars
10. Vocal Solo	Miss Addie Burnside
11. Reading	Miss Alberta Anderson
12. Quartette	Misses West, Ward, Batson, and Hemphill
13. Vocal Solo	Miss Elisa Lusk

14. Closing remarks   Lewis Walker
15. Lancaster Concert Band[47]

They gave some other concerts during the summer, but not with the same activity as before. The band was invited to play again at High Bridge in June but were unable to accept "owing to the band's crippled condition."[48] Several months later Louis Landram, editor of the *Central Record*, reported, "The Lancaster band had a severe case of too much courting, and has gone the way of most all amateur organizations."[49] In the summer of 1900 the band began practicing after a six-month hiatus, but by September "efforts to reorganize the Lancaster band have again proven futile, and the ones who worked so hard for its success have thrown up the sponge. Too much 'girl on the brain' was responsible for the band's collapse."[50]

Symbolically, by May 1901 the bandstand was "beginning to fall to pieces. It should be either painted and repaired or torn away entirely."[51] In June 1901 the stand was down: "Several public spirited citizens are talking of making a flower bed in the center of the Park, on the spot formerly covered by the old band stand."[52] Five years later, in September 1906, there was talk again of reorganizing a band, but there was no indication that they ever did before World War I.

A similar pattern emerged with what eventually became the Lancaster Orchestra.

On several occasions the women in Lancaster helped organize an orchestra. In August 1895 they practiced in the home of Miss Lula Batson,[53] but little more is heard of them until October 1897 when they once again began to meet; it flourished for at least one month because it was making nice progress "under the able direction of Miss May Hughes."[54]

Years passed, and in January 1901 the orchestra reorganized and met at the New Garrard Hotel on Friday evenings.

Mr. Long, the accommodating proprietor of the Garrard [Hotel], who is a musician of great ability and much experience, kindly consented to instruct the band, and under his able direction, the members are making fair progress. The organization will not make a tour of the great cities, but merely meet and saw away for their own enjoyment. The instrumentation is as follows: Misses Fannie Collier, Nell Johnston, Willie Belle Burnside, Mary Gill, Mr. Long and Owen Shugars, violins, Will West, clarinet, J. E. Stormes and Overman, cornets, Louis Landram, trombone and J. H. Kinnaird, bass.[55]

This orchestra played numerous times, including a charity benefit in March for fire victims in Cloverport, Kentucky,[56] and for the eighty-second anniversary of the Odd Fellows lodge in April 1901 before temporarily disbanding again. In August 1901, they reorganized and met "every Monday evening at the Garrard Hotel. Mr. Long is deeply interested in the band and devotes much time to it. The members think they will be in shape to furnish good music next winter."[57] They performed at the Garrard County Common School Contest on 25 October 1901 and for commencement at the Lancaster Graded School in May 1902, but did not perform regularly. In August 1902 they met twice weekly at the residence of Miss Mary Gill until T. B. Long left town.[58] In May 1903 they briefly continued playing under the direction of Mr. Homer, the piano tuner, but after this date there is no mention of them ever gathering together or performing again.[59]

Other local groups organized musical events and contests as well. In November 1901, the Lancaster Commercial Club sponsored a new attraction—an Old Time Fiddler Contest:

On Thursday night November 18th, twelve of the best old time fiddlers in the country, will appear at the Garrard Opera House and render the selections which delighted our ancestors, and which now gladden our hearts and make us forget our sorrows.[60]

Attractive features will be introduced for the entertainment of all ages and classes. Among them, a fine violin will be given to the best old-time fiddler; no notes but the pat of the foot, the nod of the head and the wink of the eye.[61]

GARRARD OPERA HOUSE

M. D. HUGHES, Mgr

Piano used in this Theatre is from the D. H. Baldwin & Co., Louisville. E. W. Arnold, local agent.

THURSDAY, NOVEMBER 28th, 1901,
AT 8 O'CLOCK P. M. SHARP.

OLD FIDDLERS CONTEST.

Benefit Lancaster Commercial Club.

R. L. DAVIDSON, Ch'mn.

PROGRAMME:

a Grand Chorus Old Time Fiddlers.....................
b O. T. Wallace..................................Point Leavell
   "Rough and Ready," Medley Waycsburg, "Last on the Track," Etc.
c T. S. Moore...................................Bryantsville
   "Yankee Doodle," "Rainbow Scottische."
d S. D. Merritt.................................Lancaster
   "Broadway Girls," "Boneparte's Retreat."
e Gabriel Salter...............................Paint Lick
   "Evening Star Waltz," "Soldiers Joy."
f Alexander Martin.............................Stanford
   "Wagoner," "The Girl I Left Behind Me."
g Armp H. Dawson...............................Mt. Zenia
   "Hix's Dream," "Old Pine Tree."
h Samuel Bishop................................Turnersville
   "Rush the Kettles," "Big Mule."
i Lish Forbes..................................Mc. Creary
   "Mississippi Sawyer," "Arkansas Traveler."
j George Arnold................................County at Large
   "Little Home on the Poosey," "Bring me Back my Old Coon Dog."
k C. W. Mitchell...............................Buckeye
   To be Announced.
l William Pollard..............................Cat Hole Bend
   "Old Pine Tree," "Forked Deer."
m Mrs. Alice Crutchfield.......................Bourne
   To be Announced.
n Perry King...................................Crab Orchard
   To be Announced.
o Alex Traylor.................................Gilberts Creek
   To be Announced.
p Scott Farris.................................Crab Orchard
   "Chicken Pie," "Run Nigger Run."
q Charles Grimes...............................Marksbury
   "Resin The Bow," "Barlow Knife."
   Other entries will be announced from stage.

   PRIZE—A Fine Violin. Other features will be added. Competent and disinterested committees will be appointed to award the prizes. Admission—First two rows. children 25c, next five rows will be reserved at 75c, balance of ground floor at 50c, with privilege to reserve without extra cost. Balcony 35c. Contestants free. Contestants are requested to meet at Garrard Hotel at 7 o'clock, from whence they will be conducted to the Opera House.

FRUIT STORAGE HOUSE.

Description of One Used by H. H. Hill, One of Vermont's Successful Horticulturists.

   My house for storing fruit is one that was on the premises and, not built for the purpose. But I find it quite convenient. It is a stone building 26x34 feet, with good walls two feet thick, well laid in mortar, as shown in the illustration. To make it so I could hold fruit through the winter, I lined it inside with matched lumber, making an air space of about ten inches between the wall and lin-

VERMONT FRUIT HOUSE.

ing. It is a two-story house. I protect from cold by putting straw on upper floor about four feet thick when settled. It kept the fruit well. I make a fire in it only three or four times through the winter, on account of extreme cold.

   I could, with but little expense, make it good for cold storage by putting eight or ten 12-inch galvanized iron pipes through the upper floor, letting them down three or four feet, and filling from above with crushed ice and cheap fertilizer salt; I have used it as it is, opening the doors nights to cool off and keeping it closed during the day, except when putting in more fruit. I pick and put in barrels in the orchard and store them open. In rainy weather I can sort and pack for market. I usually sell to buyers, so they are off my hands and in market or cold storage, near market, by November 15. I have seldom kept a crop over.—Orange Judd Farmer.

PLUMS FOR MARKET.

There Are Hundreds of Varieties, But Only a Few Are Adapted for General Cultivation.

   The number of known species of plums runs up into the hundreds, but among those hundreds there are only a few that it will pay to do much with. But it requires a great deal of

---

An announcement for the Old Fiddlers' Contest
(*Central Record*, 20 November 1901)

The type of music the fiddlers played is clear from the titles given in the advertisement reproduced on page 208. In reviewing the evening, Landram wrote, "It was strictly 'old-time music, none of the highfalutin' stuff sawed out by 'violinists' being allowed."[62] The event was so successful that a similar competition was arranged for black fiddlers the following month.[63]

On 25 July 1902 Lancaster hosted a vocal contest that included singers from Richmond, Mt. Sterling, London, Lancaster, Cynthiana, Bryantsville, Paris, Midway, Danville, Stanford, Flemingsburg, and other central Kentucky towns. A large crowd turned out to hear the event, and the first and second place winners won a diamond ring and a gold medal, respectively. The sponsors also awarded a popular prize decided by audience vote.[64] The contest was so popular that it was held the following year and then turned into the state tournament in voice and piano held 22-24 June 1904. The event was sponsored by the Lancaster Athletic Association, and awards were given for hurdle races, throwing a baseball, tennis, bicycle race, clay pigeon shooting, shot put, mile run, standing high jump, running high jump, and three-legged race, in addition to the musical prizes for voice, piano solo, and piano duet each separated into male and female categories.[65]

Music also was a significant part of the core curriculum of schools in the immediate surroundings, and in 1891 Garrard College in Lancaster offered "Piano, Vocal and Violin Culture, directed by Prof. Raphael Koester, from the Royal Conservatory, Berlin, Germany with eight years experience as a director."[66] From 1885 to 1891 the music class of Garrard College gave a musical entertainment at the Court House and invited the public.[67] The commencement exercises from the Garrard Female College in 1885 were quite elaborate social affairs.

> This will be the gayest week Lancaster has seen for years. This (Tuesday) evening a musicale at the college will be the attraction and Wednesday evening the college grounds will be illuminated and a lawn party given. Thursday evening the commencement exercises of Garrard Female college are held at the Christian church and will be followed by a full dress hop at the City Hop. Eichhorn's orchestra will furnish the music for the last three affairs and as 1,000 invitations have been sent large crowds of young people are expected from the neighboring towns.[68]

Students later studied in the Lancaster Graded School under Mrs. Belle Burnside. In 1902 the school had outstanding facilities, including "seven music rooms, two pianos in the primary divisions, and an organ in the chapel."[69] Many of the students entered elocution and music contests held at the Garrard Opera House[70] and provided music for the yearly musicals and closing exercises at school.[71] The most talented young ladies went off to study at the Cincinnati Conservatory of Music under the direction of Miss Clara Bauer and later returned to showcase their talents in the town. Guests trained in other musical institutions would also visit. In 1905 Miss Lena M. Phillips, a graduate of the Boston Conservatory of Music, sang and performed on the piano selections of Mendelssohn's "March" from *Athalia*, Verdi's "Miserere" from *Il trovatore*, Raff's *Cavatine*, and Chopin's Prelude, Op. 28, No. 20.[72]

In 1900 J. M. Johnson began a class in vocal music at Scott's Forks Church "with very flattering prospects,"[73] and in April 1904 Miss Jennie Swope organized a Music Club, which met monthly to discuss an important composer at each meeting (beginning with J. S. Bach).[74]

Music also played a major role in the small churches in the area. Frequently traveling musicians would use the sanctuaries as auditoriums, and during revivals soloists would perform in the church. At a revival in 1901 Professor J. Walter Wilson, the Singing Evangelist from Indianapolis, sang solos such as "The Holy City" and "The Ninety and Nine" interspersed with illustrations of "nearly two hundred magnificent steropticon views."[75] As the churches grew more prosperous they were able to purchase better, though still quite modest, instruments. In 1904, for example, the Lancaster Christian Church purchased a $1,500 pipe organ made in St. Louis.[76] Mrs. Belle Burnside and her daughter, Willie Belle, who studied organ at the Cincinnati Conservatory of Music, played for church services.

Shortly after it was installed, Mrs. Taylor of Lexington presented an organ recital at the church accompanied by local singers.[77] Seeing the success of the organ in the Christian church, the Presbyterian church only a couple of blocks away decided that they too needed to purchase a pipe organ.

In addition to fairs, dances, and hops of all types, music made up a major portion of the Civil War celebrations. In particular, confederate reunions and celebrations took place annually in Lancaster. Most spectacular were the annual birthday celebrations the United Daughters of the Confederacy held in honor of Robert E. Lee. The most extravagant was held a day after Lee's 101st birthday.

On January 18th at 2 P.M., the United Daughters of Confederacy held a memorial service for their beloved chieftain, Robert Edward Lee. The handsome home of Mrs. Fred P. Frisbie was beautifully decorated for the occasion, with potted plants and red and white draperies. A large portrait of Lee was draped with confederate flags. After a prayer by Rev. C. C. Brown the "Sword of Lee" was sung by Misses Alberta Anderson, Allie Arnold. The President Mrs. Jas. A. Roystone spoke of the object of the meeting telling eulogies pronounced on this noble character by men of note and introduced the speaker, Hon. W. I. Williams who gave an eloquent address. Mr. Williams gave a minute history of Lee's life in a most interesting and impressive manner which was greatly enjoyed by all and pronounced a masterpiece. After a song ... the president conferred Crosses of Honor on three old veterans in an impressive manner. Eld. F. M. Tinder led in prayer and all joined in singing "Old Kentucky Home." At the close of the service the old veterans, filled with enthusiasm, made the house sing as they sang "Dixie" with thoughts of days that have passed.[78]

Five months later the citizens celebrated Jefferson Davis's one hundredth anniversary:

A sextet of young girls sang "My Old Kentucky Home" and "The Sunny South" led by Miss Katherine Conn.... A flag drill accompanied the last song.... The last number on the program was a piano medley of airs arranged and rendered by Mrs. Eugenia Dunlap Potts, Historian of the Lexington Chapter U D C.... The selections were "Old Folks At Home," "My Maryland," "The Bonnie Blue Flag," and "Dixie." When the notes of the beloved old war song fell upon the ear, the Veterans arose en masse and gave the "Rebel Yell" so famous in the 60's. Great enthusiasm was manifested by assembled crowd.[79]

Local firms supplied the musicians with instruments as well, many of which could be purchased within the vicinity of Lancaster early as the mid-1880s. In 1885, S. R. and L. J. Cook in the neighboring town of Stanford were the "agents for the old and reliable John Church Co. of Cincinnati, Ohio, for the sale of Pianos, Organs, Automatic Musical Instruments and Musical Merchandise in Lincoln and Garrard counties, Kentucky."[80] They carried upright and square pianos made by William Knabe & Company, Hassled Brothers, Decker & Son, Everett and New England, as well as organs made by Clough & Warren, John Church & Company, and the "Sterling, with its patent Chime Bells Attachment. The Celesteon, an Automatic Musical Instrument, the most perfect in the world."[81]

In the late 1890s pianos were common in many of the homes. Tuners came from various cities to work on pianos in Lancaster. In 1898 R. W. Hunter of the Kimball Music House tuned instruments,[82] and W. J. Homer from Danville spent several days in April and June 1903 tuning pianos in Lancaster. "He tuned nearly every piano in Lancaster and Garrard county, and if there is the least complaint of his work, we have yet to hear it."[83]

In 1900 E. W. Arnold represented D. H. Baldwin & Company locally,[84] and in October Harding & Riehm established offices in Lancaster. They billed themselves as the "Largest Wholesale and Retail Dealers in Pianos and Organs in Central States ... and propose[d] to accommodate the music-loving people of Lancaster and vicinity with an assortment of the largest and best line of instruments in America at prices and terms that cannot be duplicated."[85] Harding & Riehm became Harding & Miller in December 1900. In 1902 W. J. Homer, representative for the Montenegro-Riehm Music Company, came to town regularly and sold instruments from that firm.[86]

In 1905, Hamilton & Dunlap opened a store on Danville Street and became the agent to sell pianos and organs for D. H. Baldwin & Company.[87] Their strongest competition was West and Herndon who advertised: "Cheer up your home by putting in an organ, piano or graphophone—they do not cost much, and West & Herndon will make you better figures than you can possibly obtain elsewhere."[88] W. B. West retired in at the end of 1906,[89] and Lewis Herndon continued operating the business. In 1907 Herndon sold "Second-hand pianos in first class condition" for only twenty-five dollars and gave "a copy of sheet music free to every visitor" who came to the store.[90]

A Lancaster County advertisement for phonographs
(*Central Record*, 10 November 1905)

Pianos and organs were not the only instruments sold in Lancaster. As early as January 1892 traveling entrepreneurs exhibited Edison's phonograph at the local McRoberts's drug store.[91] In May 1897, Joe Haselden bought a new graphophone, which he took "great pleasure in exhibiting the wonderful invention. He makes a specialty of playing for private parties."[92] In December of that year, G. S. Gains also put "a graphophone in his store which grinds out mirth and melody for his customers."[93] Many musical instruments were also sold by Thompson the jeweler.[94] A typical newspaper advertisement for such devices is reproduced on page 213.

The graphophones were so popular that in 1907 the *Central Record* claimed that "Lewis Herndon has sold graphophones to nearly every family in the county. They are a great pleasure, and cost very little money on the terms he sells 'em."[95] Soon the rage turned to the phonograph, and Herndon ran his ad for this:

> The phonograph, Mr. Edison's greatest invention, fills a place in the home which drives away care and brings joy and happiness. It isn't like the human being, for it will play at any time you wish and never refuses because it 'hasn't its notes,' or 'don't feel well.' All you have to do is wind it up and it will sing for you, play the banjo, make a speech or tell a story. The cost of these wonderful instruments is very low, within the reach of all. Lewis Herndon, the Lancaster music dealer and jeweler, is selling phonographs faster [than] he can get them in, and it looks like everybody is going to get one of the delightful instruments.[96]

Prices for the phonograph in Lancaster around 1907 ranged from $10 to $150. By 1910 ads for "Columbia Indestructible Cylinder Records" appeared frequently in the *Central Record*.[97]

Just as a variety of instruments were available, there were many different types of sheet music and book collections, including marches, patriotic tunes, folk songs, hymns, light classics, and popular songs of all types. Songwriters from the area were able to perform and publish their works. Professor Herbert of the Richmond Band composed a "Sigma Nu March," which he sold for thirty-five cents per copy.[98] The black band leader Milton Sneed composed music for a work entitled "The South Before the War," as well as a quickstep that he dedicated to the local Knights of Pythias lodge. "It is pretty, and has been sent to the John

Church Co. for publication. The piece is a good one, and the average country band could not touch it with a forty foot pole."⁹⁹ Charley Storm, a cornet player with Saxton's Military Band in Lexington, composed a number of songs that attracted "much favorable comment in the music world. They are exceedingly pretty, and are meeting with a ready sale. If you want something pretty to sing, something that will catch your hearers, secure some of this music."¹⁰⁰

The musicians in the town were also aware of the most recent classical compositions. West & Herndon had "all the latest classical and popular sheet music.... Prices cheaper than you can order. See 'em and save money."¹⁰¹ Notices and advertisements of the American Popular Music Publishing Company and the John Horn Publishing Company in the paper drew musicians' attention to diverse works ranging from Paderewski's *Menuet Moderne* to various versions of "My Old Kentucky Home." An advertisement in January 1898 offered the following under the catchy title, "What Is Home Without Music?":

104	"Silver Stars" (Piano 4 hands)......	Bohon
134	"The Raft" (Vocal)	Pinsuit
838	"Rondo Capriccioso" (Piano)	Mendelsshon [*sic*]
29	"Ask Me Not Why?" (Vocal)	Donizetti
103	"Tannhauser March" (Piano)	Wagner
157	"The Wanderer" (Vocal)	Schubert
100	"Faust," op. 35 (Piano)	Leybarch
47	"Bells of St. Mary's" (Vocal)	Rodney
101	"DeMolay Commandery March" (Piano)	Marzian
96	"Hear Me, Norma" (Vocal duet)	Bellini
110	"The Storm" (descriptive Piano)	Weber
107	"Land of the Swallows" (Vocal duet)	Massini
108	"Musical Club Waltz" (Piano)	Redman
109	"Hungarian Rhapsode" [*sic*] (Piano)	Liszt
108	"My Old Kentucky Home" (Vocal)	Foster
111	"The Flatterer" (Piano, 4 hands)	Chaminad [*sic*]¹⁰²

Certainly homegrown musicians were prominent in the area, and music-making was an everyday affair for many of Lancaster's citizens. For some, however, music was too prominent in Lancaster. A local columnist humorously suggested some restrictions on music-making:

In some countries laws have been enacted to protect the public from the piano-playing nuisance by regulating or restricting the time of practicing and playing on that instrument of torture to certain hours. I heartily wish such wise and beneficent laws could be put into immediate operation right here in Lancaster. Now, to my mind, an organ is vastly worse than a piano. The good people in the neighborhood in which I live are continuously annoyed by the screeching, vibrating discords of an organ, produced by the unskilled hands of an amateur performer. From early morn till after the shades of night have fallen, almost without intermission, this bellowing, screeching, groaning instrument is made to grind out such an endless variety of inharmonious sounds as are truly nerve-racking and soul-harrowing. At one moment the instrument is made to shriek and scream until the unwilling listener imagines he has suddenly been transported to the abode of the damned, and that it is the agonizing cries of a poor lost and tortured soul, doomed to eternal punishment, that he hears instead of a musical instrument. The next instant the organ is made to bellow and growl like an infuriated wild beast rendered insane by pain and rage. Thus the concert goes on and on in a succession of diabolical sounds that are enough to tempt a man to commit murder or drive him to drink. I believe that pianos and organs are the choicest specimens of the devil's creative genius, especially designed to punish his victims in advance for their misdeeds, but the innocent are made to suffer, with the guilty, "ah, there's the rub."
Give us a rest.[103]

In addition to local talent, Lancaster hosted numerous traveling musicians and musical groups. Perhaps, the most famous person to perform in Lancaster was the pianist Blind Boone. On 16 April 1897 Blind Boone gave a recital at the Garrard County Court House. The Knights of Pythias lodge in Lancaster had been able to bring him to Lancaster in hopes of making a good deal of money to help build the new opera house. Ads and reviews of his concert were printed in March and April building up excitement about his appearance. He was billed as the "World's Most Wonderful Musical Prodigy, so special that he "carries and uses at all concerts, his own beautiful grand piano."[104]

A week before the concert, the *Central Record* reported that "reserved seats for the Blind Boone concert are going like hot cakes. Better get one or you may have to stand."[105] The Knights of Pythias reported that he was the equal of Blind Tom and went all out to build up excitement about the concert, including bringing out the lodge goat for the parade (something they had not done for many years).[106]

> The large Hall of the Court House was packed and jammed Friday night to hear Blind Boone. It was estimated that more people were in the house than ever attended a similar entertainment in Lancaster. Boone is certainly a genius and his playing is marvelous. He differs from Blind Tom in many ways. In the first place, he is an educated man, and one of fine sense. He travels on his merits and not sympathy. He played many classical numbers and sang several of his own songs. He then played and sang several darkey pieces for the amusement of the children. His imitations were splendid. We asked a number of the best local musicians what they thought of Boone, and each expressed the opinion that he exceeded Blind Tom by far. An enjoyable feature of the evening was the singing of Miss Stella. She possesses a sweet voice, and the ease and grace with which she did her part was greatly appreciated by the vast audience. She was enchored [*sic*] several times after each of her numbers on the program. The Knights of Pythias will clear about fifty dollars on the entertainment, which goes to the building fund. The thanks of those who enjoyed the entertainment are due to Mr. Jon. M. Farra, as he made all arrangements for the performance. It is hoped that Boone will make [another visit to Lancaster soon]. In talking with him, we found Boone to be a perfect gentleman, a Christian and a man of fine intellect. He is a deacon in the Christian church and devotes half his earnings to charitable purposes.[107]

The concert itself was enormously successful.

Traveling groups had often come to Lancaster even when they did not have an opera house; but with the opening of the new opera house in 1900, musical shows became considerably more frequent. These groups brought variety and a particular novelty that local musicians could not always replicate. For example, the Gus Sun American Minstrels brought their own scenery with them: "Special scenery, something seldom carried by a minstrel show, and mechanical effects are used by this company in conjunction with the big song and dance and the finale. In equipping this company for the road Mr. Sun has gone to an enormous expense, the special Pullman car 'Nellie' alone costing $10,000—a small fortune."[108] Lancaster with its meager resources could not possibly mount something so extravagant, and nothing so extravagant could be displayed outside of an appropriate opera house. Between 1900 when the new opera house officially opened and 1902 when it burned, at least twenty traveling shows of this sort performed in the opera house:

Out-of-Town Performing Groups at the Garrard Opera House

1900	San Francisco Minstrels
	The Hawthorne Sisters
	The Western Stars
	The Kentucky Colonels
	The Williams Comedy Company
	Herald Square Opera
	Schumann Concert Company
	Harry Ward's Big Minstrels
	Barlow and Wilson's Minstrels
1901	The Gus Sun American Minstrels
	W. H. Harris' Old-Time Negro Minstrels
	Hoy's A Trip to Tramptown
	Al. G. Field
	The Big Four Minstrels
1902	Gorton's Minstrels
	Goodwal Dickerman Company
	E. J. Carpenter's "Quo Vadis" Company
	Berea College Glee Club
	The Gus Sun American Minstrels

A discussion of music in Lancaster during this time would not be complete without a detailed examination of the opera house and how essential it was in attracting traveling shows and exhibitions to Lancaster. The challenge to build an opera house for such a small town proved arduous and, in the end, often disappointing.

An early opera house was destroyed by fire in October 1891. Since the owners had only $1,000 worth of insurance on a $4,000 building, it could not be immediately rebuilt.[109] The citizens put forth little effort to see it rebuilt, although rumors surfaced periodically that it would rise again from the ashes. For five years, no serious actions were undertaken to rebuild it. In October 1896, however, the Knights of Pythias lodge began to consider seriously plans for building an opera house.[110] Louis Landram supported the idea and wrote: "Carry a stuffed club and bounce it over the head of the first croaker you hear throwing cold water on the opera house scheme. Judge Totten will not fine you for it."[111]

In June 1897, the Knights of Pythias paid Capt. W. J. Kinnaird for a 50×200 foot lot on Lexington Street. The plans at the time were for the opera house to be built on the ground floor with lodge rooms above and for it to have "elevated seats, a balcony, gallery (or 'roost'), and all modern improvements."[112] Not all the money was raised at the time, and the project fell through, largely because the title to the lot was not free and clear.[113]

A year later, in November 1898, the Knights again planned for a three-story brick building that would be "a model of convenience and beauty" and built for $15,000. Landram supported the idea and printed a picture of a rooster in the *Central Record*:

> This bird is not splitting his throat over the victory of any political party, but is crowing over the great success those working up at the hotel and opera house are meeting with. That's what we are interested in. Right here in Lancaster is where Lancaster people make their meat and bread and what we want to see is the good old town built up. The parties getting the stock have secured in black and white an even eight thousand dollars. Several other parties who want stock have not yet been seen, and all [that is] necessary is for them to sign the paper and [the] new building is assured. Each stockholder will pay two hundred dollars down and the balance in monthly installments of about sixteen dollars. Several parties not able to take a whole share have purchased jointly with others.[114]

By the first week of January 1899, the lodge had finalized plans for the opera house and hotel.

> When talk of erecting a handsome hotel and opera house in Lancaster was commenced, the most enthusiastic promoters of the town's interests could scarcely see how the required amount of capital could

be secured, but where there's a will there's a way, and the few
hustlers put their shoulders to the wheel to carry out the idea. A
drawing was ordered made ... and it was found it would take
seventeen thousand dollars to carry out the plan. The following
public spirited citizens formed a permanent organization this week:
John E. Stormes, W. H. Kinnaird, H. T. Logan, J. C. Hemphill,
Robt. Kinnaird, J. R. Ryan, of Lexington, Capt. Herndon and Mrs.
Margaret Gill. The following officers were chosen: John E. Stormes,
president, Capt. Wm. Herndon, secretary, National Bank of
Lancaster, treasurer.[115]

On 3 February 1899, the contract was closed. The Lancaster
Hotel Company paid Capt. W. S. Miller three thousand dollars for
the lot and contracted James Ryan & Son of Lexington to build
the hotel and opera house. A week later Landram printed a picture
of hotel and opera house in the paper and described the complex.

Everything is now complete and as soon as the weather will permit,
work of digging cellars and foundation will be commenced.... The
opera house will front on Richmond street. The lobby will be 14×31
with store rooms or offices on either side 16×23. Bath rooms will
be made back of one of these and ticket office in rear of the other.
The auditorium will be 47×55 with seating capacity of 400. The
stage is to be 37×48 and [the] orchestra pit 4×26. The dressing
rooms, closets, etc., will be built under the stage, and on either side
of stage will be large boxes. The balcony will seat 250 people and
will be fitted up with the same chairs as the auditorium. The scenery
will be made to draw up into a "rigging loft," the latter being 45 feet
from stage floor to top.... The entire building will be lighted by
electricity and the company will put in a dynamo of its own.[116]

Soon after Ryan began making contracts with various
businesses, including one with Lancaster Planing Mill for one
hundred thousand feet of lumber.[117] The pressed brick was made at
Zanesville, Ohio, and "cost 2 1/2 cents apiece laid down here.
They are brought to Danville over the Q. & C., and hauled here in
wagons. Mr. Ryan says by doing this he saves $2.50 per thousand,
the freight being less than that charged by the L. & N."[118] The
association purchased "seven hundred handsome, up-to-date opera
chairs"[119] from the Andrews Furniture Company of Chicago.
"Those for the lower floor are stained mahogany and the ones for
the balcony are of the finest oak. They are made with folding

seats, hat and cloak racks, and are the very latest and most improved pattern."[120]

On 22 February 1899, workers began cleaning up the lot. "Wednesday morning a line of colored men, armed with wheelbarrows, filed into the Miller corner and began removing the old bricks, stone and rubbish preparatory to digging the foundation for the hotel and opera house. As soon as this is removed the wheelbarrows will be replaced with dumpcarts and work will be pushing with the greatest rapidity."[121] "About 40 men wield picks and shovels from sun-up to dark, while at least 25 two-horse wagons haul away the dirt and debris. In a few days the foundation will have been dug and the large stones will be put in position to receive the brick walls."[122] Bad weather impeded progress during March, but by mid-May, workers had dug the cellars, laid the foundation, and began placing the joists.[123]

Construction of the opera house led to a boom in building, transforming the public square. At the same time the city council passed a new ordinance requiring all buildings built on the public square to be made of brick or stone. Landram took note of the many improvements going on in the town: "A spirit of enterprise, hitherto unknown has taken possession of our people. Six store rooms, a hotel, an opera house and ten new residences are being built. All indications point to the fact that the shrill whistle of the emblem of civilization will soon be heard running over the new route which is being surveyed for the great Southern Railway."[124]

The new storerooms were begun in May 1899 on the site of the old opera house, covering the entire lot from the National Bank to Richmond Street. This area had remained vacant for nearly nine years since October 1891. The four new rooms ran the full depth of the lots and included office rooms above the storefronts. "The front is to be of Ohio pressed brick with trimmings of cut stone, and the entire front of [the] store rooms plate glass. There are to be large fire walls between each store and the entire building constructed in the latest and most up-to-date manner. The building will cost $10,000 and is to be completed by fall. The erection of this block will be one of the greatest blessings the town has had."[125]

By the first two weeks of July, the foundation for the storerooms was laid,[126] and "the walls of the old Opera House block [were] rapidly going up.... From their appearance, contractor Ryan is putting up a building that will stand against fire and storm. The ram's horn will have to be blown seven times before the fall thereof."[127]

On 24 July "a large force of brick-layers commenced work on the hotel and opera house.... As enough material is on hand to prevent delay the walls will go up very rapidly. The corner stone at Richmond street and Square was laid Saturday, without the foolishness usually attending such occasions. A copy of he *Record*'s Christmas number and one of recent date was placed under the stone. Capt. Ryan has about a dozen houses in course of construction, but will have all completed before cold weather sets in."[128]

In August Ryan had trouble getting in certain materials,[129] slowing work considerably. Plans were made for the opening on the November 21st with Porter J. White's company presenting *Faust*.[130] By mid-November, the chairs for the opera house had arrived, but the building was not completely ready.[131] "A large force of hands are working on the Opera House and it will CERTAINLY BE READY TUESDAY NIGHT for the production of *Faust*. The chairs are ready, the stage almost complete and the furnaces will be put in Monday. If you want to see this production, you had better secure your seat. The house will be completed in a few days."[132] "Although the plasterer, the painter and the decorator are yet to do their part on the Garrard Opera House, the building was opened to amusement lovers Tuesday night, when Mr. Porter J. White presented *Faust*."[133]

Three nights later the opera house was active again.

The coming of the famous "Wright's Original Nashville Students" combined with "Gideon's Big Minstrel Carnival" will prove a gala event to all lovers of good, bright, wholesome minstrelsy. This popular attraction will appear at the Opera House, Lancaster one night only, Friday Nov. 24th, and promises to prove the fun festival of the season. Everywhere in the large cities where it appears, theatres are filled to overflowing and the press speak in the most gloving terms of the excellent performance and the merit of the many big acts presented. Forty-five of the best colored entertainers in minstrelsy appear at every performance and good rollicking fun runs riot for three solid hours. The Nashville Students Glee Club and The Occidental Quartette furnish the most beautiful of music, rendering sweet Southern melodies, and fifteen natural colored comedians create uproarious merriment with their bright, up-to-date ideas of humor. Slack wire walkers, jugglers, tumblers, acrobats, and a score of other varied features are included in the enjoyable programme. A big symphony orchestra furnishes the music for the performance and two Peerless Bands appear in the street parade that is given every day.[134]

These performances took place, however, in an unfinished opera house. The authorities had to cancel an engagement of the *Three Musketeers* in December and decided at the time that no more entertainments would be given until they had completed the opera house.[135]

The house opened again in January after the plastering had been done, but problems still remained. The lamps frequently went out because of electrical problems, forcing the installation of gas lamps in November 1900.[136] The heating also did not always work, and reports from a March 1901 concert indicated that "the house was cold as a step-mother's heart, which made it impossible to keep the instruments in tune."[137] Apparently Lancaster also had some trouble attracting groups to come to perform in the house at first.[138] By the middle of 1901, however, a variety of minstrel troupes and singers were arriving frequently and when combined with the local talent's presentations, the opera house was quite successful. In November 1901 the owners had installed an outside drop curtain, which contained advertisements of several local firms.[139]

Some problems, however, were not with the house, but with the patrons of it. As early as January 1900 articles concerning the behavior of the audience appeared in the *Central Record*: "At the Opera House, a number of young roosters who are possessed with more wind than brains, applaud certain people when they come in, much to the annoyance of patrons of the house. A gentleman will act a gentleman, at all times, while bad breeding will crop out everywhere."[140]

A month later conditions appeared to worsen:

At nearly every performance given at the Opera House there is in the audience a few misguided persons who seek to distinguish themselves by applauding late arrivals. It seems as though some people can never learn how to deport themselves with propriety in a public place. Applause when merited and properly directed is perfectly right, but to attempt to stamp the floor into the basement with your feet just because you see some one walking down the aisle to his seat is disgusting. While your sentiments may be pro-Boer, you should not allow yourself to become too extremely boor-ish in an audience which is undoubtedly neutral. And should your appreciation be elicited by developments on the stage which is probable, the suggestion is offered that it be expressed by the more seemly correct method of clapping the hands.[141]

In November, conditions had gotten to the point that the manager, M. D. Hughes, established and published rules of behavior for the opera house: "Curtain rises promptly at 8 o'clock. Stamping of feet, whistling, loud talking, unnecessary noise, eating peanuts, loafing in the lobby not allowed. No one but employe[e]s allowed behind the curtain. If you leave the house between acts, please return to your seat before opening of next act. Ladies will please remove their hats when play commences, thus conferring a favor upon those sitting in their rear. These rules will be enforced."[142]

The hats were another issue that led a member of the Kentucky legislature to introduce a bill "making it unlawful for ladies to wear high hats at theatre hall or public gatherings."[143] Landram approved this suggestion:

The anti-theatre hat law is becoming general all over the country, and man, poor man, is happy. It is an outrage to pay fifty cents or a dollar for a seat and then be compelled to sit behind a woman with a wash tub on her head.... I went down the other night and selected a good seat where I thought certainly no one would get between the speaker and me. All went well for a while, but presently a girl, about the shape of a mop stick, switched in and flopped down before me. She had on a hat that occupied a space of at least four square feet. A little neck, about as big as your wrist, ran up into the head gear, and the whole looked like a frog stool. I was wedged between two other "umbrellas" and there I sat, with only a view of the ceiling.[144]

All these small problems diminished greatly, however, when compared to the overwhelming destruction of fire. The ram's horn was not required to blow seven times before the walls fell as

Landram had boasted. The opera house and hotel complex finished in the first month of 1900, burned to the ground only two and one-half years later on 3 August 1902. Immediately attempts were made for it to be quickly rebuilt. But year after year passed with no new opera house. The numbers of events dwindled, and the courthouse was used once again for the few traveling shows that did come into town. Without the opera house and without an increase in population to support local musical groups, live music could not compete with the rapid advances in musical technology and softly declined year by year in the little town of Lancaster.

Emory University

---

[1]*Interior Journal*, 22 January 1892, 1. The members were all men: John M. Duncan, J. E. Stormes, H. W. Batson, J. C. Hemphill, R. E. Hughes, Louis Landram, J. M. Farra, L. Owsley, Charley Anderson ,and John Lear. *The Interior Journal* is the local paper of Stanford, Kentucky, a town located ten miles south of Lancaster.

[2]*Interior Journal*, 8 March 1892, 1.

[3]*Interior Journal*, 18 March 1892, 1.

[4]*Interior Journal*, 31 May 1892, 1.

[5]*Interior Journal*, 8 November 1892, 1.

[6]*Interior Journal*, 3 February 1893, 1.

[7]*Interior Journal*, 27 June 1893, 1.

[8]*Interior Journal*, 30 June 1893, 1.

[9]*Interior Journal*, 15 December 1893, 1. The Knights of Pythias is a secret, benevolent order founded in 1864 to help heal the wounds of Civil War America.

[10]*Interior Journal*, 20 February 1894, 1.

[11]*Interior Journal*, 20 March 1894, 1.

[12]*Interior Journal*, 1 June 1894, 1.

[13]*Interior Journal*, 17 July 1894, 1.

[14]*Interior Journal*, 9 March 1894, 1.

[15]*Interior Journal,* 6 April 1894, 1.

[16]*Interior Journal,* 10 April 1894, 1.

[17]*Interior Journal,* 11 May 1894, 1.

[18]*Central Record,* 5 April 1895, 1. Founded in 1890 in Lancaster, the *Central Record* has been in operation since that time.

[19]*Central Record,* 21 May 1895, 1.

[20]*Central Record,* 7 June 1895, 1.

[21]*Central Record,* 30 August 1895, 1.

[22]*Central Record,* 20 September 1895, 1.

[23]*Central Record,* 27 March 1896, 1.

[24]*Central Record,* 24 April 1896, 1.

[25]*Central Record,* 1 May 1896, 1.

[26]*Central Record,* 8 May 1896, 1.

[27]*Central Record,* 8 May 1896, 1.

[28]*Central Record,* 15 May 1896, 1.

[29]*Central Record,* 3 July 1896, 1.

[30]*Central Record,* 31 July 1896, 1.

[31]*Central Record,* 19 June 1896, 1. The band members were J. E. Stormes, director; B. D. Herndon, C. M. Owsley, J. M. Farra, O. W. Shugars, J. S. Haselden, F. R. Marksbury, M. F. West, M. A. Archer, W. L. Herndon, J. H. Kinnaird, J. C. Hemphill, H. W. Batson, H. K. Herndon, Letcher Owsley, and B. Y. Cogar.

[32]*Central Record,* 26 June 1896, 1.

[33]*Central Record,* 14 August 1896, 1.

[34]*Central Record,* 9 April 1897, 1.

[35]*Central Record,* 16 April 1897, 1. [A few obvious corrections were made to make this and other excerpts easier to read. - Ed.]

[36]*Central Record,* 23 April 1897, 1.

[37]*Central Record,* 2 July 1897, 1.

[38]*Central Record,* 25 June 1897, 1.

[39]*Central Record,* 13 August 1897, 1.

[40]*Central Record,* 27 August 1897, 1.

[41]*Central Record,* 24 September 1897, 1.

[42]*Central Record,* 3 December 1897, 1.

[43]*Central Record,* 21 January 1898, 1.

[44]*Central Record,* 25 February 1898, 1.

[45]*Central Record,* 11 March 1898, 1.

[46]*Central Record,* 22 April 1898, 1.

[47]*Central Record,* 3 June 1898, 1.

[48]*Central Record,* 3 June 1898, 1.

[49]*Central Record,* 28 Sept 1899, 1.

[50]*Central Record,* 13 Sept 1900, 1.

[51]*Central Record,* 9 May 1901, 1

[52]*Central Record,* 19 June 1901, 1

[53]*Central Record,* 30 August 1895, 1.

[54]*Central Record,* 19 November 1897, 1.

[55]*Central Record,* 31 January 1901, 1.

[56]*Central Record,* 28 March 1901, 1.

[57]*Central Record,* 22 August 1901, 1.

[58]*Central Record,* 21 August 1902, 1.

[59]*Central Record,* 22 May 1903, 1.

[60]*Central Record,* 14 November 1901, 1.

[61]*Central Record,* 10 October 1901, 3.

[62]*Central Record,* 5 December 1901,1.

[63]*Central Record,* 19 December 1901, 1.

[64]*Central Record,* 17 July 1903, 1.

[65]*Central Record,* 26 June 1904, 1.

[66]*Interior Journal,* 28 July 1891, 1.

[67]*Interior Journal,* 16 January 1891, 1.

[68]*Interior Journal,* 2 June 1885, 1.

[69]*Central Record,* 24 April 1902 2.

[70]*Central Record,* 7 March 1901.

[71]*Central Record,* 8 May 1903, 2.

[72]*Central Record,* 26 May 1905, 1.

[73]*Central Record,* 4 October 1900, 1.

[74]*Central Record,* 1 April 1904, 2.

[75]*Central Record,* 19 June 1901, 3.

[76]*Central Record,* 11 March 1904, 1.

[77]*Central Record,* 18 March 1904, 1.

[78]*Central Record,* 24 January 1908, 1.

[79]*Central Record,* 12 June 1908, 1.

[80]*Interior Journal,* 27 July 1885, 1.

[81]*Interior Journal,* 27 July 1885, 1.

[82]*Central Record,* 17 June 1898, 1.

[83]*Central Record,* 12 June 1903, 1.

[84]*Central Record,* 23 August 1900.

[85]*Central Record,* 4 October 1900.

[86]*Central Record,* 9 January 1902, 1.

[87]*Central Record,* 30 June 1905, 1.

[88]*Central Record,* 24 August 1906, 1.

[89]*Central Record,* 11 January 1907, 1.

[90]*Central Record,* 31 May 1907, 4.

[91]*Interior Journal,* 22 January 1892, 1.

[92]*Central Record,* 21 May 1897, 1.

[93]*Central Record,* 10 December 1897, 1.

[94]*Central Record,* 20 December 1904, 1.

[95]*Central Record,* 15 March 1907, 1.

[96]*Central Record,* 5 April 1907, 1.

[97]*Central Record,* 18 February 1910, 4.

[98]*Central Record,* 21 May 1895, 1.

[99]*Central Record,* 11 June 1895, 1.

[100]*Central Record,* 14 August 1903, 1.

[101]*Central Record,* 19 October 1906, 3.

[102]*Central Record,* 14 January 1898, 1.

[103]*Central Record,* 3 July 1896, 1.

[104]*Central Record,* 2 April 1897, 1.

[105]*Central Record,* 9 April 1897, 1.

[106]*Central Record,* 9 April 1897, 1. The goat was carefully guarded by twenty-five or thirty uniformed Knights.

[107]*Central Record,* 23 April 1897, 1.

[108]*Central Record,* 10 April 1902, 3

[109]*Interior Journal,* 23 October 1891, 1.

[110]*Central Record,* 23 October 1896, 1.

[111]*Central Record,* 23 October 1896, 1.

[112]*Central Record,* 4 June 1897, 1.

[113]*Central Record,* 24 November 1898, 1.

[114]*Central Record,* 8 November 1898, 1.

[115]*Central Record,* 6 January 1899, 1.

[116]*Central Record,* 10 February 1899, 1.

[117]*Central Record,* 10 February 1899, 1.

[118]*Central Record,* 25 May 1899, 1.

[119]*Central Record,* 11 May 1899, 1.

[120]*Central Record,* 11 May 1899, 1.

[121]*Central Record,* 24 February 1899, 1.

[122]*Central Record,* 2 March 1899, 1.

[123]*Central Record,* 9 March 1899, 1 and 25 May 1899, 1.

[124]*Central Record,* 13 July 1899, 1. The Southern Railroad never came through Lancaster, although for several years the citizens believed and hoped it would.

[125]*Central Record,* 25 May 1899, 1.

[126]*Central Record,* 6 July 1899, 1.

[127]*Central Record,* 13 July 1899, 1.

[128]*Central Record,* 27 July 1899, 1.

[129]*Central Record,* 31 August 1899, 1.

[130]*Central Record,* 2 November 1899, 1.

[131]*Central Record,* 16 November 1899, 1.

[132]*Central Record,* 16 November 1899, 1.

[133]*Central Record,* 23 November 1899, 1.

[134]*Central Record,* 23 November 1899, 1.

[135]*Central Record,* 14 December 1899, 1.

[136]*Central Record,* 1 November 1900, 1.

[137]*Central Record,* 21 March 1901, 1

[138]*Central Record,* 6 September 1900, 1.

[139]*Central Record,* 28 November 1901, 1

[140]*Central Record,* January 1900, 1.

[141]*Central Record,* 8 February 1900, 1.

[142]*Central Record,* 1 November 1900, 1.

[143]*Central Record,* January 1900, 1.

[144]*Central Record,* April 1897, 1.

JACOB GUTH IN MONTROSE: A TOWN BAND IN CENTRAL PENNSYLVANIA, 1888-1897

Kenneth Kreitner

In late March or early April 1889 Jacob Guth, a traveling cornetist, music teacher, and band director around northeastern and central Pennsylvania, arrived in the small town of Montrose to work with its newly formed town band. He stayed until August, teaching the players their instruments, directing the band, and playing the cornet himself, and then he moved on to the next town and the next band.

There is nothing unusual about this story; it must have been repeated thousands of times, by hundreds of musicians, in late nineteenth-century America, when the amateur-band tradition was at its height. What makes these months in Montrose stand out is something that happened, or rather failed to happen, in the following years: For one reason or another the band's founder, leader, and solo cornetist, a certain George M. Noll, did not throw his music away. Six of Noll's partbooks, at least three of them dating from the Guth era, survived to be acquired by Margaret and Robert Hazen in the early 1980s. In 1986 the Hazens donated their collection to the Smithsonian Institution,[1] where I came across them while, coincidentally, I was in residence studying the town bands of the next county over.[2]

The Montrose partbooks contain almost two hundred pieces of music: they represent, to the best of my knowledge, the largest surviving repertory of any American town band of their period. They are solo and first B-flat cornet parts, which means that even if they do not allow a complete reconstruction of the full scores, they at least give us the tunes. (There is nothing more dispiriting than an isolated second E-flat alto book.) And perhaps most intriguing of all, the contents of the Montrose books are mostly handwritten and unpublished. A substantial proportion of the compositions and arrangements they contain seem to be local products; and indeed, forty-nine pieces, a quarter of the total, are attributed to Guth himself. The stories of the Montrose band, and Jacob Guth, and these months in the spring and summer of 1889, convey to us information otherwise inaccessible not only about rural Pennsylvania, but about the music of all small-town America in the last decades of the nineteenth century.

Montrose is the county seat of Susquehanna County in northeastern Pennsylvania, about fifty miles north of Scranton and forty miles south of Binghamton, New York. In 1890 its population was 1,735 and that of the county as a whole was about 40,000.[3] Montrose has never had any significant industrial development, depending instead on county government and on its function as a market town for the surrounding dairy farms. In the 1890s it was a prosperous and vigorous establishment: It had two railroads of its own, two newspapers, a village improvement society, the beginnings of a public library, and even a Philharmonic Orchestra (in 1892 consisting of first violin, clarinet, first and second cornets, trombone, and double bass).[4]

In nineteenth-century America a population of 1,735 was "awkward" culturally—which is to say, large and culturally strong enough for people to want and expect a town band, but not quite large enough to keep one going with ease. Montrose may have had bands of some sort as early as the 1830s,[5] and probably had them off and on in the succeeding decades. By the late 1880s, however, the town seems to have been going through a musical drought. On 21 December 1888, the *Montrose Democrat* reported that the band of nearby Tunkhannock expected to attend the inaugural of Benjamin Harrison and added snidely that "The Montrose band will not be there, or any where else. There is'nt [*sic*] any such band."[6]

In fact there probably was. Ten days later the other local paper, the *Montrose Independent Republican,* reported that "The members of the new cornet band meet for rehearsal in rooms over the *Sentinel* printing office."[7] By early February the ensemble was reportedly up to twenty members;[8] and on 8 April it announced its intentions and its progress in the paper:

THE NEW BAND

The band recently organized in this place is progressing very rapidly under the efficient and thorough instruction of Prof. Jacob Guth, of Lock Haven. The Professor evidently understands his business, and it is to be hoped that he will return to this place in the fall after completing his engagement at Lock Haven, as is now his intention.

The band, which promises to be one of the best organizations of its kind in the county, consists of seventeen members as follows.

Geo. M. Noll, Leader, solo B flat [*sic*] cornet.
A.C. Uptegrove, solo B flat cornet.
J.T. Smith, E flat cornet.
I.D. Hawley, 1st B flat cornet.
Ira Calph, 2nd B flat cornet.
P.R. Noble, 3rd B flat cornet.
Geo. P. Ross, B flat clarionet.
W.C. Reynolds, baritone.
Perry Calph, solo alto.
Al. Rice, 1st alto.
Verne Frink, 2nd alto.
L.R. Herrick, 1st tenor.
W.W. Nash, 2nd tenor.
J.F. Harrington, E flat bass.
Frank Herrick, E flat bass.
Ambrose Payne, bass drum.
Bert Decker, snare drum.[9]

By early spring, then, the two main characters in our drama—George M. Noll, "Leader" of the band and solo cornetist, and Jacob Guth, visiting instructor—were on stage, and the ensemble itself was already a nicely balanced "reed band" (i.e., valved brasses plus clarinets and/or piccolos) of seventeen players. (The two basses in particular were a great luxury, and especially rare in newly formed and thus normally poor and insecure ensembles.)

The table below (pages 234-237) shows all the engagements I have been able to identify for the Montrose band[10] in local newspapers from 1888 to 1897. The list is quite typical of the kind of work these small-town bands found: a few annual events like Memorial Day, a firemen's parade in the fall, and the county fair, but also more spontaneous performances—outdoor concerts in summer, indoor dances and entertainments in winter, special occasions as necessary.[11]

Engagements of the Montrose Band, 1888-1897

Date	Location	Event
Dec. 1888		Band formed
30 Mar. 1889	Montrose	Plays in street.
1 Apr. 1889	Opera House	Lecture by Sam. Small.
15 Apr. 1889	Opera House	Entertainment, with Philharmonic Orchestra
15 May 1889	nr. Opera House	Open-air rehearsal.
30 May 1889	Montrose	Memorial Day.
10 Aug. 1889	Montrose	Open-air concert.
13 Aug. 1889	Montrose	O.O.F. picnic; serenade for citizens.
19 Aug. 1889	Mrs. E. Thomas's house	B.A.M.E. entertainment.
Sept. 1889	Fairgrounds	Susquehanna County Fair.
?23 Apr. 1889		Concert.
28 Aug. 1890	Fairgrounds	?Reunion encampment, 141st Pennsylvania Regt.
1-2 Oct. 1890	Fairgrounds	Susquehanna County Fair.
21 Jan. 1891	Montrose	Escorts Fire Co. #2 to reception of Co. #1.
21 Apr. 1891	Opera House	Performance of "Our American Cousin."
22 Apr. 1891	Montrose	Escorts Fire Co. #1 to reception of Co. #2.
30 May 1891	Montrose	Memorial Day.
5 June 1891	Montrose	Unspecified performance.
4 July 1891	Heart Lake	Fourth of July celebration.
24 July 1891	Montrose	Plays in streets.
24 Aug. 1891	L&M station	Meets 1st train on L&M RR.
Sept. 1891		Breaks up.
15 Dec. 1891	Skating rink	Plays for skating.
25 Dec. 1891	Skating rink	Plays for skating.
30 May 1892	Montrose	Memorial Day.
28 July 1892	Montrose	Welcomes home Co. G, N.G.P.
16-18 Aug. 1892	Fairgrounds	Susq. Co. Veterans Assn. camp.
3 Sept. 1892	by Post Off.	Plays in street.

Date	Location	Event
6 Sept. 1892	Mon't. Sq.	Opening of new school building.
10 Sept. 1892	Montrose	Open-air concert.
16 Sept. 1892	Montrose	Open-air concert.
23 Sept. 1892	Montrose	Open-air concert.
27-8 Sept. 1892	Fairgrounds	Susquehanna County Fair.
30 Sept. 1892	Montrose	Firemen's parade; plays in evening.
10 Oct. 1892	Chapel Hall	Concert?
21 Oct. 1892	Montrose	Columbus Day parade.
22? Oct. 1892	Armory	Meeting of Montrose & Bridgewater Township Republicans.
14 Nov. 1892	Montrose	Grand Democratic Jollification Meeting after election of Grover Cleveland.
18 Nov. 1892	Armory	First annual band reception.
28 Feb. 1893	Armory	Concert.
12 Apr. 1893	Armory	Concert.
27 May 1893	Montrose	Plays near establishments of D. V. Gardner and A. W. Lyons.
30 May 1893	Montrose	Memorial Day.
c28 June 1893	Montrose	"... out practicing marching "
28 June 1893	Montrose	Serenades J. B. McCollum for Fire Co. #2; other serenades.
4 July 1893	Heart Lake	Fourth of July picnic.
22-9 July 1893	Montrose	Encampment of 13th Regiment, N.G.P.
25 Aug. 1893	Montrose	Marches from G.A.R. hall to Capt. Beardsley's house & lawn festival.
13 Sept. 1893	Montrose	Firemen's parade.
26-7 Sept. 1893	Fairgrounds	Susquehanna County Fair.
15 Nov. 1893	Armory	2nd annual band reception.
31 Jan. 1894	Armory	Reception for Fire Co. #1.
6 Feb. 1894	Armory	Concert.
21 Feb. 1894	Tarbell House	Banquet for congressman-elect G. A. Grow.
16 Apr. 1894	Montrose	Open-air concert; serenade for Prof. Hawk and bride.
11 May 1894	Montrose	Open-air concert.

Date	Location	Event
22-23 May 1894	Armory	?Fire Co. #2's entertainment and trades display.
30 May 1894	Montrose	Memorial Day.
13 June 1894	Armory	Concert.
4 July 1894	South Montrose	Fourth of July celebration.
10 July 1894	Armory	Ice cream social, Fire Co. #2.
22 July 1894	South Montrose	Platform dance.
4-6 Sept. 1894	Montrose	Susquehanna Co. Veterans Organization encampment.
27 Sept. 1894	Carbondale	Parade (acc. Fire Co. #2).
5 Oct. 1894	Montrose	Firemen's parade.
30 May 1895	Montrose	Memorial Day.
4 July 1895	Heart Lake	Fourth of July celebration.
22-23 Aug. 1895	Fairgrounds	7-County Veteran Reunion.
5 Sept. 1895		Susquehanna Parade (acc. Fire Co. #1).
18 Sept. 1895	Montrose	Firemen's parade.
13 Apr. 1896	Montrose	Open-air concert.
13 May 1896	Blakeslee Bldg.	Opening, new YMCA rooms.
30 May 1896	Montrose	Memorial Day.
4 July 1896	Montrose	4th of July parade in town; celebration at fairgrounds.
19-20 Aug. 1896	Montrose	Susquehanna Co. Veterans Assoc. reunion: proc. from M.R.R. depot for Dept. Commander, then to fairgrounds.
15 Sept. 1896	Montrose	Firemen's parade.
c25 Sept. 1896	Montrose	Visit of J. Wanamaker for Repub. Party: torchlight parade, mtg. at Armory.
29-30 Sept. 1896	Fairgrounds	Susquehanna County Fair.
30 Apr. 1897		"Band! Dis-Band!! New Band!!!"
29 May 1897	Montrose	Memorial Day.
21 June 1897	Montrose	Parade advertising celebration, 3 July.
26 June 1897	Public Avenue	Open-air concert.
3 July 1897	Montrose	Fourth of July celebration.

Date	Location	Event
15 Sept. 1897	Owego	Parade (acc. Rescue Hook & Ladder Company).
6 Oct. 1897	Fairgrounds	Susquehanna County Fair.
6 Oct. 1897	Armory	Hop.

Note: South Montrose, Heart Lake, Susquehanna are all in Susquehanna County, Pennsylvania. Carbondale is in Lackawanna County. Owego is in Tioga County, New York.

After Guth's departure, the band had at least one other professional instructor: Professor T. G. R. Hawk, who served (at least part of each year) from 1892 to 1894.[12] The band itself broke up at least twice, in 1891 and 1897; but on the whole it managed to stay together, more on than off, as a conspicuous part of its community for at least eight years and probably more. In short, there is nothing in this ensemble's instrumentation or its known history to suggest that it was anything but a completely typical small-town amateur band of the late nineteenth century.

In early 1889, when Guth arrived in Montrose to work with this ensemble, he was nearly seventy years old; the census returns for 1900 state that he was born in Germany in 1820.[13] Apparently he learned his craft "over there"; according to a much later account, he was "band master in the Prussian Army before coming to America."[14] The date and details of Guth's immigration are not yet known, but at least by the 1880s he seems to have gained a reputation as a traveling band instructor around northern and central Pennsylvania.

At some point, possibly by the mid-1880s, Guth must have been working with the band of Milesburg, a village (1880 population 643)[15] in Centre County, near State College. Milesburg had a band at least in 1887,[16] and the titles of three pieces in the Montrose partbooks seem to allude to that area. "J. G. Uzzel's Quickstep" (No. 31/100 in the inventory; see Appendix 1, pages 264-267), for example, was named for John G. Uzzle, a hotel keeper (which probably means saloon keeper) in nearby Snow Shoe township.[17] "Moose Run Quickstep" (No. 71/98, Appendix 1; see page 247 below) was probably named for the stream that runs through Milesburg. And "Post No. 261 Quickstep" (No. 69, Appendix 1) immortalizes Dr. Geo. L. Potter Post No. 261, Grand Army of the Republic, whose headquarters were in Milesburg.[18] It was here, most likely, that Guth met George Noll. We know from the documents quoted earlier that, just before he moved to Montrose, Guth was instructing the band at Lock Haven (1890 population 7,358), in north-central Pennsylvania. At least one piece from the partbooks, attributed to "Miller of Lock Haven," doubtless entered Guth's repertory there.[19]

The circumstances of the composer's arrival in Montrose can be guessed at without much difficulty. In the spring of 1889 Noll was thirty-one years old, a painter and plasterer, probably newly moved into town and possibly newly or about-to-be-wed.[20] Noll had come from the Milesburg-Bellefonte area[21] and, if the parts in the partbooks are any indication, was already a competent cornetist. Presumably he had worked with Jacob Guth and a band in Centre County. As a recently arrived and skilled musician, Noll was probably the founder of the Montrose band and acted as its first instructor; few of his young men would have known how to play a musical instrument before the band was formed. On 25 March 1889, the *Republican* reported that "The members of the new cornet band, under the instruction of Geo. M. Noll, have made commendable progress in the art of music." And after the band found its feet, Noll must have convinced them that they could use professional help, and suggested his old acquaintance Guth.

On 15 March the *Democrat* reported that "the band boys of Montrose expect to secure an instructor soon—Prof. Guth, of Lock Haven. That's enterprise."[22] Guth was in town by 5 April, when the same paper said, "They are doing wonderfully well, and their instructor, Prof. Guth, who is here for two or three weeks for the purpose of training them, seems to be very proficient as a tutor."[23] And on 15 April the results of Guth's labors were unveiled:

The Band Concert

We are pleased to report the success of the band concert given at the opera house on Monday evening last.

The programme consisted entirely of instrumental selections, which were executed in a manner creditable indeed to the members comprising the organization and their efficient instructor, Prof. Guth, of Lock Haven.

Mr. Guth favored the audience with a number of cornet solos, which were a pleasing feature of the entertainment, and showed the performer to be well up in his profession as a musician.

The excellent music rendered by Philharmonic Orchestra was enjoyed and highly complimented.

Montrose has long needed a first-class band and is not lacking in the requisite musical talent to fill the bill, and now that our town has given birth to such an organization with no bad symptoms and bidding fair to become a healthy and robust child, it is gratifying to know that our citizens are manifesting a disposition to accord hearty and liberal support.

The receipts of the concert and festival were $82.02.[24]

Writing about the same event, the *Democrat* reports the gate as sixty dollars and quotes the professor as saying, apparently in a little speech, that the Montrose boys "tried the hardest too [*sic*] learn of any similar organization he had ever met, and spoke of them as fine young men, with the best of habits."[25] (Note the omission, perhaps tactful, of any mention of their musical accomplishments to date.)

Mention of cornet solos by Guth is of particular interest partly because we have no other evidence that he was an active performer (though it would seem inevitable, and the cornet would be the clear instrument of choice), and partly because the partbooks contain a composition (No. 103/133, Appendix 1) entitled "Es ist nicht gut daß der Mensch allein," with a splendid cornet solo (see page 254), dated 11 April—i.e., four days earlier—was surely meant as a gesture of friendship or thanks. The piece may also have been a wedding present: The title is taken from the Lutheran marriage service, and as we have seen, Noll may have been married around this time.[26] Possibly it was played by Guth at this concert, possibly by Noll himself—at any rate, it got bound into in the partbooks and was presumably meant to be played by Noll after Guth left.

Meanwhile, "two or three weeks" turned into several months: The last we hear of Guth's presence in town is from the *Democrat* of 16 August 1889:

On Tuesday evening the Montrose Band, with Prof. Guth, serenaded
some of the leading citizens. The Professor was appreciated and the
boys gratified by genial hospitality, hearty hand-shakes, and cash
nearly sufficient to pay Prof. Guth's expenses while he was here.

This sounds like a valedictory, and the professor then disappears
from the papers.

Where Guth went after Montrose is not known—possibly
Lock Haven, where (as we have seen) he was supposed to have
had obligations. But Guth soon took an important step upward. He
next surfaces in Scranton, the largest city of the area (with a
population of 75,215 in 1890), where he is listed as a musician
and/or music teacher in various city directories from 1891 to
1898 and again in 1902, and where "Guth's band" was listed
commercially from 1894 to 1899. (In 1897 and 1898, August
Miller is given as the "leader" of this band.[27]) Guth is located by
the 1900 census as living in Pittston, a smaller town (population
12,556) just south of Scranton.[28] The last reference I have yet
found is a newspaper article from Honesdale on 23 July 1902,
when the octogenarian bandmaster was making a musical tour of
the area with a small ensemble.[29] Apparently, then, in the early
1890s Guth established a professional or semiprofessional band
under his own name, retiring around 1897—by which time the
band was evidently well enough known to make his name a box-
office draw even after the leadership of his ensemble had changed.
Why he came out of retirement in 1902 is not known, but the
article suggests that his tour may have been motivated by general
hard times in the anthracite region because of the great coal strike
that had begun in May and would not end till presidential
intervention in October.[30]

It would be good to know more about the Scranton years.
Modern research on American bands from this period has so far
focused on small-town amateur bands (like the Montrose band)
and big touring professional organizations (like Sousa's); but the
territory in between—the local urban professional band—remains
all but unexplored.[31] Presumably there were a great many such
ensembles; some of them must have been impressive and locally
influential. That the story of Guth's band in particular might be
especially interesting is suggested by the one glimpse of it that has

come to light: On 17 June 1893, the *Montrose Independent Republican* reported that

> Jacob Guth, leader of Guth's band, Scranton, was arrested at that place on Tuesday charged with aggrevated [*sic*] assault and battery. Guth's band had furnished music at a picnic the previous Sunday, at which a free fight occurred. On their return the band was followed by a drunken ruffian by the name of Gilbride, who brandished a knife and attacked them. Some of the musicians, fearing for their own safety, attacked Gilbride with their music racks, gave him a severe pounding, and hence the arrest. Mr. Guth was formerly instructor of the Montrose band.

For our purposes, however, all this would be only a distraction. The Jacob Guth who arrived in Montrose in spring 1889 was not yet a locally famous bandleader nor, presumably, a felon. He was a musical figure of a kind that was common and clearly influential in his own day, though forgotten in ours: the itinerant bandmaster and music teacher, traveling from town to town to help amateur bands for a few weeks or months by teaching their members to play, by running rehearsals, and by copying out music for them to play and keep.

The Montrose partbooks are made from commercially available partbook kits, with which players could assemble a small pile of march-sized music (on the order of 5-1/2 inches tall by 7 inches wide) and lace it together with cardboard-and-oilcloth covers. Eighty-two folios of music, most with music on both sides, are bound in this way, and twenty-eight more (including at least a few, like two bassoon parts that clearly do not belong) are inserted without having been bound. Such a system allowed players to unlace their books, edit their contents, and reassemble them as their bands' repertories shifted—not between performances but perhaps, say, once or twice a season. The Montrose books show signs of such reshuffling: Quite a few pieces are given handwritten numbers, but no coherent numbering system survives intact. As a result, it is impossible to know just when the partbooks attained their present form. But a summary of their salient features, with a hypothesis about the date and provenance of each book, may be found in Appendix 2 (see pages 268-269).

The partbooks contain a total of 198 musical items, most of them complete solo or first B-flat cornet parts to entire pieces. There are also a few fragments of pieces, scales, bugle calls, and the like. Almost two-thirds of the contents (and the majority of the bound folios by far) are handwritten, in a variety of hands. A number of place names and dates from the late 1880s and early 1890s are written in, and the printed pages represent a variety of publishers and copyright dates ranging from 1872 to 1910. There are, in other words, a million stories here, but none perhaps more interesting to us than the one suggested by the forty-nine pieces attributed to Jacob Guth himself. These may also be found in Appendix 2, which is extracted from my inventory of the partbooks as a whole.

A quick glance over the titles and genres (usually presented as part of the title, as was the custom) will give a general idea of what manner of music this is. Almost half of the pieces are identifiable as members of the march family (quicksteps, marches, and dirges), and the rest are about evenly divided between dances (polkas, waltzes, schottisches, etc.) and "concert pieces" (medleys, overtures, themes with variations, etc.).[32] Nineteen of the forty-nine are listed in the books as arrangements; insofar as I can tell, however, this distinction is almost completely meaningless; the lines between "arrangement," "original composition," and "plagiarism" were, as we shall see, rather vague. Indeed, "Dessauer March" (No. 36/92, Appendix 1; see the top of page 248) is called an arrangement in Book II, but not in Book I (where it is anonymous, suggesting that a large number of otherwise-unattributed compositions in the partbooks may be largely Guth's work as well). All forty-nine pieces are handwritten, and all are found in Books I, II, and III; the other three volumes may postdate Guth's visit.

A good many of Guth's pieces seem to be named after people, places, and institutions; the titles of "Moose Run Quickstep," "J. G. Uzzel's Quickstep," and "Post No. 261 Quickstep" all refer to Milesburg and environs. To that list may now be added "Dessauer March," named for M. S. Dessauer, a Montrose clothing merchant who was having a spectacular twenty-fifth anniversary sale in the spring of 1889,[33] and "Es ist nicht gut daß der Mensch allein"—which, as I have also mentioned, is dated "Montrose, April 11th, 1889," in Book II and seems to be a soloistic gift for George Noll. (A fourth possibility, at least remotely, is "Marching Down to George," whose title, if not a misspelling, might be a pun. If so, the inclusion of "Little Brown Jug" among its melodies may represent further biographical information about the plasterer-cornetist.) At any rate, a dozen examples, including the two pieces provably written in Montrose, will perhaps suffice to show the music's quality and character in more specific terms.

"Philadelphia Quickstep" will serve as representative of Guth's quicksteps. It appears here in a legible and beautiful handwriting, the best in the partbooks and probably the composer's own; note "Quickstepp" and "von" as signs that the scribe was a native speaker of German; several other pieces in this hand, including another copy of "Philadelphia," are labeled "Solo B Cornet" (see below):

More puzzling are all the fingerings: It is hard to imagine the
cornetist who could play this piece, with its leaps and high G's,
and still have to have fingerings written under every single note—
but there they are. Possibly the fingerings were written out for a
rural player in a town formerly without a band, who had thus
learned a transposition or never learned to read music at all
(though such a description would rule out Noll). Conceivably,
especially if this piece was several decades old, its fingerings might
have been written out for a keyed-bugle player who had only
recently taken up the valved cornet.[34] There are several pieces in
the partbooks with fingerings, again all in this same handwriting,
and it is currently impossible to assign a date to any of them.

The classic form of the American march—"The Stars and
Stripes Forever," for example—consists of two preliminary
melodies in the tonic, a trio (usually the famous tune) in the
subdominant, and two bits of transitional material: an introduction
at the beginning and a "dogfight" between repetitions of the trio.
Something like this:

|| Introduction ||: 1st Strain :||: 2nd Strain :||(soft) Trio || Dogfight ||: (loud) Trio :||

This form, so ubiquitous today, seems not to have been quite
standardized until later, especially with the works of Sousa.[35]
"Philadelphia" thus shows a simplification of the archetype: The
first strain is not set off from the introduction by a double bar, so
it is a bit unclear where the first repeat, if any, goes back to; there
is no dogfight; and the trio is presented just twice, without a soft
version, thus:

|| Introduction - 1st Strain :||: 2nd Strain :||: Trio :||

The piece starts out a bit predictably, but it does have a few
features of interest: the mock bugle call at the beginning of the
second strain, for example, and the rather subtle echoing of the
endings of the second strain and trio. If not the best march in the
world, it is also nowhere near the worst.

"Philadelphia" (see page 243) is made up entirely of original,
if cliché-ridden, material, and most of Guth's quicksteps and
marches are similar in content and style. In a few pieces, however,
Guth mixes familiar tunes in with his own: For example, "Long

Ago Quickstep" (see below) incorporates T. H. Bayly's old song "Long, Long Ago" into the trio of a quickstep, writing new tunes for the first and second strain but naming the piece after the part the audience would recognize:[36]

There are a number of cases like this; see the Remarks column in Appendix 1 for tunes I have been able to identify.

Perhaps the most curious is "Fruden Quickstep" (see page 246), which matter of factly incorporates "Bringing in the Sheaves," verse and refrain both, as a third strain before the trio. "Fruden" is also distinguished by a thematic relationship between the first strain and trio, by the Scotch-snap rhythms of the trio, and by the trio's length and ambition (note also the pompous mock-classical ending):

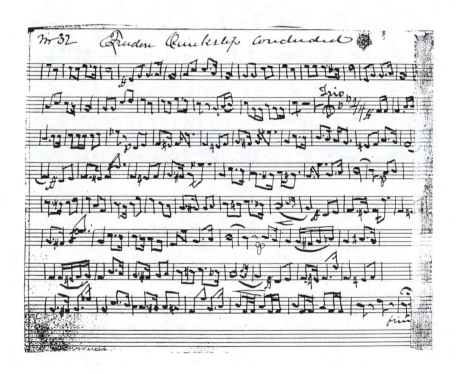

Guth's marches and quicksteps often (as in "Fruden") extend the traditional three-strain form. In the Milesburg-era "Moose Run Quickstep" (see below), here misspelled, he adds fourth and fifth strains—actually a setting of J. P. Webster's "The Sweet By and By":[37]

For a less inspiring specimen, though significant because, as we have seen, it seems to have been written while Guth was in Montrose: "Dessauer March" is short and very dull indeed; perhaps the Professor wrote it in a hurry or under duress (see the top of page 248).

Guth's twelve dances include three polkas, three waltzes, two schottisches, two reels, a galop, and a gavotte. Dances may be less conspicuous than marches in our popular image of the nineteenth-century town band today, but they were well represented there in fact:

fact: a number of the engagements of the Montrose band (see pages 234-237) are listed as dances, and still more must have actually included them. Indeed, Book IV, which has no works by Guth, consists only of dances and was probably intended for use at such events. The concert programs of bands of this time universally intersperse dances in among the marches and concert pieces without any apparent expectation that the audience would actually dance.[38]

The "Lager Polka" (see the bottom of page 248) is a typical polka. Its form is clearly derived from the march: Like "Moose Run Quickstep," it has two strains in the tonic followed by a subdominant trio (so labeled in the manuscript), a fourth strain thrown in for good measure, and a pompous coda (with an *ossia* cornet part suggestive of cornetist unable to negotiate the high G's reliably). But the dynamics, rhythms, and melodic textures immediately identify to the ear that the "Lager Polka" is a polka even if it looks to the eye like a march. It is a pleasant bit of fluff, rather demanding to play, lively and vigorous, exactly as we might expect.

"Elisen Schottisch" (see below) is in five sections:

After a plagiaristic andante introduction, the actual schottisch begins, presumably with an increase in tempo. This is even more like the classic march form, with a trio and even a dogfight. "County Waltz" (see the top of page 250) is typical of Guth's waltzes, containing not one waltz melody but four; it also uses a

variant of what I have called—perhaps a bit too glibly—the
march form, with a modulation to the subdominant and even the
marking "Trio." The melodic tritone in the first strain is a
curiosity, especially since the B's become A's in the partbooks'
other version (No. 15) of this piece; but which is correct cannot
today be determined.

Among the "concert pieces"—works of a style and form
suitable not for the parade ground or dance floor, but for a regular
sit-down concert situation[39]—medleys are the most numerous and
in some ways the most intriguing. Medleys take their life and
meaning, of course, from audience recognition of their tunes; and
with that in mind it seems odd that I recognize so few of the tunes
in Guth's medleys. A reasonable specimen is the aptly named
"Potpourri" (see page 251):

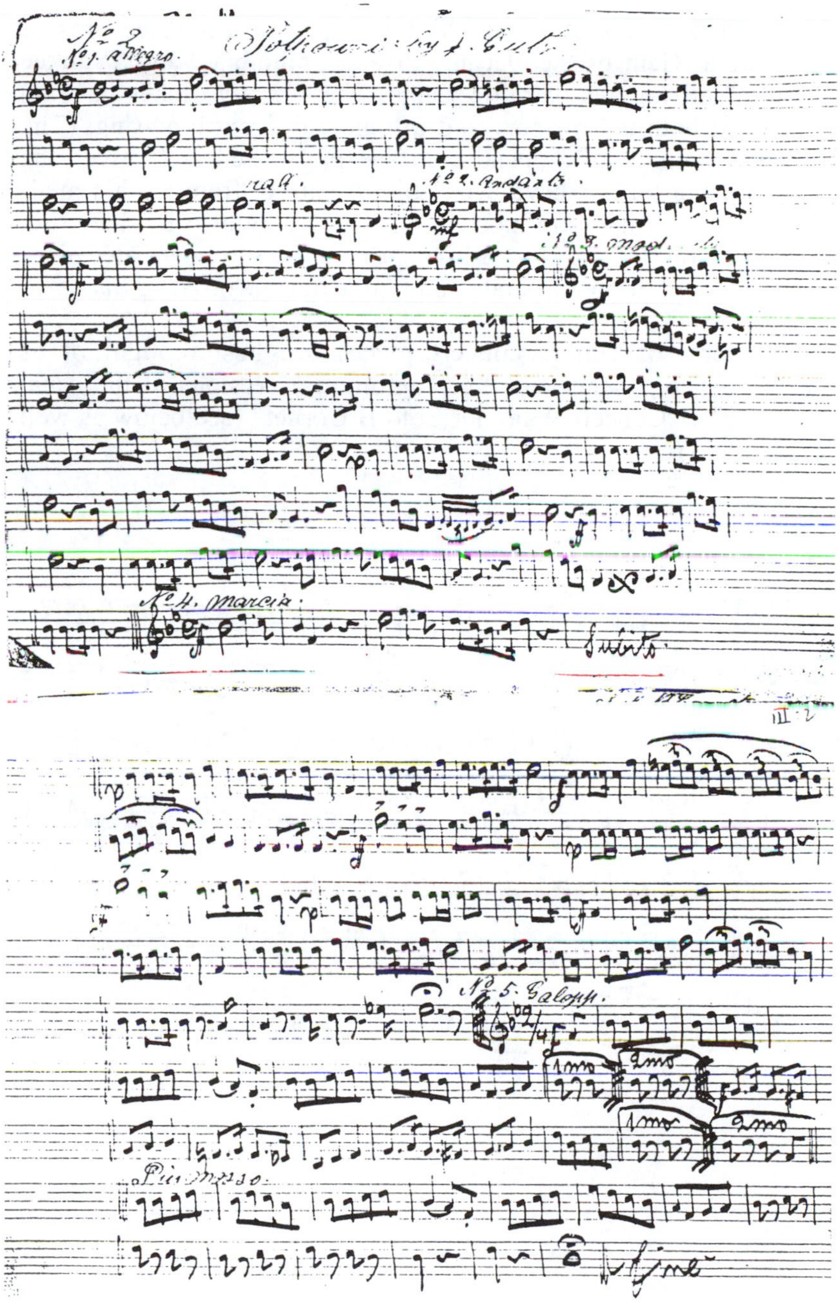
No. 2
No. 1. Allegro
rall.
No. 2. Andante
No. 4. Marcia
Subito
III · 2
No. 5. Galopp
1mo
2mo
1mo
2mo
Piu mosso
Fine

Of the five sections of "Potpourri," the last three present "Columbia, Gem of the Ocean," "Hail, Columbia," and "Yankee Doodle," all famous patriotic songs. The first two tunes have so far eluded both my memory and my most diligent browsing. (The Remarks column of Appendix 1 (see pages 264-267) gives the names of the tunes I have been able to extract from Guth's medleys; no doubt there are more. Even so, it may also be that Guth used the term "medley" in a less specific way to mean any piece sewn together from disparate tunes but not an obvious dance or march.)

Several of Guth's concert pieces are best thought of as "concert" (i.e., longer and more ambitious) versions of the usual dances. The "Concert Waltz for Solo B Cornet" (see below as well as page 253):

Cornu½ Waltz continued

Cornu½ Waltz concluded

The "Concert Waltz" strings together seven separate waltz melodies to cover almost two and a half pages in the manuscript. Others seem to combine genres: "When the Leaves Begin to Turn," for example, starts out in 2/4 time, perhaps as a sentimental song; then and at the bottom of the first page it too turns into a series of waltzes—again with a key change and a "Trio." The first waltz is to my ear one of Guth's most attractive melodies; indeed, I have noticed in general that his waltzes are the tunes that I find myself humming in odd hours of the day.

Finally, the beginning of the solo cornet part to Guth's most remarkable composition, the concert polka entitled "Es ist nicht gut daß der Mensch allein" (see below):

This is the only piece in the partbooks with a title page, in the hand that I identify as Guth's own. The music begins with a virtuosic cornet solo, followed by a concert polka with two melodies, one in the tonic and the other (as usual, marked "Trio") in the subdominant. Perhaps significantly, this piece looks more difficult to play than it is; actually, for all the spectacle, it is not particularly difficult to pull off. But it must have caused quite a sensation in a town that had not even had a band six months before.

It would be dangerous and wrong to judge a composer from only the cornet parts to twelve (or forty-nine) compositions—and especially pieces written for players who were all amateurs and mostly beginners. Unless more of his works come to light, however, it may be permissible to say, in the gentlest possible way, that the music preserved in the Montrose partbooks gives us little cause to proclaim Guth the long-awaited American Orpheus.

Insofar as they can be reconstructed or imagined from their cornet parts, Guth's compositions for band seem at best to be competent, workmanlike essays within some traditionally very stereotyped genres. In pieces like "County Waltz" (see the top of page 250) he shows an ear for a pretty tune; in "Es ist nicht gut" he shows the craft of making one's best players look good; in pieces like "Long Ago Quickstep" and "Fruden Quickstep" (see pages 245-246) he seems to show a degree of wit—it must have been good for a laugh when the band, in the middle of a march, suddenly broke into "Bringing in the Sheaves," and Guth must have known it. On the other hand, the presence of pieces like "Dessauer March" (see page 248) in the books suggests—assuming for now that we are not missing something important, like perhaps a spectacular baritone part—that he was also capable of allowing some perfect drivel to appear under his name. Mostly, this is music without much individual profile: nicely crafted and pleasant, well suited to its masculine, wholesome role in small-town life, and typical of the amateur-band repertory as I understand it.

Jacob Guth's contribution to music history, therefore, may be not so much his achievement as an individual composer as his performance in a professional role, the importance of which to

American music may have been seriously underestimated. For almost a century, from before the Mexican War to after World War I, the amateur town band was arguably the most influential musical institution in the United States: There were thousands of these bands in towns and even the smallest villages all over the country, and for most of the people in those towns the band was the biggest, most prestigious, most spectacular music they ever heard. And the existence of these bands raises a difficult question: Where did all these people learn to play?

Band instruments were not taught in school, and in a village without a band there was little impetus for a child to learn, say, the E-flat bass. Typically small-town and village bands were founded by someone who played a brass instrument reasonably well and then moved to town, discovered that there was no band, rallied support for the idea among the local young men, supervised the purchase of instruments, and began teaching the members to play. In neighboring Wayne County, for example, the Equinunk band was started in 1896 by the new Methodist preacher,[40] and in Montrose the key figure seems to have been George Noll. As anyone who has run one knows, everything about the survival of a musical ensemble, from the continued financial and moral support of the audience to the attendance of the musicians at rehearsals, depends on the quality of the performance. In such a fragile economy, the itinerant bandmaster of post–Civil War America made his living and left his mark: Those bands that were lucky or enterprising enough to hire an instructor[41] found their level of playing, and thus their reputation and chance of survival, greatly increased.

"Prof. Guth ... has been instructor of some of the best bands in northeastern Pennsylvania," says a newspaper report from 1902,[42] implying that the band "instructor" was a profession familiar in the area. Note also that Guth is not called a director or conductor, even though by that time he might reasonably have been expected to be more famous as the leader of the band under his own name in Scranton. Apparently, then, even after the rise and (apparent) fall of Guth's band, the professor was still best known for his work with amateur groups around the state. His itinerary has not yet been fully explored—we know only of Milesburg, Lock Haven, Montrose, and Scranton—but the nature of the job seems reasonably clear just from what we know about his time in Montrose. Guth came to town, I believe, on the recommendation of Noll, who had known him in previous years in Centre County; he arrived from Lock Haven, about a hundred miles away, where he had been working with another band. He came with a cornet of his own and, evidently, a trunk full of band music; he intended to spend a couple of weeks in Montrose, but ended up staying about five months. He is given much credit in the newspapers for the progress of the Montrose band under his tutelage. At the end, he was paid and moved on—as, one presumes, had happened dozens of times during a career of many decades.

For our purposes, of course, it is that trunk of music that is most important. In its day, of course, it was not the sort of thing to have been mentioned in the papers, or to have been photographed (even if any photographs had been taken of its owner) or, afterward, to have been talked about by anyone. But the collection that trunk once contained and the nature of its contents are verified by the existence of Montrose Books I, II, and III.

These three books are almost entirely handwritten, partly in the hand I have identified as Guth's own and partly in other hands (one of them doubtless Noll's), and they contain not only an abundance of compositions by Guth himself, presumably spanning his entire career as a band musician, but at least a few and probably quite a few, like the piece attributed to "Miller of Lock Haven," that he picked up from others along the way. Some may also have been copied by hand from printed parts in the professor's collection, though this is at present impossible to prove.[43] In any case, it is clear that a considerable amount of music from the library of Guth's band was given to, or copied out for, the Montrose band and remained in their possession after Guth's departure. How long that music remained in the active repertory of the Montrose band is less certain: I have found only one contemporary band program, dating from 1894, and none of the pieces mentioned on it appears in any of the Montrose partbooks.[44] The six books did stay together, however, and some of them were still in use at least into the mid-1890s.

The amount of handwritten and locally originating material in the Montrose partbooks challenges some long-held assumptions about the repertories of amateur bands in nineteenth-century

America. The conventional wisdom so far has tended to divide the
amateur band movement into two periods: "before" and "after"
the Civil War. "Before" (i.e., during the 1830s) the
instrumentation of these town bands varied so wildly that it was
impractical to try to publish music to suit all their possibilities.
Only a few printed collections from this period are known, and
some of them were presented in score, so that conductors could
write out their own parts to suit their personnel and
instrumentation.[45] At that time, then, bands must have relied on
their leadership for a great deal of their music, and the music must
therefore have had a distinctly local character.

"After," as the band movement became vastly more popular
and its instrumentation more standardized, a substantial publishing
industry developed to supply repertory nationwide. By 1881, for
example, the catalogue of the Lyon & Healy Co., instrument
dealers and manufacturers of Chicago, offered more than five
hundred selections, in parts for full brass and reed bands[46]—and
this was just one catalogue, and in a year somewhat before the
band movement reached its peak. This publishing industry, the
conventional wisdom runs, naturally tended to supplant the local
homemade arrangements, improving on them in many cases to be
sure, but also homogenizing them, making the local arranger
practically extinct, and giving the band tradition as a whole a
uniform but bland repertory, without the local color and vigor
that we so much value in the traditions of American vernacular
music.

If the Montrose partbooks are typical of the genuine
repertories of these town bands (and I see nothing in the record to
suggest otherwise), store-bought music may not have been as
important or widespread as we thought. To judge from what has
survived, the Montrose band must have had a repertory, and thus
a musical personality, quite separate from those of the bands of
neighboring communities; and the flavor of that repertory and
that musical personality must have been very largely the work of
Jacob Guth. To the people of Montrose, the professor was
probably the most distinguished musician (possibly the only full-
time professional musician) they had ever met, and at least for a
time he must have been the author, whether they knew it or not,
of a fair fraction of the music they heard. And multiplied by
thousands of towns like Montrose, for we all have Jacob Guths in

our musical past, and not many generations back, the influence of the itinerant bandmaster over the music, and the musical taste, of America has been incalculable.

Montrose today is only a bit bigger than it was in 1889. It is the kind of town that makes it easy on the historian—the kind of town where the shady back streets have hardly changed at all in a hundred years, and where the slow evolution of the main street has left the outlines of the original clear. Walking up Public Avenue toward the white Greek-revival courthouse, it is the easiest thing in the world to imagine the Montrose band marching down the other way, on its way to the cemetery for Memorial Day, or setting up folding chairs in Monument Square, alongside the courthouse, for an open-air concert on a warm summer evening. The walls of Montrose are walls against which "Philadelphia Quickstep" would echo comfortably even now. Behind them, today, the people of Montrose have forgotten Jacob Guth's name and his music, and what they owe him. Their great-grandparents had not forgotten, however, and neither should we.[47]

University of Memphis

---

[1] See Margaret Hindle Hazen, *Register of the Hazen Collection of Band Photographs and Ephemera ca. 1818-1931* (Washington, D.C.: Archives Center, National Museum of American History, Smithsonian Institution, 1990), 121; the books are numbered as Series 2, Sub-Series 3, box 15, folders 5, 6, and 7. I am grateful to Margaret and Robert Hazen, the former owners of the partbooks, for giving me free access to this collection at the time of its acquisition by the NMAH, and for their cooperation and support ever since.

[2] This study of bands in Honesdale and Wayne County, Pennsylvania, eventually became Kenneth Kreitner, *Discoursing Sweet Music: Town Bands and Community Life in Turn-of-the-Century Pennsylvania* (Urbana: University of Illinois Press, 1990); the Montrose partbooks are discussed briefly on pp. 156-57.

[3]Except as noted, all population figures are from *Report on Population of the United States at the Eleventh Census: 1890* (Washington, D.C.: Government Printing Office, 1895), Vol. I, pt. 1, pp. 288-305.

[4]*Montrose Independent Republican,* 8 October 1892.

[5]This much we know from an article by W. H. Ham (b. 1835) entitled "Honesdale Fifty Years Ago," published in the (Honesdale) *Wayne County Herald* on 15 February 1900. Reporting on Honesdale's first bands, probably in the early to mid-1840s, Ham says that "We believe that the first instruments in use here, came from Montrose and Dundaff, much older towns." See Kreitner, 22-24.

[6]The *Montrose Democrat,* 21 December 1888.

[7]*Montrose Independent Republican,* 31 December 1889 [*recte* 1888].

[8]*Montrose Independent Republican,* 4 February 1889.

[9]*Montrose Independent Republican,* 8 April 1889.

[10]Town band names at this point seem to have been rather informal: The partbooks are stamped "Montrose Cornet Band," and this name does frequently appear in the newspapers, and for awhile in 1897 the papers call them the "Keystone Cornet Band." For convenience, I have adopted the usual nineteenth-century convention (also well represented in the Montrose papers) of using the town name plus "band," with a lowercase b. See Kreitner, 74-75, n. 1.

[11]As a comparison, see the similar tables for Wayne County bands between 1897 and 1901 in Kreitner, 28, 47, 59. 87, 95, 101, 110, 111, and 116.

[12]*Montrose Independent Republican,* 25 June 1892 and following issues; 11 February 1893 and following issues; and 16 June 1894.

[13]1900 U. S. census returns for Pittston, Pennsylvania.

[14]*Wayne Independent* (Honesdale), 23 July 1902: "On Thursday and Friday last Prof. Guth and a few of his band artists, of Scranton, gave Honesdale some good music. Prof. Guth was band master in the Prussian Army before coming to America. He has been instructor of some of the best bands in northeastern Pennsylvania. The [coal] strike has rather shut off band business for excursions from Scranton so he and a few of his players started out last week on a starring trip."

[15]*Statistics on the Population of the United States at the Tenth Census (June 1, 1880)* (Washington, D.C.: Government Printing Office, 1883), Vol. 1, p. 309.

[16]*Bellefonte Republican* of 9 June 1887 reports that the Milesburg band participated in that year's Memorial Day celebrations at Milesburg; Guth is not mentioned. Another clue, though ambiguous, is provided at the bottom

of Book 1, page 18v, where "J. G. Uzzels Quickstep," a Milesburg piece (see next note), seems to be annotated "I.O.O.F. hall / 2-26-84." If this means 26 February 1884 (or, as the handwriting might indicate, "8/26/84," or 26 August 1884), that would place Guth in Milesburg in 1884.

[17] *Eleventh census of the population of the United States, published by boroughs and townships, in connection with a business directory of the same, for advertising purposes, with the addition of marginal blanks and sufficient blank pages to record changes of residence, births, and deaths in the different enumerated districts* (Bellefonte, PA: [James A. Fiedler], 1890). Uzzle's family is listed under Snow Shoe township.

[18] *Proceedings of the 34th Annual Encampment of the Department of Pennsylvania, Grand Army of the Republic, at Gettysburg, June 6-7, 1900* ([Harrisburg?]: Wm. Stanley Ray, State Printer of Pennsylvania, 1900), 103.

[19] Book I, f. 32^v; the piece is untitled.

[20] The 1900 U. S. census returns, Montrose, Pennsylvania, have him born in August 1857 in Pennsylvania, living with his wife and mother-in-law. According to the *Montrose Democrat* of 15 March 1889, Noll was at that point moving from rooms vacated in someone's house (suggesting that he had been a temporary boarder, i.e., newly arrived). No wife is mentioned at that point; the first we hear of Mrs. Noll is in the *Democrat* of 2 August 1889. Mrs. Noll was originally from Montrose, however, for in 1892 the couple, just returned from a year "near Pittsburgh" (possibly back in Centre County, which from Montrose's perspective might well be so described), were living in Montrose with her parents (*Montrose Independent Republican*, 5 November 1892). My hypothesis is that he arrived in town in, say, 1888; took some rooms; became engaged in the spring (or was engaged to a local girl before he came?) and moved into larger quarters in March; and married in the spring. Indeed, the *Democrat* of 7 June 1889 reports the band giving him a gold watch "in appreciation of his services," possibly on the occasion of a June wedding.

[21] See Appendix 2 (pp. 268-269) for inscriptions in partbooks I and III showing that Noll used them in Milesburg. *Eleventh census* ... lists a great many Nolls around Bellefonte, including at least four Georges. The *Montrose Democrat* of 2 August 1889 mentioned that a "Mr. and Mrs. Noll, of Bellefonte, Pa.," presumably George's parents, were visiting; and the same paper (7 November 1890 and 23 January 1891) reported that the Montrose Nolls were spending the winter in Bellefonte. Milesburg and Bellefonte are only a few miles apart.

[22] *Montrose Democrat,* 15 March 1889.

[23] *Montrose Democrat,* 5 April 1889.

[24] *Montrose Independent Republican,* 22 April 1889.

[25]*Montrose Democrat,* 19 April 1889.

[26]A contemporary American version of the Lutheran marriage service is found in *Auszug aus der Kirschen-Agende für Evangelisch-Lutherische Gemeinden* (St. Louis: Lutherischer Concordia-Verlag, 1890), 27-31. The phrase "Es ist nicht gut daß der Mensch allein sei" (from Genesis 2:18) is found on p. 28. On Noll's marriage, see note 20 above.

[27]*Williams' Scranton Directory* (Scranton: Williams, 1887-1894, 1904-1905); *Taylor's Scranton City Directory* (Scranton: Taylor, 1895-1900); *R. L. Polk & Co.'s Scranton Directory* (Scranton: Polk, 1904-1905).

[28]See note 13 above. Pittston's population is given in *Census Reports, Volume I: Twelfth Census of the United States, Taken in the Year 1900: Population, Part I* (Washington, D.C.: United States Census Office, 1901), 342.

[29]See note 14 above.

[30]The story of the anthracite strike is told in a number of places. For a succinct, if not exactly partial, contemporary account, see John A. Howland, *Triumphs of the Roosevelt Administration* (Chicago: Republican Publishing Co., 1904), 45-60.

[31]For a fascinating start, see the brief biography of Fred L. Grambs of Birmingham (and, coincidentally, Scranton) in Hazen and Hazen, *The Music Men,* 27-29.

[32]For comparison, see Kreitner, 152-55 and 158-60.

[33]*Montrose Democrat,* 29 March 1889. Advertisements for this sale ran for many weeks thereafter.

[34]On the replacement of keyed bugles by cornets in the 1850s and 1860s, see Hazen and Hazen, 40, 116, and elsewhere.

[35]For a recent exposition of this topic (among others), see Frank Byrne, "Sousa Marches: Principles for Historically Informed Performance," in *The Wind Ensemble and Its Repertoire: Essays on the Fortieth Anniversary of the Eastman Wind Ensemble,* ed. Frank J. Cipolla and Donald Hunsberger, (Rochester: University of Rochester Press, 1994), 141-67.

[36]On the popularity of this song (written in the 1830s) in Guth's time, see Richard Jackson, *Popular Songs of Nineteenth-Century America* (New York: Dover, 1976), 274.

[37]See Jackson, 281. Note that, as in "Fruden," Guth uses the whole song, not just the most familiar parts.

[38]See Kreitner, especially 153-55.

[39]For a contemporary usage of this term in the next county, see Kreitner, 160.

[40]Kreitner, 80-94.

[41]This was, incidentally, by no means universal. In Wayne County I found no band that actually hired a professional instructor between 1897 and 1901, but plenty of evidence that it was considered a possibility—claims by the newspaper, for example, that this or that band's homegrown leader was better than they could have hired for hundreds of dollars. See Kreitner, 135-136.

[42]See note 14 above.

[43]One tentative possibility, however: Book VI contains two printed pieces, "Bertie Waltz" and "Andante and Schottische: Home Treasures," by Jos. H. Feehrer, both published by Brophy Brothers of Philadelphia and undated; and Book I contains four handwritten pieces apparently by the same composer: "Dirge" is attributed to "Feehrer" and dated 1885, "Rally Q. S. [Quickstep]" is attributed to "J. H. Feehrer" and undated, and "Andante and Waltz" and "Superb Q. S." are attributed to "J. H. F." and dated "11.30.85" and "Dec. 1st, 1885" respectively. This may mean (a) that Feehrer was a local composer, like "Miller of Lock Haven," from whom Guth got some music in 1885 and who later got a few pieces published in Philadelphia; or (b) that Guth had a number of Feehrer prints in his possession and copied four out for the Montrose band (in which case the dates may be dates of performance by an earlier band).

[44]*Montrose Independent Republican,* 10 February 1894.

[45]For an excellent bibliography of surviving prints and manuscripts from this period (and after), see Frank J. Cipolla, "Annotated Guide for the Study and Performance of Nineteenth Century Band Music in the United States," *Journal of Band Research* 14/1 (Fall 1978): 22-40. A number of sources have of course been found since Cipolla's article (including the Montrose partbooks), but as a guide to the early material it is still to my knowledge unsurpassed.

[46]Lyon and Healy [Co.], *Band Instruments, Uniforms, Trimmings, &c.* (Chicago: Lyon & Healy, 1881), 12-22 (music section).

[47]Portions of this paper, in different form, were read at the 16th Annual Conference of the Sonneck Society (Toronto, April 1990).

APPENDIX 1

Guth Compositions in the Montrose Partbooks

Inv. no: numbers extracted from my larger inventory of the partbooks as a whole (but duplicated pieces consolidated for clarity).

Folios: the partbooks are unnumbered and unfoliated; see Appendix 1 for explanation.

Titles: punctuation and capitalization have been normalized; spellings given as they appear in original.

Remarks: "Arrangement" means piece listed as arrangement in ms.; part-names given here when provided in ms.; otherwise, solo B-flat cornet may be assumed from labels on covers.

Inv. No.	Folios	Title	Remarks
1	I:1-1^v	Ride Galop	Arrangement.
3	I:2-2^v	When the leaves begin to turn	Arrangement.
5 97	I:3^v II:5	Philadelphia Quickstepp	
6	I:4-5	When the leaves begin to fade	Arrangement; word "fade" written over "turn," ff. 4v, 5.
7	I:5^v	Ann Eliza March	
9	I:6^v-7	American National Potpourri	Arrangement; 6 numbered sections; incorporates "America" (s. 6).
10	I:7-7^v	Fruden Quickstep	Arrangement; incorporates "Bringing in the Sheaves"
11	I:8-8^v	Secret Love Gavotte	
14	I:10	Luxumburg Polka	

Inv. No.	Folios	Title	Remarks
15 23	I:10$^\text{v}$ II:15	County Waltz	
27 130	I:16-16$^\text{v}$ III:1$^\text{v}$-2	Potpourri Potpourri	5 numbered sections; incorporates "Columbia, Gem of the Ocean" (s. 3); "Hail, Columbia (s. 4); "Yankee Doodle" (s. 5).
29	I:17$^\text{v}$-18	Republican Quickstep	Arrangement.
31 100	I:18v II:6v	J. G. Uzzel's Quickstep John Uzzel's Quickstepp	Marginal note in #31: "I.O.O.F. Hall 2-26-24" [=1884?].
34	I:20	Eliza Waltz	
36 92	I:20$^\text{v}$ II:2$^\text{v}$	Dessauer March	#36 not attributed; #92 listed as an arrangement.
37	I:20$^\text{v}$-21$^\text{v}$	Concert Waltz for Solo B Cornet	7 numbered sections.
39	I:22$^\text{v}$-23	Theme with Variations by Hosleck	Arrangement; theme + 3 variations
64	I:34	Sussannen—Waltzer	
65	I:34$^\text{v}$	St. Paul's Polka	
66	I:35	Kunes Quickstep	
68 99	I:36 II:6	Moores Quickstep	
69	I:36v	Post No. 261 Quickstep	Arrangement.

Inv. No.	Folios	Title	Remarks
71 98	I:37^v II:5^v	Moose Run Quickstep Mosse Run Quickstep	Incorporates "The Sweet By and By."
73	I:38^v	Schottische	Also incorporated in #137 below.
75	I:39-40	Comic Song Selections	Arrangements; 6 numbered sections; incorporates "The Oak & the Ash" (s. 5).
79	I:B-B^v	Goodbye My Lover Goodbye Quickstep	Incorporates "Goodbye, My Lover, Goodbye" as trio.
90	II:1	Marching Down to George: Quickstepp	Arrangement; "Solo B Cornet"; incor- porates "Little Brown Jug," "Marching through Georgia."
91	II:1^v-2	Medley Overture	8 numbered sections; incorporates "The Campbells are Coming" (s. 5).
93	II:2^v	Reel	
95	II:3	Chorale	
101	II:7	Quickstepp	Half folio; "Solo B Cornet.

Inv. No.	Folios	Title	Remarks
103 133	II:8-10 III:3-4	Es ist nicht gut daß der Mensch allein: Concert Polka	#103: f. 8 is a title page; dated "Montrose, April 11th, 1889"; "Solo B Cornet"; #133 is 1st cornet part to same.
129	III:1	Listen to the Mocking-Bird: March	Setting of "Listen to the Mockingbird."
131	III:2^v	Gen'l Boulanger's March	Arrangement.
132	III:3	Grand March	"Solo B Cornet."
134	III:4^v	Salt River Quickstepp	
137	III:6	Elisen Schottische	Arrangement; "Solo B Cornet"; incorporates "Old Folks at Home" & #73 above.
130	III:6^v-7	Arie aus dem Wahnsinnigen von Donizetti	Arrangement.
139	III:7^v	Lager Polka	Arrangement.
140	III:8	Parade Quickstepp	Arrangement.
141	III:8^v-9	Sacred Overture	Titles listed: Trovatore; The Music of Heaven; Arise co[me] over Jordan; To Arms to Arms Ye Soldiers; Christ Is All.
142	III:9^v	Farewell Quickstepp	Arrangement.

APPENDIX 2

Summary Descriptions of the Montrose Partbooks

No.*	Description	Conclusions
I	First piece, "Ride Galop." Made from Wm. Reichert's Improved and Unequaled Band and Orchestra Folios (Philadelphia; advertising text contains patent date 1884). 40 bound folios, 5 unbound. All handwritten. 88 pieces (or fragments of pieces) total, 32 attributed to Guth (2 on unbound folios), incl. "Dessauer March" from Montrose period. "G.M. Noll / Milesburg — —Centre Co. Pa." hand-written inside front cover; bound folios contain dates 2-26-24 [=1884?], 11.30.85, Dec. 1st 1885.	Partbook kit, and much of repertory, probably belonged to Noll in 1885 in Milesburg, but repertory at least added to in Montrose.
II	First piece, "Marching Down to George" [*sic*]. Made from kit by unknown manufacturer (ads for various band apparatus, pasted over with bugle call and tempo chart). 19 bound folios (9 pp. printed), 7 unbound folios (7 pp. printed, 4 pp. handwritten. 40 pieces total (incl. some scales), 13 attributed to Guth (all on bound folios). "Geo. M. Noll / Milesburg / Centre Co. / Pa." handwritten inside front cover. Bound handwritten folios (Piece "Es ist nicht gut") contain date Montrose, April 11, 1889, also "Dessauer March" from Montrose period; bound prints contain copyright date 1887; bound portion occasionally stamped "Montrose Cornet Band. 1890"; unbound prints contain copyright dates 1888, 1890; unbound mss. contain date Feb. 20, 1891.	Bound portions used by Noll in Montrose band 1889-1890 at least.

No.*	Description	Conclusions
V	First piece "Harlequin." Covers from Fales Folio (Foxboro, Mass.). 3 unbound folios, all printed. 6 pieces, none by Guth. All copyright dates mutilated or missing. One page stamped "Geo. M. Noll"; back cover handwritten "O.R. Cook / Montrose / Cornet Band / 1894."	Partbook at one point did not belong to Noll, but at least one piece did. Otis Cook Leader of Montrose band in 1895 (see *Republican,* 7 September 1895) Motley collection; may not have all belonged together. Book (though not necessarily contents) in use by Montrose band, 1894. No music by Guth.
VI	First piece "Our Leader." Made from Fales' Band Folio ([Foxboro?]). 6 bound folios, all printed. 12 pieces, none by Guth. Copyright dates 1892-1896. Inside front cover handwritten "Montrose Band"; inside back cover handwritten (?) "Mar. 1st 93."	Book used by Montrose band from 1893, but added to later. No explicit association with Noll, no music by Guth.

*The partbooks are unnumbered and unfoliated; for convenience I indicate individual volumes with fictitious roman numerals and have foliated my photocopy in a way that should be easy to reconstruct (arabic numerals for bound folios, uppercase letters for unbound, in the order in which I found them in 1986).

WHEN CAIRO MET MAIN STREET: LITTLE EGYPT, SALOME DANCERS, AND THE WORLD'S FAIRS OF 1893 AND 1904

Charles A. Kennedy

In the annals of the American stage "Little Egypt" has become the generic reference for the Oriental dancer, better known in vaudeville and burlesque circles as the cooch dancer. The dance is also known by a variety of names: the couchee-couchee, houchie-couchie, koochie koochie, or even given alternate names like hoolah-hoolah and tootsie-wootsie.[1]

As a result of her numerous incarnations, considerable confusion has been raised in various publications about where and when "Little Egypt" first appeared on the American scene. Some have pointed to the "Street of Cairo" attraction on the Midway at the Chicago World's Fair and Columbian Exposition in 1893. Others place it later at the St. Louis Fair of 1904, or earlier at the Philadelphia Centennial in 1876.

The confusion arises from the various retellings of the story in which conflations have occurred. There were two "World's Fairs" (Chicago in 1893, and Saint Louis in 1904), and both had an attraction called the "Street of Cairo." The one in St. Louis was intended to replicate the success of the Chicago Fair and boasted the presence of the "Belle Fatima" and "Little Egypt" among its dancing girls. Some writers have inadvertently added to the confusion by mistakenly referring to the Centennial Exposition held in Philadelphia in 1876, or the St. Louis "Universal Exposition" of 1904 as "the Columbian Exposition." To see how the confusion arose, a little background is necessary.

The first Oriental dancers on record in America arrived for the Philadelphia Centennial in 1876, where a dancing group (three men musicians and two women dancers) performed in the Turkish Theater. After the Centennial closed, the act moved to the theater at Eleventh and Wood Streets in Philadelphia. Douglas Gilbert credits them with presenting the first "hootchy-kootchy" act in America:

> The women wore short skirts, and a silken band bound their breasts. Their feet, in fact the rest of their bodies, were bare.... Although the dance was sensationally sexual, it was received with apathy. The can-can, with the girls kicking high in ruffled drawers ... was considered far more risqué." The show folded as quickly as the proverbial Arab tents.[2]

When the Chicago World's Fair was organized, plans were made for a Midway Plaisance that would combine entertainment and edification for the delectation of the visitors. The mile-long strip was laid out in the fashion still familiar to us at Disney World or Busch Gardens.[3] Sections were designated for various countries, and "villages" were constructed in the architectural styles of those countries, featuring displays, shops, and restaurants.

The layout of the Midway, however, was far from the haphazard arrangements associated with county fairs and traveling carnivals. Allen describes the arrangements as follows:

> Officially, the Midway operated under the auspices of the exposition's Department of Ethnology, and it was planned as part of an ambitious project to introduce the science of anthropology to the American public and to bring together anthropological artifacts and data that might form the core of a great museum collection.... It is both ironic and appropriate that the cooch dance, the immediate forerunner of the striptease, should enter burlesque by way of an attempt to popularize the new science of anthropology.[4]

The "village" exhibits were arranged according to a Darwinian scheme that located the most primitive examples (Dahomey and the American Indians) farthest from the White City. The semi-civilized societies (the Middle East and Asia) came next, and the Teutonic and Celtic entries were constructed nearest the White City as the pinnacle of evolutionary development.[5]

In the middle of the Midway, across from that new marvel of engineering, the ferris wheel, stood the Cairo Street. In spite of the notoriety given to the dancing girls at the time and subsequently, the camel rides received almost as much attention in the guidebooks:

> A Street in Cairo has become a conventional adjunct of universal Expositions, but the Chicago concession was declared by competent judges to be the best of its kind that has been so far gotten together. The success of this entertainment was largely due to the characteristics of Western people, who seemingly look upon a ride on the back of a camel with favor, and certainly the same people love to see the mount [i.e., the camels rising].... On these tall beasts, ladies with their male admirers would seat themselves, and when the camel got up, there was joy in Cairo. It was the most hilarious place on the Midway.... Why this should have become such an attraction is not known; but because there were always a swain and lass together, and because the lass always repented when it was too late, the altitudinous camel was rising in sixteen parts, the dense crowd at the square would go into convulsions of merriment.[6]

For an extra fee of ten cents, visitors could go into a reproduction of the Temple of Luxor at the western end of the Street. Replicas of the mummies of Tutmose III, Sesostris, Seti I, and "a dozen others of the most important people who have yet lived on earth" were displayed. Periodically inside the Temple, a procession was staged with musicians, and "two priests of Isis, draped with leopard skins, stood erect in position, and the solemn Egyptian chants, such as Verdi has imitated in the opera of 'Aida,' were sung." For all of this wealth of Nilotic culture, the conclusion was somewhat ruefully drawn that "Egyptologists are not as plentiful as people who think they want to ride on a camel, and it was the other end of Cairo Street that was always crowded."[7]

For most historians, the reason for the crowds at the other end of the Street had nothing to do with camel rides and everything to do with dancing girls, of whom there was no shortage on the Midway. The Egyptian Theater ran a continuous performance from 10 A.M. to 10 P.M., and there were also dancing troupes at the Persian, Turkish, and Algerian Theaters. The dance itself, as described in the souvenir book *Gems of the World's Fair and Midway Plaisance,* was

> a suggestively lascivious contorting of the abdominal muscles, which is extremely ungraceful and almost shockingly disgusting. Curiosity prompted many to view the performance, but very few remained more than five minutes before this was fully satisfied. Only one girl danced at a time, but others were in reserve, so that as one retired another promptly succeeded her, thus making the performance continuous throughout the day and evening.[8]

The racist and sexist bias of the organizers is apparent in the descriptions found in the several photographic albums from the fair. The dancing girls did not get any better reviews than their dancing style. The description under a photograph of three of the women from the Egyptian Theater reads in part:

> Writers of Oriental stories have created the impression among the uninformed that houris of the East are sylph-like and beautiful; but close contact reveals them as we behold them here, destitute of animation, formless as badly-stuffed animals, as homely as owls, and graceless as stall-fed bovines. [Having said this, the author tempers his remarks with a back-handed compliment:] But truth compels us to add that the dancing girls in the Midway were not the best types of their race either in form or character, and that their abdominal muscles were the only portions of their anatomy or mind which showed any cultivation, while these, to their shame, were displayed to serve the basest uses.[9]

Sol Bloom, the impresario, press agent, and later congressman, brought a Syrian troupe from the Paris Exposition of 1889 to perform at the Algerian Theater, and it is he who is widely credited with dubbing his star performer "Little Egypt." But, in his own words, "I most emphatically deny that I had anything to do with a female entertainer known professionally as 'Little Egypt.' At no time during the Chicago Fair did this character appear on the Midway. She was later introduced at Coney Island and there and elsewhere she acquired great renown for her actual or reputed stage appearances in the nude."[10] Nonetheless the theatrical tradition lives on. Sobel says that her real name was Fahreda Mahzar, that she came from Damascus, not Cairo, and she did a dance with a lit candelabra on her head. According to Sobel,[11] "Little Egypt" single-handedly saved the Chicago Fair from bankruptcy, but, alas, this is the stuff of theatrical legends, not history.

American audiences in their enthusiasm to see the dancing did not distinguish between the Cairene, Algerian, Turkish or Persian performers and hence the confusion among later writers as to where the one-and-only genuine "Little Egypt" really performed. In the description of the Algerian Theater, *The Dream City* portfolio reports:

> [The] troop [*sic*] arrived on the 25th of April, 1893, and it was not long before nearly all the leading clubs of the city had seen the pretty Nautch girls.... The oriental dances, as performed here, were in no sense disorderly or vulgar, for the dancer scarcely lifted her feet from the floor, and her long flowing skirts were fastened about her ankles. The music which accompanied the dance was peculiarly weird to Western ears.[12]

The reference to Nautch girls in the Algerian Theater may explain why Joe Laurie Jr. in his recollections about vaudeville referred to a Nautch Theater as the venue of "Little Egypt" at the fair.[13]

One dancing girl did get her name on the marquee: Belle Baya, at the Persian Palace, was billed as "the greatest Oriental star, the prize beauty of the Paris Exposition of 1889." The other dancing girls, the guidebook noted, were "nothing more or less than young women of Paris, educated in the *cafés chantants* of that pleasure-seeking city.... The original idea of the Persian Palace [to demonstrate Persian wares and crafts] was laudable. The development which made the place profitable and popular was instructive only in deplorable things."[14] In another photo,[15] a dancer in the theater at the Street of Cairo is identified as coming from Madame Roza's Cafe Chantant in Paris.

There are mixed motivations at work in these descriptions of the dancers: by connecting the girls with Paris, the naughtiness of their performances can be suggested to attract the men and at the same time the negative "oriental" features (such as ascribed to the

Cairo Street women) could be offset with the not-so-subtle hints that the dancers were really French, not Arabic. Certainly, the frequently reproduced Culver Service photos of "Little Egypt"[16] are in sharp contrast to those of the Egyptian dancers shown in the souvenir albums: the theatricality in the pose of the former (her arms raised above her head holding a scarf, weight all concentrated on the right leg and hip with the left foot forward to the side, flesh-tight-midriff accentuated by the bolero fringe above and the low-tied skirt below) contrasts sharply with the ethnographic frontality of the Oriental dancers in the Columbian Exposition albums. One suspects the Culver Service photos, similar to one in the Museum of the City of New York, represent a dancer from New York, who, like the girl in the song, "never saw the Streets of Cairo."

Along the Midway in 1893 other and more obvious sensibilities had to be considered. "No ordinary Western woman looked on one of these performances with anything but horror, and at one time it was a matter of serious debate in the councils of the Exposition whether the customs of Cairo should be faithfully reproduced, or the morals of the public faithfully protected."[17] As far as the organizers of the Midway were concerned, the cloak of anthropological respectability was used to protect the morals of the public and insure the profits of the theater managers.

> The allure of the exotic women and their slithery dance had one other formidable barrier to surmount, the music that grated on Western ears. Notwithstanding the indignation of the Board of Lady Managers, the *danse du ventre* proceeded, and though thousands went to see it, they did not go often, for the music was too irritating....[18] The music which will accompany this performance will be of a most monotonous character, the drums, particularly, hurting the ordinary ear with their increasing sharp beats.[19]

Bloom claimed credit for the famous cooch music phrase that became synonymous with belly dancing, but this is disputed. The infamous undulating minor key sequence has been traced back to eighteenth-century French copies of an Algerian melody.[20] Certainly, the Chicago Fair was forever linked to the theme through a vaudeville song, "The Streets of Cairo," that satirized the show from the Midway. The verses repeat the cooch theme, while the chorus changes to a more familiar music hall style.[21]

Streets Of Cairo
James Thornton; © Frank Harding, 1895

I will sing you a song and it won't be very long,
'Bout a maiden sweet, and she never would be wrong.
Ev'ryone said she was pretty,
She was not long in the city,
All alone, oh, what a pity,
Poor little maid.

[Chorus]: She never saw the streets of Cairo,
On the Midway she had never strayed,
She never saw the kutchy-kutchy,
Poor little country maid.

She went out one night, Did this innocent divine,
With a nice young man Who invited her to dine.
Now he's sorry that he met her,
And he never will forget her,
In the future he'll know better,
Poor little maid.

(Chorus repeat): She was engaged As a picture for to pose,
To appear each night In abbreviated clothes.
All the dudes were in a flurry,
For to catch her they did hurry,
One who caught her now is sorry,
Poor little maid.

[Final Chorus]: She was much fairer far than Trilby,
Lots of more men sorry will be,
If they don't try to keep away from this
Poor little country maid.

Other extrapolations of Oriental music quickly appeared. In 1895 alone, in addition to the Streets of Cairo already mentioned, *Hoolah! Hoolah!* as well as the *Dance of the Midway*, the *Coochi-Coochi Polka, Danse du Ventre, Kutchi Kutchi*, and *Kutchy Kutchy* all were published. There was even a *Cairo Street Waltz* "dedicated to the managers of Cairo Street."

One song needs to be singled out from this group of post-fair exploitations because it may explain the origin of the term "hoochie coochie" from a source heretofore overlooked.

In 1898 Gussie H. Davis introduced a song, "When I Do the Hoochy Coochy in the Sky." Sam Dennison in his study of African-American music classifies the composition as a "pseudo-spiritual."[22] The song is a parody of black religious experience and especially the preacher who promises a better world hereafter. One obvious question that has not been asked is why a preacher should encourage his flock with a vision of doing an Oriental dance in the sweet bye-and-bye? Such a vision is usually associated (improperly and incorrectly) with Islam, not Christianity.

The answer is to be found in a second meaning of the term "hoochy coochy." The words "hoochee koochee koochee" first appeared in the song "The Ham Fat Man" in 1863, three decades before the Chicago Fair and Little Egypt.[23] By 1890 the term was connected with the minstrel show: William T. "Biff" Hall in his theatrical memoir mentions a certain "Hoochy Coochy" Rice, so called because he "invariably says that whenever he comes on stage."[24] The popularity of Davis's song in the 1890s may be completely unrelated to the Oriental cooch craze from the Chicago Fair but rather may be an extension of the minstrel show language that the black population of that day understood.

The topicality of Davis's song, which is typical of all these songs about the cooch dance, is illustrated by the reference to using the newly discovered (1895) X-rays to "see into the dance." The connections with the Chicago Fair are apparent in the mention of the Midway and in one of the main attractions there: the hot air balloon. What is not certain is that the Oriental dance is referred to in the song. More likely this "hoochy coochy" indicates a promenade or strutting style, not the *danse du ventre*.

The song's topicality also underlines the "separate and unequal" status of African Americans in the society of the 1890s. Prevented from full participation in this world, the hope was transferred to a celebration in the next. Dennison concludes that the song "offers a nonpareil insult to the black religious impulse,"[25] but the song could also be viewed as a protest against the exclusion of African Americans from the official events of the fair.[26] If the managers of the fair were content to exclude black Americans from their great show, the African Americans knew that there would come a time and place when they would be welcome.

When I Do the Hoochy Coochy in the Sky
Gussie L. Davis © 1898

I ain't got no money and I don't need none,
'Cos I don't expect to stay here very long;
An' old colored preacher by de name of Parson Brown,
He used to sing to me dis good ole song:
Says he, "I know you coons will stare
When I fly up thro' the air,
When I bid all of you black chromos good bye;
I will raise a big sensation with the white population,
When I do the hoochy-coochy in de sky!

[Chorus]: When you feel that funny feeling,
As it over you is stealing.
You will flop your snow-white wings and try to fly;
I know the angels they will giggle,
When I do that awful wiggle,
When I do the hoochy-coochy in the sky.

They'll turn the X-rays on me when the music plays,
So dat ev'ry one can see into the dance,
I'm goin' to do the Coochy seven thousand diff'rent ways,
An' I'll knock the Midway people in a trance.
Oh, I have got a big balloon
With a seat for ev'ry coon,
So now ev'ry nig must either go or die;
Don't you listen to strange rumors,
but go buy a pair of "bloomers,"
For to do the hoochy coochy in the sky!

After the Chicago Fair closed some of the dancers went to New York and appeared at the Grand Central Palace (opening on Saturday, 3 December 1893). The dancers were billed as Stella, Zora, Ferida, and Fatima. A raid by the New York Police

Department helped to boost ticket sales. The following Monday three dancers were arrested and brought before the judge for arraignment the next day. As reported in the *New York Times*, their attorney asked one of the women to demonstrate her dance for the court. Zelika, dressed in "red silk Turkish trousers, a blue Eton jacket, trimmed with gold, and a white gauze waist drawn in tight ... wriggled and twisted, turned, cavorted, and kicked through an exhibition in which there was not the slightest sign of graceful movement." Fortunately for the theater manager, the judge admitted, "Oh, it won't harm anybody for a few days. Out in Chicago I saw it myself." When the case came to trial, the women were fined fifty dollars each for immoral conduct, but under the watchful eye of the police a version of the show continued that was so restrained that "not even a church member could take offense."[27]

Millions had come to Chicago to see the Fair in 1893. In the years that followed at carnivals and theatrical productions everywhere millions more would have the thrill of watching the cooch dancers, and this time without the pseudo-scientific anthropological veil. It was time to take it all off. At the St. Louis Fair of 1896 (not the exposition of 1904) a "World's Fair celebrity" by the name of Omeena did a "take-off," perhaps the first striptease cooch.[28] The burlesque and vaudeville circuits picked up the attraction and packed the houses.

A theater bill from the 1890s featured a second act that heralded

> a bright and spicy program always concluding with a novel Burlesque up to the times, entitled Liberty's Reception to Uncle Sam with much females.
>
> P.S. During the Burlesque there will be introduced Songs, Dances, etc., also the latest novel craze from the Columbian Exposition, entitled THE PLAISANCE DANCERS.[29]

In his history of Coney Island, Edo McCullough has "Little Egypt" arriving on Surf Avenue in 1895. He cites a barker's spiel, perhaps of his own invention, that captures the atmosphere of the event:

This way for the Streets of Cairo! One hundred and fifty Oriental beauties! The warmest spectacle on earth! Pre-sen-ting Little Egypt! See her prance, see her wriggle! See her dance the Hootchy Kootchy! Anywhere else but in the ocean breezes of Coney Island she would be consumed by her own fire! Don't rush! Don't crowd! Plenty of seats for all![30]

On the carnival circuit the craze was no less intense. Sobel re-creates another spiel from a typical carnival performance:

"Gather up closely, gentlemen, and get a surprise. See a free show!"

As the crowd assembled, the dancer would stroll out onto the platform. Her costume was always strictly Oriental: a short bolero with coin decorations, a white chemise, harem pantaloons and a wide sash. Her hair hung loose over her shoulders, an outward indication of abandon that was somewhat startling in the nineties.

Expectancy made the crowd tense, but while the perspiring barker made his oratorical spiel the lady would glance indifferently at the heavens or push aside her draperies casually in order to emphasize the intimacies of her costume.

"And now," the barker would cry, as he tapped his cane on the ticket box, "I take pleasure in introducing Little Egypt, the famous dancer who has turned this carnival into a conflagration.

"When she dances, every fiber and every tissue in her entire anatomy shakes like a jar of jelly from your grandmother's Thanksgiving dinner. Now, gentlemen, I don't say that she's hot. But I do say that she is as hot as a red hot stove on the fourth day of July in the hottest county in the state.

"Recently a prominent society woman, attired in men's clothing, came to see her, surreptitiously. The report was that she screamed for the police. That was a lie. The fact is she screamed for the ice-man. Yes, the entertainment is hot stuff! Come in and enjoy the experience of a lifetime for ten cents."[31]

By 1903 the sensation was over in New York, and the vacated "Streets of Cairo" attraction at Coney Island was replaced by the Loop-the-Loop roller coaster ride. The success of "A Street in Cairo" at the Chicago Fair, however, was not lost on the planners of the St. Louis Exposition. A new version of the Egyptian attraction was built, and visitors were assured that they could see the "Belle Fatima" and "Little Egypt" performing daily.

In the decade between the two fairs "Little Egypt" had become the generic name for an Oriental dancer. In 1904 the St. Louis Exposition would start a new generation down the byways of the "Streets of Cairo" to meet "Little Egypt."

The next phase of the Oriental dance craze owed its beginnings to the opera and the new dance theater. Ruth St. Denis claimed to have performed an interpretation of Salome's Dance of the Seven Veils in Paris in 1906,[32] but it took a Strauss opera to spark the publicity that made for good box office. Based on Oscar Wilde's poem, Strauss's *Salome* had its premiere at Dresden in 1905. The New York debut took place on 22 January 1907, with Olive Fremstad in the title role. The Dance of the Seven Veils quickly became the center of attention. The critic for the *New York Times* gave Mme. Fremstad a rave review for her

> representation of the feline sensualist and in the growth of her passion from mere curiosity to a consuming flame of desire. She presented a figure of wonderful exotic beauty, of lithe and snaky grace, with the languor and the fire of the Orient, the passion of a perverted nature. [Not to let this passion or the veils get out of control, the review goes on to note:] In her dance, after the first of the seven veils had been cast off, [Mme. Fremstad] was represented by Miss Bianca Froehlich, who carried through the rest of it in a manner conclusively Oriental, with all its appropriate posturings and shiverings and serpentine movements, now measured, now wild, frenetic.[33]

The custom of substituting a dancer for the diva after the first veil dropped continued in later productions. As the *Victor Book of the Opera* delicately remarks, "It is highly improbable that any operatic Salomé has ever been sufficiently gifted as a dancer or sufficiently shapely to delineate the psychopathic voluptuousness of Herodias's daughter."[34] Not to be overlooked, however, is the uproar the Salome's dance caused on opening night and the repercussions this might have on a diva's career. The critic for the *Times* wrote:

It was the dance that women turn away from, and many of the women in the Metropolitan Opera House last night turned away from it. Very few men in the audience seemed comfortable. They twisted in their chairs, and before it was over there were numbers of them who decided to go out to the corridors and smoke.[35]

A startling innovation in later productions occurred when the soprano actually performed the entire Dance of the Seven Veils. Mary Garden both sang and danced the role in New York and Chicago after the directors of the Metropolitan Opera had banned future productions of the opera.[36] She was such a sensation that she did a turn in vaudeville presenting her Salome dance, but she eventually returned to opera.[37]

Joe Laurie Jr. called the Salome craze the phoniest fad to hit vaudeville, but it continued to make waves on the circuits, including versions that featured female impersonators.[38] At Coney Island, New York, fifteen to twenty cooch shows might be running at any one time. At Hammerstein's theater in New York Gertrude Hoffman's Salome dance act ran for an unprecedented twenty-two weeks.

The year 1908 marked the peak of the Salome rage. Coincidentally, that was the same year one Catherine Devine, another claimant to be the original "Little Egypt," died. Several new Salome songs appeared in shows and revues in New York, but with a twist. In these songs Salome shifted from being Oriental and biblical to being black. As Irving Ziedman phrased it, "Little Egypt was followed by Little Africa."[39] This development also coincided with the latest phase in the evolution of the "coon songs" that still were very popular in the vaudeville houses.

The first question the songwriter had to face was deciding on the pronunciation of the lady's name. Was it "Sa-lo-me" to rhyme with "Dahomey" or "Sa-lome" that rhymes with "home?" Both were used, depending on the intention of the lyricist to convey a sense of culture or the lack of it.[40] Bartley Costello in 1920 solved the issue by calling his song "Sal-O-May,"[41] but in 1908 matters were more fluid. Irving Berlin tried it both ways in

The Dusky Salome.

Lyrics by
EDWARD MADDEN.

Music by
BEN M. JEROME.

The fair___ Eva - line was a rag - time queen___ with a man - - - - ner sen - ti -
One mus - i - cal coon said to - night I'll spoon___ .where the fair_____ Sa - lo - me

The beginning of "The Dusky Salome"
(Ed Madden and Benjamin M. Jerome; 1908)

the same song: "Salomy" in the first verse, but silent-e "Salome" inthe chorus. Stanley Murphy followed suit: the rhyme pattern is "Sa-lo-me"/"Dahomey" in the verse, but "home"/"Sa-lome" in the chorus. Will Cobb preferred silent-e for his "Sunburnt Salome," adding "foam" to "home" as a rhyme.[42]

The one thing the songwriters did agree on was Salome's lack of clothing. The notoriety of the Dance of the Seven Veils prepared the audience to expect this, and the lyricists were only too happy to accommodate them. The "Dusky Salome" wore "a necklace and a dreamy smile" (see the musical example on page 284). "Sunburnt Salome" was told to leave her clothes at home in Cairo and come to America, where she would "top the bill in Vaudeville." Big Bill Jefferson, the railroad man, was tired of spending his hard-earned wages on fancy clothes for his sweetheart and saw the answer in finding a black "Salome" who would be content to wear "a yard of lace and some mosquito netting on her face." The total cost for the new outfit, "about a cent."[43] As far as the staging of the Salome dance was concerned, the women remained rather well-clothed by modern standards, with flesh-colored tights preserving the integrity of the performers. It was only when the Oriental dance moved into burlesque and striptease that the costumes decreased in coverage.

The Dusky Salome
Ed Madden and Benjamin M. Jerome
© Trebuhs Publishing, 1908

[The music begins with a habeñera rhythm]

The fair Evaline was a ragtime queen
with a manner sentimental;
But she sighed for a chance at a classical dance
with a movement oriental.
When lovesick coons with ragtime tunes
sang, "Babe, you've got to show me,"
She'd answer, "Bill, you bet I will,
I'm going to dance Salome.
Oh, oh me, that'll show me, For

[Chorus (the music shifts to ragtime)]: I want a coon who can spoon to the tune of Salome.

I'll make him giggle with a brand new wiggle that'll show me;
In a truly oriental style,
With a necklace and a dreamy smile
I'll dance to the coon who can spoon to the tune of Salome.
One musical coon said tonight I'll spoon
where the fair Salome lingers.
When she danced 'round the place he just covered his face
but he looked right thro' his fingers.
He sighed "It's grand my heart and hand
I'd give to see you do it,"
She only said: "Give me your head
I'll dance Salome to it,"
I'll woo it that'll do it. For [Chorus]

Sunburnt Salome
Will D. Cobb and Gus Edwards
© Gus Edwards Music Pub. Co., 1908

In the land of Cleopatra,
Where the palm-trees take the palm,
And the pyramids appear amid the sand,
There lives a little Sphinx
I'd give a lot to label "mine,"
And when the sun retires for the night;
Beneath her window in a turban white,
I twang a bar on my guitar,
And sing to eyes that shame the evening star.

[Chorus]: Sunburnt Salome, Sunburnt Salome,
Pack your grip and take a trip,
With me across the foam;
Don't put on your shoes and stockings,
Leave your clothes at home,
And you'll top the bill in Vaudeville,
My sunburnt Salome.
It was on the streets of Cairo,
With her dark Egyptian art,
She danced herself into my open heart one day.
Her father by the Prophet swore an Oriental "nay,"
But stolen fruits are sweet they say,
And soon across the Desert sands I'll ride;

On camel, High with my sweet stolen bride,
Though Papa swear and tear his hair,
I'll plead to her my Queen, beyond compare.

I'm Going to Get Myself a Black Salome
Stanley Murphy and Ed Wynn; © M. Shapiro, 1908

Big Bill Jefferson a railroad man,
Says "I try to save but never can.
Every month I've got to buy my babe a dress,
Then the landlord hands me out a dispossess,
She's got Brinkley hats and Gibson sacks
Long straight fronts and habit backs,
I get enough remuneration, goodness knows,
But ev'ry single cent I earn she spends on clothes. So
[Chorus]: I'm going to get myself a black "Salome"
A Hootchie-Kootchie dancer from Dahomey
All that she'll wear is a yard of lace
And some mosquito netting on her face
A whole new outfit costs about a cent, And
then she can wiggle out of paying rent,
There's no use of talking, I'm tired of my home,
So I'm going to get myself a black Salome.

Big Bill took a trip to Coney Isle,
Saw a dancer dressed up in a smile,
Oriental ear-rings and a string of pearls,
Took her up to Ethiopian Hall,
To the dark town fancy ball,
She hadn't hardly started in to wiggle about,
When ev'ry colored gentlemen [*sic*] began to shout.
Oh [Chorus]

The last variation of the Salome craze featured a Jewish Salome. This was not the biblical maiden from Judea as in the Strauss opera, but a modern young woman from the East Side of New York. Fanny Brice had been winning amateur night prizes doing other people's songs and was anxious to break into vaudeville. She needed a specialty number of her own to include in her act. She bluffed her way past a producer by assuring him she had one, and then in desperation turned to a young writer in Tin Pan Alley for a new song. Irving Berlin offered her "Sadie Salome Go Home," complete with Yiddish accent: "glasses" rhymes with "dresses" in the chorus (see the illustration on page 289). But it was her performance, wriggling to stay comfortable in a starched sailor suit that kept catching her "you know where," that started her on the road to success.[44]

Sadie Salome, Go Home!
Irving Berlin and Edgar Leslie; © Ted Snyder, 1908

> Sadie Cohen left her happy home
> To become an actress lady,
> On the stage she soon became the rage.
> As the only real Salomy baby,
> When she came to town, her sweetheart Mose
> Brought for her around a pretty rose;
> But he got an awful fright
> When his Sadie came to sight.
> He stood up and yelled with all his might:
>
> [Chorus]: Don't do that dance, I tell you Sadie,
> That's not a bus'ness for a lady!
> 'Most eveybody knows
> That I'm your loving Mose,
> Oy, Oy, Oy, Oy, Where is your clothes?
> You better go and get your dresses,
> Everyone's got the op'ra glasses.
> Oy! such a sad disgrace, No one looks in your face;
> Sadie Salome, go home.
>
> From the crowd Moses yelled out loud,
> "Who put in your head such notions?
> You look sweet but jiggle with your feet.
> Who put in your back such funny motions?
> As a singer you was always fine!
> Sing to me, 'Because the world is mine!'
>
> Then the crowd began to roar,
> Sadie did a new encore,
> Mose got mad and yelled at her once more: [Chorus]

The cover illustration for "Sadie Salome, Go Home!"
(Irving Berlin and Edgar Leslie, 1908)

After 1908 the Salome craze in vaudeville was replaced by the "Venus" dancers (Zallah, the Dancing Venus, Jessie Keller, the Venus on Wheels, etc.).[45] But a decade later Salome reemerged in the costume of the flapper dancing the shimmy. What can be said about the cooch dance craze from the Chicago Fair? On the positive side it must be admitted that the performances at the Egyptian Theater and elsewhere on the Midway were authentic ethnic activities and not the satires and burlesques of music and motion that were to follow. For all the attention given the dancers, it was the male musicians who demonstrated the music of the Middle East on horns, reeds, strings, and drums. Nonetheless, then as now, the tonalities of Middle Eastern music remained mostly noise to American ears.

For the cooch dance to become the hit of the carnivals and theater houses, the accompaniment had to be transformed into Western musical forms and rhythms. Several musical conventions became stereotyped as "oriental" for immediate audience recognition. The "cooch" theme music has already been mentioned. Besides being used in the verses of "She Never Saw the Streets of Cairo," the motif also appeared in the accompaniments of other songs to lend an "Oriental touch" to the music.

The most obvious musical device was the use of the minor key in the introduction or verse, although the chorus usually shifted to a major key. The choice of rhythmic pattern depended on the number of beats needed. In four, there was the repetition of hollow-fifth drumbeats (also familiar as the "American Indian" pattern of the accented first beat followed by three unaccented beats). This could be speeded up in two using a strong downbeat followed by two quick short beats. Another variation in two was the steady alternating of the tonic and fifth with the embellishment of an accidental on the fifth. Finally, Spanish rhythms such as the habeñera were borrowed to create an exotic mood.[46]

On the negative side, "Little Egypt" and her sisters re-enforced all the bad ethnic and gender stereotypes about Middle Eastern women: they were objects and toys, things of pleasure intended for the benefit of men. An American male could accept the development of the female abdominal muscles as noteworthy; it certainly attracted crowds of paying customers at the Chicago

Fair. The public display of such accomplishments, however, was tempered by the observation that these women represented a lower social class; they could not be expected to be any better than their origins. There was no way for the American audience to know or appreciate the status of professional dancers in the Middle East or the rigorous training required of the dancers; from the American standpoint the negative associations of the undulating movements of the torso were sufficient to denigrate the performers.

For the author of *The Dream City*, the contrast between the Oriental dancer and the dancing girl in the *Hungarian Cafe Chantant* clearly demonstrated the great differences between the European and Middle Eastern women. Photos of the two were juxtaposed on the same page with these remarks: the performer of the *danse du ventre*, the reincarnation of the dancer who doomed the first New Testament martyr, is shown in

> a close and trying study of a posture-dancer in the Street of Cairo. The Western eye was but a moment in determining, at the World's Fair, that time has wrought as great a change in the dance as in the alphabet. Whereas, men began by reading from right to left, they now mostly read from left to right; and whereas, dancing began by movements of the body rather than the lower limbs, it has now developed into the Western performance. When Western officials came to gaze on her rendition of the act by which John the Baptist lost his head, they were sorely perplexed.[47]

But when one moved to the Hungarian cafe,

> The change from a study of the Cairo girl and her frightful tambours to Listz's [*sic*] music and Western beauty and grace, is the greatest that could be furnished by feminine youth. Only Darwin could expatiate impartially on these variations of taste in the human kind.[48]

After the Chicago Fair things only got worse: the *danse du ventre* degenerated into a striptease or burlesque routine. Strauss's opera had the effect of encouraging a "chic porn" evolution of Salome's dance. There is the perception that opera productions, after all, are staged for the better classes of citizens who, by virtue of their education and social position, can appreciate the nuances of Salome's troubled psyche externalized in her dance. But the performer still takes off her clothes in front of a paying audience, and so ultimately the Oriental dance is stereotyped as a striptease rather than as an art form.[49] The hundreds of Salome dancers at carnivals, and vaudeville and burlesque houses only reinforced the stereotype.

There is a danger of judging the outlook and opinions of those living even a century ago with a moral or social yardstick invented only in recent decades. The organizers of the exhibitions on the Midway were following the intellectual program of the new science of ethnology with a strong overlay of Darwinian theory. For them the mechanical and technological superiority of Europe and America was demonstrable evidence of an intellectual and moral superiority that relegated all other cultures to lower rungs of the evolutionary ladder. This judgmental attitude continues to be reinforced whenever the criteria for evaluating another society focuses on appearances and ephemeral material objects instead of comprehending the interpersonal and community relations that hold a society together.

In our own time there is the methodological confusion on the part of observers from one culture analyzing what another culture is doing in its traditions and rituals. Even the words used to describe another people's traditions are loaded with meanings that may be alien to the observed culture. To call a non-Western society "medieval" or its social system "feudal" inevitably carries the freight these terms denote in the experiences of Western Europe. Anthropologists and sociologists have become aware of these problems of field reporting, but oversimplification and not-always-glittering generalities too often remain the norms of discourse about other cultures.

Less than two months after "A Street in Cairo" closed on the Midway at the Chicago Fair, the structures were relocated to the San Francisco Midwinter Fair. Within two years another "Streets of Cairo" had opened at Coney Island in New York. Meanwhile "Little Egypt" was reinvented in vaudeville houses and carnivals from coast to coast. Over twenty-one million people attended the St. Louis Exposition and had the chance to walk yet another "Street of Cairo" and watch "Little Egypt" and her sisters in the dance. In just over ten years the "cooch" dancer had captured the popular imagination with a stereotype that has endured ever since. In our own time of image-saturation in multiplex cinemas and cable television, it must also be remembered that all of these sisters of "Little Egypt" were live performers, not celluloid or electronic images. This collective memory of watching real people in real time cannot be easily erased.[50]

Newbury, New Hampshire

---

[1]The words of the popular song "Meet Me in St. Louis, Louis" include the well-known couplet: "We will dance the Hoochee Koochee, I will be your tootsie-wootsie," referring to the attractions of the 1904 Exposition. Most people today probably assume "tootsie-wootsie" is a variant of "toots" as a term of endearment.

[2]Douglas Gilbert, *American Vaudeville, Its Life and Times* (New York: Whittlesey House/McGraw-Hill, 1940), 16.

[3]It is said that Walt Disney's father, Elias, was a carpenter at the Chicago World's Fair and he possibly told his son (b. 1901) stories about the fantasy city.

[4]Robert C. Allen, *Horrible Prettiness: Burlesque and American Culture* (Chapel Hill: North Carolina Press, 1991), 225-26. Some of the displays became part of The Field Museum of Natural History just as exhibits from the Philadelphia Centennial had been moved to the Smithsonian Institution in Washington.

[5]Allen has made a Procrustean bed out of the Midway and allowed an unfortunate typographical error to slip by. He writes that the Japanese exhibit in the Asian section featured a people who were "closest to the American heart of all the semi-civilized races" [Allen, 227]. Actually, the Japanese exhibit was next to the Irish, and so closer to the White City than Allen allows. The original quotation was in reference to the Javanese, not the Japanese. See Robert W. Rydell, *All the World's a Fair* (Chicago: University of Chicago Press, 1984), 66, quoting *Frank Leslie's Popular Monthly* 36 (October 1893): 415. For a study of the various "villages," see Gertrude M. Scott, *Village Performance: Villages at the Chicago World's Columbian Exposition, 1893* (Ph.D. diss.: New York University, 1991).

[6]"Typical Scenes in Cairo Street" in *The Dream City: A Portfolio of Photographic Views of the World's Columbian Exposition* (St. Louis: N.

D. Thompson Publishing Company, 1983). There are no page numbers in the album; pictures are identified there and here by their titles.

[7]"The Temple of Luxor" in *The Dream City*.

[8]"A Performance in the Egyptian Theatre" in *Gems*.

[9]"Three Dancing Girls from Egypt" in *Gems*. There are no page numbers in the album.

[10]Sol Bloom, *The Autobiography of Sol Bloom* (New York: Putnam, 1948).

[11]Bernard Sobel, *A Pictorial History of Burlesque* (New York: Putnam, 1956), 55ff. An earlier version of this material was published as "The Historic Hootchy Kootchy" in *Dance Magazine* 20/10 (October 1946): 13-15, 46. In 1936 Metro-Goldwyn-Mayer released *The Great Ziegfeld*, which featured a sequence set at the Chicago Fair. The story line invented a proposed romance between "Little Egypt" and Sandow the strong man. A libel suit was filed against MGM in New York by Frieda Mahzar Spyropoulos who alleged "that she was born in Cairo, Egypt, and that in 1893 ... she was chosen for the role of "Little Egypt" on the Midway." The use of her stage name and the story of a romance with Sandow, she said, "was without her consent and has injured her reputation." (*New York Times*, 5 May 1936, p. 26, col. 4) These two references, both connected with the MGM film, are the only ones linking "Little Egypt" with the Midway Plaisance at the Chicago Fair.

[12]"The Algerian Theatre" in *The Dream City*.

[13]The use of the term "nautch girls" comes from Urdu/Hindi through the British reports of professional dancers in India. Like their American cousins, the English found the music monotonous and the dancers not very pretty. See "nautch" in the OED. The dancers in the Persian Palace were also called nautch dancers in some reports.

[14]"The Persian Palace" in *The Dream City*.

[15]"Dancing Girl in the Street of Cairo Theatre" in *The Dream City*.

[16]Sobel, *Burlesque*, 56; and Ann Corio, *This Was Burlesque* (New York: Madison Square Press, 1968), 37, show the same woman in two similar poses. Edo McCullough, *Good Old Coney Island* (New York: Scribner, 1957), 255, credits a third picture from the same series to the Museum of the City of New York.

[17]"A Dance in the Street of Cairo Theatre" in *The Dream City*.

[18]"A Performer of the Danse du Ventre" in *The Dream City*.

[19]"A Dance in the Street of Cairo Theatre" in *The Dream City*.

[20]James J. Fuld, *The Book of World-Famous Music* (New York: Dover Publications, 1985), 276. He traces the original phrase back to Kradoutja, a melody of Arabic origin known in France since 1600. Since Bloom had brought an Algerian troupe to Chicago from Paris, it would not be surprising if the tune came with them. Sobel, on the other hand, cites Hans Spialek's research that traced the dance back to the Balkans, not the orient [!] and to music "founded probably on an 18th c. shepherd song" [*Dance Magazine* (October 1946): 13-14].

[21]Douglas Gilbert, *Lost Chords* (Garden City, NY: Doubleday Doran, 1942), 291, reports the enduring legend that when Will Rossiter published "She Never Saw the Streets of Cairo," he adorned the cover of the music with a photo of "Little Egypt." All of those copies were allegedly destroyed out of fear of legal action by the dancer. For many years a bounty of $500 was offered for a copy of that nonexistent first edition.

[22]Sam Dennison, *Scandalize My Name: Black Imagery in American Popular Music* (New York: Garland Publishing, 1982), 391.

[23]Fuld (see note 20).

[24]*The Turnover Club* (Chicago: Rand McNally, 1890), 75.

[25]Dennison, 391.

[26]The continuing divide between the races in American society was evident at the fair. In the United States out of a total population of 67 million, blacks accounted for eight million nationwide, yet none was invited to participate in the opening festivities. Frederick Douglass was there in his capacity as commissioner from Haiti to the exposition. He wrote, "In contemplating the inauguration ceremonies, glorious as they were, there was one thing that dimmed their glory. The occasion itself was world embracing in its idea. It spoke of human brotherhood, human welfare and human progress. It naturally implied a welcome to every possible variety of mankind. Yet, I saw, or thought I saw, an intentional slight to that part of the American population with which I am identified" [James B. Campbell. *Campbell's Illustrated History of the World's Columbian Exposition* (Chicago: N. Juul & Co., 1894), 250]. A certain degree of recognition was accorded to "the Afro-American race" on 25 August, which was designated Colored People's Day. Frederick Douglass gave a speech on "The Race Problem in America."

[27]*New York Times*, 3 December, p. 2; 5 December, p. 8; and 7 December, p. 3. The Fatma Masgish arrested in New York may have been "Fatima" from the Persian Palace on the Midway. A film of "Fatima's Dance" made in 1896, now in the Museum of Modern Art, New York, may be the same Fatima/Fatma. Cf. G. Scott, 211 and 385, n. 20. Scott concludes that if

this assumption is correct, "then Fatima of the Persian Palace would be as good a candidate for the title of Little Egypt as Fareda Mahzar."

[28]Allen, 230.

[29]Irving Zeidman, *The American Burlesque Show* (New York: Hawthorn Books, 1967), 37.

[30]McCullough, 254-56. The attraction at Coney Island was called the "Streets of Cairo," unlike "A Street in Cairo" at the Chicago Fair. This may be the origin of the confusion of "Little Egypt" appearing in the Chicago Midway attraction. Sobel, for example, incorrectly refers to the Chicago exhibition as the "Streets of Cairo" [*Dance Magazine* (October 1946): 13].

[31]Sobel, 57, 59.

[32]In her autobiography *Ruth St. Denis: An Unfinished Life* (New York: Harper & Brothers, 1939), there is no mention of a Salome dance at this time. She did perform an Indian dance, Nautch, which she and later commentators may have conflated or confused with a Salome dance. She composed a five-part dance entitled Egypta, based on pharaonic motifs (1906, U.S. premiere in 1910), and a group of dances with Ted Shawn called Arabic Suite (1914).

[33]*New York Times*, 23 January 1907, p. 9. In 1908 a Mlle. Froelich was later hooted off the stage in Yonkers when she did the Salome dance. Was this Bianca from the Metropolitan Opera House production of Salome? Abel Green and Joe Laurie Jr., *Show Biz from Vaude to Video* (Port Washington, NY: Kennikat Press, 1951), 9; Joe Laurie Jr., *Vaudeville from the Honky Tonks to the Palace* (New York: Henry Holt, 1953), 41.

[34]*The Victor Book of the Opera,* ed. Charles O'Connell (Camden, NJ: RCA Manufacturing Co., 1929, rev. 1936), 458.

[35]*New York Times*, 23 January 1907, p. 9. Henry Krehbiel, writing in the *Tribune,* said the performance "left the listeners staring at each other with starting eyeballs and wrecked nerves." The critic had a "conscience stung into righteous fury by the moral stench with which Salome fills the nostrils of humanity." See Martin Mayer, *The Met* (New York: Simon & Schuster/The Metropolitan Opera Guild, 1983), 92.

[36]Strauss referred to "the Puritans in New York, where the opera had to be taken off the repertoire at the instigation of a certain Mr. [J. Pierpont] Morgan." "Reminiscences of the First Performance of My Operas" in *Recollections and Reflections,* ed. Willi Schuh (London: Boosey and Hawkes, 1953), 152. Oscar Hammerstein presented Salome at his Manhattan Opera House two years later with Mary Garden in the title role. Salome was not presented at the Met again until 13 January 1934.

37Sobel, 215.

38*Show Biz*, 9; "It was Eva Tanguay who really busted things wide open for Salome dancers, when she discarded all seven veils." See Laurie, 41. Eventually, this would find its way back to the opera productions: in 1988 Maria Ewing finished the "Dance of the Seven Veils" in Covent Garden totally naked, "an effect common in contemporary German productions, but not previously experienced in this country" [Derrick Puffett, *Richard Strauss Salome* (New York: Cambridge University Press, 1989), 161].

39Ziedman, 43.

40The difficulty goes back to the origins of the name itself, as Derrick Puffett remarks, speaking of Jochanaan, i.e., John the Baptist, in Strauss's opera: "Any attempt to impose linguistic consistency on a work [that is] the German version of an English transliteration of a Hebrew form of the name of a character in a German opera based on a play written in French by an Irishman is probably doomed from the outset" [Puffett, *Richard Strauss*, 9].

41Music by Robert Stolz, published by Wiener-Boheme. In 1961 Jimmy Kennedy wrote new lyrics, and under a new title, "Romeo," it was recorded by Petula Clark.

42Sunburnt Salome comes from the land of Cleopatra, whose name would become a much simpler subject for the lyricists in the mid- to late teens and into the 1920s. But even the Egyptian queen has acquired at least two variations: P. G. Wodehouse's "Cleopatterer" (1917) and Alfred Bryan's Egyptian colleen[!] "Cleopatricola" (1920).

43Johnny Burke and Jimmy VanHeusen managed the same effect with greater indirection in a chorus about Salome (three syllables) in "Personality" (©1946 in *Road to Utopia*):

> And when Salome danced
> and had the boys entranced
> no doubt it must have been easy to see
> that she knew how to use her—personality.

44The story is repeated with variations in Barbara Grossman, *Funny Woman, The Life and Times of Fanny Brice* (Bloomington: Indiana University Press, 1991), 27-33; Norman Katkov, *The Fabulous Fanny. The Story of Fanny Brice* (New York: Knopf, 1953), 50-51; and Herbert G. Goldman, *Fanny Brice, The Original Funny Girl* (New York: Oxford University Press, 1992), 35-37.

45Zeidman, 61.

[46] David Burg, *Chicago's White City of 1893* (Lexington, KY: University of Kentucky Press, 1976), 220, reproduces the coverplate of "Cairo Street Waltz" published by Signor Gugliemo Ricci, Chicago, "Dedicated to the Managers of Cairo Street, World's Columbian Exposition 1893." Sobel, 57, prints the beginning of the first violin part for "'Danse du Ventre' Polka" by Tom Clark (New York: Carl Fischer, 1912), music which illustrates how the original ethnic melodies were replaced by more familiar Western musical forms.

[47] "A Performer of the Danse du Ventre" in *The Dream City*.

[48] "Dancing Girl from the Hungarian Cafe Chantant" in *The Dream City*.

[49] See note 38 for contemporary operatic nudity. Class distinctions can also appear in the opera house. The climactic scene in the Strauss opera comes when Salome holds the severed head of John the Baptist and kisses its lips. At the New York premiere pandemonium broke out:

> But when, following the lines of Wilde's play, Mme. Fremstad began to sing to the head before her, the horror of the thing started a party of men and women from the front row, and from Boxes 27 and 29 in the Golden Horseshoe two parties tumbled precipitously into the corridors and called to a waiting employe [*sic*] of the house to get their carriages.
>   But in the galleries men and women left their seats to stand so that they might look down on the prima donna as she kissed the dead lips of the head of John the Baptist. Then they sunk back in their chairs and shuddered." [*New York Times*, 23 January 1907, p. 9]

[50] The author wishes to thank the members of the Southeastern Regional Middle East and Islamic Studies Seminar, and especially Ellen Fairbanks-Bodman, for their support in this project. Special thanks are also due to the librarians Anita Haney (at Virginia Tech) and Rosemary L. Cullen (at the John Hay Library, Brown University) for their special efforts in locating materials otherwise unreported in the literature.

INVENTING TRADITION: SYMPHONY AND OPERA IN PROGRESSIVE-ERA LOS ANGELES

Catherine Parsons Smith

For most of the present century, symphony and opera have been viewed as cornerstones of America's elite cultural establishment. The two genres achieved this status via widely divergent paths with roots extending well before the Civil War; neither had held so exalted a position even at the end of Reconstruction. Each was differently affected by the economic, social and political currents of the Progressive Era, and each played a role in contemporary contests involving ethnicity, class, and gender. Each took a place in America's newly forming self-image after the turn of the century, emerging as a newly adopted emblem of an aspiring, characteristically "American" upper class. Both became parts of a new tradition, invented in the Progressive Era and accepted for several generations thereafter. This is a pair of stories about the institutionalization of two musical genres derived from nineteenth-century Western European cultural practice in the service of an American-born, white, capitalist, Protestant, English-speaking, male-dominated society, as well as for the aesthetic satisfaction of its participants.

Opera and symphony each developed slightly differently in different parts of the country. In this essay, Los Angeles will provide a case history for tracking how these two genres assumed their twentieth-century roles. Specific features of Los Angeles as a new Progressive-Era city influence the details of the story. One detail is especially convenient for an essay of limited length: a century's history of music in pre–World War I, Anglo-dominated

America was, for Los Angeles, compressed into a few decades. Only in the 1880s was the older Native American and Mexican population of the Los Angeles basin marginalized by an influx of American-born Anglos and other European Americans.

Another characteristic of Los Angeles was its geographic isolation from the rest of the United States. Until 1886, when the Santa Fe Railroad reached southern California, the city depended for overland transportation and communication with the East Coast on a spur of a Southern Pacific rail line whose inland route from San Francisco (a much larger and richer city) to Vera Cruz, Mexico, bypassed the city some sixty miles to the east. (The rail connection with Mexico had specific importance for Los Angeles's operatic history, since it meant that traveling Italian companies such as the Del Conte troupe visited Los Angeles via Mexico City rather than through New York or San Francisco.)

Los Angeles's continuously explosive growth is important to the story as well; the population soared in the Progressive Era, from 11,000 in 1880 to 100,000 in 1900 and 500,000 in 1920. The nature of its growth is also relevant. Most of the city's new citizens were American-born whites, plus a handful of African Americans who came by rail from somewhere back East. (Seaport cities like New York or San Francisco, by contrast, had a higher proportion of immigrants from other countries.) European-born immigrants were nevertheless quite numerous; 25 percent of Los Angeles's population in 1890 was foreign-born. Nor was it a stereotypical "frontier" western city with many more men than women, as San Francisco had been in Gold Rush days. There was still a significantly higher proportion of females among Los Angeles's adult population than was the case in San Francisco: 47 percent in 1890, compared to San Francisco's 39 percent.[1]

Nationwide, the population of musicians and music teachers grew much faster than the general population in the Progressive Era. Between 1880 and 1920, the census reported that musicians tended to be predominantly male, with a higher proportion of foreign-born than the general population; and that music teachers tended to be predominantly female and mostly American-born. This national trend is reflected in census figures for Los Angeles, where there were many working musicians and music teachers almost from the moment of Anglo domination. By 1910, even before full-length silent films came in, Los Angeles had the highest number of musicians and music teachers per unit population of any American city, including New York City and Boston. (The figures were also high for other far western cities such as Oakland, Portland, Seattle, and Denver.) Musical literacy—the ability to read the notes at some level—was widespread all across the population. By 1900, women outnumbered men in Los Angeles by a three-to-two margin in the census category "musicians and teachers of music." These features and others set Los Angeles apart from eastern U.S. cities that were forming elite traditions of high culture at the same time.

These population characteristics help provide a context for the city's musical life, and in some cases for American musical life across the board. They add some elements that complicate and confuse when it comes to using any sort of music—and the musicians that go with it—by one group, say, for example, older Anglo-Americans, as a societal sorting device. The main "problem" was that music-making and music teaching were so widespread that a hierarchical structure had to be cultivated (or reinforced) in order for music to be understood as an indicator of social position. The gender of the participants—male performers, female teachers—supplied one such marker.[2] Another, contradictory marker was country of origin: foreign-born for many male performers and teachers, American-born for most female teachers and performers.

Indeed, there was always some inherent contradiction in the proposition that foreign-born musicians performing repertoires of opera and symphony that were overwhelmingly European-dominated should become emblems of an elite, characteristically "American" culture. In general, musicians have been, and still are identified as the "other" in American society, a potential problem when it came to sacralizing their art. While music was considered an acceptable profession for foreign-born males, it was questionable for American-born men, who were sometimes considered effeminate if they were musicians. Women had been encouraged in the nineteenth century to study music superficially, as an "accomplishment"; by the turn of the century, many women had gone beyond this limitation to pursue careers as teachers, composers, and performers. The rather uneasy process by which the sacralization of symphony and opera took place in the context of these societal crosscurrents will be described first for opera, then for symphony.

In *Highbrow/Lowbrow: The Emergence of Cultural Hierarchy in America*, Lawrence Levine describes the changing roles of opera and Shakespeare in nineteenth-century America.[3] In the first half of the century, he points out, audiences for both opera and theater included members of all social and economic classes. Well acquainted with their Donizetti, their Verdi, and their Shakespeare, they relished even abridged and imperfect performances and participated in them immediately and noisily, even raucously. They behaved more like the audience at a sports event than like today's sedate concert audiences. Only in the latter part of the century, Levine argues, was everyman distanced from a newly sacralized Shakespeare, the audience tamed into polite submissiveness and segregated by class in different performance venues. Thus both opera and the Bard were elevated to the newly invented, elite status of "high culture," where both were pressed into service as symbols of social class distinctions. By arguing the association between "high" culture and class distinctions, Levine offers potential insight into the puzzling question of how it came about that, by the mid-twentieth century, there was such a chasm between the categories of "classical" and "popular" music.

Opera was in fact a troublesome quantity as far as its role in American life is concerned. It was introduced earlier, and was, in one form or another, as Katherine Preston describes, a very well-traveled, widely patronized form of popular entertainment in the United States before the Civil War.[4] Preston makes the points that opera in fully staged form and in staged burlesques was patronized by audiences of mixed socioeconomic rank; that operatic music dominated the repertoires of theater and dance orchestras; and that the music was widely circulated in sheet music form and was heard in concert and in the street. Such ubiquitousness tends in her view to challenge the validity of categorizing music as either "vernacular" or "cultivated" through much of the nineteenth century, even though this kind of classification is appropriate to much of the twentieth.[5] The pervasiveness of its presence and popularity across social classes was in fact the biggest problem presented by opera as a potential signifier of social stratification. While it was being sacralized for elite audiences on one hand, it continued on as a form of popular entertainment, ingrained in the popular memory well into the twentieth century. Its echoes turn up repeatedly, in unexpected places. For example, L. E. Behymer, just starting to establish himself as an impresario, wrote of the remarkable hold *Il trovatore* held on the population in small western towns as late as 1899:

> The songbirds are doing nobly tonight. Famous old *Il Trovatore*. Verdi was a wonder. That is all they want through the one-night stands. We have two casts now made up, so we can sing *Il Trovatore* every night if they want it.... In all the operas, there is nothing sweeter than the dear old "Miserere" scene in the last Act.[6]

This popularity wasn't limited to the West, and continued into the new century. Three arias from *Il trovatore* appear in a large 1909 collection of "best-loved songs" chosen by surveying magazine readership and published in Boston as *Heart Songs*. The early songs of Irving Berlin (especially before 1925) reveal the composer as a frequenter of opera; some are extended burlesques on well-known operatic scenes; recorded jazz improvisations by Louis Armstrong during the later 1920s contain melodic lines from these same Italian operas, barely recognizable in their radically new context.[7] Yet by the 1920s, opera in its fully staged form was so elitist that there were only three permanent companies in the United States, and two of these had relatively short seasons.[8]

Efforts to make opera a sacralized symbol of elite, highbrow culture did not succeed in Los Angeles for a long time; instead, it continued as a regular element of popular culture and commercial entertainment. From the 1870s on, visiting opera companies were an integral part of Los Angeles's theatrical life.[9] In 1875, when the city's population was still less than 10,000, two small troupes came from San Francisco. Sig. Marra's Grand Opera Company offered excerpts from *Don Pasquale* (Donizetti) and *Il trovatore* (Verdi); the Inez Fabbri Company offered excerpts from *Linda di Chamounix* (Donizetti), *Norma* (Bellini), *Der Freischütz* (Weber), and *La traviata* (Verdi).[10]

In 1887, a dozen years later, there was much more commercial entertainment, including more opera. The celebrated Adelina Patti, perhaps the most famous diva of the nineteenth century, and the Campanini Operatic Company each offered programs with operatic excerpts. The Bijou, Pyke, and the Emma Abbott English Opera Companies all had been well enough received to pay return visits to Los Angeles. The Abbott company, which had first visited in 1885, offered *La traviata*, *Lucretia Borgia*, *Mikado*, *Martha*, *Il trovatore*, *Mignon*, *La Somnambula*, *The Bohemian Girl*, *Faust*, *Linda di Chamonix*, *Crispino e la Comare* (Federico and Luigi Ricci, 1850), and *The Carnival of Venice*. The Carlton Opera Company came for the first time; it played *Nanon*, *Erminie*, and one other on its first visit, then added *Fra Diavolo* and *The Drum Major's Daughter* for a second run. These companies played the five-hundred-seat Grand Opera House or the somewhat larger Los Angeles Theater in their turn along with traveling minstrel shows, legerdemain artists, and other theatrical entertainments (including, from late 1894, vaudeville.) Later in the 1880s and the 1890s, the Arcaraz Spanish Grand Opera Company, the Bostonians, the Calhoun, Columbia, Del Conte, Emma Juch, Lambardi, and Salvini companies also visited. Several of them came three times or more. Their repertoire extended from Donizetti, Verdi, and Gounod to Gilbert and Sullivan and de Koven.

Since Los Angeles was small and remote and these companies were self-supporting, their productions were highly variable in scope and quality, especially in the early years. They depended on the local theater orchestras for instrumental support. Even by 1900, these orchestras were quite small, providing part-time work for no more than twenty-five musicians in all.

Four of the more specialized companies that arrived over several decades will be discussed in more detail: one with distinctly nationalist and elite aspirations; one that played to a specific ethnic population; and two with self-consciously "popular" intentions. These were the National Opera Company (1887), the Del Conte Italian Opera Company (1897), the Lambardi Company (1899 and 1906), and the Bevani Company (1910). Each offers a different perspective on the complex role played by opera in the community's cultural life.

The National Opera Company (1887)

One opera company that visited in 1887 was quite different from the others. The National Opera Company under Theodore Thomas was much larger than the usual small commercial company; it required its own train to haul its extensive costumes, scenery, large orchestra, and chorus. The company was founded by Jeannette Thurber of New York for the purpose of raising the standard of operatic performance and domesticating opera as self-consciously "American" by including Americans in the casts and singing in English. The hoped-for result was to achieve a more elite status for the genre in the United States. (Despite its lofty aspirations and extravagant size, the company was expected to pay its own expenses on the road, just as the smaller companies did.)

Having reached San Francisco, where it lost money, its managers demanded the enormous guarantee of $20,000 before it would head south for Los Angeles. (The guarantee was posted by a wealthy Los Angeles wine merchant of German extraction, Otto Weyse.) Instead of playing the small Grand Opera House, the local presenters settled on a cavernous new all-purpose auditorium. Hazard's Pavilion acquired a temporary stage and seats for between 3,500 and 4,000 people for the occasion. The venture was wildly successful, a high point in the National Opera Company's short and rather troubled career. The five promised performances were expanded to seven, including a Saturday afternoon ballet. The opera repertoire included *Lohengrin*, *Lakmé*, *Faust*, *The Merry Wives of Windsor*, *Aïda*, and *Nero*; newspaper reports suggest that only the matinée (Délibes's *Coppelia*) did not fill the house.[11] For seven performances, then, the total possible audience was between 24,500 and 28,000 people. It seems likely from newspaper reports that between 22,000 and 25,000 tickets were actually sold, in a town whose total population, age fifteen and over, was probably no more than 21,000 at the time.

Some "elite" event! While it is true that some of the audience came from neighboring towns, and that many people attended more than once, the response to the National Opera Company indicates that its visit to Los Angeles was a grand community happening rather than an exclusive event.[12] At least half the town's adult population was "elite" for the week. The newspapers made every effort to report it as a major social happening, making a fuss over the splendor of the ladies' attire and listing out-of-towners from Pasadena and elsewhere who came for the performances; they also cultivated it as a "high-class" music event. Summaries of the opera plots appeared before each performance. The *Los Angeles Times* obligingly supplied a lengthy and wonderfully Darwinian account of the history of music as it led directly to the week of opera:

> In the [National] Opera Company we find the consummation of what Jubal in the world's younger days reached toward so eagerly with untaught hand; what the Egyptian, in his pride of power and pleasure, so longed to attain; what Greece hewed the way for, and with ready ear was listening for adown the line of ages. Let us rejoice in our triumph and be glad. All the ages have been at work to give us what we now enjoy.[13]

Theodore Thomas later wrote in his scrapbook for this tour of 1887: "Travel with opera from April 10th, going to San Francisco, ended tour in Buffalo June 15th, 1887. Of all experiences in my life, this was the most trying."[14] While he may have been responding to specific problems with management and productions, the comment may also relate to the far greater complexity of changing and "improving" the taste of Americans for opera than for symphony.

The *Times* discussed the relative success of the National Opera Company in San Francisco, where it lost money, and Los Angeles, one of the few places where it prospered, in these terms:

> The [San Francisco] city papers attribute this fact to the high prices at which tickets were sold, which excluded virtually the great middle-class of well-to-do people, who, while they have enough upon which to live in comfort, have not enough to pay three and four dollars for as many hours amusement. There is doubtless something in this. These high prices result in exclusiveness, shutting out that large class in the community who are able to pay only a fair price for being entertained, but whose combined contributions would make a much better showing than the larger sums paid by the wealthy. Many people thus deprived of attending are people of musical taste and fine culture—people who would be as appreciative listeners as could be desired. It would be no loss to

any operatic company if their schedule of prices were placed within the reach of this class in every community. The time is coming when the wisdom of such a course will be more fully appreciated.[15]

In this case, we have an "elite" opera company that turned out to be, in at least one place, distinctly popular.

The Del Conte Company

A decade later, after any number of smaller companies had played Los Angeles, the Del Conte Italian Opera Company arrived in Los Angeles for two weeks of performances at the Los Angeles Theater. Circumstances had changed. The population was, of course, at least twice what it had been in 1887. The nature of entertainment had also changed. The older and smaller Grand Opera House was now the Orpheum, part of a new chain of successful vaudeville houses; Talley's modest kinetoscope parlor also drew a steady audience for one-reel silent movies. The Los Angeles Theater, where the Del Conte Company appeared, struggled to hold its former, broad-based audience in the face of this "low-end" competition. The company, whose tour was underwritten by Ricordi, the Italian publishing firm, offered five Verdi operas (*La Forza del Destino, Aïda, Rigoletto, Ernani,* and *Otello*); two by Ponchielli (*La Gioconda* and *I promessi Sposi*); the twin bill of *Cavalleria rusticana* and *I Pagliacci* (Mascagni and Leoncavallo); and the U.S. premiere of one of the most popular of all grand operas—snubbed for decades by musicologists because of its very popularity—Puccini's *La Bohème*.[16] (See the illustration reproduced on page 308.)

In this case, the company could not find an audience, probably because it lacked a label as clearly "elite" entertainment, or because the label was understood as flawed. It drew poorly, attracting neither the general, "popular" Anglo audience for theatrical events nor those who sought the "elite" label. Newspaper publicity said that the company had come by rail via Mexico City rather than from some other American city. It was said that the company chose this route because political problems made it impossible for it to play in Havana, as it had planned. The orchestra was described as "31 ... professors from the National Conservatory of the City of Mexico."[17]

LOS ANGELES THEATRE

H. C. WYATT, MANAGER.

PROGRAMME

Thursday Evening and Saturday Matinee,

First time in this city of the Sublime Opera in Four Acts, by
G. Puccini, words by G. Giacosa and L. Illse,

LA BOHEME

CAST.

Rudolfo, poet... ....Signor Giuseppe Agostini
Schaunard, musician..................Signor Luigi Francesconi
Benoit, inn keeper....................Signor Antonio Fumagali
Mimi.................................Senorita Linda Montanari
Marcello, painter.....................Signor Cesare Cioni
Coleine, philosopher..................Signor Victorio Girardi
Alcidoro, counsel of estates.........Signor Antonio Fumigali
Musetta..............................Senorita Cleopatra Vicini
Parpignol............................Signor Aristide Masiero
Sergeant-at-Arms......................Pedro Lopez
Students, Bergers, Commercial Merhants, Modistes, Venders,
Soldiers, Singers, Walters, etc., e.c.

Scene—Paris, France.   Time—A. D. 1800.

ACT I.—Attic, top floor Latin Quarter.
ACT II.—In the Latin Quarter.
ACT III.—The Boulevarde and Gate of d'Enter.
ACT IV.—Attic on top floor in Latin Quarter.

Friday Evening—*Verdi*.........................Ernani
Saturday Evening—*Verdi*.................. Il Trovatore

STAFF.

Signor Alfonso Del Conte.........................Director
Mr. Al. Harris,................................... Manager
Signor Palocio..................................Treasurer
Mr. Ed. Bageard ....General Agent
Signor Ettore Drog............................Stage Manager

The Great Saloma Quartette appears in the Orchestra.
Signor Pietro Vallni...................Leader of Orchestra
Luis E. Saloma........................Violin Concertante

A contemporary advertisement for the Del Conte Company and
Puccini's *La Bohème*

All these points emphasized the "otherness" of the troupe's identity as Latino/Italian ethnic. Although opera was always understood and accepted as an event of "foreign" origin, this company was apparently a little too foreign. The *Los Angeles Herald* reported of the premiere performance of *La Bohème*, that there were 532 people in the audience, less than half the theater's capacity: "The opera [company] did not attract the people of wealth. Italian and Mexican citizens were conspicuous in the audience throughout the engagement, but the bon-ton of American society sought its pleasure elsewhere."[18] In Los Angeles and other large American cities, the Del Contes were apparently not "elite" enough to attract major support as a social event, nor were they able to attract the usual "popular," Anglo-dominated theater audience that had kept other traveling companies in business over the years. Thus the promise of the well-sung Italian repertory, an American premiere, and low prices could not overcome what was, in Los Angeles at that time, a handicap. The "elite" audience is here revealed as not only European American, but specifically Anglo.

The Lambardi and Bevani Companies

Other efforts to bring elite, "high-priced" opera to Los Angeles were also less than successful, however, in this short end-of-century period of uncertain class identity for opera. In 1899, the Ellis Grand Opera Company came from Chicago with Melba as its featured star; its performances of *Faust* and *Carmen* were not well attended, and the company left in a flurry of claims about who lost how much on the venture. In the same year, the Wakefield, a modest repertory company playing at the Burbank, likewise failed.

Later in the same season, the Lambardi Company attracted large audiences for a run of several weeks. *La Bohème* now drew an overflow audience, and the company's stay was extended twice. (Despite its reported success, a final return run in August resulted in the financial difficulties that led to L. E. Behymer's letter about nightly performances of the "Miserere" in Kansas small towns quoted earlier.) This time the weekly *Western Graphic* noted with approbation the behavior of the ethnic (minority) presence in the crowd: "It was noticeable that the cheers and bravos came from those auditors whose dark complexions indicated the warm southern blood that is impulsive and hearty."[19] Perhaps this observer regretted that many in the audience lacked the "impulsive and hearty" involvement in the action.

In 1906, the Lambardis were selected to open the newly completed Temple Auditorium, a monument to the success of a new order of things that recognized "elite" entertainment as an institution separate from other entertainment. Temple Auditorium was built on the site of Hazard's Pavilion, the twenty-year-old structure that had accommodated prizefights, flower shows, and the National Opera Company, in favor of a more specialized hall built by a newly organized congregation for the dual purposes of sectarian worship and "high culture" events. (The hall's boosters hoped it would house at least one national political convention, but prizefights were presumably excluded.)[20] The Lambardis played to audiences similar in size to those for the National Opera Company's visit two decades earlier. In a now much larger city, the audience no longer represented such a large portion of the community.

Even (perhaps especially) after larger, self-consciously elite and certainly more expensive companies began to extend their tours to Los Angeles more often (the Ellis Company in 1899; the Met in 1905), the populist desire to retain opera as an affordable people's entertainment accessible to all remained. A locally organized group, the Bevani Opera Company, offered a season in 1910 at Temple Auditorium aimed at filling this need. Described as "dollar opera," it offered gallery seats at twenty-five cents, the price of a vaudeville ticket. Julian Johnson reported in the *Pacific Coast Musical Review* that there were 70,950 paid admissions for thirty-two performances of ten operas:

> The question of grand opera in Los Angeles has been solved—the company has made money and goes on its way rejoicing; the local impresario has vindicated his assertions; the Auditorium has shown the practicability, with a large seating capacity and a huge stage, of giving grand opera at popular prices, and there is no reason why a series of from eight to twelve weeks of grand opera could not be financed and given in a most artistic manner if the right kind of brains, energy and determination is behind it.[21]

The critics spoke too soon about "solving" the "problem" of popular opera in Los Angeles, for the Bevani company did not repeat this venture. Nevertheless, a clear distinction between opera as an elite social event and opera as a "popular" event had been established.

Music and business joined forces in an innovative attempt to establish American opera for a middle-class and elite audience not long afterward. A locally raised prize of $10,000 was offered for a new American opera whose premiere would coincide with a convention of the National Federation of Music Clubs in 1915. *Fairyland* by Horatio Parker (1863-1919) won the prize but was not successful even though the first performance was greeted ecstatically by the audience that had helped bring it about.

The sequel to the Progressive-Era opera story in Los Angeles, one that lasted for decades, was occasional visits by relatively low-budget Italian companies such as Bevani and the long-running San Carlo Company, balanced by annual one-week visits by the San Francisco Opera, with high prices and a socially elite audience. This pattern became established in the mid-1920s and continued until well after World War II. It was increasingly leavened with various low-budget, homegrown productions, including some quite spectacular outdoor operas at the Hollywood Bowl. Local productions, both by university music departments and small nonprofit independent companies thrived especially after the operas produced by the Federal Music Project between 1936 and 1938 were well received. No large resident company was actually established until near the end of the century, in the 1990s.

Opera and symphony brought widely divergent histories from their European origins to their American careers; each has followed a separate path in the U.S. The symphony orchestra was scarcely known firsthand in the United States before the mid-nineteenth century; it came to this country already wrapped in a Romantic, sacralized tradition, which it has most definitely retained, despite many attempts to appeal to a wider audience. Michael Broyles has recently shown that the aesthetic basis for the American Romantic vision of the inherent superiority of instrumental music, specifically music unaccompanied by any text, performed by an orchestra, and the foundation for its elite social role was laid, in Boston, well before the 1850 dividing line offered by Levine in *Highbrow, Lowbrow*.[22]

Small bands and orchestras (often not clearly distinguished) were commonplace in the nineteenth century; they played (operatic excerpts more often than symphonies) in theaters, for dancing, and for other public and private entertainments. But the conductor Theodore Thomas is credited, through extensive touring with his own orchestra from 1869 on, with establishing "the popularity of the symphony orchestra in the USA today."[23] More than any other individual, Thomas taught American audiences to accept symphonic music on its most elite terms. Thomas's autobiography, published very shortly after his death, proposes this status distinction between symphony and opera:

> A symphony orchestra shows the culture of a community, not opera. The man who does not know Shakespeare is to be pitied; and the man who does not understand Beethoven and has not been under his spell has not half lived his life. The master works of instrumental music are the language of the soul and express more than those of any other art. Light music, "popular" so called, is the sensual side of the art and has more or less devil in it.[24]

Later in the century it was Thomas who did for the symphony orchestra what a whole succession of touring companies and divas had achieved decades earlier for opera: that is, spread his preferred genre to many American towns rather than restrict it to a few large cities.

In Los Angeles, the symphony story does not extend as far back as does opera; moreover, it involves a rather different cast of characters. The first public performance of symphonic music took place only in 1888, part of a series of four concerts by a group called "The Philharmonics" that combined choral and instrumental forces (and probably included women as well as men), under the leadership of German-born and trained Adolph Willhartitz.[25] It is probably significant that the "Philharmonics" organized their season following the appearance of Thomas's National Opera Company with its large orchestra. The push to organize these performances, and later ones more specifically symphonic, came from the participants themselves, who wanted the satisfaction of performing the "serious" repertoire for these large forces. Many of the performers, as well as some of the audience, had become familiar with this tradition in the course of their European training or travel, and wanted to reclaim it for themselves and the community. In addition, the hymn-singing tradition, widespread among Protestant congregations, and the secular tradition of men's singing societies among German-speaking immigrants contributed to the interest and involvement of both singers and audience.[26] The Ellis Club, a men's chorus, had also organized in 1888.

Audiences for two of the four programs were reported as small.[27] As in Theodore Thomas's model, audience-taming was part of the agenda even for an elite audience. According to newspaper reports, the concerts introduced

> several novelties ... of so excellent a character that they could, with lasting benefit, be generally introduced. The doors were kept locked during the performance of each number on the programme. No[thing] was permitted to disturb the thorough enjoyment of the audience, and the programmes ... were dainty specimens of the printer's and binder's art.[28]

The music was reported as "of the highest class"; likewise, the eliteness of the audience was recognized as embracing "some of the nicest people of our musical city and of Pasadena."[29]

This series was abandoned after one season. The next Philharmonic, an orchestra of some forty musicians that gave four concerts in each of two seasons beginning in 1893 under A. J. Stamm, was discontinued for lack of financial support. "Stamm's Philharmonic" was composed entirely of men, leading one to conclude that it was no accident that the Los Angeles Women's Orchestra was also organized in 1893.[30] A third, more successful attempt to organize a symphony orchestra followed in 1897. Despite the city's rapid growth and the greater number of musicians available, the new Los Angeles Symphony Orchestra struggled, settling for afternoon concerts because its members played in the local theaters and cafes by night.

In each of these cases, the motivation was not commercial. It came from the musicians themselves, who were happy, up to a point, to play this repertoire for their own satisfaction. The activity was understood as elite; newspaper criticism assumed that the concerts represented a higher kind of music, having a strong component of moral uplift rather than the merely entertainment value of the usual theater music. The audience remained small, largely female and middle- to upper-class, its membership limited by the weekday afternoon performances. The separate gendering of audience and performers remained characteristic of concert music for decades to come. The Women's Orchestra, which lasted into the 1950s, was marginalized as an amateur group for most of that time.

In the Los Angeles Symphony's third season, L. E. Behymer, who by this time wanted to cultivate an elite audience as part of his campaign to become the dominant impresario in town, began to promote the Symphony as an institutional civic obligation as well as a cultural advantage:

> There will be a meeting of the Board of Directors of the Los Angeles Symphony Orchestra next Tuesday morning.... We are ashamed to report that a shortage of funds for the next season is the reason.... It is as much the duty of the citizens of Los Angeles to see that the Symphony Orchestra is supported as it is to keep up good roads and a public library.... It is the duty of every merchant, every capitalist and every property owner to secure at least one season ticket.[31]

Symphonic music was increasingly marginalized as an elite activity in Los Angeles after 1900 in the context of both the rising population and of the explosive growth of commercial mass entertainment. Its aristocratic nature was accepted from the start, but the restriction of the Symphony's concerts to an exclusive, largely female, Thursday afternoon audience was always resisted, especially given the very wide potential audience for its concerts among Los Angeles's extensive musically literate population. The argument for making the concerts more widely available by giving more of them, at lower prices, in the evenings or on weekends, was generally based on their moral and educational value to the community. These arguments came most strongly from music store operators and music teachers.

In Los Angeles, resistance to the symphonic monopoly surfaced twice, with differing results. A People's Orchestra gave weekly Sunday afternoon concerts, starting in November 1912.

Financial mismanagement led to its failure by early 1914; however, its example forced the Los Angeles Symphony to reorganize and offer its own popular concerts. The second act of resistance was enormously successful. By 1922, the present Los Angeles Philharmonic, whose financial stability was then guaranteed by a single individual—the ultimate elitism—had replaced the Symphony.[32] However, in that year, the newly organized Hollywood Bowl summer concerts, the "Symphonies Under the Stars," offered forty concerts in a span of ten weeks—67 percent more performances than took place over the entire winter season—at twenty-five cents a ticket.[33] These concerts, with which the Philharmonic was soon identified, continue to this day. The Bowl concerts in Los Angeles, and other summer symphony concerts in other places, have always attracted larger, less elite audiences to locations at least somewhat different in character from the more formal ones of winter seasons.

In Lawrence Levine's terms, the symphony was indeed "sacralized" by the start of the twentieth century. The aesthetic basis for that sacralization was present well before such concerts were ever presented in Los Angeles. Symphony was presented as a sacralized, elite activity from the start—but the elitist winter audience was soon leavened by mass outdoor summer concerts, where the forms and customs of the sacralized performance were, and are, at least somewhat different. The debate over its proper repertoire, and over how exclusive its audience would be, is an ongoing one.

The process by which the European concert music tradition was marginalized and formally separated from both popular and commercial mass culture before World War I in Los Angeles, involves a third strand, not discussed so far in this essay—namely, the performances of traveling virtuosi. In that strand, intertwined with both the history of the symphony and of "elite" opera productions, the visits of the traveling virtuosi (who early on were part of the generally undifferentiated commercial theatrical tradition) were consistently packaged and commodified for an elite public only in 1905, after a period of intense competition among local impresarios. (This competition followed very quickly after the emergence of theater chains controlled by a few hands in New York City.) During the six-year competition that began around 1899, the issue was not whether such traveling virtuosi would appear, and not only who would present them locally; it was over the fundamental cultural question of the identity and size of the audience—that is, over the issue of elitism, the social role that these concerts would play.[34]

The title of this essay, "Inventing Tradition," refers to a concept from historian Eric Hobsbawm. Hobsbawm's definition: "'Invented tradition' is taken to mean a set of practices, normally governed by overtly or tacitly accepted rules and of a ritual or symbolic nature, which seeks to inculcate certain values and norms of behavior by repetition.... In fact, where possible, they normally attempt to establish continuity with a suitable historic past." He writes of "attempts to fix certain aspects of the shifting landscape of modernity into an unchanging relationship with a symbolic past," and "a set of symbolic ritual practices that function to inculcate values and behavior patterns signifying continuity with the past."[35] As examples, Hobsbawm cites the Pilgrim Fathers, George Washington and the cherry tree. Levine argues that such invented tradition extends far beyond the merely political: "the creation of the institutions and criteria of high culture was a primary means of social, intellectual, and aesthetic separation and selection" (p. 229).

Hobsbawm wrote about notions of patriotism and nationalism that emerged in the late nineteenth century in Western Europe, but his phrase applies as well to the process of sacralization of opera and symphony in America generally outlined by Levine and described for Los Angeles here. The connection between the developing sense of American nationhood and music is confirmed in W. Mitchell Chappie's introduction for the 1909 collection mentioned earlier in this paper, *Heart Songs*: "This book represents the history, the sentiment of the American people of today, as well as of the various European races who, in this new world, have been moulded into a great and powerful nation."[36]

To conclude, the central issue in Los Angeles's musical life in the Progressive Era and, indeed, in American musical life had to do with settling the social role that European-based art music would play, in reference both to the commercialized mass culture that took shape in those decades, and to the formation of an elite model for a specifically "American" culture. Such a culture might provide a firm basis from which to meet the impending novelties of the new century—novelties driven by the movement for women's rights, the waves of immigration, continuing economic growth and technological change, the emergence of the eight-hour workday and an entertainment industry based on the availability of leisure time, and the rest.

Both symphony and opera presented some specific problems that made them awkward and sometimes recalcitrant tools for asserting the hegemony of an economic and social hierarchy. From the specifics, especially the frequent uncertainties of the Los Angeles picture, one draws the uncertain conclusion that the outcome of the sacralization process was in doubt for much longer than one might have otherwise guessed and that, had things happened just a little differently, the social role assigned to symphony and opera would be, perhaps, just a little different today.

University of Nevada, Reno

---

[1]A much larger proportion (42%) of the population of San Francisco was foreign-born, according to census reports. San Francisco was a major seaport and a much larger and wealthier city at the start of the Progressive Era. In 1890, the population of Los Angeles was 50,395; of San Francisco, 298,997. In Los Angeles, there were 12,752 foreign-born; in San Francisco, 126,811. In 1900, 50% of the population over age fifteen in Los Angeles was female, as compared to 43% for San Francisco.

[2]As an aside, I would suggest that the high level of participation by women in the music profession in Los Angeles heightened concern about the "feminization" of music, and could be one hidden reason behind the frequently heard comment that Los Angeles had no music history, or that it was a musical vacuum, before the late 1930s.

[3]Cambridge: Harvard University Press, 1988. For his findings about opera, Levine drew heavily on the work of Katherine Preston (see note 4 below).

[4]Katherine K. Preston, *Opera on the Road: Traveling Opera Troupes in the United States, 1825-1860* (Urbana: University of Illinois Press, 1993).

See also Preston, "The Multifaceted Audience for Operatic Music in Antebellum America: or, Do the Terms 'Vernacular' and 'Cultivated' Really Apply to All Music of the Early Nineteenth Century?": a paper presented to the 1992 national meeting of the Sonneck Society for American Music, Baton Rouge, 14 February 1992.

[5]H. Wiley Hitchcock, *Music in the United States: A History* (Englewood Cliffs, NJ: Prentice-Hall, various editions) depends on oppositions such as "vernacular" and "cultivated" to achieve its elegant organizational structure.

[6]The entire letter:

Lawrence, Kansas, 7 Oct., 1899

Dear Wife, Babies and Dad:

I do wish I were with you tonight. The songbirds are doing nobly tonight. Famous old 'Il Trovatore.' Verdi was a wonder. That is all they want through the one-night stands. We have two casts now made up, so we can sing 'Il Trovatore' every night if they want it. With the city people, it is different. 'Carmen' is the first cry, 'Rigoletto' next. 'Faust,' 'Aida,' 'Norma' are on a par. But in all the operas, there is nothing sweeter than the dear old 'Miserere' scene in the last Act of 'Il Trovatore.' When I get back home, I am going to write a book on what I don't know about Italian opera.

Letter, L. E. Behymer to Minette Sparkes Behymer. Quoted in Minette Sparkes Behymer's typed memoir, courtesy of Lynn Hoffman.

[7]*Heart Songs Dear to the American People, And by them Contributed in the Search for Treasured Songs Initiated by the National Magazine* (Boston: Chapple Publishing Company, Ltd., for World Syndicate Company, New York, 1909.) It is not entirely clear whether the assortment of 404 songs in this volume were actually chosen by or for the public, nor how broad a range of public taste might be sampled through the readership of the *National Magazine*.

Charles Hamm, "Irving Berlin's Early Songs as Biographical Documents": a paper presented to the Sonneck Society for American Music, Baton Rouge, 16 February 1992; and Joshua Berrett, "Louis Armstrong as Opera Buff: Of Breaks, Bravura, and the Creative Process": a paper presented to the American Musicological Society, Oakland, CA, 9 November 1990.

[8]The Metropolitan Opera of New York; companies in Chicago and San Francisco had shorter seasons.

[9]Sue Wolfer Earnest, *An Historical Study of the Growth of the Theatre in Southern California* (Ph.D. Diss: University of Southern California, 1947), contains a Day Book, in Vol. 3, Part II, pp. 1-178, which I have used as a source for the information in the following paragraph. Other sources on Los Angeles include Howard Swan, *Music in the Southwest, 1825-1950* (San Marino, CA: The Huntington Library, 1952); and various articles by Robert

Stevenson. See especially Stevenson, "Music in Southern California: A Tale of Two Cities," *Inter-American Music Review* 10/1 (1988): 51-111.

[10]Both groups came from San Francisco; Marra returned to Los Angeles in 1882; Fabbri in 1876, 1881, and later.

[11]The most prominent singer in the company was Emma Juch, who later toured with her own English opera company, visiting Los Angeles in 1889 and 1890. The price of individual seats ranged from $1 to $4; the original series of five was sold at $15. The *Times* reported the gate for the first three performances as $17,000. Reports of attendance, like those of the number of seats in the house, are not consistent in the newspaper sources.

[12]The census recorded for Los Angeles 11,000 people in 1880 and 50,000 in 1890. That means an average growth rate between 16% and 17% per year. In 1887, there were about 32,000 persons in Los Angeles; 65%, or 20,800, were age fifteen and over. At a 16% growth rate, the population in 1887 was 31,088, and 48,525 in 1890; at a 17% growth rate, it was 33,014 in 1887 and 52,875 in 1890. The 1890 census gives the population for each year of age statewide; approximately 35% was age fourteen and under. That is probably a conservative estimate for Los Angeles, since much larger San Francisco had a smaller proportion of women and, presumably, fewer children.

[13]*Los Angeles Times* (17 May 1887): 4, "The World's Musical Advance." Unsigned; possibly by W. F. Kubel.

[14]Theodore Thomas, handwritten note in scrapbook, Vol. 25, Theodore Thomas collection, Music Division, Library of Congress, p. 148. I am grateful to Wayne Shirley for calling this to my attention.

Ezra Schabas, "Thomas, Theodore," *Grove Dictionary of American Music*, ed. H. Wiley Hitchcock and Stanley Sadie, (London: Macmillan, 1896), Vol. 4, pp. 380-83, reports that the American/National opera companies "failed dismally, however, through poor performances and bad management."

[15]*Los Angeles Times* (19 May 1887): 4.

[16]*Los Angeles Capital* 6/14 (2 October 1997): 11. The first U.S. performance of *Bohème* took place on Wednesday, 13 October 1897. This Los Angeles premiere is omitted in histories of opera in America. In "An Operatic Odyssey: Hypocrisy and Revisionism in the Gilded Age (a paper read to the Sonneck Society for American Music, 9 March 1997), JoAnn Taricani documents opposition from the *New York Sun*, critic Henry Krehbiel, and rival diva Nellie Melba as reasons for this historical omission.

[17]*Capital* 6/15 (9 October 1897)

[18]*Los Angeles Herald*, 24 October 1897, as quoted in Swan, 188.

[19]*Western Graphic* [Los Angeles] No. 21 (27 May 1899).

[20]For the role of at least one woman in the construction of Temple Auditorium, see Catherine Parsons Smith, "'Popular Prices will Prevail': The Social Role of European-based Concert Music in the Progressive Era," *Selected Reports in Ethnomusicology X: Musical Aesthetics and Multiculturalism in Los Angeles*, ed. Stephen Loza (Los Angeles: University of California, 1994), 207-21. Temple Auditorium eventually became Philharmonic Auditorium and was used for symphony concerts until 1964.

[21]Julian Johnson, "An Idea of Dollar Opera in Los Angeles," *Pacific Coast Musical Review* 19/13 (24 December 1910): 8.

[22]Michael Broyles, "Music and Class Structure in Antebellum Boston," *Journal of the American Musicological Society*, 44 (1991), pp. 451-493; and *Music of the Highest Class: Elitism and Populism in Antebellum Boston* (New Haven: Yale University Press, 1992).

[23]See the article by Schabas cited in note 14 above. Thomas (1835-1905) emigrated from Germany in 1845 with his parents. He conducted in Brooklyn, Cincinnati, New York and finally (from 1891) Chicago, where a full-time, permanent orchestra was established for him to conduct.

[24]*Theodore Thomas: A Musical Autobiography*, ed. George P. Upton, (Chicago: A. C. McClurg, 1905), Vol. 1, p. 3.

[25]Stevenson, "Los Angeles," *New Grove Dictionary of American Music*, ed. Hitchcock and Sadie (New York and London: Macmillan, 1986), Vol. 3, pp. 107-15, mentions another "Philharmonic" organized in 1878. It may be that Willhartitz's experience with the "Philharmonics," or perhaps the later refusal of the Los Angeles Symphony to accept women as members, led him to write *Some Facts About Woman in Music* (Los Angeles: Press of Out West, 1902), a monograph on women as musicians in nineteenth-century Europe. The policy of excluding women was contrary to the practice of the musicians' union when it was organized in Los Angeles in the 1890s.

[26]Concerts and entertainments by both local and visiting artists and companies were offered from the 1870s at the local Turnverein Hall, and later in the Grand Opera House (from 1884) and the Los Angeles Theater (from 1886). These often drew a wide audience, but did not involve a large orchestra. A secular men's choral society, the Ellis Club, was also founded in Los Angeles in 1888. The Women's Lyric Club was not organized until 1904; a second men's club, the Orpheus Club, was formed in 1905.

[27]Reviews in the *Los Angeles Times*, *Express*, and *Herald*, quoted in Burton Karson, "Music Criticism in Los Angeles, 1881-1895" (M.A. thesis: University of Southern California, 1959). The other two performances are not reported.

[28]*Los Angeles Times* (28 September 1888), quoted in Karson, 155-56.

[29]A list of subscribers is given in the newspaper account, along with the members of the orchestra.

[30]Harley Hamilton, an American-born violinist who directed the orchestra at the Los Angeles Theatre, organized the Women's Orchestra from his own violin students. He became conductor of the Los Angeles Symphony a few years later, and resigned both positions in 1914.

[31]"The Los Angeles Symphony Orchestra," *Los Angeles Graphic* 10/21 (19 November 1904): 12.

[32]William Andrews Clark Jr. founded the present Los Angeles Philharmonic in 1919 and single-handedly paid its deficit until his death in 1934. The Symphony competed with the new Philharmonic for one season, and then disbanded.

[33]Smith, "'Something of Good for the Future': The People's Orchestra of Los Angeles, 1912-1913," *Nineteenth-Century Music* 16 (1992): 147-61; and "Founding the Hollywood Bowl," *American Music* 11 (1993): 206-43.

[34]See "Popular Prices will Prevail," note 20 above.

[35]Eric Hobsbawm, "Introduction: Inventing Traditions," in *The Invention of Tradition*, ed. Hobsbawm and Terence Ranger (Cambridge, Eng: Cambridge University Press, 1983), p. 1. See also Hobsbawm's essay in the same collection, "Mass-Producing Traditions: Europe, 1870-1914," 263-307.

[36]*Heart Songs*, ix.

THE OPERETTAS OF
CHARLES HUTCHINSON GABRIEL

Clyde W. Brockett

Charles Hutchinson Gabriel (Wilton, Iowa; 18 August 1856 –
Los Angeles, California; 14 September 1932) became one of our
most beloved gospel song composers.[1] (A likeness of Gabriel
appears on page 325.) His music is inalienably associated with
urban revivalism. At the zenith of his career between 1911 and
1925, he was editor-in-chief for Homer Rodeheaver, Billy
Sunday's gospel voice and publisher. Gabriel's books about the
genre were all published during those years. Yet while his hymn-
composition talent was largely recognized only in the twentieth
century, his career began and bore fruit in the milieu of secular as
much as religious music during the nineteenth century. Even many
compositions prepared for religious institutions throughout his
career have almost surprisingly secular texts.[2] Indeed, although
the first composition for which Gabriel received acceptance for
publication was a hymn, the first of his own words and music he
ever submitted, when age thirteen or fourteen, was a duet for
soprano and alto with chorus, representative of the nineteenth-
century American song tradition. George F. Root, its publisher,
years later "remembered the circumstances surrounding the
manuscript although thousands of songs had passed through his
hands since that time."[3]

The extent of Gabriel's nineteenth-century secular
composition is not known. Gabriel himself, only months before
his death, exclaimed, "Yes, I have composed more than 7,000
songs, mostly hymns, and I haven't stopped yet."[4] Many date
from after his settling in Chicago in 1892. He himself numbered
his collections published after 1890; this information appeared in
three sources—the first by a different author, J. H. Hall, to whom
Gabriel had, however, forwarded information.[5] The secular music
inventories appear in Table 1 (see page 324):

TABLE 1

An Inventory of Gabriel's Work

Works	Hall (*Biography*), 1914 (pp. 350-51)	Gabriel (*Personal Memoirs*), 1914 (p. 49)	Gabriel (*Sixty Years*), 1921, (p. 74)[6]
Juvenile Cantatas	7	8	10
Operettas	3	4	4
Reed Organ Instruction Books		2	2
Piano Instruction Books		2	2
Piano Duet Books		2	2

In these inventories, we see no secular songs, but Gabriel does add, in his *Personal Memoirs,* "several hundreds of pieces of sheet music, vocal and instrumental." A friend's testimonial notes that certain such songs were printed "in sheet form."[7]

Gabriel was an experienced scorer for band. He programmed his instrumental as well as vocal secular works on concerts. One such program included the "Medley Overture" and a "selection from [Henry] Farmer's Mass" scored by Gabriel for the Union Band. Incidentally, rendered also in this concert were the choral "Hail, O Hail," the duet "Happy Thou Pale Moon," the trio "Evening Chimes," the classed Jubilee Song, the piano duet "Silvery Moonlight," the women's quartet "When the Birds Wake the Morn," the solo "Little Gipsy Girl," the duet "Beside the Throne," the piano solo "Voices Among the Trees," and the song [solo] and chorus "Nora Madain."[8] Gabriel recognized his specialization in band music; he credited his melodic skill to his work with military bands, which he was to instruct and lead in the late 1870s and the 1880s.[9]

Charles Hutchinson Gabriel at about age sixty

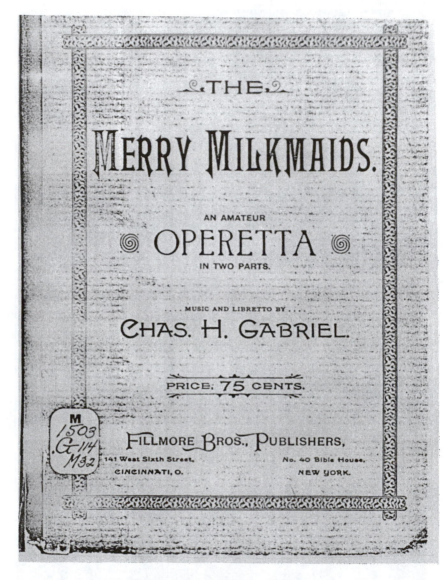

The cover of *The Merry Milkmaids*
(somewhat reduced in size)

Part of the Waltz from *The Merry Cyclers*

No. 40. CYCLERS OUTING, GRAND MARCH

*Ladies and gentlemen file in at back of stage from opposite sia.s, passing around the stage in opposite directions.
As they meet at the back of the stage they march to the front in couples,   Alternate couples then right and left pass
around, meet at the back of the stage and advance in fours.   Alternate fours right and left pass around, meet and advance in eights.   Alternate eights right and left pass around and advance in sixteens, and so on according to the size of
stage and company.   This to be done to the music of the following march.*

Copyright, 1896, by Fillmore Bros.

The opening of the
"Grand March" from *The Merry Cyclers*

The cantata, possibly designed to be staged, was another
veritable proving ground for Gabriel's operettas. Such "juvenile"
works were performed with adult complements.[10] In reality,
Gabriel's operettas also belong to the stratum of church-social
music and the tradition of singing schools. And yet, his first
operetta is billed "operetta for adults" in the cantata
advertisements on the back covers of *Heart Songs* (1893) and
Male Choir (1896), both published by Fillmore Brothers in
Cincinnati. Although the cantatas contain spoken dialogue, with
rare exception they sport no overture. The fundamental
difference between staged "day-school" cantatas, like *A Day in the
Woods* (1889), *A Visit to Grandpa* (1890), *The Jolly Picnic Party*
(Cincinnati: John Church, 1893), or (for Christmas) *How We
Waited for Santa Claus* (1889-1890), and the operettas seems to

be length. Cantatas consulted were on the average only a third as long as the operettas.

Gabriel's three extant operettas are *The Merry Milkmaids*, *The Merry Cyclers or Love, The Golden Key*, and *Pauline or An Eventful Day*. That four unnamed operettas are counted by Gabriel himself after 1918 presents an enigma. Hall's list of 1914 numbers only three, and it is conceivable that the fourth, unlocated, was published between these listings. This assumes that Gabriel is not counting as operetta some shorter playlet like his twenty-three-page *Love Finds the Way* or *The Detective That Father Hired* (1912). Gabriel did claim two of his own operetta librettos,[11] both of which we have in *The Merry Milkmaids* and *Pauline*. On the cover and title page of *Pauline* one reads that Gabriel is accorded *The Merry Milkmaids, The Merry Cyclers*, etc. One may strongly suspect, then, that his fourth operetta, not being advertised, does not pertain to the nineteenth century. If so, it was published by some other firm. In any event, nothing to the contrary has surfaced in response to calls for information and the check of the firm of Carl Fischer that acquired Fillmore Brothers, the house that published Gabriel's other operettas. Even the three known works are sparsely preserved; their repositories, identified in Table 2, are few (see page 330).

Mrs. Geragi's example of *Pauline*, in fact, appears to be unique. The conclusion, that these are Gabriel's only purely theatrical works from the nineteenth century, may stand, even if by default.

The Merry Milkmaids, copyrighted by Fillmore Brothers in 1891, not only ushers in the 1890s as a decade of song for Gabriel, but also the Fillmore imprint of it is the most elegant of his trio of operettas (see page 326).[12]

Gabriel relates that he wrote both the libretto and music of *The Merry Milkmaids* in ten days.[13] It was for the King's Daughters of Grace Methodist Church in San Francisco (21st and Capp Streets), where Gabriel was in 1889-1890. Conceivably, Gabriel, whom the directory lists as "music teacher"[14] had secular contacts. There is no information concerning the first performance, nor evidence that his first operetta has ever been revived. This is, unfortunately, the unanswered question adumbrating the other two dramas.

TABLE 2

Repositories

The Merry Milkmaids:
Library of Congress, Occidental College, University of
Illinois, University of Texas, University of Wisconsin-
Madison (The Tams-Witmark/Wisconsin Collection)

The Merry Cyclers, or Love the Golden Key:
Library of Congress, University of Wisconsin-Madison (The
Tams-Witmark/Wisconsin Collection)

Pauline, or An Eventful Day:
Privately owned, Paulette T. Geragi, Newport News,
Virginia

The plot bears a personal stamp in its locale, characters, and
daily activities. Gabriel, raised on an Iowa farm, evokes memories
with both characters, down to the very accent of their speech, and
events, like the evening milking. The real value of the background
for this and the other librettos issues from the vignette of life in
the 1890s that they provide. In the background is Gabriel's own
involvement, as in youth concerts, accompanied by a small Estey
organ,[15] on the Fourth of July,[16] or reckoning the status of the
amateur singer, right up to the 1920s.[17] The ephemeral character
of all three librettos ("a day in the life of") conveys a certain
experiential tone too. Despite his lack of formal musical training,
seen in expressions like "fol la la," Gabriel's words are carefully,
even at times symbolically, graced by his music. Typical is the
religiosity of his cadential harmonies in No. 26, a lovely duet
about "blessed hope." The words, more illustrative of this
sentiment than the music, are quoted below:

> When in the silent midnight hour,
> That whisp'ring voice of sondrous pow'r
> Impel'd by doubt and fears prevail,
> Oh, how our hearts in terror quail;
> But hope dispels the doubt and fear,
> And sweetly dries the mourner's tear
> Oh, blessed hope, thou are divine,
> Forever fill this heart of mine![18]

Beginning the second half of the 1890s is Gabriel's second operetta, *The Merry Cyclers, or Love, the Golden Key*.[19] Its libretto is by Palmer Hartsough (1844-1932). About him Gabriel records definitively, "Palmer Hartsough is a name familiar to those who sing gospel songs. He is one of the few remaining of the 'old school' type, into whose writing commercialism did not enter."[20] Hartsough was educated at Plymouth, Ypsilanti, and Kalamazoo, Michigan, and was among the pupils of George F. Root, whom he impressed with his verse writing.[21] In 1893 Hartsough associated with the Fillmore Brothers, and in 1915 he was teaching vocal music in Ontario, Wisconsin. His picture also appears in Gabriel's *The Singers and Their Songs*, published in 1916.

In its Part I, this libretto is inferior to *The Merry Milkmaids*. The music follows suit with more repetitions of entire sections, sometimes with changed key, sometimes uncharacteristically leitmotivic, and with doubling in the harmony. But the music of Part II improves along with the text and at times is exquisite with a waltz (see page 327)[22] and Sousa-like march (see the top of page 328).[23]

Gabriel's style is better articulated in *The Merry Milkmaids*, which often shows a preference for sixteenth-note embroidery on final or weak beats and frequent transitory minor harmonies. Symbolism is more apparent also: the diamond note-heads and series of augmented fourths associated with the devil, whose name the women of the trio are not allowed to utter (see page 332, beneath the *A tempo ad lib* direction).[24] Symbolic too are running thirds, skipping grace notes, and trills associated with spinning tricycle wheels.[25]

The ensembles and instrumental sections are well developed too with an artful sextet, No. 33 (mislabeled "trio and octet" in the table of contents) developed out of the aforementioned "bedeviled" trio. This sextet, incidentally, is reduced in size in the printed score.

Pauline, or an Eventful Day represents the late 1890s—it appeared in 1899—in a number of details, that is, in some indistinctive features in its score.[26] There are now metronomic prescriptions and, happily, measures are no longer divided between braces of score, half a measure on one level, half on another.

Symbolism through "shaped notes" in *The Merry Milkmaids*

Polyphony and Bells in *Pauline*
(incorporating "Nearer My God to Thee")

While the country life of milkmaids and town life of cyclers is earlier featured, this latest work emphasizes national pride. Patriotic expression, like "all honor to the Stars and Stripes Forever!" (No. 14) and "hip, hip, hooray," and figures, like Uncle Sam, are illustrative. *Pauline* is also clothed with a more noticeable garb of religiosity, seen in its lullaby (No. 23) and "Evening bells" whose invisible chorus intentionally quotes "Nearer My God to Thee" (see page 333).[27] Different, too, in *Pauline* are black roles with dialect.

As to special directions for musical interpretation, the scores are most usefully detailed. A capella ensembles are designated "sing without accompaniment," indicating that for all other unaccompanied passages the accompanist might play the vocal score. On occasion, passages for the accompaniment alone, which dot the score, contain clear prescriptions for supplementary instruments: a "violin obbligato," for instance.[28] Gabriel also calls occasionally for bells, which are limited to a descending G-major scale at the beginning of the number (No. 29). Cadenzas flourish; one of them, printed into the score of *The Merry Milkmaids*, is optional for flute, symbolic of morning (see page 335).[29]

A more enigmatic direction, "Basses," overlays bass octaves in a march refrain of *The Merry Milkmaids*. Here, the men having been designated "brigade" and no words being present, Gabriel seems to imply some borrowed "military brass" rather than men's voices.[30] See Page 336.

A gavottelike instrumental "interlude" in *Merry Cyclers*, Part I, finale, was separately published as *"The Merry Cycler's Minuet, C. H. G. ..."* in Gabriel's *Perfect Organ Method* (1900, page 63). Indeed, the reed organ would have provided a serviceable accompaniment for Gabriel's operettas, as it normally did for voices in Sunday school and auditorium.[31] Stage directions, nevertheless, refer only to "instrument."[32]

In *The Merry Cyclers* there are no fewer than thirty-two different singing roles, as opposed to twenty in *The Merry Milkmaids* and eighteen in *Pauline*. With soloists pragmatically doubling in the choruses, modern organizations could probably assure each Cycler's cast member a solo! Even without as large a cast as the others, *Pauline* is indicative of this sort of wholesale

An optional flute cadenza in *The Merry Milkmaids*

maid to the mead-ow hies, Each maid to the mead-ow hies.
hom-age we pay to you, All hom-age we pay to you!

maid to the mead-ow hies, Each maid to the mead-ow hies.
hom-age they pay to—who? All hom-age they pay to—m-m-m. (*tap breast.*)

CAPTAIN:—*Attention, battalion! Shoulder arms! Forward march!*

Basses.

ff

Exit Farmers' Brigade.

DOROTHY.—Oh, that irresistible captain, is n't he sweet?

MAIDS.—Is n't he sweet?!

DOROTHY.—Yes, yes, my heart is all in a flutter, and I'm in a high fever of admiration. Oh, is n't he sweet!

MYRTLE.—Well, yonder they are—brigade, rakes, pitchforks, hoes, shovels, captain and all, and—as I live, he is drilling his men with a corn-knife!

DOROTHY.—Ah, so he is! let me go, for I must be near him. Oh, is n't he sweet! (*Exit.*) .

MYRTLE.—Poor Dorothy!

MAUDE.—Yes, "poor Dorothy" better be getting ready for the milking: she loses her head, as well as her heart, to every vagabond that comes along, and goodness knows that the man who finds either will not find much. Farmer Jim must have a superabundance of patience to tolerate her nonsense as he does.

"Basses" as instruments in *The Merry Milkmaids*

CHARACTERS.

PAULINE..Daughter of Cassady.
CULLIE..Servant maid.
CHICKIE.............................A spinster sister of Cassady.
NAINE...A village belle.
KIOMI....................................An Indian fortune teller.
MOTHER.....................................A widow lady and her
CHILD.......................... A boy, five to seven years of age.
FABER......................................A New York journalist.
SHADY.............................. Faber's valet, a colored boy.
CASSADY..........................Landlord of the Dalles—an inn.
PROFESSOR.........................A middle-aged school teacher.
CHILKOOT IKE......................An eccentric village character.
RUBEN...A farmer boy.
THE VILLAGE PHYSICIAN.
UNCLE JOE...............Former slave of the widow lady—colored.
SORROW   ⎫
BORROW   ⎬..............................Three insurrection spies.
MORROW   ⎭
Chorus of picnickers.   Chorus of grenadiers.   Chorus of villagers, etc.

CONTENTS.

No. 1. — Overture...................................*Instrumental.*
No. 2. — Hail the Morning........................*Opening Chorus.*
No. 3. — The Reporter.........................*Solo and Chorus.*
No. 4. — A Serving Maid am I.................................*Solo.*
No. 5. — Bum Bums..*Trio.*
No. 6. — A Charming Morning...........................*Recitative.*
No. 7. — Chilkoot Ike..*Solo.*
No. 8. — Could the Flowers Speak.............................*Duet.*
No. 9. — He's a Jonah ....*Solo.*
No. 10.—Laugh and Sing....................................*Chorus.*
No. 11.—Fortune Telling.......................*Solo and Chorus.*
No. 12.—Shadow Land...*Solo.*
No. 13.—The Grenadiers.........................*Soli and Chorus.*
No. 14.—The Stars and Stripes..................*Soli and Chorus.*
No. 15.—The Village Physician...............................*Solo.*
No. 16.—The Robin's Song....................................*Duet.*
No. 17.—The Aboriginal Swell ....*Solo.*
No. 18.—The Whole Thing ....*Solo and Chorus.*
No. 19.—When Life is Young................................*Chorus.*
No. 20.—Flower Song..................................*Ladies' Chorus.*
No. 21.—The Flower's Secret.....................*Solo and Chorus.*
No. 22.—Pauline...*Solo.*
No. 23.—Lullaby ....*Solo and Invisible Chorus.*
No. 24.—It's All Er Comin' Right, By-m-by..........*Solo and Chorus.*
No. 25.—Hail! Our Landlord......................*Solo and Chorus.*
No. 26.—Hip, Hip, Hooray........................*Solo and Chorus.*
No. 27.—The Discomfitted Bums...............................*Trio.*
No. 28—Evening Bells ....*Trio.*
No. 29.—The Light of Love.................... ....*Sextet.*
No. 30.—Hail to the Queen........................*Closing Chorus.*

The characters and partial contents of *Pauline*

An ideal fugue subject, as it appears in *The Merry Milkmaids*

role assignment, as named in the *dramatis personae*, followed on the same introductory page by most of the sequence of numbers of the playlet (see page 337).[33]

Pauline also may serve informatively as the summary of Gabriel's scene complex with all its amateur silliness.[34] Naive and saccharine as this "Argument" reveals the action to be, Gabriel's operetta is typically for "furnishing the young people (in and out of the church) an altogether pure, chaste and wholesome entertainment."[35] Taken as the contribution of principally one fashioner of one genre, its aesthetic potential, however, lies above and beyond what the foregoing commentary may relate. Real artistic worth resides in Gabriel's perception of the values of music and verse, for which music should be composed, not the reverse,[36] and his regard for others' work. Although an occasional reflection of Balfe[37] or an ideal fugue subject[38] (see page 338) may steal into his music, Gabriel is inventive throughout. In fact, Gabriel reproves the plagiarist, "a most contemptible thief."[39]

Gabriel pays his highest respects to composers of history, from Ambrose to Puccini. Almost telepathically he writes "If someone's work arouses scorn or derision, it is entirely safe from mediocrity.... While thousands worshipped at the throne of Bayreuth, the few whom Wagner dethroned call him impostor. Mediocrity is neither envied nor emulated."[40] A champion of "good" music, in the vilification of mediocrity, Wagner, Gabriel claims, "caught and transcribed the echoes of the divine music sung by the morning stars at the creation of the world." Chopin, he continues, "carries us into the worlds yet to be."[41]

The man who so admired his musical forebears but whose own successes made him the "Irving Berlin of Gospel song"[42] is left to perorate on his educational shortcomings with the inspiration and facetiousness of a libretto:

> If not [the result of study and determination] then I am inclined to credit Madame Blavatsky's theory and claim the reincarnation of some long-haired fossil of the dim past ages. I never studied theory, harmony, composition, or counterpoint under a teacher. I never studied rhetoric, phraseology or poesy with an instructor ... I urge upon you to make the most of your privileges.[43]

His posthumous reward is to stand beside American colleagues who have enriched our musical culture.[44]

Christopher Newport University

---

[1]There are three known photographs of the composer. Shown here is the pose in profile copied, enlarged, from Chas. H. Gabriel, *Personal Memoirs* [*Gospel Choir* (ed., C. H. Gabriel, n.p., 1918)], hereafter, *Memoirs*, title page. The other two reveal the face at an angle, the second, also with glasses, facing left, and the third, larger, without glasses, facing right. The last, found in Jacob Henry Hall, *Biography of Gospel Song and Hymn Writers* (New York: Fleming H. Revell, 1914, 348) is so much in shadow that reproduction was found unsatisfactory.

[2]Terry Wayne York, "Charles Hutchinson Gabriel (1854-1932): Composer, Author, and Editor in the Gospel Tradition," (D.M.A diss.: New Orleans Baptist Theological Seminary, 1985), 54. The only source for the middle name is Hall, 349, where it is spelled without the first n. This letter has been restored apparently on the strength of Gabriel's tune titles that refer to family names, including HUTCHINSON (York, 54).

[3]Chas. H. Gabriel, *Gospel Songs and Their Writers* (Chicago and Philadelphia: Rodeheaver, 1915; © 1913 and 1914 by Gabriel), 38.

[4]*Los Angeles Examiner*. Quoted in York, 74,

[5]Hall, 349.

[6]Chas H. Gabriel, *The Singers and Their Songs* (Chicago, Philadelphia: Rodeheaver © 1916 by Gabriel).

[7]*Memoirs*, 30.

[8]York, 46-47.

[9]*Memoirs*, 33.

[10]York, 95.

[11]*Memoirs*, 50.

[12]The facsimile here and in all examples of *The Merry Milkmaids* and *The Merry Cyclers* taken from score into this article are from copies of original imprints preserved in the Library of Congress. The decoration at both ends of the paperback scores of *The Merry Milkmaids* and *The Merry Cyclers* and the fineness of the music typography is quite handsome, while the printed score to *Pauline* is altogether plain. It may be telling of the industry that the buyer paid the same price for all three, seventy-five cents each,

throughout the nine-year period, whereas those possibly costlier, earlier printings totaled, respectively, 128 and 186 pages and the unadorned, latter one only 124.

[13] *Memoirs*, 34.

[14] A. Merrill Smoak Jr., "Charles H. Gabriel: The Turning Point," *The Hymn* (July 1983): 160-64.

[15] *Memoirs*, 24.

[16] *Memoirs*, 27.

[17] Gabriel, *Church Music of Yesterday, Today and for To-morrow* (Chicago and Philadelphia: Rodeheaver), 22-35.

[18] *The Merry Milkmaids*, Score, pp. 100-01.

[19] *THE MERRY CYCLERS... / OR / Love, the Golden Key. / AN / OPERETTA / IN TWO PARTS* / Libretto by... / PALMER HARTSOUGH. / Music by... / Chas. H. Gabriel (Cincinnati: Fillmore Brothers, 1896).

[20] Gabriel, *The Singers*, 29.

[21] *Ibid.*, 30.

[22] Gabriel, *The Merry Cyclers*, No. 35; Score, pp. 118-19.

[23] Gabriel, *The Merry Cyclers*, No. 40; Score, pp. 135-37.

[24] Gabriel, *The Merry Cyclers*, No. 32; Score, p. 107.

[25] Gabriel, *The Merry Cyclers*, No. 28; Score, pp. 82 and 88.

[26] *An Amateur Operetta / PAULINE / OR / AN EVENTFUL DAY. / IN TWO PARTS* / Music and Libretto by Chas. H. Gabriel (Cincinnati: Fillmore Brothers, 1899).

[27] *Pauline*, No. 28; Score pp. 109-10.

[28] Gabriel, *The Merry Milkmaids*, No. 21; Score, pp. 79-80.

[29] Gabriel, *The Merry Milkmaids*, No. 9; Score, p. 33.

[30] Gabriel, *The Merry Milkmaids*, No. 4; Score, p. 17.

[31] See Barbara Owen, "Reed Organ," *The New Grove Dictionary of Musical Instruments* (London: Macmillan, 1984), III, 223, 225-226.

[32] As to the modern production possibilities, the Tams-Witmark exemplars are heavily annotated with 60-odd suggestions for staging and musically realizing *The Merry Milkmaids* but only five for *The Merry Cyclers*. Typescripts are in the author's possession, with thanks to Jean Bonin, formerly at the Tams-Witmark Archives.

[33] Gabriel, *Pauline*, [4].

[34] Gabriel, *Pauline*, [3].

[35] Gabriel, *The Merry Milkmaids*, 4

[36] Gabriel, *Gospel Songs*, 12.

[37] Frederick's Solo, "How sweet, how fair" in *The Merry Cyclers* (No. 27; Score, p. 75) resembles the opening notes of Thaddeus's air "Then you'll remember me" in Act III of Michael Balfe's *The Bohemian Girl*.

[38] Gabriel, *The Merry Milkmaids*, No. 10; Score, p. 37.

[39] Gabriel, *Church Music*, 58 ("DON'TS").

[40] Gabriel, *The Singers*, 72.

[41] *Memoirs*, 46.

[42] Robert M. Stevenson, *Protestant Church Music in America: A Short Survey of Men and Movements from 1564 to the Present* (New York: Norton, 1966), 91.

[43] Gabriel, *Church Music*, 60.

[44] This article began as research for the inaugural Jean B. Falk Seminar at Christopher Newport University. The project was begun by Paulette T. Geragi through whose efforts this photograph along with much of the bibliography was gained. To her, Dr. Harry Eskew and his student Terry W. York, Jack L. Ralston, Special Collections Librarian at Regent University, Jean Bonin representing the Tams-Witmark/Wisconsin Collection of Mills Music Library at the University of Wisconsin, William Kearns, Deane L. Root, Carl Fischer, Inc., New York, and the Iowa State Historical Library, Des Moines, go my sincere thanks for their contributions.

THE MISSING TITLE PAGE: DVOŘÁK AND THE AMERICAN NATIONAL SONG

John C. Tibbetts

There is a sweet scene in *A Song Is Born*, a Samuel Goldwyn film from 1948, in which a group of musicians present a radio broadcast about the evolution of jazz. A stellar cast of performers—Benny Goodman, Lionel Hampton, Gene Krupa, Mel Powell, Charlie Barnet, Tommy Dorsey, Louis Bellson, and members of the Golden Gate Quartet—subject a simple tune to a series of riffs, casting it as an African tribal dance, a Latin samba, a black spiritual, a popular song, and, finally, a swing piece for jazz combo. Even if the movie failed at the box office, this sequence is of major interest to the rest of us: The "folk" melody, never credited, is in fact the "Largo" from Antonín Dvořák's Symphony in E minor (*From the New World*), written during the composer's American sojourn of 1892-1895.[1]

Dvořák (1841-1904) would have appreciated the Hollywood tribute immensely. At the time of his American visit, the Czech composer had predicted that the appearance of an American national song would be a model of the nation itself—that is, an expressive conjoining of disparate ethnic and cultural elements transcending any one individual type. It is no exaggeration to say that through his own example, precept, and influence, Dvořák helped stimulate important turn-of-the-century currents in modern American music: the ragtime dance, the popular songs of Tin Pan Alley, the classical spiritual, and concert jazz. Ironically, it was he, the foreigner, who was in a position to raise the musical consciousness of Americans, promoting the desirability of a native style. And, as we have seen in *A Song Is Born*, Dvořák's own music was, in turn, absorbed into the American cultural mainstream. Of all the "classical" composers of his day, Dvořák would have taken the least umbrage that his music should be thus transformed into a pop song. "I've enjoyed everything I have done," he once told a friend, "I always wrote a polka, or any silly trifle at all, with the same zest, the same delight, as I wrote an oratorio."[2]

When Dvořák came to New York in the fall of 1892 at the invitation of cultural entrepreneur Jeannette Meyer Thurber to assume the directorship of the newly formed National Conservatory of Music of America, he was well aware of his mission. "The Americans expect great things of me," he wrote to a friend back in Prague, "and the main thing is, so they say, to show them to the promised land and kingdom of a new and independent art, in short, to create a national music."[3] Critic Henry E. Krehbiel hailed the arrival of the famed Czech composer and predicted that he would bring together "popular elements and classical forms" to serve as an example for a new kind of American music:

> The phrase that music is a cosmopolite owing allegiance to no people and no tongue is become trite.... [Rather,] the originality and power in the composer rest upon the use of dialects and idioms which are national or racial in origin and structure.[4]

Dvořák, then fifty-one years old, was at the height of his international popularity, and American audiences had already had ample opportunities to hear his music. Thirteen years before, several of his *Slavonic Dances*, Opus 46, had been performed in New York under the baton of Theodore Thomas. In 1884-1886 Dvořák's *Stabat Mater*, his Seventh Symphony, and his opera *The Spectre's Bride* were heard, respectively, in Boston, New York, and Providence, Rhode Island. Promoting his cause in America were leading musicians of either German or Austrian ancestry, particularly Thomas, Emil Paur, Anton Seidl, and Frank van der Stucken. And it was two Americans—composer Dudley Buck and opera entrepreneur Jeannette Thurber—who first suggested Dvořák might come to America to succeed Jacques Bouhy as director of the National Conservatory.

Unlike other prominent composers who had previously visited America—including Russian piano virtuoso Anton Rubinstein, who arrived in 1872 for a lucrative twenty-month tour; Jacques Offenbach, who celebrated the 1876 American Centennial with a series of concerts; and Peter Ilych Tchaikovsky, who lent his prestige to the opening festivities of Carnegie Hall in May 1891[5]—Dvořák actually lived and worked here. He remained for almost three years, taught many students of exceptional ability, traveled extensively, commented publicly on the cultural scene, and composed ten major works.[6] American pupils and colleagues under his guidance at the Conservatory included African-American composers Harry T. Burleigh, Maurice Arnold, and Will Marion Cook, as well as white composers Horatio Parker and Rubin Goldmark.

The ever-inquisitive Dvořák was supremely sensitive to the sights and sounds of America. From the windows of his Conservatory offices at 126-128 East 17th Street, he looked on in astonishment at the bustling parades celebrating the Columbus Quadricentennial. An indefatigable walker, he left his flat at 327 East 17th Street on daily rambles all over Manhattan Island, savoring the street life and frequenting the opera houses, churches, train stations, coffeehouses, and saloons. With his family he traveled by train and wagon across the country to Niagara Falls; Chicago; Spillville, Iowa; and Omaha, Nebraska.[7] He met Buffalo Bill and Annie Oakley, conducted his own music at the 1893 Chicago World's Fair, and, in general, listened to "the music of the people," as he put it—the "Negro melodies, the songs of the creoles, the red man's chant, the plaintive ditties of the German or Norwegian... the melodies of whistling boys, street singers and blind organ grinders."[8] As a result, Dvořák's own music, as well as that of his American pupils, took on "American" characteristics—a controversial point to be dealt with presently.

America was changing from an essentially rural-agrarian vision of paradise to an imperialist world power. Transcontinental rail lines and telegraph wires spanned the continent—provoking young Frederick Jackson Turner to proclaim that the frontier was now closed.[9] With further westward expansion halted, America was suffering an implosion of its energies and peoples. A restless population, swelled by recent waves of immigrants, was spilling into the city streets and across the plains. Ethnic groups like

Native Americans were being displaced by other, newly arrived peoples, like the Czechs.[10]

Inevitably, Dvořák was caught up in an ongoing debate over American cultural identity that had been raging for half a century. Ralph Waldo Emerson had predicted in his essay "The American Scholar" that Americans must renounce their former dependence upon European cultural models and "walk on our own feet [and] speak our own minds." Obviously, this meant acknowledging America's own ethnic and racial diversity. This process began with language itself, said Walt Whitman in the preface to *November Boughs* (1885). He wrote that speech would become our universal "absorber and combiner." English as a living speech was assimilating contributions from every ethnic group, rejecting none. Slang, he further insisted, was renewing language. Vernacular speech is the kind of process that is "not made by dictionary makers" but "by the masses, people nearest the concrete, having most to do with actual land and sea."[11]

Music had already become a part of this process. In the parlors of Stephen Foster's day there were few distinctions between American and Old World music, popular and classical. Operatic arias rubbed shoulders with Scots-Irish tunes and African-American "plantation songs."[12] However, by the time Dvořák arrived in 1892, there were signs of a retrenchment, a "sacralization of culture," that reopened the gap between highbrow and lowbrow music (now expressed, variously, as "cultivated" versus "vernacular" and "genteel" versus "popular"). From certain quarters, including the New England conservatories and the hallowed pages of *Dwight's Journal of Music*, came attacks on what editor John Sullivan Dwight described as the "musical babble" of eclecticism. Dwight, a Bostonian, alleged that vernacular music appealed only to a "commonplace majority" rather than a "higher plane of spiritual aesthetic gratification."[13]

Part and parcel of this late nineteenth-century attitude was the emergence of a more tightly stratified class structure. There were political and racist agendas at work here, namely, that one body of music—especially that of the German academies—was superior to all others and could be understood and "appreciated" only by a small, privileged segment of the population. This cultural divide corresponded to ethnic and national divisions: Most of the so-called elite were of Anglo-Saxon descent, while the outsiders were Irish, Italian, African-American, Scandanavian, and, soon, Central European and southern Mediterranean.[14]

Until the publication of my own volume *Dvořák in America* (Amadeus Press, 1993), together with a few articles by other authors confined to specialty music journals, Dvořák's American sojourn has been only superficially examined, regarded at most as a footnote to his life and to America's cultural history.[15] This neglect is, in part, understandable: Few physical traces of his sojourn remain, excepting a tiny but charming Dvořák Museum in Spillville, Iowa, and an area along New York City's East 17th Street between First and Second Avenues that has been recently designated "Dvořák Place."[16] The Conservatory and most of its papers disappeared after the 1929 stock market crash. And the Dvořák residence in New York was demolished in 1992.[17] Dvořák left no journal or comprehensive written record of his activities, save a handful of articles and letters that have been neglected or, at the least, misleadingly excerpted and/or misquoted. (Indeed, their very authorship has been questioned.[18]) And Dvořák's most important African-American pupils, Harry T. Burleigh, Will Marion Cook, and Maurice Arnold, have, up to now, received little popular exposure and scholarly scrutiny.[19]

Yet Dvořák's American adventure is fraught with significance and controversy. The most modest of men, he himself was a creature of contradictions: Born a Czech villager, a minority figure in a German-dominated musical establishment, Dvořák became a cosmopolitan artist feted in all the musical capitals of Europe, Russia, and America. Many of his countrymen accused him of turning his back on his own roots; and, conversely, the German musical establishment criticized him for his inordinate employment of folk idioms in his music. The truth is, he lived in both worlds, exploiting the idioms of his own culture in a vocabulary befitting the academic, or classical style. He was precisely the right person to assume the leadership of the National Conservatory.

Established in 1885, the Conservatory had become, by the time of Dvořák's arrival, the most outstanding institution for professional musical preparation in the United States, boasting a faculty that included lecturer Henry T. Finck, pianist Rafael Joseffy, pianist and journalist James Gibbons Huneker, cellist and composer Victor Herbert, conductor Anton Seidl, and composers

Rubin Goldmark and Horatio Parker. In recognition of its artistic and educational attainments, the Conservatory won a Congressional Charter in 1891, the only such acknowledgment ever conferred on a school of the arts in America. However, its admission policies were most unorthodox: It was the first institution in the United States to make a special mission of seeking out and encouraging women, minorities, and the handicapped.[20] This was at a time, it must be remembered, when women were not employed by "respectable" orchestras, and nonwhite musicians had difficulty gaining recognition in the concert world.

During his tenure at the Conservatory, Dvořák spoke out on what he regarded as America's cultural shortcomings. "It is a difficult task at best for a foreigner to give a correct verdict of the affairs of another country," he admitted in 1895. "It would ill become me, therefore, to express my views on so general and all-embracing a subject as music in America, were I not pressed to do so." But comment he did, and the newspapers and magazines constantly hounded him for quotes. While he admired the enthusiastic patriotism that tended to pronounce every building and new invention the finest in the world, and while he applauded "the American push" that propelled his pupils to stop at nothing in their pursuit of goals—"they are inquisitive to a degree that they want to go to the bottom of all things at once"—he deplored the lack of public support of the arts:

> When I see how much is done in every other field by public-spirited men in America—how schools, universities, libraries, museums, hospitals, and parks spring up out of the ground and are maintained by generous gifts—I can only marvel that so little has been done for music.

It was not so in the Old World, Dvořák continued, documenting an extensive catalogue of instances of public and government support. "The great American republic alone, in its national government as well as in the several governments of the States, suffers art and music to go without encouragement." His arguments seem remarkably pertinent today—as is their failure to enact governmental response.[21]

Nothing among his pronouncements aroused more heated debate and controversy, however, than his attitudes toward the musical possibilities of certain ethnic groups. In "The Real Value of Negro Melodies," published in the *New York Herald* on 21 May 1893 as his first public utterance as the new Director of the National Conservatory, Dvořák wrote:

> I did not come to America to interpret Beethoven or Wagner for the public. This is not my work and I would not waste any time on it. I came to discover what young Americans have in them and to help them express it.... The new American school of music must strike its roots deeply into its own soil.

Moreover, he admonished composers that an American national style should be based on the music of African Americans. "In the [N]egro melodies of America I discover all that is needed for a great and noble school of music."[22] At the time of the premiere of the "New World" Symphony on 15 December 1893, in New York City, he amplified his statement to include also the music of Native Americans.[23] And in his last comment on the subject, in *Harper's New Monthly Magazine* of May 1895—as he prepared to leave America and return to Prague—he admitted that his original prescription was based on incomplete knowledge of musical traditions in America. All ethnic groups, he now believed, should be included: "The germs for the best in music lie hidden among all the races that are commingled in this great country."[24]

Protest was immediate. Members of the New England musical establishment reacted with bitter scorn to the contention that a truly American music might be based on the music of socially and politically marginal groups. "We have here in America been offered a pattern for an 'American' national musical costume by the Bohemian Dvořák," responded Edward MacDowell, America's most distinguished composer; "—though what Negro melodies have to do with Americanism in art still remains a mystery." Writing in the pages of the *Boston Herald* of 28 May 1893, John Knowles Paine stated flatly, "In my estimation, it is a preposterous idea to say that in the future American music will rest upon such a foundation as the melodies of a yet largely undeveloped race." Amy Beach, the most prominent female composer of the day, said the "[N]egro melodies of which Dvořák speaks" are "not fully typical of our country." The blacks, moreover, "are no more native than the Italians, Swedes or Russians." George Whitefield Chadwick, an important colleague of Paine and Beach, deplored the use of such melodies as models for serious composition, declaring, "I should be sorry to see [them] become the basis of an American school of musical composition." Somewhat later, Arthur Foote wrote that African-American music was either of the music hall variety or, regarding spirituals, indistinguishable from white models. He asked if there could be better models than "composers from Bach to Wagner." Finally, Adrienne Fried Block has concluded that

> [i]f Paine and some others dismissed Dvořák's ideas outright, it was because they had for some time been hoping to purify their music of the very American provincialisms now being urged on them by Dvořák.[25]

Two related issues were at stake: the survival of "classical"— read that, elitest—music in the face of the growing threat of popular music; and the maintenance of an Anglo-American identity in the face of increasing tides of immigration from non-British lands. Thus, classical music was first and foremost the province of upper-class Anglo-Saxons (though Germanic elements dominated in other parts of the country), and popular music was the province of the lower classes, mostly of non-British descent. It is clear that the split between classical and popular music also had racial and ethnic implications. Historian Charles Hamm has even suggested that behind these objections was a not-so-subtle aversion to Dvořák's selection of New York City as a residence. New York was regarded as a "foreign" city overrun by hordes of immigrants from undesirable national backgrounds. They could not speak English and were not even Protestant! "The fact that Dvořák went to that city rather than to Boston, and that he soon suggested that American composers might draw on the culture of ethnic groups outside the traditional New England establishment, surely had something to do with the suspicion directed toward him in certain conservative musical quarters, particularly in New England."[26]

Clearly, Dvořák believed there was such a thing as nationalism in music, that each country should encourage its own unique musical expression, and that American composers should therefore immerse themselves in the folk traditions of their own land. These notions grew out of the conviction that music is essentially a "realistic," or programmatic art—a belief that ran counter to the opposite view that music is a "universal," or absolutist phenomenon that bore no relationship whatever with extramusical elements. In Europe these camps were epitomized by, respectively, the adherents of Richard Wagner and Johannes Brahms (especially the critic Eduard Hanslick). Dvořák's own music, written in America, was a test case: To what extent was it uniquely "American," or descriptive of national traits, and to what degree did it remain in the European absolutist academic tradition?

On the one hand, Dvořák did not literally appropriate "negro" and Native American melodies for his own use. That was never his practice, and he never advocated it in his teachings. Rather, he saturated himself with these materials until he became "thoroughly imbued with their characteristics," as he put it, so that he could "make a musical picture in keeping with and partaking of those characteristics."[27] Thus, for example, melodies in the "New World" Symphony that seemed to resemble the spiritual "Swing Low, Sweet Chariot" and the patriotic ditty, "Yankee Doodle," were, in actuality, little more than general allusions. Thus, we might conclude that his music remained centered in the European academic tradition, filtered somewhat through his American impressions.

On the other hand, Dvořák was undeniably fascinated by specific rhythmic and melodic features he attributed to an indigenously African-American and Native American music—that is, "Scotch" snaps (a short note value occurring on the beat followed by a longer note value lasting through the remainder of the beat—producing a kind of whiplash crack to a musical phrase), pentatonic scales (in Dvořák's case, a stack of four perfect fifths, e.g., FCGDA), flatted sevenths in minor and major keys, and syncopations. While historians and musicologists John Clapham, David Beveridge, and Gerald Abraham admit that these characteristics occur in Dvořák's music prior to his American visit, they insist that they occur more frequently, even persistently, in his American works, particularly in the "New World" Symphony, the "American" Quartet and Quintet, and the

Sonatina.[28] Moreover, the composer himself declared in a *New York Herald* article, dated 28 May 1893, that the second and third movements of the symphony utilized musical materials originally intended for an opera based on Longfellow's *Song of Hiawatha* (an opera that was never completed).[29] This has been confirmed by recent researches by Michael Beckerman.[30]

Dvořák himself was inconsistent in his stated intentions. One moment, in a letter written from Spillville, Iowa, to his friend, Dr. Kozánek, in Kromeriz, on 15 September 1893, he declared:

> I am very well off here, God be praised, I am in good health and am working well and I know that, as for my new Symphony, the F major String Quartet and the Quintet (composed here in Spillville)—I should never have written these works "just so" if I hadn't seen America.[31]

On another occasion, however, he contradicted himself in a later statement recorded by his secretary, J. J. Kovařík: "So I am an American composer, am I? I was, I am, and I remain a Czech composer. I have only showed them the path they might take— how they should work. But I'm through with that! From this day forward I will write the way I wrote before!"[32] Perhaps James Gibbons Huneker had the most amusing and insightful observation on the presumed American character of the "New World":

> Dvořák's is an American symphony: is it? Themes from negro melodies; composed by a Bohemian; conducted by a Hungarian and played by Germans in a hall built by a Scotchman [*sic*]. About one third of the audience were Americans and so were the critics. All the rest of it was anything but American—and that is just as it can be....[33]

Dvořák's precepts and examples had an immediate, decided, and longlasting effect on American composers. "Not only was his influence still strong two decades after he left the United States," Block writes, but there is also considerable evidence that his definition of Americanism in music determined the parameters of the debate over nationalism for almost half a century."[34] The list of examples, apart from the work of his own students, is endless; the merest sampling will have to suffice.

Despite his initial objections to Dvořák's suggestions, Edward MacDowell's most ambitious orchestral work, his *Suite* No. 2, Opus 48, which was premiered in 1896, utilized Native American idioms and was subtitled "Indian." George Chadwick incorporated vernacular elements evocative of Dvořák's "American" Quartet into his own Fourth String Quartet; and Amy Beach composed a "Gaelic" Symphony—her first and only symphony—as a "Celtic response" to Dvořák, premiering it in Boston on 30 October 1896, almost three years after the "New World" symphony's premiere in that city. Henry F. Gilbert was perhaps the first American to draw directly upon Negro spirituals in orchestral pieces like *Americanesque on Negro-Minstrel Tunes* (1903), Dance in the Place Congo (1906-1908), and Negro Rhapsody ("Shout") in 1912. Charles Ives introduced various vernacular elements into many works, among them *Ragtime Pieces* (1902-1904), Third Symphony ("The Camp Meeting"), completed in 1904, *Central Park in the Dark* (the second of his *Two Contemplations*, 1906), the First Piano Sonata (completed in 1909), and the *Three Places in New England* (1911-1914). And, hard on the heels of Dvořák's statements and based on recent research by ethnologists at the Smithsonian Institution and the Peabody Institute of Archaeology and Ethnology, the so-called Indianist movement soon developed. Collectors and researchers H. E. Krehbiel and Alice Fletcher published volumes of Native American melodies. In 1901 Arthur Farwell became, in his own words, "the first composer in America to take up Dvořák's challenge ... in a serious and whole-hearted way," establishing his Wa-Wan Press to publish his groundbreaking *American Indian Melodies*.[35]

Dvořák's own pupils and colleagues, particularly Burleigh, Arnold, Goldmark, Cook, and Franko Goldman, played their part in the formation of a new American song. Although it is unclear to what extent Burleigh (1866-1949) was Dvořák's pupil (he entered the Conservatory a few months before Dvořák took up the directorship), there is no doubting that they became close associates, personally and professionally. Perhaps more than anyone else, contends Jean M. Snyder in her study of Burleigh, he extended by example and spirit his teacher's musical legacy.[36] Burleigh, an African American, introduced Dvořák to the black spiritual tunes he had heard from his grandfather, Hamilton

Waters, like "Swing Low, Sweet Chariot" (which, Burleigh claimed, provided thematic materials for the "New World" Symphony), and to the music of Stephen Foster, which he had learned from his mother (who, it is alleged, may have met Foster). He was present at the genesis of the "New World," for which he not only did much of the manuscript copying, but made suggestions about the orchestrations.[37] He sang the baritone solo at the premiere of Dvořák's arrangement of Foster's "Old Folks at Home," which the composer had dedicated to him.[38] He confirmed that Dvořák's fascination with "Negro songs" bore musical fruit in his own compositions: "[He] literally saturated himself with Negro song.... I sang our Negro songs for him very often, and before he wrote his own themes, he filled himself with the spirit of the old Spirituals."[39]

For his part, at Dvořák's urging, Burleigh brought the traditional spiritual into the arena of the art song:

[Dvořák] left behind a richer appreciation of the beauties of Negro song," wrote Burleigh, "of its peculiar flavor, its sometimes mystical atmosphere, its whimsical piquancy, and its individual idiom, from all of which many other artists have already drawn inspiration.... Under the inspiration of Dvořák, I became convinced that the spirituals were not meant for the colored people, but for all people.[40]

Thus, in addition to the hundreds of "art songs," romantic ballads, and sacred anthems that he composed between 1901 and 1918, Burleigh arranged many traditional spirituals for various vocal combinations. To the latter group belonged *Plantation Melodies, Old and New* (1901), arrangements for Henry E. Krehbiel's *Afro-American Folksongs* (1914), and the ever-popular "Deep River" (1916).

As these spirituals became standard fare for concert performers, both white and black, controversies inevitably arose. Although some African Americans were gratified at their performance and reception—certainly a far cry from the prevailing popular minstrel and coon song tradition—others saw a "distasteful irony" in the performance of white slave songs by white performers. Moreover, Burleigh's blend of black musical materials with European musical practices incurred the same sort of criticism that had greeted Dvořák years before: "Spirituals had derived originally from group performance in particular contexts," explains Snyder,

> and were the product of artistic procedures rooted in an African music aesthetic. European solo performance practices, like the ritualized protocol of the concert stage where the distance between performer and audience is preserved, violated that aesthetic.[41]

Nonetheless, Burleigh's seminal position in a burgeoning awareness and celebration during the first two decades of the new century of the black aesthetic is assured. As James Weldon Johnson wrote in the *Second Book of American Negro Spirituals* (1926), the rediscovery of black spirituals, "coupled with a consciousness of innate racial talents and powers ... gave rise to a new school of Negro artists." H. L. Mencken claimed that Burleigh was "one of the few Americans who have ever learned how to write ... an American song—not a limp reboiling of a German song or French song or a Russian song, but an American song, race of the soil in its whole cut and color."[42] In 1941 Burleigh himself, on the occasion of the commemoration of Dvořák's one hundredth birthday, publicly acknowledged the composer's lasting influence in this black renaissance, thanking him not only for having the "black folk melodies" capable of artistic rendition, but for making them into "spokesmen" of the black people, standing firmly "against oppression and humiliation."[43]

African Americans Maurice Arnold and Will Marion Cook applied Dvořák's teachings into the realms of, respectively, the popularization of creole folk music and the development of ragtime and jazz. Arnold built upon the precedent of the late virtuoso pianist/composer Louis Moreau Gottschalk, who, a half-century previously, had incorporated the French- and African-tinged Caribbean folk songs he heard while growing up into many of his piano pieces. Clara Gottschalk Peterson, the pianist-composer's sister, declared in 1902,

> If as Dr. Dvořák has claimed there is in time to be a native school of American Music based on the primitive musical utterances of the

Red Man and the black among us, then truly these melodies of the
Louisiana Negroes ... are ... of some interest.[44]

As if in response to this charge, Arnold's suite of "Creole Dances"
was premiered a year later in the summer of 1893. Dvořák
publicly performed the work with Arnold in a two-piano version
and pronounced him "the most promising and gifted of [my
composition] pupils." He described the suite as "contain[ing]
material that he has treated in a style that accords with my
ideas."[45]

Will Marion Cook (1869-1944) was a musical phenomenon
whose important place in the development of modern American
musical theater has yet to be carefully examined and clarified.
After studies at Oberlin Conservatory and later in Berlin with
Joseph Joachim, he entered the Conservatory to study under
Dvořák. Inspired by the new "ragtime" craze—and recently
popularized on Broadway by May Irwin's renditions of "The Bully
Song" and "Mister Johnson Turn Me Loose"—Cook left the
Conservatory in 1898 to compose and produce the all-black
production *Clorindy; or, the Origin of the Cakewalk*. It played at
the Casino Roof during the 1898 Broadway summer season, and
its hit ragtime songs, like "Emancipation Day" and "That's How
the Cakewalk Is Done" (lyrics by Paul Laurence Dunbar) were an
immediate success. Three years later Cook brought another all-
black musical show to Broadway, *In Dahomey*. "Negroes were at
last on Broadway," said Cook, "and there to stay.... We were
artists and we were going a long, long way."[46]

James Weldon Johnson, a member of the Cole and Johnson
Brothers songwriting team and a major historian of black culture,
praised Cook as "the first competent composer to take what was
then known as rag-time and work it out in a musicianly way."
Although ragtime historian Edward A. Berlin disputes the fact that
Cook was the first black composer to thus develop ragtime on the
stage—Bob Cole's *A Trip to Coontown* was playing at the same
time as *Clorindy*—he avers that Cook's shows were an important
part of ragtime's development, spawning many more productions,
both black and white.[47] After producing a succession of ragtime
shows, Cook joined what historian Macdonald Smith Moore called
the "jazz invasion" of 1919. He formed his all-black Syncopated
Orchestra (for which he arranged a jazz version of his mentor's

"Largo," by the way) and mentored many younger musicians, including Harold Arlen and Duke Ellington.

Another student, Rubin Goldmark, establishes an intriguing link between Dvořák and the "Americanist" movement of the 1930s and 1940s. First a student of Dvořák's and then a teacher at the National Conservatory, he composed several works reflecting his master's precepts. While a large portion of his music is virtually unknown today, the *Hiawatha Overture* (1900) and the *Negro Rhapsody* (1919) are still occasionally performed. The latter contains quotations from various spirituals and features elements characteristic of black folk music, like syncopations, flatted sevenths, and an emphasis on subdominant harmonies. Later, Goldmark became one of the most respected composition teachers in America, numbering among his students George Gershwin and Aaron Copland. Referring to Goldmark, with whom he studied for four years, Copland asserted that he "really should get more credit than he has been given for my early training."[48]

Yet another student, Edwin Franko Goldman, ventured off into a wholly different but no less significant direction. With Sousa, he became an important figure in the flowering of the repertoire of the concert band. After winning a scholarship to the National Conservatory and studying with Dvořák, he joined the faculty of Columbia University as a teacher of band instruments. In 1911 he founded the famous Goldman Band and composed many staples in the band repertory, including "On the Mall," "On Parade," and "The Pride of America."

Despite the glory of students like these and their mentor from Bohemia, the National Conservatory began to fade from the scene with the dawning of the new century. Alas, according to Emanuel Rubin, who has conducted the most extensive research to date, information is scant, since most of the Conservatory's records have been scattered and lost.[49] After Dvořák's departure in 1895, three years passed before a new director, Emil Paur, began his tenure. More skilled as a conductor than Dvořák, he drew more polished public performances from the students and elicited favorable reviews from the New York critics. Paur was succeeded by Vassily Safonov in 1906, who in turn yielded the position to Engelbert Humperdinck in 1913. After that date, reports Rubin, no one can be identified as director, and many of the daily management decisions must have been relegated to

Thurber, who was nearing age seventy. The Conservatory's address, meanwhile, had changed several times by 1920. But the *Musical Blue Book* of 1921-1922 has no listing at all for a "National Conservatory," although there is a reference to it under Thurber's name at 621 West 79th Street. Unfortunately, that was the last *Blue Book* to be issued. The Manhattan telephone directory for the winter of 1929-1930 provided the last known address, 53 West 74th Street. No record of its operation exists after 1930.

According to Rubin, the Conservatory's decline can be explained in part by the rise of competitor institutions like the Institute of Musical Arts of the City of New York, chartered on 27 June 1904, with Frank Damrosch as director and Andrew Carnegie, one of Thurber's original backers, as a patron. Under Damrosch's imaginative guidance the Institute received an award of $23 million from the Juilliard Foundation in 1923, when it was renamed the Juilliard School of Music. At the same time, the hopes of a federally funded conservatory, for which Thurber, supported by Dvořák, fought so strenuously all her life, and which fueled useful public debate, dwindled. One of her supporters had been Oscar Sonneck, head of the Music Division of the Library of Congress, who in 1904 declared that "such an institution [as] an outlet for thousands of home-trained musicians would become imperative—symphony orchestras and chamber music organ-izations would spring up everywhere by sheer force of economic necessity."[50]

The opposing view, which, of course, ultimately won out, had been expressed in an editorial in May 1895 in the *New England Conservatory Quarterly*: "Indeed, we do not think that a single musical school in America is endowed in the way and to the extent that many in Europe are. Nor do we today think that state aid is the method best suited to the American nation."[51] Meanwhile, concludes Rubin, the directors of private music schools and conservatories across the country did not find the prospect of a centralized, federally supported institution in the least attractive: "They were, in fact, appalled at the spectre of federally funded competition, resenting the downgrading of their schools to 'feeder' status."[52]

The Conservatory's precedent was far-reaching. Aside from bringing Dvořák to America, concludes Rubin, "it set the pace and standard for post-secondary music education in the United States; it established a curricular philosophy that still remains the infrastructure of every American music school; it assailed the barriers that kept minorities and women from advanced education and professional engagements in music."[53]

The issues and debates sparked by Dvořák's visit a hundred years ago—public support of the arts; the rights of minority groups to public education; the assimilation of immigrant and minority groups into American culture (the conflicting priorities of diversity and centrism); the racist/elitest agendas behind the boundary lines separating "pop" and "classical" art; and the implications of "nationalism" in the arts—remain today as lively and controversial as ever. Moreover, as outlined earlier, his influence on the music of his students and their contemporaries was considerable, although it is only now being fully documented and assessed.

Ironically, while Dvořák is being recognized as a major influence on the formation of an American national song, his name has disappeared from many of his own melodies, like the "Largo," as a result of their entering the mainstream of American pop music and the movies. For example, by the time the "Largo" tune was sung by a tearful Deanna Durbin in the 1941 film *It Started with Eve* (featuring the lyrics of William Arms Fisher, another Dvořák pupil), jazzed up in *A Star Is Born*, and, most recently, performed in a wordless choral arrangement in Bruce Beresford's World War II epic *Paradise Road*, it has left the specific contexts of history to become a part of an "anonymous" folk tradition. Dvořák seems to have come full circle: He came to America to partake of a folk tradition, and he ultimately has contributed to it.

The Czech writer Karel Capek has eloquently described this process:

> Every copy of [a writer's work] would travel from hand to hand, from hands marked by pinpricks and corrosive laundry detergents, reddish with kitchen cleansing powder, soiled by inkspots, into hands bruised by some other kind of hard life, until finally the title page of all copies would be lost and nobody would know any more

who the author was. And it would be unnecessary to know because
everybody would find himself in the book.[54]

In this same way Dvořák's music has thus gone out to the people,
been absorbed, "lost its title page" (as it were), and returned
bearing the marks of its new owners.

University of Kansas

---

[1]The sequence was devised by lyricist Don Raye and composer Gene
DePaul. In the cue sheets of the Goldwyn Archives it is listed as the "Long
Hair Jam Session Production Routine." For production information about *A
Song Is Born*, see Alvin H. Marill, *Samuel Goldwyn Presents* (New York:
A. S. Barnes and Company, 1976), 258-60.

[2]Quoted in Josef Skvorecky, "Every Silly Trifle," *Iowa Dvořák Centennial
Symposium Abstracts* (Iowa Center for the Arts, 1993), 5-6.

[3]Dvořák letter to Dr. Emil Kozanek, 12 October 1892; in Otakar Sourek,
Ed., Trans. Roberta Finlayson Samsour, *Antonín Dvořák: Letters and
Reminiscences* (Prague, Artia, 1954), 152.

[4]Henry E. Krehbiel, "Antonín Dvořák," *Century Illustrated Monthly
Magazine* 44/5 (September 1892), 657.

[5]For accounts of the Offenbach and Tchaikovsky American visits, see,
respectively, *Orpheus in America: Offenbach's Diary of His Journey to the
New Worlds*, ed. and trans. Lander MacClintock (Bloomington: Indiana
University Press, 1957); and Elkhonon Yoffe, *Tchaikovsky in America*,
trans. Lidya Yoffe (New York: Oxford University Press, 1986).

[6]The ten works are, in chronological order of composition: *Te Deum*, Opus
103 (1892); *The American Flag Cantata*, Opus 102 (1893); Symphony No.
9 in E minor ("From the New World"), Opus 95 (1893); String Quartet in
F Major ("American"), Opus 96 (1893); Sonatina in G Major for Violin and
Piano, Opus 100 (1893); Suite in A Major ("American"), Opus 98 (1894);
Cello Concerto in B Minor, Opus 104 (1895); *Humoresques*, Opus 101
(1894-1895); *Biblical Songs*, Opus 99 (1894); and "Old Folks at Home"
[arrangement of a Stephen Foster song for solo voices, chorus, and full
orchestra], 1894. A sketch for a twelfth piece, an "American Anthem," was
begun in New York in 1892 but never completed (although its thematic
ideas surfaced in the Opus 97 Quintet).

[7]The trip to Spillville, Iowa, in the summer of 1893 was suggested by
Dvořák's secretary, J. J. Kovarik, who had grown up in that Czech-
American community. See John Tibbetts, "Dvořák in the New World: A
Spillville Adventure," *Classical Magazine* 3/2 (February 1991), 32-36. For

a thorough history of the Czech presence in the Iowa region, see Cyril M. Klimesh, *They Came to This Place: A History of Spillville, Iowa, and Its Czech Settlers* (Sebastopol, CA: Methodius Press, 1983).

[8]Antonin Dvořák [assisted by Edwin E. Emerson Jr.], "Music in America," *Harper's New Monthly Magazine* 90/537 (February 1895), 433.

[9]For an especially lucid examination of the various historical and social currents of the day, see Paul F. Boller Jr., *American Thought in Transition: The Impact of Evolutionary Naturalism, 1865-1900* (New York: University Press of America, 1981).

[10]See Klimesh, *They Came to This Place*, 13-18.

[11]Whitman's essay is discussed in F. O. Mathiessen, *American Renaissance* (New York: Oxford University Press, 1941), 519. For a discussion of Emerson's address, see Gay Wilson Allen, *Waldo Emerson* (New York: Viking, 1981), 198-202.

[12]Opera in the first half of the nineteenth century had both popular and elite appeal, arias and popular airs being common staples on the concert stage and in the parlor alike. Amusing examples of these juxtapositions are catalogued in Lawrence Levine, *Highbrow/Lowbrow: The Emergence of Cultural Hierarchy in America* (Cambridge, MA: Harvard University Press, 1988), 85-101; and in Charles Hamm, *Yesterdays* (New York: Norton, 1979), 62-88.

[13]Quoted in Levine, *Highbrow/Lowbrow*, 119-22. For a more sympathetic discussion of Dwight, see William W. Austin, *"Susannah," "Jeanie," and "The Old Folks at Home": The Songs of Stephen C. Foster from His Time to Ours* (New York: Macmillan, 1975), 55-60.

[14]See Hamm, "Dvořák, Stephen Foster, and American National Song," in Tibbetts, *Dvořák in America* (Portland, OR: Amadeus Press, 1993), 149-56. Hereafter "Tibbetts."

[15]The distinguished music historian John Clapham wrote about Dvořák's American sojourn in the following articles: "Dvořák on the American Scene," *19th Century Music* 5/1 (Summer 1981): 16-21; "Dvořák and the American Indian," *Musical Times* 107/1484 (October 1966): 863-67; "Dvořák's Musical Directorship in New York," *Music & Letters* 47 (1967): 40-51; "Dvořák's Musical Directorship in New York: A Postscript," *Music & Letters* 59 (1978): 19-27; and "Dvořák on the American Scene," *19th Century Music* 5/9 (Summer 1981), 16-21. The only book-length study of Dvořák's Spillville sojourn is a poetic effusion by Patricia Hempl entitled *Spillville* (Minneapolis: Milkweed Editions, 1987).

[16]The area in the Stuyvesant District where Dvořák lived was designated "Dvořák Place" in February 1992. Plans are afoot to place a Dvořák statue in Stuyvesant Park, directly across the street from 327 E. 17th Street, the site of Dvořák's residence.

[17]The fate of the Dvořák house, a four-story brick row house at 327 E. 17th Street, is a sad testament to public neglect of historical sites. It had been honored in 1941, on the occasion of the 100th anniversary of the composer's birth, as a symbol of Czech-American relations. Mayor Fiorello La Guardia and Minister of Foreign Affairs for the Czechoslovak government Jan Masaryk, participated in the ceremonies. At that time La Guardia promised to secure landmark status for the structure. Such was not to be, however, and the home was purchased in 1989 by the Beth Israel Medical Center and, after a bitterly divisive debate, subsequently torn down in late August 1991, just a few days short of the composer's 150th birthday. An AIDS hospice is presently being built on the site. For a detailed account of this rather sad story, see Tibbetts, *Dvořák in America*, 341-54.

[18]Just after the completion of his "New World" in the spring of 1893, Dvořák began to write articles and consent to interviews regarding issues relevant to a national "American" music. He read English perfectly, but wrote it in a highly idiosyncratic fashion. Thus, it has been suggested that an "invisible voice" assisted in the translations and/or rewritings—perhaps colleague James Gibbons Huneker, critic and ethnomusicologist Henry E. Krehbiel, or journalist James Creelman. In an address delivered to the Iowa Dvořák Centennial Symposium, 4-7 August 1993, Michael Beckerman of the University of California, Santa Barbara, claimed to have discovered the authorial identity behind Dvořák's most controversial article, "The Real Value of Negro Melodies," 16 December 1893. The individual in question was one James Creelman, editor of the *New York Telegram*, the *Herald*'s sister paper at the time. Creelman, a friend of Dvořák, was in perfect sympathy with the composer's attitudes about "negro melodies" and was in a position to articulate it. "Know what we do now about Creelman, we might want to be careful about how we attribute this material to Dvořák," said Beckerman. "Perhaps we shall never know precisely what Dvořák said himself and what Creelman did with it, but certainly we have a charismatic new character introduced into this drama" (See *Iowa Dvořák Centennial Symposium Abstracts*, 14; and Michael Beckerman, "The Master's Little Joke: Antonín Dvořák and the Mask of Nation," in *Dvořák and His World*, ed. Beckerman (Princeton, NJ: Princeton University Press, 1993), 134-53.

[19]A doctoral dissertation about the life and music of Burleigh has recently been completed by Jean E. Snyder at the University of Pittsburgh. See her chapter on the subject, "A Great and Noble School of Music," in Tibbetts, 123-48.

[20]For the most detailed history of the Conservatory extant, see Emanuel Rubins's "Dvořák at the National Conservatory" in Tibbetts, *Dvořák in America*, 53-81.

[21]Dvořák, "Music in America," 430-31.

[22]Ibid., 28.

[23]Dvořák's first references to Native American music appear in "Dvořák on His New Work," *New York Herald,* 15 December 1893, 11; and "Dr. Dvořák's Great Symphony," *New York Herald,* 16 December 1893, 8.

[24]Dvořák, "Music in America," 433.

[25]MacDowell's statement is quoted in Hamm, *Music in the New World* (New York: Norton, 1983), 415. Dvořák's article in the New York *Herald* of 21 May 1893 was reprinted in the *Boston Herald,* 28 May 1893. The *Herald* editor, Frederick Bacon, solicited reactions by prominent Boston musicians. An invaluabale documentation of the New England response to Dvořák's pronouncements is contained in two articles by Adrienne Block: "Boston Talks Back to Dvořák," *I. S. A. M. Newsletter* 18/2 (May 1989), 10-11, 15; and "Dvořák, Beach, and American Music," in *A Celebration of American Music: Words and Music in Honor of H. Wiley Hitchcock,* ed. Richard Crawford et al. (Ann Arbor: University of Michigan Press, 1990), 256-80. The quotation is from "Boston Talks Back to Dvořák," 15.

[26]Hamm, "Dvořák, Stephen Foster, and American National Song," in Tibbetts, 149-50.

[27]Dvořák, "For National Music," *Chicago Tribune,* 13 August 1893. The article is quoted in its entirety in Tibbetts, 361-62.

[28]An investigation into the supposedly "Indian" aspects of Dvořák's String Quintet appears in John Clapham, "Dvořák and the American Indian," 863-67. For a discussion of Dvořák's pentonicism, see David Beveridge, "Sophisticated Primitivism: The Significance of Pentatonicism in Dvořák's 'American' Quartet," *Current Musicology* 24 (1977): 25-35. And Gerald Abraham concludes that these traits of American music "attracted him because they were closely related to something already present in him, something which they helped to clarify and crystallize." See Gerald Abraham, "Dvořák's Musical Personality," *Antonín Dvořák, His Achievement,* ed. Abraham (London: Lindsay Drummond, 1942), 204.

[29]"Dvořák on His New Work," *New York Herald,* 15 December 1893, 11.

[30]Beckerman, "The Dance of Pau-Puk-Keewis and the Song of Chibiabos: Reflections on the Scherzo of Dvořák's Symphony 'From the New World'," in Tibbetts, 210-27.

[31]The letter is quoted in its entirety in Tibbetts, 399-400.

[32]Quoted in Beckerman, "The Master's Little Joke: Antonín Dvořák and the Mask of Nation," in *Dvořák and His World,* 141.

[33]*Loc. cit.*

[34]Block, "Dvořák's Long American Reach," in Tibbetts, 157. An excellent overview of this subject is in Hamm, *Music in the New World,* 410-13. Speaking at the Dvořák Conference in New Orleans, 10-14 February 1991,

Crawford presented a list of eight music histories from Elson (1904) to Hitchcock (1988) in which Dvořák's influence is discussed.

[35]Evelyn Davis Culbertson, "Arthur Farwell's Early Efforts on Behalf of American Music," *American Music* 5/2 (Summer 1987): 167.

[36]Although Victor Herbert and James Gibbons Huneker would claim Burleigh had been Dvořák's composition pupil, Burleigh himself denied this, stating that he studied with Rubin Goldmark, because he was not advanced enough to be admitted to Dvořák's composition class: "I didn't even dream of being a composer—at least not out loud. I was going to be a singer." See Jean M. Snyder's discussion of Burleigh and Dvořák in "A Great and Noble School of Music," in Tibbetts, 123-48. The quotation is from page 132.

[37]Dvořák changed his orchestration of the famous "Largo" melody from clarinet and flutes to English horn "because of all the instruments it resembled the quality of Burleigh's voice most closely." Quoted in John Clapham, *Antonín Dvořák: Musician and Craftsman* (New York: St. Martin's Press, 1966), 90.

[38]Dvořák's choral arrangement premiered under his baton on 23 January 1894 at the Madison Square Garden Concert Hall. Among the all-black performers were the soloists Burleigh and Sissieretta Jones. The work was not published and was not performed publicly again until 18 April 1990, when the University of Pittsburgh and its Department of Music presented it in concert in Pittsburgh, Pennsylvania. It was finally published in facsimile by Sixty-Eight Publishers in August 1991. The manuscript is preserved today in the Stephen Foster Memorial Archives in Pittsburgh. See Dean L. Root, "The Stephen Foster–Antonín Dvořák Connection," in Tibbetts, 243-54.

[39]Harry T. Burleigh, "The Negro and His Song," in *Music on the Air*, ed. Hazel Gertrude Kinscella (New York: Viking, 1934), 186-89.

[40]Quotations from Burleigh, "The Negro and His Song," 189; and "Harry Burleigh Returns to Erie for Sunday Concert," *Erie Times*, 9 June 1944.

[41]Snyder in Tibbetts, 137.

[42]Quoted in Snyder (Tibbetts, 139-41).

[43]Originally quoted in Anne Keye Simpson, *Hard Trials: The Life and Music of Harry T. Burleigh* (Metuchen, NJ: Scarecrow Press, 1990), 141.

[44]Clara Gottschalk Peterson, *Creole Songs from New Orleans in the Negro Dialect* (New Orleans: L.W. Greenewald, 1902), Preface.

[45]Quoted in "For National Music: Dvořák, the Great Bohemian Composer," *Chicago Tribune*, 13 August 1893, 29. Information about Maurice Arnold is scant at this writing. Much is yet to be done about this pioneering, yet neglected figure in American music.

[46]Quoted in Edward Jablonski, *The Encyclopedia of American Music* (New York: Doubleday, 1981), 123.

[47]James Weldon Johnson, *Black Manhattan* (New York: Knopf, 1930), 103; quoted in Edward A. Berlin, *Reflections and Research on Ragtime* (I. S. A. M. Monographs: No. 24, 1987), 24.

[48]David Beveridge, "Dvořák's American Pupil Rubin Goldmark," 5. Unpublished paper quoted in Block, "Dvořák's Long American Reach," 171.

[49]Rubin's pioneering essay, "Jeannette Thurber and the National Conservatory of Music," appeared in *American Music* 8/4 (Fall 1990), 294-325. It was extensively revised for Tibbetts, 53-81.

[50]Oscar Sonneck, "Should Our Government Establish a National Conservatory of Music?" *Musical America*, 4 September 1904, 17.

[51]Claude M. Girardeau, "Editorial," *New England Conservatory Quarterly* (May 1895): 90.

[52]Rubin in Tibbetts, 81.

[53]Rubin in Tibbetts, 75.

[54]Quoted in Josef Skvorecky, "Every Silly Trifle," *Iowa Dvořák Centennial Symposium Abstracts*, 5-9. Mr. Skvorecky is also the author of a novelization of Dvořák's life, *Dvořák in Love* (New York: Knopf, 1987). For his own account of the writing of this book, see his "How I Wrote *Dvořák in Love*" in Tibbetts, 320-31.

INDEX

Asterisks (*) indicate composers and performers whose first names can no longer be determined. Quotation marks indicate literary characters or stereotypes.

Abbot, John M., 18
Abbot, Marie, 18
Abbot Opera Company, 132, 304
and opera performed, 304
Abraham, Gerald, 351
Abt, Franz (and works by), 93, 119, 121, 123
Academy of Music (Boston), 154
Academy of Music (New York), 8, 16, 20, 34-5, 37-8, 42, 83, 95-6
Adam, Adolfe, 13, 16-7
Adams family, 144
Adams, John, 32-3
Addison, Joseph, 29-33, 35, 38, 41, 45
Ahlquist, Karen, 383
Albani, Emma, 171, 175
*Albites (conductor), 16
Aldrich, Richard, 154, 160
Allemania Männerchor (New York), 10
American Mechanics Fair (New York), 3
American Musical Journal, 34

Anschütz, Carl (and company), 13, 15, 17
Apollo Club (Boston), 157-58
Apthorp, William Foster, 151, 153
Arcaraz Spanish Grand Opera Company, 304
Aristophanes, 11
Arlen, Harold, 357
Arion Männerchor Society (New York), 10, 16-7, 84-6, 89-90, 96, 126
performances by, 107-09
Arnold, Ben, 383
Arnold, Matthew, 35-6, 39-40
Arnold, Maurice, 345, 347, 353, 355-56
Aschenbrödel Verein (New York), 10
Auber, Daniel-François-Marie (and works by), 13, 17, 80
"Aunt Jemima," 73

Baccei, Pietro, 176
Bach, Johann Christoph (and works by), 123

Balatka, Hans, 116, 121-23,
    131
Baldamus, Gustav, 115
Balfe, Michael William (and
    works by), 14, 16-7, 339
Barnet, Charlie, 343
Barnum, P. T., 34
Barnum's Museum (New
    York), 16
Barus, Carl, 120-22, 133
Barus Symphony Orchestra,
    133
Bateman, H. L. (and
    company), 8, 18
Batson, Flora: see "Flora
    Batson Bergen"
Baya, Belle, 275
Bayly, T. H., 245
Beach, Amy, 349, 353
Becker, Constantin Julius, 128
Beckerman, Michael, 352
Beethoven, Ludwig van (and
    works by), 9, 14-5, 17-8,
    41, 43, 91, 93, 114, 119,
    126, 128, 133, 190, 312
Beethoven Männerchor (New
    York), 84-5, 95
Behymer, L. E., 184, 303,
    309, 314
Bellini, Vicenzo (and works
    of), 13, 15-6, 60, 80, 175-
    76, 303
Bellson, Louis, 343
Belluiger, Franz, 116
Bender, Thomas, 35, 37, 40
Benoit, Peter, 129
Bergen Concert Company, 57,
    60-1
Bergen, Flora Batson, 60
Bergen, James, 61

Bergmann, Carl, 8
Berlin, Edward A., 356
Berlin, Irving (and works by),
    288-89, 339
Bevani Opera Company, 304,
    309-11
Beveridge, David, 351
Bidwell, Marshall S., 21
Bijou Opera Company, 304
Billings, William, 141, 144
Birge, Edward Bailey, 129
Bischoff, Mr. (tenor), 121
Bishop, Anna, 132, 174-77
Bishop, Henry Rawley, 80
Bispham, David, 125-26,
    132, 152
Black Patti Troubadours, 62
Blavatsky, Madame, 339
Block, Adrienne Fried, 350,
    352
Bloom, Sol, 274, 276
Bochsa, M., 132
Boekelmann, Bernardus, 5
Boildieu, François-Adrien (and
    works by), 14, 17, 80, 120
Boston Conservatory, 155
Boston Herald, 349
Boston Philharmonic, 154,
    158
Boston Philo-Harmonic
    Society, 154
Boston Symphony Orchestra,
    144, 151, 155, 161
Boston University, 160
Bostonians (opera company),
    304
Bouhy, Jacques, 344
Boylston Club (Boston), 157-
    58
Bradford, Joseph, 63

Bradstreet, Anne, 144
Brahms, Johannes, 93, 159, 351
Breitkopf & Härtel (publishers), 115
Brice, Fanny, 287-88
Brignoli, Pasquale, 8
Bristow, George F., 9, 142
Brockett, Clyde W., 384
Bronson, Carl, 185
Brooklyn Philharmonic, 10
Brooks, Van Wyck, 29, 149
Brown-Mitchell, Nellie E., 57, 59-61, 63, 68
Broyles, Michael, 311
Bruch, Max (and works by), 93, 126, 128
Bryant's Minstrels, 12
Buck, Dudley, 344
Buffalo Commercial Advertiser, 58
Bull, Ole, 91, 142
Bülow, Hans von, 9
Burleigh, Harry T. (and works of), 345, 347, 353-55
Busch Gardens, 272

Cadman, Charles Wakefield, 114
Calhoun Opera Company, 304
Cameron, Joseph, 114
Campanini Operatic Company, 304
Campbell, Jno. B., 114
Campbell, Mrs. W. C., 178
Candidus, William, 12
Capek, Karel, 359
Carlton Opera Company, 304
Carpenter, John Alden, 160
Casals, Pablo, 134

Cecilia Club (Boston), 157-58
Chadwick, George Whitefield, 143, 145, 147-48, 151, 153, 156-61, 350, 353
Chapman, John Jay, 151
Chappie, W. Mitchell, 316
Chicago Grand Opera, 190
Chicago Symphony Orchestra, 156
Chicago Tribune, 123-24
Chicago World's Fair (1893), 271-76, 278-81, 290-92
Chickering & Sons, 6, 9, 19
Chickering, C. Frank, 6
Chisholm, Kate, 178
Chopin, Frédéric, 339
Cincinnati Commercial, 124
Clapham, John, 351
Coakley, Mary, 72
Cobb, Will D., 285-86
Cody, William (a.k.a. Buffalo Bill), 345
Colby, Frank H., 184-85
Colby, G. W., 19
Cole, Bob, 63, 356
Cologne Männergesangverein, 115
Colored American Opera Company, 72
Columbia Opera Company, 304
Columbia University, 146-47, 161, 357
Concone, Giuseppe, 113
Concordia Männerchor (Chicago), 123
Converse, Frederick Shepherd, 160
Cook, Will Marion, 345, 347, 353, 355

Copland, Aaron, 357
Copley, John Singleton, 144
Costello, Bartley, 283
Curtis, George William, 29,
  39-45

Daily Alta California (San
  Francisco), 176
Daily Picayune (New Orleans),
  97-9
Damrosch family, 30
Damrosch, Frank, 358
Damrosch, Leopold, 42, 96-7,
  126
Damrosch, Walter, 97, 126-28
Damrosch Opera Company,
  126
Dannreuther, Edward, 5
Darby, W. Dermot, 141
Darwin, Charles (and ideas of),
  291-92, 306
David, Félicien, 11
Davis, Gussie H., 278-79
Davison, Archibald, 160
Deaville, James, 386
Deiler, J. Hanno, 97-8, 129
De Koven, Archibald, 304
Del Conte Italian Opera
  Company, 300, 304, 307-
  09
  and operas performed, 307
Délibes, Leo, 305
De Meyer, Leopold, 5, 19
Dennis, John, 31-2, 41
Dennison, Sam, 278
Despa, Anton, 113, 118
Devine, Catherine, 283
Dickens, Charles, 19
Disney World, 272

Donizetti, Gaetano (and works
  by), 13, 15-7, 43, 60,
  302-04
Donner, Walther, 116
Dorsey, Tommy, 343
Downes, Olin, 160
Dream City, 275, 291
Dresel, Otto, 155-56
Dressler, William, 18
Drury, Theodore, 72
Dunbar, Paul Laurence, 356
Duncan, Kenneth, 135
Dupree, William, 60
Durbin, Deanna, 359
Dvořák, Antonín, 151, 159,
  343-65
Dwight, John Sullivan, 36, 39,
  41, 151, 153, 169, 346
Dwight's Journal of Music,
  153, 346

Edwards, Gus, 286
Ehrenritter Gesangsverein
  (New York), 89
Ehrgott, Louis, 126
Eichberg, Julius, 72, 151, 155-
  56
Eliot, Charles William, 160
Ellington, Duke, 357
Ellis Club (Los Angeles), 313
Ellis Grand Opera Company,
  309-10
Elson, Louis C., 153
Elzer, Annie, 176
Emerson, Ralph Waldo (and
  writings of), 144, 346
Engelhardt (or Engelhard),
  Henry, 3
Equinunk band (Pennsylvania),
  256

Erard (piano manufacturers), 9
Ernestinoff, Alexander, 126-
28
Evans, George T., 176

Fabbri, Mulder, 177
Fabbri Opera Company,
303
and operas performed, 303
Farrell, Mrs. Charles H., 190
Farwell, Arthur, 160, 353
Fay, Amy, 145
Federal Music Project, 311
*Ferranti (bass), 8
*Ferrari (composer), 16
Fields, Annie, 143
Fields, James T., 143
Fillmore Brothers (publishers),
328-29, 331
Finck, Henry, 146, 154, 347
Fischer, Carl (publisher), 328
Fischer, Emil, 125
Fisher, William Arms, 359
Fisk Jubilee Singers, 63, 70-1
Fisk University, 70
Fiske, John, 152
Fletcher, Alice, 353
Flonzaley Quartet, 134
Flotow, Friedrich von (and
works by), 13-4, 17, 133-
34
Foote, Arthur (and works by),
143, 145, 147-48, 153,
156-61, 350
Forbert, Otto (publisher), 114
Fortuna (baritone), 8
Foster, Stephen, 141, 346, 354
Fremstad, Olive, 282
Frenzel, John P., 134
Froehlich, Bianca, 282

Frohsinn (Mobile, Alabama),
117
Frohsinn (New Orleans), 89-
90, 97
Fry, William Henry, 141-43

Gabriel, Charles Hutchinson,
323-42
and works by, 324
Gade, Niels W., 11, 131
Garden, Mary, 283
Gardner, Isabella Stewart, 153,
155
Gatewood, Willard, 69-70
Gehl, Anna, 113
*Gems of the World's Fair and
Midway Plaisance*, 274
Geragi, Mrs. Paulette T., 329-
30
Gericke, Wilhelm, 155-56
Germania Männerchor (New
York), 10
Germania Musical Society, 154
Germania Society (Chicago),
121, 123
Gesangsektion Turnverein
(New Orleans), 116
Gershwin, George, 357
Giddings, Paula, 65
Gilbert, Douglas, 272
Gilbert, Henry F., 353
Gilbert and Sullivan, 304
Gilman, Lawrence, 154
Gluck, Christoph Williband,
119
Goethe, Johann Wolfgang, 111
Goldbeck, Robert, 5
Golden Gate Quartet, 343
Goldman Band, 357

Goldman, Edwin Franko, 353,
357
Goldmark, Rubin, 345, 348,
353, 357
Good, Edwin M., 384
Goodman, Benny, 343
Gordon, MacKenzie, 190
Gottschalk, Louis Moreau (and
works by), 5, 9, 114, 142-
43, 355, 384
Gounod, Charles (and works
by), 13-4, 16-7, 20, 304
Grand English Opera
Company, 132
Grau, Hermann (and
company), 17
Graupner, Gottlieb, 154
Greenfield, Elizabeth Taylor,
54-6, 58-61, 68, 72
Groschel, Sophie, 9
Grotrian, Helfferich, and
Schultz, 4
Grover, Leonard, 15
Gublin, Max, 131
Guilmette Method, 68
Guth, Jacob, 231-33, 237-41,
255-59
works by, 232-55, 264-67

Habelmann, Theodor, 12, 20
Hadley, Henry Kimball, 185,
190
Hale, Philip, 153, 158
Halévy, Jacques-François-
Fromental (and works by),
16, 80
Hall, J. H., 323, 329
Hall, William T. (Biff), 278
Halttunen, Karen, 39
Hamm, Charles, 350, 387

Hampton Institute, 70
Hampton, Lionel, 343
Handel, George Frederick, 30,
32-3, 36, 119
Handel and Haydn Society
(Boston), 154-55, 157
Hanslick, Eduard, 351
Harding, Frank, 277
Harmony Society
(Indianapolis), 113
Harper's Magazine, 39-40,
349
Harrison, Benjamin, 62, 232
Hartford Fire Insurance Co.,
170
*Hartmann (composer), 114
Hartsough, Palmer, 331
Harvard Musical Society, 155,
158
Harvard University, 144, 146,
151-52, 160
Hatton, John Liptrot, 8
Haupt, Karl, 145
Hawk, T. G. R., 237
Hawthorne, Nathaniel, 144
Haydn, Franz Joseph, 93, 119
Haydn, Michael, 111
Hazen, Margaret and Robert,
231
Heart Songs, 303, 316
*Hegar (composer), 128
Henschel, George, 155
Herbert, Victor, 347
Herold, Louis-Joseph (and
works by), 80
*Heyne (composer), 114
Higginson, Henry Lee, 155,
160
Hill, Edward Bulingame, 160
Himmer, Franz, 12, 20

Hobsbawm, Eric, 316
Hoffman, Gertrude, 283
Holmes, Oliver Wendell, 143
Holst, Gustav, 114
Homer, Louise, 152
Hopkinson, Francis, 141
Houseworth's Photographic
  Parlors (San Francisco),
  170
Howe, Julia Ward, 151
Howe, M. A. DeWolfe, 160
Howell, Mrs. H. B., 178
Howells, William Dean, 40,
  152
Humperdinck, Engelbert, 357
Huneker, James Gibbons, 154,
  347
Hutchinson, Marr & Smith
  (insurance agency), 170
Hyde, F. A., 169, 179
Hyers, Anna, 63
Hyers, Emma, 63-5
Hyers Sisters, 63-5, 68

Indianapolis Daily Journal,
  119, 122-23, 125
Indianapolis Männerchor, 111-
  13, 115-18, 120-35
  carnivals of, 131
  1867 Sängerfest of, 118-25
  1908 Sängerfest of, 125-29
Indianapolis Musical Review,
  124
Indianapolis News, 127, 129
Indianapolis Star, 129
Indicator (Chicago), 184
Institute of Musical Arts (New
  York), 358
Irwin, May, 356
Isham, John, 65

Isouard, Nicolò, 80
Ives, Charles (and works by),
  353

Jacksonian era, 35
James, William, 152, 155
Jefferson, Big Bill, 285
Jefferson, Thomas, 35
Jerome, Benjamin M., 284-85
"Jim Crow" laws, 66
Joachim, Joseph, 356
Johnson, James Rosamund, 63
Johnson, James Weldon, 355-
  56
Johnson, Julian, 310
Johnson, W. R., 19
Jones, Matilda Sissieretta
  Joyner, 61-2
Jose, Nicholas, 112
Joseffy, Rafael, 347
Juch Opera Company, 304
Juilliard Foundation, 358
Juilliard School, 358
Jullien, Antoine, 142

Kalliwoda, Johann Wenzel, 93
Kanner, D. (publisher), 114
Keller, Jessie, 290
Kellogg, Clara Louise, 12
Kemble, Adelaide, 34
Kempton, Jenny, 19
Kennedy, Charles A., 384
Kersands, Billy, 64
King, Wallace, 63
*Kipper (composer), 14, 133
Klein, Francisca, 119
Klein, George, 119
Kneisel, Franz, 155-56, 159
Kneisel Quartet, 155, 159
Kopta, Wenzel, 19

Kotzschmar, Hermann, 145
Kovařík, J. J., 352
Kozánek, Emil, 352
Krebs, Marie, 5
Krehbiel, Henry E., 161, 344,
 353-54
Kreisler, Fritz, 96
Kreitner, Kenneth, 385
Kreutzer, Conradin, 117, 123
Krupa, Gene, 343

Lachner, Franz, 115
Lambardi Opera Company,
 304, 309-10
Lambord, Benjamin, 144
Lang, Benjamin, 151-52, 158
Laurie, Joe Jr., 275, 283
Lawrence, Vera Brodsky, 21
Leckner, Max, 131
Leichtentritt, Hugo, 160
Leon and Kelly's Minstrels, 12
Leoncavallo, Ruggero, 307
Leppert, Richard, 31
Leslie, Edgar, 288-89
Leuckart, F. E. C. (publisher),
 114
Levine, Lawrence, 60, 302,
 312, 315-16
Library of Congress, 358
Liederkranz Männerchor (New
 York), 84-5, 89-90, 93,
 96
 performances by, 107-09
 works performed by, 94
Liederkranz Society
 (Indianapolis), 113
Liedertafel Männerchor (New
 Orleans), 86-9, 97-8
Life Illustrated, 37, 39
Lincoln, Abaraham, 85

Lind, Jenny, 96, 142
Liszt, Franz, 9, 93, 121, 128,
 291
 and studies of, 383, 385-86
"Little Egypt" (pseud. Fahreda
 Mahzar), 274-76, 278,
 281, 283, 290, 292
Locke, Ralph, 29-30
Longerich, Eduard, 112-13
Longfellow, Henry
 Wadsworth, 143, 145, 352
Los Angeles Herald, 309
Los Angeles Philharmonic
 Orchestra, 313-15
Los Angeles Symphony
 Orchestra, 313-15
Los Angeles Times, 306-07
Los Angeles Women's
 Orchestra, 313-14
Louisville Volksblatt, 124
Louis XIV, 130
Luca, John, 63
Lucas, Sam, 64
Ludecus, Miss, 20
Lumley-Blath, Eliza, 19
Lyon & Healy Co. (Chicago),
 258

MacDowell, Edward, 125, 143-
 44, 146-47, 151-52, 154,
 156-57, 159, 161, 187,
 349, 353
 and family, 146-47
Madah, Anna, 65
Madden, Ed, 284-85
Mahzar, Fahreda: see "Little
 Egypt"
*Mangold (composer), 128
Männerchor Society
 (Indianapolis), 113

Männerchöre of New Orleans:
works performed by, 82
Männerchöre of New York:
works performed by, 81-2,
94
Manuscript Club of Boston,
153
Mapleson Grand Italian Opera
Company, 132
Maretzek, Max (and
company), 13, 15-6, 20,
34
Marra's Grand Opera
Company, 303
and operas performed, 303
Mascagni, Pietro, 307
Mason, Daniel Gregory, 160
Mason, William, 5, 9, 12, 20,
152
Massé, Victor, 14, 16
Matthews, W. S. B., 154
Mayor, S. D., 178
McCullough, Edo, 280-81
McGinty, Doris, 66
Mehlig, Anna, 5, 20
Melba, Nellie (pseud. Helen
Porter Armstrong) 125
Mencken, H. L., 355
Mendelssohn, Felix, 10-11,
114, 119, 123, 128, 132
Metropolitan Opera Company
(New York), 8, 42-5, 62,
74, 85, 132-33, 152, 283
Metzger, Arthur, 182, 184,
187, 190-91
Meyerbeer, Giacomo (and
works by), 13, 15-7, 60,
62, 80, 98, 119, 123
Miller, Lena, 72

Mills, Sebastian Bach, 5, 8-9,
20
Montresor, Giocomo, 33
Montrose Band (Montrose,
PA), 231-32, 240
and partbooks for, 231, 241-
43, 257, 264-69
engagements of, 234-37
list of members, 233
Montrose (Pennsylvania)
Democrat, 232, 238-40
Montrose (Pennsylvania)
Independent Republican,
232-33, 238, 241
Moore, Macdonald Smith, 356
Moore, Mary Carr, 386
Morgan, George W., 18
Morrow, Mary Sue, 385
Moscheles, Ignaz, 114
Mossell, Mrs. N. F., 53
Moulton, Louise, 151
Mozart, Wolfgang Amadeus
(and works by), 9, 13, 15-
7, 33, 91, 93, 96, 114,
119, 126, 128, 167, 177,
190
Mozartverein (New York), 89,
91
"Mrs. Potiphar," 29, 40-1
Muehlmann, Adolf, 126
Murchison, Gayle, 386
Murphy, Stanley, 285, 287
Museum of the City of New
York, 276
Music Fund Society (Boston),
154
Musical America, 190
Musical Blue Book, 358
Musical Courier (New York),
182, 184

Musical Herald (Boston), 144-45
Musical Quarterly, 168
Musical Times (London), 169
Music Teachers National Association, 153

National Conservatory of Mexico City, 307
National Conservatory of Music (New York), 160, 344-45, 348-49, 353, 356-59
National Federation of Music Clubs, 311
National Opera Company, 304-07, 310, 312
and operas performed, 305
Neue Zeitschrift für Musik, 168
New England Conservatory of Music, 145, 160
New England Conservatory Quarterly, 358
New Orleans Quartett Club, 97-8
New Orleans States, 98
New Orleans Times, 124
New York Allgemeiner Sängerbund, 10
New York Herald, 349, 352
New York Liederkranz, 10-12, 19-20
New York Männergesang-verein Eichenkranz, 90-1
New York Musik-Zeitung, 124
New York Oratorio Society, 42, 96
New York Philharmonic Society, 8-10, 18, 36, 83, 96, 158

New York Symphony (Society), 42, 96-7, 126-27
New York Times, 10, 96-7, 280, 282
New York Tribune, 96-7
New Yorker Sängerrunde, 10, 90-1, 93
works performed by, 95
Newark (New Jersey) *Advertiser*, 124
Nicolai, Otto (and works by), 14-5, 17
Nilsson, Kristina, 12, 20
Noll, George M., 231, 233, 238, 244, 256-57
Nordica (pseud. Lillian Norton), 125
North American Sängerbund, 92, 111, 115-17, 120
member organizations, 117-18
Sängerfeste of, 111, 115-16, 118, 121
Norton, Charles Eliot, 150-51

Oakley, Annie, 345
Oberlin Conservatory of Music, 356
Odell, George, 8, 17
Offenbach, Jacques (and works by), 13, 16-17, 345
Olivet College, 145
Omeena (dancer), 280
Oregonian, 65
Orpheon Français Choral Society (New Orleans), 98
Ottendorfer, Oswald, 85
Otto, Julius, 93

Paasch, Wilhelm, 93
Pacific Coast Musical Review, 168, 179, 181-82, 186-91, 310
Pacific Coast Musician, 168, 179-80, 182-86
Paderewski, Ignacy Jan, 125
Paine, John Knowles (and works by), 143, 145-47, 151, 153-54, 156-57, 159-61, 349-50
and family, 146-47
Parepa-Rosa Company, 16-7
Parepa-Rosa, Euphrosyne, 8, 12, 19
Paris Exposition (1889), 274-75
Parker, Henry Taylor, 153
Parker, Horatio (and works by), 143, 145-49, 152, 156-61, 311, 345, 348
and family, 146-47
Patti, Adelina, 42-3, 61
Patti, Carlotta, 12, 20
Pattison, John Nelson, 5, 18, 20
Paur, Emil, 344, 357
Peabody Institute of Archeaology and Ethnology, 353
Pease, Alfred H., 5, 18
Pedrotti, Carlo, 34
People's Orchestra (Los Angeles), 314-15
Peretti, Burton, 41, 43
Peri, Achille, 14
Persons, Stow, 44
Peterson, Clara Gottschalk, 355
Petrella, Errico, 14

Pfeiffer, Oscar, 5, 19
Philadelphia Centennial Exposition (1876), 271-72
Philadelphia Sängerbund, 10
Philharmonic Orchestra (Montrose, PA), 232
Pickney, Estelle, 72
Pickwick Club (New Orleans), 89
Plato, Desseria, 72
Pleyel, Ignaz Josef, 9
Pollak, Ignatz, 19
Ponchielli, Amilcare (and works by), 307
Ponte, Lorenzo da, 33
Potiphar Papers, 40
Powell, Mel, 343
Presto (Chicago), 184
Preston, Katherine, 302
Progressive Musical Union (Boston), 67
Puccini, Giocomo (and works by), 128, 307-09, 339
Pyke Opera Company, 304

Raff, Joachim, 147
Rappold, Marie, 126
Recker, Gottfried, 112
Recker, Hubert, 112
Révue et Gazette Musicale de Paris, 168
Rembusch, N. R., 114
Rheinberger, Joseph (or Josef), 93, 147
Ricci, Federico and Luigi, 14
Richardson, C. S., 386
Richings, Caroline (and company), 15, 17
*Rigo (singer), 176

Riis, Thomas L., 385
Ritter, Theodore, 20
Rodeheaver, Homer, 323
Rogers, Clara Kathleen, 151
Rogers, Henry Munroe, 151
Romantic movement, 149
Roos, Regina Steinway, 3, 19
Roosevelt, Theodore, 85
Root, George F., 323, 331
Rosa, Carl, 19
Rossini, Gioachino (and works
    by), 13-4, 16, 114, 120
Rotter, Johanna, 12, 19
Rousseau, Jean-Jacques, 54
Rubin, Emanuel, 357
Rubinstein, Anton, 127, 345
Rubinstein, Arthur, 125
Ruskin, John, 142

Saar, Louis Victor, 126
Saffle, Michael, 383, 385-86,
    387
Safonov, Vassily, 357
Saint-Saëns, Camille, 114, 128
Salem Gazette, 145
Salvini Opera Company, 304
San Carlo Opera Company,
    311
*San Francisco Daily
    Examiner*, 175-77
San Francisco Opera, 311
San Francisco Pacific Appeal,
    65
San Francisco Symphony
    Orchestra, 185
Scarlatti, Domenico, 29
Schenk, Johann, 133
Scherrer, Anton, 113
Schiller, Friedrich, 91, 123
Schirmer, G. (publisher), 115

Schmidt, Arthur P., 155-56
Schmidt, Louis, 178
Schnabel, Artur, 134
Schnellschmidt, Adolph, 112
Schoenfeld, F., 20
Schubert, Franz Peter, 11, 93,
    119, 126
Schuberth (Edward) & Co., 114
Schuberth, J., & Co., 122
Schultze, Edward, 113
Schumann-Heink, Ernestine,
    126, 132
Schumann, Robert, 93, 114,
    132, 168
Schurz, Carl, 85
Schwarz, Joseph, 115
Sears, J. Montgomery, 152
Seelig, Nathalie, 8
Seidl, Anton, 344, 347
Selby, William, 154
Selika, or Madame Selika
    (pseud. Marie Smith
    Williams), 59-61
Shakespeare, Joseph, 98
Shakespeare, William, 29, 91,
    302, 312
Shepherd, Arthur, 160
Sheppard, Ella, 70-1
Sherman & Hyde Music Co.
    (San Francisco), 170-73,
    178-79, 182
*Sherman & Hyde's Musical
    Review*, 168-79, 182, 184
Sherman, Leander S., 169,
    179, 182
Sherman, William T., 129
Sibelius, Jean, 185
Siegel, C. F. W. (publisher),
    114
Simond, Ike, 65

Singer, Marian, 174
Smallwood, Agnes Gray, 72
Smart, Sir George, 58
Smith, Catherine Parsons, 386
Smithsonian Institution, 231,
    353
Snyder, Jean M., 353
Snyder, Suzanne G., 386
Société des Beaux Arts
    (France), 7
Sonneck, O. G., 358
Sousa Band, 240
Sousa, John Philip (and works
    of), 244, 357
Southern, Eileen, 65
Spectator, 35 (see also
    "Addison" and "Steele")
Spicker, Max, 114
Spirit of the Times (New
    York), 33-4
Staatszeitung (New York), 84
Stamm, A. J., 313
Steele, Richard, 30-1, 33, 35,
    38, 41, 45
Steins, Fred, 18-9
Steinway, Albert, 4
Steinway & Sons, 3, 7-9, 19-
    20
Steinway, Charles, 3
Steinway, George, 19
Steinway, Henry, Jr., 3, 6
Steinway, Henry, Sr., 3-4
Steinway, Paula Theoda, 18-9
Steinway, Theodore, 4, 6-7
Steinway, William, 3-27, 85
    and the New York
        Liederkranz, 10-11
Steinway, William (cont.)
    and Steinway Hall, 8-9
    operas attended, 13-7

Steward, Theodore, 71
Still, William Grant, 160, 386
St. Ambrose, 339
St. Denis, Ruth, 282
St. Louis Fair (1896), 280
St. Louis Westliche Post, 124
St. Louis World's Fair (1904),
    271-72, 280-82, 292
St. Paul's School, 159
Stobaios, Miss, 20
Stoeckel, Carl, 158
Stowe, Harriet Beecher, 58
Strakosch, Max (and
    company), 13, 16, 34
Strauss, Johann Jr., 41
Strauss, Richard (and works
    by), 96, 126, 282, 291
Strong, Charles E., 21
Strong, George Templeton, 21
Stucken, Frank van der, 344
Sulgrove, Berry Robinson, 132
Sunday, Billy, 323
Suppé, Franz von (and works
    by), 17
Swift, Jonathan, 31
Syncopated Jazz Orchestra,
    356
Szigeti, Joseph, 134

Tägliche Deutsche Zeitung
    (New Orleans), 86, 92, 98
Talbot, Howard, 132
Tanner, Jo, 65
Tawa, Nicholas E., 386-87
Tchaikovsky, Peter Illich (and
    works by), 9, 114, 128,
    345
Teich, Otto, 93
Temple Emanu-El (San
    Francisco), 178-79

Teutonia (New York), 10
Thaxter, Celia, 151
Théâtre Français (New York), 16
Thiemer (Steinway), Julianna, 3
*Thiessen (composer), 113
Thomas, J. R., 19
Thomas, Theodore, 5, 8, 12, 30, 44, 96, 156, 306, 312-13, 344
    and the National Opera Company, 312
    orchestra of, 10, 18-9
Thornton, James, 277
Thurber, Jeannette Meyer, 305, 344, 357-58
Tibbetts, John C., 387
Tick, Judith, 53
Tickner, Howard Malcom, 153
Tinel, Edgar, 131
Tippett, J. E., 178
Toedt, Matilda, 18
Tonger, P. J., 115
Topp, Alida, 19
Trotter, James Monroe, 55, 58-9, 72
Truhn, Friedrich, 114
Tucker, Henry, 18
Turner, Frederick Jackson, 345
Turner Singing Club (Indianapolis), 113
Twain, Mark (pseud. Samuel Clemens), 40

Ulmann, Bernard, 34
Upton, George P., 154

Van Hagen family, 154
Van Horn, A. R., 130

Verdi, Giuseppe (and works by), 13, 15-7, 38, 60, 113-14, 123, 131, 273, 302-04, 307
Verstovsky, Alexey Nikolayevitch, 17
Victor Book of the Opera, 282
Vogel, Wilhelmine (Steinway), 12
Vonnegut, Bernard, 133
Vonnegut, Kurt Jr., 133

Wachtel, Theodor, 12
Wagner, Richard (and works by), 13, 15-7, 41-3, 45, 96, 114-15, 119-20, 123, 126, 128, 131, 133, 339, 351
Wakefield Opera Company, 309
Walker, Aida Overton, 63
Walker, George, 63
Wallace, William Vincent, 14, 16
Walpole, Robert, 31
Waltenspiel, A., 124
Wandesforde, Joy, 177
Washington, George, 130, 316
Waters, Hamilton, 352-53
Webb, George, 154
Weber, Carl Maria von (and works by), 13-4, 16, 113, 120, 303
Webster, J. P., 247
Wehli, James, 5, 9, 20
Weinzierl, Max von, 115
*Wengert (composer), 128
Wesleyan University, 40
Western Graphic (Los Angeles), 309

Wharton, Edith, 30
Wheatley, Phillis, 55, 73
White, George, 70-1
Whiting, Arthur, 159
Whitman, Walt, 36-9, 346
Wieprecht, Wilhelm, 145
*Wiesner (composer), 128
Wilde, Oscar, 282
Willhartitz, Adolph, 312
Williams & Walker, 65
Williams, Bert, 63
*Wohlgemuth (composer),
  114
Wolfssohn, Carl, 5, 8, 18
Wood, Colonel, 58
Woolf, Benjamin Edward, 153
Woolf, Mr. (Rabbi), 178
Wright, Josephine, 65-6
Wulschner & Son
  (Indianapolis), 114

Wynn, Ed, 287

Yale University, 146-47, 161
Yorkville Männerchor (New
  York), 91

Zallah (dancer), 290
Zelika (dancer), 280
Zelter, Carl Friedrich, 111
Zerrahn, Carl, 154-55
Ziedman, Irving, 283
Zimbalist, Efrem, 134
*Zimmermann (composer),
  114
Zollner, Heinrich, 115
Zöllner, Karl (or Carl)
  Friedrich, 93, 123
Zoellner Männerchor
  (Brooklyn), 10

CONTRIBUTORS

Karen Ahlquist teaches music at The George Washington University in Washington, D. C. She received her Ph.D. from the University of Michigan, where she was awarded the Horace H. Rackham Distinguished Dissertation Award in 1992. A student of vocal music in nineteenth-century European and American culture, Professor Ahlquist has presented papers before the American Musicological Society, the Society for Ethnomusicology, and the Sonneck Society for American Music. Her book, *Democracy at the Opera: Music, Theater, and Culture in New York City, 1815-60*, was prepared for publication under a grant from the National Endowment for the Humanities and published recently by the University of Illinois Press. She has written articles for the *Journal of Musicological Research*, the *Journal of American History, Criticus Musicus*, and *In Theory Only*, and has served on the board of the Sonneck Society as well as on the editorial board of *Women in Music*.

Ben Arnold received his Ph.D. in musicology from the University of Kentucky in 1986. He joined the Emory College faculty in 1987 and currently serves as Chair of the Music Department there. Professor Arnold is the author of *Music and War: A Research and Information Guide* (1993) and has contributed articles related to music and war to *The Musical Quarterly*, the *International Review of the Aesthetics and Sociology of Music, Holocaust and Genocide Studies,* and the *Emory Journal of International Affairs*. He has also contributed essays to Michael Saffle's *Franz Liszt: A Guide to Research* (1991), to *Analecta Lisztiana I* and *II*, and to the *Journal of the American Liszt Society*, for which he was Visiting Editor in 1989-1990. Other of his articles have appeared in *The New Grove Dictionary of American Music*, the *Carl Nielsen Companion*, and Garland's *Encyclopedia of Keyboard Instruments*.

Clyde W. Brockett earned M.A. and Ph.D. degrees in musicology at Columbia University, where he studied under Edward A. Lippman, Erich Hertzmann, Walther Wiora, and Paul Henry Lang. Professor Brockett holds the Falk Professorship of Music at Christopher Newport University (Newport News, Virginia), where he teaches world musics, music history, and paleography and directs the Falk Seminar and the Christopher Newport Collegium Musicum. He has published studies of Gregorian chant, liturgical drama, and aspects of Louis Moreau Gottschalk's career in Europe and South America. He has also prepared an edition of the eleventh-century Pseudo Odonion *De modorum formulis et tonarius*.

Edwin M. Good is Professor Emeritus of Religious Studies at Stanford University and Research Collaborator at the Smithsonian Institution, Washington, D.C., where he is currently researching the diary of William Steinway. Author of *Giraffes, Black Dragons, and Other Pianos* (1982) and *The Eddy Collection of Musical Instruments: A Checklist* (1985), Professor Good has also contributed articles and reviews on musical subjects to *Notes*, the *Early Keyboard Journal*, Garland's *Encyclopedia of Keyboard Instruments*, the *Business History Review*, the *Journal of the American Liszt Society*, and the *Journal of the American Musical Instrument Society*. In the Washington area he has served as pianist for the Rock Creek Chamber Players and for Quantum, a group specializing in twentieth-century chamber music.

Charles A. Kennedy is Professor Emeritus of Religious Studies at Virginia Polytechnic Institute and State University, where for several years he served as Head of his department. His undergraduate work was in fine arts, and he completed his doctorate in Near Eastern Languages and Literatures at Yale. Professor Kennedy's musical interests range from choral performance to the composition of church music and football marches. Periodic trips to the Middle East, combined with post-doctoral researches, have heightened his concerns over cultural misunderstandings between the Arab world and the United States and also led him to undertake *The Religious Music of Asia*, which he produced several years ago for Scholastic/Folkways Records.

Kenneth Kreitner received his Ph.D. degree from Duke University and currently works as an Associate Professor and Coordinator of the Division of Music History at the University of Memphis. His book, *Discoursing Sweet Music: Town Bands and Community Life in Turn-of-the-Century Pennsylvania,* was published by the University of Illinois Press in 1990. Professor Kreitner has also published articles about music in Renaissance Spain in several periodicals, including *Early Music, Early Music History,* and *Musica Disciplina.*

Mary Sue Morrow is Associate Professor of Music History at Loyola University in New Orleans. Her book, *Concert Life in Haydn's Vienna: Aspects of a Developing Musical and Social Institution,* was published by Pendragon Press in 1989. Professor Morrow has also published articles and reviews in *19th Century Music, The Musical Times,* the *Journal of Musicological Research, The Southern Quarterly,* and *The Eighteenth Century: A Current Bibliography.* She has held a Fulbright-Hays Fellowship for work in Vienna, as well as a Summer Seminar Grant from the National Endowment for the Humanities and a Research Fellowship from the Alexander von Humboldt-Stiftung. A former president of the Southern Chapter of the American Musicological Society, she has also served on the AMS Council.

Thomas L. Riis holds degrees from Oberlin College and the University of Michigan. He has taught at the Interlochen Center for the Arts, Northern Illinois University, and the Universities of Michigan and Georgia. In 1987 Professor Riis served as Senior Fellow at the Brooklyn College Conservatory's Institute for Studies in American Music. He is the author of numerous articles as well as two books on American music: *Just Before Jazz* (1989) and *More than Minstrel Shows* (1992). In 1992 he was appointed Professor of Music and Director of the American Music Research Center at the University of Colorado, Boulder.

Michael Saffle completed his Ph.D. in music and humanities at Stanford. He has published two books on the life and music of Franz Liszt, and his articles and reviews about Liszt and Wagner have appeared in *Acta Musicologica, Notes, The American Music Teacher, The Musical Quarterly,* the CRME *Bulletin* (which he served as an Editorial Associate from 1985-1995), the *Programmhefte* of the Bayreuth Festival, and other periodicals. From 1987-1991 he edited the *Journal of the American Liszt Society*, and he currently co-edits *Criticus Musicus* with James Deaville. Professor Saffle has received fellowships from the American Philosophical Society, the German Academic Exchange Service, the Fulbright Foundation, and the Alexander von Humboldt-Stiftung.

Catherine Parsons Smith holds degrees from Smith, Northwestern, and Stanford Universities and is currently Professor of Music at the University of Nevada, Reno. Her work on the formation of concert life in Los Angeles—supported by a fellowship from the National Endowment for the Humanities as well as several smaller grants from the Graduate School, University of Nevada—has resulted in the publication of a series of essays. With C. S. Richardson, Professor Smith is working on a biography of Mary Carr Moore; with Gayle Murchison, she is currently editing a collection of essays on cultural aspects of the career of William Grant Still. Among other activities Smith has presented papers at national meetings of the American Musicological Society.

Suzanne G. Snyder holds degrees in performance and music history from Butler University in Indianapolis, as well as a Ph.D. in musicology from the University of Iowa, where she received the Rita Benton Dissertation Award for her research into "The Männerchor Tradition in the United States: A Historical Analysis of its Contribution to American Musical Culture." In addition to contributions to the *Sonneck Society Bulletin*, her publications include ten articles commissioned by the POLIS Research Center for *The Encyclopedia of Indianapolis* (1994). Dr. Snyder has presented papers on aspects of nineteenth-century German-American music at meetings of the College Music Society, the Sonneck Society for American Music, the Society for German-American Studies, and the American Musicological Society. She is currently employed as an editor with Macmillan Publishing USA.

Nicholas E. Tawa, Professor Emeritus of the Department of Music, University of Massachusetts, Boston, received his Ph.D. in musicology from Harvard University. He has written eleven books, among them *The Coming-of-Age of American Art Music* (1991), *Mainstream Music of Early Twentieth-Century America* (1992), and *American Composers and Their Public: A Critical Look* (1995). Professor Tawa also edited and wrote critical commentaries for *American Solo Songs Through 1865* and *American Solo Songs, 1866 Through 1910*, published respectively as Volumes I and II of "Three Centuries of American Music" (1989). His essay on the history of American art music after 1865, together with essays by Charles Hamm and Michael Saffle, will appear together in a forthcoming volume of the new *Die Musik in Geschichte und Gegewart.*

John C. Tibbetts received his Ph.D. from the University of Kansas in Multi-Disciplinary Studies: art history, theater, photography, and film. From 1976-1985 he edited the bimonthly magazine *American Classic Screen*, and for years he has been a regular contributor to *The Christian Science Monitor* and its radio network. He has also contributed to such reference works as *The New Film Index, The Oxford Companion to Mystery and Crime Writing*, and *American Cultural Biography* and is the co-editor of the forthcoming *Encyclopedia of Novels into Film.* Professor Tibbetts's book *Dvořák in America* was published by Amadeus Press in 1993. He teaches as an Assistant Professor of Film at the University of Kansas.

GLUCK AND THE OPERA

GLUCK AND THE OPERA

A STUDY IN MUSICAL HISTORY

by

ERNEST NEWMAN

GREENWOOD PRESS, PUBLISHERS
WESTPORT, CONNECTICUT

Library of Congress Cataloging in Publication Data

Newman, Ernest, 1868-1959.
    Gluck and the opera.

    Reprint of the 1967 ed. published by V. Gollancz,
London.
    1. Gluck, Christoph Willibald, Ritter von,
1714-1787. 2. Opera--History and criticism.
I. Title.
[ML410.G5N3   1976]   782.1'092'4   76-7579
ISBN 0-8371-8849-0

This is a re-issue of the edition published in 1895 by Bertram Dobell. The book has never been re-published.

This edition originally published in 1967 by Victor Gollancz Ltd., London

Reprinted with the permission of Victor Gollancz Ltd.

Reprinted in 1976 by Greenwood Press, Inc.,
51 Riverside Avenue, Westport, Conn. 06880

Library of Congress catalog card number 76-7579

ISBN 0-8371-8849-0

Printed in the United States of America

10 9 8 7 6 5 4 3 2

PREFACE

So far as I am aware, there is no English biography of Gluck. The article by M. Gustave Chouquet in Grove's " Dictionary of Music and Musicians " is grossly inadequate, and little more can be said of the late Dr. Hueffer's article in the " Encyclopædia Britannica " (9th ed.) For English readers, by far the best account of the musician and his work is that in Naumann's " History of Music," translated by Mr. Ferdinand Praeger.

Apart from the usual articles in the French and German Dictionaries and Histories, and the treatment of Gluck in books and articles dealing with the history of the opera, there are several foreign studies of the life and works of the master. Anton Schmid's " C. W. Ritter von Gluck, dessen Leben und Wirken " (Leipzig, 1854), is a very detailed biography, containing almost everything that is known of the life of Gluck. By far the best of all books on the subject, however, is the celebrated " Gluck und die Oper " of Adolph Bernhard Marx (2 vols., Berlin, 1863, afterwards published in one volume as " Gluck's Leben und Schaffen "), which, besides narrating the life of the composer, and supplying details that have been overlooked by Schmid, gives a minute analysis of almost all his works. It is marred, however, by undue hero-worship, and is scarcely critical enough to be considered final. A. Reissmann's "Christoph Willibald von Gluck, sein Leben und seine Werke" (Berlin and Leipzig, 1882), is an admirable and well-balanced work of history and criticism, thoroughly sound in every respect, as far as it goes. A good piece of patient research is that of the French antiquarian, M. Gustave Desnoiresterres, "Gluck et Piccinni, 1774 – 1800 ; La Musique Française au 18me siècle" (2nd ed. Paris, 1875), a work which has served as basis for Barbedette's "Gluck, sa Vie, son Système, et ses Œuvres" (Paris, 1882). Heinrich Welti's "Gluck," in Reclam's "Musiker-Biographien," is small but good.

A goodly number of works exist for a history of the opera up to and including the time of Gluck, such as the "Mémoires pour servir à l'histoire de la révolution operée dans la musique par M. le chevalier Gluck" (Paris, 1781), and Arteaga's "Le rivoluzioni del teatro musicale italiano dalla sua origine fine al presente" (2nd ed. Venice, 1785, 3 vols.), of which a translated and abridged form was published in London in 1802. Marcello's "Il Teatro alla moda" is of course indispensable, though, as a satire, it has to be read with caution ; it is easily accessible in the French version of

M. Ernest David (Paris, Fischbacher, 1890). One of
the most suggestive writers of the epoch was Algarotti,
whose various essays on the arts were translated into
German under the title of "Versuche über die Architectur, Mahlerey, und musicalische Opera" (Cassel,
1769).* Noverre's "Lettres sur la danse et sur les
ballets" (Lyons, 1760), and Planelli's "Dell' Opera
in musica" (Naples, 1772) are also useful.

For an accurate estimate of Gluck and the music of
his time the general intellectual life of the eighteenth
century has to be studied, especially in the works of
those who wrote on music, such as Diderot, Rousseau,
Grimm, Marmontel, Suard, La Harpe, Goldsmith,
Harris, Du Bos, and others. Some of these men knew
little of music in a practical sense, but they knew at least as
much as Sonnenfels, whose "Briefe über die Wienerschaubühne" are always quoted approvingly. For a
general survey of the music of the time by a competent
musician, Burney's various works are of course indispensable; while the general musical life of the eighteenth
century is well illustrated in Vernon Lee's "Studies
of the Eighteenth Century in Italy."

Berlioz' "A travers chants" contains some interesting articles on *Orfeo* and *Alceste*, and articles on Gluck
are scattered about the *Revue des deux Mondes*, the
Revue Contemporaine, and the *Revue Germanique*.

---

* English translations of his Essay on the Opera were published in
1767 and 1768.

Schuré's "Le drame musical" treats cursorily of Gluck and the opera, but the book is too *à priori* in its method to be of much value. Ludwig Nohl's "Gluck and Wagner, ueber die Entwicklung des Musikdramas" (Munich, 1870) is Wagnerian in feeling, while an anti-Wagnerian counterpoise is to be had in C. H. Bitter's "Die Reform der Oper durch Gluck, und R. Wagner's Kunstwerk der Zukunft" (Brunswick, 1884). This gives a good account of the opera previous to Gluck, with copious musical examples.

A few words remain to be added as to the general method and purport of the present volume. So far as the biographical portion of it is concerned, I have, of course, been entirely dependent upon the recognised authorities, whose united labours have covered the whole field exhaustively. In the critical portions I have attempted to sum up the measure of Gluck's achievement in relation to the intellectual life of his day. As the book is meant rather as a tentative contribution to culture-history from a side hitherto painfully neglected, than as a mere narration of a thrice-told tale, I have thought it well to dispense with the history, in detail, of the technical side of the opera. This can be had in many excellent works, and it were superfluous to devote another volume to the task. I have rather endeavoured to view the subject philosophically, and to bring the opera of the eighteenth century in general, and Gluck's work in particular, into line with the whole intellectual tendencies of the time. Thus in the sketches in Part II. of the rise and development of the opera in Italy, France, and Germany, I have dealt only with such historical phases of it as fall within the province of culture-history. This seemed to me the more important and the more pressing work in view of the present condition of musical culture in England; while those who wish to supplement the account of the intellectual development of music in the seventeenth and eighteenth centuries by an account of the formal development of the expressive side of music and of musical structure, will find this without difficulty in any of the numerous histories of the art.

．　　．　　．　　．　　．　　．

My grateful acknowledgments are due to my friend Mr. F. H. Woollett for his constant assistance and advice.

CHRONOLOGICAL LIST OF
GLUCK'S WORKS

? De profundis.
1741 Artaserse.
1742 Demofoonte.
Demetrio (Cleonice).
Ipermnestra.
1743 Siface.
Artamene.
1744 Fedra.
1745 Alessandro nell' Indie
(Il Re Poro).
1746 La caduta de' Giganti.
Piramo e Tisbe.
1747 Le nozze d' Ercole e
d'Ebe.
1748 La Semiramide ricon-
osciuta.
1749 Tetide.
Telemacco.
1751 La Clemenza di Tito
1754 Le Cinesi.
L'orfano della China.
Il trionfo di Camillo.
Antigono.

1755 La Danza.
L'innocenza giustifi-
cata.
Les amours cham-
pêtres.
1756 Il Re Pastore.
Le Chinois poli en
France.
Le déguisement pas-
toral.
1758 L'île de Merlin.
La fausse esclave
1759 Cythère assiégée.
? L'arbre enchanté.
1760 Tetide.
L'ivrogne corrigé.
1761 Don Juan.
Le cadi dupé.
? Le diable à quatre.
1761 Il trionfo de Clelia.
1762 On ne s'avise jamais
de tout.
Orfeo.

1763 Ezio.
1764 La rencontre impré-
       vue.
1765 Il parnasso confuso.
       La corona.
1767 Alceste.
1769 Paride ed Elena.
       Prologo delle Feste
       d'Apollo.

1769 Bauci e Filemone.
       Aristeo.
  ?   Klopstock's Oden und
       Lieder.
  ?   Hermannsschlacht.
1774 Iphigénie en Aulide.
1777 Armide.
1779 Iphigénie en Tauride.
       Echo et Narcisse.

*** In the case of some of the early operas, of which it is impossible to learn the real year of the first performance, the above dates are merely approximative.

CONTENTS

INTRODUCTION

The comparative method in criticism—Deficiencies of
musical criticism in England—Need of wider culture
—The development of musical form—No form absolute—Necessity of an historical view—The influence
of Wagner on criticism—Weakness of the Wagnerian
method—Contrast between the metaphysical and the
scientific methods—Failure of the metaphysical method
to account for the changes in music—The historical
explanation the true one—Correlation between the
music and the general culture-conditions of any
epoch—The historical method as applied to the
eighteenth-century opera—Gluck and "nature"—
A new musical criticism wanted—Histories of music
should be physiological, not merely anatomical . p. 1

PART I

LIFE

CHAPTER I. 1714-1746

Ancestry and birth of Gluck—Early years—Education at
Kommotau and at Prague—At Vienna—At Milan

under Sammartini—The *De Profundis*—*Artaserse*— *Demofoonte*—*Demetrio*, *Ipermnestra*—*Artamene*—*Siface* — *Fedra*—*Alessandro dell' Indie*—In London—*La Caduta de' Giganti*—Relations with Handel—*Piramo e Tisbe*—The supposed awakening of Gluck . p. 16

CHAPTER II. 1746–1762

At Hamburg and Dresden—*Le Nozze d'Ercole e d'Ebe*— At Vienna—*La Semiramide riconosciuta*—At Copenhagen—*Tetide*—Rome—*Telemacco*—At Vienna again —Marriage—At Naples—*La Clemenza di Tito*—At Vienna—*Le Cinesi*—At Rome—*Il Trionfo di Camillo* —*Antigono*—*La Danza*—*L'innocenza giustificata*—*Il Re Pastore*—*Tetide*—*Don Juan*—At Bologna—*Il Trionfo de Clelia*—Durazzo and Favart—Gluck's work in light opera—*L'arbre enchanté* . . . p. 29

CHAPTER III. 1762–1769

Gluck's intellectual life—His studies—Influence of the system of patronage upon eighteenth-century music— Lack of esteem for musicians in the eighteenth century —Gluck's early environment harmful—Strength of nature required to rise above it—Growing perception in Europe of the need for a reform in opera—The deepening of Gluck's ideas—His meeting with Calzabigi—Their collaboration in *Orfeo ed Euridice*— Gluck's probable share in the libretto—The first performance—The poem of *Orfeo*—The music—*Ezio*

Contents

—*Les Pèlerins de la Mecque*—The engraving of *Orfeo*
—Philidor and the aria of Gluck—*Il parnasso confuso*
—*La corona*—Short visit of Gluck to Paris—Produc-
tion of *Alceste* at Vienna—The Italian and French
forms of the opera—The music of *Alceste*—*Paride ed
Elena*—The dedicatory epistle—*Prologo delle Feste
d'Apollo*—*L'Atto di Bauci e Filemone*—*L'Atto d'Aristeo*
—Gluck's life at Vienna—Burney's visit—Klopstock's
Oden—The *Hermannsschlacht* . . . . p. 46

CHAPTER IV. 1769–1787

Gluck's desire for an opening in Paris—Collaboration with
Du Roullet—Letter of Du Roullet to Dauvergne—
Gluck's letter—*Iphigenia in Aulis*—The story accord-
ing to Euripides—According to Racine—Modifications
by Du Roullet—The opera—Gluck's position in Paris
—His relations with Rousseau—State of the opera in
Paris at that time — Gluck's conversations with
Corancez—Profits from *Iphigenia in Aulis*—Produc-
tion of *Orfeo*—Changes necessitated in it—*L'arbre
enchanté*—Return to Vienna—Meets Klopstock at
Strasburg — Specimen of Gluck's letter-writing —
Cythère assiégée—*Armida* and *Roland*—Intrigues at
Paris — Piccinni — Gluck's letter to Du Roullet —
Journey to Paris—Production of the French *Alceste*—
Gluck and Corancez—Rousseau on *Alceste*—"La
soirée perdue à l'Opéra"—Gluck's explanations of his
method—Death of his niece—Bust of him by Houdon
—*Iphigenia in Aulis* reproduced—The literary war—

Arrival of Piccinni—*Armida*—Gluck and Piccinni at dinner—At work on *Iphigenia in Tauris*—Gluck's letter to Guillard—Piccinni and the directors of the Opera—Production of *Iphigenia in Tauris*—Its balance and proportion—*Echo et Narcisse*—The arrangements for *Hypermnestra*—Gluck's enfeeblement—*Les Danaïdes*—Letter of Calzabigi to the "Mercure de France" —Gluck's life in Vienna—Visit of Klopstock—*Le Jugement dernier* — Death of Gluck — Proposal of Piccinni to found an annual concert in his honour—His portrait, physique and character   . . p. 111

PART II

GLUCK'S RELATIONS TO THE INTELLECTUAL LIFE OF HIS EPOCH

CHAPTER I

1. COURSE OF THE OPERA IN ITALY. An outgrowth of the Renaissance—The Florentine reformers—Artificial from the beginning—The "music of the Greeks"—Imitation of the antique—Evil influences of the Renaissance in Italy—Declamation in the opera—Mythological subjects—Italy too weak to produce genuine drama—Gorgeous decoration in the opera—It passes from the Courts to the public—Growth of the lyrical element—Rise of the singers—The domination of the singers not wholly harmful—Need for lyrical uplifting

—Absence of dramatic feeling in Italian audiences—
The *Commedia dell' Arte* and the *opera buffa* . p. 200

2. COURSE OF THE OPERA IN GERMANY. Popularity at the
Courts—Took root in Italian—Intellectual condition
of Germany at the end of the 17th century—Absence
of an indigenous literature—Improvement in the 18th
century—Simultaneous awakening in music—Emotional effect of the Thirty Years' War—Gradual
humanising of music through Bach and Handel, culminating in Gluck—Growth of the native German
spirit in opera—Kusser—Keiser—His seriousness of
purpose — Based his airs on the *Lied* — Wrote to
German words—His preface to *Almira and Octavia*—
Telemann — Growth of the scenic element — En-
croachment of the Italians—Steffani—Zeno—Metastasio — Hasse, Graun and Naumann followed the Neapolitan school—Growing vogue of *pasticcio* operas—
The strength of Germany up to this time in ecclesi-
astical rather than in operatic music . . p. 211

3. COURSE OF THE OPERA IN FRANCE. Development from
the ballet—Le ballet comique de la rayne (1581)—
Perrin and Cambert—Lully in France—The French
opera restricted in purpose and method—Comparative
unimportance of music in it—Lully's mode of working—Absence of lyrism in his music—His basis poetical and declamatory—Prominence of the *danse*—
The *ouverture*—Louis and Jean Louis Lully—Colasse
—Marais improved the aria—The French opera ap-

proaching the Italian—Brought back by Rameau—His
advance on Lully—Visit of the Bouffons—The *opera
buffa* a healthier and more natural growth than the
opera seria—Its influence on the French opéra comique
—General European contempt for French music—
Opinion of Burney—Evil condition of opera in Europe
at the time Gluck's career began .   .   . p. 217

CHAPTER II

Gluck's ideas not of sudden origin—National and physiological factors in music—His development retarded by
social conventions—Aristocracy in art—The patronage
of music in the 18th century—Gluck not alone in his
demand for reform in opera—Algarotti, Addison,
Marcello, D'Alembert, La Bruyère, Boileau, Panard,
St. Evremond, La Fontaine, Dryden—Importance of
Algarotti's book—His main ideas—Reform in the
libretto—The overture to anticipate the opera—
Recitative—Trills and ornaments—Pauses in the
music—Repetition of words—Ritornelli—Display of
technique—The aria—Had Gluck seen Algarotti's
Essay? .   .   .   . p. 228

CHAPTER III

The preface to *Alceste*—The music to second the poetry—
Banishment of abuses from the opera—The overture
to prepare the spectators for the coming action—His
main purpose "to seek a noble simplicity"—His

assistance from Calzabigi—Gluck's other writings and conversations — Contradictions in his ideas — The attempted reconciliation of Marx futile Gluck's ideas varied at different times—Necessity of judging his theories by the general æsthetic of his epoch—Basis of his theory—The appeal to "nature"—General revolt against the artificiality of the stage—Art and "imitation" in the 18th century—Influence of Aristotle—Confusion of artistic media—"Reason" in philosophy and art—Mistaken view of the function of the imagination—Comparatively low stage of evolution of music—The theory of the "imitation of nature"—Diderot's advice to the artist—The "nature" principle in Algarotti, Avison, Rameau and others—Illustrations of 18th century æsthetic from Grimm and Rousseau—D'Alembert on "painting" in music—Harris on music —Du Bos—Attempts to make music an imitative art—Its dependent position in the 18th century relatively to poetry paralleled in Greek culture—Aristotle and Plato — Chastellux — Evidence from Gluck's own writings of the subordinate position of music—Absence of appreciation of music for its own sake—Rousseau—Melody and harmony—Form and colour—Baumgarten —Winckelmann—Rousseau on *vraisemblance* in opera —"Imitation of nature" in the ballet—Noverre—General drift of opinion in the 18th century as to the function and nature of music—Beattie and Twining on music as a mimetic art—Burney—Gluck's ideas merely the ordinary æsthetic of his time   . p. 238

CHAPTER IV

The practical working of Gluck's theory—Subordination of music to poetry—"Painting" in music—His differentiation of character by "painting" depends mainly on the physical elements of music—His theory fails of itself—Is only efficient to define types, not characters—The theory breaks down where strong passion comes into play—Gluck's theory constantly contradicted by his practice—Difference between Romantic and pre-Romantic art in their attitudes towards music and poetry—Criticism of Berlioz—The divergence of poetry and music in evolution—The higher imaginative existence of music—Herder's anticipation of modern musical æsthetic—Foreshadowing of it in Rousseau—Externality of Gluck's mind—The opinion of Michael Kelly—Marmontel disparages Gluck by comparing him with Shakespere—Neural differences between the 18th century and the 19th—The correlation between art and physique—Music no longer the handmaid of poetry in our day—The real value of Gluck's achievement—His immortality

p. 275

GLUCK AND THE OPERA

INTRODUCTION

To make a plea in these days for the use of the comparative method in criticism would seem to be a work of supererogation. That method, so distinctive of our century in its purposes and results, has, through the labours of a number of men, raised the historical criticism of literature almost to the rank of a science. Apart from the question as to whether the comparative method covers the whole field of criticism ; apart, indeed, from the main question as to what the purpose and function of criticism really are ; it is indisputable that certain forms of literary criticism have, in our own day, attained to something like the certainty and the comprehensiveness of physical science ; and even in the minds of those who disclaim the method and deny its validity, there is an underlying conviction of its truth, and an unconscious application of its principles. While, however, the use of the historical method is thus at the present time practically universal in the criticism of literature and of art in general, there is one department which is as yet almost inno-

cent of scientific treatment ; we look in vain for any
attempt to bring the criticism of music within the
scope of method.

Up to a comparatively recent epoch it was, indeed,
scarcely possible for the scientific criticism of music to
make even a beginning.   It is a truism to say that in
any art or any literature the epoch of criticism must
be of late evolution ; it implies, as the very conditions
upon which it can exist, a fairly complete and multi-
form body of data to go upon—data furnished by
preceding epochs of great and varied creative activity.
It is only within quite recent times that music has
become important enough in itself, and sufficiently
rich in the material it presents, to render possible a
comprehensive and penetrating criticism of it.   Thus
it is not surprising that, until now, music has known
no other criticism than that of personal taste, unaided
by reflection and lacking in basic principles.   Even
yet we are, for all practical purposes, in the lowest
stages of musical culture.   The appreciation of music
is almost universal ; reflection on it is the greatest
rarity.   In the criticism of literature and art we have
attained to some measure of civilisation ; in our judgments on music we are for the most part still un-
tutored barbarians.   While in other departments we
have progressed beyond the static conditions of previous ages to the dynamic criticism of art and letters,
in the musical world we are yet centuries behind the
time ; we are still with the scholiast, the commentator,
the expositor, the pedagogue.   Nothing is more disappointing to the general student of culture than the
dead stop that is given him as soon as he reaches

music. He reads the culture-history of a given epoch, and learns not only what men thought and felt in those days, but why men so thought and so felt ; and when, after having surveyed the poetry, philosophy, social customs, art and literature of the epoch, he wishes to see what shape these ideas assumed in music, he finds his glass darkened. Not being, in all probability, a musician by training or in technical knowledge, it is impossible for him to get more than the barest idea of what the music of such an epoch was, and his culture suffers correspondingly ; for no help is afforded him by the works on musical history or biography he may consult. The complaint is common among liberal-minded men of letters that there is no rational criticism of music, considered as an expression of what men have thought and felt ; our criticism, such as it is, exerts itself for the most part on technical matters alone. This, of course, has its value, and perhaps a greater psychological value than its very exponents are aware of ; but it goes for comparatively little in a survey of human history. Out of the whole library of English writings on music it would be impossible to name ten works, to make an extremely liberal estimate, that could bear comparison for one moment with good contemporary literary criticism. Almost the only help the student gets is from the writings of scientists or philosophers who are treating of the arts, and who do indeed apply a scientific method to the phenomena of music. But from the very nature of the case the knowledge of these men cannot be extensive enough to cover the whole field of music ; so that the art finds itself in some such

dilemma as this : the men who can look at musical
creations in the same way as at other products of the
human mind—which is the indispensable basis of
rational criticism—have not a sufficient knowlegde of
music at first hand to assist them in the application of
the comparative method in anything more than a suggestive way ; while the men who have this knowledge,
whose whole lives have been spent in the attainment
of it, are quite devoid of any critical faculty, and
ignore, with monotonous consistency, every opportunity for applying to their own art the methods that
have alone given coherence to, and thrown light upon,
the being and growth of other arts.*

Part of the general inefficiency of musical criticism
is undoubtedly due to that peculiarity which music
shares with none of the other arts ; the peculiarity that,
owing to its greater indefiniteness of utterance, it has
to seek a greater and more conventional definiteness of
form. This depends upon a psychological necdssity

---

* The imperfect musical culture of even eminent
literary men in England is seen in Mr. John Morley's
painfully inadequate treatment of music in his volumes on
Rousseau and Diderot, and in his omission from his translation of *Le Neveu de Rameau* of "the technical points of
the musical discussion," on the ground that these cannot
interest now. On the other hand, the haphazard and inconclusive method of professed musical æstheticians is
typified in Professor Knight, who in his "Philosophy of
the Beautiful" not only omits any discussion of the late
Edmund Gurney's brilliant book on "The Power of
Sound"—the ablest of all works on music—but even fails
to mention Gurney's name.

of our nature, by which we attempt to gather from certain structural devices the completeness and the symmetry that will bind the abstract musical tones into a consistent whole. Thus ever since the birth of modern music, composers have been unconsciously reaching out to certain structural forms with the object of getting the maximum of expression possible to music unaided by poetry.* These forms have gradually become crystallised and rigid, and their very excellence as modes of musical expression under certain conditions has led to their being regarded as unalterable laws which no future composer must disobey. Some such state of affairs as this has existed in every epoch in which an art has attained to great efficiency of expression. The Greeks of the Periclean age probably argued that the current form of drama was the one inherent in the nature of things, just as our modern pedants affirm that Beethoven has said the last word in the symphony, and that " all we can ask of those who follow him is not to come too far short of that inimitable model."† In the case not only of the symphony but of all other art-forms, there is as

* On the development of the sonata-structure, the reader may consult the excellent article of Dr. Hubert Parry in Grove's Dictionary. I may also refer to an article of my own on "Women and Music" in the *Free Review* for April 1895, in which the psychological meaning of the evolution of musical form is correlated with the general logical movement of the mind in other departments.

† See M. Arthur Coquard, "La musique en France depuis Rameau," p. 175.

yet apparently not the slightest perception of their relativity, and of the peculiar historical conditions under which each of them grew up. And unfortunately the evil does not end here. Not only have we to submit to the ignorance of pedantry in the literature of music, but the imperfect condition of our criticism reacts upon musical culture in general. Music has been at all times an art in which it was possible to produce a pleasing effect by mere imitation, and to the mistaken idea of the absolutism of certain musical forms we owe not only a vast quantity of third-rate music written in imitation of the masters, but the much more serious evil of a hindrance to our future development along more natural and more contemporary lines.

The method of procedure thus followed in the criticism of the more abstract forms of music may be taken as typical of the whole tenor of our criticism at present. It is perfectly futile to go on discussing the æsthetic of music *in abstracto*, without reference to the historical conditions under which the art has lived and by which it has been moulded from century to century. And it must be sorrowfully confessed that the loftiest musical genius of our own day has contributed more than any other man to darken our counsels and to lead us into the wrong path. An examination of his theoretical writings, had we the space to attempt it here, would furnish the most convincing proof of the inefficacy of any other method than the historical in the criticism and æsthetic of music. Wagner was typically German in his metaphysical bias and his *à priori* manner of treating history ; and just as we need hardly look to Germany to say the last word in philosophy or in sociology, we need not expect from it a scientific treatment of music—the most abstract of all forms of human expression, and therefore the one that lends itself most to bastard analysis and spurious generalisation. The method followed by Wagner in his æsthetic writings is typical of the labour that begins in assumption and ends in futility ; and if we can further lay to his charge all that has been perpetrated by disciples such as M. Edouard Schuré, his guilt is heavy indeed.* The Wagnerian method is just that which has been proved time after time to be utterly inefficacious in all other fields of thought ; it is the metaphysical method that first erects spurious entities, and then proceeds to deduce from these entities precisely what has already been put into them ; in opposition to the genuinely scientific method that traces results to causes, and comprehends the whole sphere of human thought and action as a perpetually mobile system of interacting forces. The Wagnerian method is the counterpart of the method we are just beginning to surrender in history and sociology generally, whereby we used to discover the causes of

---

* I hasten to appease the anger of any Wagnerian who may feel aggrieved at this attack on the master's prose writings, by assuring him of my profound admiration for Wagner as a musician. I think it possible to demonstrate, however, that while his music at its best is unmatchable, a good three-fourths of his theoretical æsthetic is the merest Teutonic speculation, with no historical validity whatever, and simply holding the attention, as does the dialectic of Hegel, by its factitious air of symmetry and conclusiveness,

certain historical changes in the " national character " of this or that people, and endow abstract terms with the qualities of concrete forces, and generally explain everything most learnedly in terms of itself. In the Wagnerian dialectic we still have the metaphysical method in all its pristine glory and all its primitive irresponsibility. The problem for Wagner is, how to unite poetry and music in such a way as to procure the maximum of expression with the minimum of friction between the two specialised arts. To see most plainly the futility of any but the historical method in the treatment of such a problem as this, we have only to look at a parallel case in sociology. Copying the æsthetic formula, it may be said that the industrial problem of the present age is how to strike a balance between socialism and individualism, so as to maintain all the desirable advantages of each, and at the same time to increase the total sum of the efficiency of labour. We are not likely to come to any valuable conclusion on such a question as this by taking one entity called " individualism " and another called " socialism," and arguing downward from these to the concrete conditions of life, in the Hegelian style, painting a fancy picture of the mortal combat between these two principles throughout the ages, and their final reconciliation in some form that includes them both, as " unity in diversity." What we shall have to do is to take each country by itself to begin with, trace the historical and other conditions that have led to its present structure being precisely what it is, estimate the relative value of the various internal and external forces that shape its industrial constitution at present, attempt to forecast the relative values of these forces in the immediate future, and then make our provisional alterations accordingly. Any other method than this may be interesting as an essay in the Hegelian manner, but is likely to throw very little light upon the past and still less upon the future.

It is practically the Hegelian method that Wagner and his disciples have followed. One entity is called "poetry," the other "music," and history, by a process of ingenious eclecticism, is re-written to suit the supposed gyrations of these two entities about a common centre. They begin by being united ; then the earth-spirit, in the plenitude of his wisdom, sees fit to separate them for many a century, but solely with an eye to their ultimate reunion. You have your thesis, antithesis and reconciliation ; and all you have to do is to take so much history as suits your purpose and quietly ignore the rest, reading, of course, your own preconceived meaning into everything. Ever since poetry and music became separated, thinks Wagner, each has been yearning in secret for the other ; and though each has gone a-holidaying at times and come to mishap, still on the whole their paths have been gradually converging, and now, of course, have met. It is a curiosity of the metaphysical method that though it deals so manfully with the past, it seems to take little or no account of the future ; it generally appears to imagine that after the threads have once been tied in a particular manner they will remain so tied to all eternity. But inefficient as the method is with regard to the future, it is not less so with regard to the past. There never has been such an entity as " poetry," nor such an entity as " music," nor have these two been turning each an eye on the other throughout the ages. Art has not developed on any preconceived plan, nor has the evolution from form to form been according to the logical necessities of a dialectic. How painfully inadequate the metaphysical method is to explain the vicissitudes of music may be seen by any one who takes the trouble to compare the Wagnerian history of poetry and music with the actual history of those arts. To take Gluck or Rossini, for example, and treat them as stages in the evolution of a dialectical idea, is simply to ignore the actual social and æsthetic conditions that went to shape their music and their relations to poetry. To call the symphonic form " absolute " music, and to write of it as an inevitable stage in the development of music, is to ignore the peculiar conditions under which that form grew up and rose to such perfection. There has been no musical expression that has not owed its origin to the historical circumstances of the time. The internalism of the music of Bach, for instance, was mainly due to the shrinking-in of the German intellect after the political troubles of the seventeenth century, and its religious preoccupation with itself, thus generating in music a psychological state similar to that which underlay the contemporary mysticism in philosophy ; while the later internalism of the symphonic forms, as I shall attempt to show, is due to the comparative exclusion of the composer from the outer world, the consequent atrophy of his dramatic sense, and his disposition to construct musical thought on purely inward lines. The climax of metaphysical absurdity comes in the making of analogies between Gluck and Wagner on the basis of a supposed similarity between their methods of reform, unmindful of the fact that while Gluck and the eighteenth-century thinkers in general held that music should be wholly subordinate to poetry, and should strive to express not musical but *poetical* ideas, the practice of the nineteenth century, whatever its theories may occasionally be, is to subordinate poetry to music in any combination between them, and to use the poetry merely to supply the definiteness that is lacking in music.

Thus by the comparative method alone can we hope to understand the changes that have come over music since the end of the seventeenth century, and the varying attitudes it has assumed towards poetry. Everywhere we see that music has not developed along its own lines without reference to the other arts, but that these and the general culture of the times have helped to shape its course. The long controversy about aria and recitative would in all likelihood have never begun but for the fact that the time when the old polyphonic system was beginning to break up coincided with the reign of a purely derivative culture, that looked back to Greece for guidance in the arts, and that strove to model the new relations between poetry and music upon the antique. Thus began that system of declamation which, helped out by the desire to make music a mimetic art, and to make practice square with the precept of Aristotle, by the relatively low stage of development to which music had then attained in comparison with poetry, and by the general cast of thought of an age that was essentially objective, in philosophy as in art, in science as in sociology, dominated the dramatic music of the eighteenth century, and has not been without influence on the music of the nineteenth. The very vehemence of Wagner's revolt against the florid Italian music of his early years could never have been, but for the political troubles of centuries previous, that crushed the native spirit of Italy, and made it impossible for her to envisage life with freedom and vigour and spontaneity of expression. Look where we will, we find an invariable correlation between the music and the general culture-conditions of any epoch.*

One other point bearing on this matter is suggested by the immediate subject of this book. I do not

---

* A curious evidence of this correlation may be had from the early Byzantine music. "At Constantinople . . . . they were a dainty and fastidious people. Hair-splittings and niceties of thought and language absorbed their attention and engaged their partisanship. The mystery of the Trinity, the precise length of the Incarnation, etc., were debated and defined with the greatest acumen, and the subtlety of their thinking went through the other parts of life as well. Their art was mosaic painting, which consists in piecing innumerable little fragments of tiles together and making a picture out of them; their literary style was the style of exactitude and dainty choice of words; and in their music they delighted in hair-splitting scales, employing not only the chromatic and the enharmonic, but the Soft chromatic, which went by one-thirds of tones, and the Hemiolian chromatic, which went by three-fourths, turns, trills, and shakes innumerable, of which a whole literature survives." See Mr. J. F. Rowbotham's "History of Music," pp. 209, 210.

think that in all the many treatises on Gluck and the opera there is a single reference to that principle of the "imitation of nature" which played so large a part in the æsthetics, politics, morals, and sociology of the eighteenth century, and which really accounts for so many of Gluck's ideas and so much of his method of working. The nearest approach to the recognition of it is by Marx, who does indeed speak of those arias in which Gluck attempts to suggest the external aspects of nature (*Gleichniss-Arie*); but even in Marx it leads to nothing further; he does not even try to discover *why* Gluck held this opinion as to the imitative function of music. Yet the principle stares the student of the eighteenth century in the face at every turn. He can scarcely take up a book of the time without meeting it; in France he finds it in Du Bos, in Voltaire, in Rousseau, in Diderot, in Grimm, in D'Alembert, in Marmontel, in Suard, in Arnaud, in La Harpe, in Beaumarchais; in Italy in Algarotti; in England in Avison, in Harris, in Beattie. Nay, even if the importance and universality of the principle at that time might be missed by the musical historian, owing to his lack of culture beyond the department of music, it is inexplicable how it could have been passed over in the writings of Gluck himself. The famous preface to *Alceste*, round which so much discussion has centred, is absolutely nothing more than the application to the opera of principles that were universal in the thought of the time; just as the later romantic view of music is paralleled in the later German philosophical movement under Kant and Schelling and the æsthetic movement under Lessing and Herder. The real

B

meaning of Gluck's music and its relative importance
in the history of the opera can only be estimated by a
study of the culture-conditions in which he lived.

And if the comparative method has thus never been
applied to one of the most striking of figures and one
of the most obvious ideas in the history of music, it
is futile to look for its application to the history of
the art as a whole. One has only to compare any
genuinely scientific history of nations with the usual
histories of music to realise the great gulf that is set
between them. In the treatment of music there
seems to be little grasp on the part of the historian of
the unity and totality of the conditions that go to
shape the form and determine the utterance of art ; if
his work has any organic connection whatever it is on
the side of the technical development alone. But that
is not enough. What is really wanted is an explanation
of how these various changes and developments in
form were rendered possible. The earlier opera of the
late Renaissance period, the French opera of Lully
and Rameau, the opera of Gluck, the romantic opera
of Weber, the modern opera of Wagner, the fugue,
the sonata, the symphony, the song—all are directly
explicable by reference to their surroundings. Some
day a real history of music will have to be written ;
not an anatomical history, merely marking out the
lines these forms have taken, but a physiological
history, having reference both to structure and to
function. Here, as in every other department of
knowledge, it is synthesis that illuminates ; it is the
spectacle of one mental phenomenon bound up causally
with another that widens knowledge and gives it

certainty and coherence. And when this physiological method of musical criticism comes, it will be found that no intellectual matter can surpass it in interest or value. Music is just as important a factor in the history of civilisation as poetry or philosophy ; and to elucidate it by scientific criticism will be a service to culture as valuable as any other that can be rendered.

PART I

LIFE

CHAPTER I

1714–1746

As the Bach family seems to have had a hereditary predisposition to music, the hereditary strain of the family of the Glucks appears to have run in the direction of game-keeping and forestry in the service of princely houses; for besides the musician's father and grandfather, two of his uncles were engaged in these occupations. The composer's grandfather, Johann Adam Gluck, the second son of one Melchior Gluck, was born in 1650 and died in 1722. He had nine children, one of whom, Alexander, married Anna Walburgis, and was the father of the musician, Christopher Willibald. Four sons and two daughters were afterwards added to the quiver of Alexander Gluck; one of the sons, Anton, born in 1716, probably died young. The youngest of the daughters married a certain Klaudius Heller, a riding-master; their daughter Marianne was subsequently adopted by her uncle, the composer, and usually accompanied him on his various journeys, until the time of her premature death.

It seems to be settled conclusively that Christopher Willibald was born on the 2nd of July, 1714,* at Wiedenwang, in the Upper Palatinate. At this time his father was gun-bearer to Prince Eugene of Savoy. His father's life, however, was at all times unsettled. In 1717 he was at Neuschloss, in Northern Bohemia, in the service of Count Kaunitz ; in 1722 he was master of the forest to Count Kinsky, at Kamnitz, and in 1724 he held a similar office with Prince Lobkowitz, at Eisenberg. He died at Reichstadt, in 1747, in the service of the Grand Duke of Tuscany.

The young Christopher accompanied his father on all these journeys. Alexander seems to have been a stern, hard-natured man, with little power of attraction for his children, who generally found their mother a much more sympathetic friend. In his later days of prosperity, Gluck used to relate how he and his brother Anton would accompany their father into the woods, bearing the implements of his craft for him, and undergoing much physical hardship ; even in midwinter they always went bareheaded and barefooted. Throughout their childhood, indeed, physical comfort seems to have been rare with them. It is no doubt to the rough life he led at this time that Gluck owed the

---

* It was formerly a matter of uncertainty whether Gluck first saw the light in 1700, 1712, 1714, or 1717, a certificate of baptism of a certain Christopher Gluck having led to some confusion, until it was discovered that this referred to an uncle of the composer. See Desnoiresterres, pp. 2–5.

vigorous constitution, the gross good health, and the stubbornness of temper that subsequently distinguished him, and that certainly influenced his intellectual creations. Whether, as imaginative biographers have loved to fancy, his boyish soul was all the while drinking deeply of the mysterious beauty of the woods, and receiving impressions that were ultimately to be re-produced in his music—as in the garden-scene in *Armida* —may reasonably be doubted. Against this pleasingly fanciful theory it must be remembered that a senti-ment of the beauty of nature is rarely roused in those who are only brought into contact with her by the necessities of painful toil, and that in the garden of Armida, as Gluck depicts it, there is rather more of Versailles than of Bohemia.

After some little education at Eisenberg, the young Gluck was sent in his twelfth year to the Jesuit seminary at the neighbouring town of Kommotau, where he remained for six years (1726–1732). Here he learned to sing and to play the violin, 'cello, and organ. Although his father intended him to be a forester like himself, he was commendably bent on giving him as good an education as possible, and in 1732, probably being dissatisfied with the instruction his son was receiving at Kommotau, he sent him to Prague. Here the boy had his first experience of the sterner necessities of life. The parental purse was never too full, and with a large family dependent upon him, the poor forester had little to spare in the way of remittances to his son. Christopher found himself compelled to eke out his livelihood by giving lessons in singing, the violin, and the 'cello, and by playing in the churches.　At the Teinkirche, which was then under the control of Czernohorsky, a musician of some celebrity in his day, he was in receipt of a small monthly salary.　This he managed to supplement by vacation-tours in the surrounding villages, where he charmed the rustic ear with waltzes and polkas, and was paid in eggs—the only available mode of payment for the villagers ; and he exchanged the eggs for cash, if possible, at the first town he came to.　These tours were not altogether valueless even from an artistic point of view, for he brought away with him many rustic melodies that afterwards did duty in his lighter operas.　Later, he passed on to the towns, giving concerts there that brought him in rather more substantial returns than eggs.　In 1736 he went to Vienna, where he was befriended in a very cordial manner by the princely house of Lobkowitz.　His patron introduced him to the musical circles of the capital, and made him acquainted with the group of musicians that adorned the court of Charles VI. at that time—Caldara, Porsile, Fux, and the Conti.　It was in this cultured circle that he met an enthusiastic amateur, Count Melzi, who, becoming attached to the promising young musician, engaged him in his own service and carried him off to Milan, where he placed him under the tuition of the celebrated Sammartini. Here Gluck remained four years, until 1741.　The influence of the Italian master is said to be plainly discernible in Gluck's early operas, more especially in the prominence given to the string quartet, which was a characteristic of Sammartini's "symphonies." Whether he received from his master any profitable instruction in counterpoint is a question difficult to decide. The whole bent of Gluck's essentially dramatic mind was opposed to any mere display of technical proficiency in the opera, and his one work in the contrapuntal style—the *De profundis*—is too inconclusive to prove much. Nor is it definitely known when the work was written ; Marx is inclined to date it about the period of *Iphigenia in Tauris*, as it bears an occasional resemblance to parts of that opera.*

Gluck was now in his twenty-seventh year, and, fully confident of his own powers, he resolved to begin his career as an operatic composer. He chose for his subject the *Artaserse* of Metastasio, probably obtaining the commission for the work through the good offices of Count Melzi. He worked at the opera in a very independent way, without even taking Sammartini into his confidence. At the rehearsals, prophecies of the failure of the work were frequent ; for although, like almost every operatic composer of the time, Gluck wrote as far as possible in the Italian manner, he had not entirely succeeded in veiling his northern origin, and the epithet *Tedesco*, at that time a very damaging one, was sarcastically applied to him and his work. According to the orthodox story, he inserted in the opera an aria of such grace and roundness of form that the connoisseurs at the rehearsals declared it to be superior to the rest of the music, and thought it the composition of Sammartini himself. When *Artaserse* came before the public, however, it turned out that the

* Marx, i. 25–30.

whole opera was a success with the exception of this one aria, that seemed utterly out of place.*

In the following year (1742) he produced, also at Milan, and with equal success, a new opera, *Demofoonte*, the libretto again being by Metastasio. This led to his receiving commissions from several theatres. In the same year two of his operas were produced at Venice—*Demetrio* at the San Samuele theatre, and *Ipermnestra* at the San Giovanni Crisostomo. *Demetrio* at first appeared under the title of *Cleonice ;* in it sang the celebrated Felice Salimbeni, a pupil of Porpora.

In 1743 Cremona saw the production of *Artamene,* while *Siface* was produced at Milan. Thus in two or three years Gluck had composed no less than six operas. During the next two years he worked in a more leisurely way, giving *Fedra* to Milan, and *Alessandro nell' Indie*, produced under the title of *Il Re Poro,* to Turin. It is unfortunate that these earliest operas of Gluck have not come down to us in their entirety ; they were never engraved, and some of the original scores perished in a fire. Gluck so frequently borrowed from his earlier operas that it would have been interesting to observe, as we are able to do in other cases, how he adapted his old ideas to his new requirements. The most successful portion of *Alessandro nell' Indie,* according to Marx,† was a ballet of Indian sailors.

The number of operas thus produced by Gluck— eight in five years—in a country swarming at the time with facile musicians, indicates the existence in his music of elements that appealed strongly to the

* Schmid, pp. 24, 25. † Marx, i. 107.

B*

popular taste. His fame was now extending over
Europe, and in 1745 he received an invitation from
Lord Middlesex, who controlled the opera in London
at that time, to visit England and write a work for
the Haymarket Theatre. Gluck accordingly set out
from Turin with Prince Lobkowitz, passing through
Paris on his way here. He came to London at an
inopportune moment. Independently of the great
vogue of Handel just then, which rendered it exceedingly difficult for any other composer to make head-
way, political troubles combined to disorganise the
theatrical world ; the Rebellion of 1745 had only just
been put down.* Gluck's opera, *La Caduta de'*
Giganti—having reference, in the custom of those
days, to the Duke of Cumberland's recent victories—
was produced on the 7th January, 1746, but was quite
unsuccessful, and was withdrawn after only five performances. It was sung by Italians, and the dances
seem to have won more applause than the vocal portions, on account of the imperfect rendering of the
latter ; the music itself does not appear to have been in
any way above the ordinary Italian standard of the
time, the airs being monotonous, forced, and over-
loaded with senseless ornament.† Handel is said to
have expressed himself contemptuously of Gluck's
attainments, in the well-known phrase that the latter

* See Burney : " Present State of Music in Germany,"
etc., 1773 ; i. 263.

† Marx, i. 110, 111. Burney gives a fair account of
the opera, and adds : " Something might be expected from
a young man able to produce this opera, imperfect as it
was." (" History of Music," iv. 453.)

knew no more of counterpoint than Handel's cook.
But an anecdote is told by Reichardt that seems to
indicate rather more cordial relations between the
two musicians. He says that Gluck, in despair at the
bad reception of his opera, went to Handel for consolation and advice, bearing the score with him for
the master's inspection. "You have taken too much
trouble over your opera," said Handel ; "that is quite
out of place here. If you want to work for the
English you must give them something tumultuous,
like the rattle of drum-sticks on a drum."* Gluck is
said to have so far profited by the advice as to have
added trombones to his orchestra. And Reichardt's
anecdote, as against the cook-story, is borne out by
the gossipy Michael Kelly, who relates how Gluck,
in the evening of his life, one day showed him the
portrait of Handel hanging in his bedroom. "One
morning, after I had been singing with him, he said,
'Follow me upstairs, sir, and I will introduce you to
one whom, all my life, I have made my study and
endeavoured to imitate.' I followed him into his bedroom, and opposite to the head of his bed saw a full-
length picture of Handel, in a rich frame. 'There,
sir,' said he, 'is the portrait of the inspired master of
our art ; when I open my eyes in the morning, I look
upon him with reverential awe, and acknowledge him
as such, and the highest praise is due to your country
for having distinguished and cherished his gigantic
genius."†

* See Desnoiresterres, pp. 13, 14 ; and Reissmann, pp.
9, 10.
† "Reminiscences of Michael Kelly," 1826 ; i. 255.

The Giants having fallen, in a sense not anticipated by Gluck, he produced, on the 4th March 1746, his *Artamene*, written three years previously for Cremona, which met with more success and ran to ten performances. This, of course, was thoroughly in the popular Italian style.* One air in particular, *Rasserena il mesto ciglio*, which had been sung by the *castrato* Monticelli, had become immensely popular.† Many years afterwards Gluck charmed Burney by singing it to him. "I reminded M. Gluck of his air *Rasserena il mesto ciglio*, which was in such great favour in England so long ago as the year 1745 ; and prevailed upon him not only to sing that, but several others of his first and most favourite airs." ‡

Then came the incident out of which so much has been made by the historians of music. Gluck, the story runs, was invited to make a *pasticcio* out of the most popular airs of the operas he had already written, which, it was thought, would catch the popular taste. He did so ; but the pasticcio, *Piramo Te isbe*, fell utterly flat. Then, according to the current theory, which probably owed its propagation in the first place

---

* See Marx, i. 108.

† Some indication may be had of the great success of the airs from this opera from the fact of their being published in 1746—a thing that rarely happened with the operatic music of that day. Six airs were printed—"The favorite songs in the Opera call'd *Artamene*, by Sgr. Gluck. London. Printed for J. Walsh." See Reissmann, pp. 9, 10.

‡ Burney: "Present State of Music in Germany," etc., i. 263.

to Suard, Gluck had his eyes miraculously and almost instantaneously opened to the true problem of the opera ; he saw " that all efficient music must be the peculiar expression of some situation ; that in spite of the splendour of the melody and the richness and originality of the harmony, this is its principal merit ; and that if this vital quality is lacking, the rest is only a vain arrangement of sounds, which may tickle the ear agreeably, but never move people deeply. The consequence of such a discovery led Gluck to subordinate music to the sincere interpretation of nature, and to prefer the smallest cry from the heart to the most ingenious and most learned combinations. So that it was to a failure that he owed this happy transformation in his ideas ; and far from feeling the least rancour towards his critics, he declared himself later to be indebted to the people of London." *

There does not seem much probability of ever getting at the truth of the matter. In spite of the plausible appearance of the story, we cannot place much reliance on it. Several facts tell against it, not the least significant being the number of operas in the Italian style written by Gluck between this date (1746) and the year 1762, in which the reform of the opera actually began with *Orfeo.* If Gluck could really have had his mind roused in this way to a sense of broader issues in music during his stay in London, he would hardly have needed sixteen years to elaborate so convincing and self-evident a principle. Besides, as Schmid has pointed out, he had already, during the

* Desnoiresterres, p. 16.

earliest years of his career in Milan, conceived the idea of making the music conform closely to the words.* According to the full version of the story, he was influenced by the music of Rameau, of Handel, and of Arne. Something in support of the theory might be based on Rameau, were it not that the objection already made holds good here also—that the length of time that elapsed between 1746 and 1762, and the quality of the works that occupied these years, are almost conclusive against the idea of new seed being sown in Gluck's mind at this particular juncture ; while there was little in Handel's operatic music, and still less in that of Arne, on which so essentially dramatic a genius as Gluck could base any operatic reform. Further, that he always held strong opinions as to the functions of dramatic music being something more than the mere giving of sensuous pleasure, is shown by his customary phrase on the usual " pathetic " airs of the Italian composers—" It is all very fine, *but it doesn't draw blood*." Altogether, there seems to be little in the story that is of any real importance. Some colour has been lent to it, however, by a passage in Burney : " He told me that he owed entirely to England the study of nature in his dramatic compositions ; he went thither at a very disadvantageous period ; Handel was then so high in fame, that no one would willingly listen to any other than to his compositions. The rebellion broke out ; all foreigners were regarded as dangerous to the state, the opera-house was shut up by order of the Lord Chamberlain, and it was with

* See Marx, i. 112.

great difficulty and address that Lord Middlesex obtained permission to open it again, with a temporary and political performance, *La Caduta de' Giganti.* This Gluck worked upon with fear and trembling, not only on account of the few friends he had in England, but from an apprehension of riot and popular fury, at the opening of the theatre, in which none but foreigners and papistry were employed.

" He then studied the English taste ; remarked particularly what the audience seemed most to feel ; and finding that plainness and simplicity had the greatest effect upon them, he has, ever since that time, endeavoured to write for the voice, more in the natural tones of the human affections and passions, than to flatter the lovers of deep science or difficult execution ; and it may be remarked that most of his airs in *Orfeo* are as plain and simple as English ballads." *

But there is an air of insincerity about this also. Gluck merely says, in effect, that he wrote in London, as he had done in Italy, what he thought would please the public most ; and the compliment to the taste and discernment of the English audiences—which, only a generation previously, were enraptured with the farce of Hydaspes and the lion—was almost certainly a piece of heavy flattery for the worthy Burney, for Gluck was an adept in the art of managing men. The London spectators of that time were assuredly not the admirers of Spartan severity which he pretends

* Burney : " Present State of Music in Germany," etc., i. 264.

they were; it was decidedly not "plainness and simplicity that had the greatest effect upon them." And in his girding at the partisans of "deep science and difficult execution," and his profession of a desire to "writefor the voice in the natural tones of the human affections and passions," he was probably on the one hand alluding to Handel and his hold over musical London, and on the other endeavouring to make light of his own lack of contrapuntal ability in favour of the forms of dramatic expression more peculiarly suited to him. The ingenuity of Burney in skipping at once from *La Caduta de' Giganti* to *Orfeo* in his effort to vindicate Gluck's new-found passion for simplicity, is a further indication that the story is untrustworthy. It may be noted, too, that Burney says nothing of *Piramo e Tisbe*, but makes the awakening of Gluck's mind follow upon the failure of *La Caduta de' Giganti*.

Rameau, of course, may have had and probably did have some influence on Gluck. When in Paris he had heard the French master's *Castor et Pollux*, and could not have failed to be struck by the dramatic power of the work, the well-defined dramatic rhythm, the clear declamation, and the usual French practice of subordinating the music to the words.

CHAPTER II

1746–1762

TOWARDS the end of 1746 Gluck left England to return to Germany, passing through Hamburg, a town then celebrated for its operatic performances, and where Handel himself had worked in days gone by. The opera, at the time Gluck visited Hamburg, was in the hands of a very competent Italian troupe, led by one Pietro Mingotti, whose wife figured as first soprano. Mingotti was in the habit of taking his company to Dresden for occasional performances, although an Italian troupe was already established there ; and it is an indication of the vogue of opera at that time, more especially of the Italian opera, that the Saxon capital should have been thus able to support two companies. Gluck is supposed to have received an appointment as Kapellmeister about this time, but in November 1746 he left Hamburg, probably feeling himself constrained and hindered in his work with Mingotti.

On June 13th, 1747, the marriage of Princess Anna, daughter of August III., with the Electoral Prince of Bavaria, took place in Dresden, and the usual festivities were necessary. On the day of the wedding an opera by Hasse, *Archidamia*, was performed ;

meanwhile Mingotti had had a libretto put together, which was handed to Gluck to be set to music. It was produced on the 29th June, on a newly erected stage in the Schlossgarten at Pillnitz, under the title of *Le Nozze d'Ercole e d'Ebe*. Nothing much need be said about the music, which seems to have been Italian in style throughout. The Jupiter was a tenor and the Hercules a soprano, but as there was no *castrato* available for the latter part it was taken with great success by Madame Mingotti. The performance resulted in her being engaged at the Hoftheater, as *prima donna*, at a salary of 2000 thalers.

About this time Gluck's father died, leaving him a small inheritance—an inn in Johnsdorf; this he sold, and then settled down in Vienna, early in 1748. The Austrian capital was henceforth his chief dwelling-place. Vienna had been for generations a music-loving city ; the hedonistic tastes of the inhabitants had led to the firm establishment of Italian music there, and the Emperors had long fostered and protected it, retaining in their service the most celebrated composers and poets, such as Hasse and Metastasio. Here Gluck found the highest circles of art and letters opened to him. His fame as a composer had by this time spread over Europe ; and not only his musical ability but his general intellectual powers made him a welcome and respected guest in any society of culture. He had not been long in Vienna before he was called upon to provide an opera for the festivities attending the celebration of the Empress's birthday, and working again on a poem of Metastasio, he produced *La Semiramide riconosciuta* on the 14th May, in the newly erected

Opera-house. The success of the work was complete, though it gave very few indications of the future
reform of the opera. The characters, of course, are
only court characters, and their sentiments only court-
gossip.* The overture is the customary one in three
movements, separated entirely from the opera itself.
The middle section—*andante maestoso*—is marked by
real feeling and earnestness, though its beauty is somewhat marred by monotony of rhythm.† Most of the
airs belong to the *bravura* order, with long and prolix
ritornelli ; even the fine dramatic air of Scytalco, *Voi,
che le mie vicende,* is spoiled by trills and *fioriture.* One
peculiar sign of the difference between the intellectual
world of the composer in the eighteenth century and
that of the composer in the nineteenth, is to be seen
in the many attempts of Gluck and his contemporaries
to treat a musical situation from the point of view of
the plastic arts—to *describe* or *paint* a situation, by
giving to the spectator's ear an impression somewhat
similar to that given to the eye by a picture. Nothing
shows more clearly than these attempts the really
objective way in which the operatic composers of that
time looked at music and the emotions ; and evidences
of this kind, taken in conjunction with the evidence
afforded by contemporary writing on æsthetics, cannot
be neglected in any attempt to arrive at the real meaning of operatic forms in the last century or in this. In

* For a copious analysis of the Opera see Marx, i. 158–
175.
† The andante is given at the end of the second volume
of Marx, No. 8.

several airs of *La Semiramide riconosciuta* we find
Gluck trying to imitate the external aspects of nature
—the brook flowing calmly through the valley, or
meeting with obstacles in its course, and so on.*
This method of "painting" in music, as will be
shown later, was a consequence of the general æsthetic
ideas of the eighteenth century; in our own time,
though it survives in an attenuated form in "pro-
gramme-music," the method is generally abandoned,
as being essentially inartistic and opposed to the real
nature of music as an art of inner imagination.

According to Marx, Gluck gives a foreshadowing of
the future dramatist in the scene between Scytalco and
Semiramis, which is distinctly above anything else in
the work.†

In the course of his visits to Vienna, Gluck had
become acquainted with and enamoured of Marianne
Pergin, the daughter of a rich banker and merchant,
Joseph Pergin ; but though both the mother and the
daughter were favourably inclined towards Gluck, the
father, who seems to have been something of a
Philistine, looked coldly on the suit, he not having a
very high opinion of the financial resources of musicians.
Finding it impossible to carry out his plans just then,
Gluck departed from Vienna, obeying a call to Copen-

* For an interesting light on the eighteenth-century
view of musical "imitation," see Harris's "Discourse on
Music, Painting, and Poetry ; " *Works*, vol. i. pp. 33–60
(*edit.* 1801). The "Discourse" was first published in
1744.

† The aria *Tradita, sprezzata*, to which he refers, is
given as No. 9 at the end of his second volume.

hagen, where a Crown Prince (afterwards King Christian VII.) had been born on the 29th January 1749. Gluck was welcomed with open arms in the Danish capital, and lodged in the royal palace. On the 12th March he gave a " soirée musicale," and on the 9th April his " serenade " in two acts, *Tetide,* was represented at the Charlottenburg Theatre. The libretto seems to have attained the full degree of stupidity customary on these occasions, the chief object, of course, being to make plenty of references to the royal infant. There is neither overture nor symphony, the work being opened simply by an Introduction ; according to Marx, the score contains passages of great power, the influence of Handel being evident. The " serenade " was very successful, and Gluck's excellent business sense made him seize the opportunity to give another concert for his own benefit on the 19th April. It was announced in the *Post-Rytter* of the 14th : " On Sunday, the 19th April, Herr Kapellmeister Gluck will give, in the Italian Theatre at Charlotten-burg, a concert of vocal and instrumental music—a very brilliant and remarkable concert, worthy of great applause—in which he will perform, to the great pleasure of the audience, on a glass instrument hitherto unknown. Tickets may be had in the said Castle from the Kapellmeister himself." *

Towards the end of April, Gluck left Copenhagen

---

* See Desnoiresterres, p. 19, and Marx, i. 179. The " glass instrument " was the *verillon.* During his stay in London, Gluck had probably heard the performance of Puckeridge, an Irishman, upon it.

for Rome, travelling for some reason or other under the garb of a Capuchin ; either, as is imagined, for economical reasons, or to avoid passport difficulties. At Rome he produced at the Argentina Theatre a new two-act opera, *Telemacco, ossia l'Isola di Circe,* which met with the greatest success both at Rome and at Naples. The score is preserved at Vienna ; it shows Gluck to be really trying to shake off the yoke of the Italian opera ; he aims at greater unity of handling, a truer dramatic expression in the airs, and a more continuous interest in the recitative ; in one part he has nine numbers following each other in one dramatic sequence.* Probably the opera would have shown still further excellences had the libretto been more inspiring. Gluck thought a great deal of *Telemacco* in later years, judging from his employment of portions of it in his maturer works.†

In the beginning of 1750 the Philistine Pergin died, and Gluck returned to Vienna, where he espoused Marianne on the 15th September. This was for him the beginning of what seems to have been a wedded life of uninterrupted happiness. His wife, an accomplished and intellectual woman, accompanied him on most of his wanderings ; she survived him several years and died in 1800. Almost immediately after their marriage the pair travelled to Naples, where Gluck had to produce his opera *La Clemenza di Tito,* the

---

* For an analysis of the opera see Marx, i. 189–202.

† Gluck's borrowings from his earlier works are detailed with German thoroughness by Bitter ; see " Die Reform der Oper durch Gluck," pp. 231–243. He gives ten instances in which Gluck has used *Telemacco* in his later operas.

words of which were by Metastasio.* At Naples,
Gluck signalised himself by a successful combat of
obstinacy with the celebrated *castrato,* Caffarelli, who
was at that time the idol and spoiled child of the
Neapolitan public. The opera, like almost all the
productions of Gluck's first period, was very successful.

Field-Marshal Prince Joseph Frederick of Saxe-
Hildburghausen, a favourite of Maria Theresa, had
been captivated by an air in *La Clemenza di Tito—
Se mai senti spirarti sul volto*—and on Gluck's return
to Vienna in 1751, he appointed him director of the
concerts which were given every Friday in his palace
of Rofrano. There Gluck wrote several works for
him, and frequently led the violins in the concerts.
Dittersdorf, the composer of *Doctor and Apothecary,* was
also in the service of the Prince.

In 1754, the Prince was entertaining the Emperor
and Empress and other members of the Imperial family
at his château of Schlosshof, near the Hungarian
frontier, and the usual musical performances were
required in the festivities. Gluck was commissioned
to set to music Metastasio's *Le Cinesi,* which was
produced on the 24th September, the work being
magnificently staged by Quaglio. It was intended as
a prologue to a ballet, which bore the title of *L'Orfano
della China.* The following winter it was given again
in the Court Theatre, with Gabrielli in the chief
part.

In July 1754, Count Jacob von Durazzo was

---

* Mozart set the same poem to music forty years later.

appointed by Maria Theresa to the post of Director
of the Court Theatre. Durazzo, who was favourably
inclined towards Gluck, made him Kapellmeister of
the Opera at a salary of 2000 florins ; and in this
capacity he wrote a number of works for the Vienna
Theatre. Towards the end of 1754 he was invited to
Rome for the production of two operas, *Il Trionfo di
Camillo* and *Antigono*. Both were successful, in spite
of a cabal that was formed against him. He was
further honoured by having the title of " Chevalier of
the Golden Spur " bestowed upon him by the Pope—
a title which henceforth was greatly affected by the
composer. He was always very careful in the future
to style himself " Ritter von Gluck."

In 1755 he set to music, for performance at the
Imperial Château Laxenburg, a " Pastorale " of Metastasio, entitled *La Danza*, consisting of a Symphony in
three parts, four airs, and one duet.* On the 8th
December he produced another *pasticcio*, made up of
selections from various works of Metastasio, under the
title of *L'innocenza giustificata*, in one Act ; it was
repeated at the Court theatre in August of the next
year. This work shows another step in advance in
dramatic power, especially in the portions where the
libretto affords him genuine dramatic moments. Although, however, in *Telemacco* he had abandoned the
conventional symphony in three pieces in favour of an
Introduction, he here makes a retrograde step to the
symphony-form again. " Nevertheless, the symphony
of *L'innocenza* indubitably bears, at least in the first

* Marx, i. 215.

and third sections, the signs of striving after character-indication ; and it is the first symphony of which this can be said. The poem has evidently seized upon Gluck, and roused in him an idea of the ancient Romans. He has not yet succeeded in making a plastic representation of them ; as yet we only see the bare thought of something warlike ; the music consequently only gives an impression of common formalism and of a colouring that aims at the representation of character." *

In 1756, for the celebration of the Emperor's birthday, he set to music a three-act opera of Metastasio, *Il Re Pastore.* Here again, as in *Telemacco,* there is no symphony ; the work begins with an "overture," which finishes in the dominant and leads immediately into the opening aria. Gluck, however, is not yet quite at home in the overture form ; though he uses two themes in contradistinction, the contrast between them is insufficient not merely for dramatic purposes, but even for pure musical treatment. And here, as elsewhere, he hovers between dramatic intensity and conventional weakness. He begins with a finely expressive air, but soon degenerates into mere bravura ornamentation ; and everywhere throughout the work good intentions are seen to go along with lack of power to realise them adequately.

In the autumn of 1760 the marriage of the Grand Duke Joseph (afterwards Emperor) with Isabella Bourbon, Duchess of Parma, took place, and the usual operatic festivities were required. Reutter, the first

* Marx, i. 222.

Kapellmeister, was passed over, and the commission for the new opera was given to Gluck. He wrote a "serenade," *Tetide* (his second work of that name), to words by Giannambrosio Migliavacca, which was produced on 10th October. The work is of little value. It commences with a fairly good three-section symphony, which here receives the name of overture.

The following year, 1761, saw the production of a ballet, *Don Juan, oder das steinerne Gastmahl* (*Don Giovanni, ossia il convitato di pietra*), the words being by Angiolini. It was successful, though it is unfortunate in challenging comparison with the opera of Mozart. Gluck afterwards utilised portions of it for *Armida* and *Iphigenia in Aulis*.

Some time previously the opera-house at Bologna had been burnt down, and a new one erected by Count Bevilacqua. To celebrate the opening of this, a work was demanded from Gluck's pen. He chose again a three-act opera by Metastasio, *Il trionfo di Clelia*, and went to Bologna to conduct it in person. He took with him Dittersdorf, who claimed to be a favourite in the great man's eyes, and who has left in his *Lebensbeschreibung*,* written by his son, a lively account of the journey. "One day Gluck told me that he had been invited to Bologna to compose an opera for that place. He asked me at the same time if I would care to go to Italy with him, but, it was to be understood, on the condition of my paying half the expenses of the journey and half of our daily expendi-

* Leipzig, 1801.

ture ; as to leave of absence, he undertook to procure that from Count Durazzo. 'Oh ! with infinite pleasure,' I answered, in the highest enthusiasm (a sentiment which a man like Gluck, who knew my love for art, as well as my circumstances, ought to have been able to appreciate above everything) ; 'but,' I added sadly, 'I have no money.' 'Then,' replied Gluck coldly, turning his back upon me, 'that is an end to the matter.' " However, Dittersdorf managed to find a generous patron to pay his expenses, and the time of their departure was fixed upon, when a request came from Signora Marini, a celebrated young Venetian singer, that she and her mother might be allowed to join the party. She had been singing in Prague for two years, and was now anxious to return to Italy ; and Gluck being willing, the four set off together.* They passed through Venice, and Gluck and Dittersdorf reached Bologna during Easter week. There Gluck made the acquaintance of Farinelli, the singer, and of the celebrated Padre Martini. He found the Bolognese orchestra very incompetent in comparison with those he had been accustomed to at Vienna, and his new opera had to go through seventeen complete rehearsals before he was sufficiently satisfied with the rendering to venture on a public performance. The opera was successful, however, though it has little interest or value for the modern student. After the third performance Gluck and Dittersdorf made preparations for departure on a tour of pleasure, that was to include Venice, Milan,

* See Desnoiresterres, 32–34.

Florence and other cities.   At this juncture, however,
they received a summons from Durazzo to return
immediately to Vienna for the approaching coronation
of Joseph II.   They accordingly made their way back
through Parma, Mantua and Trent, only to find on
reaching Vienna that the coronation had been postponed to the following year.

For some time previously Count Durazzo, in his
capacity of director, had been negotiating for the performance at Vienna of select specimens of the French
light opera.   This was a species of composition in
high favour in Paris at this time, the music being
usually by Duni and Monsigny, while Favart supplied the texts that were most sought after.   In December 1759, Durazzo had written to him : "When
M. Favart writes a comic opera for Paris, there is
nothing to hinder his sending it to Vienna.   Count
Durazzo will have it set to music by the Chevalier
Gluck or other able composers, who will be delighted
to work on such agreeable verses.   The poet and
musician will thus extend their reputations by mutual
assistance, and will doubly profit by working one for
the other ; and M. Favart will obtain new music
without expense."   Gluck had already written several works of this order—*La fausse esclave* (1758),
L'arbre enchanté (1759), *L'ivrogne corrigé* (1760),
Le cadi dupé (1761), and *Le diable à quatre* (1761);
while to six others—*Les amours champêtres* (1755),
Le Chinois poli en France, *Le déguisement pastoral*
(1756), *L'ile de Merlin* (1758), *Cythère assiégée*
(1759), and *On ne s'avise jamais de tout* (1762)—he
at various times added *airs nouveaux*.   Some of these

were sent by Durazzo to Favart, to enable the latter to obtain an idea of what was required for a Viennese audience. Favart replied : " It seems to me that M. le Chevalier Gluck has a perfect understanding of this kind of composition. I have examined and had performed for me the two light operas *Cythère assiégée* and *L'île de Merlin* ; I find they leave nothing to be desired in point of expression, taste and harmony, and even with regard to the French prosody. It would flatter me to have M. Gluck exercise his talent upon my works ; I would be indebted to him for their success." *
It has to be said that Favart had previously forwarded to Durazzo several scores of Duni and Monsigny, and it is probable that Gluck, with his customary faculty of adapting himself to any circumstances, had modelled his light-opera style on that of the French composers.†

The French light-opera seems to have been almost as popular in Vienna as in Paris ; in the latter city it was looked upon as an agreeable refuge from the " psalmody " of the old opera of Lully and his successors. Gluck's style, as already stated, was modelled upon that of Paris, and it is astonishing with what ease he reproduces their characteristic ideas, turns of melody, and modes of working. It is one more illustration of the difficulties of criticism in dealing with an age of

* Desnoiresterres, p. 28. Favart's letter is dated 24 Jan. 1760.

† Fétis (" Biog. univ. des Mus." ; art. " Gluck "), mentions another comic opera by Gluck, *Le chasseur en défaut*. Neither Marx nor Schmid knows anything of this work, and Marx supposes Fétis to have met with it in the Library at Paris. See Marx, i. 259, note.

artistic imitation like the eighteenth century, where in many cases the traces of the individual handling are almost as nothing compared with the incessant sinking of the artist's personality to comply with the fashionable demands of the time.

To many who must have been weary of the conventionality and inanity of the current Italian opera, of impossible and uninteresting Greek and Roman personages, all cut to the same unvarying pattern, these comic operas may have been an intellectual relief, and a symbol, however faint and imperfect, of a life that was at all events, in spite of its own theatrical formalism, nearer to them than that of Rome or Athens or Bagdad. There is a freshness about some of these works that brings a little warmth to the student's breast after much groping among the dry and dusty stupidities of eighteenth-century Italian opera. They stand nearer to the possibilities of genuine dramatic development than the conventional opera according to Metastasio and the courts ; just as at the time of the Renaissance, as, indeed, before and after it, there were more possibilities of dramatic development in the songs of the people than in the futile antiquarianism and scholarly exclusiveness of the seekers after "the music of the ancient Greeks." The very titles and themes of the comic operas of the eighteenth century are indicative of a frame of mind, on the part of artist and of audience, more clearly bearing on the actual life of the day than the hollow stage-imitations of antiquity that made up the average *opera seria*. *L'arbre enchanté*, for instance, is a fairly amusing story, based on a well-known tale of Boccaccio

("Decameron," 7th Day, 9th Novel); while *La ren-contre imprévue,** by Dancourt, is taken from a farce of Le Sage, the subject being similar to that of Mozart's *Entführung aus dem Serail.* In each of these works some opportunity is given to the composer really to delineate character, and Gluck's treatment of the old man Thomas in the first-named opera is decidedly humorous. And insignificant as they may appear to our eyes, these works in all probability played no unimportant part in the development of Gluck's genius. For Gluck was at heart no mere imitator of a supposed antiquity ; frequently as he blunders in æsthetic theory, like so many of his contemporaries, through a too-conscious reaching back to the past, his own really great work is most characteristic of his epoch, of its thoughts, its emotions, and its life. That he constantly read a wrong meaning into his own artistic meditations and intentions is not a characteristic of him alone ; in our own century Wagner has frequently worked rightly and reasoned wrongly, arguing, like Gluck, from premises that, if worked out logically, would negate the value of his own work. And in spite of Gluck's aspirations after antiquity, he was unconsciously performing a much greater service than that of reproducing "the music of the Greeks" ; he was expressing for us the thought of his own day. To do this adequately, to express himself and the men he lived among as they really were, it was necessary that he should break loose

* For a consideration of these two works, see Marx, i. 260–279.

from the conventionalities, the slothful spirit of imitation, that were this curse of the operatic music of that time ; and in this effort after greater intellectual freedom, his essays in musical comedy were not without importance. That he took much trouble over them is undeniable. The old man in *L'arbre enchanté* is a genuine creation of humour, and the orchestration is at times very fine. Though the opera commences with the usual "symphony" in three portions, Gluck is really endeavouring to make it bear upon the subject of the coming play, and he employs the oboe very effectively to give a rustic colouring to it. "What is of greater importance is the fact that Gluck enters into this new field quite conformably to his real character. Wherever he finds the least support, he attains to dramatic truth and characterisation ; where this support is not to be had, he writes music in the sense and according to the taste of his time ; so that a thoughtful reader who knew nothing of Gluck's future would feel the question urged upon him— what will this lead to, if ever he gets a really dramatic foundation ? It is noteworthy, too, that what we have called in the abstract 'music' (not music *) in antithesis to the dramatic moments, has always the colouring of the rustic melody to which it is linked ; this abstract music is in the Italian style in the Italian opera, and in the French operettas, so far as we know, quite French ; no one would take Lubin's ariettas—for example, the first one, *Près de l'objet*—for Italian music.

---

* This is a subtle German distinction which, I am afraid, none but compatriots can appreciate.

" When we look more closely, however, at *L'arbre enchanté*, we see that even in such a trifle as this, Gluck's originality is undeniable. In the Italian comic opera—for example, Piccinni's *La buona figliuola*, the compositions of Galuppi in this *genre*, the later works of Cimarosa and Paisiello—the main object is to write easy and pleasant melodies with an appropriate accompaniment ; the comic man, the buffo, must delight the audience with endless cascades of chatter ; the French have almost the same bent in their vaudevilles and operettas, except that they make the music much less exuberant and bring it nearer to their popular songs—these latter being more witty and pointed than characteristic or emotional. In Gluck, the effort after definite characterisation is undeniable." *

La rencontre imprévue seems also to have been very popular in its time. In it occurs the air, *Unser dummer Pöbel meint, dass wir strengen leben* (*Les hommes pieusement pour Catons nous prennent*), upon which Mozart afterwards wrote a set of variations. The opera was reproduced at Vienna in 1807, but by that time a great change had come over the public taste, and it fell rather flat.

* Marx, i. 269.

c

CHAPTER III

1762–1769

GLUCK was now in his forty-eighth year, and in full vigour of body and mind. His residence in Vienna and his constant association with men of genius and culture were now beginning to bear fruit. We know, besides, that during the ten years from 1750 to 1760 he had been an assiduous student of literature and art, and his virile intellect was now commencing to bear more strongly and more consciously upon æsthetic questions, and in particular upon the question of the natures of poetry and music and their combination in opera. It is inconceivable that he should not have been struck from the earliest years of his career with the complete fatuity of the current Italian opera, though he might well feel himself powerless to do anything to alter the existing condition of things. His early necessity of earning his bread and making his way in the world, as well as the later necessity of ministering in the accustomed way to the musical pleasures of the Court to which he was attached, would make it impossible for him to step far out of the common circle of conventionality. No estimate can be too great of the deadly evil done to music in the eighteenth century by the system of patronage in

courts and noble houses ; it is one of the points in the
history of music that has not yet had a tithe of the
consideration it deserves.   A truly scientific criticism
would investigate the system of patronage in its
inevitable effects upon the composer's nature, and its
equally inevitable effects upon his art ; when we examine the character of the pacific and timorous Haydn,
for instance, and reflect how much of this was due to
long-continued subservience to the wishes and habits of
his patrons, it is impossible to avoid the conclusion
that much of the out-of-the-world repose that pervades
his music is the expression of a spirit almost emascu-
lated by undue seclusion from the active life of men—
a spirit of weak complaisance and unambitious compromise, turned away from the outer world to the
inner, rarely venturing to touch upon a phase of life of
which, indeed, it was almost wholly ignorant.

In the eighteenth century it was a matter of the
greatest difficulty for the musician to see the world as
it shaped itself to other men, by reason of his having
to look at it from the salon of his patron.   The
musician was in many cases less a man than a human
song-bird.   Thus a true historical study of the development of musical form would have to take account
of the influence upon the musician's art of his dependence upon kingly or princely patronage.   It was
partly by reason of this that pure instrumental music
attained to such extraordinary perfection in the last
century.   A musician like Haydn was of necessity shut
up with himself to a very large extent, and the
inevitable consequence was a development of *absolute*
musical forms, that bore little relation to the moving

life of men, rather than of the forms of dramatic music ;
and in spite of Gluck's reform, it is quite possible that
opera as an independent growth would have languished
in Europe in another quarter of a century—would
have merely escaped the Scylla of Italian absurdity or
the " imitation of antiquity " to have fallen into the
Charybdis of the absolute forms of instrumental music
—had it not been for the Revolution and the new
Romantic movement. There are not wanting signs
of this danger threatening dramatic music from the
side of pure instrumental music in the later work of
Gluck himself. In every department except that of
farcical comedy—placing Gluck's six great operas on
one side—the musical imagination was distinctly below
the imagination of other men of that day. Compare
the relation between poetical comedy and musical
comedy in *Die Meistersinger*, or in any of the Gilbert-
Sullivan operas, or in any one of Auber's best works,
where they stand on the same plane, with the relation
between the verbal comedy of Beaumarchais in *Figaro*
and Mozart's musical comedy in his setting of that
play, and it will be realised how far below contemporary thought the best eighteenth-century music was,
with the exception of that of Gluck. Mozart's *Figaro*,
of course, is a work of immortal beauty, but the significant point is that this beauty is far more akin
to the symphonic work and the chamber-music of
the time than to the drama it professes to illustrate.
All that is interesting to the student of eighteenth-
century manners in the comedy of Beaumarchais
vanishes in this setting of it by Mozart. This interest
is replaced by another, that of absolute esoteric musical

enjoyment.   Not only the characters but the world they live in is changed.   Everything takes an artificial and conventional air ; the opera itself, intellectually almost ridiculous, lives in our minds, not, like the comedy of Beaumarchais, as a picture of eighteenth-century life, but as a piece of pure impersonal music. It is the world, not of Beaumarchais' Paris but of Haydn's salon.

One more fact may be noted, as being related both as cause and effect to this exclusiveness of music ; the fact that the musician was generally held in small esteem in the eighteenth century, just as the actor was despised in the sixteenth century in England. The musician had very little actual relation to the world ; his main concern was with his employer or his patron.   He produced his works, not through the stress of humanistic feeling urging him to express the thoughts within him—in cases like those of Haydn and Mozart, this feeling practically did not exist— but in obedience to the wishes of his employer or the necessities of some theatrical performance.   Piccinni, for instance, to take one of the best specimens of the class to which he belonged, was perfectly willing and perfectly able to turn out operas in abundance for any occasion that might arise, adapting the style of them to the conventional models for each kind of composi- tion—for a royal wedding or coronation, for a pleasure party at a noble house, and so forth ; but on scarcely a single occasion would he feel compelled to utter him- self in music through any burning, imperative need within him.   And so we find him hustled about from one court or one patron to another, never regarded as a man or a thinker, but as a mere machine to grind forth music when it was required of him. Could there be produced, under such circumstances as these, music that should be of any permanent value, music that would survive after its own immediate day had closed? Deprive the artist of his independence, his individuality, his very essence as a man, distinct from his capacity as servant to a court or a prince or any system of convention, and you take away from his art all bearing upon the life and thought of the world. He may still produce art, but it will be for the most part simply art for the chamber or the church, not art that can stir men, not art that can give them new impulses and new lights on life. The opera of the eighteenth century was undignified, and paltry, and servile, because the men who wrote it were undignified, and paltry, and servile. Social conditions in which the artist is regarded as a mere means of ministering to the enjoyment of the ignorant and selfish wealthy, must inevitably result in the degradation of himself and the emasculation of his art.

It was under such conditions as these that Gluck passed his years of apprenticeship; from the very beginning he found himself in that dignity-destroying atmosphere of patronage. The son of a poor forester, dependent from his earliest years upon himself for support, forced to receive his musical education through the charity of princes and noblemen, introduced into their houses as an object of their protection, where a thousand silent influences would be constantly at work to sink his soul in nerveless acquiescence in the spiritless course of things around him—a system

of patronage on the one side and of dependency upon
the other ; then finding employment in writing for
Italian theatres where everything original had to be
sacrificed to the dominant taste for slothful conventions, where the musician's sole function was that of
an embroiderer, to adorn weak and foolish libretti with
figures and colours all of one invariable kind ; then
attached to the Imperial court, the petted protégé of
the emperors, where again, as in the houses of his
princely patrons, every original conception must be
stifled in embryo, where deep thought and true
imagination and serious feeling were hampered and
vitiated by the one great necessity of doing nothing
to offend the ears of his noble protectors, of putting
nothing in his compositions that would be above their
small capacity ; the wonder is how he managed to do
good work in spite of all.   Nothing can be said in
greater praise of Gluck than that he lived through
these conditions and outgrew them.   Nothing is more
conclusive of his claim to honour than the way in
which, by virtue of his strong physical and mental
organisation and his genuine humanism of feeling, he
set himself with iron will to express *himself* in his
music, and in the teeth of all the opposition of foolishness, and conventionality, and sham, to make his music
manly, truthful and sincere.   This firmness of will
and purpose, often amounting to dogged obstinacy, led
him frequently to the commission of injustices and to
a harshness of attitude towards other men ; but we
can pardon this and more in him.   To do the
magnificent and courageous work he did, he required
a strength of nature that perhaps necessarily led him

into an attitude of uncompromising roughness towards other and weaker men. But without this dogged self-sufficiency of character he would never, in the age in which he had the misfortune to live, have been at all equal to the reformation of the opera. During all these years of servitude and imitation he must have frequently realised with shame and self-contempt that he was pandering to meanness of spirit and unintelligence of soul. He himself is reported to have said that he had wasted thirty years of his life in imitating Jomelli and Pergolesi. Critics have tried to compromise the matter by saying that these thirty years were not wholly wasted ; that they had given ease and facility to his imagination, and so prepared the ground for his later reforms ; as if any ease and facility that came of servile and unintelligent imitation of an art that was itself divorced from the deeper meanings of men's lives, could be of any value to a man of native strength of soul ; as if thirty years of a strong artist's life spent in mean and pitiful pandering to the desires of men who had no part in the thoughts and movements of actual life, could be anything less than thirty years taken from the study of men as they actually were outside the salon or the opera-house ; as if the musician who could create real and breathing men and women could be anything else but weakened and degraded by thirty years' association with the nerveless dolls and bloodless puppets of Metastasio and the Viennese and Italian theatres. The ease and facility that Gluck gained from the Italian style, if indeed he gained any, could have been acquired in something less than thirty years. But that after such a length of time his soul and spirit should not have become as emasculate as those of his contemporaries, that after this time he should still have strength of mind and force of will enough to bring his music to bear upon the expression of what men really felt and thought— this it is that makes him so magnificent and so statuesque a figure. He dwarfs the Piccinnis and all around him ; the same generic name is hardly applicable to them both.

Of late years Gluck had been earnestly studying ancient and modern literature, and the thoughts within him were slowly ripening to fruit and flower. He could not have failed to be struck years earlier by the inanity of the Italian stage. Others beside him in the eighteenth century had turned away in disgust from its weaknesses and its lack of human interest. " How is it the Italians have not a good serious opera ? " asks Grétry ; " for during the nine or ten years I have lived in Rome I never saw one succeed. When any- body went there it was to hear this or that singer ; but when the latter was no longer on the stage, every- one retired into his box to play cards and eat ices, while the pit yawned." * The Président de Brosses had said the same thing about the time Gluck was maturing his plans for the reformation of the opera ; once in the Della Valle Theatre, he says, he found chess an excellent pastime " for filling the void in these long recitatives," and music equally excellent " for interrupting one's too great passion for chess."†

* " Mémoires et Essais sur la Musique," i. 114.

† "La Président de Brosses en Italie," ii. 357, 358. Quoted in Desnoiresterres, p. 48.

c*

Forty years before, Marcello had satirised the inanities of the Italian stage in his celebrated " Il Teatro alla moda ; " while Addison in England and Algarotti in Italy, besides a number of other writers, had called attention to the great degradation into which the opera had fallen.

Thus Gluck by no means stood alone in his perception of the crying need for reform in the Italian opera. His crowning merit is not that perception, but the realisation of it in work, the translating it into actual reform. A thousand weary and sated hearers of the opera might see the foolishness and the hollowness of it all ; Gluck alone could create something better to take its place. Already in some of his works he had shown flashes of that rich creative energy that was at the foundation of his nature. In *Semiramide*, *Telemacco*, and elsewhere, he had given proofs of a strong dramatic capacity, waiting only for a favourable opportunity for the employment of it. Naturally the first requisite was a reform in the verbal groundwork of the opera. Nothing could be done with the ordinary libretto, with its sham personages, its conventional airs and situations, its rigidity of structure, and its wearisome reiteration of words destitute of the barest dramatic or even intellectual signification. Gluck believed himself to have chosen rightly when he fixed upon Raniero di Calzabigi to be his coadjutor in the reform of the opera. Calzabigi was an Imperial Councillor who had already earned some reputation in Europe as a critic and a man of taste ; at Paris he had edited an edition of Dante, to which he had written an introduction. Gluck apparently had found in his conversation evidences of culture and understanding, and had settled upon him as the man most fitted to work with him in his new project. The result of their collaboration was the opera *Orfeo ed Euridice.* It is not known precisely what was Gluck's share in the composition of the libretto, though it was certain to be a large one. Probably we shall not be far wrong in saying, with Marx, that he would insist on the sense and dramatic interest of the recitative, on the lyrical portions being really lyrical, and not the conventional " arie " of Metastasio, and on the importance of the work to be given to the chorus. In this last connection, he would in all likelihood have in his mind a vivid image of the choruses of Rameau, which he had heard in Paris, and of those of Traetta, whose *Iphigenia,* containing a fine chorus of Furies,* had been performed at Vienna in 1760.

The new work was produced on the 5th October 1762. The ballet was arranged by Angiolini ; the machinist was Quaglio. The part of Orpheus was given to Guadagni, a *castrato* who stands out in refreshing contrast to his fellows of that age by being the possessor of two qualities not usually found among them—intelligence and modesty. He entered into the spirit of Gluck's work with perfect comprehension, and refrained from defacing the music allotted to him with any of the customary " embellishments," the employment of which, due in the first instance to the vanity and vulgarity of the singers, had been so long consecrated by custom. Gluck's exacting spirit showed itself at

* See Bitter, pp. 164–177.

the rehearsals.   More than once he came into conflict
with the instrumentalists, to appease whom the Emperor's personal influence had to be exerted : " You
know, my children, what he is !   But he is a worthy
man at bottom."   Calzabigi himself had taken in
hand the training of the singers in the action and
expression necessary to the realisation of his play.
The first performance naturally created astonishment
and some opposition, but these gradually declined,
until at the fifth rendering the position of the new
work was assured.   It passed out of Germany into
Italy, and " at Parma itself, Traetta, one of the greatest
masters of that time, certainly the most pathetic and
the most ' German ' of Italian composers, was unable
to have his *Armida* performed ; the public wished only
to hear *Orfeo*." *

Much as Gluck wished to emancipate himself from
the traditional conventionalities of the opera of this
day, he was bound by these conventionalities in his
choice of a subject.   It was the almost universal custom
to take the stories for grand opera from "classical"
life, and it is from this ancient world that Gluck drew
his subject ; a pre-historic sun-myth was to serve
as groundwork for the reformation of the opera.

He has given up the old " symphony " form of
introduction ; he begins the opera with an overture,
which is, however, disappointing and inconclusive both
from the dramatic and from the musical standpoint ;
from the former, because the great defect of construction of the poem of *Orfeo* is its absence of any strongly

---

* Desnoiresterres, p. 51.

marked dualism of subject, which leaves the composer
without the opportunity of employing two forcibly
contrasted themes ; and from the latter, because it has
not sufficient strength or beauty or interest to be
pleasing in itself, purely as a piece of music, apart from
any dramatic associations. It might have been written
by Gluck in his apprentice days, when he was under
the tuition of Sammartini, traces of whose influence
are clearly discernible in it. Broadly speaking, he
may be said to be aiming tentatively at duo-thematic
treatment, but his themes are neither interesting
in themselves, nor sufficiently strong in contrast to
produce dramatic effect. The overture, in fact, is perfectly supererogatory ; the opera would not be appre-
ciably affected if it were removed altogether. How
inconclusive and unnecessary it is, becomes strikingly
evident on hearing the *real* introduction to the drama
—the short orchestral prelude that precedes the opening chorus of the First Act. The stage shows an
open plain with the tomb of Eurydice; round it are
moving the shepherds and girls, bearing flowers and
twigs of myrtle, and singing a chorus of mourning.
Here the orchestral introduction breaks away from the
characterless spirit of the overture ; here the pervading
spirit is unmistakably dramatic at every point. The
chorus take up the same broad, sad theme, and for a
moment the voice of Orpheus blends with theirs in
the cry " Eurydice ! " twice repeated as the mournful
song continues ; and a peculiarly poignant effect is
created at the third utterance of the name by the
singer's voice taking a tone higher than on the two
previous occasions, and by its standing out against a

moving background of chords of diminished intervals, instead of blending, as before, with the chord of the minor third of the dominant. Thus in the first few moments of the opera, Gluck had shown his extraordinary faculty for realising the most striking dramatic effect by the most simple and most natural means.

The chorus conclude their sorrowful appeal to Eurydice to return, and Orpheus addresses them in a recitative, " Enough, my companions ! your grief increases mine. Strew flowers about the marble tomb, and leave me ; here will I remain, alone with my sorrow." They make silent processions round the tomb, crowning it with flowers, while the orchestra gives out solemn music ; then they break again into the first chorus, to the strains of which they make their exit, leaving Orpheus alone. In a short but extremely beautiful air he calls upon Eurydice to return to him. The air is more in the voluptuous Italian fashion than are the later arias we are accustomed to associate with the idea of Gluck, but is not without dramatic significance, more especially on the words, " Vain is my lament ! my beloved one answers not ! " Three times during the course of the aria an echo of the theme is heard from a small orchestra behind the scenes. The most serious flaw in the aria is the constant alternation of *piano* and *forte*, almost chord by chord ; it is at once unnecessary and undramatic, and by forcing the expression tends to render the aria insignificant. This is one of those instances of Gluck's employment of the usual trickery and frippery of his contemporaries, which show how hard it was for him to break completely away from the conventional style. The following recitative, " Eurydice ! Eurydice ! dear shade, where art thou ? " is of the " accompanied " order, and more dramatic. Not only is the expression sought most carefully and patiently in the vocal part, but the orchestra is given its share in producing the general effect. Then Orpheus repeats his aria to slightly different words. A third time he sings it, and a third time breaks into recitative, this time of a more passionate character, and in parts almost lyrical. He has just declared his resolve to descend into the under-world and win back Eurydice, when Cupid appears, tells him that he has the sympathy of the gods, and that Jupiter pities him ; and advises him to descend to the kingdom of the shades, where by the magic of his harp he may win back his wife. Short as this piece of recitative is—only fifteen bars—it exemplifies the studied way in which Gluck was now handling the implements of his craft. Where the least significance is given in the words, over and above their mere ordinary indicative quality, he attempts to illustrate their meaning through the orchestra, as on the words, " Lethe's dreadful strand," where a suggestion of the gloom of the river is given in the accompaniment.

The following recitative, in which Cupid tells him the conditions on which he will be allowed to bring Eurydice from the underworld—that he is not to look upon her face until they have come into the light of day again—is dry, unlyrical, and uninteresting. " Think over it," says Cupid ; " Farewell ! " Before making his departure, however, he sings an aria, which affords an interesting illustration of the eighteenth-century method of "painting" in music; where the sense of the words changes, a complete change is made in the material characteristics of the music. Thus the first part of the aria, depicting the happiness of the man who bows patiently to the will of the gods, is a rather broad melody in $\frac{3}{4}$ time, in the key of G, *sostenuto* ; in the second part, Cupid tells Orpheus of the joys that await him, and to paint this Gluck converts the *sostenuto* into an *andante* (*piano*), changes from the former key to that of D and from the $\frac{3}{4}$ time into a very tripping $\frac{3}{8}$ time, made even more dactylic in character by the strong accent on the first note of each phrase, and prefixes to almost every bar an ornamental triplet figure ; the purpose of all this being to convey through the ear a *picture* of the joys that are spoken of in the words. This change from one theme to another takes place five times, the same theme being always used to accompany the same words. That occasional imperfection of the lyrical sense also that is noticeable in Gluck betrays itself here. There is a peculiar awkwardness about the conclusion of the second theme ; by setting the words to this $\frac{3}{8}$ time he finds himself, at the end of them, just one step off the tonic conclusion of his theme, considered as a musical phrase. The consequence is, that he has to conclude a symmetrical sweep of four bars with another bar that seems to need still another to balance it ; and the effect of this make-weight conclusion is inexpressibly awkward ; it suggests the pedestrian difficulties of an animal encumbered with an extra and superfluous leg.

Cupid retires, and Orpheus debates within himself, in a recitative that is both dramatic in intention—the intervals between the notes being greater than in any of the previous recitatives—and accompanied in a descriptive way by the orchestra, which also concludes the act.

The Second Act shows the under-world; the ground is broken by abysses; heavy clouds come floating down, riven every now and then by lurid bursts of flame. After a ballet, the Furies break into a chorus, in octaves—"Who is the mortal who dares approach this place of dread?"—strongly and decisively written. Then follows another ballet, the music to which is amongst the most effective ballet-music Gluck has written; after which the question of the chorus is repeated, this time with an extension; while through the orchestral accompaniment is heard incessantly the howling of Cerberus. Without any pause, the music leads into a short prelude for the harp, to which accompaniment Orpheus lifts up his voice in passionate entreaty. This is the marvellous scene that after the lapse of a century and a quarter has not lost one atom of its original force and beauty: that is among the most remarkable dramatic productions of that or any other age; and which alone would suffice to give to future generations some indication of the wonderful power of Gluck, if all were lost of his work but this. It is almost impossible to speak with undue admiration of this supple, fluent melody, with its piercing anguish of entreaty, the admirable leading up, time after time, to the word of supplication, and the dramatic decision of the *No!* of the Furies, which, in the middle portion of the air, where the word is pronounced on the B natural, is positively appalling. Nor is the succeeding chorus one whit inferior. There is something of the highest psychological expression in the passage in which, after warning the wretched intruder of the horrors that infest the place, they ask, " What wouldst thou, poor youth ? What wouldst thou ? " The orchestra takes up a short theme that seems by unconscious and subtle suggestion to lead us out of the immediate present, to throw our minds forward into the later development of the scene ; it is one of those rare psychological moments that are the triumph of dramatic art. Repeating the word " What ? " the suppressed rage of the Furies breaks out again in lurid passion. The reply of Orpheus, " In my breast are a thousand torments ; hell itself is within me, its fires are burning in my heart," is as fine and as pregnant with musical beauty and as significant with dramatic meaning as his previous entreaty. The Furies reply in subdued tones, expressive of the power his song is beginning to exert on them, " What magic in him overcomes our rage ? " Finally they throw open the gates to him, and their voices die down to exhaustion and submission, while the orchestra continues their previous theme.

The scene changes to the Elysian fields. Some of the happy spirits are performing a ballet, in accordance with eighteenth-century ideas of the occupations of happy spirits |in Elysium, while Eurydice and the chorus sing of the quiet joys of their abode. Meanwhile Orpheus has entered, and expresses his wonder at the beauty of the scene ; " How pure the light ! "

His melody is something between aria-form and that of recitative (Gluck has marked it *quasi recitativo*) ; and, considered from a purely musical standpoint, it is among the finest of his creations ; it has that unity and consistency that are so noticeable in his later works, especially in the scene in Armida's garden and in the first scene of *Iphigenia in Tauris.* Particularly fine is the effect of the constant modulation of the beautiful theme for the oboe.

On his asking the chorus for Eurydice, they reply, in a charming *ensemble*, that she is now approaching. The Act draws to a close with a beautiful ballet, reminding us in parts of the sweetest ballet-music in *Paris and Helen,* and a chorus. Seizing the hand of Eurydice, but without looking into her face, Orpheus hastens away with her.

The Third|Act shows the pair in a labyrinthine cave. Orpheus is still leading her by the hand, and his face is still turned away from hers ; he will answer nothing to her questions, but reiterates his entreaty to hasten onward. But her suspicions have been aroused by his averted face ; she is beginning to doubt his passion, and all his entreaties are of no avail. It is curious to notice how Gluck is hampered here by the material he has chosen to work in. Time after time there seem to be struggling through the bald recitative a passion and a dramatic power that cannot find their full realisation in such a medium. As it is, just where the feelings of the personages demand lyrical treatment, Gluck is tied down, by a convention from which he cannot free himself, to a form of musical speech that is the very negation of all lyrical expansion.

Thus at one point of the dialogue we have the following :—

> EURYDICE. But my delight at beholding you again,—you, alas, share it not.
>
> ORPHEUS. O doubt not, but . . . . know . . . . hear me . . . . Oh sad fate ! Dear Eurydice, tarry no longer here.
>
> EURYDICE. Why are you sad, when rapture surrounds us ?
>
> ORPHEUS. It has happened as I foresaw ! And yet I must keep silence !

Now this speech of Orpheus is a kind of crisis of feeling in the dialogue, and no expression that the composer could put into it could be too deep or too sorrowful. Yet by reason of having chosen to write this part in recitative, Gluck can do no better than set to these important words the well-known conventional form of recitative conclusion, a fall of the voice from the tonic to the dominant, followed by a close, in the accompaniment, from dominant back again to tonic. His neglect of the emotional possibilities of this passage, and his abandonment of it to the most meaningless formalism that recitative can offer, is the more inexplicable in view of the fact that his setting of the very next words of Eurydice, "Wilt thou not embrace me ? not speak to me ? " etc., is strongly dramatic and passionate, and the recitative is on its way again to lyric warmth and fervour. The remainder of the recitative in this scene is alternately passionate and conventional, and on the two occasions on which the words, "O follow and be silent," are repeated, Gluck, as previously, puts no dramatic force whatever into them.

The lovers now break into open rupture. The voices, which commence in dialogue, soon blend in a duet, which, from a musical point of view, is one of the best numbers in the opera, but the dramatic significa- tion of which is incessantly waxing and waning, some passages of meaning being neutralised by unnecessary repetition. Gluck, in fact, was here unconsciously in the dilemma that always attended his later consciously- pronounced theory of the opera ; he was hovering irresolutely between an essentially *musical* method that made more exclusively for formal æsthetic gratification, and an essentially *dramatic* method in which purely musical gratification was to be sub- ordinated to the more intellectual effects of decla- mation.

Eurydice breaks loose from Orpheus, and bursts into an aria, in which Gluck again alters the external characteristics of the music at every moment ; the aria is alternately *allegro, lento, allegro, andante,* 2nd *andante, allegro.* Yielding to her entreaties, however, he at length looks at her, and immediately she feels the pangs of death upon her again. Her cry, "O ever beloved ! O great gods, I tremble, I sink, I die !" is very fine. A recitative for Orpheus leads into the well-known *Che farò senza Euridice?* in which we have something of a reminiscence of the Orpheus of the first act. Then, just as he is about to slay himself, Cupid again appears, and tells him that the gods have had sufficient proof of his fidelity. Eurydice rises again, and ballets celebrate the happy issue of their trials. The ballet-music is not specially noticeable, with the exception of the charming gavotte —which may be a reminiscence of the composer's early days of wandering among the country people—and the rather pretty opening phrase of the succeeding *andante* in D. The work concludes with a trio and chorus of rather commonplace character.

Such was the opera with which Gluck began his great reform. It is a mixture of extraordinary strength and extraordinary weakness. The beginning and the end, the overture and the finale, are especially vacuous and futile ; and Berlioz is right in speaking of the " incroyable niaiserie " of the overture. Within the opera itself, again, as has been pointed out in the foregoing analysis, scenes of deathless interest and beauty exist side by side with passages almost devoid of either musical or dramatic significance. Gluck, in fact, was in a double dilemma, that of effecting a compromise between the musical and the dramatic interests in the lyrical portions, and that of striking a genuine balance between ordinary speech and pure lyrism in the recitatives. Thus his practice, like his subsequently-expressed theory, was vitiated from the outset by fallacy and contradiction ; as will appear later, these were necessary results of his hovering irresolutely between two courses of action—between real expression of the emotional life of his own day in lyrical forms, actually and naturally created by this emotional life, and a fictitious expression, forced on him by the usual practice at that time of imitating a supposititious antiquity. Under such circumstances as these it was inevitable that Gluck's opera-style should be always contradictory both of itself and of his written theories.

In spite of this, however, he had really achieved much in *Orfeo*. Though he preserved the old antagonism between aria and recitative, he yet aimed straight and strongly at the improvement of the latter, and at giving it a real place in the development of the opera, instead of making it, as in the conventional style, mere padding to fill up the spaces between the airs. This, of course, was a reform he had really in part attempted much earlier. In *Telemacco* he had already given a hint of what he could do in accompanied recitative. In *Orfeo*, however, he applies the principle more rigorously, by writing accompanied recitative throughout, and thus giving increased significance to the orchestra. A similar reform was effected in the aria by relinquishing, in most cases, the stereotyped *da capo* form, which, although not without its usefulness and its meaning in many places, was so palpably artificial in its ordinary employment as to be quite against the possibility of dramatic effect. That Gluck uses it occasionally here and in other places, and with success, is a proof that there is nothing essentially undramatic in the *da capo*, but that its employment must be strictly regulated by the contents of the aria. Nothing, for instance, could exceed the impressive effect of the return to the first subject in the aria of Iphigenia, *O toi qui prolongeas mes jours*. But Gluck's increasing perception of the possibilities open to free emotional outpouring, and his growing seriousness in relation to his art made him employ the *da capo* form very sparingly, and substitute for it a form that was more unfettered, more direct, and more continuous. This reform almost necessarily begat another : the giving of greater unity to the drama by linking each successive piece to its predecessor ; not, as formerly, by a mere juxtaposition, but causally, each dramatic moment growing out of that which preceded it. Here, again, Gluck had reached out tentatively to this reform on previous occasions, notably in *Telemacco.* That even in *Orfeo* he was prevented from carrying out each of these new methods to completer excellence, was due, in part at least, to the weaknesses in the construction of the libretto. No composer can write dramatic music to an undramatic situation, and it is the misfortune of *Orfeo* that the interest of the play degenerates at the end. Apart from the absurdity of Cupid's whole existence and appearance in the opera —for no study of character whatever is possible in the case of a mere allegorical personage such as this—his final coming as *deus ex machinâ* to give the completing touch to the drama is weak in the extreme. The ending of *Orfeo* is an " excursion in anti-climax ; " the real end of the interest of the play is at the swooning of Eurydice.

Gluck, of course, had still his position to maintain at the Court at Vienna, and he found himself compelled, time after time, to fill up the intervals between his greater operas with the customary ephemeral works intended for performance at some imperial ceremony or at some country house. About a year after the performance of *Orfeo* he is supposed to have set to music *Ezio*,* a three-act opera by Metastasio, of which only part of the second act is known.

In the following year he received from Dancourt an adaptation of a farce by Le Sage, entitled *Les Pélerins de la Mecque*, which he set to music as a comic opera in three acts.† "I have suppressed the licentious in it," writes Durazzo to Favart, "and I have only preserved the more noble portion and such comic scenes as could go along with it; I have no doubt that the poem, thus arranged in accordance with the actual taste of the nation, will make its mark, especially as it is supported by the music of M. Gluck, a man incontestably unique in his sphere. I would like the piece you are to adapt to be treated in this spirit. I think I have already, in my preceding letters, communicated to you my ideas on this matter; but I do not hesitate to repeat them, being anxious for them to have their full effect." ‡

Durazzo meanwhile had set about having the score of *Orfeo* engraved, and had sent it to Favart at Paris, begging him to take the matter in hand. Favart handed it to Mondonville, who, on being applied to, estimated the probable cost at about 800 livres. On coming to the engraving of it, however, it was found

---

* It is not certain whether this opera was really written at this time (Dec. 1763), or twelve years earlier (1751), the work performed on the present occasion being a resuscitation of the older one. See Marx, I. 331–2.

† This is the work which has already been described as *La rencontre imprévue*.

‡ Lettre du Comte Durazzo à Favart, 19 Nov. 1763, in Desnoiresterres, p. 52.

to be full of errors and omissions,* and Favart passed the score on to Duni for correction. The latter, however, thinking it an opportunity to gain some profit for himself, gave Favart what was probably an exaggerated account of the confusion of the score. "Duni," writes Favart to Durazzo on the 19th April, 1763, "has made a mountain of the score of *Orfeo ed Euridice;* he says he could only undertake the task of correcting the copyist's errors for 500 livres. I have shown the score to Philidor, who is not nearly so difficult to deal with; he offers to correct the false notes gratis, and to superintend the engraving of the work personally; he only asks a single copy from Your Excellency. He has examined the opera attentively; he finds that the copyist's errors are not very numerous; he is enchanted with the beauty of the work; in several places he has shed tears of pleasure. He has always had a great admiration for the talent of the Chevalier Gluck; but his esteem has grown into veneration since he has become acquainted with *Orfeo.* So we can go on immediately with the engraving without the necessity of waiting for M. Gluck."† After some little trouble Favart managed to obtain a remittance from Durazzo, who had apparently overlooked this preliminary, and the work was taken in hand. Philidor has been accused of appropriating the melody of the air, *Chiamo il mio ben cosi*, and, by

---

* Berlioz has pointed out in detail the almost incredible carelessness of Gluck in the matter of his scores. See "A travers chants," pp. 201, 202.

† Desnoiresterres, pp. 53, 54.

means of a little dexterous manipulation, converting it to his own uses for an air, *Nous étions du même âge*, in his comic opera *Le Sorcier*. The fraud was pointed out by Sevelinges, and later by Berlioz. Fétis defended the French musician, on the ground that a comparison of dates proves the opera in question to have been performed before the publication of the score of *Orfeo*; to which it is replied that the above-quoted letter of Favart to Durazzo shows that some nine months had elapsed between the time when Philidor received the *Orfeo* and the performance of *Le Sorcier*. The curious in these matters of literary squabbling will find the subject thrashed out by Berlioz and Desnoiresterres.

At the coronation of the Archduke Joseph as King of the Romans at Frankfort-on-Main, on the 3rd April, 1764, *Orfeo* was produced with great success. Shortly after, Gluck severed his official connection with the Court, although in the beginning of 1765, for the marriage of Joseph II., he set to music *Il Parnasso confuso*, which was produced at Schönbrunn. Four archduchesses sang in it, and Archduke Leopold conducted. On the 30th of the same month (January) *Telemacco* was again produced. Another work, *La Corona* (words by Metastasio) which was intended for the celebration of the name-day of the Emperor, was rendered unnecessary by the monarch's sudden death. Meanwhile the engraving of the score of *Orfeo* was approaching completion, and Durazzo was astonished to find that the expenses had run to nearly 3000 livres. Gluck himself, in the meantime, had made a short visit to Paris, Durazzo begging Favart to give him all the information he might need about the taste of Paris at that time. "I will send you also," he wrote, "the letter I wish to be put in front of the score of *Orfeo*, which must be corrected as soon as Gluck reaches Paris; and to this I beg you to force him, for he is naturally indolent and very indifferent about his own works."

The score of *Orfeo* sold very badly; in 1767, three years after its publication, only nine copies had been sold, and it is not known whether or not Durazzo indemnified Favart for the expense he had been put to.

Five years after *Orfeo*, Gluck gave to the world the second of the great works that were destined to immortalise his name; *Alceste* was produced at the Vienna Court Theatre on the 16th December 1767. Here again Calzabigi had co-operated with him, and the result was a libretto greatly superior to that of *Orfeo*, and, of necessity, leading to a finer opera. At a later period, when the work was given in Paris, Gluck altered it in some particulars, notably at the end, where Calzabigi's conclusion is dispensed with and a new character—Hercules—is introduced as *deus ex machinâ*, the words being supplied by Du Roullet. It will be best, however, to consider the opera in this place, as notwithstanding the alterations subsequently made, its true place is after *Orfeo* and before the works of Gluck's French period.

The overture to *Alceste* is a notable triumph of dramatic expression, and is all the more remarkable by its complete contrast with the aimless futility of the overture to *Orfeo*. Gluck's hold upon dramatic feeling is admirable at all times, and nowhere, perhaps, has he maintained this hold with such consummate power as in the overture to *Alceste*. A short sombre phrase in D minor (*lente*) leads into an *andante* of a dolent expression, which in its turn glides into what may be called the second subject in A minor, a dolorous phrase of peculiar form, giving to the ear something of the same impression as a pyramid gives to the eye; it commences broadly and smoothly on the chord of the dominant, and then strikes upward to the pointed chord of the minor ninth,* producing a transition from absolute breadth of harmony to the most poignant contrast possible. This leads on into a passage of storm and stress, that finally dies down as if in exhaustion, leading again into the *lento* prelude, this time in A minor, and then into the *andante* again. The pyramidal theme now recurs in D minor, and here the ascent to the culminating note is even more dolorous, and the discord of the minor ninth even more poignant, by reason of its occurrence four notes higher in the scale, the minor ninth being this time based on A. The rest of the overture follows the order already described.

Here Gluck has given up all ideas of writing a formal "overture" in the customary style ; and in endeavouring to strike out a new path for himself he is again unconsciously confronted by that irony of structure which we formerly observed in *Orfeo*. There he found himself—or, to speak more correctly, we found him—in a dilemma between speech-like recitative

---

* That is, the minor ninth from the dominant (E–F).

and passionate lyrism. Here the dilemma is between the dramatic form and the forms of pure instrumental music. Gluck is really aiming, in a tentative kind of way, at a primitive form of sonata-structure. But in music written in this form the themes should be strongly contrasted. Now Gluck does indeed employ two themes, looking at the overture broadly, but the contrast between them is exceedingly faint. The contrast, indeed, is mainly one of melody and harmony; the idea expressed in both is the same passionate grief and despair. And it was Gluck's true dramatic sense that kept him to this uniformity of idea, for *Alceste* is pre-eminently a drama of one idea ; the burden of the play is sorrow and lamentation, which simply shifts from Admetus at the beginning of the drama to Alcestis in the subsequent acts. This then was the unconscious dilemma of Gluck. There can be no reasonable doubt that had the subject of the opera been more varied, had it been duo-thematic instead of mono-thematic, he would have written an overture representing both these aspects, and anticipating in some degree such a composition, for instance, as Mozart's *Magic Flute* overture, though he would of course have treated it less symphonically and with less wealth of technical display.

It is noticeable, too, that this overture has no formal close, but leads forthwith into a short chorus of five bars, "O gods, restore to us our king, our father ! " The scene is at Phera, in front of the king's house, and the people are gathered there, awaiting news of the death of Admetus. A trumpet fanfare is heard ; a herald steps forward and announces that the king is now at the point of death, human aid being of no avail to save him. The recitative in which this is spoken is finely expressive, and the following chorus is almost equally so, its dignity, however, being slightly marred by a suspicion of artificiality in the treatment of the second portion. Evander, the confidant of Admetus, exhorts * the people to suspend their lamentations ; the palace doors open, and Alcestis herself comes forth with her children and attendants. She is greeted with a double chorus, " O unfortunate Admetus ! O unhappy Alcestis ! O destiny too cruel ! O fate too heavy ! " treated somewhat in the manner of the strophe and antistrophe of the chorus in the Greek drama. The chorus is in the minor, and a very sombre and yet piercing effect is given to it by the constant employment of the chord of the diminished seventh. Alcestis replies in a recitative that again shows an advance on *Orfeo*, and then breaks out into an aria (*adagio*), " O gods, relax the rigour of my fate ! " which after a short *moderato* passage leads abruptly into a more passionate *allegro*, " Nothing can equal my despair," which is perhaps Gluck's finest achievement up to this time. It is full of fire and mobility, and both the downward modulations on the words addressed to her children, and the agitated orchestral figure as she presses them to her bosom, show the completer mastery the composer has now attained over the vocabulary of his art.

The attendants and people repeat the previous chorus, " O unfortunate Admetus ! " and Alcestis summons

* In the French score.

them to attend her in the temple, there to offer their supplications to the gods ; and they quit the stage to the accompaniment of the first chorus.

The next scene is in the temple of Apollo, showing the statue of the god and the sacred tripod. The High Priest and the attendants are preparing for a sacrifice ; their preparations are interrupted by the entrance of Alcestis and her people. The "pantomime" that takes place in the temple, with its exquisite simplicity of scoring—strings and flutes—is well known. The following chorus and solo of the High Priest are in some respects the finest passages in the whole opera. To an agitated accompaniment he implores the god to have mercy on the dying man, and to remember the time when Admetus had sheltered him in the days of his trouble and banishment. Not the least noteworthy thing is that the piece is in $\frac{6}{8}$ time, which it is usually difficult to treat gravely and impressively. There is something terrible in this music, with its agonising theme and its feverish repetitions ; it reminds us somewhat of the scene with the priests of Baal on the mountain in Mendelssohn's *Elijah*, except that Gluck's scene has more of wild abandonment of passion, of almost unspeakable excitement striving to make itself articulate. Dramatically it is as fine as anything he ever wrote. It gives way for a moment to a recitative for the High Priest, and is then taken up again. A remarkable effect is produced by the contrast between all this intensity of human frenzy, the moving and gesticulating swarm of men and women, and the statuesque immobility of the image of Apollo ; the mere contrast of itself is full of dramatic effect.

After a repetition of the previous pantomime Alcestis herself speaks, imploring the intercession of the god. Then follows another pantomime of a much more excited nature than the first, and the High Priest declares that the god has heard. In a recitative of the "accompanied" order, and of a chameleon variety of expression, he commands the queen to vail her pride of station, and to listen to the oracle in fear and trembling. She prostrates herself, her brow upon the ground, while the oracle utters its famous reply, "Admetus must die to-day, if no other will die in his stead!" No one requires to be told of the terror-striking effect of this wonderful utterance, with its dreadful monotone for the voice, and the shifting colour of the orchestra. It is interesting to note that the form in which it is so well known is that of the later French, not of the earlier Italian score, and that Gluck has changed it decidedly for the better, by making the downward progression in the orchestra more gradual, and thus introducing perhaps the most striking chord of all— that of the third inversion of the dominant seventh, which gives the passage most of its air of inexorable severity. "A fearful oracle!" sing the chorus, while the voice of the High Priest is heard asking, "All silent? which of you will offer himself to death!" The people are seized with terror; shouting "Fly! Fly!" they hasten out of the temple, leaving Alcestis alone with her children. She resolves to sacrifice herself for her husband; the air in which she announces this determination is subject to many changes of time—as was the habit of Gluck—according to the dominant emotion to be expressed. Here

D

again the orchestra has a part of the utmost importance to play ; it emphasises the vocal utterance at every point in the most varied manner. In a vigorous recitative Alcestis calls upon the gods to accept her sacrifice, and the High Priest, taking it in their name, tells her that Admetus is now restored to health again, and that at the close of day her sacrifice will be demanded of her. "I will hasten to fulfil a duty so dear to me," replies Alcestis, and breaks out into the celebrated aria, *Divinités du Styx.* Berlioz has pointed out how the peculiarities of the French translation compelled Gluck to alter the arrangement of the syllables in the Italian score, by which the dramatic effect he had primarily achieved was somewhat weakened. "Is it possible to believe that Gluck, in order to comply with the exigencies of French versification or the impotence of his translation, should have consented to disfigure, or, to speak more justly, to destroy the marvellous arrangement of the opening of this incomparable air, which he has for the rest so advantageously altered ? Yet this is the truth. The first verse of the Italian text is this :

Ombre, larve, compagne di morte !

"The first word, *ombre,* with which the air begins, being set to the two long notes, of which the first can and ought to be swelled out, gives the voice time to develop itself, and makes the response of the infernal gods, represented by the horns and the trombones, much more striking, the song ceasing just as the instrumental cry is heard. It is the same with the two sounds written a third higher than the first two, for the second word *larve*. In the French translation, instead of the two Italian words, which might have been translated entire by simply adding an *s* to each, we have *Divinités du Styx*; consequently, instead of one organic phrase, excellent for the voice, and with the sense contained completely in one bar, the change renders necessary five insipid repetitions of the same note for the five syllables *di-vi-ni-tés du*, the word *Styx* being placed in the succeeding bar, at the moment of the entry of the wind instruments and the fortissimo of the orchestra, which crush it and prevent its being heard. So that, the sense being incomplete in the bar where the melody is free to show, the orchestra appears to enter too soon, and to be responding to an unfinished interpellation. Further, the Italian phrase *compagne di morte*, on which the voice can deploy itself so finely, being suppressed in the French, and a silence substituted for it, leaves a lacuna in the melody which nothing can justify. The fine idea of the composer would be reproduced without any alteration, if, instead of the words I have noted, we were to adopt the following :

Ombres, larves, pâles compagnes de la mort ! " *

In this aria, again, Gluck constantly changes the time (*andante, adagio, andante, un poco andante, lento, andante, lento, andante expressivo, presto, andante, adagio, andante*). From this it will be seen how strongly such an aria partakes of the character of

---

* " A travers chants," pp. 172, 173.

painting.   Although he had partly given up the old
attempt to imitate nature (*gleichniss-Arie*), he was still
making the attempt at a kind of descriptive survey of
the passions by means of changing *tempi* and rhythms.
How far this was rendered necessary by the nature of
the groundwork afforded him in the words it is, of
course, impossible to say ; what we can be certain
about is the masterly manner in which Gluck has
accomplished this descriptive survey of the emotions.

In the Italian score, the second act opens with a
scene in a gloomy forest near Phera, sacred to the
powers of the under-world.   It is night.   Alcestis is
hastening through the forest, accompanied by Ismene,
who, suspecting her purpose, enquires of her why she
thus leaves her husband and children.   Alcestis commands her to be silent and obey, and after further
wandering dismisses her.   Left alone, she realises to
the full all the horrors, the fearful sights and sounds of
the forest, but her purpose is unchangeable.   She calls
on the ghostly powers, and is answered by the invisible
Thanatos, "What wouldst thou ? "   Gradually through
the darkness she begins to discern his fearful form and
ghastly livid face; but nothing now can turn her back,
and to his question whether she is resolved to die, she
boldly answers " Yes ? "   Her sacrifice is accepted by
Thanatos, who invites her to descend into the gloom
with him ; the ghostly steersman waits for her on the
banks of Styx.   But she obtains permission first to
return to Phera, to bid Admetus and her children
farewell ; and her exit is made to the accompaniment
of a horrible pantomime by the spirits.

It will at once be understood what an opportunity

such a scene as this afforded to those powers of gloomy realism that Gluck possessed in such abundance; and in omitting the scene from the French version of the opera, and making the second act commence with the festivities attending the recovery of Admetus, he has decidedly weakened the opera in one way, although the joyful commencement of the second act, as it now stands, has the merit of a clear and vivid contrast with the end of the first. This, however, is barely a compensation for the loss of so fine a scene as that in the forest. In any case, the contrast obtained by the festal chorus was equally obtainable later on ; while it is quite certain that the dramatic structure of the opera has been weakened by reason of the fact that the recovery of Admetus is not led up to with due gradation. It cannot follow consistently, at the beginning of the second act, the mere resolve of Alcestis at the end of the first ; it can only consistently come after the voluntary offer of herself to the powers of the under-world.

The opening chorus, "Let transport take the place of grief," is charmingly beautiful, and is followed by the regulation ballet, of which the two most noticeable sections, from the point of view of musical feeling, are the final *andante* (in G), and the second *andante* (in G minor), the latter especially being most characteristic of Gluck. It is a peculiarity of some of his ballet music that the mere perusal of it in the score, quite independently of any theatrical performance, suggests the most definite pictures of the dancers' movements ; they scarcely require actual human representation, so pronounced and so definite is their character ; an indication of the extremely realistic manner in which Gluck was able to conceive not only the mental states of his characters, but the proper physical correlatives of these states.

After a repetition of the chorus, greetings take place between the recovered king and his subjects. Nothing could well be finer than the beautiful recitative of Admetus, " O my children ! O my friends ! " with the dolorous wailing phrase in the orchestra (in D minor ; repeated later in F minor), that seems to link itself by association with the poignant " second subject " of the overture. Admetus inquires the meaning of his restoration to life, and hears for the first time of the unknown one who has voluntarily gone to death for him. " O fearful oracle ! " he exclaims ; but the chorus break in again, interrupting his words of protest. The chorus is especially noticeable for a charming quartett in the middle portion. Then, just as Admetus is wondering at the absence of Alcestis, the queen herself appears, slowly and mournfully, and in gloomy contrast with the general appearance of festivity. The chorus again exhort to merriment, interrupted for a moment by Alcestis with a poignant cry of pain, that seems wrung from her secret heart, " Their songs remind me of my grief ; " and after another short recitative by Admetus, who is happy in the love of his people, there follows the exquisite chorus which also does duty in the first scene of *Paris and Helen*, " Deck your brows with garlands new." The short intercalary passage given to Alcestis during a momentary cessation of the chorus is one of Gluck's highest dramatic efforts ; " O gods, sustain my

courage ; my excess of grief I cannot hide. In spite
of myself, the tears fall from my eyes." It is in his
best manner throughout ; the voice part, which is
confined within very narrow limits, suggests utter
weariness and despair of soul ; while the finely
graduated sway and undulation of the orchestra about
the voice add a further element of sorrow. Admetus
now questions her as to the meaning of her sadness,
but she can only answer, " Alas ! " and his exhorta-
tions to joy are vain. His fears increase : he asks her
in accents of passionate rapidity to tell him the meaning
of it all. " Do you no longer love me, then ? " he
asks her ; and she replies, " The gods who have heard
my vows and my sighs, they know I love you ! "
Her short aria, " Never have I cherished my life but
for you alone," is unnecessary in this place, and is a
weakening of the dramatic texture ; it retards and
hinders the full sweep of passion on to the scene
where she is forced to tell him that it is she who has
offered herself to the gods for him, and she who must
die in his stead. This scene Gluck manages very
finely, bringing the catastrophe to a head in a duet in
recitative, increasing in intensity every moment, up to
the slow despairing cry of the queen, " And who but
Alcestis should die for you ? " The chorus add their
strain of astonishment and sorrow to that of Admetus,
who breaks out into passionate denunciation of her
act, and declares his resolve to offer himself again to
the gods as a victim, or failing that to take his own
life, that he may not be parted from Alcestis. It is
difficult to characterise the music to this scene. It
is hardly recitative ; perhaps it more nearly approaches

declamation, in the general sense of the term. Gluck is at his highest pitch of abandonment here ; never in his recitative have the heart-beats been so violent, the pulse so feverish ; he is carried away on a flood of passion so swift and so turbulent that no time is left him to collect and arrange his ideas according to any definite forms. He is hardly writing music, in the signification that word usually carries ; he is eloquent, rhetorical, forensic. This spirit is carried on even into the aria, "O cruel one," where an additional poignancy of expression is imported into the orchestra as, towards the end, Admetus, having lashed himself into a fury of grief and anger, rushes wildly from Alcestis.

When he is gone she prays for him, while the people mourn her too early death in a chorus of exquisite simplicity and beauty. Bidding them not to mourn for her, she herself bewails her setting sun in an aria long and justly celebrated for its pathos, its beauty, and its deep dramatic power. Then her regret becomes more mordant ; she breaks into a passionate cry in the manner of the previous recitative of Admetus. Interrupted for a moment by the chorus, "Oh how the dream of life flies rapidly away ! like a dying flower withered by the wind !" to the philosophical meaning of which Gluck has given an extraordinarily fine expression, she breaks forth again into her delirious ecstasy of grief and despair.

At the beginning of the third act, in the Italian score, Admetus is wandering about distractedly in the decorated hall of his palace. He has made them inquire of the oracle once more ; Evander enters and tells him that all has been in vain, and that Alcestis must die. She herself comes in to him with her children and attendants. Her strength is slowly passing away, but before she dies she implores Admetus (as in the play of Euripides) not to take another wife, which he faithfully promises. Then the powers of death come to claim her. Admetus offers himself to them in vain ; Alcestis swoons and sinks into their midst, murmuring " I die ! " and is taken from under the very eyes of the terrified and sorrow-stricken people. Admetus, who has temporarily left the hall, rushes in distractedly, followed by a number of his attendants. He endeavours to kill himself that he may be united with her again, but before he has time to accomplish his purpose, Apollo appears seated in the clouds, Alcestis with him ; and the husband and wife are once more united.

Gluck changed entirely this ending to the opera in arranging it for the French stage. " After the first four representations," says Berlioz,* " according to the journals of the day, Gluck, having received the news of the death of his niece, whom he loved tenderly, set out for Vienna, whither he was called by his domestic grief. Immediately after his departure *Alceste*, with which the *habitués* of the opera were becoming less and less pleased, disappeared from the bill. To recompense the public, they thought of mounting a new ballet at great expense. The ballet fell flat. The directors of the Opera, not knowing what to do next, had the hardihood to produce Gluck's

* " A travers chants," pp. 185, 186.

D*

work again, but with the addition of this *rôle* of Hercules, which, coming in towards the end of the drama, had no interest and no purpose ; the *dénoûment* being possible simply with the intervention of Apollo, as Calzabigi had written it. . . . . It was an unfortunate idea that had been suggested to Du Roullet for this *reprise*, and we may suppose that Gluck, to whom it was no doubt submitted in letters to him at Vienna, only adopted it reluctantly, since he obstinately refused to write an air for the new character. A young French musician named Gossec was therefore commissioned to write it."

There is really not much to choose between the two endings in point of dramatic, or undramatic, effect ; each is essentially weak. But the French *Alceste* has been decidedly vulgarised by the introduction of the swashbuckler Hercules.

The act begins with Evander and the chorus mourning the untimely end of Alcestis, the chorus " Weep, O Thessaly ! " being that which in the Italian score was sung as Alcestis disappeared with the ministers of death. It is deeply and painfully impressive, and its sombre effect is heightened by an inner chorus repeating it as a kind of sorrowful echo. Then Hercules enters, announcing in an affable way that having seized a moment's rest from the toils imposed on him by the implacable Juno, he has come to revisit his friend Admetus. On being informed by one of the attendants of the sacrifice of Alcestis, and of the resolve of Admetus to follow her into the shades, he declares his ability and his determination to rescue her, setting forth his views on the subject in a very

ranting aria, " In vain Hell reckons on its victims."
This is the aria which, we are glad to be assured, is
not from the pen of Gluck but from that of Gossec.

Meanwhile Alcestis is groping about painfully and
fearfully in the gloom of the under-world, her soul a
prey to all the dreadful horrors of the place.   Her fine
recitative is interrupted by the chorus of spirits :
" Unhappy one, where goest thou ?   Thou shalt
descend to the dark river at the close of day.   Not
long shalt thou tarry here ! "—in which the voices
maintain a single note throughout, while the orchestra
weaves its sombre harmony about it in passionate
unrest.   The scoring—strings, horns, trombones,
clarinettes—is particularly impressive.   The whole
passage has an iron rigidity, something chilling,
terror-striking, inexorable, that makes it even a finer
utterance than that of the oracle in the first act.   The
succeeding aria is distinctly lower in conception and in
execution ; it is thoroughly cold and artificial.   Here
Alcestis meets her husband, whose prayer has been
rejected by the gods, and who has come to perish with
her.   The aria in which she conjures him to return
and guard his children is, like the previous one,
inexpressibly poor and glacial.   It is strange that after
this should come a scene that has many claims to be
regarded as the finest in the opera.   " What ! live
without thee ! " exclaims Admetus.   " Live to abhor
the light of heaven and the cruel gods, authors of all
our ill ! to drag life on through terrible days, torn by
new torments !   Oh Heaven !   Alcestis ! "   And then
he breaks out into that wonderful air, " Alcestis, in
the name of the gods, behold the fate that is crushing

me ! " in which Gluck attains a mastery of his materials such as he has nowhere surpassed ; in which voice and orchestra blend and separate and re-unite, each giving life unto the other, till the spirit that animates them is absolutely one and indivisible. Nowhere has he treated the orchestra so organically ; he gives it a writhing theme, similar in expression, though of course not in actual form, to the well-known one at the commencement of "Tannhäuser's Pilgrimage," which weaves in and out among the vocal themes with a peculiar sinuous motion, while the climax comes in the marvellous ascending cry at the end of the aria, where wave seems to follow wave, passion to press on passion.

Unfortunately the succeeding scenes between them are almost commonplace, and when Thanatos appears, telling Alcestis that Charon awaits her, and warning her of the consequences to Admetus if she fails in courage now, his aria is banal and undramatic in the extreme, belonging to the same showy and superficial class as the previous air of Hercules. " Let him live ! " cries Alcestis, in spite of the protest of Admetus, and the chorus breaks in sombrely, till the voice of Admetus rises above them in one last passionate cry. Just as he is about to follow her, however, Hercules appears on the scene, and the powers of death are vanquished. But the opera has already degenerated sadly, and we are not now surprised at the thoroughly Gallic exchanges of compliments between the god and the king :

HERCULES. From the hands of friendship receive, my dear Admetus, the worthy object of thy passion.

ADMETUS. Ah ! my felicity is all the more complete
when I reflect that it is from my friend I
receive the happiness.

The inevitable *deus ex machinâ* appears ; Apollo
descends in a cloud, and addresses the pair of heroes in
this wise : " Pursue thy course, oh worthy son of the
sovereign of heaven, and immortality will be thy
portion. Heaven, that regards thee, admires thy
courage, and thy place is already marked out by the
side of the gods ! Hail, happy husband ! and let this
hideous place disappear at the sound of my voice, to
serve as an example to mortals enchained under the
laws of Hymen ! " And the opera finishes with a
commonplace terzett, a short recitative between
Alcestis and Admetus, and a final chorus of almost
incredible banality. The usual ballets bring up the
rear.

Thus Gluck had deliberately spoiled his opera in
his concessions to Parisian taste. The ending with
Apollo was bad enough dramatically in all conscience,
but with the introduction of Hercules everything
became degraded and vulgarised. It is almost impossible to imagine how a work that began so
finely should end in such sad commonplace. After
the commencement of the last act, every genuine
human passion vanishes, and we are left with the
absurd conventions and artificialities of the worst
part of the French society of that time. The
degeneration is all the more regrettable in view of the
fact that the promise of the first two acts had been
something exceptional ; parts of them, indeed, were
never surpassed by Gluck at any time. But all unity

of conception, all high strenuousness of purpose, were
utterly inefficacious when the librettist was allowed to
perpetrate his manifold inanities unchecked; the
greatest subject for wonder is that both in the last
century and in this, composers have managed to
produce so much fine work under circumstances of
such unmitigated stupidity on the part of their col-
laborators.

The tenor in the Viennese performance of *Alceste*
was Tibaldi, who had sung at Bologna in Gluck's
Il Trionfo di Clelia in 1762. We are told that his
upper notes had deteriorated somewhat, but that he
more than made up for this by his superb acting
and his intelligent facial expression. The Alcestis
was Madame Buonascosi, who till then had only sung
in comic parts. Her impersonation of Alcestis was
so fine that she became the recognised exponent of
Gluck's music.* The opera does not seem to have
been at once successful; it was probably too gloomy
and too severe for the Italianised Viennese sense of
that day. "What!" they cried, "the theatre is
closed for nine days, and then on the tenth we simply
assist at a requiem!" Others said they had come to
weep through compassion, not through *ennui*. One
wanted his money back; "another, more cynical,
asked what pleasure one could find in the jeremiads of
an idiot who died for her husband."† On the other
hand, among more enlightened hearers, *Alceste* met
with a recognition that would easily console Gluck

---

* Marx, i. 392.
† Desnoiresterres, pp. 63, 64.

for the disparagement of the Philistine element. "I
am in the land of marvels," wrote Sonnenfels in his
Briefe über die Wienerschaubühne, a day or two after
the battle, the result of which for a little time appeared
uncertain ; "a serious opera without *castrati,* music
without solfeggi—or to speak more correctly, without
gurgling—an Italian poem without bombast and
without attempts at wit—such is the triple prodigy
with which the Court Theatre has opened." * And
perhaps the best measure of the success *Alceste* won is
the fact that it ran for two years in Vienna.

The score was engraved in 1769, and in the celebrated dedicatory epistle to the Grand Duke of
Tuscany, Gluck formulates that theory of his art
which has been the starting-point of so much æsthetic
discussion. It will be quoted and considered later.†

Two years after, the third of the great operas,

* See Nohl, "Gluck und Wagner," p. 65.

† Desnoiresterres has the following : "A note by Brack,
the translator of Burney, attributes the redaction of this
epistle to the Abbé Coltellini. 'This preface,' he says,
'which is a masterpiece of taste, erudition, and musical
reasoning, was written by the Abbé Coltellini, a distinguished poet who was then at Vienna. The English
author, who attributes it to Gluck, was surely ignorant of
this circumstance, as was, in France, the author of the
Mercure of 1769, who gives this composition to the German composer, whose ideas and dramatic conceptions the
poet was no doubt only transcribing.'" Desnoiresterres,
p. 66, *note.* Gluck's own style was, indeed, so truly exe-
crable that there is no difficulty in believing the preface
to *Alceste* to have been written for him.

Paride ed Elena, was produced at Vienna. The poet's name does not appear on the title-page of the score; but it is evident from a letter by Gluck to the *Mercure de France,* four years later, that Calzabigi was again the librettist.* Here again Gluck prefixed to the score an epistle dedicatory; it may be quoted here: " I only determined to publish the music of *Alceste,*" he says, " in the hope of finding imitators; I was bold enough to flatter myself that in following the path I had opened out, people would be moved to destroy the abuses that had been introduced into Italian opera to the dishonouring of it. I confess with sorrow that up to the present I have tried in vain. The *demi-savants,* the professors of taste—a species unhappily too numerous, and at all epochs a thousand times more pernicious to the progress of the fine arts than that of the ignorant—have banded themselves together against a method which, if it were once established, would annihilate their pretensions.

" It has been thought possible to criticise *Alceste* after chaotic rehearsals, badly directed and still more badly executed; they have calculated in an apartment the effect the opera might produce in a theatre, with the same sagacity as in a Greek town they once tried to judge, at the distance of a few feet, the effect of statues destined for the summits of lofty columns. One of those delicate amateurs who put their whole soul into their ears will have found an air too harsh, a transition too strongly expressed, or badly prepared, without considering that, in the situation, this air or

* Marx, i. 397.

this transition was the sublime of expression, forming the happiest contrast. A pedantic harmonist will have remarked an ingenious negligence or a fault in the score, and will have hastened to denounce the one and the other as so many unpardonable sins against the mysteries of harmony ; soon after, several voices will unite to condemn the music as barbarous, savage and extravagant.

"It is true that the other arts are scarcely better off, and that they are judged with neither more justice nor more intelligence ; and your highness can easily comprehend the reason ; the more we are bent on seeking perfection and truth, the more necessary do precision and exactitude become . . . . I wish no other proof of this than my air in *Orfeo—Che farò senza Euridice ?* Make the least change in it, whether in the movement or in the turn of expression, and it becomes an air of marionettes ; in a work of this kind, a note more or less sustained, an increase of tone or of time neglected, an *appoggiatura* out of place, a trill, a passage, a roulade, can destroy the effect of an entire scene. And when it is a question of executing music written according to the principles I have laid down, the presence of the composer is, so to speak, as necessary as the sun is to the works of Nature ; he is its life and soul ; without him all remains in confusion and chaos. But we must expect to meet with these obstacles when we see in the world men who, because they have a pair of eyes and ears, no matter of what kind, think themselves in a position to judge of the fine arts." *

* Desnoiresterres, pp. 68, 69.

Such was the dedication of *Paris and Helen* to the Duke of Braganza, in the score published at Vienna in 1770. Helen, it is necessary to premise, is not the later heroine of Troy ; the story deals with her in the time before she had become the bane of Ilion ; and although Menelaus is incidentally mentioned in the course of the work, he does not appear in it as an actual character. The opera is simply concerned with the wooing of the Spartan by the Phrygian, his pleading and her final surrender.

The overture is in three sections, but of a totally different nature from the old "symphony." Besides being musically interesting, each of the sections has reference to and is preparatory to the opera itself, and one or two suggestions from the overture actually reappear later on. Especially noticeable is the middle piece, *moderato con expressione*, in A minor, of an exquisitely languorous expression.

The first act opens on the sea-coast near Sparta ; all around are the tents of the Trojans, while their ships are visible in the distance. They are making offerings to Venus, singing the beautiful chorus *Non sdegnare, o bella Venere*, which Gluck has also employed in *Alceste*. There, however, it is as essentially out of place as in *Paris and Helen* it is appropriate and harmonious. Paris interrupts his followers with an aria in which the contrast with the rigid form and heavy-laden atmosphere of *Alceste* is at once noticeable. Gluck's hand in *Paris and Helen* was so much freer than in either of his previous works, that he could surrender himself luxuriantly to his more purely lyrical impulses, that only required a fitting occasion to burst the iron gates of formality and reserve. It is curious to reflect how

greatly the composer who writes only vocal compositions is dependent for his fame upon the nature of the
verbal material that is supplied to him. We have only
to consider Gluck never having had such a libretto
as *Paris and Helen* within his reach, to see how we
would thereby have missed the evidence of this lyrical
side of his genius ; for *Paris and Helen* stands quite
apart, even away from *Armida,* among his operas.
It is the product of a frame of mind so widely different
from that which gave birth to the others, that it is
with something of bewildered delight that we surrender
ourselves to this stream of pure and engaging lyrism.
And it is further noticeable that in this opera Calzabigi
himself has also written verse of a more genuinely
poetical nature than any he had previously produced ;
verse with something of the real "lyrical cry," that
found an echo in Gluck's beautiful music. When we
think of the often false and tawdry sentiment of *Alceste,*
for instance, we can understand how the composer
would feel an added stimulus to write good music to
such words as those of Paris' first aria :

> Oh del mio dolce ardor
>   Bramato oggetto,
> L'aure che tu respiri
>   Alfin respiro.
> Ovunque il guardo io giro,
> Le tue vaghe sembianze
> Amore in me dipinge ;
> Il mio pensier si finge
> Le più liete speranze,
> E nel desio che cosi
> M'empie il petto,
> Cerco te, chiamo te,
> Spero e sospiro.

After the aria, the first chorus is repeated in another key as a ballet, and Paris again breaks forth into song; he is interrupted by a Trojan, who comes to tell him of an approaching messenger from Sparta. The messenger, in fact, is our old friend Cupid, who comes disguised in Spartan garb, and followed by a Spartan train; the god passes under the name of Erasto. To the question of what brings him to Sparta, Paris disclaims any intention of seeking riches, honour or aggrandisement, and recounts his experiences as judge between Venus, Pallas, and Juno in the tournament of beauty. Erasto quickly tells him he has "read his heart," that the motive impelling him to come to Sparta has been love for Helen, and that the aid of Venus herself will be given him in his undertaking. Then follows a charming duet, in which Paris asks in astonishment how Erasto has been able thus to discover his intentions, while the god assures him that love is so plainly written on his countenance as to be legible by all. Again he promises in recitative that Helen shall be his, ratifies the contract in an aria, and departs. Meanwhile, more Spartans have been flocking in, and stand amazed at the luxurious presents that are being arranged in order by the Trojans; at length, encouraged by their reception, they join the visitors in festive dances.

The ballet music of *Paris and Helen* is remarkable throughout for beauty and elegance. Here the second piece (in C major), is a pleasing snatch of melody, more in the style of Mozart than in that of the Gluck of *Alceste* and *Iphigenia in Tauris*; but the most noticeable section, perhaps even the most remarkable lyrical outpouring in a work that is lyrical from beginning to end, is the beautiful fourth movement (*amabile moderato*). One does not quite know what to make of this music, meeting it thus in the score of a man usually associated with all that is sternly and rigidly dramatic. It seems to stand away from the ordinary world of Gluck's dramas, to come as an echo from distant cloud-capped mountains ; it has the elusive beauty of a summer night, faintly odorous with the perfume of hidden flowers. It is the Romantic spirit crying in the womb of time, as yet unborn ; it is the utterance of a mind that is already swinging slightly round from the broad-based, externalised life of its own day, towards a life more inward, more fugitive and more mysterious ; its note is *Sehnsucht*, not the *Sehnsucht nach Sehnsucht* of later Romantic art, but the first incomprehensible stirrings of a new *genre* of emotion, too vague for concrete expression, and unable to find voice in any art but music. In *Armida*, too, he touches chords that thrill more with the life of this century than of his own, notably in that moment of languorous rapture when Rinaldo looks up into the face of the enchantress, murmuring "Armida!" If only the master had given us a little more of the "harmonious madness" that was in him ! A student of the music of the eighteenth century, so formal, so precise, so regular, and frequently so impersonal, is inexpressibly grateful for these few moments when he lights upon a passage that seems to be warm with blood or moist with tears, some healthy abandonment to feeling, some taste of cool fresh water in the bitter brine.

But to return to the opera, the first act of which is closed by these ballets. The second act opens in a room in the palace at Sparta, where Helen is seated in the midst of her attendants, and with Erasto by her side. Erasto enumerates in recitative the charms of Paris, till the colloquy is cut short by the entry of the Trojan youth himself. Then comes a dialogue of " asides " in recitative :

Paris. O queen ! (Ye gods !)
Helen. (What do I see ?)
Paris. (What loveliness !)
Helen. (What a countenance !)
Paris. (Oh ! what anguish seizes my soul !)

Further compliments pass between the pair, Paris singing the praises of Helen's beauty ; and finally Paris, Helen and Erasto indulge in a terzett, in which Paris is rather bantered by the young queen. His next aria " Sweet images of Love," in which we again hear suggestions of the later Romantic art, is one of the most beautiful melodies Gluck ever wrote. This finishes the second act.

At the beginning of the third, the scene is in the courtyard of the palace ; Paris and Helen enter to watch the games that are to be given in honour of the stranger. There is a fine chorus of athletes, followed by a tenor solo, and this again by an " aria of athletes " for the orchestra—a bold and vigorous composition. Finally, the games are over, and all leave the stage but Paris, Helen and Erasto. Helen begs that Paris will sing to her, as a contrast to the rude Spartan strains, some melody of Troy, and Paris gladly seizes the

opportunity thus to express his love for her. The harp
is brought to him, and he sings a passionate song in
praise of her eyes, that approaches both in feeling and
in treatment the love-songs of the later Italian schools.
It is marred, however, by a slight monotony in the
harmony, the ear being sometimes led to expect a
modulation where none is forthcoming. Ever through
the aria Helen interrupts him, as she gradually sees that
it is she whom he is endeavouring to reach through
the song.

Helen's abrupt termination of the aria has a disastrous
effect on Paris; he is on the point of swooning, so that
Helen has to despatch Erasto for assistance. Her
recitative here is extremely fine and expressive, digni-
fying and ennobling of itself this poor play of mario-
nette-passion. In the midst of it Paris recovers, and
Helen debates within herself whether she ought to
stay or fly. "O stay and hear me!" cries Paris, and
begins the first part of a duet that is the finest psychological expression in the whole opera; the opposition
of Helen's sense of duty to the passion of Paris, and
her vacillating moods of feeling, are skilfully portrayed.
Probably Gluck never again had such a truly lyrical
moment as this; at times we seem quite transported
out of the pre-Romantic opera, so easy and so free is
the movement, so genuinely passionate the feeling, so
truly does the musical form cling to and obey the
poetical emotion. And again when, at the conclusion
of the duet, Helen flies from him, the following aria of
Paris is equally true and nervous in expression. This
was indeed music that drew blood, in Gluck's own
significant phrase. It is the master at his greatest ease

and most consummate power; there is less divorcement here than in much of his finest music between the idea and the manner of expressing it; he has struck the perfect balance between dramatic intensity and emotional beauty and artistic objectivity of form.

The act closes with the return of the athletes, and ballets in honour of the victors.

At the beginning of the fourth act, Helen is sitting in her chamber, holding in her hand a letter from Paris. She reads it in recitative; he is begging her to fly with him. Undecided for a time whether simply to answer his letter by scornful silence, she finally resolves to reply, and sitting down writes a letter to him, reproaching him for having come to Sparta to induce her to leave her husband, and advising him to seek elsewhere for another love. She considerately imparts to the audience, in recitative, the words as they flow from her pen. Calling Erasto, she bids him deliver the letter, but before he has time to depart Paris himself enters and Erasto hands the note to him. Then comes a terzett, at the conclusion of which Erasto disappears, and Paris and Helen break out into one of the loveliest snatches of duet imaginable; its only defect is that it is too short. In a long recitative he continues his attack on her wavering resolution, till, almost vanquished, she implores him to leave her and forget her. " Forget thee ! " he cries, and bursts into an aria not without passion, though it is disfigured by an absurdity that might be taken as a matter of course had we met with it in an opera of the Italian school, but that is inexplicable in Gluck, especially in the light of the dedicatory epistle to *Alceste*. The aria is of the *da capo* form ; and Gluck, either because he thinks it a sign of passion to be unable to finish one's words, or because he did not know how to get the full number of syllables in with his music, makes Paris cut the second part of the aria summarily short in the middle of a word in order to begin the *da capo;* thus : "La tue celeste immagine fra l'ombre ancor l'avrò sempre d'avan. . . . . Di te scordarmi," etc. (Dein holdes, zartes Götterbild wird noch an Lethe's Strand mich treu umschwe. . . . . Ich dich vergessen ! etc.)

Having finished his aria, Paris rushes off the stage, while Helen, left alone, again hovers between love and duty, finally appealing, in a fine aria, to the gods for help.

In the third act Erasto, in the garden of the palace, rouses Helen's grief by telling her that Paris means to return to his own country, being disappointed at her harshness ; and in an air of exquisite simplicity and breadth she warns all maidens not to give ear to the voice of man : "All his words are but mockery." Then, as Paris himself enters, and Helen turns furiously on Erasto, the latter discovers himself : " I am not Erasto but Cupid ; " and at last Helen yields to the entreaties of Paris to fly with him. Suddenly a peal of thunder is heard, and looking up they see Pallas descending from the clouds. The angry goddess pours out the vials of her wrath upon them, prophesying the future evil that shall come of their love ; here Gluck employs in the orchestra the theme that figures at the end of the first section of the overture. Then comes the second theme of the overture, during which the pair hover for a moment

between doubt and resolution, and then the third
theme, when, rushing into each other's arms, they
cast the evil prognostications of Pallas to the winds.
Thus the overture has direct reference to, and is
closely bound up with, the later course of the opera.
Cupid now appears, promising them support and
happiness in spite of Pallas ; and after a florid duet the
pair set out for the shore. The scene changes to the
coast. It is night ; in the distance are seen the Trojan
ships. Sailors and attendants of Paris and Helen come
down to the shore, and in an exquisite chorus call on
them to embark while the sea is tranquil. Then
follows an aria by Cupid and a duet between Paris and
Helen, and the three enter the ship and leave the shore
to the strains of the former beautiful chorus.

It will be seen at once how different all this is from
Alceste. The contrast may be stated in Gluck's own
words :

" Your highness," he wrote in the dedication of the
score, " will have read the drama of *Paris and Helen,*
and will have noticed that it does not provide the
composer with those strong passions, those great
images, those tragic situations which, in *Alceste,* move
the spectators so deeply, and give such great opportunities for artistic effect. So that in this music one
must not expect to find the same force and energy ;
just as, in a picture representing a subject in full light,
one would not expect the same effects of chiaroscuro, the
same contrasts, as in a picture painted in half-light.

" Here we have not to do with a wife, who, on the
point of losing her husband, finds courage to evoke

the infernal divinities in the depths of the tenebrous night, in a savage wood, and, in the anguish of her agony, trembles for the fate of her sons and cannot tear herself away from the husband she adores. Here we are dealing with a young lover, who stands in contrast with the strange humours of a proud and virtuous woman, and who, with all the art of ingenuous passion, ends by triumphing over her. I have had to seek truth of colouring in the different characters of the Phrygians and the Spartans, setting in parallel to the rudeness and savagery of the latter the delicacy and softness of the former.

"I have thought that, song in my opera being only a substitute for declamation, I ought, on occasion, to imitate the native rudeness of my heroine ; and I have also thought that, in order to preserve the character of this music, it would not be a fault sometimes to descend to the trivial.

"When one wishes to keep to the truth, one's style must be adapted to the subject that is being treated ; the greatest beauties of melody and harmony become imperfections when they are out of place in the whole.

"I do not hope for my *Paris* a greater success than that of *Alceste*. As for my endeavour to lead musical composers towards a reform so greatly to be desired, I am sure to meet with the greatest obstacles ; but I will not cease to make new efforts to realise my design." *

Thus it is evident, both from the words of Gluck

* Barbedette, pp. 76, 77 ; Reissmann, pp. 130, 131 ; Marx, i. 445, 446. Barbedette mistranslates grossly at

and from his treatment of the opera itself, with its strong contrasts between Phrygian luxury and Spartan plainness, how thoroughly pictorial his method was. He aimed at presenting to the ear, as if to the eye, two different pictures, painted in entirely different colours, the distinction between which constituted, for him, the greater part of the dramatist's function. As an opera, *Paris and Helen* has fallen into undeserved neglect; Gluck himself apparently did not care to tempt the French taste with it at the time he was giving *Alceste* and *Orfeo* to Paris as a preparation for his later works. The story of course is weak, and the one attenuated emotion is dragged out to an inordinate length; and further, the appearance of Pallas at the end of the opera and her prophesyings of future misfortune are essentially undramatic, seeing that these must find their fulfilment at some later time outside the scope of the opera itself. But as a purely lyrical work *Paris and Helen* stands in many respects even above *Orfeo* and *Alceste*. Its neglect has been inexcusable, and we may agree with Naumann that its restoration to public favour is only a matter of time. Nowhere else has Gluck written so freely and with such clear impulsion of genuine, heartfelt passion; and thus it has for our ears perhaps more charm than it had for the men of its own day. It stands nearer in motive and treatment to the lyrical fervour of our own

times, and his version of the above is full of liberties; for instance, by omitting "my" in the sentence, "song in my opera being only a substitute for declamation," he perverts the meaning entirely.

time.   In his other works Gluck rarely loses himself in the pure artistic joy of musical expression ; almost the only instance in *Alceste*, for example, is that fine scene in the last act, where Admetus bursts into such a torrent of feverish eloquence.   Here in *Paris and Helen* he continually sinks himself in his art, and loses his rigidity of method and his formalism of expression. Time after time he surrenders himself, like a modern poet or musician, to his purely lyrical impulses ; and it is with a surprised sense of artistic gladness, of freedom, of genuine æsthetic joy as distinguished from melo-dramatic satisfaction, that we listen to the free and sincere flow of melody and the expressive harmony. It was one more of the contradictions between Gluck's theory and his practice that where he occasionally relaxed the rigidity of some of his theories, his practice became proportionately finer.   "When composing," he once said to Corancez, " I strive before all things to forget I am a musician ; " that is, he felt at times that if he was to follow inexorably the poetical groundwork given him by his librettist, he must check the musician's impulse to burst forth into sheer lyrism for its own sake.   But here, in *Paris and Helen*, his work is actually finest and most enduring where he dis-regards his own precept about forgetting that he was a musician.   Where he does regard it, as in the recita-tive and one or two of the arias, his music is already out of date and a dreary affliction to the ear ; when, on the contrary, he gives his musicianly impulses freer play, he writes music that may confidently be pronounced immortal.   It was not that there was no truth and no æsthetic principle involved in his dictum

to forget that he was a musician ; every dramatic composer who genuinely strives to write dramatic music
recognises the need of checking, at times, the impulse
to develop the music unfettered along its own non-
verbal lines ; but Gluck pushed the principle to an
illogical extreme, making no allowance for the more
exclusively æsthetic side of us that craves artistic
enjoyment as well as dramatic enforcement, and that
in the extreme case, would rather have a wrong thing
exquisitely said than a right thing said crudely and
uninvitingly.   Thus Gluck's theory failed to correlate
with his practice, and the situation was further complicated by the fact that there were really two Glucks
—the Gluck of *Alceste* and *Iphigenia in Aulis,* typical
of the eighteenth century in his ideas, and the Gluck of
Paris and Helen and *Armida,* constantly reaching out
to the Romanticism of our own century, losing his
externalism of thought and emotion in exquisite suggestions of wider issues ; the motive force being not
so much the bare dramatic insistence upon the verbal
facts of the scene, as a purely lyrical delight in giving
wing to his art.   But Gluck was only a Romanticist
at times, and it is probable that, standing alone in this
respect as he did at that epoch, he would tend to have
misgivings about these more entirely lyrical impulses,
identifying them erroneously with the ways of the
fatuous Italian school against which he so resolutely
set his face ; and the more external, pictorial manner of
the eighteenth century predominated in his transcriptions of emotion.   It was this manner again which,
being the accompaniment of those moods when he was
calmer and more consciously master of himself, gave

its form and colour to his æsthetic theories. Hence
their shortcomings in relation to modern art. They
are almost entirely of the eighteenth century. Had
he allowed for the more lyrical side of his nature,
wherein existed Romanticism in embryo, had he
judged the æsthetic problem of the opera in the light
of this also, and incorporated it in his survey of the
necessaries of dramatic composition, he would have
done even more for musical art than he has done. But
we can but take the best a man can give us and be grateful for it ; and Gluck would have been superhuman had
he so transcended the thought of his own time as to have
based an æsthetic theory upon the dim stirrings of the
newer impulses that only came to actual birth some
thirty or forty years later.

In the same year which saw the production of *Paris
and Helen* (1769), Gluck was called upon to furnish
the necessary music for the festivals attending another
royal marriage, the celebrations beginning in Vienna
on the 27th June, and in Parma a couple of months
later. Gluck provided the Court with three new
works—a *Prologo delle Feste d' Apollo, L' Atto di Bauci e
Filemone,* and *L' Atto d' Aristeo,* all in the old style, and
of no more merit than such an occasion demanded.
The second of these works contained a solo and chorus,
the theme of which bears an extraordinary resemblance
to that of the opening chorus of *Paris and Helen—
Non sdegnare.*

In addition to these three compositions, a version of
Orfeo was produced, the opera being compressed into
one act. The singer cast for the part of Orpheus, at
Parma, was the celebrated Millico, who is said to have

undertaken it with many misgivings ; closer study of
the work, however, having roused his enthusiasm for
it, he became one of the most devoted adherents of
Gluck. Taking up his residence afterwards in Vienna,
he became the personal friend and companion of the
composer, and undertook the further vocal education
of Gluck's young niece, Marianne, who was at this
time a girl of about thirteen years of age.

Gluck had now won for himself a position of assured
respect at Vienna. His fine house was the place of
resort of all who were distinguished in art, music or
letters, and an introduction to him had become an
honour difficult to obtain. It was about this time that
Dr. Burney visited him, procuring the introduction
through Lord Stormont, the English ambassador at
Vienna, who made use of the good offices of Gluck's
friend, the Countess Thun. She had been, he says,
" so good as to write a note to Gluck on my account,
and he had returned, for *him*, a very civil answer ; for
he is as formidable a character as Handel used to be ;
a very dragon, of whom all are in fear. However, he
had agreed to be visited in the afternoon ; and Lord
Stormont and Countess Thun had extended their
condescension as far as to promise to carry me to him
. . . . He was so good-humoured as to perform almost
his whole opera of *Alceste ;* many admirable things in
a still later opera of his, called *Paride ed Elena ;* and in
a French opera, from Racine's *Iphigenia*, which he has
just composed. This last, though he had not as yet
committed a note of it to paper, was so well digested
in his head, and his retention is so wonderful, that he
sang it nearly from the beginning to the end, with

as much readiness as if he had a fair score before him.

" His invention is, I believe, unequalled by any other composer who now lives, or has ever existed, particularly in dramatic painting and theatrical effects. He studies a poem a long time before he thinks of setting it.   He considers well the relation which each part bears to the whole, the general cast of each character, and aspires more at satisfying the mind than flattering the ear.   This is not only being a friend to poetry, but a poet himself ; and if he had language sufficient, of any other kind than that of sound, in which to express his ideas, I am certain he would be a great poet ; as it is, music, in his hands, is a most copious, nervous, elegant, and expressive language.   It seldom happens that a single air of his operas can be taken out of its niche and sung singly with much effect ; the whole is a chain, of which a detached, single link is but of small importance.

" If it is possible for the partisans of *old French music* to hear any other than that of Lully and Rameau with pleasure, it must be M. Gluck's *Iphigénie*, in which he has so far accommodated himself to the national taste, style and language, as frequently to imitate and adopt them.   The chief obstacles to his fame, perhaps, among his contracted judges, but which will be most acceptable to others, is that there is frequently *melody*, and always *measure*, in his music, though set to *French words*, and for *a serious French opera*." *

* "Present State of Music in Germany, the Netherlands, and United Provinces," 1773, p. 255, etc.   Burney is

E

It was at this time that Gluck did such a signal service to Salieri, then a young man about the age of twenty, by procuring the performance of his comic opera, *Le donne letterate*, written to words by Boccherini. The young Italian became one of his closest and most trusted friends.

Meanwhile Gluck was employed on some works more intimately connected with the thoughts of the Germany of his time than any to which he had formerly written music. He had taken a liking for the work of Klopstock, and published a collection of his *Oden und Lieder, beim Klavier zu singen, in Musik gesetzt von Gluck*. They are, says Marx,* "sehr declamatorisch," indicating once more the careful, perhaps too careful, attention he was paying to the verbal basis of his art. A more extensive undertaking was the setting of the *Hermannsschlacht*,† of the music to which, however, nothing is known. The choice of the work shows Gluck in a new light, that of German patriot.

wrong in saying that *Iphigenia in Aulis* was not yet written in score ; it appears from a letter of Du Roullet to Dauvergne, about a month before Burney's visit to Gluck, that the opera was already completed.

* Marx, ii. 11.
† *Ibid*. ii. 12, etc.

CHAPTER IV

1769–1787

BUT the Alexander of the opera was now longing for a fresh kingdom to conquer. His eyes were turned on Paris, for it was there he believed a great success might be won. He was impelled to court the suffrages of the Parisians by the consideration that his work was really more after the French model than any other ; by a study of the works of Lully and Rameau, that convinced him of the similarities between his style and theirs, and of the certainty of success with the French public on that account ; and by the knowledge that Paris was at that time the centre of the intellectual world. Gluck at all times showed himself an adept in the art of obtaining his ends by skilfully working upon others, and with characteristic address he now began to create an impression in his own society that he bore a particular affection towards France and the French school, by making dexterously flattering references to Lully and other French favourites. The Comte d'Escherny narrates the manner in which Gluck worked through M. de Sevelinge :

" A certain M. de Sevelinge was recommended to me at Vienna in 1767. This M. de Sevelinge was a melomaniac, and, without actually being a musician, was the soul of the music of Paris and the president of all the concerts of that time. I thought it well to do honour to the recommendation, and invited M. de Sevelinge several times to dine with me, inviting at the same time the chevalier Gluck. It need hardly be said that music was talked of. Gluck laid himself out to praise Lully most highly—praise which no doubt was merited in many ways, but which M. de Sevelinge did not expect from a composer of Italian operas. He (Gluck) praised in Lully a noble simplicity, a natural melody and dramatic intentions. He had studied Lully's scores, he said, and this study had been a revelation to him ; through this he had perceived a real basis for pathetic and theatrical music, and the true genius of the opera, which only required to be developed and brought to perfection ; and that if he should receive an invitation to work for the Opéra at Paris he would hope, by preserving the style of Lully and the French cantilena, to create in this manner the true *lyrical tragedy*.

"M. de Sevelinge, with his enthusiasm for music, was inflamed by these hopes of the chevalier Gluck, and I had no need to urge him to mention at Paris the desire and the projects of M. Gluck. M. de Sevelinge, on his return to Paris, did not fail to do so, and worked efficiently for M. Gluck."*

Gluck, however, was setting further machinery at work to attain his ends. He had been for some time

* Le Comte d'Escherny, "Mélanges de Littérature, etc.," Paris, 1811, II. 356–358. In Desnoiresterres, pp. 77, 78.

past on terms of special intimacy with the Bailli du Roullet, an amateur whom he had formerly met at Rome, and who was now attached to the French Embassy at Vienna ; and a partnership had been formed between them similar to that which had previously existed between the composer and Calzabigi. They resolved to make an opera upon the subject of *Iphigenia in Aulis,* taking as their model the tragedy of Racine. Gluck set to work at once upon the words that were given him, and portions of the opera were performed privately with great success before a few of the men of taste connected with the Court.

Du Roullet now made overtures for the production of the new work in Paris, himself addressing the following letter to Dauvergne, at that time Director of the Académie Royale de Musique :

"VIENNA, 1 *Aug.* 1772.

"SIR,—The high esteem I have for your person and your distinguished talents, as well as for your well-known honourable character, has prompted me to inform you that the famous Gluck, who is celebrated throughout all Europe, has written a French opera, which he earnestly desires to have brought out in Paris.

"This great man, after having written more than forty Italian operas which have had the greatest success in every theatre where that language is admitted, is convinced, through thoughtful study of the ancients and moderns, and by profound meditation on his art, that the Italians in their dramatic creations have departed from the true path; that the French style is the true one for the musical drama; that if this has not yet attained to perfection, it is less because of the talents of the French musicians, which are indeed estimable, than through the authors of the poems, who, not understanding the capacity of music, have in their compositions preferred wit to sentiment, gallantry to passion, the charm and colour of versification to the pathos of style and situation. After Gluck had communicated his ideas on these matters to a man of taste, talent and understanding, he received from the latter two Italian poems which he set to music. They were brought out in Parma, Milan, and Naples with incredible success, and wrought in Italy a revolution in operatic matters. One of these operas,* which was produced at Bologna last winter during Gluck's absence, drew more than twenty thousand spectators, and yielded to the management about 80,000 ducats.

"When Gluck returned to Vienna he became of the opinion that the Italian language was certainly fitted for that swarm of notes that goes by the name of 'passages,' but had nothing like the clearness and strength of the French tongue, so that this excellence in relation to vocalisation, which we are the first to concede, is pernicious in relation to truly dramatic music, since in the latter these 'passages' are inappropriate, or at any rate weaken the expression.

"According to these observations, Gluck was roused against the bold assertions of those of our famous writers who have dared to calumniate the French

* *Orfeo.*

tongue, saying that it could not lend itself to great musical creation. Nobody can be more competent to judge of this matter than Gluck, who has a complete knowledge of both languages ; and although he speaks French with difficulty, he comprehends it thoroughly ; he has made a particular study of it ; he understands the *finesses*, especially the prosody of it ; on the latter, indeed, he has made some profound observations. He has, besides, for a long time tried his talent in both languages and in various styles, and has been successful at a Court where both tongues are spoken fluently, although the French is preferred in society—a court the more capable of judgment in this field, as ears and taste are continually in use. Since he thought of these matters he had been desirous of having his opinions of the efficacy of the French language justified by actual proof, when an opportunity was afforded him by the receipt of the tragic opera *Iphigenia in Aulis.* He believed he had found in this work what he had been seeking.

" The author, or, to speak more correctly, the adapter of this poem, has followed with scrupulous exactness the poet Racine, whose tragedy he has wished to work up into an opera. To attain this end it was necessary to restrict the action somewhat and to eliminate the part of Eriphile. In the first act Calchas appears instead of the *confidant*, Arcas ; in this way the unfolding of the situation has been changed, the subject has been simplified, and the action has received greater animation. The interest has not been lost by these changes ; it is as complete as in Racine's play. Since with the omission of the episode invented by Racine, his conclusion of the poem could not be preserved in the opera, the end has been altered for the sake of a finer effect.

" The opera falls into three acts, a division which appears to me the best for a species of composition the action of which requires a rapid progression. In each act there has been arranged, without doing violence to the piece, a brilliant *divertissement*, in such wise that the action is thereby only heightened and completed. Care has also been taken to contrast the situations and characters in such a way that they afford a piquant and necessary variety, which will hold the spectator's attention, and that the interest of the piece is fully maintained throughout. Without having recourse to machinery or incurring any great expense, it has been found possible to provide a noble and sumptuous display for the eye. I hardly think a new opera was ever staged in which so little expenditure was necessary and yet so fine a spectacle afforded. The author of the piece, the representation of which, including *divertissements*, should not take more than two hours and a half, has made it his duty to preserve the thoughts and even the verses of Racine, so far as was permitted in an opera which is not really a tragedy. Racine's verses are welded in with care sufficient to prevent any mark of division being perceptible in the style of the whole. The choice of *Iphigenia in Aulis* appears to me so much the happier as the transcriber, by following Racine as far as possible, has secured the success of his undertaking ; this being ample compensation for any loss of individuality.

" Gluck's name would relieve me of the necessity

of saying much about the music to this opera, if the pleasure I had experienced at so many rehearsals would permit me to be silent. It appears to me that this great man has exhausted in his creation all the powers of art. Simple, natural song, supported throughout by a genuine and interesting expression and an enchanting melody ; an inexhaustible variety of ideas and devices ; the loftiest effects of harmony, whether in the portrayal of the terrible, the sublime or the tender ; a rapidly moving and at the same time noble and expressive recitative, similar to the best of the French recitatives ; the greatest versatility in the dance pieces, which are of a quite new kind, full of the most alluring freshness ; choruses, duets, terzetts, quartetts, all alike expressive, moving, and well declaimed with a scrupulous regard to the prosody ; in short, everything in this composition appears suitable to the taste of the French, while there is nothing in it which could seem to them peculiar. And all this is the work of the creative talent of a Gluck, in whom we everywhere see poet and musician at once, everywhere the man of genius and taste ; nothing is common, nothing neglected.

"You know, sir, that I am no enthusiast, and that in all the wars over this new music I have preserved a decided impartiality ; and so I flatter myself that you will not be suspicious of the praise I have been moved to give to the music of *Iphigenia*. I feel myself the more certain of your assent as I am certain that nobody is more anxious for the progress of art than you. Have you not shown this by your own words, and by the approbation that has long been bestowed

E*

on you by men themselves distinguished in music?
As man of talent and as honest citizen, you will certainly not misjudge the advantage that lies in so
famous a foreigner as the Chevalier Gluck thinking it
worth his while to concern himself with our language,
and defend it against the calumnious accusations of
our own authors.

" Gluck only wishes to know whether the Académie
de Musique can place so much reliance on his talent
as to decide on producing his opera. He is ready to
undertake the journey to France, but he must have a
thorough assurance both that his opera will be produced, and at what time. If you have nothing fixed
for the winter, for Lent, or for after Easter, I think
you could not do better than arrange with him for one
of these periods. Gluck has a pressing invitation to
Naples for May next ; for his part, he has not been
willing to accept any engagement, and is determined
to sacrifice all these advantages if he can be assured
that his opera will be taken by your Academy, to
whom I beg you to communicate this letter." *

Dauvergne did not answer this letter immediately,
but published it in the October (1772) number of the
Mercure de France; and some months afterwards
Gluck himself addressed to the editor of that journal a
letter, which was published in the number for February
1773. It ran as follows :—

" Sir ! Others might with justice reproach me, and
I too would not spare myself, if, after seeing in your

* Marx, ii. 25-30.

October number a letter to one of the directors of the Académie de Musique on the subject of my opera *Iphigenia*, I did not hasten to thank the author of this letter for his high praise of me, and yet at the same time to point out that his friendship and his undoubtedly too great prepossession for me have led him to say too much, and that I myself am very far from believing that I have really deserved this flattering eulogium. Still more would I reproach myself if I permitted the invention of the new style of Italian opera, the attempts at which have been justified by success, to be attributed to me alone. It is to Signor Calzabigi that the chief praise is due, and if my music has found some approbation, I think I must gratefully recognise that I am indebted to him, since he it was who gave me the opportunity to pour forth the waters of my art. This writer, who is possessed of the greatest genius and talent, has, in his poems *Orpheus*, *Alcestis*, and *Paris*, struck out a path that was little known to the Italians. These works are full of the happiest situations, of the most terrible and sublime traits, which serve the composer in the expression of deep passion, and in the writing of strong and seizing music ; since however great the talent of the composer may be, he will only write indifferent music if the poet does not rouse in him that enthusiasm without which all the forms of art are dull and lifeless. The imitation of Nature is the aim both must set themselves, and it is this I have sought to attain. Simply and naturally my music always strives, as far as it is possible to me, after the highest power of expression and the strengthening of the declamation in the poetry. On that account I never employ trills, passages and cadenzas, with which the Italians are so liberal. Your tongue offers me nothing in that respect. Born in Germany, and reasonably conversant with the French and Italian languages through diligent study, I do not believe myself capable of appreciating the delicate shades which might make one preferable to the other, and I think every stranger should abstain from judging between them ; but I think it is permitted me to say that the language which will always suit me best will be that in which the poet furnishes me with the most varied means of expressing the passions. This is the advantage I believe I have found in the words of the opera of *Iphigenia*, the poetry of which appears to me to have all the energy proper to inspire me with fine music. Although I have never been in the position of offering my works to any theatre, I cannot be displeased with the author of the letter to one of the directors for having proposed my *Iphigenia* to your Académie de Musique. I avow that I would be glad to see it produced in Paris, because by its effect, and with the aid and the advice of the famous M. Rousseau of Geneva, we may perhaps together be able, by seeking a melody noble, sensible and natural, together with a declamation following exactly the prosody of each language and the character of each people, to find the means to effect my purpose of producing a music appealing to men of all nations, and eliminating the ridiculous distinctions of national music. The study I have made of this great man's writings on music—among others the letter in which he has analysed the monologue in

Lully's *Armida*—proves the depth of his knowledge and the reliability of his taste, and has filled me with admiration. I have been convinced that if he had chosen to apply himself to the exercise of this art, he would have been able to realise the prodigious effects which the ancients have attributed to music. I am delighted to take this opportunity to render him publicly the eulogies which I believe he merits." *

Dauvergne now entered into correspondence with Du Roullet, who sent him the first act of the new opera. The directors were favourably impressed with it, and wrote to the attaché : " If the Chevalier Gluck is willing to pledge himself to write six operas of this kind for the Academy, well and good ; otherwise it cannot be played, for such a work as this is calculated to kill all the old French operas ; " which was undoubtedly true. Evidently nothing more was to be done in this direction, and in a moment of happy inspiration Gluck remembered Marie Antoinette, who had formerly been his pupil. The young princess used her influence to have the work brought out, and in the end an invitation was sent to Gluck to come to Paris and attend personally to its production.

The libretto of *Iphigenia in Aulis*, as appears from the above-quoted letter of Du Roullet, is based on the tragedy of Racine ; this in its turn was founded on the play of Euripides. In the Greek the story is as follows :—In the course of their campaign against Troy, to avenge the rape of Helen by Paris from her husband Menelaus, the Greeks find themselves sud-

* Marx, ii. 31–33.

denly becalmed at Aulis. Consulting the oracle, they
are informed by Calchas, the priest, that favourable
winds will spring up again only on condition that
Iphigenia, the daughter of Agamemnon, is sacrificed
to Diana. Thereupon Agamemnon is urged by
Menelaus and Ulysses to send for Iphigenia, giving as
his motive his desire to see her wedded to Achilles ;
and the king yields to their wishes, being impelled by
the desire of glory and of fulfilling the pledges he had
made when undertaking the expedition. When left
to himself, however, Agamemnon is overcome by his
affection for his daughter, and in agony lest she should
obey the command of his letter and come to Aulis to
meet her death, he secretly sends an attendant to
Clytemnestra, his wife, bidding her defer her coming
and that of Iphigenia, as the nuptials of his daughter
have been put off to a later time. This letter,
however, is intercepted by Menelaus, who upbraids
Agamemnon for his perfidy, and the customary
Euripedean scene ensues in which the two characters
abuse each other roundly. The warning message
having miscarried, Clytemnestra and Iphigenia arrive
in the Grecian camp and are greeted sadly by
Agamemnon. Achilles, coming to the house of
Agamemnon to inquire of him why the Greek host
does not set sail for Ilium, meets Clytemnestra, who,
accosting him as the affianced of Iphigenia, thus
acquaints him for the first time with the manner in
which Agamemnon has made use of his name to draw
his daughter thither. During their mutual question-
ings and explanations, however, the same attendant
enters who had been entrusted with the note inter-

cepted by Menelaus; he, being an old servant of
Clytemnestra, tells her of the plot against the life of
Iphigenia, and of Agamemnon's strategies, first to
bring her to Aulis and then to avert her coming.
Clytemnestra is overcome with grief and despair,
while Achilles swears to save her daughter from the
sacrifice. Agamemnon soon learns that his wife and
child are acquainted with all the train of circumstances,
but declares himself unable to fight against the will of
the gods; while Iphigenia, after a moment's weakness,
proffers herself calmly and bravely for the sacrifice, in
spite of the entreaties and protestations of Clytemnestra
and Achilles. She goes forth, indeed, to the altar;
soon after, word is brought to Clytemnestra that a
miracle had happened. Just at the moment when the
victim's neck was bared, and Calchas had raised the
sacred knife to strike, Iphigenia was taken from their
presence, and in her stead was seen panting

> " a hind of largest bulk,
> In form excelling; with its sprouting blood
> Much was the altar of the goddess dewed; "

and the gods being thus appeased, the winds spring up
again and the Greeks make their way forth to Troy.

Racine altered this scheme of the drama materially.
In one point he improved it, from the modern
dramatic point of view, by making Achilles the lover
of Iphigenia, and ardently expecting her coming;
instead of being, as in Euripides, merely a counter in
the hands of Agamemnon. But Racine brought in
the inevitable *confidant* and *confidante*; the "attendant"
in the Greek play becomes Arcas, and a further

domestic, Eurybates, is introduced ; Clytemnestra also is enriched with a *confidante*, Ægina. He further thought to give additional interest to the drama by introducing a totally new character, Eriphile, with, of course, her *confidante*, Doris. This Eriphile was the daughter of that rather abandoned lady, Helen, by Theseus ; and Racine supposes her to have been captured in war by Achilles, brought up in ignorance of her true name and birth, and delivered as a companion to Iphigenia. In this condition she is a prey to two emotions—the desire to learn her name and her parents, and, of course, a secret passion for Achilles. With the exception of the scenes in which Eriphile and Doris appear, Racine conducts the drama on much the same lines as those of Euripides, allowing for the fact that here Achilles is the expectant lover of Iphigenia. He makes Agamemnon, however, scheme more for the deliverance of his daughter by sending her and Clytemnestra out of the camp, but his design is frustrated by Eriphile, who informs the soldiers of what is passing. When the time comes for the sacrifice, Achilles and Patroclus beat back those who would slay Iphigenia, and suddenly Calchas learns from the oracle that there is present in the crowd one of the blood of Helen, who must be immolated for Iphigenia. Eriphile does not wait for the attack, but plunges the sacrificial knife into her own bosom. She plays the part of " the hind of largest bulk " of Euripides ; while Iphigenia, instead of being translated by Diana into the clouds and deposited at Tauris, is happily wedded to Achilles.

This is the form of the story upon which Du

Roullet worked, though, as he says in his letter to Dauvergne, he omits the part of Eriphile entirely.

The overture to *Iphigenia in Aulis* is perhaps the most elaborate of Gluck's instrumental compositions, and at the same time the most successful. It begins at once with a mournful theme (*andante*) which had formerly figured in *Telemacco*. This is succeeded by a *grave* passage, leading into an *allegro maestoso*, which after some heavy octave passages for the strings leads into the dolorous subject in G minor, with its contest between the flute and the oboe—altogether a passage of profound dramatic characterisation. The rest of the overture follows the same general plan, each of the themes being reiterated. It has no formal ending,* but leads at once into the opening air of Agamemnon, O "pitiless Diana, in vain dost thou command this fearful sacrifice," in which the first theme of the overture appears again. He has sent Arcas to turn back Clytemnestra and her daughter, and declares his anguish at the thought of sacrificing Iphigenia.

He is interrupted by a chorus of Greeks, demanding of Calchas the reason of the god's displeasure. Calchas, without replying to them, bemoans the awful nature of the sacrifice, and inquires of the gods if no other victim will content them; he is finally joined by Agamemnon in a short duet, "O terrible divinity, have mercy upon us." The Greeks burst into a ferocious chorus, "Name us the victim, and at once we will slay him," ending with a solemn and impressive appeal

---

* Endings for concert purposes have been written by various composers, the best being that of Wagner.

to the gods to be propitious. Calchas dismisses
them with the assurance that a victim shall be found
that day.

Left alone with Agamemnon, Calchas urges him to
bow to the will of the gods. " Can they wish a father
to bring his daughter to the sacrifice ? " asks Agamemnon, and gives agonised expression to his grief ;
the air, broad and noble, is accompanied by strings
pianissimo, while alternate long notes for the oboe and
bassoon form a kind of wailing comment on his words.
Finally he avers he will not obey the gods, and on being
asked by Calchas whether he intends to break the oath
he has taken, he replies that all he had promised was
to give his daughter up to death if she should set foot
in Aulis—secretly relying on the clandestine message
he had sent to warn her against the journey. But
this of course has miscarried, and just as Calchas is
replying to him, shouts are heard in the camp,
announcing the arrival of Clytemnestra and Iphigenia.
Solemnly the priest admonishes him that he is nothing
to the gods, and that he must bend before them ; and
the sorrowful king inclines his head in resignation.
The chorus add new poignancy to his grief by singing
of the beauties of his wife and daughter, and his
happiness in possessing them.

Clytemnestra goes in to seek the king, leaving
Iphigenia to receive the homage of the Greeks in the
customary ballets, and a chorus in praise of her beauty ;
Iphigenia herself interjecting a short lament that
Achilles does not appear to gladden her eyes. But
Clytemnestra hastily re-enters. Agamemnon, with
the purpose of getting her and her daughter away from

Aulis, has told her that Achilles has proved false ; and in a magnificent aria she calls upon Iphigenia to cast from her heart every remembrance of her betrayer—an aria of clear, strong, sinewy passion that is all the more powerful by contrast with the somewhat weak ballet music and chorus that went immediately before. Iphigenia bewails her fate in an aria now tender, now passionate, those portions of it being finest where anger against Achilles bursts forth. But at this moment Achilles himself enters, in transports at the sight of his betrothed. "Can I believe my eyes ? " he asks. "Thou in Aulis, my princess ! " Iphigenia becomes immediately as freezing as a *grande dame*. "Whatever it may be that brings me here, at least I cannot reproach myself with being here to seek Achilles." Explanations and reproaches follow, the music being uninterruptedly expressive ; and the final duet, in which they are reconciled, has in it some anticipatory suggestions of the manner of Mozart or Weber.

The second act begins with the congratulations of the chorus to Iphigenia, whose heart, however, is ill at ease. Achilles has heard of Agamemnon's report that he was false, and Iphigenia dreads an encounter between them. Clytemnestra urges her to rejoice on her wedding-day, and Achilles himself, after introducing Patroclus to her in courtly wise, leads a chorus in her praise—the chorus "Sing and celebrate your queen," which was applied during the performance of the opera to Marie Antoinette ; after which the usual congratulatory ballets and so forth proceed. Just, however, as Achilles is about to lead Iphigenia to the altar, Arcas, the attendant, steps forth and discloses the purpose of Agamemnon to have slain her when she arrives there. All are horror-stricken; the Thessalians swear they will not permit the sacrifice, while Clytemnestra, clinging to Achilles, implores him to save her daughter. This Achilles promises to do, but Iphigenia somewhat coldly begs him to remember that Agamemnon is still her father, though condemned by fate to slay her.

In the following scene Achilles meets Agamemnon, and the two abuse each other in the orthodox style, Achilles finally declaring that they shall only reach Iphigenia through him. When he has gone, Agamemnon, in a fine recitative and aria, hovers in anguish between love for his daughter and fear of the gods; in the end he sends Arcas to Clytemnestra with orders to proceed with Iphigenia to Mycenæ at once.

In the third act the Greeks are clamouring for their victim. Achilles implores Iphigenia to fly with him, but she entreats him to leave her, assuring him of the uselessness of the attempt, yet protesting her eternal love. Her aria " Farewell ! " is one of the most perfect emotional utterances of the eighteenth century; in it can be seen the gradual amalgamation that was taking place in Gluck's mind between the two styles of *Alceste* and *Paris and Helen*.

Achilles swears to strike down the priest himself at the altar, and to slay Agamemnon if he comes in his way. This is the aria that fired the audience to such enthusiasm at the first performance; the officers, we are told, rose in their seats, grasping theirs words, and scarcely able to refrain from rushing on the stage.

Then follows a scene between Iphigenia and Clytemnestra, followed by another chorus of the Greeks demanding the sacrifice. Iphigenia is taken off ; Clytemnestra, held back by the attendants, bursts into a passionate recitative, seeing in imagination her daughter under the knife of the priest ; her following aria, "Jove, dart thy lightning," is in some respects the most modern expression ever attained by Gluck. It is perfect in feeling and in form, and might have come from the pen of Mendelssohn himself.

A beautiful hymn of the Greeks is now heard, imploring the favour of the gods and the acceptance of the sacrifice ; it is cut short by the sudden onslaught of Achilles and the Thessalians. For a time the contest rages between the two parties ; then comes the inevitable anti-climax of eighteenth-century opera. Calchas bids the combatants cease ; the gods are satisfied, the altar is consumed, and Iphigenia is restored to Achilles and her parents. There follow a quartett and chorus, and the usual ballets. It is noticeable that Gluck has repeated in the ballet, though in a slightly changed form, the exquisite *amabile moderato* from *Paris and Helen.* A Greek woman lifts up her voice to exhort the warriors to set sail for Troy, there to achieve greatness ; the melody is that of *Donzelle semplice* in *Paris and Helen.* There, however, it is appropriate and pathetic ; here it is utterly out of place. The opera ends with an unharmonised chorus of Greeks.

Fine as *Iphigenia in Aulis* is in parts, it is unsatisfactory as a whole. It is true that Gluck here is working on a larger canvas than he had yet attempted. In *Orfeo* the dramatic interest was small; there were only two real personages and only one emotion. Exactly the same criticism applies to *Paris and Helen*, allowing for the difference in the phase of love that is there under treatment. In *Alceste*, the strongest of his operas up to this time, there were similarly only two real characters and only one real emotion; that of a wife for a dying husband and of a husband for a dying wife. Much of the space of the canvas in both *Orfeo* and *Alceste* is taken up with representations of the unearthly—scenes that are in their very essence incapable of psychological treatment in the sense in which that phrase applies to scenes of human life and character; they are simply designed to add pictorially to the general effect of terror in a scene. But in *Iphigenia in Aulis* the supernatural is wholly eliminated, if we except the very small part it plays in the final announcement of Calchas; and even in that case it only enters by way of narrative; it plays no pictorial part itself, as do the Furies and Shades in *Orfeo*, or the oracle and powers of the under-world in *Alceste*. Nor are there in *Iphigenia in Aulis* any merely abstract or mythological persons, such as Cupid in *Orfeo*, Pallas and Erasto in *Paris*, Hercules and Apollo in *Alceste*. Here all the characters are actual human beings, and Gluck has a greater variety of them to study than in any other opera—Agamemnon, Clytemnestra, Iphigenia, Achilles, and Calchas, excluding such minor personages as Arcas and Patroclus; besides which, the choruses of Greeks and Thessalians are so treated as to become additional acting characters in the drama. Moreover, the story itself is more intrinsically interesting, more varied, more moving, more human, than any he had previously treated.   As there are more personages, there are more states of mind to be depicted, and the psychological scope of the drama is proportionally widened.

Yet in spite of all this, and in spite of the many magnificent strokes of genius in it, *Iphigenia in Aulis* is disappointing as a whole. Gluck too rarely rises above and out of himself ; where he does so, as in many passages in his previous operas, his work is invariably finest and most convincing. But here the opportunities of this forgetfulness of self are not frequent. Now and again, as in his treatment of the mental anguish of Agamemnon, the rage and fury of Clytemnestra, and the passion of Achilles, he is firm and clear and touching ; but he cannot maintain this high level throughout the opera, in all probability because of the frigid tone of the libretto. The stimulus to pure and lovely lyrism that had at times been given him by the really poetical words of Calzabigi, was absent from the cold and formal libretto of Du Roullet. What could any composer do, for instance, with such words as these ?—

> Iph. Ah ! you essay in vain to repress my alarm ;
> Achilles has heard that the king, my father,
> thinks that he my charms despises, meaning to
> break his faith. His honour resents the sus-
> picion, and to him, it appears, mortal offence is
> given. I have read in his eyes all the anger he
> feels, and, as you know, very proud is my
> father. The two have met this very hour.

A Woman in the Crowd. See the fierce raging lion,
untamed, roaring with anger, by his love overcome, crouching low on the ground : submissive,
full of sighs, scarcely his eyes uplifting, he
caresses the godlike hand that gave the wound.

Chorus of Women. Be sad no more, &c.

Iph. You try in vain to bring my alarms to an end,
for love has only feeble weapons where a hero
thinks his honour is hurt.*

A libretto like this accounts for many of the shortcomings of *Iphigenia in Aulis,* though not for all.
There are scenes where Gluck is inexpressibly dull
and tedious, scenes unlit by the faintest ray of passion
or beauty—where yet existed in the libretto the possibility of finer treatment. And it is noticeable that
some of the best and some of the worst specimens
of Gluck's aria-writing here exist side by side. There
are moments when he has surpassed himself, when we
catch the breath in amazement at some fine stroke of
art ; there are other moments when our senses fall
asleep under the heavy burden of dull and meaningless
sequences of notes. While the melody thus hovers

* I quote these passages from the really admirable
translation of the Rev. J. Troutbeck, in Novello's edition
of the opera. I have tried, but ineffectually, to set forth
the woman's speech, "See the fierce lion," in rhyme and
rhythm, as in the French text, *colère, altière—terrassé,
blessé ;* but although there is evidently a most courageous
attempt at rhyme in "ground, wound," the passage defies
all ordinary rules of prosody, and I am reluctantly compelled to print it as prose, with profound apologies to the
translator.

between excellence and mediocrity, the recitative is almost everywhere true and dramatic. Gluck's command of recitative as a dramatic instrument is here almost at its height ; and at times it rises to the rank of lyric beauty.   Perhaps the finest scenes, after those descriptive of the torment of Agamemnon's mind, are those two in which Clytemnestra bursts forth in passionate anger, first against Achilles, then against the murderers of her daughter.   Gluck too rarely worked himself up to such self-abandonment as this.   Wherever he does so, as here and in the aria of Admetus in the third act of *Alceste*, he is almost unapproachable.   And exactly here, where he is finest and strongest, his theory of " forgetting that he was a musician " breaks down.   It is where he *is* a musician that he is most interesting and most beautiful ; where he forgets that he is a musician he is too often dull and turgid.

Gluck's position in Paris was at first not an easy one.   As yet his music was unknown there, and the amateurs of music, ever inclined to take sides in matters of art, were preparing for a new war, similar to that of the Buffonists and Anti-Buffonists—which had been occasioned by the advent of an Italian troupe in 1752, performing some of the works of the Italian *buffo* order, such as the *Serva Padrona* of Pergolese. The immense contrast between the free and open melody of these operas and the style of Lully and Rameau, that necessarily seemed crabbed and rigid in comparison, had set all Paris by the ears, the Buffonists swearing by Pergolese, and the Italians, the Anti-

Buffonists, making a virtue of dullness in the sacred cause of patriotism, remaining faithful to the French composers. Immediately upon Gluck's advent into Paris, the musical world began to range itself for or against him. Unfortunately for a clear understanding of things, Gluck, though he was not of the school of Italy, certainly was not altogether of the school of France; which was unfortunate, as it complicated what might have been a very clear state of affairs, making nicely for a settled antithesis between Italian music and French, and puzzled many amiable and enthusiastic heads that would have been glad to range themselves on one side or the other, had they only been certain of their side. However, two parties were soon formed—Gluckists and Anti-Gluckists; and it must have been a consolation for the latter party to cast the skin of negativism and wriggle forth as something positive when the later advent of Piccinni as antagonist to Gluck gave them the opportunity to style themselves Piccinnists. Such is the consolatory virtue of names.

The consternation of the old playgoers was great at the appearance of Gluck upon the scene. He saw that it would be necessary to make influential friends in the French capital, and to conciliate some of the more powerful among the writers who might range themselves against him. He began with Rousseau, who was well known as a persistent opponent of French music and an advocate of the Italian, and whose main thesis in his *Lettre sur la musique française* (1753) had been that France could never have a genuine music of her own, because her

language was fundamentally unfit for it and opposed
to everything musical. Rousseau, of course, was not
easily accessible, but Gluck managed to procure an
introduction to him through Corancez, who was at
one time part director of the *Journal de Paris*. He
afterwards narrated a conversation between Rousseau
and himself relative to the German composer :

" Rousseau said to me one day (it was before the
initial performance of Gluck's first work), ' I have
seen many Italian scores in which there are some fine
dramatic pieces. M. Gluck alone appears to set
himself the aim of giving to each of his personages
the style that is proper to them ; but what I think
most admirable is that this style, once adopted, never
changes. His scrupulousness in this respect has even
made him commit an anachronism in his opera *Paris
and Helen.*' Astonished at this expression, I asked
him to explain himself. ' M. Gluck,' he continued,
' has expended upon Paris, in the greatest profusion,
all the brilliance and softness of which music is capable ;
to Helen, on the contrary, he has given a certain
austerity that never abandons her, even in the expression of her passion for Paris. This difference
doubtless arises from the fact that Paris was a
Phrygian and Helen a Spartan ; but Gluck has forgotten the epoch in which they lived. Sparta only
received the severity of its manners and language from
the laws of Lycurgus, and Lycurgus belonged to a
much later age than Helen.' I repeated this observation to M. Gluck. ' How happy should I be,'
he replied, ' if any number of the spectators could
understand and follow me in this way ; pray tell

M. Rousseau that I am grateful to him for the attention he is good enough to bestow on my works ; observe to him, however, that I have not committed the anachronism of which he accuses me. If I have given a severe style to Helen, it is not because she was a Spartan, but because Homer himself gives her this character ; tell him, in short, to sum the matter up in a word, that she was esteemed by Hector.' " *

Such was the remarkable brilliance of operatic criticism in the eighteenth century. One hardly knows whether Rousseau or Gluck was the more absurd.

Affairs between these two, however, came to a rather strange pass. Gluck had sent the philosopher a score of the Italian *Alceste* for his perusal and the expression of his opinion. In spite of his musical attainments, the study of the score was probably no easy matter for Rousseau. He himself writes : " M. Gluck pressed me so much that I was unable to refuse him this favour, although it was as fatiguing for me as it was useless for him." But Gluck brought matters to a head by suddenly taking the score away from him. " I had commenced the task," writes Rousseau to Dr. Burney, " when he withdrew his opera, without asking me for my remarks, which were only just commenced, and the indecipherable confusion of which made it impossible for me to send them to him."

Gluck found the task of producing *Iphigenia* harder than any he had yet undertaken. Nothing was in a condition to please him ; the orchestra, singers, chorus, ballet, all were inefficient, and had to go

* *Journal de Paris*, No. 231, p. 398, 18th Aug. 1788. In Desnoiresterres, pp. 86, 87.

through a course of the most rigorous training under his iron hand and watchful eye. The state of the Paris opera at this time was almost incredible. " Disorder, abuse, caprice, routine, and inertia were despotically enthroned there, without a protest from any one. If reform was urgent, so many people were interested in the *statu quo* that there was scarcely any hope of obtaining from the administration and from this ignorant and prejudiced crowd any improvement that was at all practical. In the midst of all this pomp and expenditure was a carelessness, an anarchy, a disorder past all credence. Actors and actresses pushed indecency to such a point as to appear outside the scenes, the latter in white camisoles with *une culotte d'argent* and a band across the forehead, the former in a simple dressing-gown. It was not a rare thing, while the foreground was occupied by Jupiter or Theseus, to see, through the scenery, the dancers moving and fluttering about, they having actually chosen the background of the stage to practise their steps and make their *jetés-battus.* Five or six years before this time, masks were still in use, and the choruses drew themselves up in a row, the two sexes carefully sorted out, impassible, without a gesture, like grenadiers on duty. . . . . However, at the time of the coronation of Louis XV., almost all the actors of the opera had been sent to Villers-Cotterets and Chantilly, and it had been necessary to substitute for the usual choruses other provisional ones, acting without singing, while musicians who could not or would not appear in public sang in the wings." * He was

* Desnoiresterres, pp. 89, 90.

confronted with similar difficulties in the case of the orchestra, which had been compared to "an old coach drawn by consumptive horses, and led by one deaf from his birth." The "Lettre de l'amant de Julie à Madame d'Orbe," in Rousseau's *Nouvelle Heloïse*, (lettre xxiii., part ii.) gives an equally bad picture of the condition of the singers: "I will not speak to you of this music; you know it; but what you can have no idea of are the frightful cries, the long roars with which the theatre resounds during the performance. One sees the actresses, almost in convulsions, violently tear the yelps out of their lungs, their fists clenched against the chest, the head thrown back, the face inflamed, the veins swollen, the stomach heaving; one does not know which is the more disagreeably affected, the eye or the ear; their exertions give as much suffering to those who see them as their singing does to those who hear them; and the astonishing thing is that the spectators applaud hardly any thing but these howlings. By the way they beat their hands together one would take them for deaf people, delighted to catch a piercing tone here and there . . . ."

The Iphigenia in Gluck's opera was the celebrated Sophie Arnould, a fine dramatic soprano, though with a tendency to sing out of tune. The Achilles was Legros, who made up in voice what he lacked in intelligence. The thorn in Gluck's side was Larrivée, to whom had been entrusted the part of Agamemnon. Once the composer was forced to tell him that he seemed to have no comprehenson of his part, and to be unable to enter into the spirit of it. "Wait till I get into my costume," said Larrivée; "you won't recognise me then." At a later rehearsal the singer reappeared in his costume, but his interpretation remained the same. "Oh, Larrivée, Larrivée!" cried Gluck; "I recognise you!"

With the ballet Gluck's troubles began again. He found himself compelled to struggle with the stupidity of Vestris—*le diou de la danse*—who once said that there were only three great men in Europe—Frederick II., Voltaire and himself. Full as the opera was of ballets, Vestris wanted yet another, in which to introduce his son. Gluck peremptorily refused. "Quoi!" stammered Vestris; "moi! le diou de la danse!" "If you are the god of the dance, monsieur," replied Gluck; "dance in heaven, not in my opera." The great man lamented that there was no chaconne at the end of the opera. "A chaconne!" said Gluck, "whenever did the Greeks dance a chaconne!" "Did they not?" was the compassionate reply of Vestris; "then so much the worse for them!"

More than once the composer threatened to withdraw his opera and proceed to Vienna; and Marie Antoinette had to exercise her power to remove the difficulties from his path. Finally, the performance was fixed for 13th April 1774; but almost at the last moment Legros announced that he was too ill to appear. Gluck demanded the postponement of the opera, but as every arrangement had been made, and the Royal family itself was to be present, it was attempted to induce him to allow another singer to take the place of Legros. It was impossible, however, to shake Gluck's resolution; he swore he would rather throw his work into the fire than submit to see it murdered by an inferior rendering ; and the opposition was forced to give in. The opera was at length produced on the 19th April with great success, though parts of it pleased better than the whole ; the overture was encored. The opera grew in favour with each repetition. No better proof could be given of its popularity than the fact that the ladies began to wear " a head dress in the form of a coronet of black flowers surmounted by the crescent of Diana, whence escaped a kind of veil that covered the back of the head ; it was called *à l'Iphigénie.*" *

It is unnecessary to quote here all the letters and articles by the littérateurs of the day on *Iphigenia in Aulis ;* a fair selection of them will be found in Desnoiresterres and in the second volume of Marx. One quotation, however, may be given from Corancez, as it illustrates Gluck's own ideas of dramatic composition :

"One day the passage, *Peuvent-ils ordonner qu'un père,* from *Iphigenia in Aulis,* was being sung at my house. I perceived that in the line *je n'obéirai point à cet ordre inhumain* there was a long note to *je* the first time it occurred, and a short note when it was repeated. I observed to M. Gluck that this long note had been unpleasant to me in the melody, and I was the more astonished at his employing it the first time seeing that he had dispensed with it afterwards, he himself apparently not making much of it.

"'This long note,' he said, 'which has displeased

---

* Desnoiresterres, p. 100.

you so much at your own house—did it equally
displease you in the theatre?' I answered 'No.'
'Well,' he added, 'I should be contented with that
reply, and as you will not always have me near you, I
beg you to look at the matter in the same way whenever such a case occurs again. When I have succeeded in the theatre I have done what I set myself
to do; it can matter little to me, and I assure you it
affects me very little, to create a pleasant effect in a
drawing-room or at a concert. If you have often
noticed that good concert-music has no effect in a
theatre, it is surely in the nature of things that good
theatrical music should frequently be unsuccessful in
a concert-room. Your question resembles that of a
man who, being in the high gallery of the dome of
the Invalides, should cry out to the painter below,
" Sir, what was your intention here—a nose, an arm?
it looks like neither." The painter would with more
reason say to him, " Sir, come down here and judge
for yourself."

" 'I ought to add, however, that I had very good
reasons not only for setting a long note to *je* the first
time Agamemnon pronounces it, but also for suppressing it each time it is repeated. Remember that the
prince is between the two most potent of all forces—
nature and religion; nature finally gains the victory,
but before articulating this terrible word of dis-
obedience to the gods he must hesitate; my long
note marks this hesitation; but when once this word
has been spoken, let him repeat it as often as he may,
there will no longer be hesitation; the long note
would in that case be only an error in prosody.'

F

"I also complained to M. Gluck that in this same opera, *Iphigenia in Aulis*, the chorus of soldiers who advance so many times to demand loudly that the victim be given up to them, not only has nothing striking in itself, in point of melody, but that it is repeated each time, note for note, although variety seems so necessary.

"'These soldiers,' he replied, 'have quitted all they hold most dear—their country, their wives, their children—in the sole hope of pillaging Troy. The calm surprises them in the middle of their progress and keeps them bound in the port of Aulis. A contrary wind would be less harmful, since then they could at least return home. Suppose,' he added, 'that some great province is in famine. The citizens gather together in crowds and seek the chief of the province, who appears on the balcony: "My children, what do you wish!" All reply at once, "Bread!" "My friends, we are . . . ." "Bread! bread!" To everything he says they will answer "Bread!" Not only will they utter nothing but this laconic word, but they will utter it always in the same tone, because the great passions have only one accent. Here the soldiers demand their victim; all the circumstances count for nothing in their eyes; they see only Troy or else a return to their own country; so they ought only to employ the same words and always with the same accent. I might perhaps have written something more beautiful from a musical point of view, and varied it so as to please your ears; but in that case I would only have been a musician and would have been untrue to nature, which I must never abandon. Do

not imagine, however, that in that case you would
have had the additional pleasure of hearing a fine piece
of music ; I assure you to the contrary ; for a beauty
out of place has not only the disadvantage of missing a
great part of its effect, but it is really pernicious,
because it distracts the spectator, who is no longer in
the necessary disposition for following the dramatic
action with any interest.'

" My absolute ignorance of the art of music did not
repel M. Gluck ; I did not fear to interrogate him,
especially when it was a question of criticising some
apparent faults. His replies had always an air of
simplicity and truth which only made my esteem for
his person increase day by day.

" I begged him afterwards to explain to me why the
number in *Iphigenia*, describing the anger of Achilles,
sent a shiver through me, and transported me, so to
speak, into the situation of the hero himself : while if
I sang it myself, so far from finding anything terrible
or menacing in it, I only saw in it a melody pleasing
to the ear.

" 'You must recognise before all,' he said, ' that
music is a very limited art, especially in that part
of it which is called *melody*. You would seek in vain,
in the combination of notes which compose the air, a
character proper to certain passions ; it does not exist.
The composer has the resource of harmony, but that
is frequently insufficient. In the piece you speak of,
all my magic consists in the nature of the air which
precedes it, and in the choice of the instruments that
accompany it. For some time previously you have
heard nothing but the tender regrets of Iphigenia and

her adieux to Achilles ; the flutes and the mournful tones of the horns play the greatest part there. It is no wonder that when your ears, after being thus lulled to rest, are suddenly struck with the sharp tone of all the military instruments together, an extraordinary effect is produced on you—an effect, indeed, which it was my aim to produce, but which yet depends principally upon a purely physical sensation ' " *

Iphigenia in Aulis, besides the honour and adulation it brought Gluck, benefited him also in a more material sense. In Vienna, whereto reports of his triumphs had spread, Maria Theresa made him her *Kammer-Kompositeur* ; in Paris he received 20,000 livres for this and for each succeeding opera. When he had produced three operas for the French stage he was to have a pension of 1000 livres, which was to be increased to 1500 livres after the fourth and 2000 after the sixth.

He at once set to work upon his second opera, having resolved to produce *Orfeo* upon the Parisian stage. Several alterations were necessary ; as there were no *castrati* in Paris, the title-part had to be recast for a counter-tenor instead of a contralto, and, as Fétis remarks, it thereby lost " that character of profound melancholy that suited the subject so well." This change, by altering the key throughout the music of Orpheus, necessarily altered the meaning and the impression throughout. In the opening chorus, the effect of the exquisite call " Eurydice ! " was utterly

* *Journal de Paris*, No. 234, 21st August 1788, pp. 1009, 1010. In Desnoiresterres, pp. 101–104.

spoiled. The beautiful aria in F, in the first act, was transposed into C, and *Che farò*, conversely, from C into F ; while the chorus of the Furies in the second act was altered from C minor into D minor. Moreover, as Legros refused to sing the part of Orpheus unless he had the opportunity of making a brilliant exit in the first act, a new aria was inserted for him—*L'espoir renaît dans mon âme*—by a composer named Bertoni.

Orphée et Eurydice was produced 2nd August 1774, and met with a success surpassing even that of *Iphigenia in Aulis*, by reason of its simpler and more emotional character. The journals, letters, and memoirs of the time are filled with eulogies of it. Corancez, Rousseau, Voltaire, Mlle. de Lespinasse, all recorded their opinions in enthusiastic language.* "'I know nothing more perfect,'" says the *Journal de Paris* in 1788, quoting Rousseau, "''in what is called congruity, than the *ensemble* of the Elysian Fields in the opera *Orphée*. Throughout there is the enjoyment of pure and calm happiness, but with such a character of equality that there is not a trait, either in the song or in the ballet, that in any way rises into exaggeration.' Praise so well merited in the mouth of a man like Rousseau appeared to me too flattering to be kept from the chevalier Gluck. 'My lesson,' he replied, is written in the picture Eurydice makes of the abode of the blest :

* See *Journal de Paris*, No. 231, 18th Aug. 1788. Rousseau, " Œuvres," xii. 413–420, etc. ; Voltaire, "Œuvres—Lettre au Chevalier de Lisle," 27th May, 1774, etc.; " Lettres de Mlle. Lespinasse," p. 148, etc.

Rien ici n'enflamme
l'âme,
Une douce ivresse
laisse
Un calme heureux dans tous les sens.

"'The happiness of the just,' he added, 'must chiefly consist in its continuity, and therefore in its equableness ; that is why what we call pleasure can have no place there ; for pleasure is susceptible of different degrees ; it becomes blunted, too, and in the end produces satiety.'"*

The opera had a long run at Paris, and even passed again into Germany in its Gallicised form.

Gluck was in high favour at the Court, and as the young Archduke Maximilian was visiting Paris at this time, an opera was requested of the German composer. He produced, on 27th February 1775, his old work, *L'arbre enchanté*, slightly altered from its previous form ; its success, however, was not very great. Shortly after, he left Paris for Vienna, calling on his way at Strasburg, where he met Klopstock. Some correspondence passed between them afterwards, and Gluck's letter is worth quoting as a specimen of his epistolary style. It must be given in German ; it would be impossible to do justice to the orthography and punctuation in a translation :

"Ich hoffe sie werden Von dem Hrn. Graffen Von Cobentzl die Verlange Arien richtig Erhalten haben,

---

* *Journal de Paris* as above. See Desnoiresterres, p. 112.

ich habe selbige durch diese gelegenheit wegen
Erspahrung der Postspesen ihnen geschickt, die anmer-
kungen habe ich müssen wecklassen, weilen ich nicht
wuste, mich auszurucken, wie ich Es Verlangte, ich
glaube, Es würde ihnen Eben so schwer vorkommen,
wan sie sollten jemanden durch Brieffe belehren, wie,
und mit was vor Einen aussdruck Er ihnen Messias
zu declamiren hätte, alles dieses besteht in der
Empfindung, und kan nicht wohl explicirt werden,
wie sie bässer wissen, als ich ;—Ich Ermangle zwar
nicht zu pflantzen, aber handlen habe ich bis dato
noch nicht können, dan kaum war ich in Wien
angekommen, so verreiste der Kaiser, und ist noch
nicht zurücke gekommen, über dieses muss man
annoch die gutte Virtlstunde beobachten, umb Etwas
effectuiren zu können, bey grosen Höffen findt man
selten gelegenheit, Etwas guttes anzubringen, indessen
höre ich dennoch, das man will Eine Academie der
Schönen Wissenschaften allhier Errichten, und das
der Eintrag Von den Zeitungen, und Calendern soll
Eine portion des fondi aussmachen, umb die Kosten
zu bestreitten ; wan ich werde bässer Von der sache
unterrichtet sein, werde nicht Ermangeln ihnen alles
zu berichten. Indessen haben sie mich Ein wenig
lieb, bis ich wiederumb so glücklich bin sie zu sehen.
Mein Weib und Tochter machen ihnen Ihre Compli-
menten und freyen sich sehr Von ihnen Etwas zu
hören, und ich Verbleibe dero,

"Ihnen Ergebenster,

" Gluck."*

* Marx, ii. pp. 144, 145.

Evidently the introductions to *Alceste* and *Paris and Helen* were not the work of the composer himself.

Meanwhile another opera was wanted for Paris, and Gluck gave them his *Cythère assiegée*, which he had written in 1759, and which was now somewhat altered for the French stage.   Passages were inserted in it from *Paris and Helen* and *Iphigenia in Aulis*, and Berton himself composed some of the new music for it.*   It was produced on the 11th August 1775, but was received with little else but laughter. Even Gluck's own adherents were forced to admit the failure, and to console themselves with the *mot* of Arnaud, that " Hercules was more at home with the club than the distaff."

He had received from the Directors of the Opera a commission for two new works, as well as for an adaptation of *Alceste*.   The two works were Quinault's *Armida*, and an opera, *Roland*, based on a poem of Quinault, though not following it entirely.   But in his absence from Paris the Italianist party had been steadily working to undermine his influence, which could best be done, they thought, by bringing another musician to write in opposition to him.   Accordingly they brought to Paris the Neapolitan Piccinni (born 1728), at that time one of the most celebrated and most popular composers in Europe ; a facile writer, whose operas, says his biographer Ginguené, had already mounted up to the respectable number of one hundred and thirty.   One fine morning Gluck received the information that to Piccinni also had been entrusted the composition of a *Roland*.   His

* See Marx, ii. pp. 148–155.

anger was great ; according to his own account, he immediately cast the score of his opera into the fire. His letter to Du Roullet will give an idea of his state of mind :

" I have just received your letter of the 15th January, in which, my dear friend, you exhort me to work diligently at the opera *Roland.* This is no longer possible, for as soon as I heard that the Directors, who were not ignorant that I was at work on this opera, had given the same text to Signor Piccinni, I cast into the flames all I had completed of it. Perhaps it was not worth much, and in that case the public will be greatly obliged to M. Marmontel, who in this way has spared them the misfortune of hearing bad music. Moreover, I do not feel fit to enter into a contest. Signor Piccinni would have too great an advantage over me ; since, besides his personal merit, which is undoubtedly great, he would have the advantage of novelty, for Paris has already had from me four operas—whether good or bad matters not ; in any case, they exhaust the imagination. Moreover, I have marked out the path for him, and he has only to follow it. I say nothing of his patrons ; I am sure that a certain politician of my acquaintance * will have three-fourths of Paris to dinner and supper, in order to make proselytes, and that Marmontel, who is so good at stories, will acquaint the whole kingdom with the exclusive merit of Signor Piccinni. I pity M. Hébert † sincerely for

* Marquis Caraccioli, the Neapolitan ambassador at Paris, a patron of Piccinni.

† A director of the Opéra.

F*

having fallen into the clutches of such people, one of whom is a blind admirer of Italian music, and the other the author of so-called comic operas; they will make him see the moon at midday.

"I am truly put out about it, for M. Hébert is a worthy man, and that is why I do not hesitate to give him my *Armida*, on the conditions, however, which I mentioned to you in my previous letter, and of which the essential points are, that when I come to Paris I must have at least two months in which to train my actors and actresses; that I shall be at liberty to have as many rehearsals as I think necessary; that no part shall be doubled; and that another opera shall be in readiness, in case any actor or actress shall fall sick. These are my conditions, without which I will keep *Armida* for my own pleasure. I have written the music of it in such a way that it will not soon grow old.

"You say in your letter, my friend, that none of my works will ever compare with *Alceste*. This prophecy I cannot agree with. *Alceste* is a perfect tragedy, and I do not think it often fails of its full perfection. But you cannot imagine how many shades and manners music is capable of, and what varied paths it can follow. *Armida* is so different from *Alceste*, that one would hardly believe they were by the same composer; and I have put into it what little power remained to me after *Alceste*. I have striven to be, in *Armida*, more painter and poet than musician; of that, however, you will be able to judge yourself when you hear the opera. With it I think to close my career as an artist. The public, indeed, will take as long to understand *Armida* as they did to understand *Alceste*.

There is a kind of refinement in the former that is not in the latter ; for I have managed to make the different personages express themselves in such a way that you will be able to tell at once whether Armida or another is singing. I must end, or you might think me either a charlatan or a lunatic. Nothing sits so badly on a man as praise of himself ; it only suited the great Corneille. When I or Marmontel blow our own trumpets, people laugh in our faces. For the rest, you are right in saying that the French composers are too greatly neglected ; for I am very much in error if Gossec and Philidor, who understand the style of the French opera so well, could not serve the public better than the best of Italian composers, if people were not too enthusiastic over whatever is new. You say further, dear friend, that *Orfeo* loses in a comparison with *Alceste*. But, good heavens ! how is it possible to compare two works that have nothing in common ? The one can please as well as the other ; but put *Alceste* on the stage with your worst players and *Orfeo* with your best, and you will see that *Orfeo* will bear away the prize ; the best things become insupportable in a bad performance. Between two works of a different nature there can be no comparison. If, for example, Piccinni and I had both composed a *Roland*, then people would have been able to judge which was the better ; different libretti must necessarily produce different compositions, each of which might be the most beautiful of its kind ; in any other case—*omnis comparatio claudicat*. Indeed I must almost tremble at the idea of a comparison between *Armida* and *Alceste*—two poems so diverse, of which one moves to tears and the other stimulates exquisite sensations. If such comparisons are made, I do not know what to do, except to pray God to give the worthy city of Paris its sound common sense again." *

This letter subsequently appeared in the *Année Litteraire* for 1776, "without the participation," it was said, "either of M. Gluck or of the person to whom it is addressed ; " but we may discount that statement considerably. Gluck evidently intended the letter for publication.

Now, however, he thought it time to do something himself, and accordingly he set out for Paris with the altered score of *Alceste*. This was produced on 23rd April 1776 ; † and though the first and second acts were applauded, the third fell flat. It is related that Gluck, who had been watching the house from the wings, rushed despairingly into the street, where he happened upon the Abbé Arnaud. "*Alceste* is fallen!" moaned the composer. "Fallen from heaven!" replied the consoling Abbé. Corancez wrote at a later date :

"*Alceste* was not successful at the first representation. I met Gluck in the corridor, and found him more occupied in seeking the cause of an event that seemed to him so extraordinary, than affected by the small success of the opera. 'It would be a joke,' he said to me, 'if it were to fail ; it would be an epoch in the history of taste of your nation. I can conceive

---

* Marx, ii. pp. 156–159. Desnoiresterres, p. 124.

† The title runs—"Represented for the first time by the Académie Royale de Musique, *30th* April 1776."

that a piece composed in a purely musical style should succeed or not succeed ; I can conceive even that a piece of this kind should be passionately admired at first, and then die in the presence of, and, so to speak, with the consent of its first admirers ; but that I should witness the failure of a piece modelled wholly on the truth of nature, and in which all the passions have their true accent—I admit that this amazes me. *Alceste,*' he added proudly, ' can only displease now when it is new ; it has not yet had time ; I say that it will please equally in two hundred years, if the French language does not change ; and my reason for saying so is that I have built wholly on nature, which is never subject to changes of fashion.' " *

But Gluck might have remembered that *Alceste* had at first met with a similar reception at Vienna, and that the non-success of the opera at its first hearing there, as at Paris, was due to the unrelieved sombreness of its colouring, and the uniformity, amounting almost to monotony, of its subject. Rousseau, indeed, pointed this out in his " Fragments d'observations sur l'Alceste italien de M. le chevalier Gluck " :

" I know no opera in which the passions are less varied than in *Alceste;* almost everything turns on two sentiments, affliction and terror, and the prolonged employment of these two sentiments must have cost the composer incredible pains to avoid the most lamentable monotony. Generally speaking, the more warmth there is in the situations and expressions, the more prompt and rapid should be their passage ;

* Desnoiresterres, p. 130.

otherwise the force of the emotion decreases in the hearers; and when the proper limit is passed, the actor strives in vain, for the spectator grows cold and finally impatient.

"It results from this fault that the interest, instead of being quickened by degrees in the course of the piece, dies away to the end, which, with all respect to Euripides himself, is cold, dull, and almost laughable in its simplicity."

As Gluck had passed over Sophie Arnould on account of her inferior physique, and confided the part of Alcestis to Rosalie Levasseur, the cry was heard that a cabal had been raised against the work by the friends of the slighted singer. But there was little truth in the charge, the best refutation of it being the fact that the success of *Alceste* grew with each performance. Gluck's friends were not idle in proclaiming the merit of the work: the Abbé Arnaud in particular distinguished himself by his *Soirée perdue à l'Opéra*—a controversial piece in the form of a dialogue, in which the Gluckist had an easy triumph over his opponent. Once more it may be worth while to quote a passage, as showing what contemporary criticism of music was like:

"'One moment, one moment, Sir Eternal-admirer,' cried angrily a man who wept with rage when every sensible person was weeping with compassion; 'now you will hear a piece I challenge you to undertake to praise . . . . There it is: well, what say you, gentlemen? four entire verses on the one tone, on the same note! Could anything be more wretched? is it not the very negation of music?' 'It is true that the

function of music, and especially theatrical music, is to
seize the accent of the passions, to embellish it, fortify
it, and render it more palpable ; but these are *shades* on
the stage, and there are no passions beyond this life ;
these verses are not susceptible of any other declamation ;
and it is in depriving them of even their natural and ordinary accents that the chevalier Gluck proves his fine
sense of the congruous.   However, as it is not simply a
matter of imitation, and as imitation ought to have place
in music, keep one ear open for the orchestra, and you
will see that the composer supplements this monotonous declamation by a most varied, most expressive,
and most picturesque harmony—a harmony that will
affect all sensible persons, and at the same time move
with terror and admiration those who have not only
sensibility but a knowledge of art.' " *

This defence of the part of the music in question was
undoubtedly suggested to Arnaud by Gluck himself,
for we find it reappearing in Corancez :

" The chorus of the infernal deities struck me with
terror, but I could not conceive what had led M.
Gluck to make these four verses be sung to a single
note.

" ' It is not possible,' he said to me, ' to imitate the
language of fantastic beings, since we have never
heard them ; but we have to try to approach the ideas
inspired in us by the functions with which they are
charged.   Devils, for instance, have a conventional
character that is well known and very pronounced ;

* " La Soirée perdue à l'Opéra," pp. 53, 54, in
" Mémoires pour servir," etc.

they ought to be dominated by excess of rage and madness. But the infernal gods are not devils ; we regard them as the ministers of destiny ; they are not swayed by any peculiar passion ; they are impassible. Alcestis and Admetus are indifferent to them ; all they have to do with them is the accomplishing of destiny. In order to delineate this special impassibility of theirs, I thought I could not do better than deprive them of all accent, reserving for my orchestra the task of painting all that is terrible in their announcement.'"

And again Corancez writes :

" I was at the first rehearsal of *Alceste ;* I thought myself alone in the amphitheatre, which was in darkness. The execution of the march of priestesses probably drew from me some external sign of approbation. M. Gluck was almost at my side without my seeing him. 'So this march pleases you,' he said, coming up to me. ' It does indeed,' I replied ; ' it has a religious character which at once pleases and surprises me.' ' I will explain it to you,' he said. ' I have observed that all the Greek poets who have composed hymns for the temples have made a certain metre predominate in their odes ; I have thought that this metre had in it something sacred and religious ; I have composed my march in conformity with the same succession of longs and shorts ; and now I see that I was right.' Then, striking me on the shoulder, ' They were fine fellows, those Greeks !' " *

* *Journal de Paris*, No. 237, 24th Aug. 1788. In Desnoiresterres, pp. 134–137.

The opera, of course, as has been already stated, was altered from its first Italian form, sometimes for the better, sometimes for the worse. Marx discusses the question fully,* but his bias against French taste and French feeling makes him depreciate unnecessarily the later form of the opera ; *Alceste* was certainly improved in some respects by the change, although it has to be as freely admitted that Du Roullet's version † weakened the poem in parts. The Hercules especially was a concession to French tastes, being a reminiscence of the *Alceste* of Quinault and Lully. Grimm points out the defects in the character of Admetus in the second act, and the faults of construction in the third : " What a difference between this poem and that of Quinault ! "

Meanwhile a misfortune had befallen the composer ; his niece Marianne had died on the 22nd April, the day before the production of *Alceste.* At Vienna, whither he now repaired, he had the satisfaction of hearing that *Alceste* had at last captured the French taste. Further honours crowded in on him. "Certain actors, musicians, men of letters and of society, at the head of whom we may name Berton, Legros, Gélin, Larrivée, Gossec, Leduc, Langlé and Rollan, agreed, by a private act before a notary of Paris, on the 17th July 1776, to bear the whole expense of a marble bust of the German composer, the execution of which was entrusted to Houdon. The author of

* Marx. ii. 160–170.

† It is certain, from the testimony of Grimm and Reichardt, that the French version is by Du Roullet, and not, as was formerly supposed, by Guillard.

Orphée was treated as the author of *Zaïre* had been treated six years before ; and it is this bust which, after having been exhibited at the Salon of 1777, was placed by the order of the king in the grand *foyer* of the Opéra, by the side of that of Rameau." *

After *Alceste*, *Iphigenia in Aulis* was again brought out, with Sophie Arnould in her original part. And now La Harpe, one of the enemies of Gluck, unburdened himself, in his *Journal de politique et de littérature*, in a passage that is worth quoting as another light on the manner of eighteenth-century criticism :

"Those who reproach M. Gluck with frequent lack of melody, remark, to the advantage of Italian composers, that their airs when separate from the accompaniment still have great beauty. But at least one cannot deny that M. Gluck repairs this lack of melody, as far as possible, by his profound knowledge of harmony and the effects of which it is capable.

"Another observation has been made *à propos* of the duet of Achilles and Agamemnon in the second act. It is, that it is in no way consistent with the dignity of two heroes to be speaking at the same time, as when two vulgar people are quarrelling ; and indeed this conflict of menaces and clashing cries is absolutely lacking in the nobility that should characterise this scene, and does not inspire the terror one ought to feel when in the presence of two such men as Achilles and Agamemnon. One might go still further, and say that the music hardly lends itself thoroughly to the

* Desnoiresterres, pp. 147, 148.

main expression of this scene.   The accent of pride is
hard and anti-harmonic ; and this dialogue of Achilles
and Agamemnon is of a kind of recitative at which
the ear is at any rate astonished.   It should not rise
even into declamation, in which style, nevertheless,
the attempt has been made to write it ; and perhaps
Achilles and Agamemnon could not brave each other
in music.   What is certain is that the effect of this
scene, when sung, is very inferior to the effect of the
same scene when declaimed ; and although it may be
true in general that music can render everything,
perhaps it is as well not to employ it on objects to
which it cannot be felicitously applied." *

This brought upon La Harpe, who was undoubtedly
the most stupid of all the stupid littérateurs who wrote
about music in those days, an attack in the *Journal de
Paris* by the celebrated "Anonyme de Vaugirard."
The contest went on for some time, arousing an extraordinary amount of interest in the musical world.   La
Harpe was no match for his antagonist, who easily
convicted him of being as weak in his reasoning as he
was superficial in his knowledge of the subject.   But
the war went raging on in other quarters.   It was
about this time that Marmontel's "Essai sur les révolutions de la musique en France" appeared—a work not
without merit, having for its object to demonstrate
that while the French stage was incontestably superior
to the Italian, its music was as incontestably inferior,
and that a true opera would only be obtained by trans-

---

* *Journal de politique et de littérature,* 5th March 1777.
In Desnoiresterres, pp. 149, 150.

planting Italian melody into the really dramatic poems
that were in favour in Paris. Innumerable pamphlets
sprang forth in reply to Marmontel and La Harpe,
—" Lettre d'un gentilhomme allemand à qui l'on avoit
prêté l'Essai sur les révolutions de la musique : " " La
Brochure et M. Jérôme, petit conte moral ; " " Lettre
d'un hermite de la forêt de Sénart ; " and so on.*

Piccinni, the intended rival of Gluck, had left
Naples on 16th November 1776, arriving in Paris on
the 31st December. At this time he was a man of
about forty-eight years old ; pale, thin, weak, and
impressionable ; evidently no fit antagonist for the
vigorous Gluck. Piccinni had to set to work to learn
the French language, and had little time for anything
but continuous reading of Voltaire, Rousseau and
Racine. Marmontel had adapted Quinault's *Roland*
for the Italian composer, and spent three or four hours
a day with him, trying to endow him with a just
appreciation of accent and quantity.

All this time Gluck was working at the fifth of the
great works by which he was to be remembered.
On this occasion he had gone straight back to Quinault, accepting the libretto of *Armida* as the poet had
written it and as it had been set by Lully. In a
notice of the opera in the *Journal de Paris* the following reasons were given for Gluck's retention of the
original poem : " The plan of Quinault's poems is
not the most favourable for dramatic music ; M.
Gluck might have been able to avoid some of the
difficulties by suppressing in *Armida* several feeble, or

* See Desnoireterres, p. 163.

incongruous details, as has been done in some late reproductions of Lully's opera. He has been desirous of preserving in its entirety this masterpiece of our lyric theatre, and has been convinced that in his art there are resources sufficient not only to make admirable the beauties of this poem, but further, to cover or even embellish its faults. Time will show how far he has succeeded in this attempt, which deserves at least the gratitude of admirers of Quinault." * Probably this laudable motive, however—to preserve in its entirety the masterpice of the lyric theatre—was not the real one ; it seems likely that Gluck had had a suspicion that some of the success of his former works was due to the libretti of his collaborateurs ; and he may further have thought that by working upon the unaltered poem of Quinault he might propitiate beforehand many who were formerly against him. The work was given on the 23rd September 1777, to a crowded and not very appreciative house.

In *Armida* Gluck has left classical antiquity for a time ; in choosing for his new opera a poem the central idea of which was drawn from Tasso and the East, he was making one more uncertain and unconscious movement towards the Romanticism that characterised the later epochs of music.

The overture is a modification of the one he had written to *Telemacco* and afterwards used for *Le feste d'Apollo.* This was not the only instance of the employment in *Armida* of themes from his earlier

* *Journal de Paris,* Sept. 1777. In Desnoiresterres, pp. 206, 207.

operas; the air of Hate, *Plus on connaît l'amour*, is an adaptation of one of Jupiter's airs in *Bauci e Filemone*; while other portions of the opera are taken from *Le nozze d'Ercole e d'Ebe*, from *Telemacco*, from *L'innocenza giustificata*, and from *Don Juan*. The overture begins with a pompous subject in C major, that leads after a few bars into a theme of a more agitated character, which may be taken to denote the mental anguish and irresolution of Armida; when prefixed to *Telemacco* it had reference to Circe. The next theme is thoroughly dramatic and pointedly referable to the opera itself, and is handled with more skill and persistency than is generally the case in Gluck's music; keeping the opening theme of this section running almost throughout, he cleverly interweaves others with it and draws new meanings from it; then, with a repetition of the "Armida" theme of the first section in a modified form, the overture leads at once into the opening scene of the first act.

Armida is seen in the garden of her palace with her *confidantes*, Phénice and Sidonie, who are urging her to banish care and melancholy. No regular aria is assigned either to Phénice or to Sidonie; they carry the flood of melody on by turns in a rather charming manner. The music is soft and gentle and languorous, one fine trait being noticeable—the disturbing element that is introduced into the harmony as soon as the war is mentioned; we hear a reminiscence of the theme that is so well worked out in the second section of the overture. A different colour is diffused over the music when Armida speaks; she complains that whatever may be her power over the other warriors it fails to subdue Rinaldo, and this although he is in the maytime of youth, when he should be most susceptible to love. Phénice and Sidonie endeavour to console her with the philosophical reflection that one victory more or less can make very little difference to her, and that the proper way to make Rinaldo conscious of his shortcomings is to treat him with contemptuous disregard. Again the pictorial change comes over the music when Armida replies. In rapid and vigorous tones she reminds them of the prophecy that her power would be vain against this hero ; and the accents rise and quicken as she exclaims : " How I hate him ! how his scorn wounds me ! in spite of myself, incessantly the thought of him disturbs my rest." Then in a recitative she narrates her dream, in which Rinaldo had vanquished her, and Sidonie tries to console her in an aria that is an adaptation of one in *Paris and Helen.*

A few bars of music of a pompous character are now heard—the kind of pretentious nullity that was always employed to signify the arrival of some important personage—and Hidraot, the uncle of Armida, enters. He wants her to choose a husband, that when his own days end he may know that Armida will leave others to inherit the kingdom. She replies, in the language of the Court of Louis XIV., that she " dreads the alluring tie of Hymen : "· " Ah ! how unhappy does the heart become when liberty abandons it." Hidraot admonishes her again, singing the praises of wedded life, and reminding her that she has only to look in order to conquer ; but she reiterates her resolve to live alone, adding that she admires before all things valour,

and that she would bestow her hand upon no one but
the conqueror of Rinaldo. Then the chorus sing the
praises of her power and beauty, their song being
interspersed with stanzas for Phénice and Sidonie, and
a very pretty ballet. It is noticeable how Gluck
maintains the pictorial method he had spoken of in
his letter to Du Roullet, where he speaks of each
character having a music of its own that at once
distinguishes it from all the rest. Each time Phénice
or Sidonie or Armida sings, the music undergoes a
total change.

Just as all are celebrating the might of Armida,
however, and her power to vanquish heroes and armies
with a smile, Arontes enters, bleeding from his
wounds, and bearing the news that as he was conducting his captives thither they were taken from
him by the prowess of a single warrior. " A single
warrior ! " all exclaim ; while Armida ejaculates, " O
heaven ! it is Rinaldo ! " " It is he," replies Arontes ;
and in a fine chorus, full of movement and passion, all
swear to pursue the victor and have vengeance.

The second act opens in a woody country, where
Rinaldo is taking farewell of Artemidoro, who is
returning to the Christian camp after having been
rescued from his captors by the hero. Artemidoro
wishes to accompany him in his adventures, but
Rinaldo urges him to return to the camp ; he, for his
part, having incurred the wrath of Godfrey, must
pursue his undertaking alone. Artemidoro warns him
against the blandishments of Armida ; Rinaldo replies
that he is indifferent to her charms, his only passion
being for liberty.

In the next scene, Armida and Hidraot, in a duet that sometimes rises into sublimity, call upon the spirits of hate and rage to deliver Rinaldo into their hands. Hidraot wishes to ensnare him by means of an ambuscade, but Armida claims the right to take him captive in her own way and to slay him herself.

Rinaldo now appears in the garden which Armida and Hidraot have just quitted. In the orchestra is heard a gliding, voluptuous strain, rising and falling, swelling and dying away ; gradually his voice blends with it, but the voice-part is a thing apart from and independent of the accompaniment, which flows on unceasingly in the orchestra, a perfect instrumental picture of languorous delight. Nothing that Gluck had written up to this time was so uninterruptedly perfect as this ; its voluptuous, cloying beauty is in marked contrast to much of his music, with its usual qualities of rigidity and reserve. The spell is maintained to the end, when Rinaldo, overcome by the magical enchantment of the place, lays down his arms one by one, and finally sinks into slumber. Naiads sing about him, and a ballet is danced ; especially noticeable is the tender final song of the naiad.

A spirited theme in the orchestra announces the presence of Armida ; she rushes forward, dagger in hand, contemplating the sleeping form of Rinaldo. But her exultation is marred by an undercurrent of weakness, cunningly denoted in the orchestra, before there is a suspicion of it in the words, by a hesitating phrase interpolated in her recitative ; time after time she approaches him to plunge the dagger in his breast, yet always finds herself overcome at the sight of him.

Finally, in an aria of magnificent expression, she
yields herself regretfully to love, and invokes the
powers of earth to transport her with Rinaldo to the
bounds of the universe. It is strange what a passion
of profound regret quivers through this music, which
is ostensibly a confession of love ; Gluck was at the
height of his psychological power in thus pourtraying
the struggle of Armida against her sudden engulfing
passion.

Equally fine is her aria at the beginning of the
third act, where she again laments her weakness, and
the contrast between the deep, moving passion of the
music and the frigid formalism of the words is most
noticeable. More than once Gluck has written some of
his finest and most enduring music to words that, apart
from the music, are intellectually almost ridiculous.

Close upon Armida's lament is heard the lighthearted frippery that serves to designate Phénice
and Sidonie. They attempt to console her in the
usual way, but she is inconsolable ; Rinaldo has
rejected her love, and in a frenzy she calls upon the
spirit of Hate to appear. Hate sings an aria descriptive of his power, and then, after a chorus and a
strange ballet of Furies, conjures Love to yield to him
his place in Armida's heart ; and there follows another
ballet. Armida however finally lifts up her voice
in protest, in a duet with Hate. While he sings
" Love, break thy chain ; leave Armida's bosom," she
cries, in the language of the time, " Cease, oh dreadful
Hate ! leave me under the laws of so charming a
conqueror ; leave me ! I renounce thy fearful aid !
No ! it is impossible to take Love from me without

tearing out my heart." Then Hate turns on her, telling her, seconded by the chorus, that since she has chosen Love, Love she shall have, but that in the end Love will prove her bane ; and in a short monologue, Armida, left alone, abandons herself to the tender god as her only solace.

The fourth act is both ridiculous in itself and wholly undramatic and unnecessary as far as the opera is concerned. Ubaldo and the Danish knight are first beheld struggling among the horrors and pitfalls of the scene ; but they disperse the demons and emerge into the open country by the charm of Ubaldo's magic wand. Joining in a duet, they warn each other against the seductive influences of the place. Ubaldo points out the palace of the en-chantress, wherein lies captive the hero they have been deputed to rescue. An evil spirit however appears, under the form of Lucinda, the beloved of the Danish knight, and by the aid of song, a chorus of spirits like-minded with herself, and a ballet, works upon the susceptible warrior's feelings ; and in spite of his companion's protestations, he is about to wander off with the fair one, when Ubaldo's magic staff breaks the spell, Lucinda disappears, and the scales fall from the eyes of the Danish knight. Congratulating each other and moralising profoundly over these things, they pass on, when, to complete the farce, a second spirit appears as Melissa, the beloved of Ubaldo, and the same performance is gone through again, the Danish knight this time brandishing the magic staff. Then they go on their way rejoicing, singing yet another duet to fortify each other's soul against the seductions of the enchantress, the pauses in the duet being filled with a languorous phrase carrying the mind significantly back to the scene of their temptation.

The fifth act opens in a room in the palace, where Armida is taking leave of Rinaldo ; he clings to her, begging her not to quit him. This scene is the most voluptuously beautiful that ever came from Gluck's pen. Well might he say in after-years, according to Grétry, that if ever he was damned it would be for this scene. The enchantment of the garden is upon us, cloying our taste and sealing up our eyes ; the very air seems heavy-laden with subtle narcotic fragrance ; and for once we are out of the formal salons of the eighteenth century, in the wind-swept valleys of Romanticism. Here Gluck rises for once above the grinding commonplaces of his age ; here he has communion with more secret voices, hears more secret whispers of imaginative beauty, than were ever his before or after. One wonders what strange new stirring of unknown depths of soul was in this old man of sixty, when, in the midst of labour that so often required the merest mechanical unimaginativeness, there came over him this wondrous breath of emotions unknown to him before. In the garden scene, indeed, he had sunk his senses in voluptuous delight in romantic beauty, so that the music almost seems filled with the placid murmur of the waters and the odour of the falling rose-leaves ; but here the enchantment is even more subtle, more imaginative, more romantic. It is a foreshadowing of all that was most beautiful and most seductive in Romantic art.

Weighed down with presentiments of evil, Armida

wishes to leave Rinaldo to consult the powers, but he reproaches her with lack of love. The only fault in their beautiful duet is the long passage on the word *flamme*, towards the end, traversed by the voices in concert. Leaving him at last, she calls the spirits together to charm him with their play, which they do in the customary choruses and ballets—the choruses showing more grace and flexibility of imagination than is customary with Gluck on these occasions. Rinaldo, weary of everything if Armida is not there, finally drives the spirits away ; and the next scene shows him with Ubaldo and the Danish knight, who rouse him to his better senses and persuade him to accompany them. Just as they are leaving, however, Armida returns. All her protestations of love are vain ; and Rinaldo takes leave of her in the courtliest language of the time : " Armida, it is true I flee from the too charming peril I find in seeing you ; glory demands that I leave you, and orders love to yield to duty. If you suffer, rest assured that it is with regret I disappear from your sight ; you will always reign in my memory, and, after glory, it will be you I shall love most." Her reply is less elegant and more impetuous, striking chords of genuine passion. Sincerity of feeling, again, breathes through the regret of Rinaldo as he sees her fall at his feet ; but beholding this last sign of weakness in him, Ubaldo and the Danish knight promptly rush in, and, exhorting him to be steadfast, lead him off. In the final scene, where Armida, left alone, calls upon the demons to destroy her palace about her, Gluck is once more almost at his best and highest.

As was said above, *Armida* was not altogether successful at the first performance, while the customary *sottises* were perpetrated in the journals at the first opportunity. La Harpe especially had scarcely a good word for the opera. "There was no melody in the new work; everything was carried on in recitative. The part of Armida, almost from one end to the other, was a monotonous and fatiguing shriek; the musician had made his heroine a Medea; he had forgotten that she was an enchantress, not a sorceress. In *Orphée* the melody was perceptible; there it was treated with a superiority which it would be bad grace to deny; but that was an exception; M. Gluck appeared to have made it his purpose to banish song from the lyrical drama, and seemed to be persuaded, as his partisans said, that song is contrary to the nature of the dialogue, to the progress of the scenes, and to the *ensemble* of the action." *

"I will say then to M. Gluck, in conclusion, 'I prefer your *Orphée*. It has pleased you, since that time, to write as little melody as possible. You have given up that truly lyrical plan of a drama interspersed with airs, which you yourself have expounded to us. You have come back to *Armida*, which is a very fine poem and a bad opera, to establish the reign of your melopœia, sustained by your choruses and your orchestra. I admire your choruses and the resources of your harmony. I could wish you to be more prodigal in your melopœia, and that it were more adapted to the French phrase; that it were less broken and

* Desnoiresterres, p. 209.

less noisy ; and above all, I could wish for some arias. For I like the music one sings and the verses one carries away.

"' I am not unaware that this opinion is strongly opposed to that of several of your friends, whom I like and esteem infinitely. But as, in order to like and esteem each other, it is not necessary to hold the same opinions on music, I hope they will pardon my ignorance, and that they will be content to regard me as a free lance, who, being of good faith, can never be sectarian, and whose heresy is not dangerous.' " *

This criticism roused the ire of Gluck, who replied with extraordinary bitterness in a letter to the *Journal de Paris* of 12th October :

"It is impossible, sir, for me to do anything but agree with the intelligent observations on my opera that appear in the number of your journal for the fifth of this month ; I find in it nothing, absolutely nothing, to contravene.

"I have been simple enough to believe, till now, that music, like the other arts, embraces the whole sphere of the passions, and that it cannot please less when it expresses the troubles of a madman and the cry of grief, than when it paints the sighs of love.

"Il n'est point de serpent ni de monstre odieux,
    Qui, par l'art imité, ne puisse plaire aux yeux.

"I have thought that this rule should hold in music equally as in poetry. I have persuaded myself that

* *Journal de politique et de littérature*, Oct. 1777. In Desnoiresterres, pp. 209, 210.

song, when it thoroughly takes the colour of the feeling it is to express, should be as various and as many-sided as feeling itself; in fine, that the voices, the instruments, the tones, even the pauses, should strive after one end—expression—and the agreement between the words and the song should be such that neither the poem should seem to be made for the music nor the music for the poem.

" However, this was not my only error; I thought I had noticed that the French language was less rhythmical than the Italian, and that it had not the same definiteness in the syllables; I was astonished at the difference between the singers of the two nations, as I found the voices of the one soft and pliable, those of the other stronger and more suited for the drama; and so I had decided that Italian melody could not link itself with French words. Then, when I came to examine the scores of their old operas, I found that in spite of the trills, runs, and other inappropriate devices with which they were overladen, there were yet so many genuine beauties in them that I was prompted to believe that the French had within themselves all that was required to do good work.

" These were my ideas before I had read your observations. Now, however, you have lightened my darkness; I am wholly astonished that in a few hours you have made more observations on my art than I myself in a practical experience of forty years. You prove to me that it is sufficient to be a well-read man, in order to speak on everything. Now am I convinced that the Italian is the most excellent, the *true* music; that the melody, if it is to please, must be regular and periodic, and that even in a moment of confusion, where we have to do with the vocal utterances of several persons swayed by varying passions, the composer must still maintain this regularity of melody.

"I agree with you that of all my compositions *Orfeo* alone is supportable; and I sincerely beg the forgiveness of the gods of taste for having deafened the hearers of my other operas; the number of their representations and the applause the public has been good enough to bestow on them do not prevent my seeing how pitiable they are. I am so convinced of it that I wish to re-write them; and as I see that you are passionate for tender music, I will put in the mouth of the furious Achilles a song so tender and so sweet, that all the spectators will be moved to tears.

"As for *Armida*, I will be very careful to leave the poem as it is; for, as you very perspicaciously observe, 'the operas of Quinault, although full of beauties, are yet not well adapted for music; they are fine poems but bad operas.' So that if they are written to bad poems, which, according to your view, will make fine operas, I beg you to introduce me to a poet who will put *Armida* in order, and give two airs to each scene. We will between us settle the quantity and measure of the verse, and when the syllables are complete I will take the rest on my own shoulders. I, for my part, will go over the music again, and conscientiously strike out, according to reason, all the loud instruments, especially the kettle-drums and trumpets; I will take care that nothing shall be heard

G

in my orchestra but oboes, flutes, French horns, and muted violins. And there will be no more question whence the text of the airs was taken; this can no longer matter, since we have already taken up our position.

"Then will the part of Armida no longer be a monotonous and fatiguing shriek; she will no longer be a Medea, a sorceress, but an enchantress; I will make her, when in despair, sing an aria so regular, so periodic, and at the same time so tender, that the *petite maîtresse* most afflicted with the vapours will be able to listen to it without the least damage to her nerves.

"If some wicked person should say to me, 'Sir, be careful that Armida mad does not express herself like Armida amorous,' I will reply: 'Sir, I do not wish to frighten the ear of M. de La Harpe; I do not wish to contravene nature; I wish to embellish it; instead of making Armida cry out, I want her to enchant you.' If he insists, and shows me that Sophocles, in the finest of his tragedies, dared to show to the Athenians Œdipus with his bloody eyes, and that the recitative or noted declamation by which the eloquent plaints of the unfortunate king were rendered must have expressed the deepest sorrow, I will retort that M. de La Harpe does not wish to hear the cry of a man in suffering. Have I not well grasped, sir, the meaning of the doctrine laid down in your observations? I have done some of my friends the pleasure to let them read your remarks.

"'We must be grateful,' said one of them as he handed them back to me; 'M. de La Harpe has given you excellent advice ; it is his confession of faith in music ; do thou likewise. Get all his works in poetry and literature, and search out in them everything that pleases you through your friendship for him. Many people maintain that criticism does nothing more than upset the artist ; and to prove it, they say, the poets have at no time had more judges than now, and yet were never more mediocre than at present. But get the journalists here together in council, and if you ask them, they will tell you that nothing is so useful to the State as a journal. One might object to you, that, as a musician, you had no right to speak about poetry ; but is it not equally astounding to see a poet, a man of letters, who wants to have despotic opinions on music ? ' " *

And not content with this, he published soon after, in the same journal, an entreaty to the " Anonyme de Vaugirard " (Suard) to take up the cudgels on his behalf against La Harpe.

" It seems that these gentlemen (the journalists) are happier when they write on other matters ; for if I may judge by the welcome the public has given to my works, the said public does not lay much store by their phrases and their opinions. But what think you of the new attack which one of them, M. de La Harpe has made on me ? He is a humorous doctor, this M. de La Harpe ; he speaks about music in a way that would make all the choir-boys in Europe shrug their shoulders ; he says, ' I wish,' and he says, ' my doctrine.'

Et pueri nasum rhinocerotis habent.

* Marx, ii. pp. 236–239; Desnoiresterres, pp. 210, 211.

"Will you not say a few words to him, sir, you who have already defended me so well against him ? Ah ! I beg you, if my music has given you any pleasure, give me the opportunity of proving to my friends in Germany and Italy that, among the men of letters in France, there are some who, in speaking of the arts, at least know what they are talking about." *

Suard was not long in publishing a reply to La Harpe, in which he had no difficulty in demonstrating that writer's entire lack of qualifications for the criticism of music. This brought out another letter from La Harpe, and this another from the Anonyme ; and the contest becoming general—a kind of musical Donnybrook—any one who had a little wit to spare employed it in writing comic and serio-comic letters and treatises to M. de La Harpe. There were the " Letter of one ignorant of music to M. de La Harpe ; " "Letters to M. de La Harpe from the Sieur Thibaudois de Gobemouche ; " " Letters from a Serpent de paroisse to M. de La Harpe ; " "Letters from a lady to M. de La Harpe ; " "Verses by a man who loves music and every instrument except la harpe ; " and so on. † The "Serpent de paroisse " letter is especially amusing.‡

Nevertheless, *Armida* grew in favour as time went on. It was about this time that Berton, the director of the opera, managed to get Gluck and Piccinni to dine together, and a curious anecdote is told

* *Journal de Paris*, Oct. 1777. In Desnoiresterres, pp. 211, 212.

† Desnoiresterres, pp. 213, 214.

‡ It is given in Barbedette, pp. 40–42.

respecting them. Gluck, so the story goes, had imbibed rather freely, and in the end leaned over to his rival in vinous generosity of confidence, and favoured him with his private opinion of the French. "The French," he said, "are worthy people, but they make me laugh; they want song, and they don't know how to sing. My dear friend, you are a man celebrated through all Europe. You think only of sustaining your glory; you give them fine music; are you any better for it? Believe me, here you must think of making money, and of nothing else." * Such is the profundity of after-dinner philosophy. The story is narrated by Ginguené, the biographer of Piccinni, his authority being the musician himself; and there is no reason to doubt the authenticity of it.

After a sojourn in Vienna, whither he had retired to write his next opera, Gluck made his preparations for another descent on Paris, sending word to Arnaud to make everything ready for him. An interesting letter is that to Guillard, the author of *Iphigenia in Tauris,* in which the composer discusses the construction of the opera :

". . . . Do you wish me to reply as to the essential points ? Gladly. In the first place, I will say that the changes you have made in your fourth act are to no purpose, because I have already finished the duet between Orestes and Pylades, and the final air of the act—*Divinité des grandes âmes !*—and I do not wish to alter anything in them. In what you call the fifth act, you must cut down the third strophe of

* Ginguené, "Vie de Piccinni," pp. 45–46.

the hymn, or else write a more interesting one ; people would not understand the words, *le spectre fier et sauvage*, which, besides, scarcely make the situation any more pathetic. Your verses also must be of the same style, *quatre à quatre* ; I myself have arranged the second strophe thus :

> Dans les cieux et sur la terre
> Tout est soumis à ta loi ;
> Tout ce que l'Érèbe enserre
> A ton nom pâlit d'effroi !

" If then you wish to write a third strophe, it must go like the second ; and an important thing that must not be forgotten, is, that the ceremony takes place while they are singing, and that the same air must suit the ceremony. I also want Thoas, the high priest, to enter in a fury, in the fourth scene, singing an air of invective ; and every verse must be written without recitative, so as to be sung right up to the catastrophe. By this means the dénouement would be richer by a decisive emotion and warmth, which would penetrate the actors and chorus with an irresistible effect. So, as far as you approve my idea, hasten to send me your words ; if not, I will keep to the words already written.

" Now we come to the great air that ends the act during the sacrifices. Here I want an air in which the words explain the music at the same time as the situation. The sense must terminate at the end of each verse, and not be repeated either at the beginning or end of the following verses. This is an essential condition for the verses ; though it may be disregarded in the recitative, and so much the more happily as this mode of division is a certain means for distinguishing the lyric portion from the recitative, and for relieving the melody.

" At the same time, for the words I ask of you, I want a verse of ten syllables, taking care to put a long and sonorous syllable wherever I indicate it ; your last verse must be sombre and solemn, if you wish it to be congruous with my music.

" After these four verses—or eight, if you wish, provided they are all in the same metre—will come the chorus, *Contemplez ces tristes apprêts !* and this appears to me to suit the situation very well. I want the air here to have pretty nearly the same sense. After the chorus, the air will be resumed *da capo,* or else there will simply be the four verses you have written. I explain myself rather confusedly, for my head is excited with music ; if you do not understand me, we will leave the thing till my arrival, and then it will be soon done ; the rest, I think, we will leave as it is, cutting down the recitatives here and there, wherever they seem to be too long and mere repetitions. This will not damage the work, which ought I think, to have an astonishing effect."*

About the end of November he returned to Paris with the score of *Iphigenia in Tauris.* Piccinni, meanwhile, had received rather questionable treatment. According to his own account, the poor Italian had been called in to Devismes, who asked him to set *Iphigenia in Tauris* to music, mentioning

* Desnoiresterres, pp. 250–252.

at the same time that Gluck was writing an opera upon what was practically the same poem, and giving him the assurance that his work would be produced before that of Gluck. Relying on this assurance, Piccinni had actually written two acts of the work, when he heard of the return of Gluck and the preparations for the production of the German master's *Iphigenia*. The Italian hastened to Devismes and reminded him of his promise, but in vain; and when, thinking himself now at all events released from his promise of secrecy, he told Ginguené and Marmontel of the circumstances, and showed them the poem upon which he had been working, they saw that it was utterly foolish and worthless.

Gluck's *Iphigenia in Tauris* was produced on the 18th May 1778.

The mature hand of the master is seen at once in the beginning of the overture, so broad, so free, so firm is the handling. The first theme is peaceful and flowing, representing, as the score itself says, the calm of the elements; after a few bars it breaks into the storm-music; this increases in intensity until it culminates in some piercingly high tones, and with a descent from these the voice of Iphigenia at once strikes in, without the slightest break of the stream of music in the orchestra. She implores the gods to cease their thunders and be merciful to them; the chorus of priestesses takes up the prayer, while all the time the storm goes rushing on in the orchestra, swelling to fiercer intensity; then, when Iphigenia and the priestesses have again besought the gods to be propitious, the storm dies gradually down to an exhaustion that in itself is subtly dramatic. In a magnificent recitative, filled with every variety of expression, Iphigenia relates her dream of the burning palace and the death of Agamemnon, the vision of her mother, and the turning of her own knife against the breast of Orestes. The chorus again implore the mercy of the gods, and Iphigenia resumes her lament over the woes of her house in another fine recitative, that rises into quivering passion as she cries, "O dear Orestes! O my brother!" She sees no hope of escape from the Nemesis that is pursuing the house of Agamemnon, and in an aria of the finest expression she calls upon Diana to take away her life, that has already been too long; and the chorus add yet another shade of colour to the sombre scene—"Is there no end to our tears? Are they then unquenchable? In what a circle of sorrow have the gods set our life!" No words can do justice to the superb power of the whole of this scene, through which one dramatic spirit runs from the commencement to the end. Here was that unification of parts, for which Gluck so strenuously contended, at its finest and fullest; the recitative is at times a marvel of expression, and the orchestra plays a part in it the importance of which can only be realised by a comparison of it with even Gluck's best recitative up to this time; while the chorus works into the picture so appropriately and so dramatically, with such reticence of colour and such simple directness of feeling, that it forms a perfect background to the master-passion that flashes and quivers in the central figure of Iphigenia. And equally remarkable with the technical perfection of the scene is the firm hold Gluck

G*

has upon the dramatic passion of it. At once, when the curtain rises, showing the storm-swept coast and the terror-stricken priestesses, Iphigenia becomes as tragically statuesque as in the Greek drama; she is one with the wind and the lightning; the storm of nature seems to burst again in dolorous passion from her own breast. From beginning to end, the characters stand in perfect setting, perfect harmony, with the scene around them.

The terror and outcry of the priestesses have brought Thoas to the spot, asking in superstitious fear what answer the gods have given. "Alas, they have been silent to our prayers!" replies Iphigenia, and Thoas rejoins, "It is not tears they wish, but blood!" and he tells of his haunting dread that the gods are angry with him, and how he must appease them; the earth seems to open to engulf him; in the night the thunderbolts of the gods play about his head. His aria is a finely psychological expression; Gluck, who excelled in these representations of superstitious terror, never fails to rouse fear and horror with his priests and oracles.

The Scythian followers of Thoas call in frenzied tones for a victim; and they burst out again when a Scythian enters and tells that two young strangers have been captured, one of them with despair graven on his countenance, and calling pitifully for death. Thoas bids Iphigenia prepare for the sacrifice, and commands his people to thank the gods; they break out into another savage chorus, followed by some strangely expressive ballets. Thoas demands of the captives who they are and what their mission;

Pylades answers that they cannot make themselves known. Thoas orders them to the altar, and with a cry of wild regret from Orestes, " O my friend, it is I who bring thee to death ! " and with the fierce shouts of the Scythians, the first act comes to an end.

The second act opens with a scene between the two young Greeks. Orestes is refusing the con-solations of Pylades, bemoaning his evil fate and the maleficence of the gods. In a fine aria he abandons himself to grief and despair ; most remarkable is the independence of the part allotted to the orchestra. The following aria of Pylades, in which he exhorts his friend to patience, and glories in their common suffer-ing, is one of the broadest and most uplifted melodies that ever came from Gluck's pen ; high-mindedness and simple dignity breathe through every bar of it. An attendant of the temple now enters, bidding Pylades alone follow him ; and the two friends burst into a duet of passionate declamation, that is really recitative applied to two voices instead of to one. In spite of their protests Pylades is taken away, and Orestes, left alone, calls in frenzied tones upon the gods to slay him ; then an appalling silence spreads over everything, and in deep, pathetic accents he moans " Where am I ?   What calm is this succeeding the horror that held me ? " and breaks into that masterpiece of dramatic expression, that alone would be enough to hand down the name of Gluck with honour to all time, " Now is my heart at peace again ! " Every one knows the story of Gluck's passionate answer to the critic who objected to the tumult in the orchestra as being contradictory of the

words of Orestes—" He lies !   He lies !   He has been
the murderer of his mother ! "   Pity-moving indeed is
this great aria, where the voice of the tortured man
hangs painfully and with weary complaint upon the
long-drawn notes, while the orchestra surges and
pulses beneath like an angry sea.   " My heart grows
calm again ! " moans Orestes ; " have my pains at last
outwearied the anger of the gods ?   Is the end of my
suffering at hand ?   Shall the parricide Orestes breathe
again ?   O just gods !   Avenging heaven !   Yes! my
heart grows calm again ! " and all the while, under-
neath the accents of the singer—in themselves so
weary and so pitiful—the orchestra presses forward in
a slow, inexorable march, seeming to hold the voice in
a grip of iron.

After a terrible ballet, the Furies break into a surg-
ing and regurgitating chorus—the finest Gluck ever
wrote—" Let us avenge nature and the gods ; let us
invent torments for him ; he has slain his mother ! "
On these last words the chorus pauses each time in its
rapid movement, and draws the words out in hushed
horror ; then, on the word " mother," it swells out
again with startling emphasis. And in the pauses of
their hellish song is heard the pitiable moan of Orestes,
driven to madness by their hideous speech and gestures.

While the torture is at its height Iphigenia enters ;
both she and Orestes start at the sight of each other.
Iphigenia questions him as to whence he comes, and
what purpose had brought him to those inhospitable
shores.   He replies, " I come from Mycenæ ; " where-
upon she demands of him news of Agamemnon.   In a
recitative that is constantly heightening in passion, he

replies that Agamemnon has been murdered. In hasty tones Iphigenia asks who has slain him. " In the name of the gods, ask me not ! " replies Orestes ; but she presses the question home upon him, till she falls back in horror as she hears from his lips of the treachery of Clytemnestra ; and when he further tells her that Clytemnestra has been slain by Orestes, and that Orestes himself is now dead, she is crushed beneath the misfortunes of her ill-fated house. The chorus break into a song of mourning of exquisite and noble simplicity, and Iphigenia herself pours out her grief in the well-known aria, " O unhappy Iphigenia ; " then she sings with the priestesses a lament for her brother.

In the third act, Iphigenia resolves to free one of the victims, sending him with a message to Electra. She has been seized with pity, more especially for Orestes, feeling drawn towards him by hidden movings of sympathy. In dolorous tones she reminds herself that all regrets for her brother are useless ; only in the land of night can they meet again. Orestes and Pylades are brought to her, and after disclosing to them that she also is a Greek, she announces her intention of saving one of them, for the purpose of taking her letter to Argos ; each eagerly craves the boon of life for the other. Her speech becomes grave and sad as she laments her impotence to save them both ; finally she fixes upon Orestes as the one to bear her message. When she has departed, the friends contend with each other, Pylades rejoicing in the choice of the priestess, and Orestes refusing to accept life on such conditions. In a noble aria, Pylades pleads his love for his friend, but all is vain ; and on the re-entry of Iphigenia, Orestes, swearing to immolate himself if Pylades be slain, is accepted for the sacrifice, and Pylades entrusted with the letter to Electra. He departs, vowing to return and rescue his friend.

In the fourth act, Iphigenia is on the rack of irresolution ; something within her forbids her to slay this prisoner. In an aria of magnificent passion of abandonment she calls upon Diana to steel her heart at the moment of sacrifice, that she may fulfil her duty as her priestess ; and the chorus offer up a prayer that this victim may appease the anger of the goddess. Orestes urges her to deal the fatal stroke, and in some of the most touching and pathetic music in the whole opera thanks her for her pity of him— pity he had received from no one else. The priestesses raise their voices in a solemn hymn to Diana, and Iphigenia, taking the sacrificial knife in her hand, is about to plunge it into Orestes' heart, when he cries out, at the last moment, " So didst thou die in Aulis, oh Iphigenia, my sister ! " Then Iphigenia recognises him ; but in the midst of their transports a Greek woman enters with the news that Thoas is approaching to urge on the sacrifice of Orestes ; the orchestral accompaniment here rises to an unusual height of significance. Thoas appears, reproaches Iphigenia for allowing Pylades to escape, and commands the guards to seize Orestes and re-conduct him to the altar. In vain Iphigenia pleads that the victim is her brother ; roused to frenzy, Thoas is about to slay both Orestes and Iphigenia, when he is struck down by Pylades, who has returned with a

company of Greeks.   After a short scene of terror on
the part of the priestesses and the flight of the guards
of Thoas, Diana appears and orders the Scythians to
restore her image to the Greeks ; and Iphigenia and
Orestes return to their native land.   The opera ends
with a chorus, the theme of which is based on the
final chorus of *Paris and Helen ;* but in its employment here all the tender poetry and fragrance have
fled from it.

Such was *Iphigenia in Tauris,* the last of Gluck's
great operas and the finest.   Here his imagination
and his technical craft are at their highest maturity ;
he seems to have struck a balance between the two
moods that were always in him, and that found
expression on the one side in *Orfeo, Paris and Helen*
and *Armida,* on the other in *Alceste* and *Iphigenia in
Aulis.*   There were always two separate tendencies in
Gluck—one to neglect all sensuous æsthetic pleasure
for the attainment of dramatic intensity through
declamation, the other to attempt to realise his
purpose through emotional pleasure, to which dramatic meaning should be subsidiary, though not
entirely alien.   In *Iphigenia in Tauris* he combined
these two tendencies and made them one.   It is true
that nothing need be looked for here that shall be like
the charm of *Paris and Helen,* while there is much
that bears the seal of the mood that incarnated itself in
Alceste and *Iphigenia in Aulis ;* but that is because of
the nature of the subject.   Its tragic tone lends itself
at once to that strenuous dramatic treatment that
characterises the two latter works, while at the same

time it makes a complete return to the aromatic style of *Paris* and *Armida* out of the question. But this style is still seen, though less distinctively, in union with the other ; and in the greater harmony of colour that is here spread over Gluck's earlier dramatic manner, and in a certain ease and grace and sure-footedness that make his style more telling and more artistic than it had been in the early days when he first set himself to reform the opera, *Iphigenia in Tauris* is unique among Gluck's works. It has in the highest degree the combination of high dramatic power with genuine musical sufficiency. And his thought had become by this time both more concentrated and more continuous. He gives greater unity to his scenes, carrying out one dramatic idea in them from beginning to end ; while at the same time each individual part of the music—recitative, air, chorus, accompaniment, ballet—is finer and stronger. How completely at his ease Gluck had now become in music is most clearly evident in his orchestral accompaniments, which here attain greater independence and more ample meaning than in any previous opera. What strikes us in much of his earlier work is that his mind was in some respects non-musical—that it worked on other lines, rather poetical than musical, trying to infuse into music a life that was partly alien to it. This it was, indeed, that prompted his utterance about forgetting that he was a musician ; for Gluck was at times undoubtedly non-musical in his imagination, and shared the fallacy of his century that the spheres of the arts were interchangeable. This tendency in him, however, was corrected by that more purely lyrical tendency that found its outlet in *Armida* and in *Paris*, and in *Iphigenia in Tauris* he has amalgamated these two, has taken so much of the one as was necessary to give form and colour to the other, and produced a result that is at once vigorously dramatic and enjoyably musical. And here the final victory over the Italian school was achieved. Grimm was right when he said, "I don't know whether that is melody, but perhaps it is something better. When I hear *Iphigénie* I forget I am at the opera; I seem to be listening to a Greek tragedy, with music by Lekain and Mdlle. Clairon."

The first performance was a fine one and thoroughly successful, the parts being taken by singers accustomed to Gluck's music. Mdlle. Levasseur was the Iphigenia, Larrivée the Orestes, Legros the Pylades, and Moreau the Thoas.

Gluck was of course in greater favour than ever with the Court by this time, and within a few months of the production of *Iphigenia* a new opera was demanded of him. He set to music *Echo et Narcisse*, the words of which were by the Baron Tschudi. It was produced on the 21st September 1779, but with only a moderate success; it even failed to please the following year, when it was brought out in a shorter form. According to Noverre, however it was not without merit; "the music," he says "was fresh, able, and agreeable; gorgeous scenery, charming ballets, and dresses as pleasing as they were happily contrasted, helped the opera." *

* Marx, ii. 287.

According to his custom, Gluck travelled back
to Vienna again. Age now began to tell upon him,
and a fit of apoplexy was a warning that the end was
near. He was still willing to write, however, and
arrangements were actually concluded between him
and the Paris Opéra for a new work, *Hypermnaestra*,
which was to be ready by October 1782. Then
came the rather disreputable incident of *Les Danaïdes*,
which Gluck tried to sell to the Opéra for 20,000
livres, declaring that he himself had composed the two
first acts, the remainder being by Salieri. After much
negotiation and haggling about the price, the opera
was really produced on the 26th April 1784. After
it had become a success, Gluck confessed that the
whole of the opera had been written by Salieri, he
having taken no further part in it than advising his
pupil ; this was confirmed by Salieri in a letter to the
Journal de Paris. *

The circumstances, however, were made interesting
by a letter to the *Mercure de France* from Calzabigi ;
who complained of having been pillaged in the construction of the opera, and who, after making good his
claim with some asperity, went on to say :

" I should have ended here, but I have yet more to
be unburdened of. In speaking of the music of *Les
Danaïdes* you say that ' it is easy to recognise in the
general spirit of the composition the great, firm, rapid,
and sincere manner that characterises the system of
the creator of dramatic music.'

" Here is what I have to say on the subject.

* 18th May, 1784.

"I am not a musician, but I have given great study to declamation. I am credited with a talent for reciting verses, particularly tragic verses, and more especially my own.

"Twenty-five years ago, I thought that the only music suitable for dramatic poetry, especially for the dialogue and for the airs we call *d'azione*, was that which would most nearly approach natural, animated, energetic declamation ; that declamation itself is really only an imperfect kind of music ; that it could be noted, if we could find sufficient signs to mark so many tones, so many inflexions, so many outbursts, so many softenings, and the infinitely varied shades given to the voice in declaiming. Music, then, to any verses, being in my opinion only a cleverer kind of declamation, more studied, and more enriched by the harmony of the accompaniment, I thought that here was the whole secret of writing excellent music to a drama ; that the more compact, energetic, passionate, touching, harmonious, the poetry was, the more would the music that should express it thoroughly, in accordance with its true declamation, be the genuine music of that poetry, music *par excellence.*

"It was in meditating on these principles that I believed I had found the solution of this problem. Why are there airs like *Se cerca, se dice* of Pergolesi's *Olympiade, Misero pargoletto* of Leo's *Demofoonte,* and many others, of which you cannot change the musical expression without becoming ridiculous ; without, in fact, being driven back to the expression these great masters have given them ?   And why also is there an infinite number of other airs that do admit of variations, although already noted by several composers ?

"I think the reason is that Pergolesi, Leo, and
others have achieved the true poetical expression, the
natural declamation of these arias, so that they are
spoiled by being changed ; and if there are others
susceptible of alteration, it is because no one has hit
upon their true declamatory music.

"I arrived at Vienna in 1761, filled with these
ideas. A year after, Count Durazzo—at that time
Director of the theatre of the Imperial Court, and
now ambassador at Venice—to whom I had recited
my *Orfeo*, invited me to give it at the theatre.
I consented, on the condition that the music
should be written to please me. He sent me to
M. Gluck, who, he said, would lend himself to my
ideas.

"M. Gluck was not at that time considered—
wrongly no doubt—among our greatest masters.
Hasse, Buranello, Jomelli, Pérès and others occupied
the first rank. No one understood the music of
declamation, as I call it, and it would have been
impossible for M. Gluck, not pronouncing our language well, to declaim many verses in succession.

"I read my *Orfeo* to him, and declaimed several
parts of it to him, indicating the shades I put in my
declamation, the suspension, the slackening of the
time, the rapidity, the sounds of the voice—now
forcible, now feeble and unstressed—that I desired him
to employ in his composition. At the same time I
begged him to banish the passages, cadenze and
ritornelli, and everything that was Gothic, barbarous,

and extravagant in our music. M. Gluck shared my views.

" But declamation is lost in the aria, and frequently not found again : it would be necessary to preserve an equal animation throughout, and this constant and uniform sensibility does not exist. The most striking features are lost when the fire and the enthusiasm grow feeble. That is why there is so much diversity in the declamation of different actors of the same tragic piece; or in the same actor from day to day, and from one scene to another. The poet himself sometimes recites his verses well, sometimes badly.

" I sought for signs with which at least to mark the most striking features. I invented some of these, and placed them under the words throughout *Orfeo*. It was on such a manuscript, accompanied by notes in those passages where the signs did not make themselves completely intelligible, that M. Gluck composed his music. I did the same with *Alceste*. So true is this, that, the success of *Orfeo* having been undecided at the first few performances, M. Gluck threw the blame on me.

" As regards *Semiramide* and *Les Danaïdes*, not being able to declaim these tragedies to M. Gluck, nor to make use of my signs, which I have forgotten, and which he kept along with my original papers, I contented myself with sending him ample instructions in writing. Those for *Semiramide* alone filled three entire sheets. I have kept a copy, as well as a copy of those relating to *Les Danaïdes*. I may some day publish them.

" I hope you will agree, sir, after this statement,

that if M. Gluck has been the creator of dramatic music, he has not created it out of nothing. I furnished him with the matter—the chaos, if you will; so the honour of this creation must be shared by us.

"Connoisseurs have been delighted with this new style. From this general approbation I draw a conclusion that seems to me just, that the music written by M. Millico to my *Danaïdes* should be infinitely superior to that given at Paris with my drama.

"The author of this music (whoever he may be, for I hear M. Gluck disavows it) has not followed the declamation I wrote at Vienna, while M. Millico, when composing his music, saw me every day, and even declaimed with me the pieces he had in hand. If I did not fear to occupy your precious time to no purpose, I would send you my instructions, my notes on the only monologue of Hypermnestra (act iv. scene ii.) If you should desire it, I will send them to you.

"There is only one opinion as to the excellence of the music of M. Millico; I hope that it will appear some day. I dare flatter myself that the public will think of it as the *élite* of the Neapolitan and foreign nobility has done, who heard it at the house of Count Rasoumowsky." *

Evidently Calzabigi represented the most extreme section of eighteenth-century amateurs, who wished to wed poetry to declamation instead of to music, and to imitate antiquity in all things. He certainly exaggerates his influence on Gluck, his share in *Orfeo*,

* Desnoiresterres, pp. 353–355.

and his pretensions to equal rank with Gluck as the creator of the musical drama.   Gluck did much more in *Orfeo* than follow Calzabigi's notes indicating the declamation ; if he had not, his music would have already gone the way of Millico's.

Gluck's career as an artist had already closed, and all that was left was for the magnificent physical strength of the man to die slowly out.   Since October, 1779, when he left Paris for the last time, he had taken up his residence at Vienna, in the Alte Wieden, opposite the Paulaner-kirche.   Here he lived a life of quiet artistic pleasure, eagerly sought after by visitors to the town, from whom he, in his turn, was glad to hear news of the outside world, especially news of the success of his own works.   In 1783, he had a visit from Reichardt, who, like himself, was intimate with Klopstock, and Gluck insisted on opening his piano and singing, in his always harsh and now feeble voice, some of the *Odes* and the *Hermannsschlacht*. The conversation afterwards ran on France, and the bitterness of Gluck's references to the French showed that he never forgave them for the slight they had offered him in the rejection of *Echo et Narcisse*.

One more work, *Le Jugement dernier,* he did enter upon with Salieri, but the end was near.   Three times already he had been seized with apoplexy, and he had been leading a valetudinarian existence for some time, drinking the waters and observing a strict régime. He took a pathetically broken farewell of Salieri in 1786, the old man's speech breaking helplessly into three languages :

" Ainsi, mon cher ami . . . . lei parte domani per

Parigi . . . . Je vous souhaite . . . . di cuore un bon voyage . . . . Sie gehen in eine Stadt, wo man die fremden Künstler schätzt . . . . e lei farà onore . . . . ich zweifle nicht . . . . Ci scriva, mais bien souvent."

The end came in November 1787. On the 15th of that month he was entertaining two friends from Paris; during the absence of his wife, who had gone to prepare the carriage for his daily drive, he insisted on drinking liqueurs that had been forbidden him, and within half an hour of that time he was seized with a fourth attack, and died without recovering consciousness, at the age of seventy-three. On the 17th he was interred in the cemetery of Matzleinsdorf, in a plain and humble grave, that was discovered in 1844, bearing the simple inscription : " Here lies an honest German, a good Christian, and a faithful husband, Christopher, Chevalier Gluck, master in the art of music; died 15th November 1787." By his side his widow was afterwards laid ; her epitaph is curiously in contrast with the brevity of his :

" Here lies, by the side of her husband, Marie Anna Elde von Gluck, née Pergin. She was a good Christian and the secret friend of the poor. Loved and appreciated by all who knew her, she ended her life at the age of seventy-one, not without having generously rewarded those who merited it. She died, 12th March 1800. This monument to her has been erected by her grateful nephew, Charles von Gluck, in testimony of his profound veneration." Evidently Frau Gluck's reputation for charity eclipsed that of her husband; his will runs : " I leave to the Institu-

tion for the needy, one florin ; to the General Hospital, one florin ; to the Town Hospital, one florin ;
to the Normal School, one florin ; in all four florins."
Whether this curious testament was prompted by his
desire to leave the disposition of his fortune in the
hands of his wife, or merely by pure miserliness, cannot
be known ; certainly Gluck was not lacking in worldly
goods.

The last act in the drama in which Gluck and
Piccinni had figured as antagonists was the proposal
by the latter to do honour to the memory of his
illustrious rival by founding an annual concert, at
which nothing should be performed but the German
master's music. "You know," he wrote in the
Journal de Paris, * " that this art, which owes perhaps
its charms to its mobility, and which requires, I dare
to say, a kind of inconstancy in its forms, changes in
a nation in proportion as it becomes perfected or
diffused. Perhaps that need of variety, that has so
corrupted art in Italy, will seize upon you here, and
your music of forty years hence will no longer
resemble that which pleases you to-day. The institution I propose will have the further advantage of
recalling to our composers the principles of the arts
and the kind of truth that is required in music. The
image of the grand models Gluck has left us will
preserve for those who shall succeed him the character
and method of dramatic music, in which the genius
of this great composer especially lay." † The pro-

---

* 15th December 1787.
† Desnoiresterres, p. 393.

posal, however, after much discussion, came to nothing.*

Gluck's personal character shows itself both in his music and in his physical structure. To the last he was the hardy, virile peasant, trained to rough and sturdy habits of life. In his face can be clearly seen those qualities that appear again in his music and in his correspondence ; the head is thrown back proudly and confidently ; the large and mobile mouth has an air of quick intelligence ; and the eyes look out straight and fearlessly upon the beholder. He was a man whose native strength often showed itself un-

---

* An interesting light on the relative estimates in which Gluck and Piccinni were held by the lovers of Italian music is to be had in Grimm's remarks on this letter of Piccinni. One phrase in the letter was to the effect that " the lyrical theatre owes to this great composer what the French stage owes to Corneille." On this Grimm remarks : "If the revolution effected by the Chevalier Gluck on our lyrical stage, if the character of his genius, the asperity of his productions, the sublimity of his ideas, the incoherence, the triviality, we may say, of these at times, offer strong points of resemblance between him and the father of the French theatre, it is not less true that the opera owes to Piccinni what the French stage owes to the inimitable Racine ; that purity, that uninterrupted elegance of style, that exquisite sensibility so characteristic of the author of *Phèdre*, which we do not find either in Gluck or in the great Corneille, and which constitutes the charm of the compositions of Piccinni, as it will eternally constitute the charm of the verses of Racine." (Grimm's " Mémoires," 1813, vol. iv. pp. 120–126.)

pleasantly, as in his frequently harsh relations with other men ; but this native uncompromising strength was absolutely necessary to the man who should effect the reform of the opera.   Different from Wagner, less nervously constituted, less self-conscious, he yet did a work which, though it cannot be compared to Wagner's in real depth of importance, yet marks him out far above any musical figure of his time.   How closely he shared the ideals and the fallacies of his age will be shown in the following analysis of his method.

PART II

GLUCK'S RELATIONS TO THE INTELLECTUAL LIFE OF HIS EPOCH

CHAPTER I

GLUCK's career began at an epoch when the opera had already run a comparatively lengthy course; at the time of his death it had been in existence in Europe for nearly two hundred years. In that time many changes had come over it, many new impulses had sprung up within it, and it had been modified from without by many social and intellectual forces; in less than a century, in fact, after its birth in Florence, it had altered so completely that it would scarcely have met with recognition from its founders.

1. The art-form that was subsequently to develop into the modern opera had sprung up in Italy among a set of refined scholars, imbued with all the antique erudition of the Renaissance, who wished to give to music something of the living dignity it was thought to have possessed in connection with the Greek drama. Antiquarians are now agreed that it was towards the

end of the sixteenth century that the opera, in the sense in which we employ the term, really had its birth. It is true that for generations previously there had been entertainments of which music formed an essential part; our knowledge of performances of this kind goes back at least to 1350. But the musical portions of these entertainments were for the most part merely intermezzi inserted casually between different parts of the spoken portion, and were, of course, entirely in the madrigal style then so much in vogue. It was appropriately enough in Florence, which had a healthier and more secular intellectual life than either Rome, Venice or Naples, that the spirit of revolt against the older religious forms had birth. In 1579, during the festivities attending the marriage of Francesco I., Duke of Tuscany, and Bianca Capello, some music by Merullo and Gabrieli was performed, which impressed many people by the utter incongruity between its own slow solemnity and the dithyrambic words to which it was set. It was at the house of Count Bardi that a number of enthusiasts gathered together, from whose meditations sprang the ancestor of the modern opera. Galilei set the "Ugolino" section from Dante's Purgatorio to music for one voice with a viola accompaniment, and followed this up with a setting of the Lamentations of Jeremiah. It was, however, in 1594 that Jacopo Peri and Caccini set to music the *Dafne* of Rinuccini, and laid therein the foundations of modern opera. In 1600, the same scholars collaborated in *Euridice*, which was even more successful than the previous work. The new music found a goodly number of imitators; and

how deeply the musical world was stirred by the new
style may be seen from the controversial literature that
at once sprang up about it. *   Peri's avowed purpose
in the new dramatic monodies which he wrote was
stated in the preface to *Euridice*, published at Venice.
There he tells us " how he was led to the discovery of
the new and vital style in music.   He says that in
studying the drama of the ancients he felt convinced
that they had adopted a tone of expression other than
that of everyday speech, which, though never rising
into song, was nevertheless musically coloured.   This
induced him to observe carefully the various manners
of speaking in daily life, and these he endeavoured to
reproduce in music as faithfully as he could.   Soft and
gentle speech he interpreted by half-spoken, half-sung
tones on a sustained instrumental base ; feelings of
a deeper emotional kind by a melody with greater
intervals and a lively tempo, the accompanying instrumental harmonies changing more frequently.   Sometimes he employed dissonance." †

From this time the opera advanced with almost
incredible rapidity, owing, perhaps, more to Monteverde than to any other man since Jacopo Peri.
Monteverde, besides increasing the dramatic scope of
the recitative, gave new life to the orchestra, and
introduced several new effects, such as the *tremolo* and
the *pizzicato* in the strings.   His *Orfeo* (1607) contains
the first musical dramatic duet.   Cavalli (1599–1676),

* See Naumann, " History of Music " (English translation), vol. i. p. 521.

† Naumann, i. 524.

a pupil of Monteverde, "introduced word-repetition into his ariettas—a proceeding hitherto disapproved of by the Florentine school."

It is evident from this rapid sketch that the opera from the very beginning, and by the very nature of its beginning, was a form of art destined to many and peculiar vicissitudes. It was strained and artificial from the start ; it owed its origin to no contemporary stress of feeling, but was simply a conscious and deliberate attempt to cast the Renaissance thought and emotion into the mould of the antique. How much harm, in the midst of so much good, was actually wrought by the Renaissance, it is not easy to estimate. It is certain that the virile art and literature of Greece, bursting as they did upon the weaker æsthetic sense of the Europe of that day, tended to some extent to impede the growth of the very spirit they themselves had roused. It was the adoration of the antique that was the least satisfactory part of the Italian Renaissance ; and it was of this adoration that the opera was born. It was not an art springing from the desire to express new moods in a form born of the moods themselves, but a calm attempt on the part of a few scholars, saturated with the antique, to revive what they were pleased to call "the music of the Greeks." Study of the Greek dramatists and scholiasts had convinced them that music, in some form or other, was an integral part of the dramas of Æschylus, Sophocles, and Euripides ; and as these works represented to them the highest achievements of dramatic art, no attempt to resuscitate the drama in their own day could be thoroughly successful without a resuscitation at the same time of that music which had been so inseparable from the drama at Athens. The members of the Florentine Academy never paused to consider whether the dramatic work of the Europe of the sixteenth century had anything in common with the Greek drama; whether the music of modern Europe was music at all in the sense which that word bore for an Athenian of the fifth century B.C.; whether, therefore, the relation between the poetry and music of Athens was anything like the relation between the poetry and the music of their own day; and finally, whether anything could be really known of the music of the Greeks. These considerations did not occur to them; they were less artists than scholars, and their sole aim was to bring upon the stage of the sixteenth century a form of union of poetry and music which they believed to have been the form of union between these arts in the drama of the Greeks.* And this

---

* Peri, in his preface to *Euridice*, says that the object of the Florentine reformers was " to try the power of this species of melody, which they imagined to be such as was used by the ancient Greeks and Romans throughout their dramas." And Guidotti, the editor of Cavaliere's *Dell' anima e del corpo*—another of the works in the new style— says it consists of " singular and new musical compositions, made in imitation of that style with which the ancient Greeks and Romans are supposed to have produced such great effects by their dramatic representations." (See Burney, " History of Music," iv. 18.) Even in the eighteenth century the question was still laboriously discussed whether the ancient or the modern music created the greater effect.

union mainly resolved itself, for them, into an accompaniment of the words of the drama by musical declamation.*

The spirit of imitation of the antique, that had thus called the opera into being in Italy, controlled also its choice of subject, causing this to be taken, as a rule, from the scenes and personages of the Greek mythology. Dealing as it thus did with the ghostly forms of dead antiquity, it was bound to suffer both in content and in expression. Had there been sufficient originality of thought in Italy at that time to give any life to dramatic poetry, the intellectual conditions would have been such that opera, in the sense of imitation of the antique, would have been unable to maintain itself for long ; but Italy was too weak to give birth to any original dramatic art, and there was no healthier native product to drive out this bastard growth, the offspring of weak modernity upon misunderstood antiquity. So that the opera, growing as it did out of a purely stagnant culture, took the only course that was open to it, and became the toy first of the Courts, afterwards of the public. It was necessarily monotonous and inexpansive in the vocal portions ; and so, almost from the very first, recourse had to be had to magnificent

* The abbé Grillo wrote to Caccini in 1609 : " You are the father of a new order of music, or rather of a style of melody which is not melody, a recitative-melody, noble in character and surpassing the songs of the people ; not altering the words nor depriving them of their life and sentiment, but, on the contrary, augmenting them and giving them great meaning and force." (See Ludovic Celler, " Les Origines de l'Opéra," p. 334.)

H

decorations and scenery, to atone for the lack of sensuous excitement in the story itself.*

Then, in process of time, the opera passed from the Courts to the public ; instead of being a spectacle used merely on the occasion of princely festivities, it became the amusement of the ordinary theatre-goer. And at this point of its development it underwent a change that was of vital importance in its subsequent history. It began, as we have seen, as a form of art in which a kind of musical declamation, with a simple instrumental accompaniment, was superimposed upon the words of the play. Had the learned theorists of the Florentine Academy been less intent upon the music of the Greeks, they might have seen among the country people around them a form of union between poetry and music that was much more natural, more modern, and more pleasing to the ear than the carefully reasoned system of declamation of Jacopo Peri and his fellows. There, if anywhere, was the germ of a genuine musical drama, that should take *modern* poetical feeling and *modern* musical feeling and technique, and by a spontaneous co-ordination of them should give birth to an art that would be related as naturally to modern dramatic ideas as the

* See Algarotti, " Versuche über die Architectur, etc.," p. 227. The decorations of course found their way into the opera in the first place from the masque, and were the inevitable amusement of an idle Court in a relatively low stage of culture. On the magnificence of the display in the early operas see Grove's " Dictionary of Music," art. "Opera ; " and on the masques see Burckhardt's "Civilisation of the Renaissance in Italy," pp. 415–418.

Greek dramatic form was related to Greek ideas. It was really no more consistent of the Italian scholars to attempt to force upon modern emotions the forms of antiquity, than it was of the English university scholars of the same epoch to attempt to crush our growing English tongue into the fetters of the antique prosodial rules. The same danger that had beset Italy beset England also. Here too the Renaissance threatened for a time to make literature derivative and imitative in quality rather than native and spontaneous; but from various causes England escaped the danger of a slavish admiration of antiquity. The student of the Shakespearian drama knows how, for a time, the finest intellects of the nation spent themselves in endeavouring to mould English tragedy in the fashion of the antique; and how criticism, such as that of Sir Philip Sidney in his "Defence of Poesie," equally looked upon Greek and Latin dramas as the only models worthy to be followed, and regretted the signs of an unruly tendency in English dramatists to set the classical rules at nought. The growing romanticism of feeling in England, however, made it finally impossible for contemporary art to restrict itself within the formulas of antiquity; while the wave of classical imitation that England struggled through and rose triumphant from, entirely swamped the weaker spirit of Italy. Yet though to the shaping of the opera at the commencement there went only the fastidious preferences of antique-souled scholars, and though the union of poetry and music that was already among the people was passed by in contemptuous indifference, it was this form of union—or rather the spirit of it—that ultimately prevailed. The Nemesis came when the opera passed from the courts to the public at large. From the very nature of the case, this system of arid declamation could only hope for length of days among scholars who would be content to forego the sensuous delights of music, in consideration of the greater satisfaction they felt at the idea of having resuscitated the long-lost "music of the Greeks."

But the general theatrical public, Gallio-like, cared for none of these things. They were indifferent to Euripides and Seneca, and knew nothing of Aristotle and Longinus. They demanded simply pleasure from the theatre, and as their healthy instincts began to assert themselves, the Florentine declamation gave way to a form of union between music and poetry more like that which had always existed among the people, who did not breathe the musty air of libraries, and to whom the Greek drama was a thing uncared-for and unknown. At a later time this naturalistic spirit actually came to play a considerable part in shaping one of the most delightful species of musical art—the *opera buffa;* for this was in reality the musical analogue of the *Commedia dell' Arte*, a form of rural comedy that had existed from time immemorial among the people, and that had been absolutely untouched by the new spirit of the Renaissance. And when, in the seventeenth century, the opera was settled upon the theatrical stage, it was inevitable that the old ideal of declamation should be partly put away, and that both composers and audience should take delight in new melodic freedom and harmonic richness. To this another circumstance contributed. The director of a theatre, not having at his command the vast pecuniary resources of the Courts, and being thus unable to provide the same magnificence of scenic display, was compelled to hold out to his patrons a bait of equal or greater attractiveness in the shape of superb singing.* Thus began what musical historians have called " the reign of the singers." This movement, which has generally been regarded as a retrogression of the musical drama, a falling from the high and rigorous ideal of the Florentine Academicians, was in reality a much-needed movement towards freedom and spontaneity of expression. The musical drama needed this ; for, as has already been shown, the form of opera projected by Peri and his associates was both imitative and artificial in itself, and had the further demerit of passing over the more fundamentally natural form of union between poetry and music that was already in existence among the people. That this movement towards naturalism and lyric freedom, which probably had its origin in Naples, was carried too far, and ultimately became thoroughly vicious and harmful, is regrettable from the point of view of a later time ; but the fact remains, that had the much-abused " reign of the singers " not come, or, to speak more accurately, had the lyrical principle implied by this domination not asserted itself, the opera would have missed one great motive force that gave it incalculable assistance in its movement towards modernity and freedom. It was not that the lyrical flood was evil in itself ; the evil consisted in losing sight of the grain of truth that

* See Algarotti, p. 229.

was really contained in the plan of the founders of the opera—the truth that some provision must be made for an exceptional kind of union between poetry and music in those cases where the words do not demand, or indeed suggest, a copiousness of lyrical fervour ; that is, some other musical form, interesting in itself, would have to be devised for carrying on the main business of the opera between the soli, duets and *ensembles.* The great defect of the lyrical movement was that it became too exclusively and too facilely lyrical ; it cared for sensuous pleasure and for little more ; and recitative became in consequence unutterably degraded. Here, of course, we have to seek the explanation in the social and political circumstances of the time. The Italy of that and later days was utterly incapable of such an interest in life as would have led to the creation of a genuine humanistic drama. The letters from Italy of the Président de Brosses show all too clearly the flaccid intellectual life of the time, and convince us that in such an environment it was impossible for the opera to be more than a fashionable lounge for the idle public.* The desire for a musical drama that should be poetically interesting throughout would have implied an audience capable of taking a continuous dramatic interest in the play ; and such an audience did not then exist in Italy. To take an intellectual interest in opera would have been an almost unheard-of thing for either composers or

* See De Brosses : " L'Italie Galante et Familière," *passim ;* and the testimony of Algarotti, *op. cit.* pp. 261, 267.

audience ; they asked for nothing more than passive
sensuous enjoyment. *

2. In Germany the course of the opera had been
for the most part similar to its course in Italy. It
quickly became popular there, more especially at the

---

* In the foregoing brief *résumé* of the course of the
opera in Italy, the culture-side of the development has
alone been looked at. The reader who wishes to supplement this with a view of the formal evolution of music
per se during this epoch, and the changes from the
madrigalesque style to the specifically modern manner,
may consult Dr. Parry's excellent account in his "Art of
Music," or any of the good histories of the opera. As
bearing on the question of the sudden lyrical orgasm that
seemed to come upon Italy in the early years of the
seventeenth century, and the subsequent development of
the buffo forms of opera, it is noticeable that an analogous
sociological situation had come about at an earlier epoch
in the *Commedia dell' Arte*—the ancient comedy of the
people, the real antiquity of which can scarcely be estimated. It is certain that the great vogue of the *Commedia
dell' Arte* in the sixteenth, seventeenth, and eighteenth
centuries was due to its affording the down-trodden Italian
populace a refuge from their political and social sorrows.
They played at gaiety in order not to realise that they
should be sad. Thus in the second quarter of the sixteenth century we have one of the players and writers
of the Comedy of Masks—Angelo Beolco, surnamed
Ruzzante—giving his reasons for adopting this rude form
of dramatic representation. "The world is no longer
what it was," he writes. "There is nothing but slaughter
and famine ; in the fields there is no longer any sound of
laughter and singing ; the young people no longer make

Courts ; and it was one sign of the intellectual weakness of Germany at this time that the opera took root there in Italian, instead of in the native tongue.* Artistic princes and dilettante barons thought their possessions incomplete without an Italian opera-troupe. The performances were generally in Italian, the singers and conductors were for the most part Italians ; the poets

love and marry ; we seem choked by the plague in our throats ; the very nightingale no longer sings as in former days ; happy are the dead quiet underground. Let us therefore, since we cannot cry freely, laugh in our misery." (Quoted in Vernon Lee's "Studies of the Eighteenth Century in Italy," p. 235.) On the sociological side of the dramatic forms in Italy, see also Burckhardt's "Civilisation of the Renaissance in Italy," pp. 315–321 ; and on the condition of the Italian people in the seventeenth century, see an eloquent passage in Vernon Lee's book, pp. 241, 242. The great growth of the *buffo* forms in the seventeenth century, and the rapid rise of the melodic style, were phenomena intimately related to the social life of the time ; and this popular element in music certainly did more for opera than the efforts after the antique on the part of the Florentine academicians. On the greater naturalness of the *buffo* order, see Algarotti, pp. 251, 252.

* In 1627 the drama of *Dafne* was translated from the Italian, set to music by Schütz, and performed at Dresden. The first German performance of opera on a public stage was in 1678, when Theile's *Adam and Eve* was given at Hamburg in the German language. For the most part, however, the recitatives alone were in German, and the arias, which were looked upon as the really important parts of an opera, were sung in Italian. See Burney, "History of Music," iii. 577.

and composers were either Italians or men who had been educated in Italy, and who had acquired so much of that fatal facility of imitation as enabled them to turn out work after work of merely mechanical construction ; and the subjects in Germany, as in Italy, were mainly drawn from classical mythology. The northern nations were no more capable than the southern of creating and maintaining a contemporary drama ; in every direction they spent such energy as they possessed in imitation and convention.

At the end of the seventeenth century, indeed, Germany could not be credited with the possession of an indigenous literature. Hindered by the difference in local dialects and by a general lack of intellectual stamina, she could attain to nothing more than a few cold and spiritless imitations of the French and the Greek. A new wave of intellectual energy passed over the country at the beginning of the eighteenth century, and the literature that grouped round Leibnitz gave some promise of the richer flood that was shortly to pour over northern Germany. Gottsched, though he detested the English drama and modelled his style on Racine, yet had the merit of wishing to see a truly national literature in Germany ; and the celebrated controversy between him and Bodmer—the leader of the opposite party and the champion of Milton— though puerile enough in our eyes, gave a noteworthy stimulus to literary discussion and to culture. And with a quickening intellectual life in the universities, the way was being prepared for the great revival in the middle of the century under Winckelmann, Lessing, Herder, and Kant. With this awakening in

H*

literature came a simultaneous awakening in music, and a similar note of humanistic culture is heard in both of them.   One result of the Thirty Years' War had been to throw the German mind more thoroughly upon itself; a deeply emotional nation, in its hours of depression, develops an internal world of melancholy and pious resignation.   Hence the literature was for a long time intensely religious and the philosophy wholly mystical ; and the spirit that blossomed into the hymnals of the seventeenth century lived on into the eighteenth, and culminated in the work of John Sebastian Bach.   He, indeed, was dominated almost entirely by this mysticism, which gave to his music throughout a character of intensive, melancholy longing.   Beyond all other composers he is the psychologist of the soul in its moments of placid claustral seclusion.   Handel, with more virility of temperament, and a mind strengthened and braced by constant intercourse with the world, helped to make music more thoroughly humanistic.   He is less of the cloister than Bach ; he has the strength that comes from the buffetings of nature ; there is a tension, a fibre of oppugnancy in his music, that is absent from the work of the quiet old Cantor.   Handel, though his finest compositions were written to religious words, yet gives to all his music a broader and more genuinely humanistic character than appears in the work of Bach.   In Handel, although his own operas were destined to be held in little more account than the current opera-writing of his day, music reaches out so superbly to human life, and gives such strong and vibrant utterance to the deeper emotions, that it was receiving the best possible preparation for its later task of dramatic expression.* And what was religious mysticism in Bach, and religious humanism in Handel, became in Gluck the broadest secular humanism : his artist's eye was turned solely on men as men, on human passion solely as human passion.

Even in the dark times of the Italian domination, Germany had not been lying idle ; even then the firm, sincere, musical sense of the nation had been groping after a saner ideal than that of the south. It was natural, of course, that French and Italian methods should underlie most of the German opera-work of that day ; but in several places, notably at Hamburg, various men set themselves the task of making German opera more completely German. Kusser, at the end of the seventeenth century, did good work at Hamburg, although his style was mainly foreign in intention ; and he must have greatly influenced Keiser (1673–1739), who made more for earnestness in opera than any German before Gluck. Keiser shared his countrymen's passion for the oratorio and cantata, and the seriousness of purpose and of execution required by these forms of art imported itself also into his

* It is curious to what a slight extent Handel influenced the later forms of music. As Mr. A. J. Balfour has well expressed it, "his works form, as it were, a monument, solitary and colossal, raised at the end of some blind avenue from which the true path of advance has already branched ; a monument which, stately and splendid though it be, is not the vestibule through which art has passed to the discovery and exploration of new regions of beauty." ("Essays and Addresses," p. 122.)

dramatic work. He based his airs less on the Italian form than on the German *lied*, at the same time giving greater care to the recitative ; and as he wrote operas to German words, he had all the more opportunities to give a characteristically German expression to his music. He pondered much over his art, somewhat in the manner of Gluck, and expounded his views in a preface to a collection of airs from his *Almira and Octavia*, published at Hamburg in 1706.* Like Gluck, he set his face against the abuse of contrapuntal devices in opera, and avowed his desire to deliver German music from the influence of the "protzigen Italiener und prahlerischen Franzosen." Characteristically, German is his dictum that "nicht durch Kunst, wohl aber durch Erfahrung," can the composer alone hope to do enduring work.

Keiser, however, and his successor Telemann (1681–1767), were greatly hindered by the scenic display of the opera, which in Germany, as in France and Italy, went to such proportions as almost to eclipse the work of both poet and musician, the true lords of the opera frequently being the decorator and the machinist. The gravity and naturalness of Keiser were, in fact, only importations from the *lied* and the oratorio, and were powerless for good in face of the increasing popularity of Italian music. Italians like Agostino Steffani

---

* The preface is not actually by Keiser, but by Feind. The ideas, however, are Keiser's, in the same way that the ideas in the preface to *Alceste* are Gluck's. For an excellent account of the opera in Germany, see Reissmann's "Illustrirte Geschichte der deutschen Musik."

(1650–1730) settled themselves in Germany, and won riches and position as composers and conductors; Italians like Zeno and Metastasio provided the libretti; while the most popular German operatic writers before Gluck—Hasse, Graun and Naumann—modelled their style upon that of the Neapolitan school, which was then the most brilliant in Europe. Graun, indeed, had something of Keiser's depth and seriousness, and his airs sometimes showed the influence of the earlier master. He had a training in technique equal to that of Handel, but his talent was predominantly lyrical, and his aria-writing was the finest and most expressive portion of his work. Graun, however, was unable to break away from the current Italian tradition; and not only the bulk of his operatic compositions, but even the greater part of his oratorio *Der Tod Jesu*, is in the style of the Italian opera.

A further sign of dramatic degradation was the growing vogue of *pasticcio* operas, made by patching together a number of airs and duets, sometimes from the works of one composer, frequently from the works of several. The time for the German emancipation had not yet come. All the real strength of the nation spent itself in religious music; secular art was left to French and Italian degradation. It was reserved for Gluck to bring high seriousness of purpose from the church into the theatre.

3. In France, the course of the opera was different from what it had been either in Italy or in Germany. The ballet—a medley of dances, song, dialogue and chorus—had long been a popular French form of

entertainment, particularly at the Courts; and the French opera had really sprung up out of this.

As early as 1581, on the occasion of the marriage of the Duc de Joyeuse with Mdlle. de Vaudemont, a work of this kind was given, entitled *Le ballet comique de la rayne, rempli de diverses divises, mascarades, chansons de musique et autres gentillesses;* the words were by Baltazarini, the music by Beaulieu and Salomon. The first French opera, in the ordinary sense of the word, was *La pastorale* (1659), the words of which were by the Abbé Perrin, and the music by Cambert; and so successful does this appear to have been that it was quickly followed by others by the same composer. Some impetus was given to dramatic composition in France by the king's letter of 1668, giving Perrin the exclusive right of these performances; three years after, the first opera-house was built in Paris, and opened with a pastoral, *Pomona,* the words again being by Perrin and the music by Cambert. A new craftsman, however, had by this time appeared upon the scene; one who was destined to give so forward an impulse to the French opera as to have his name erroneously coupled with it as its founder. In the same year that saw the production of *Pomona,* Perrin delegated his privilege to Lully, an Italian by birth, but a Frenchman in feelings and ideas. He opened his reign at the theatre with *Les fêtes de l'Amour et de Bacchus,* the words being a pasticcio from the ballets of Quinault. Then, in 1673, came the first real step towards the consolidation of the opera, in the production of *Cadmus,* —a *tragédie lyrique* in five acts; the poetry by

Quinault, the music by Lully. They co-operated in several other works : *Alceste* (1673), *Theseus* (1675), *Carnaval* (1675), *Atys* (1676), *Isis* (1677), *Persée* (1682), *Phaëton* (1683), *Amadis* (1684), *Roland* (1685), *Armida* (1686), &c. ; while for some time Lully worked with Thomas Corneille, producing *Psyche* (1678), and *Bellerophon* (1679).

From the beginning French opera was peculiarly hampered both in form and in expression. Its courtly origin imposed some strangely rigid necessities upon it. Its subjects it of course drew from classical mythology or from the romances of chivalry, following the fashion of the time ; and though the opera was everywhere employed as a medium for flattery of potentates, in France this adulation was so gross, and dominated the opera so completely, that it may almost be said that everything was sacrificed to this. * The mode of working followed by Lully is an indication of the prevailing taste in opera in the Paris of the seventeenth century, and at the same time a revelation of the difficulties with which French opera had always to contend. In selecting the story from Greek or Roman mythology, special care of course had to be taken that everything should be favourable to flattery of the monarch. To this end, several subjects were submitted to the judgment of Louis ; the one selected

---

* On the influence of Louis' " protection " upon the French intellect of the time, the reader may consult Buckle's " History of Civilisation," vol, i. chap. xi. Buckle is historically right in his condemnation of the protective spirit, though his sociological conclusion is of course open to question.

by him was then passed on to Lully, whose first business was to plan out the decorations and the dances. It next came into the poet's hand, and after his portion of the work had been approved by the Academy, Lully set it to music, making, however, any change that suggested itself to him. Thus music was really quite a secondary thing in the early French opera. Dances and decorations played a very large part in it, and when we consider the tone of French social and intellectual life at that time, and the high contemporary development of the specialised art of poetry, it is easy to conceive how the verbal substratum came to bulk more largely in importance than the music. There was in France none of the sensuous lyrical outpouring that had so strangely and so rapidly transformed the Italian opera. In his recitative, Lully reduced music almost to a minimum. He did not attempt to dominate it, either in time, in rhythm, or in intervals, by specifically musical feeling ; he characterised it instead by a method that consisted in accentuating the metrical and prosodial elements of the words themselves. It is a well-known peculiarity of music that it makes light of the relationship of words and syllables and accents as these occur in ordinary speech or in poetry, claiming to do this by the fact of its addressing a higher rhythmical and accentual sense than is appealed to in poetry or in prose ; and this music does even in usual recitative, where at least some pretence is made to give a musical pleasure over and above the mere intellectual significance of the words. There is very little of this in Lully ; what he does in recitative is to follow closely

the accent of the words, and even rigidly to retain the
verbal rhythm by frequent changes of time—moving
from common time to ¾ time and back again, every
few words, thus : | Vous passez sans me | voir ;
craignez-vous ma pré | -sence ?   Je vous aime Thé |
-one, et ce soupçon m'offense.   Que ma veuë aujourd-
huy vo' cause d'embar | -ras, Avouëz qu'en ces | lieux
vous ne me cherchiez | pas ?   Je cherchais la Reyne,"
&c.*

Naturally, a similar method of procedure was
employed in the airs.   There was little or no feeling
in them ; being often intended mainly for the adulation of the monarch or his favourites, they were
lavishly besprinkled with witty or sententious sayings
that defied emotional treatment.   The aria was thus
restricted to more or less conventional forms, and the
music was added to the words with little thought of
their essential inappropriateness for it.   So characterless, indeed, were Lully's melodies, that they were
easily applicable to the most dissimilar circumstances ;
and it is related of Guion that when in prison at
Vincennes, he employed his time in writing mystical
hymns to these operatic melodies of Lully.†   The
relations of the composer towards music in the opera
were in fact very ill-defined.   The art being still
almost in its infancy, it was difficult for it to struggle

---

* Scene from *Phaëton*, quoted from Reissmann, " C. W.
von Gluck," p. 94.   Reissmann erroneously prints *sous* for
vous as the first word.   The recitative commences in common time, and then successively changes to ¾ time and
back again.

† Reissmann, p. 96.

against the combined influences of a society that was essentially anti-musical in culture, and a powerful and well-developed poetical drama.*

Yet something of the same inevitable change which we noticed in Italy took place here also. For some time recitative remained where Lully had left it, and the opera was on the whole conducted on the lines laid down by him. It was in this spirit that his sons Louis and Jean Louis worked, as well as his pupil Colasse. But Marais (1650–1718) improved the aria slightly, giving it a greater lyrical expansiveness and a closer dramatic coherence ; and a similar tendency was apparent in the other men who took up the opera at that time—Desmarets, Campra, Destouches and others. In process of time the French aria began to assume the Italian style, and from such dangers to dramatic expression as lay in this assimilation the French aria was delivered by Rameau (1683–1764), who commenced his operatic career at the age of fifty-one. Rameau as a musician was in every way superior to Lully. He gave greater significance to the recitative, and brought the aria round from its seductive Italian form to the older French style, only retaining so much of the Italian method as was necessary to give a finer freedom to the melody. That he consciously strove to produce a more truly national aria is shown by his

* For a brilliant study of the intellectual world of the time of Louis XIV., see Taine's article on Racine in his "Nouveaux Essais." Naumann ("History of Music," i. 597, 598) summarises Lully's qualities and defects very well, but fails utterly to correlate them with the intellectual conditions of his time.

use of the phrase *Air italien* whenever he uses the Italian form in its entirety. Added to this, his orchestration, his counterpoint, his rhythm, and his treatment of the chorus all showed an advance on Lully ; and it was probably the dramatic nature of his rhythm that attracted the attention of Gluck during his Parisian visit of 1745.

The performances of the Italian Bouffons in Paris in 1752 revealed to the astonished ears of the French a kind of music of the possibilities of which they had previously had little conception.

As we have seen, the Italian *opera buffa* was in many respects a healthier and more natural growth than the *opera seria* ; it was more cognate with the real feelings of that portion of the Italian people that had escaped the impulse of classical imitation during the Renaissance ; and it steered clear of much of the solemn and inflated absurdity of the serious opera. What recommended the work of Pergolesi, Atella, Jomelli and their fellows to the French public of 1752, however, was their free, expansive and seductive melody, and the genial atmosphere that pervaded the whole music ; it must have been felt as a dear-bought relief from the turgid declamation or the monotonous plain-song of many of the native compositions. The literary war that sprang up over the Bouffons, as, at a later time, over the music of Gluck, was an indication of how deeply the sense of the French theatrical public was stirred ; and the new impulse communicated by the visit of the Italians undoubtedly influenced French music for good. The French were already possessed of an *opéra comique* with many pleasing points, and the warmer style and more spontaneous handling of the Italians were now communicated to it ; the work of Duni, Monsigny, and Grétry would certainly not have been so charming as it was, had the war of the Buffonists and anti-Buffonists never taken place.* And the healthier and more spontaneous spirit that thus gave life to the comic *genre* found its way also into the department of serious opera, influencing it for good. French music on the whole was, however, in the latter half of the eighteenth century, a subject of scorn for all Europe, which was then fascinated by the Italian style. "The long and pertinacious attachment to the style of Lulli and his imitators in vocal compositions," writes Burney, "to the exclusion of those improvements which were making in the art in other parts of Europe during the first fifty years of this century, have doubtless more impeded its progress than want of genius in this active and lively people, or defects in their language, to which Rousseau and others have ascribed the imperfections of their music." And again : "When the French, during the last century, were so contented with the music of Lully, it was nearly as good as that of other countries, and better patronised and supported by the most splendid prince in Europe. But this nation, so frequently accused of more volatility and caprice than

---

* The war between the Italian and the French schools was really much older than 1752. Fifty years before that time there had appeared a "Parallèle des Italiens et des Français en ce qui regarde la Musique et l'Opéra," by the Abbé Raguenet, which was answered furiously by Freneuse. See Burney, "History of Music," iv. 608.

their neighbours, have manifested a steady persevering constancy to their music, which the strongest ridicule and contempt of other nations could never vanquish." *
And again : " Indeed, the French seem now the only people in Europe, except the Italians, who, in their dramas, have a music of their own. The serious opera of Paris is still in the trammels of Lully and Rameau, though every one who goes there either yawns or laughs, except when roused or amused by the dances and decorations. As a *spectacle*, this opera is often superior to any in Europe ; but as *music*, it is below our country psalmody, being without time, tune, or expression that any but French ears can bear ; indeed, the point is so much given up by the French themselves, that nothing but a kind of national pride, in a few individuals, keeps the dispute alive ; the rest frankly confess themselves ashamed of their own music."†

Such was the verdict given upon French music by a cultured *bon vivant* of the last century.

Surveying the whole field of opera at the time, it is evident that it had come to an *impasse*. The comic opera was too restricted in subject and method, and too far removed from the deeper thought of the time, to win for itself any great place in the intellectual world ; while the serious opera was such a mass of absurdities and anomalies, so vitiated by bad libretti and degraded by the unhappy facility of numberless insignificant

---

* Burney, " History of Music," iv. 607, 610.
† Burney, " Present State of Music in Germany, &c.,"
1773, i. 54.

composers, that it was almost everywhere a byword
and laughing-stock to the wise, an object of contempt
for those who were not musical by nature, and an
object of regret for those who were.*

* In the *Revue des deux Mondes* for 15th July of this
year there is an article by M. René Doumic on " L'Opéra
et la Tragédie au xviime Siècle," *à propos* of a recently
published volume on the " Histoire de l'Opéra en Europe
avant Lully et Scarlatti," by M. Romain Rolland. M.
Doumic's article is an excellent study, from the non-
musical side, of the connection between the opera and the
drama in the seventeenth century. He notes the artificial
nature of the opera-cult of the time : " Le goût de l'opéra
est au xviime siècle une forme de la manie de l'exotisme.
Il rallie tous les 'snobs' de l'époque. . . . . Une cour
galante, le monde élégant, les femmes et les marquis, tous
les doucereux et les enjoués, ceux qui préfèrent le 'vain
plaisir' aux jouissances de l'esprit, ceux qui ne demandent
à l'art que de les amuser, tels sont ceux pour qui se prépare
et au gré de qui se façonne le divertissement de l'opéra.
C'est le triomphe de l'influence mondaine." He shows
that the opera even infected the poetical tragedy of the
time, and led to aberrations on the part of Corneille and
Racine, and quotes Grimm in evidence of the unpsycho-
logical nature of opera and its inferiority to tragedy : " Le
merveilleux visible," says Grimm, "n'aurait-il pas banni
tout intérêt de la scène lyrique ? Un dieu peut étonner,
il peut paraître grand et redoutable ; mais peut-il
intéresser ? Son caractère de divinité ne rompt-il pas
toute espèce de liaison et de rapport entre lui et moi ? "
(Compare also Dryden's preface to "Albion and Albanius,"
and a surprisingly good statement of the weakness of the
early opera on the psychological side in Rousseau's
" Dictionnaire de la Musique," art. " Opéra.") Saint-

Evremond also had fears for the drama: "Ce qui me fâche le plus de l'entêtement où l'on est pour l'opéra, c'est qu'il va ruiner la tragédie, qui est la plus belle chose que nous ayons, la plus propre à élever l'âme et la plus capable de former l'esprit." M. Doumic grows somewhat pessimistic over the future encroachments of the opera, and is inclined to lay to its charge some faults of the modern stage in general and of Victor Hugo's dramas in particular. M. Rolland promises a further volume, showing the influence of the opera on the tragedy of the eighteenth century.

CHAPTER II

As we have seen, the one musician who had it within him to reform the opera spent almost half a century of his life before he moulded into enduring concrete form the ideas that had been so gradually taking shape in his brain. It is, of course, impossible to say with any certainty when these ideas first became definite ; in all probability they were of quiet and imperceptible growth. It is essential to bear in mind the physical constitution of Gluck, as well as his intellectual surroundings, if we would arrive at an understanding of his work. From all we know of him— his birth, his ancestry, the early conditions of his life, his later relations with men—it is clear that much of his forthright spirit of innovation was simply the intellectual expression of a healthy, vigorous, independent, unsophisticated nature, forcing itself, in spite of all opposition and of every seduction, into the way that was most natural to it ; Gluck was merely following the line of least resistance. If his system, to take the most idealistic view of the case, was the outcome of his reflection, this reflection, for the most part, was in turn simply the formulated and conscious expression of the impulses of his physical nature. It was as impossible for a man of his temperament to take up finally with anything but an honest and natural dramatic system, as it would have been for a Newman to prefer Rationalism to Roman Catholicism, or for a Rossetti to become a devotee of the classics. Physiological necessity was at the bottom of Gluck's rejection of the tawdry unreality of the Italian opera-style of his day.

So that it is as unwise as it is impracticable to attempt to fix any one moment for the genesis of Gluck's reformatory ideas. Co-operating, too, with the personal element of his nature would be the factor of nationality, which would give him, in common with his great German contemporaries, a leaning to earnestness and directness in music rather than to the floreate and aromatic sensuousness of the southern composers. We saw that even in his first opera, composed for the Italian stage, there was a certain northern rigidity and reserve that marked it out as the work of a *tedesco;* and we have had to chronicle, in the operas of his early and middle periods, many indications of the later Gluck —passages where the serious, intensive Teuton showed himself under the counterfeit presentment of an Italian mask. And allowing for the deliberateness of motion of Gluck's mind—for his six great works indicate that his was a cautious, slowly moving intellect—it is certain that he would have attained to greater freedom and naturalness at an earlier period of his career, had it not been for the soul-deadening system of artificiality and commonplace under which he had the misfortune to live. The advocates of aristocratic patronage of art have only to turn their eyes to the music of the eighteenth century to see the evils such a system can work, unless directed by men of the widest knowledge

and utmost catholicity of culture. Music, being the
art that ministers most exclusively to sensuous pleasure,
found greater difficulty than the other arts in throwing
off the burden of commonplace convention that was
imposed upon it by its protectors. In the philosophy
of the time, the tendency was to break the intellectual
fetters that held men in subjection to constituted
authority, and to restore to human nature something
of the dignity that was thought to be its natural condition. But this spirit of intellectual revolt found
scarcely an answering echo in the world of music.
The generally degrading system of aristocratic
patronage, that almost inevitably sets up false and
tawdry ideals in the artist and his public, and is a direct
incentive to servility, was in full force in the musical
world of the eighteenth century, holding the artist
down, narrowing and degrading his ideal, making him
more careful to write in accordance with the taste of
his patron than with regard to his duties to himself as
an artist, and forcing him into the groove of conventionality and facile artifice. It has already been
pointed out how this system of patronage left its mark
on the composers of the eighteenth century, and how
the fact that Gluck gradually rose above it, bears eloquent testimony to his innate independence and virility.
Under a happier system, whereby he would have been
less dependent for his daily bread upon the pleasure of
a patron, he would in all probability have outgrown the
follies of the current opera at a much earlier date ;
that he ever managed to outgrow them, that he ever
learned to strike a chord of sincerity in that world of
hollow artifice, makes his figure bulk like that of some

solitary giant above the dwarfish forms of his contemporaries.

He was not alone, of course, in his perception of the absurdities and the shortcomings of the opera of the time. Other men before him had called attention to these, some with satirical contempt, like Marcello, others, like Algarotti and Addison, with a genuine desire to base the musical drama on better principles. Marcello's brilliant satire, *Il Teatro alla moda*, is well known; it is an unmerciful exposure of the imbecility of the opera of his day, down even to the minutest details. Every one, again, has heard of the *mot* of the French wit, that when anything was too silly to be said, they sang it; and some of Addison's happiest irony is directed against the follies that strutted the boards in such bombastic pride. D'Alembert, La Bruyère, and Boileau had laughed at the absurdities of the opera, and Panard had thrown them all together into exquisitely humorous verse in his poem, "What I saw at the Opera,"* which for delicacy of satire surpasses Addison. Saint-Evremond, speaking of the opera, had said : " If you wish to know what an opera is, I answer that it is a strange production of poetry and music, where the poet and the musician, each bored by the other, take the utmost possible trouble to produce a worthless performance. A piece of nonsense packed with music, dances, machines, and decorations, is magnificent nonsense, but nonsense all the same." Dryden had stigmatised it in a couplet wherein

* For Panard's poem see Crépet, "Les Poètes Françaises," vol. iii. p. 195.

the opera is made to stand as the type of foolish
work :

> For what a song or senseless Opera
> Is to the living labour of a play,
> Or what a play to Virgil's work would be,
> Such is a single piece to history.

La Fontaine also satirised the scenic display of the
opera, and the occasionally ludicrous miscarriages of
the machinery, somewhat in the style of Panard :

> Souvent au plus beau char le contrepoids résiste ;
> Un dieu pend à la corde et crie au machiniste ;
> Un reste de forêt demeure dans la mer,
> Ou la moitié de ciel au milieu de l'enfer.

The most remarkable book on the opera, however,
was that of Algarotti,* which deserves detailed consideration because of its temperate exposure of the
weaknesses of the opera, its anticipation of many later
theories, including one or two of Wagner's, and the
great similarity between the reforms proposed by him
and those actually effected by Gluck, and detailed by
the composer in his various papers and letters.   The
book is consequently of some importance in a comparative study of the æsthetic ideas of the time.

After reviewing the history of the opera from its
origin to his own day, Algarotti considers in detail all
the component parts of the opera—the libretto, the
music, the art of singing and of recitative, the ballet
and the decorations ; offering suggestions in each

* "Saggio dall' Opera in Musica," Livorno, 1763.   It
was translated into English in 1767, and again in 1768.

case as to the reforms that are needed. He saw, like Gluck and like Wagner, that the first reform must be in the libretto, since no good dramatic music could be written to stupid or uninteresting words. " All these abuses must be abolished, and the helm again given into the hands of the poet, from whom it has been wrongly taken "; * and the musician, having received a good poem to work upon, must follow the poet faithfully. After referring to the ancient union of music and poetry and their subsequent disruption, he goes on to say : " This great evil can only be remedied by the taste and understanding of the composer, by his keeping in view the purpose of the poet, and by agreeing to be guided by him, before even a note has been set on paper—as Lully by Quinault and Vinci by Metastasio ; for this alone is the true and proper theatre-discipline." †

The overture was to anticipate the opera : " Among the other abuses and imperfections of the present-day opera one must be first considered, that strikes the ear immediately the opera commences. This is the symphony. It always consists of two *allegro* movements and one *grave*, makes as much noise as it can, is of the same invariable pattern, and is always conducted in the same manner. . . . Its chief function may be said to be the annunciation of the subject, and the preparing of the hearer for impressions that shall

* P. 225. I quote from the German translation of Algarotti's book : "Versuche über die Architectur, Mahlerey, und musicalische Opera," Cassel, 1769.

† Pp. 238, 239.

arise from the drama that follows ; it must consequently have a form suited to the whole, like the beginning of a good orator's speech. At the present day, however, the symphony is looked upon as something absolutely unconnected with the drama—a mere piece for trumpets and drums, whereby the ears of the audience may be temporarily captured and stunned." *

A better recitative was wanted, together with a greater cultivation of *obbligato* recitative. " It appears as if our composers thought the recitative not worth any trouble ; it gives little pleasure, and can therefore expect little honour " ; † then he gives an account of the careful manner in which Jacopo Peri wrote his recitative. " It was manifold and varied, and modelled itself on the words. Now it was as rapid as speech itself, now it went slowly, bringing out significantly the inflexions and accents that spring from the might of passion. It was listened to with pleasure, because it was written with such diligence ; and frequently some trait in the recitative affected the hearer more powerfully than any aria of our own time has been able to do. Even to-day it pleases when it is in the *obbligato* form, accompanied by the orchestra ; and it would be better if it were more frequently so written." ‡ Like Gluck, he wished to minimise the great disparity between the aria and the recitative. " Another good effect would result from the more usual employment of the *obbligato* form ; the marked contrast between the recitative and the arias would be lessened, and a finer agreement between the various parts of the opera

* P. 240.   † P. 240.   ‡ P. 242.

would result." *   Trills and ornaments were incompatible with dramatic expression in the historical opera, where actual passions were supposed to be represented on the stage ; † and he pointed out, as Addison had done, ‡ the absurdity of pausing in the music when such a word as *padre* or *figlio* occurred, in order to give a tender expression to these words, quite irrespective of the general tenor of the music.   " These gentlemen fancy by such means to give to these words their proper *sentiment*, and at the same time to import a pleasing variety into their music.   I take leave to say, however, that this is a *dissonance of expression*, unbearable to any rational being ; that the composer must not express the sense of single words, but the sense of the whole passage. . . . . " §   In the same way he protested against the too frequent use of the *da capo* and the repetition of words : " And how long-winded and unbearable are those eternal repetitions and that unintelligent piling-up of words, simply for the pleasure of the music ! These words should only be repeated where they are required by the circumstances of passion, and where the whole sense of the aria is at an end. The first part of the aria should seldom be reintroduced ; this is a modern discovery, and quite contrary to the natural course of speech and passion, which never return on themselves ; and when once

---

* P. 243.   † P. 231.

‡ See *The Spectator*, No. 18 : " History of the Italian Opera."

§ Pp. 248, 249.   See also Du Bos : " Réflexions Critiques sur la Poésie et sur la Peinture," 5me ed., 1747, vol. i. p. 452.

the end is reached, and the fire is at its height, it is difficult to maintain this if what has gone before is repeated." *

The ritornelli are "too long, and generally superfluous. In a passionate aria, for instance, it is in the highest degree improbable that the actor should stand with his arms crossed, waiting for the ritornello to come to an end before he can give his passion play. And further, when the vocal part has actually begun, what use are the four violins in the accompaniment, except to drown it and make it unintelligible?" †

Better orchestration is needed, and resort must not be had to a too pedantic technique ; counterpoint is of no value when the composer's purpose is the expression of passion, though it has its uses in church music. ‡ A thorough reform is wanted in the aria : "Seldom does any one trouble himself to make his airs natural in method and conformable to the sentiment of the words ; and the many variations that are used to turn and wind about in them are rarely related to a common point of unity. The first thought of all our composers at the present time is to flatter and delight the ear in any way, and to be constantly surprising it. To move the heart, to keep the imagination on fire—what care they about this?" § Finally : "All these irregularities will never disappear, however, until the time when composers and singers shall no longer ignore the very foundation of music ; when the recitative, the most essential part of the drama, shall no longer be so

* P. 248.   † P. 244.
‡ P. 254.   § Pp. 246, 247.

sadly disfigured and neglected, and when the arias themselves shall be delivered in a better manner." *

These extracts will be sufficient to show the close similarity between the reforms suggested by Algarotti and those actually carried out by Gluck, as well as formulated by him in his writings and conversations. Altogether, Algarotti's book is well worth the attention of the historian and the student ; it is one of the best of the eighteenth-century treatises on the opera.

It only remains to ask the question—Had Gluck seen Algarotti's work ? † It seems at least probable that he had become acquainted with it, for the book was well known in France, Germany and England ; ‡ and the close similarity between Algarotti's ideas and his own is remarkable.

* P. 261.

† Gluck, of course, began the reform of the opera with *Orfeo* in October 1762 ; Algarotti's essay was published in the beginning of 1763. What constitutes the great importance of the essay, however, is the almost literal agreement between the ideas expressed therein and those of Gluck's preface to *Alceste*. It will be remembered that this preface was published with the opera in 1769 (two years after the first performance of *Alceste*), and it is quite possible that Gluck had read Algarotti's essay before then.

‡ A translation was published in Glasgow in 1768.

I

CHAPTER III

WE are now in a position to look at Gluck's own ideas as set forth by himself. His great manifesto was the celebrated preface to *Alceste*, which ran as follows :—

"When I undertook to set the opera of *Alceste* to music, the object I had in view was to avoid all those abuses which the misapplied vanity of singers and the excessive complaisance of composers had introduced into the Italian opera, and which had converted one of the finest and most imposing of spectacles into one of the most wearisome and most ridiculous. I sought to reduce music to its true function, that of supporting the poetry, in order to strengthen the expression of the sentiments and the interest of the situations, without interrupting the action or disfiguring it with superfluous ornament. I imagined that the music should be to the poetry just what the vivacity of colour and the happy combination of light and shade are to a correct and well-composed design, serving to animate the figures without altering their contours.

"So I have avoided interrupting an actor in the warmth of dialogue, to make him wait for a wearisome ritornello, or stopping him in the midst of his discourse, in order that on some suitable vowel he may exhibit the agility of his fine voice in a long passage, or that the orchestra may give him time to take breath again. I have not thought it my duty to hasten through the second part of an air when this second part was the most passionate and the most important, in order to repeat the words of the first part four times ; nor to finish the aria when the sense is not complete,* in order to give the singer the opportunity of showing in how many ways he can vary a passage. In a word, I have sought to banish from music all the abuses against which good sense and good taste have so long protested in vain.

" I have thought that the overture should prepare the spectators for the character of the coming action, and give them an indication of its subject ; that the instruments should only be employed in proportion to the degree of interest and of passion involved, and that there should not be too great a disparity between the air and the recitative, in order not to spoil the flow of the period, to interrupt the movement inopportunely, or to dissipate the warmth of the scene.

" I have thought, again, that my main task should be to seek a noble simplicity, and I have avoided parading difficulties at the expense of clearness ; the discovery of any novelty has seemed to me precious only in so far as it was naturally called forth by the situation, and in harmony with the expression ; lastly, there is no rule I have not thought it my duty to sacrifice willingly in order to make sure of an effect.

* Gluck himself has committed an equal absurdity to this in the aria in *Paris and Helen*, in which he finishes a three-syllable word on the second syllable, in order to end the musical phrase there. See p. 101.

"These are the principles by which I have been guided ; happily, the poem lent itself admirably to my design ; the celebrated author of *Alceste*, Signor Calzabigi, having conceived a new plan for the lyrical drama, in the place of flowery descriptions, useless comparisons, and cold and sententious moralizing, had substituted strong passion, interesting situations, the language of the heart, and a continually varied spectacle. Success has justified my views, and the universal approbation of a city like Vienna has convinced me that simplicity and truth are the only principles of beauty in works of art.

" At the same time, I know all the risks one runs in combating prejudices that are deeply and strongly rooted."*

The preface to *Paris and Helen* has already been quoted, as well as various observations on his art made by Gluck in conversations with Corancez and others, and in letters to the French journals.

It will be observed how distinctly the statement in the letter to the *Journal de Paris* (12th October 1777), as to the equality of poetry and music, clashes with the above theory, that music should merely be the handmaid to poetry. In his argument with La Harpe, Gluck had said that music and poetry should stand in a relation of equality to each other, so that neither should appear to dominate the other. Marx notices the contradiction, and tries to explain it away.† "We

---

* Marx, i. 440–442 ; Desnoiresterres, pp. 65, 66 ; Barbedette, pp. 74, 75.

† Marx ii. 240. See also i. 447–450.

have to notice here what Gluck says of the relations between poetry and music in the opera ; the relation between them must be such that neither the music shall appear to have been made for the poetry, nor the poetry for the music ; that is to say, that each is to have its full rights, neither being subordinated or sacrificed to the other. This seems to be the complete theory, and affords the necessary correction to the mistaken representation of the Dedicatory Epistle. At the same time it may be pointed out to those who love to argue that in Gluck's work the music is sacrificed to the words, that here we have a weighty proof of his holding just the opposite opinion." The defence of Marx, however, is sophistical and unscientific, being dictated solely by the spirit of hero-worship, and a dim consciousness that Gluck must at any cost be made to appear self-consistent. It is more reasonable to look upon the two contradictory statements simply as expressions of Gluck's ideas at two different epochs. Every æsthetic theory must undergo modification at some time, and the relation between poetry and music that suggested itself to Gluck in the first days of his reforming zeal was different from that conceived by him when the earlier crudities had been softened down, and when, in the composition of *Armida,* he felt his power as a musician to be greater than it had ever been before. To try to harmonise Gluck's contradictory statements by a process of ingenious dialectic, and by reading into his theories the æsthetic of our own day, is to ignore the fundamental similarity between Gluck's own early ideas and those of almost every æsthetician of his time, and to forget that the old

theory of the subordination of music to poetry was due
historically, as in the personal case of Gluck, to the
relatively imperfect stage of development to which
music had then attained.   To understand completely
the genesis and the working of Gluck's ideas we shall
have to go very far afield into the æsthetic literature
of the time.   In dealing with him we are met with
the difficulty that, unlike Wagner, he wrote very little
in a systematic manner upon his art; and though with
a little analysis we can discover in his music the
mental characteristics and the æsthetic theories that
helped to give it its distinctive quality, this is both
more difficult and more unsafe than the deductions we
could make from a reasoned system argued out in
prose.   Nevertheless, by bringing together the ideas
that underlay the ordinary writings on music in the
eighteenth century, we shall be able to recognise in
these the theories that controlled Gluck's system of
composition.   Rarely has there been an epoch in
which such æsthetic unanimity has prevailed as in the
eighteenth century.   Italy, France, Germany, and
England turned out almost precisely the same ideas
.upon the function of music and its relations to poetry;
and by reducing these to something like fundamental
principles and comparing them with what we know of
Gluck's verbally-expressed ideas, we shall be in almost
as good a position to apply them to his principles of
musical composition as if he had expressed himself
voluminously upon his art.

Starting from the preface to *Alceste*, as the first
revolutionary manifesto of the composer, we find that
this resolves itself into two main factors.   There is

on the one side the revolt against artificiality, the resolve to curb the power of the singers, to denude music of the foolish and superfluous ornaments by which it had been defaced, the desire to return to nature, to be simple and sincere—what, in fact, we may designate the destructive and polemical part of Gluck's faith. On the other side there is the declaration of what he held to be the true æsthetic function of music, its relation to poetry, to the other arts, and to nature. All his writings, indeed, group themselves round these two main points. On the one hand he wars with the abuses of the conventional opera; on the other he reveals his own views upon the æsthetic of music. Let us look at the intellectual and the social genesis of these two factors in his work.

In the preceding chapter we have seen that for many years before Gluck's reform, various writers had been calling attention to the absurdities and failings of the opera. This revolt against the folly of the music of the time was part of a wider feeling of dissatisfaction at the artificialities of both art and life. In France there was a strong feeling against the conventionality of the stage, to which voice was given by Diderot. In Italy the serious opera had degenerated into a mere lounge, where any amusement was permitted, and where the last thing that was thought of was to listen to the performance. Algarotti represents a numerous body of writers to whom this flaccidity was becoming more and more distasteful. On the other hand, the new intellectual life that was springing up in Germany was accompanied by a protest against mere formality and imitation, and a desire to conduct both philosophy and art upon original lines.

Thus while the abuses of the current opera and the artificialities of contemporary life accounted for the revolutionary portion of Gluck's ideas, the same abuses and the same artificialities would in turn partly account for the cry of a "return to nature" and "imitation of nature," which was heard so plainly throughout the musical controversies of the time. But with this doctrine of the imitation of nature we step upon the ground of æsthetic theory, and have to examine the intellectual world of the eighteenth century upon that side of it that dealt with the relations of nature and art.

The theory that art imitates nature had been taken over in its crudest form from Aristotle's *Poetics;* and happening to coincide with a strong contemporary desire for greater simplicity and naturalness of life, the theory was carried to the grossest excess not only in the poetry and painting of the time, but also in the music. There was, in fact, little or none of that discrimination between the spheres and media of the various arts that underlies all our modern systems of æsthetic. Not only was the one faculty of the mind supposed to look at all the arts from the same standpoint, and to appreciate them all for the same qualities, but this faculty itself was thought to be more rational than imaginative. To the eighteenth-century mind, indeed, the world seemed to unfold itself in perfect clearness. The destructive work of the century in theology was mainly based on the idea of a primary delusion of the human race through priestcraft, and in their abhorrence of any social structure that bore the marks of conscious human instrumentality from without, the philosophers fell into the fallacy of supposed "natural rights" and "natural beauty." In art, again, the best and most beautiful was necessarily that which was best and most beautiful in nature, and since the faculty that appreciated this primordial goodness or beauty was simply reason, this faculty became elevated into the one criterion of art and philosophy. That alone was valid which was capable of being brought within the focus of the reason ; and anything lying beyond this sure and well-defined ground was a possible field for delusion and imposture. An æsthetic shape to be conjured up, a philosophical idea to be accepted, must come in the first place armed with a certificate of validity from the rational judgment ; and ideas were valued less for their ministration to the hidden desires and unvoiced aspirations of men, than for their satisfaction of that general craving for external clearness which made their philosophy so pre-eminently objective. Of the mystic heights and depths beyond the full-visioned conception of the moment, of those fields of tremulous light where the eye is charmed with the very indistinctness of the objects it sees, the typically eighteenth-century mind knew little and cared little. It was ill at ease in the world of the fugitive and the mysterious.

Among such a people, art of necessity stood upon a lower plane than in times when the current of life is warmer and more vaguely emotional. Since their ideal of philosophy was the free exercise of reason on things inward and outward, they naturally sought in art

1*

another mode of presentation of those ideas which
formed their basis of satisfaction in philosophy. That
art springs from a different side of man's nature, and is
directed towards a different end, never suggested itself
to them. Its function was to cast upon the working
of the mind, through concrete forms, that light which
was cast through abstract forms by philosophy ; and
the sensuous medium of the art, through which it
speaks, instead of being recognised as something that
helped to determine the utterance and define the scope
of the idea, had its claims set aside in favour solely of
the idea itself. Thus their art, instead of being a
series of presentations, through varying media, of
varying impressions of life and nature—the variations
being determined by the respective scopes of the arts—
was a series of representations of the same impression
through different media—variations, as it were, upon
the same theme. It did not occur to them that a
poetical idea, a pictorial idea, a musical idea, are
essentially diverse things, neither of which can be
properly expressed in the language of the others. The
border-lines between the arts, and between thought
and imagination, were not marked out or even supposed
to exist ; hence their confusion of æsthetic purposes.
The poet was supposed to paint in words, the musician
in sounds ; the painter represented poems on his
canvas ; Michel Angelo was a great poet and Shakespeare a great painter. A distorted Aristotelianism
invaded æsthetic criticism, and increased the confusion
that already existed there. " The French of that time
approached Poetry, as they approached Religion, as
they approached the State, with the conviction that the

organ of understanding was able to produce intentionally and consciously what in reality has always been the product of other human faculties acting almost unconsciously ; they believed in inventors of religion as in inventors of constitutions. Hence a confusion of all the activities of the human mind. People believed that the Fine Arts could serve to explain abstract thought, which is allegory, and again that words might paint objects, which produced descriptive Poetry. The simple explanation that words, sounds, forms and colours are different languages for different orders of mental activity had been entirely lost sight of. Experience taught that none of these mental faculties could work when isolated, without the aid of the others ; the inference was drawn that each might do the work of the others. People wanted to express in forms and colours, that is, in the language of the Fine Arts, what can only be expressed in words ; and they wanted to express in words what can only be expressed in sounds, *i.e.,* Music." *

There was along with this rational tendency in art a slight feeling here and there that the imagination had a more important function than was usually ascribed to it, but the objective tendency was much the stronger. With all their deep-reaching interest in art, and an analysis that was often acute and penetrating, the men of the eighteenth century for the most part missed the true centre of artistic creation—its pure synthesis of imagination. The remarks of every writer on the subject of music—Algarotti, Gluck, Rousseau, Diderot,

* Hillebrand, " Lectures on German Thought," p. 94.

Du Bos, Harris, Beattie, as well as the lesser journalists
—indicate a complete inability to construct a musical
cosmos on the lines of music *per se.* In part, of
course, we may attribute this to the comparatively low
stage of evolution to which music as an independent
art had then attained.   The subordinate position which
Gluck assigned to music in comparison with poetry is
paralleled almost everywhere in the writings of the
first three-quarters of the century, and was fundamental
in the art-theories of the time.   It was only natural
that while the purely imaginative qualities of poetry
were comparatively neglected, the imaginative
quality of the still more intensive art of music should
have fallen into even greater disregard.   The imagination, as such, had small rights in the æsthetic of that
epoch, being imperfectly understood and imperfectly
defined from the reason ; and Baumgarten expressed
the opinions of his time when he held that the faculty
that apprehended beauty was just a lower phase of
reason itself.

While music thus suffered from an imperfect sense
of the true functions of the artistic imagination, it
suffered still more from the theories that attempted to
make it, like poetry and like painting, an imitation of
nature.   The return to nature itself was on the whole
a healthy sign in the art of the time, though it was
frequently carried to excess, and though it reacted
harmfully upon the arts.   " How can you learn to
draw," cries Diderot to the student in his *Essai sur la
Peinture,* " by paying a poor devil so many francs per
hour to imitate the action of drawing water ?   Go to
the well, and watch the man who has no thought of

posing, and you will see how nature disposes of his frame." He returns to the same theme in the Essay on Dramatic Poetry: " A courageous actress has just got rid of her hoop-petticoat, and nobody has found her any the worse for it. Ah ! if she would one day only dare to show herself on the stage with all the nobility and simplicity of arrangement that her characters demand ; nay, in the disorder into which she would be thrown by an event so terrible as the death of a husband, the loss of a son, and the other catastrophes of the tragic stage, what would become, near her dishevelled figure, of all those powdered, curled, frizzled, tricked-out creatures ? Sooner or later they would have to put themselves in unison. O nature, nature ! we can never resist her." * A similar adoration of nature is observable throughout the æsthetic literature of the time. Algarotti incessantly urges the artist—the musician included—to imitate nature ; † and sends him back to the " beautiful simplicity of nature." ‡ Avison praises the " noble simplicity " of Marcello, simplicity being considered an inalienable character of nature. Rameau took " la belle et simple nature " for model.§ The word is constantly in the mouths of men on each side of the musical war, Gluckist and Piccinnist—Suard, Arnaud, La Harpe, Rousseau and Marmontel.‖

---

* " La poésie dramatique," sec. 21.
† Algarotti, p. 236.   ‡ Ib. p. 251.
§ Preface to " Les Indes Galantes," Paris, 1745. See Reissmann, p. 98.
‖ The revolt from the eighteenth century veneration for

This doctrine of a return to nature, commendable in itself when not pushed to an extreme, wrought infinite harm through an imperfect understanding of the meaning of the word and of the relations of nature and art. In the musical history of the eighteenth century we have particularly to note how music was placed in the

"nature," and the contrast between their æsthetic and ours, may be incidentally illustrated from Diderot's "Paradoxe sur le Comédien," the thesis of which, to express it briefly and somewhat crudely, is that strong emotion, and a belief that he is the character he is representing, will make a bad actor, while the good actor has judgment and self-possession, but no sensibility. Falling into line with the general precept to imitate nature as she is, the more primitive opinion of the eighteenth century was that the best actor of any part would be he who had the most natural affinities with it. Thus Sainte-Albine, who may be said to have originated the discussion on the art of acting by his essay "Le Comédien," in 1747, held what we may call the nature-theory in its most outrageous form. Here are some of his propositions in evidence : (1) "Gaiety is absolutely necessary to comedians, whose business is to excite our laughter;" (2) "No one but a man of elevated soul can represent a hero well;" (3) "Only those who are born of an amorous temperament should be allowed to play the parts of lovers." (Quoted in Mr. William Archer's "Masks or Faces?" p. 13.) Diderot himself leaned at one time to the extreme emotionalist position; but about 1770 he appears to have gone over to the opposite camp, and in the " Paradoxe " (which was probably written about 1773, though not published until 1830) he maintains that the essential qualification of the good actor is lack of sensibility. Here we have him expressing, in relation to the art of acting,

same category as the other arts, having for its supposed
purpose the imitation of nature. The musician, true
to Gluck's dictum that the music was to be to the
poem what colour is to a picture, had to illustrate a
subject given to him by a poet ; the one furnished the
design, the other added the colour ; and the music was

just what we are now accustomed to say in the other arts
as to the place of " nature " in the total effect. He argues
that on the emotionalist theory a drunken man should give
the best representation of drunkenness, and an athlete the
best representation of a gladiator ; on the other hand,
that the good actor is always master of himself ; that his
tones and gestures in the moments of greatest passion are
never precisely what they would be in a similar situation
in real life, but are always carefully timed and modulated
by the reason ; that the function of the theatre is not to
show things as they are in nature, but that the " truth " of
the representation lies in " the conformity of the actions,
the speeches, the expression, the voices, the movements,
the gestures, with an ideal model imagined by the poet,
and frequently exaggerated by the player." The advance
in æsthetic that is represented by the " Paradoxe " may
be seen by comparing it with any of Diderot's earlier
panegyrics on " nature ;" for example, with the passage in
the " Poésie dramatique," in which he contends for closer
imitation of actual life, and imagines the effect of " a real
scene, with real dresses," and so on. In the " Paradoxe "
his virile intellect was really anticipating the later theories
of æsthetic. For the divergence of these from the theory
of the excellence of nature-imitation see Goethe's remarks
on Diderot's " Essay on Painting." As Mr. Morley has
said, " the drift of Goethe's contention is, in fact, the
thesis of Diderot's ' Paradox on the Comedian.' " (See
his " Diderot," vol. i. pp. 331–347, and vol. ii. pp. 72–77.)

to be a picture in sounds. As this attitude of the musician towards nature was the most important element in the musical æsthetic of the day, and as it has vital bearings on the theory of Gluck, it will be advisable to illustrate it still further, by quotations from contemporary literature.

Writing on March 1st, 1770, in reference to the opera *Silvain*, by Marmontel and Grétry, Grimm attributes the weakness of the former's libretto to his "small dramatic talent; for it is much easier to be outrageous than to be simple ; *to imagine romantic manners and events than to find true events and paint manners as they are*, in an interesting fashion ; " * a theory that would quickly place out of court all imaginative art and literature. Again, in 1780 he speaks of a great success at the Tuileries—the Carmen Seculare of Horace, set to music by Philidor—and praises the careful manner in which the musician follows and illustrates the successive pictures of the poet, as if the sole function of the composer were to supply the utterances of the poet with an illustration in sound, appealing to the reason through the ear, just as a representation of the scenes on canvas would appeal to the reason through the eye. Throughout the writings of the eighteenth century, again, we find the claims of melody constantly thrust forward before everything else, for in melody the idea was expressed, while harmony to them was nothing more than the accentuation or support of the idea. "The Abbé Du Bos is very anxious to credit the Low Countries with

* Grimm's "Correspondance littéraire," 1813, ii. 191.

the honour of the musical Renaissance ; and this could
be admitted if we gave the name of music to a con-
tinual piling-up of chords ; but if harmony is merely
the common basis, and melody alone constitutes the
character, not only was modern music born in Italy,
but it appears that in all our living languages, Italian
music is the only one that can really exist." * The
whole argument of Rousseau's " Lettre sur la musique
française "—which was evoked by the Buffonist war—
is based on the assumptions that the opera has to
depict life as it finds it, that to do this it must express
in the aria, and still more in the recitative, the
similarity between the passion and the object that has
called it forth, and that the medium of this expression
is melody, supported by harmony and varied by rhythm.
The musician must simply give more elaborate utterance to the ideas contained in the words ; and the
musical range of words, if only they are sonorous and
melodious, is as wide as if they were being employed
in poetry or in prose. Thus the French, he says, will
never have good music of their own, because their
language has not the sweetness and limpidity of the
Italian ! †

Evidently in such a musical system as this there is
little scope for that quality of the music of our later

* Rousseau, " Lettre sur la musique française," 1st ed.,
1753, p. 45, note.

† One is reminded of the saying of Charles V. that the
German language was only fit to use in addressing horses.
On Rousseau's theory, music should be an impossibility in
Germany. See also a similar dissertation in Burney's
" History of Music," vol. iv.

opera, which interprets a character or a situation not alone on the skeleton lines presented by the poet, but with a height and breadth and depth of intuition which, while necessarily linked to the verbal substratum, is yet born of a separate order of imagination ; the final expression being a joint product of the poetical and musical intuitions fused into one. For the musician to turn his thoughts inward and evolve an organism whose articulation should have been wholly esoteric, would have been an unheard-of aberration in the France of the eighteenth century. Hence the outcry against those purely instrumental compositions which, having no verbal basis, and therefore no appeal to the rational faculties and no similarity with " nature," must be judged by an esoteric imagination whose synthesis is not less complex and not less coherent than the synthesis of the understanding, though less palpable and less communicable. Since these exercises of the pure musical imagination had no connection with any objective form outside the musician's mind, they were destitute of utility, and fit only for a race of barbarians ; this was the frame of mind that saw " barbarism " in Gothic architecture. " Another thing, which is not less contrary than the multiplication of parts to the rule I have just established, is the abuse, or rather the use, of fugues, imitations, double designs, and other *arbitrary and purely conventional beauties,** which have scarcely any merit beyond that of difficulty vanquished,

* As if blank verse, or the sonnet form, or the simulation of round bodies on a flat canvas, or the pictorial device that gives the illusion of distance, were not also

and which have all been invented in the early periods of art in order to make science pass for genius. I do not say it is quite impossible to preserve the unity of melody in a fugue, by cleverly conducting the attention from one part to another in pursuit of the subject; but this toil is so painful that few can succeed in it, and so ungrateful that even success can hardly compensate for the fatigue of such a work. All that which only seeks its purpose in noise, as well as the greater number of our much-admired choruses, is equally unworthy of occupying the pen of a man of genius or the attention of a man of taste. As for counter-fugues, double fugues, inverted fugues, and other difficult fooleries which neither the ear can suffer nor the reason justify, these are evidently relics of barbarism and bad taste, which only exist, like the porticoes of our Gothic churches, for the shame of those who had the patience to make them." *

Rousseau's whole argument, indeed, goes upon the assumption that the aim of the musician is to embody in sound a creation intrinsically the same as that embodied by the poet in words, or by the painter in lines and colours. It is the function of music, he implies, to place the hearer in communication with those external facts which give birth to the idea, by representing this idea in processes corresponding to

"arbitrary and purely conventional." Rousseau's theory cuts its own throat, for all art is arbitrary in the sense that it employs certain extra-natural devices to obtain certain effects.

* "Lettre," p. 44.

those of the other arts. A music which should neglect
to do this, and should choose instead to occupy itself
with matters entirely of its own concern, " would be
languishing and expressionless, *and its images, denuded
of force and energy, would paint few objects in a great
many notes,* like those Gothic writings, the lines of which,
filled with figured letters and characters, contain only
two or three words, and enclose very little meaning in
a great space." * Since the intellectual application of
the opera comes entirely from the words, to which the
music supplies an accentuation and a kind of imitation,
the musician must not depart from either the verbal
sense or the verbal rhythm. Thus according to Rousseau, the best music would be that in which the prosodial and rhythmic form of the verses exactly coincides
with the time and rhythm of the melody.† Hence

* " Lettre," p. 16. In the preface to the Encyclopedia,
D'Alembert, after discussing poetry, painting and architecture as arts of imitation, says of music : " Finally music,
which addresses itself at the same time to the imagination
and to the senses, occupies the third position in order of
imitation; not that its imitation is less perfect in those
objects which it proposes to represent, but because it seems
limited in this respect to a small number of images;
which we should attribute not so much to the nature of
the art as to the want of invention and resource in the
greater number of those who cultivate it. . . . . All music
that does not paint something is merely noise, and were
it not for custom, that unnatures everything, would give
scarcely more pleasure than a succession of harmonious
and sonorous words, denuded of order and connection."
(" Discours sur l'Encyclopédie," ed. Bibl. Nat. pp. 43, 45.)
    † *Ib.* pp. 9, 10.

also the importance attached to declamation, which imitates, under a more or less artistic form, the accents, intervals, rhythm, cadence, and progression of actual passion, in opposition to the theory and practice of our own day, where the comparatively undeveloped poetical form becomes merged in the infinitely more developed musical form. And *obbligato* recitative, which to the eighteenth-century ear expressed so much, was in part a further development of the principle of imitation, by means of the continuance in the orchestra of the illustrative function momentarily suspended by the voice.

We shall see still more clearly the comparatively low estimation in which music was held in the eighteenth century, the subordinate function which it was supposed to perform in reference to poetry, and the extent of the false æsthetic that tried to make music an art of imitation, by looking at the opinions of contemporary belletrists who instituted comparisons between the arts.

In 1744 Harris published a " Discourse on Music, Painting and Poetry," in which he works out a comparison between the three arts on the basis of the question, "Which imitates nature most effectually ? " They agree, he says, by being all mimetic or imitative, and he states the mimetic powers of music thus : " In the natural or inanimate world, music may imitate the glidings, murmurings, tossings, roarings, and other accidents of water, as perceived in fountains, cataracts, rivers, seas, &c. The same of thunder, the same of winds, as well the stormy as the gentle. In the animal world, it may imitate the voice of some animals, but chiefly that of singing birds. It may also faintly copy some of their motions. In the human kind, it can also imitate some motions and sounds ; and of sounds those most perfectly, which are expressive of grief and anguish.",* The doctrine of the excellence of nature-imitation could not further go than this.

He sums up the case as between painting and music in the sentence, "that musical imitation is greatly below that of painting, and that at best it is but an imperfect thing ;"† while of poetry and music he remarks that, "inasmuch as musical imitations, though natural, aspire not to raise the same ideas, but only ideas similar and analogous ; while poetic imitation, though artificial, raises ideas the very same, inasmuch as the definite and certain is ever preferable to the indefinite and uncertain, and that more especially in imitations, where the principal delight is in recognising the thing imitated—it will follow from hence that— even in subjects the best adapted to musical imitation, the imitation of poetry will be still more excellent."‡ Here the characteristic note of the eighteenth century is clearly heard.

The palm is finally given to poetry, because it can imitate more important things, and imitate them better. "Poetry is therefore, on the whole, much superior to either of the other mimetic arts ; it having been shown to be equally excellent in the accuracy of its imitation ; and to imitate subjects, which far surpass,

* "A Discourse," &c., in Harris's "Works," 1801, vol. i. p. 40.
† *Ib.* p. 41.   ‡ *Ib.* pp. 47, 48.

as well in utility as in dignity."* And we seem to be listening to Gluck himself when we hear that the value of music is that it raises the same mood as that of the poetry, and so strengthens the effect of the latter. Harris, indeed, seems to be nearer the modern æsthetic of music when he deprecates too strong an insistence on the merely imitative function of the art, and says that the power of music "consists not in imitations, and the raising ideas, but in the raising affections, to which ideas may correspond."† But that in this also he is the true offspring of his century is seen in his next argument, that the music must still be the handmaid of the poetry, and that its chief value is the aid it gives the mind in the comprehension of the poetical idea. "And here indeed, not in imitation, ought it to be chiefly cultivated. On this account also it has been called a powerful ally to poetry. And further, it is by the help of this reasoning that the objection is solved, which is raised against the singing of poetry (as in operas, oratorios, &c.), from the want of probability and resemblance to nature. To one, indeed, who has no musical ear, this objection may have weight. It may even perplex a lover of music, if it happen to surprise him in his hours of indifference. But when he is feeling the charm of poetry so accompanied, let him be angry (if he can), with that which serves only to interest him more feelingly in the subject, and support him in a stronger and more earnest attention ; which enforces, by its aid, the several ideas of the poem, and gives them to his

* "A Discourse," &c., in Harris's "Works," 1801, vol. i. p. 55.   † *Ib.* p. 58.

imagination with unusual strength and grandeur ; "* there being apparently no perception of the value of the music for its own sake in this apology for its union with poetry.

And once more we hear the note of the eighteenth century in Harris's dictum that instrumental music is lower than vocal music, because in the former the mind has no concrete suggestions from poetry to carry it along. "From what has been said it is evident that these two arts can never be so powerful singly, as when they are properly united. For poetry, when alone, must be necessarily forced to waste many of its richest ideas, in the mere raising of affections, when, to have been properly relished, it should have found those affections in their highest energy. And music, when alone, can only raise affections which soon languish and decay, if not maintained and fed by the nutritive images of poetry. Yet must it be remembered, in this union, that poetry ever have the precedence ; its utility, as well as dignity, being by far the more considerable."† Thus Harris perpetrates the common fallacy of his epoch, and fails to perceive that music and poetry are arts occupying different spheres, employing different media, and appealing to different

* "A Discourse," &c., in Harris's "Works," 1801, vol. i. pp. 58, 59.

† *Ib.* pp. 59, 60. Compare also Webb : "If painting is less mimetic than poetry, music, as a mimetic art, must rank below painting; since it cannot specify the subjects of its various movements, its imitation of the passions must be extremely uncertain and indefinite. For example, the tender, melting tones that can indeed express love, suit

orders of imagination ; that the achievements of music, and more especially of instrumental music, must not be judged by a criterion drawn from poetry ; and that while certain musical creations have no need of words, there are correspondingly many orders of poetry that are insusceptible of musical accompaniment.

Earlier in the century, the abbé Du Bos had published his " Réflexions Critiques sur la Poésie et sur la Peinture," and in a few chapters at the end of his first volume had tried, somewhat in the manner of Harris, to express the relation between poetry, painting and music. " It remains now," he begins, " to speak of music, as the third of those means which men have invented to give a new force to poetry, and to render it capable of making a greater impression on us ; " * thus again exhibiting the current idea that the sole function of music was to assist the mind in apprehending the ideas of poetry. "Wherefore as the painter imitates the strokes and colours of nature, so the musician imitates the tones, accents, sighs, and inflexions of the voice ; in short, all those sounds by which nature herself expresses her sentiments and passions. These, as we have already observed, have

also the expression of the related emotions of kindness, friendship, pity, &c. And how can we distinguish the hasty motions of anger from terror and other violent disturbances of the soul ? As soon, however, as poetry and music combine, we are no longer in uncertainty; we recognise the consonance of the tones and the idea, and the dual expression serves to illustrate a particular passion." Quoted in " Algarotti," pp. 237, 238.

* *Op. cit.* vol. i. sec. 45.

a surprising power of moving us, because they are the signs of passions, instituted by nature, from whom they receive their energy." Like Harris, he argues that music is a mimetic art. "In the next place, the rhythm gives a new *vraisemblance* to the imitation in a musical composition, because it adds to that imitation of the progression and movement of natural sounds and noises which has already been achieved by the melody and the harmony. Music therefore forms its imitations by the help of melody, harmony and rhythm; just as painting makes its imitations by means of lines, chiaroscuro, and local colours." *

He even manages to say a good word for instrumental music, on the ground that it is really mimetic. "Though this kind of music is purely instrumental, yet it contains a true imitation of nature. . . . . The truth of the imitation in a symphony consists in its resemblance to the sound which it is intended to imitate. There is truth in a symphony composed to imitate a tempest, when the melody, harmony and rhythm convey to our ear a sound like the noise of the wind in the air, and the roaring of the waves dashing against each other or breaking on the rocks." And he sums up boldly thus: "The first principles therefore of music are the same as those of poetry and of painting. Music, like the other two arts, is an imitation; and it cannot be of any value unless it conforms to the general rules of these two arts as to the choice of its subjects, its probability, and other matters;" which is the eighteenth-century theory in its most naked and unashamed form. Yet Du Bos, who

* *Op. cit.* vol. i. sec. 45.

thought acutely about his subject, and to whom
Lessing was under obligations, throws out one or
two good hints to the composer about imitating
the general sentiment of a passage rather than a particular word ; and answering the objection against the
probability of the opera, rightly says that the same
objection holds against the use of Alexandrines in
tragedy ; and that the want of probability in opera is
atoned for by the pleasure the music gives us. He
has the penetration, too, to observe what so many
of his contemporaries and successors had overlooked,
that not all poetry is suitable for music, and that
the kind most easily allied with it is that which
deals with sentiments rather than with images and
descriptions.

It is evident from what has been said that music in
the eighteenth century stood on a lower plane relatively to the other arts than it does in our own day.
Being comparatively undeveloped, it occupied much
the same relation to the poetry of the times as did the
music in the Greek world to the contemporary poetry.
Aristotle held that music was the most " imitative "
of all the arts ; although with him its imitative function lay rather in the domain of feelings and ethical
qualities than in the world of natural objects, as in the
writings of the eighteenth century. Its dependent
position in Greek culture is shown in Plato's objection
to instrumental music : " When there are no words it
is difficult to recognise the meaning of harmony or
rhythm, or to see that any worthy object is imitated
by them " ;* a sentence which might have come from

* Laws, ii. 669 E.

some æsthetician of the eighteenth century. It was nothing less than inevitable that in the time of Gluck music should be looked upon simply as a pigment for the adornment of the poetry. The purely sensuous side of art was in no case, and least of all in that of music, appreciated at its full value.* The analogy of Gluck, that music bears the same relation to poetry as the colour of a picture bears to the design, finds its counterpart in the widely held contemporary theory that it was in the form that beauty really found its expression, and that the colour was at best an additional ornament, serving to heighten the effect of the

* Madame de Staël may be taken as expressing the more modern ideas on the question of words and music in the following passage from her "De l'Allemagne": "The fine arts require instinct rather than reflection; the German composers follow too closely the sense of the words. This is a great merit, it is true, in the eyes of those who like the words more than the music; and of course it is indisputable that a disagreement between the sense of the one and the expression of the other would be unpleasant; but the Italians, who are the true musicians of nature, make the airs conform to the words in a general manner only. In romances and vaudevilles, where there is not much music, one can submit to the words; but the great effects of melody must go straight to the soul by an immediate sensation. Those who have not much appreciation of painting in itself attach great importance to the subjects of pictures; they want to get from them the same impressions that are produced by dramatic scenes. So is it with music. When one is not greatly susceptible to it, one exacts a faithful conformity to the slightest shades of meaning in the words; but when it moves us to the

design.* Perhaps the most characteristic feature of the æsthetic of the eighteenth century is this insistence on the ancillary nature of music, and the attempt to make it pictorial in manner and effect.† Look, for illustration, at some passages from Gluck's own writings :

"I sought to reduce music to its true function, that of seconding the poetry."

"I held the opinion that the music should be to the poem what the lights and shades are to a good design,

foundations of our soul, the attention given to anything but the music is merely an importunate distraction ; and provided that there is no opposition between the poem and the music, we abandon ourselves to what is always the more expressive art. For the delicious reverie in which it plunges us annihilates the thoughts which the words would express, and the music awakening in us the sentiment of the infinite, everything that tends to particularise the object of the melody must diminish its effect."

* This was the opinion of Winckelmann and of Kant. See Knight's "Philosophy of the Beautiful," i. 53, 59.

† As an exception to the general theory of the inferiority of poetry we may note that in 1765 the Chevalier de Chastellux published an "Essai sur l'union de la Poésie et de la Musique," in which he held that the music should dominate the poetry in opera. The essay drew forth the commendations of Metastasio, who held the current theory; and it was quoted by the anti-Gluckists in the literary war. See Burney's "Memoirs of Metastasio," ii. 316–335. Burney is wrong in saying that Algarotti's essay had not then appeared. It was published two years before that of Chastellux.

serving to animate the figures without altering their contours."

" I had to seek truth of colouring [in *Paris and Helen*] in the different natures of the Spartans and the Phrygians, by contrasting the rudeness and savagery of the former with the delicacy and effeminacy of the latter."

" Holding, as I do, the opinion that the melody in my operas is merely a substitute for declamation, it was necessary at times to imitate the native rudeness of my heroes ; and I have thought that in order to maintain this character in the music, it would not be a fault to descend occasionally into the trivial."

" The imitation of nature is the end which both poet and composer should set before themselves ; that is the goal after which I have striven. . . . . My music tends only to greater expressiveness and to the enforcement of the declamation of the poetry."

" I have tried [in *Armida*] *to be painter and poet rather than musician.*"

" I have discovered the means of making each character express himself in such a manner that you can recognise at once, from the style of expression, who it is that is speaking, Armida or a *confidante*, &c."

" In composing, I try to forget that I am a musician."

" I might perhaps have written something more beautiful from a musical point of view, and varied it so as to please your ears ; but in that case I would only have been a musician, and would have been untrue to nature, which I must never abandon."

Everywhere there was this tendency to restrict the

sphere of music as an independent art, to clip its wings
and prevent its soaring above the sister arts of poetry
and painting.   Men seemed to have a nervous horror
of purely musical pleasure for its own sake, and felt a
difficulty in moving about among the shadowy creations of absolute music.   They were almost strangers
to the esoteric delight that future generations were to
feel in music as a self-existent art.   " How does the
musician obtain his grand effects ? " writes Rousseau.
" Is it by dint of contrasting movements, multiplying
harmonies, notes and parts ?   Is it by heaping design
on design, instrument on instrument ?   All this hurly-
burly, which is only a clumsy attempt to atone for the
lack of genius, would strangle the melody instead of
animating it, and would destroy the interest by dis-
tracting the attention.   Whatever harmony may be
produced by several parts being well sung together,
the whole effect of these beautiful melodies vanishes as
soon as they are all heard at once, and the only effect
remaining is that of a succession of harmonies, which,
whatever one may say, is always cold when not en-
livened by a melody ; so that the more one clumsily
heaps up melodies, the less agreeable and flowing is
the music, because it is impossible for the ear to entertain several melodies at the same time, and because
from the effacement of one impression by another
there results nothing but confusion and noise.   If
music is to be interesting, if it is to bear to the soul
the sentiments intended to be roused there, every part
must concur in fortifying the expression of the subject ; the harmony must only serve to render the
subject more energetic ; the accompaniment must em-

bellish it, without either obscuring or disfiguring it ; the bass, by a uniform and simple progression, must in some manner guide both the singer and the hearer, without either of them being conscious of it ; in a word, the whole effect must at each moment bear to the ear but one melody, and to the mind but one .idea."* The theory that the melody conducted the intellectual current of the music, and that the harmony was simply an agreeable colouring to it, is an indication of the backward state of music as an art, and falls into line with the argument of Baumgarten and of Winckelmann, as applied to the pictorial arts, that the beauty and the meaning of a picture lie in the design, to which the colour is wholly subordinate.

Rousseau proceeds with a remark that throws some light on the many unison passages we meet with in Gluck's music. " This unity of melody appears to me an indisputable rule, and one not less important in music than unity of action in a tragedy : for it is founded on the same principle and directed towards the same object. Further, all the great Italian composers observe it with a care that sometimes degenerates into affectation ; and to any one who reflects it is evident that from their observance of this rule their music draws its greatest effect. It is in this great rule that we must seek the explanation of those frequent unison accompaniments which we remark in Italian music, and which, strengthening the idea of the melody, at the same time render its tones more gentle, more dulcet, and less fatiguing for the voice." † And since

* " Lettre," pp. 34–36.   † " Lettre," pp. 36-37.

this unity of melody must be the great aim of the composer, harmony must play a subsidiary part, and content itself with merely enforcing the main idea above it. " If the melody is of such a nature as to exact some additions, or, as our old musicians would say, some *diminutions*, which add to the expression or the pleasure without thereby destroying the melodic unity, so that the ear, which would perhaps censure these additions if supplied by the voice, approves of them in the accompaniment and is greatly affected by them, without ceasing to attend closely to the melody —then the skilful musician, by managing them carefully and employing them with taste, will embellish his subject and render it more expressive without destroying its unity ; and even if the accompaniment were not exactly similar to the voice part, in combination they would form but one melody. . . . But to make the violins play a part on one side, the flutes on another, the bassoons on another, each with a different strain, and with scarcely any connection between them, and to call this chaos ' music,' is to insult equally the ears and the judgment of the auditors." *
The duet, he gravely tells us, " *is not according to nature ;* for nothing is less natural than to see two persons speaking at the same time, either to say the same thing or to contradict one another, without even listening to or answering each other ; and even if this supposition might be admitted in some cases, it certainly could not be admitted in Tragedy, *where such indecency is consistent neither with the dignity of the*

* " Lettre," pp. 40, 42.

K

persons speaking, nor with the education we may suppose them to possess." * And therefore the only safe rule is to follow the primordial principle of the unity of melody—to make the parts of the duet *follow* each other and thus constitute a single melodic idea ; or, if it is absolutely necessary for the parts to combine, they should proceed by simple intervals, such as thirds or sixths ! it being presumably not indecent and not inconsistent with the dignity of the heroes and the education we may suppose them to possess, to sing in simple intervals, though it might be to sing in any others. And whatever dissonance, Rousseau goes on, occurs to imply that the actors are momentarily transported by their passion beyond the bounds of reason, must not last more than a moment ; " for when the agitation is too strong it cannot last, and whatever is beyond nature no longer touches us." †

In the treatment of the overture the same desire for

---

* " Lettre," p. 48 ; see also his " Dict. de Musique," art. " Duo." The brilliant La Harpe, it will be remembered, was also struck with this idea. The more primitive opinion of the French *littérateurs* was that the opera as a whole is not according to nature. Saint-Evremond had been shocked that in the opera "they sang throughout the whole piece ; as if the persons represented had made a ridiculous agreement to treat in music both of the commonest and the most important affairs of life. Can any one imagine a master calling his valet, and *singing* his orders to him ? "—and so on. (" Au duc de Buckingham sur les Opéras.") See Castil-Blaze, " De l'Opéra en France," Paris, 1820, vol. i. p. 97.

† " Lettre," p. 49.

pictorial treatment became evident, as witness Rousseau's suggestion to Gluck for the overture to *Alceste.*
" To remedy all this I would have suggested that the
overture should be composed of two parts of different
character, but both treated in a sonorous and consonant
harmony ; the first, bearing to the heart a sweet and
tender gaiety, would have represented the felicity of
the reign of Admetus and the charms of the conjugal
union ; the second, with a more broken rhythm, and
by more agitated movements and more interrupted
phrases, would have expressed the anxiety of the people
as to the malady of Admetus, and would have formed
a very natural introduction to the herald's announcement at the beginning of the work." *

The ballet, again, affords an illustration of their
passion for the "imitation of nature." The object of
their art being to stimulate ideas rather than emotions,
this function could to a certain extent be performed by
the ballet, which was a kind of musical commentary
on a theatrical situation. The eighteenth century
mind seemed to be able to *think* in the ballet, to
arrange movements, as the poet arranges words, the
musician sounds, the painter forms and colours, so as
to exhibit a microcosm of thought and action. "Jean
George Noverre (1727–1810) in his *Lettres sur la
Danse et sur les Ballets,* in 1760, strove for a reformation in the ballet on the same principles which Gluck
employed for the opera. He condemned stereotyped
forms of set dances, and demanded a plot for the
ballet ; expression should be the task of the dancer,

* Rousseau, "Œuvres," 1793, vol. ix. p. 587.

with nature for his model, and the ballet-master should be both poet and painter." * These were practically the conditions which Gluck tried to realise in his ballets.

Thus the ideas exhibited in Gluck's prefaces and in his music were the almost universal ideas of the time. From the foregoing quotations it has been abundantly shewn that the whole of the eighteenth-century æsthetic of music was based upon a few fundamental principles that were inwoven with the very texture of their culture. Almost without exception, every writer upon the arts held that music, like poetry and painting, is a mimetic art, and that its function is to imitate nature ; that simplicity should be the aim of the composer ; that music should be subordinated to poetry ; that the melody expressed the idea, while the harmony added a little agreeable colouring ; that music without poetry was ineffectual because it lacked the concrete and definite ideas which poetry afforded ; all confused art with nature ; all were lacking in the most characteristic feature of our modern æsthetic, the appreciation of musical beauty and musical delight for their own sakes. Some held all these ideas, others held part of them ; but there is an unmistakable similarity between

---

* Otto Jahn, " Life of Mozart," ii. 21. Compare also Algarotti : " The dance must be an imitation of nature, painting the passions and affections of the mind by means of the body's motions to an accompaniment of music. It must speak to the eyes, and offer them a picture. The dance, moreover, must have its exposition, its entanglement, and its *dénouement;* it must be the quintessential representation of an action." (" Versuche," &c., p. 270.)

the opinions of all the musical æstheticians of the epoch.   Even Beattie, who published a very intelligent essay on poetry and music, and who criticised the theory of " nature-imitation " with some acuteness, agreed with his contemporaries that music could only be heard to fair advantage in conjunction with poetry ; and this not because the musical pleasure was thus increased, but because the poetry could narrow down the more expansive art to the gauge of the every-day understanding.   " I grant that by its power of raising a variety of agreeable emotions in the hearer, it proves its relation to poetry, and that it never appears to the best advantage but with poetry for its interpreter." *
Again : " Yet it is in general true, that poetry is the most immediate and most accurate interpreter of music.   Without this auxiliary, a piece of the best music, heard for the first time, might be said to mean something, but we should not be able to say what. It might incline the heart to sensibility ; but poetry, or language, would be necessary to improve that sensibility into a real emotion, by fixing the mind upon some definite and affecting ideas." †   The æsthetic of

* " An Essay on Poetry and Music, as they affect the Mind."   3rd ed., London, 1779 ; p. 119.
† *Ib.*, pp. 149, 150.   Twining, the editor of Aristotle, is also noticeable as having surrendered the imitation theory of music, in his dissertations on poetical and musical imitation prefixed to the " Poetics"   (1789). (See Phillimore's edition of Lessing's " Laokoon," p. xlvii.) At the end of the third volume of Burney's " Memoirs of Metastasio" there is a rather rambling dissertation on the question of whether music is an imitative art or not.

music in the eighteenth century, look where we will, was essentially the same.

Burney notices the remarks of Twining, who "confines musical imitations to the raising emotions and ideas. And I think the former will include the passions. There are mere instrumental movements which awaken ideas of joy, sorrow, tenderness, melancholy, &c. Thus far it may be allowed the title of an imitative art" (pp. 364–367). Of course this is really not "imitation" at all in the sense which that word currently bore in the eighteenth century. Such passages as these of Twining and Burney show the difficulty felt even at that time in shaking off the influence of Aristotle. They were conscious that music is not really a mimetic art, yet felt bound somehow or other to square their ideas with the words used by Aristotle in his "Poetics." In the 1812 edition of his book, Twining himself calls attention to the confusion created by calling all the arts "imitative."*

* See note at end of the book.

CHAPTER IV

WE are now in a position to look at the practical working of Gluck's theories. According to his own confession he tried, in the greater part of his later operatic career, to subordinate music to poetry; and this tendency, as well as the attempt to "paint" in music, is perfectly discernible in his work. The desire to be pictorial, indeed, frequently led him and his contemporaries into the perpetration of absurdities. Although Gluck had too much sense of artistic fitness to think he could give the hearer a picture, for example, of the sea, by writing a rolling species of accompaniment, as some musicians have tried to do, he yet aimed frequently at impressing the ear less with reference to the imagination, by calling up emotional reminiscences of scenes similar to those he wished to suggest, than with reference to purely external characters of the scene, that might indeed affect the eye, but were essentially incapable of any imaginative suggestion through the medium of the ear. We saw how in an early work he had aimed at a kind of pictorial representation in the aria; and in his six great operas there are many instances of the same tendency. All this, of course, was simply part of the "nature" delusion, and of the consequent confusion of æsthetic ideology and the lack of recognition of the boundaries between the arts ; it was thought that since the object existed in nature it could be represented by art, and by music as well as by any other art. Even in the case of *Armida*, where Gluck, probably with a reminiscence of the warmth of the music he had written, tried to formulate, in his letter to the *Journal de Paris*, a theory of equal co-operation between poetry and music, he had also declared that his method was more that of the painter and the poet than of the musician. The result of this was that he attempted to define his characters by giving each of them music of a different order, this difference being manifested in the *tempi* and the rhythms. But these, it will be observed, are the most *physical*, and, so to speak, the most external of the varieties of which music is capable ; yet Gluck would have found it impossible to " paint " character in the way he intended except by these purely physical means. For music, as an art of esoteric emotion, affects us in intension rather than in extension ; that is, the composer trusts to the playing upon our emotional experience by the music, and the evocation by sympathy of the mood he wishes us to feel, rather than to the projection upon the mind, through the ear, of the images of those external shapes which a picture would exhibit to the eye. Gluck himself comes to grief over his theory. Where his boasted differentiation of character reveals itself in *Armida* is mainly in the characters of Phénice and Sidonie, and there need be no hesitation in saying that here the differentiation is utterly puerile. One can only smile at the almost childish trust of the composer in this clumsy way

of marking out one character—or rather one type of
character—from another ; for his method after all
does not really define the characters of Phenice and
Sidonie as persons, but merely as types. And where
he is at his best, as in the treatment of the more
passionate portions, where Rinaldo and Armida are
the actors, his theory of " painting " character breaks
down utterly. Here, where the differentiation should
be strongest and most decided, there is absolutely none
of that pictorial difference between the characters such
as he had aimed at in depicting Phénice and Sidonie ;
each speaks the natural musical language of passion, and
no attempt is made to " paint " either of them by a
superficial distinction of rhythms and *tempi*. The
roughest examination of Gluck's theory serves to
discover the weakness of it. If such a method of
musical procedure can serve to distinguish a light and
sportive character from one that is serious and passionate—as that of Phénice from that of Armida—it
ought to be possible to distinguish in the same way
two different phases of the same passion, which it is
obviously incapable of doing ; and still less can it give
distinctiveness and definition to such external differences as those of sex and station. " You announced,"
we might say to Gluck, " that in *Armida* it could at
once be understood, from the varying styles of the
music, which character was speaking. We admit that
by giving to Phénice and Sidonie a style of music that
is lighter, more sportive, and more tripping than that
allotted to Armida, you have indicated the difference
between a serious character and a gay one. But that
in itself does not prove the possibility of painting in

K*

music. If there is anything in your theory, you ought to be able not only to distinguish in your music a passionate character from one that is not passionate, but also one variety of the same passion from another. No doubt by writing pompous and measured strains for a soldier, and gay and tripping music for a country girl, you could suggest the difference between them in some such manner as the painter would. But let us take Rinaldo and Armida in their love-scenes. How, by your method, will you give us to understand which of the two is singing at any time? In no way can you do this. The natural language of passion is the same in Rinaldo as in Armida; there is no melody and no harmony, no time and no rhythm, no intervals and no modulations, that are more appropriate to the man than to the woman; and even in your own music they speak the same tongue. Your theory is inapplicable to music in its higher forms; and where it partially succeeds is in those purely physical characteristics that, by association, bring music for the time being to the lower level of the pictorial arts."

Thus the analogy with painting, when pushed beyond the merest externalities, breaks down entirely; and as a matter of fact Gluck's theory is here again contradicted by his practice, for he has frequently, in his later operas, employed in one connection music that had primarily been written years before in quite another connection. Yet on his own pictorial principles this should be impossible. It would follow from his theory that the musical representation of a situation or a character should represent that situation or that character, and none other; and it should be as impossible, if the imitation of nature had been successfully performed, to employ the representation in quite other circumstances as it would be in a parallel case in painting. It was not Gluck's practice that was wrong, but his theory ; he did right in taking an emotional expression from one work and applying it to another ; but he was wrong in not seeing how his procedure failed to square with his theory. Had his analysis of the nature of music gone further, he would have recognised the truth that is so evident in our own day, that music is an art of generalised expression, in which the one inward emotion may be equally applicable to a thousand concrete situations, and that it is useless to attempt to give to music the definiteness that belongs to poetry or painting. The analogy with the pictorial arts, used as Gluck used it, is the most glaring of fallacies. It was not his error alone ; it was the error of his century to regard the spheres of the arts as interchangeable, and to look upon music mainly as the colour that filled and beautified the outline given by the words. This tendency to regard music as the inferior of poetry, which we meet with everywhere in the writings of the pre-Romanticists, is, it need hardly be said, wholly at variance with Romantic theory and practice. The French of the eighteenth century had no conception of that fluidity of mind that is so characteristic of our own day, when music exists in an intellectual world of its own, in which the composer can live and move and have his being, and create complete and coherent forms, without the slightest aid from poetry. To Rousseau and Harris, to Du Bos and Algarotti, to Beattie and Metastasio, poetry was the more important factor in opera. We have seen how both Calzabigi and Gluck plunged headlong into an arid theory of declamation—a theory from the consequences of which Gluck was saved, in practice, by his more essentially musical nature. But this fact, taken in conjunction with a host of others, indicates that the first impulse to musical composition came from a definite poetical idea, to which the musician consciously and deliberately tried to add a kind of coloured commentary.

Critics and historians have remarked in a general way upon this peculiarity of Gluck's system of æsthetic, and upon its inconsistency not only with our musical methods but with those of Gluck himself, without, however, tracing the matter scientifically to its historical causes. In this category falls the criticism of Berlioz, which is worth quoting, in spite of its haphazard character, as a statement of the antagonism between the musical æsthetic of the eighteenth century and that of the nineteenth, and of the internal inconsistencies between Gluck's theory and his practice.

After quoting the preface to *Alceste*, Berlioz proceeds as follows :

" Setting aside some which we shall specify later, these principles are so excellent that they have been for the most part followed by the majority of the great composers of all nations. Now in promulgating this theory, the necessity of which ought to have been apparent to any one with the smallest artistic feeling or even the simplest common sense, has not Gluck rather exaggerated the consequences of it here and there ?

We can scarcely resist this conclusion after an impartial examination of it, and even he himself, in his own works, has not applied it with rigorous exactitude. Thus in the Italian *Alceste* we find recitatives accompanied merely by the figured bass and probably by the chords of the cembalo (harpsichord), as was the custom at that time in the Italian theatres. Yet there certainly results from this species of accompaniment and recitative a *very marked disparity* between the recitative and the aria.

"Several of his airs are preceded by a fairly long instrumental solo : then the singer had perforce *to keep silence, waiting for the termination of the ritornello.* Further, he frequently employs a form of aria which, on his own theory of dramatic music, ought to be proscribed. I refer to those repetition-airs of which each part occurs twice, without any reason for the duplication, just as if, in fact, the public had demanded the *encore.* Of this kind is the air in *Alceste* :

> Je n'ai jamais chéri la vie
> Que pour te prouver mon amour;
> Ah! pour te conserver le jour,
> Qu'elle me soit cent fois ravie!

"When the melody comes to the cadence on the dominant, why recommence, without the least change either in the vocal part or in the orchestra :

> Je n'ai jamais chéri la vie—&c.?

"Most assuredly the dramatic sense is spoilt by such a repetition ; and if any one should have refrained from sinning in this way against naturalness and probability it is Gluck.   Yet he commits the same error in almost all his works.   We do not find examples of it in modern music, and the composers who succeeded Gluck have been less lax in this respect than he.

" Now when he says that the music of a lyrical drama has no other function than that of adding to the poetry just what the colour adds to a design, I believe him to be fundamentally mistaken.   The task of the composer in an opera, it seems to me, is of quite another importance.   His work contains both design and colour, and, to continue the comparison of Gluck, the words are the *subject* of the picture, and little more.   Expression is not the sole aim of dramatic music ; it would be as maladroit as pedantic to disdain the purely sensuous pleasure which we find in certain effects of melody, harmony, rhythm or instrumentation, independently of their connection with the painting of the sentiments and passions of the drama. And further, even if it were desired to deprive the hearer of this source of delight, and not to permit him to re-animate his attention by turning it away for a moment from its principal object, we would still be able to cite a goodly number of cases where the composer is called upon to sustain alone the interest of the lyrical work.   In the *danses de caractère*, for example, in the pantomime, in the marches, in every piece, in short, in which the instrumental music takes the whole of the work upon itself, and which consequently have no words, what becomes of the importance of the poet ?   In these cases the music must necessarily contain both design and colour. . . . .

" Here again (in his theory of the overture), in

exaggerating a just idea, Gluck has gone beyond the real facts; not, this time, to restrict the power of music, but on the contrary to attribute to it a virtue which it will never possess; it is when he says that the overture ought to indicate the *subject* of the piece. Musical expression cannot go so far as that; it can certainly depict joy, sorrow, gravity, sportiveness; it can mark a decided difference between the joy of a pastoral people and that of a nation of warriors, between the sorrow of a queen and that of a simple village girl, between a calm and serious meditation and the ardent reveries that precede an outburst of passion. Again, borrowing from different nations the musical style that is proper to them, it can make a distinction between the serenade of a brigand of the Abruzzi and that of a Tyrolese or Scotch hunter, between the evening march of pilgrims, sunk in mysticism, and that of a troop of cattle-dealers returning from the fair; it can contrast extreme brutality, triviality, the grotesque, with angelic purity, nobility and candour.* But if it tries to overstep the bounds of this immense circle, music must of necessity have recourse to words —sung, recited or read—to fill up the gaps left by the purely musical expression in a work addressing itself at the same time to the intellect and to the imagination.

* Berlioz is of course over-stating the case for music here, in the very act of arguing against Gluck's over-statement. No purely instrumental piece can "paint" marches in such a way as to acquaint the hearer with the fact that it is a band of pilgrims or a crowd of cattle-drovers that is marching. See his own following remarks on the *Alceste* overture.

Thus the overture to *Alceste* will announce scenes of desolation and of tenderness, but it cannot inform us either of the object of the tenderness or the cause of the desolation ; it will never tell the spectator that the husband of Alcestis is a king of Thessaly condemned by the gods to die unless some one gives his life for him ; yet this is the *subject* of the piece. . . . . " *

The truth of what Berlioz has thus crudely expressed may be seen by comparing the æsthetic of the eighteenth century at any point with that of the nineteenth. In music the contrast is particularly striking. To state it briefly, it may be said that while Gluck and his contemporaries regarded music as the inferior of poetry in any union of the arts, we in this day regard it as the superior. The fundamental error of the last century was in imagining that music could amalgamate with any kind of poetry. It may be that with the relatively imperfect development of music at that time, it was difficult for them to conceive it as anything more than just a new colour on the poet's palette. The future evolution of music has demonstrated their error. Whatever may have been the connection between the two arts in their infancy, both poetry and music have now learned to stand alone. Thus by far the greater quantity of poetry is in no need of music, and a great quantity of music is in no need of words. If the two arts are to combine in one expression, it must be on the borderland between them.

* Berlioz, " A travers chants," pp. 154–157.

The qualities that poetry shares with painting and with prose speech in its more concrete aspects, are for the most part not merely in no need of musical accompaniment, but utterly inimical to music ; while, on the other hand, the state of mind into which we have to be transported in order to enjoy a purely instrumental composition like a symphony, is one with which the concrete utterances of prose or poetry are wholly inassimilable. But between the two extreme poles of the arts there is a neutral field where each has something in common with the other, and it is here alone that they can combine artistically. The musical faculty is indeed a further growth of the faculty that is evidenced in poetry ; this is the explanation of the fact that the ordinary devices of poetry, such as rhyme, rhythm, and alliteration, are quite superfluous in words intended for music, because the æsthetic pleasure and coherence given by these devices are met with in a much more specialised form in the music itself. Music really implies a higher and subtler nervous condition than that implied in poetry ; and an age in which the more concrete ideas of poetry are held fit to dominate the music in any combination of the two arts, is one of lower nervous activity than an age in which the stream of thought is carried on in music alone, without suggestion from words. It is noticeable, in this connection, how pre-Romantic thought in Germany was tending to recognise, even in the eighteenth century, the higher imaginative existence of music. Lessing, in his " Laokoon," threw new light on artistic ideology, showing that modes of procedure peculiar to one art were inadmissible in another, though he did not include

music in his analysis.* Herder, however, who had a
good knowledge of music, looked forward to a combination of the arts in which the maximum of expression
would be achieved with the minimum of contest
between the individual idiosyncracies of each ; it was
to be an ideal union, between a *new* poetry and a *new*
music ; that is, he saw the error of Gluck and his
fellows in supposing that music could be artistically
united to words of every kind. In Herder's ideal combination, each art was to adapt itself to the other ;
poetry, in fact, was to " stand truly in the middle,
between painting and music." " A poem must be
what the inscription is to a picture or a statue—*an
explanation, a guide to lead the stream of music by means
of words interspersed in its current. It must be heard,
not read; the words must only breathe life into the
emotional frame of the music, and this must speak and
act, work on the emotions, and utter the thought, only
following the spirit and general idea of the poet.*" †

* It appears to have been Lessing's intention to discuss
music in the second part of the " Laokoon," and he has
left a few posthumous notes on the art. (See Phillimore's
edition, pp. 328–332.) For Lessing's views of the function
of music between the acts of a tragedy, and the earlier
opinions of Scheibe, a German musician who wrote on
music and the drama some twenty years before Gluck
began the reformation of the opera, see the *Hamburgische
Dramaturgie*, Nos. 26, 27.

† See Haym's " Herder," I. ii. 476. The passage
occurs in a letter sent by Herder to Gluck in 1774, along
with the former's drama, *Brutus*. Mr. Nevison (" Life of
Herder," p. 188) suggests that Herder minimised the

That is the practical wisdom of the whole theory of musical and poetical combination ; and, curiously enough, Rousseau seems to have had a foreshadowing of it when he wrote : " It is a deep and important problem to resolve, *how far we can transmute language into song, and music into speech. On a true solution of this question depends the whole theory of dramatic music.*" * But this was not destined to come within the scope of the pre-Romanticists ; and it is a far cry even from this to Gluck's " I sought to reduce music to its true function, that of supporting the poetry. . . . . I imagined that the music should be to the poetry just what the vivacity of colour and the happy combination of light and shade are to a correct and well-composed design." Gluck's definite, almost concrete imagination, impelled him away from the synthesis both of pure subjectivity, as in the later symphony, and of the modified subjectivity of esoterically definite musical thought permeated with exoterically definite poetical thought, as in the modern opera ; his intellectual world was definitely indicative poetry, helped out by an indefinite suggestion of music. The outside world impressed itself upon him, not, as with later musicians, as something to be imaginatively infiltrated in the reconstructive soul, and then re-expressed in terms not of the pure representation of externality,

claims of poetry in order to ingratiate himself with Gluck; but besides there being no evidence of such an intention, it is clear that Herder's letter revealed a system of æsthetic quite at variance with that of the composer.

* " Œuvres," ix. 578.

but of the imaginative transformation of externality, but rather as something whose outward life for the reason and inward life for the imagination were one. In Romantic art the impression is one thing, the expression another ; with Gluck and the pre-Romanticists generally they were thought to be one and indivisible. Romantic art knows there are multitudes of things not susceptible of imaginative representation, and in the things it does represent, the final form is less an image of these themselves than of something rich and rare into which they have been transmuted by the inner consciousness. Gluck, with his admiration for "nature," saw nothing that could not be represented in art, and, in his attempted representation, failed to perceive the part that should be played by the imagination. Thus his art inevitably tended to such a representation of life as is given in painting. His contemporary, the ebullient Michael Kelly, unconsciously hit upon the psychological truth when he wrote : "For describing the strongest passions in music, and proving grand dramatic effect, in my opinion no man ever equalled Gluck; he was a great painter of music ; perhaps the expression is far-fetched, and may not be allowable, but I speak from my own feelings, and the sensation his descriptive music has always produced on me."* It was this externality of purpose and conception that made the eighteenth century despise Gothic art as "barbarous"; and Marmontel thought to deal a decisive blow of disparagement at

* "Reminiscences of Michael Kelly," 1826, vol. i. p. 256.

Gluck by comparing him with Shakespeare ; an insult which, we may note, was promptly resented by Gluck's adherents.*

We have seen how closely Gluck's ideas and practice were related to the current æsthetic conceptions of his epoch ; and if we now ask the main reason for the enormous difference between the music of the eighteenth century and that of the nineteenth, we shall find it in the great nervous change that has come over western Europe in the last century and a quarter. The whole art of the epoch of Gluck indicates a slower beating of the pulse in that day than in this. Great nervous excitation in poetry tends to give birth to the lyrical qualities that are more cognate with music, and while it may be said that in our time poetry is trying to reach forward into music, in the last century music seemed to be anxious to live on the lower slopes of poetry. Gluck's temperament, as we have already had occasion to think, seems to have been at bottom more poetical than musical. It was only occasionally that he was so profoundly moved as to lose that calm command of self that usually distinguished him ; when he does so lose himself, his music begins to approach romantic music in warmth of colour. Even while he was writing his later works, there was a new movement beginning in Germany which was destined to break quite away from the semi-classical world of the middle of the eighteenth century, and find its ultimate expression in music. The morbid world of *Werther* was typical of a new element that was being

* See Desnoiresterres, pp. 159, 160.

introduced into the life of Europe, an element of vague unrest, of boundless longing, of overwrought nerves and of pessimistic philosophies of life ; and it was in music alone, the most nervous and most expansive of all the arts, that this new spirit could find its adequate expression.* Simultaneously with the general intensifying of nervous life, there came an extraordinary development of what may be called the vocabulary of music, and when the later romantic school came to its operatic work, it found ready to its hand the most varied and the most expressive language that art has ever breathed through.

The result was that music and poetry began to change places, and that from being the mere handmaid of poetry, music came to be by far the richer and

---

* The correlation between the changes in literature or art from age to age, and the simultaneous modifications of the nervous system, has not yet received all the attention it deserves. The question is of course primarily one for medical science, and in the present state of criticism we can only speculate as to these correlations. At any rate, so long as we admit that the individual's mental world is coloured by his physique and habits of life, there seems no reason for denying that a general type of nervous system may predominate in a certain epoch, and that the current art or literature may be the expression of this type. See, for example, a valuable passage in Maxime Du Camp's " Souvenirs littéraires," in which he attributes the morbid literature of his early days to the depleted vascular systems that were then so prevalent. " Often . . . . I have asked myself whether this depression may not have

the more emotional art. It is impossible to discuss in this place the development of the opera since the time of Gluck ; but it may suffice to point out how completely his æsthetic is contradicted by the practice of our own day. We have no thought now of following with faithful humility the concrete meanings of the words ; we aim rather at generalising as far as possible the emotional expression of the music, only employing the words as so many points of crystallization and support. To take an extreme case in order to show the divergence between the music of Gluck and that of the modern opera, there are times when we are so indifferent to what the characters are actually saying that the words might almost be dispensed with ; the

been the outcome of physiological causes. The nation was exhausted by the wars of the empire, and the children had inherited their fathers' weakness. Besides, the system of medicine and hygiene then prevalent was disastrous. Broussais was the leader of thought, and doctors went everywhere lancet in hand. At school they bled us for a headache. When I had typhoid fever I was bled three times in one week, sixty leeches were applied, and I could only have recovered by a miracle. The doctrines preached by Molière's Diafoiruses had lasted on to our day, and resulted in the anæmic constitution so frequently met with. Poverty of blood combined with the nervous temperament makes a man melancholy and depressed " (" Souvenirs," Eng. trans. i., 113). On the general question see a very suggestive essay by Dr. Verity, " Changes produced in the Nervous System by Civilisation," published in 1837.

music of itself is competent to express all that the situation requires. The passionate duet at the end of *Carmen* might be sung to mere vowels and would be just as passionate ; for when music is at its greatest height the less nervous art of poetry can add no new suggestion of beauty or of meaning. This of course is an extreme illustration, and is only meant to show the existence in modern music of elements Gluck never dreamed of. In the very nature of things it is impossible for music ever again to hold that subordinate relation to poetry which it held at times in the opera of the eighteenth century.

And yet, when all has been said that comparative criticism can say, when we have reduced Gluck to his proper place among the thinkers and artists of his own time, and despoiled his theories of any absolute significance for the musical drama of the present or the future, one finds it hard to maintain to the end the attitude of sober, unmoved science towards him. It is difficult to hold back the impulse to *lâcher l'admirable* in speaking of the giant who did so much that was honest and sincere in an age of degradation and conventionality. Though his ideas are paralleled in the writings of other men of his day, his service to art is yet incomparably greater than anything that was done by even the greatest of his contemporaries. It was one thing to say the reform of the opera was necessary ; it was another and more admirable thing to achieve the reform in reality. Philosophers and theorists and satirists might have written for ever without the slightest effect on music itself, had not Gluck found

the means to incarnate the new ideas in living art.
The philosophers and theorists and satirists, in fact,
had been writing for generations, and the condition of
the opera was simply becoming worse day by day.
It was the happy combination in Gluck of thinker
and artist that enabled him to convert good theory into
equally good practice ; and it was the robust pugnacity
of his nature that enabled him to override all the
opposition of conventionality and prejudice, and not
only do good work in music himself, but force it by
sheer strength of purpose upon the consciousness of
the public that music had higher purposes than those
of merely sensuous gratification. To have changed
and consolidated the whole structure of the opera ; to
have insisted on the necessity of making the verbal
basis sound and sane ; to have repressed the vanity and
egotism of the singers, and to have galvanized the
lazy, languid orchestra into life ; to have aimed at
breaking down antagonism between the aria and the
recitative, and making the latter an instrument more
worthy of playing its part in the musical drama ; to
have struck away all the pernicious excrescences that
disfigured the aria, and to have made it a genuine
expression of passion ; to fill the accompaniment
with a significance as great as that of the voice-
part itself; to make the opera dignified and humanistic,
giving music its worthy place as a factor in the lives or
thinking men ; to make the overture elucidatory of the
coming drama ; to work with a coherent principle
throughout the whole opera, giving unity to what had
formerly been a mere *pasticcio* of irrelevant elements,

this was no small labour for the life of one man in such an age.

And he has had his reward. The musician speaks a language that is in its very essence more impermanent than the speech of any other art. Painting, sculpture, architecture and poetry know no other foe than external nature, which may indeed destroy their creations and blot out the memory of the artist. But the musician's material is such that, however permanent may be the written record of his work, it depends not upon this but upon the permanency in other men of the spirit that gave his music birth, whether it shall live in the minds of future generations. Year after year the language of the art grows richer and more complex, and work after work sinks into ever-deepening oblivion; until music that once thrilled men with delirious ecstasy becomes a dead thing which here and there a student looks back upon in a mood of scarcely tolerant antiquarianism. In the temple of the art a hundred statues of the gods are overthrown ; and a hundred others stand with arrested lips and inarticulate tongues, pale symbols of a vanished dominion which men no longer own. Yet here and there through the ghostly twilight comes the sound of some clear voice that has defied the courses of the years and the mutations of taste ; and we hear the rich canorous tones of Gluck, not perhaps with all the vigour and the passion that once was theirs, but with the mellowed splendour given by the touch of time. Alone among his fellows he speaks our modern tongue, and chants the eternal passions of the race. He was indeed, as Sophie Arnould called him, "the musician of the soul;" and if we have added new strings to our lyre, and wrung from them a more poignant eloquence than ever stirred within the heart of Gluck, none the less do we perceive that music such as his comes to us from the days when there were giants in the land.

NOTE TO PAGES 273, 274.

The note on Twining is, as it stands, somewhat misleading. It would appear from it that Twining's opinions on the imitative function of music had altered between the date of the first edition of his book (1789), and that of the second edition (1812). As a matter of fact, Twining always protested against a too slavish interpretation of Aristotle's words in reference to music, and held that the term "imitative," in the sense that it applied to Greek music, was quite inapplicable to much of the music of modern times. The error in the note in question was due to my being misled by the note on Twining in Sir Robert Phillimore's edition of the "Laokoon." He apparently had only seen the 1812 edition of Twining's "Aristotle." Twining, as I have said, protested against the "imitation" theory in his 1789 edition. Not possessing this edition at the time the passage in the text was written, I was led astray by Sir Robert Phillimore's quotation from the edition of 1812; but a copy having come into my hands in the interval, I saw that it was wrong to attribute to Twining any desire to make out music to be an imitative art, from a slavish adherence to Aristotle. Twining's position may be seen from the following passage :—" The ideas and the language of the ancients on this subject were different. When *they* speak of music as imitative, they appear to have solely, or chiefly, in view, its power over the affections. By imitation they mean, in short, what we commonly distinguish from imitation, and oppose to it, under the general term of expression " (p. 46).

I may mention, in passing, that Sir Robert Phillimore errs when he writes that " It was early in the nineteenth century that Mr. Twining became acquainted, through a French translation, with the ' Dramaturgie ' of Lessing, and, in his own admirable translation of, and dissertation upon, Aristotle's poetry (!) Twining remarks upon the ' many excellent and uncommon things ' which Lessing's work contained . . ." The note in question occurs in the 1789 edition of Twining.

INDEX

ADDISON, 54, 231, 235

Algarotti, 13, 54, 231, 232–237, 243, 247, 249, 272n

Angiolini, 38, 55

"Anonyme de Vaugirard," 159, 175

Archer, William, 250n.

Aristotle, 11, 244, 263, 273n

Arnaud, 13, 148, 152, 154, 249

Arne, 26

Atella, 223

Avison, 13, 249

BACH, 10, 214, 215

Balfour, A. J., 215n

Baltazarini, 218

Bardi, Count, 201

Baumgarten, 248

Beattie, 13, 248, 273, 274

Beaulieu, 218

Beaumarchais, 13, 48

Beolco, Angelo, 211

Berlioz, 66, 70, 71, 78, 79, 85, 86, 280–284

Berton, 148, 157, 176

Bertoni, 145

Boccaccio, 42

Bodmer, 213

Boileau, 231

Bouffons, The, 223

Buckle, 219n

Buffonist War, 133

Buonascosi, Madame, 90

Burney, 24, 26, 28, 108, 224, 225

Byzantine music, 12n

CACCINI, 201, 205n

Caffarelli, 35

Caldara, 19

Calzabigi, 54, 72, 92, 95, 119, 190–195

Cambert, 218

Campra, 222

Cavaliere, 204n

Cavalli, 202

Chastellux, 265

Cimarosa, 45

Colasse, 222

Coltellini, Abbé, 91n

"Commedia dell'Arte," 208, 211n

Comparative method, 1, 2, 11–15

Conti, The, 19

Coquard, Arthur, 5n

Corancez, 105, 135, 140, 145, 152, 155, 156

Corneille, 198n, 226n

Czernohorsky, 19

D'ALEMBERT, 13, 231, 256n

Dancourt, 43, 69
Dauvergne, 113, 118, 121
De Brosses, 53, 210
Desmarets, 222
Destouches, 222
Diderot, 4n, 13, 243, 247, 248, 250n
Dittersdorf, 35, 38, 39
Doumic, René, 226n
Du Bos, 13, 235n, 248, 252, 261–263
Du Camp, Maxime, 290n
Duni, 40, 41, 224
Durazzo, 35, 36, 39, 40, 41, 69–72
Du Roullet, 72, 113, 121, 149, 157
Dryden, 226n, 231

Euripides, 85, 121, 122

Farinelli, 39
Favart, 40, 41, 69–71
Fétis, 41n, 144
Freneuse, 224n
Fux, 19

Gabrieli, 201
Gabrielli, 35
Galilei, 201
Galuppi, 45
Gluck. (See analytical table of contents.)
Gluck's borrowings from his earlier works, 34n
Gluck's reforms, 293, 294
Gluck, Marianne, 16, 85, 108, 157
Goethe, 251n
Gossec, 86, 151, 157
Gottsched, 213

Graun, 217
Grétry, 53, 224
Grillo, Abbé, 205n
Grimm, 13, 157, 189, 198n, 226n, 252
Guadagni, 55
Guidotti, 204n.
Guillard, 157n, 177
Gurney, Edmund, 4n

Handel, 22, 23, 26, 28, 214, 215
Harris, 13, 248, 257–261.
Hasse, 29, 30, 217
Haydn, 47, 49
Herder, 13, 213, 286, 287
Houdon, 157
Hugo, Victor, 227n

Imitation of nature, 13, 14, 119, 244, 248, 257–272

Jomelli, 52, 223

Kant, 13, 213, 265
Keiser, 215, 216
Kelly, Michael, 23, 288
Klopstock, 110, 146, 195
Knight, Professor, 4n, 265n
Kusser, 215

La Bruyère, 231
La Fontaine, 232
La Harpe, 13, 158, 160, 170, 174–176, 249
Lee, Vernon, 212n
Leibnitz, 213
Le Sage, 43, 69
Lespinasse, Mdlle. de, 145
Lessing, 13, 213, 263, 285, 286n

Light opera, 40–45
Lully, 14, 112, 121, 157, 218–223, 225
Lully, Jean Louis, 222
Lully, Louis, 222

MARAIS, 222
Marcello, 54, 231, 249
Marmontel, 13, 149, 159, 160, 180, 249, 288
Martini, 39
Mendelssohn, 76
Merullo, 201
Metastasio, 20, 21, 30, 35–38, 52, 68, 71, 217, 265
Migliavacca, 38
Millico, 107, 194
Mingotti, 29, 30
Mondonville, 69
Monsigny, 40, 41, 224
Monteverde, 202
Morley, John, 4*n*, 251*n*
Mozart, 38, 43, 45, 48, 49, 74, 96, 127
Music of the Greeks, 42, 43, 203, 204*n*, 208, 263
Music and Poetry, 8–10, 119, 120, 204, 205*n*, 206, 248, 251–273, 275, 279, 280, 284–287, 290–292
Musical criticism, 1–15, 47
Musical form, 4–6, 47

NAUMANN, 217
Nervous conditions in music, 285, 289, 290*n*
Nevison, 286*n*
Noverre, 189, 271

OPERA IN FRANCE, 217–226
—— Germany, 211–217
—— Italy, 200–211

"PAINTING" IN MUSIC, 13, 31, 59, 60, 103, 104, 163, 164, 246, 275–278.
Paisiello, 45.
Panard, 231
Parry, Dr. Hubert, 5*n*, 211*n*
Patronage in the Eighteenth Century, 46–50, 219*n*, 229, 230
Pergin, Marianne, 32, 34
Pergolesi, 52, 133, 223
Peri, Jacopo, 201, 202, 204*n*, 206, 234
Perrin, 218
Philidor, 70, 71, 151.
Piccinni, 45, 134, 148, 160, 176, 179, 197
Plato, 263
Porsile, 19
Puckeridge, 33

QUAGLIO, 35, 55
Quinault, 148, 157–160, 161, 173, 219, 220

RACINE, 115, 116, 121, 123, 198*n*, 226*n*
Raguenet, Abbé, 224*n*
Rameau, 14, 26, 28, 55, 222, 225, 249
Reichardt, 23, 157*n*, 195
"Reign of the Singers," 209
Renaissance, The, 200, 203
Reutter, 37
Rinuccini, 201
Rolland, Romain, 226*n*
Romanticism, 97–99, 106, 107, 161, 168, 279, 288
Rossini, 10

Rousseau, 4*n*, 13, 120, 134–136, 145, 153, 226*n*, 247, 249, 253–257, 267–271, 287
Rowbotham, J. F., 12*n*

SAINT-EVREMOND, 226*n*, 231, 270*n*
Sainte-Albine, 250*n*
Salieri, 110, 190, 195
Salimbeni, Felice, 21
Salomon, 218
Sammartini, 19, 20, 57
Scheibe, 286*n*
Schütz, 212*n*
Sevelinge, M. de., 111, 112
Sidney, Sir Philip, 207
Social position of the musician in the eighteenth century, 49, 50
Sonnenfels, 91
Staël, Mme. de, 264*n*
Steffani, 216

Suard, 13, 25, 175, 176, 249

TAINE, 222*n*
Tasso, 161
Telemann, 216
Theile, 212
Tibaldi, 90
Traetta, 55, 56
Troutbeck, Rev. J., 132*n*
Tschudi, Baron, 189
Twining, 273*n*

VERITY, DR., 291*n*
Voltaire, 13, 145

WAGNER, 6–11, 43, 125*n*, 199, 232, 233, 242
Webb, 260*n*
Weber, 14, 127
Winckelmann, 213, 265*n*
Women and music, 5*n*

ZENO, 217